WE^{THE}RESISTANCE

Documenting a History of Nonviolent Protest in the United States

Edited by Michael G. Long

Foreword by Chris Hedges

Afterword by Dolores Huerta

City Lights Books | San Francisco

Library of Congress Cataloging-in-Publication Data
Names: Long, Michael G., editor.
Title: We the resistance : documenting a history of nonviolent protest in the
    United States / edited by Michael G. Long ; foreword by Chris Hedges ;
    afterword by Dolores Huerta.
Description: San Francisco, CA : City Lights Books, 2018.
Identifiers: LCCN 2018031526 | ISBN 9780872867567
Subjects: LCSH: Protest movements—United States—History. | Social
    reformers—United States—History. | Government, Resistance to—United
    States—History. | Nonviolence—United States—History.
Classification: LCC HN57 .W3595 2018 | DDC 303.48/40973—dc23
LC record available at https://lccn.loc.gov/2018031526

City Lights Books are published at the City Lights Bookstore
261 Columbus Avenue, San Francisco, CA 94133
www.citylights.com

Somewhere I read that the greatness of America
is the right to protest for right.
—Martin Luther King, Jr.

For Karin and the Resisters Long

CONTENTS

FOREWORD *xxv*
Nonviolent Revolt
Chris Hedges

INTRODUCTION *xxxi*
We the Resistance
Michael G. Long

ONE

Early Roots of Resistance *1*

We Cannot Condemn Quakers (1657) *1*
Edward Hart
Buy Slaves to Free Them (1693) *4*
George Keith
I am but a poor SLave (1723) *7*
Anonymous Slave
I Have No King (1727) *10*
Loron Sauguaarum
The People Are the Proper Judge (1750) *14*
Jonathan Mayhew
Tea Overboard (1773; document date, 1834) *17*
George Hewes
Unjustly Taxed (1774) *21*
Isaac Backus
No Money for the Revolutionary War (1776; document date, 1797) *23*
Job Scott

TWO

The Abolitionist Movement and the Struggle for the Rights of Free African Americans 27

They Do Not Consider Us as Men (1813) 27
  James Forten
Women Overthrowing Slavery (1836) 29
  Angelina Grimke
Escape on the Pearl (1848; document date, 1855) 34
  Daniel Drayton
Resistance to Civil Government (1849) 41
  Henry David Thoreau
I Won't Obey It! (1850) 44
  Jermaine Wesley Loguen
What to the Slave Is the Fourth of July? (1852) 49
  Frederick Douglass
He Took Hold of Me and I Took Hold of the Window Sash (1854) 52
  Elizabeth Jennings
Was John Brown Justified? (1859) 54
  William Lloyd Garrison

THREE

Removing Native Americans, Dethroning Hawaiians 57

First Lords of the Soil (1830) 57
  Theodore Frelinghuysen
The Audacious Practices of Unprincipled Men (1836) 60
  Chief John Ross
The Return of the Winnebago (1873) 64
  S.
We Ask to Be Recognized as Men (1879) 65
  Chief Joseph

My Downtrodden People (1898) *68*
  Queen Liliuokalani

FOUR

Striking Against Industrialists *75*

Petition Against Terrorism (1871) *75*
  Colored National Labor Union
Will You Organize? (1877) *80*
  Albert Parsons
We Have 4,000 Men (1891) *83*
  African American Waterfront Workers of Savannah
A Petition in Boots (1894) *84*
  James Coxey
The Wail of the Children (1903) *88*
  Mother Jones
Negro Workers! (1912) *91*
  Committee of Defense, Brotherhood of Timber Workers
Wage Slavery (1912) *94*
  Textile Workers of Lawrence, Massachusetts

FIVE

Fighting for Women's Rights *101*

All Men and Women Are Created Equal (1848) *101*
  Elizabeth Cady Stanton and Others
Keep the Thing Going (1851, 1867) *105*
  Sojourner Truth
Robbed of Citizenship (1873) *108*
  Susan B. Anthony
Marriage and Love Have Nothing in Common (1910) *114*
  Emma Goldman

Why Women Want to Vote (1913) *118*
    Anna Howard Shaw
For the Sake of Consistency (1915) *122*
    Mary Church Terrell

SIX

World War I *125*

I Denounce the Governing Class (1915) *125*
    Kate Richards O'Hare
Strike Against War (1916) *128*
    Helen Keller
The Darker Races and Avaricious Capitalists (1917) *133*
    A.Philip Randolph and Chandler Owen
A Deliberate Violator (1918) *136*
    Roger N. Baldwin

SEVEN

Workers' Rights and the Great Depression *141*

Industrial Slavery, Murder, Riot, and Unbelievable Cruelty
(1919) *141*
    W. E. B. Du Bois
Organization of the Negro Workers (1925) *144*
    A. Philip Randolph
A Bolshevik Revolution in Lawrence? (1919; document date,
1958) *146*
    A.J. Muste
Brother, Can You Spare a Dime? (1932) *151*
    Yip Harburg and Bonus Marchers
Down with the Sweatshops! (1933; document date, 1945) *155*
    Rose Pesotta

Death Watch (1935) *161*
  League of the Physically Handicapped
The Flint Sit-Down Strike (1937) *163*
  United Auto Workers
Women of the Cotton Fields (1938) *165*
  Elaine Ellis
Picketing Is Exercising Free Speech (1940) *169*
  Frank Murphy

EIGHT

World War II *173*

Jim Crow and National Defense (1941) *173*
  A.Philip Randolph
I Cannot Honorably Participate (1943) *177*
  Robert Lowell
A Racist Charge of Mutiny (1944) *179*
  Thurgood Marshall
The Internment of Japanese Citizens (1944) *182*
  Fred Korematsu and Frank Murphy
Japanese American Draft Resisters (1944) *186*
  The Voice of the Nisei
Against Dropping Atomic Bombs on Japan (1945) *188*
  Leo Szilard
Judgment on Jubilation (1945) *190*
  Dorothy Day

NINE

The Civil Rights Movement *193*

BUILDING THE FOUNDATION *193*
Human Holocaust Under the Stars and Stripes (1909) *193*
  Ida B. Wells-Barnett

We March for the Butchered Dead (1917) *197*
  Charles Martin and the Negro Silent Protest Parade
We Return Fighting (1919) *201*
  W. E. B. Du Bois
It Brings a Sense of Shame (1947, 1960) *204*
  Baltimore Afro-American and Jackie Robinson
Jim Crow in the Armed Forces (1948) *207*
  Bayard Rustin
The Courage of These People in Clarendon County
(1951) *211*
  Thurgood Marshall
Dogs, Cats, and Colored People (1955) *214*
  George Grant

FROM ROSA PARKS TO THE BLACK PANTHERS *215*
Don't Ride the Bus (1955) *215*
  Jo Ann Gibson Robinson
We Shall Have to Lead Our People to You (1957) *217*
  Southern Negro Leaders Conference
SNCC and Nonviolence (1960) *220*
  *Ella Baker and the Student Nonviolent Coordinating
  Committee*
We're Going to Keep Coming (1961) *224*
  Jim Zwerg
A Living Petition (1963) *229*
  Bayard Rustin
I Didn't Try to Register for You (1964) *234*
  Fannie Lou Hamer
Our Free Speech Fight (1964) *238*
  Mario Savio
The Right to Throw Off Such Government (1966) *243*
  Huey Newton and Bobby Seale

TEN

The Threat of Atomic Bombs and the Vietnam War *249*

Statement on Omaha Action (1959) *249*
  Marjorie Swann
The Cruel Deception of Civil Defense (1961) *252*
  The Civil Defense Protest Committee
The Cuban Missile Crisis (1962) *256*
  Women Strike for Peace
The March on Washington to End the Vietnam War
(1965) *260*
  Students for a Democratic Society
A Draft for the Freedom Fight in the U.S. (1966) *265*
  Student Nonviolent Coordinating Committee
A Call to Resist Illegitimate Authority (1967) *268*
  Marcus Raskin and Arthur Waskow
Our Apologies, Good Friends (1968) *272*
  Daniel Berrigan and the Catonsville Nine
If the Government Doesn't Stop the War, We'll Stop the
Government (1971) *275*
  Mayday Tribe

ELEVEN

The Movement Expands *281*

RED, BROWN, AND YELLOW POWER *281*
Fish-Ins (1964; document date, 1967) *281*
  Janet McCloud and Robert Casey
The Occupation of Alcatraz (1969) *285*
  Indians of All Tribes
The Longest Walk (1978) *288*
  American Indian Movement

La Huelga and La Causa Is Our Cry (1966) *293*
    Dolores Huerta
Blowouts—Baby—Blowouts!! (1968) *296*
    Chicano Students in East Los Angeles
To Resist with Every Ounce (1969) *299*
    Cesar Chavez
Hasta La Victoria Siempre! (1970) *304*
    Young Lords Party
The Yellow Power Movement (1969) *307*
    Amy Uyematsu
From Colonies to Communities (1969) *311*
    Asian Community Center

LGBT RIGHTS, WOMEN'S RIGHTS, AND DISABILITY
RIGHTS *313*
Ejected from Dewey's (1965) *313*
    Janus Society
Homosexual American Citizens Picket the White House
(1965) *316*
    Frank Kameny
Christopher Street Liberation Day (1970) *319*
    Gay Liberation Front
Underground Abortion (1969) *321*
    Jane
We Call on All Our Sisters (1969) *325*
    Redstockings
Welfare Is a Women's Issue (1972) *329*
    Johnnie Tillmon
Sitting Against Nixon (1972) *333*
    Judy Heumann
The Vegetables Are Rising (1977) *336*
    Ed Roberts

TWELVE

Environmental Justice and Animal Liberation *341*

Earth Day (1970) *341*
  Gaylord Nelson
Oppose, Resist, Subvert (1981) *344*
  Edward Abbey
Occupy the Forest (1985) *346*
  Earth First
Rescuing the Monkeys (1981) *348*
  People for the Ethical Treatment of Animals
A Necessary Fuss (1984) *351*
  Animal Liberation Front
Avon Killing (1989) *353*
  People for the Ethical Treatment of Animals

THIRTEEN

Anti-Nukes, The Reagan Years, Anti-Gulf War *357*

NUCLEAR POWER AND NUCLEAR WEAPONS *357*
I Can Find No Natural Balance with a Nuclear Plant
(1974) *357*
  Sam Lovejoy
Declaration of Nuclear Resistance (1976) *359*
  Clamshell Alliance
Making the World Truly Safe (1979) *363*
  Randall Forsberg
Nuclear Waste on Our Homeland (1995) *366*
  Lower Colorado River Tribes

THE REAGAN YEARS: UNION BUSTING,
APARTHEID, AND WARS IN CENTRAL AMERICA *369*
You Are Not Alone (1981) *369*
  Lane Kirkland

End UM Investments in Apartheid (1977) *371*
    South African Liberation Committee
Boycotting Shell (1986) *374*
    United Mineworkers of America
We Join in Covenant to Provide Sanctuary (1982) *377*
    Bay Area Sanctuary Movement
Pledge of Resistance (1983) *380*
    Pledge of Resistance Campaign
I Sat on the Tracks (1987; document date, 2011) *382*
    S. Brian Willson

THE GULF WAR *387*
I Will Refuse to Fight (1990) *387*
    Jeff Paterson
One Billion Dollars a Day (1991) *390*
    June Jordan
Demonstrate, Demand, Disobey (1991) *395*
    Michael Albert and Stephen Shalom

FOURTEEN

LGBT Rights, AIDS, and Women's Rights *399*

LGBT RIGHTS AND AIDS *399*
I Am Proud to Raise My Voice Today (1979) *399*
    Audre Lorde
The Right to Lesbian and Gay Sex (1987) *401*
    The March on Washington for Lesbian and Gay Rights
We Take That Fire and Make It Our Own (1993) *405*
    New York Lesbian Avengers
Transphobia Is at the Heart of Queerphobia (1993) *409*
    Phyllis Randolph Frye
Why We Fight (1988) *412*
    Vito Russo

Stop the Church (1989; document date, 2009) *416*
      Michael Petrelis

WOMEN'S RIGHTS *418*
Women's Fast for the ERA (1982; document date, 1987) *418*
      Sonia Johnson
Clarence Thomas, Sexual Harasser (1991) *422*
      Anita Hill
March for Women's Lives (1992) *427*
      Sarah Schuster and Jewel Jackson McCabe

FIFTEEN

The Anti-Globalization Movement *433*

NAFTA Is Economic Hemorrhage (1993) *433*
      Jesse Jackson
Close Down the WTO (1999) *439*
      Russell Mokhiber and Robert Weissman
Students Against Sweatshops (1999) *443*
      SOLE
Defund the Fund! Break the Bank! Dump the Debt!
(2000) *445*
      Mobilization for Global Justice

SIXTEEN

The War on Terror *449*

Isn't This Really About Oil? (2002, 2016) *449*
      Medea Benjam
Calling All Americans to Resist War and Repression
(2002) *452*
      Not in Our Name
Bring Our Troops Home (2005) *456*
      Cindy Sheehan

Eleven Reasons to Close Guantánamo (2015) *461*
    Naureen Shah
Shut Down Creech (2016) *465*
    Anti-Drone Activists

SEVENTEEN

Emerging Movements in the New Century *469*

MINING, PIPELINES, AND GLOBAL WARMING *469*
Boats Float, Bears Don't (2008) *469*
    Greenpeace International
End Mountaintop Removal (2010) *472*
    Appalachia Rising
The Keystone Pipeline Revolt (2011) *473*
    Bill McKibben

LGBTQ RIGHTS *480*
Chained to Serve Openly (2010) *480*
    Get EQUAL
Our Love Is Equal (2013) *482*
    Anthony Kennedy and James Obergefell

OCCUPYING WALL STREET AND WASHINGTON *485*
Killing Big Insurance (2009) *485*
    Mobilization for Health Care for All
Occupy, I Love You (2011) *488*
    Naomi Klein
Moral Mondays (2013) *494*
    William Barber II
Time to Withdraw Big Money from Politics (2016) *497*
    Democracy Spring and Democracy Uprising

PRISON ABOLITION AND BLACK LIVES MATTER *501*
Life Beyond the Prison (2003) *501*
    Angela Y. Davis

Justice for Trayvon! (2012) *505*
  Tracy Martin and Sybrina Fountain
Riding to Ferguson (2014) *508*
  Black Lives Matter
Freeing Slaves in Prison (2016) *512*
  Support Prisoner Resistance

PROTECTING AND LEGALIZING IMMIGRANTS *515*
Freedom Rides for Immigrant Workers (2003) *515*
  Patricia A. Ford
We Want a Legalization Process (2006) *519*
  Luis Gutierrez, Gloria Romero, and Others
Stopping Another Deportation (2013) *522*
  United We Dream

EIGHTEEN

The Trump Era Begins *525*

Not a Legitimate President (January 2017) *525*
  John Lewis and Others
Our Pussies Ain't for Grabbing (January 2017) *528*
  The Women's March and America Ferrera
Together We Rise (March 2017) *532*
  Dave Archambault II
Fearless Girl (April 2017) *536*
  Susan Cox
And So We Resist Global Warming (June 2017) *539*
  Bill McKibben
Dying for Health Care (June 2017) *543*
  ADAPT
A White Nationalist Rally in Charlottesville (August 2017) *545*
  Brendan Novak

Targeting Transgender Troops (November 2017) *549*
    Jennifer Peace
Hunger Strike at Guantánamo Bay (December 2017) *552*
    Khalid Qassim
We Pledge to Resist for Immigrants (2017) *554*
    Alison Harrington
The Human Impact of the Muslim Ban (December 2017) *557*
    Dina El-Rifai
DACA: Depression, Anxiety, Frustration (January 2018) *561*
    Korina Iribe Romo
Marching for Our Lives (March 2016) *564*
    Patrick Northrup
We Do Not Want the Wall (March 2018) *567*
    Dulce Garcia
#MeToo Is About Restoring Humanity (2018) *569*
    Tarana Burke

AFTERWORD
Resistance Past, Present, and Future *575*
    Dolores Huerta

SOURCES AND PERMISSIONS *582*

NOTES *599*

ACKNOWLEDGMENTS *609*

19   The Boston Tea Party, 1773. *(Library of Congress)*

37   Runaway slave traveling by river. *(Schomburg Center, New York Public Library)*

47   Slave hunters seizing fugitives. *(Schomburg Center, New York Public Library)*

48   An Underground Railroad rescue. *(Schomburg Center, New York Public Library)*

63   Chief John Ross, c. 1843. *(Library of Congress)*

67   Native Americans petitioning U.S. Congress, c. 1860s. *(National Archives and Records Administration)*

87   Coxey's Army, Washington, D.C., 1894. *(Library of Congress)*

89   Women striking against child labor, New York City, c. 1900. *(National Archives and Records Administration)*

95   Striking textile workers in Lawrence, Massachusetts, 1912. *(Walter P. Reuther Library, Wayne State University)*

97   Parents sending children to safety during Lawrence strike, 1912. *(Library of Congress)*

111   Women suffragists, New York City. *(New York Public Library)*

119   Suffrage parade, New York City, 1912. *(New York Public Library)*

127   Anti-conscription march, New York City, 1916. *(Swarthmore College Peace Collection)*

137   Anti-Enlistment League flyer calling for pledges to protest WWI, 1915. *(Swarthmore College Peace Collection)*

139   Women's Peace Parade, New York City, 1914. *(Swarthmore College Peace Collection)*

153 Bonus Army at the U.S. Capitol, Washington, D.C., 1932. *(Library of Congress)*

157 International Ladies Garment Workers handbill in support of dressmakers' strike, Los Angeles, 1933. *(National Archives and Records Administration)*

175 Flyer for the March on Washington Movement, 1941. *(Public domain)*

187 Handbill of demands made by the Voice of the Nisei, Poston, Arizona, 1942. *(National Archives and Records Administration)*

189 Leo Szilard's petition to President Harry S. Truman, 1945. *(Harry S. Truman Presidential Library)*

195 African Americans march near U.S. Capitol to protest lynching of four African Americans in Georgia, 1946. *(Library of Congress)*

199 Children march in the Silent Protest Parade, 1917. *(Schomburg Center, New York Public Library)*

203 W.E.B. Du Bois, second from left in front line, marches in the Silent Protest Parade, New York City, 1917. *(Schomburg Center, New York Public Library)*

219 African Americans turn out to vote in Peachtree, Alabama, 1966. *(National Archives and Records Administration)*

223 Greensboro sit-in, North Carolina, 1960. *(Library of Congress)*

225 Freedom Riders John Lewis, left, and Jim Zwerg, Montgomery, Alabama, 1961. *(Library of Congress)*

225 Freedom Riders depart for Washington, D.C., 1961. *(Library of Congress)*

231 Labor leader A. Phillip Randolph, center, at the March on Washington for Jobs and Freedom, 1963. *(National Archives and Records Administration)*

232 March on Washington for Jobs and Freedom, 1963. *(National Archives and Records Administration)*

232 Washington, D.C. march, led by the Congress of Racial Equality, in

memory of African American girls murdered in the bombing of Sixteenth Street Baptist Church in Birmingham, Alabama, 1963. *(Library of Congress, photographer Thomas O'Halloran)*

245 Flyer for Black Panther Party health clinic, Berkeley, California, 1971. *(Itsabouttimebpp.com)*

259 Hiroshima Day protest, New York City, 1968. *(David McReyolds)*

261 Students for a Democratic Society flyer for the March on Washington to End the War in Vietnam, 1965. *(Public domain)*

263 University of Michigan students march against Dow Chemical, Ann Arbor, Michigan, 1969. *(Jay Cassidy Photo Collection, Bentley Historical Library, University of Michigan)*

269 Marchers protest the draft at Yale University, New Haven, Connecticut, 1968. *(National Archives and Records Administration)*

277 Women Strike for Peace die-in, New York City, 1972. *(Swarthmore College Peace Collection)*

279 Women Strike for Peace protest against the Vietnam War, Washington, D.C., 1972. *(Swarthmore College Peace Collection)*

283 Marlon Brando, left, and Robert Satiacum hold fish-in, Puyallup River, Washington, 1964. (MOHAI, Seattle Post-Intelligencer Collection, 1986.5.4414)

287 "We will not give up." Indian Occupiers moments after the removal from Alcatraz Island on June 11, 1971. *(Ilka Hartmann)*

291 Poster supporting the Wounded Knee occupation, South Dakota, 1973. *(Library of Congress)*

295 United Farm Workers and their allies march from Delano to Sacramento, 1966. *(Walter P. Reuther Library, Wayne State University)*

301 Cesar Chavez leads demonstration for United Farm Workers, San Francisco, c. 1970s. *(Walter P. Reuther Library, Wayne State University)*

303 Dolores Huerta with grape harvesters, California, c. 1969. *(Walter P. Reuther Library, Wayne State University)*

309 Amy Uyematsu's influential article on Yellow Power, 1969. *(Densho Digital Repository)*

321 Gay Activist Alliance at the Christopher Street Liberation Day March, New York City, 1970. *(New York Public Library, photographer Kay Tobin)*

323 From the Film "Jane: An Abortion Service," 1995. *(Courtesy of Women Make Movies)*

327 Women on "Relay for ERA," from Seneca Falls, NY, to Houston, TX, c. 1977. *(National Archives and Records Administration)*

335 Protesters at the Capitol Crawl, calling for passage of the American Disabilities Act, 1990. *(Tom Olin)*

339 The 504-sit outside San Francisco's City Hall, 1977. (Anthony Tusler)

347 Early tree-sitting by Earth First, c. 1985. *(Earth First/Public Domain)*

352 Rabbits liberated by the Animal Liberation Front. *(The Animal Liberation Front)*

361 Anti-nuclear march, Seabrook, New Hampshire, 1978. *(Swarthmore College Peace Collection)*

371 Solidarity Day March, Washington, D.C., 1981. *(Library of Congress)*

373 Poster calling for international boycott of South Africa, 1976. *(Library of Congress, creator Racheal Romero)*

379 Sanctuary activist Jose Artiga, left, protesting at U.S. Capitol, 1980s. *(Courtesy of Jose Artiga)*

381 Demonstration against the training of Nicaraguan Contra rebels, Fort Walton, Florida, 1986. *(National Archives and Records Administration)*

391 About 200 University of Wisconsin-Madison students marched in early 1991 to protest the Persian Gulf War. The students called for university

leaders to devote one school day to education about the war. *(University of Wisconsin, photographer Jeff Miller)*

403 ACT-UP die-in at City Hall, New York City, 1989. *(New York Public Library, photographer Douglass Rowell)*

407 First New York City Dyke March, 1993. *(Carolina Kroon)*

417 Poster for ACT-UP protest at St. Patrick's Cathedral, New York City, 1989. *(New York Public Library)*

429 Pro-choice march, New York City, 1992. *(Sandra Lee Phipps)*

441 Police fire pepper spray at protesters against the World Trade Organization, Seattle, 1999. *(Wikimedia Commons, photographer Steve Kaiser)*

447 Mobilization for Global Justice march against World Bank, Washington, D.C., 2006. *(Creative Commons)*

455 Marchers protest war against Iraq, Washington, D.C., 2007. *(Wikimedia Commons)*

459 Cindy Sheehan sits in front of Daniel Ellsberg speaking at protest calling for withdrawal of U.S. troops from the war against Iraq, Washington, D.C., 2006. *(Creative Commons)*

467 Rize Oliveira of Shut Down Creech protests against U.S.-led drone attacks, Creech Air Force Base, Clark County Nevada, 2016. *(Shutdowncreech. com)*

471 Greenpeace protest of global warming, U.S. Department of Interior, Washington, D.C., 2008. *(National Archives and Records Administration)*

491 Day 14 of Occupy Wall Street, New York City, 2011. *(Wikimedia Commons)*

499 Democracy Spring sit-in at U.S. Capitol, Washington, D.C., 2016. *(Wikimedia Commons)*

511 March to support Black Lives Matter and boycott of Black Friday, NYC, 2014. *(Wikimedia Commons, photographer All-Nite Images)*

523 Protest against eliminating DACA, New York City, 2017. *(Wikimedia Commons)*

531 The Women's March, Washington, D.C., 2017. *(Wikimedia Commons)*

535 Solidarity with Standing Rock march, San Francisco, 2016. *(Wikimedia Commons)*

547 Cornel West, second from right in back, and others protesting "Unite the Right" rally in Charlottesville, Virginia, 2017. *(Anthony Crider via Flickr)*

559 Muslim Ban Protest at San Francisco International Airport, 2017. *(Quinn Norton via Flickr)*

565 Protesters at March for Our Lives, Washington, DC, 2018. *(Mobilus in Mobili via Flickr)*

573 Tarana Burke leading #MeToo March, Hollywood, California, 2017. *(The Corsair, photographer Jakob Zermeno)*

Nonviolent Revolt

Chris Hedges

The ideas that sustain the corporate state—neoliberalism, the free market, globalization—have lost their efficacy across the political spectrum. The ideas that are rising to take their place, however, are inchoate. The right has retreated into Christian fascism, xenophobia, racism, a dangerous hyper-individualism and a celebration of the gun culture. The left, knocked off balance by decades of fierce state repression in the name of anti-communism, is struggling to rebuild and define itself. Popular revulsion for the ruling elite, however, is nearly universal. It is a question of which ideas, which vision, will capture the public's imagination.

Revolutions, when they erupt, appear to the elites and the establishment to be sudden and unexpected. This is because the real work of revolutionary ferment and consciousness is unseen by the mainstream society, noticed only after it has largely been completed. Throughout history, those who have sought radical change have always had to first discredit the ideas used to prop up ruling elites and construct alternative ideas for society, ideas often embodied in what is dismissed by the ruling elites as a utopian revolutionary myth. Once ideas shift for a large portion of a population, once the vision of a new society grips the popular imagination, the old regime is finished.

"Did you ever ask yourself how it happens that government and capitalism continue to exist in spite of all the evil land trouble they are causing in the world?" the anarchist Alexander Berkman wrote in his essay, "The Idea Is the Thing." "If you did, then your answer must have been that it is because the people support those institutions, and that they support them because they believe in them."

Berkman was right. As long as most citizens believe in the ideas that justify global capitalism, the private and state institutions that serve our corporate masters are unassailable. When these ideas are shattered, the institutions that buttress the ruling class deflate and collapse. The battle of ideas is percolating below the surface. It is a battle the corporate state, which no longer has a coherent counterargument, is steadily losing. An increasing number of Americans are getting it. They recognize that we have been short of our most basic and cherished civil liberties, and live under the gaze of the most intrusive security and surveillance apparatus in human history. Half the country, because of deindustrialization and automation, can no longer find work that pays a sustainable wage and lives in poverty or near poverty.

The historian Crane Brinton in his book, *Anatomy of a Revolution*, laid out the common route to revolution. The preconditions for successful revolution, Brinton argued, are discontent that affects nearly all social classes, widespread feelings of entrapment and despair, unfulfilled expectations, a unified solidarity in opposition to a tiny power elite, a refusal by scholars and thinkers to continue to defend the actions of the ruling class, an inability of government to respond to the basic needs of citizens, a steady loss of will within the power elite itself and defections from the inner circle, a crippling isolation that leaves the power elite without any allies or outside support and, finally, a financial crisis. Our corporate elite, as far as Brinton was concerned, has amply fulfilled these preconditions. But it is Brinton's next observation that is most worth remembering. Revolutions always begin, he wrote, by making impossible demands that, if the government met, would mean the end of the old configurations of power.

I reported for two decades on revolts, insurgencies and revolutions, including the insurgencies in the 1980s in Central America, the civil wars in Algeria, the Sudan and Yemen, the two Palestinian uprisings and the revolutions in East Germany, Czechoslovakia and Romania as well as the wars in the former Yugoslavia. George Orwell wrote that all tyrannies rule through fraud and force, but that once the fraud is exposed, they must rely exclusively on force. We have now entered the era of naked force. The vast million-person bureaucracy of the internal security and surveillance state will not be used to stop terrorism but to try and stop us.

Despotic regimes in the end collapse internally. Once the foot soldiers who are ordered to carry out acts of repression, such as the clearing of parks or arresting or even shooting demonstrators, no longer obey orders, the old regime swiftly crumbles. When the aging East German dictator Erich Honecker was unable to get paratroopers to fire on protesting crowds in Leipzig in the fall of 1989, the regime was finished. The same refusal to employ violence doomed the communist governments in Prague and Bucharest. I watched in December 1989 as the army general that the dictator Nicolae Ceausescu had depended on to crush protests condemned him to death on Christmas Day. Tunisia's Ben Ali and Egypt's Hosni Mubarak lost power once they could no longer count on the security forces to fire into crowds.

The process of defection among the ruling class and security forces is slow and often imperceptible. These defections are advanced through a rigid adherence to nonviolence, a refusal to respond to police provocation and a verbal respect for the blue-uniformed police, no matter how awful they can be while wading into a crowd and using batons as battering rams against human bodies.

Revolution usually erupts over events that would, in normal circumstances, be considered meaningless or minor acts of injustice by the state. But once the tinder of revolt has piled up, as it has in the United States, an insignificant spark easily ignites popular rebellion. No persons or movement can ignite this tinder. No one knows where or when the eruption will take place. No one knows the form it will take. But it is certain now that a popular revolt is coming. The refusal by the corporate state to address even the minimal grievances of the citizenry, along with the abject failure to remedy the mounting state repression, the chronic unemployment and underemployment, the massive debt peonage that is crippling more than half of Americans, and the loss of hope and widespread despair, means that blowback is inevitable.

"Because revolution is evolution at its boiling point, you cannot 'make' a real revolution any more than you can hasten the boiling of a tea kettle," Berkman wrote. "It is the fire underneath that makes it boil: how quickly it will come to the boiling point will depend on how strong the fire is."

Max Weber wrote, "What is possible would never have been achieved if, in this world, people had not repeatedly reached for the impossible."

It is the visionaries and utopian reformers such as the socialist Eugene V. Debs and the abolitionists who brought about real social change, not the "practical" politicians. The abolitionists destroyed what the historian Eric Foner calls the "conspiracy of silence by which political parties, churches and other institutions sought to exclude slavery from public debate."

Foner writes:

> For much of the 1850s and the first two years of the Civil War, Lincoln—widely considered the model of a pragmatic politician—advocated a plan to end slavery that involved gradual emancipation, monetary compensation for slave owners, and setting up colonies of freed blacks outside the United States. The harebrained scheme had no possibility of enactment. It was the abolitionists, still viewed by some historians as irresponsible fanatics, who put forward the program—an immediate and uncompensated end to slavery, with black people becoming U.S. citizens—that came to pass (with Lincoln's eventual help, of course).

By the time ruling elites are openly defied, there has already been a nearly total loss of faith in the ideas—in our case free market capitalism and globalization—that sustain the structures of the ruling elites. And once enough people get it, a process that can take years, "the slow, quiet, and peaceful social evolution becomes quick, militant, and violent," as Berkman wrote. "Evolution becomes revolution."

An uprising that is devoid of ideas and vision is never a threat to ruling elites. Social upheaval without clear definition and direction, without ideas behind it, descends into nihilism, random violence and chaos. It consumes itself. This, at its core, is why I disagree with some elements of the Black Bloc anarchists and antifa. I believe in strategy. And so did many of the older anarchists, including Berkman, Emma Goldman, Pyotr Kropotkin and Mikhail Bakunin. And I know that non-violence is the *only* route we have to radical social and political change.

I prefer the piecemeal and incremental reforms of a functioning democracy. I prefer a system in which our social institutions permit the citizenry to nonviolently dismiss those in authority. I prefer a system in which institutions are independent and not captive to corporate power. But we do not live in such a system. Revolt is the only option left. Ruling elites, once the ideas that justify their existence are dead, resort to force. It is their final clutch at power. If a nonviolent popular movement is able to ideologically disarm the bureaucrats, civil servants and police—to get them, in essence, to defect—nonviolent revolution is possible. But if the state can organize effective and prolonged violence against dissent, it spawns reactive revolutionary violence, or what the state calls terrorism. Violent revolutions usually give rise to revolutionaries as ruthless as their adversaries. "Whoever fights monsters should see to it that in the process he does not become a monster," Friedrich Nietzsche wrote. "And if you gaze long enough into an abyss, the abyss will gaze back into you." Violent revolutions are always tragic. I, and many other activists, seek to keep our uprising nonviolent. We seek to spare the country the savagery of domestic violence by both the state and its opponents. There is no guarantee that we will succeed, especially with the corporate state controlling a vast internal security apparatus and militarized police forces. But we must try. Once violence becomes the language of resistance, the state, which can speak in the language of force with a ruthlessness that the opposition can never match, can triumph. The state uses violence to demand "law and order" and demonize the opposition, isolating it within the wider society and making it easier to crush.

The corporate state seeks to maintain the fiction of our personal agency in the political and economic process. As long as we believe we are participants, a lie sustained through massive propaganda campaigns, endless and absurd election cycles and the pageantry of empty political theater, our corporate oligarchs rest easy in their private jets, boardrooms, penthouses and mansions. As the bankruptcy of corporate capitalism and globalization is exposed, the ruling elite are increasingly nervous. They know that if the ideas that justify their power die, they are finished. This is why voices of dissent—as well as spontaneous uprisings such as the Occupy movement—are ruthlessly crushed by the corporate state. Revolutions are not only fundamentally nonviolent, because they never succeed unless the ruling apparatus self-destructs, but they are won around the battle of ideas. The ideology that sustained corporate power is dead. It is our job to fill the vacuum with an articulated socialism. And it is our job to use the tool of nonviolence to bring enough of the population and those who administer power to our side. If we fail, a Christianized fascism will be ascendant.

"[M]any ideas, once held to be true, have come to be regarded as wrong and evil," Berkman wrote in his essay. "Thus the ideas of the divine right of kings, of slavery and serfdom. There was a time when the whole world believed those institutions to be right, just, and unchangeable. In the measure that those superstitions and false beliefs were fought by advanced thinkers, they became discredited and lost their hold upon the people, and finally the institutions that incorporated those ideas were abolished. Highbrows will tell you that they had 'outlived' their 'usefulness' and therefore they 'died.' But how did they 'outlive' their 'usefulness'? To whom were they useful, and how did they 'die'? We know already that they were useful only to the master class, and they were done away with by popular uprisings and revolutions."

We the Resistance

Michael G. Long

"The politics of dissent is back in the United States," says scholar Erica Chenoweth. "Since 2011, the country has witnessed the resurgence of popular action—from Occupy Wall Street to Flood Wall Street to Black Lives Matter to Standing Rock."

Chenoweth may be right, but it's not that the politics of dissent was ever absent. Dissent played an important role in our history long before the right to dissent—that is, the right to free speech, the right to assemble peacefully, and the right to express grievances to the government—was guaranteed by the Bill of Rights, and it has consistently appeared throughout the course of our history, even though its popularity has ebbed and flowed along the way. It ebbed in the early 1950s, for example, and now it's flowing.

In light of the recent resurgence, Chenoweth and her colleagues have started counting political crowds on a monthly basis, and beginning with the Women's March on January 21, 2017, they have found that monthly protests in the United States have numbered in the hundreds and that the most common type of political protest today is "civil resistance," acts in which "unarmed civilians confront opponents using protests, strikes, boycotts, stay-aways and other forms of nonviolent contention."

In defining civil resistance, Chenoweth, as well as many others who write on this subject, draw from Gene Sharp, founder of the Albert

Einstein Institution, whose work on nonviolent action has created a rich legacy for all of us who believe in the right to protest for right.

Sharp defines nonviolent action as "a technique of action for applying power in a conflict by using symbolic protests, noncooperation, and defiance, but not physical violence."

It's different from pacifism because it refers to a technique of action rather than a wholesale rejection of violence based on one's religious or philosophical beliefs. Historically, nonviolent action has been employed by pacifists and non-pacifists alike, and it's not a stretch to say that most U.S. citizens who participate in nonviolent actions are far from pacifists.

Nonviolent action is different from passivity, too, because it actively resists, challenges, defies, and confronts governing authorities. It's not for slackers or the surrendering type.

Sharp has also classified nonviolent action into three broad categories: nonviolent protest and persuasion (like public speeches, marches, and teach-ins), noncooperation (strikes, boycotts, and sanctuaries), and nonviolent intervention (occupations, filling jails, and parallel governments). Although most of these methods—he's identified more than 190 of them—are unlike those employed in conventional politics (voting, running for office, and other forms of electoral politics), his category of nonviolent protest and persuasion does include tactics, such as group lobbying, that do not altogether avoid standard political channels.

We the Resistance follows Sharp's general lead, but there are a few differences to note. As it appears here, "nonviolent protest" refers to the use of nonviolent methods, including social, psychological, political, and economic ones, for resisting governing authorities—for example, speeches, petitions, opinion editorials, lobbying, picketing, marches, parades, teach-ins, walkouts, boycotts, strikes, sit-ins, sit-downs, speak-outs, civil disobedience, parallel governments, seizure of property, and occupations. In other words, nonviolent protest is a large umbrella term that includes all the methods included in Sharp's three categories of nonviolent action.

In addition, although Sharp's work addresses nonviolent action as it occurs throughout the world, *We the Resistance* tends to the context of the United States and especially to the nonviolent methods used to resist governing authorities whose attitudes, actions, policies, and systems seek to undermine the democratic ideal of equal justice under law or to trample the rights to life, liberty, and the pursuit of happiness.

The last point is especially significant because there have been significant nonviolent protests throughout our history that have directly and intentionally sought to squash democratic principles and values.

On August 8, 1925, for example, more than 30,000 members of the Ku Klux Klan paraded down Pennsylvania Avenue in Washington, D.C., in a public display of racism, anti-Semitism, and anti-Catholicism. Wearing white Klan robes, unmasked men and women carried U.S. flags in a three-hour march that ended at the Washington Monument. However historically significant it may be, the 1925 Klan parade, as well as similar nonviolent rallies, is not a proper subject for this book.

Nor are demonstrations that have been socially or politically conservative. This book does not include, for example, nonviolent protests that have targeted *Roe* v. *Wade*, the landmark U.S. Supreme Court decision granting women the right to abortion, even though these protests have shown massive strength.

We the Resistance aims to document nonviolent protests that have been leftist—socially, politically, and economically—within the context of U.S. history. These include protests for the separation of church and state, the abolition of slavery, the enfranchisement of women, the right to free love and unregulated sex, the basic need for livable wages, the elimination of Jim Crow customs and laws, first-class citizenship for people of all colors and abilities, the right to abortion, the preservation of the environment, the liberation of animals, the citizenship of immigrants without legal standing, the right to same-sex marriage, the regulation of Wall Street, the elimination of police brutality against people of color, and so much more.

Although *We the Resistance* is not comprehensive in its documentation of leftist nonviolent protests, the documents included here will introduce readers to some of the most significant protests, individual and collective, that have advanced equality, freedom, and justice. Taken together, the historic documents suggest that nonviolent protest is at the heart of what it means to be a U.S. American.

Violence, too, is at the heart of what it means to be part of our country, and if we have any doubt about that, all we have to do is read standard history books. There we will discover that historians have used conflicts and wars to order, explain, and give meaning to our past and present lives. Sometimes these histories even seem to suggest that the capacity to maim and kill for democratic values and principles is what it means to be American.

Perhaps this is the reason that nonviolent protests often feel so marginal, so peripheral, so out of the ordinary. But they're not. If we look closely, we will see countless individuals and groups throughout history who have wielded the powerful weapons of nonviolence in order to "redeem the soul of America," as Martin Luther King, Jr. put it. We will see slaves, Native Americans, Quakers, abolitionists, sharecroppers, suffragists, union members, immigrants, people of color, people with disabilities, pacifists, environmentalists, animal-rights activists, and LGBT folks, among so many others—all of them using nonviolent weapons to advance equality, justice, and freedom.

It's simply impossible to understand U.S. history without tending to nonviolent protests and the creative ways they have deepened and advanced our commitments to democratic values and principles. Nonviolent protests have been so pervasive and constant that we can even use them, rather than conflict and wars, to order, explain, and give meaning to our collective history. The critics who suggest that protest against the governing authorities is un-American simply don't know their own history.

My hope is that *We the Resistance* will inspire and educate readers about nonviolent protests, and help them discover that they're part of a wider community of resisters, even ones who date back to the pre-Revolutionary War era. I also hope that this book will help readers make connections between their own protest actions and those of the recent past, and between those of the recent past and those of long ago—connections, for example, between the Black Lives Matter movement, the black civil rights movement, and the abolitionist movement.

Martin Luther King, Jr., rightly noted that the black civil rights movement did not emerge out of nothing but that it was deeply connected to the past. King felt especially indebted to Jackie Robinson and his nonviolent shattering of the color barrier in Major League Baseball. He even described Robinson as "a sit-inner before the sit-ins, a freedom rider before the Freedom Rides."

Robinson, too, recognized his own indebtedness to nonviolent resisters of the past. Indeed, before Robinson, A. Philip Randolph organized the Brotherhood of Sleeping Car Porters and the 1941 March on Washington movement. Before Randolph, African American WWI veterans marched with the Bonus Army to demand payments that would help them survive during an awful depression. Before the Bonus Army, Ida B. Wells and the NAACP campaigned against lynching, as did those who marched in the Negro Silent Protest Parade of 1917. Before the parade, Elizabeth Jennings refused to leave a whites-only streetcar in New York City, and before she did that, African Americans in the North organized themselves to resist the 1850 Fugitive Law. And these brave folks had roots extending way back to the pre-Revolutionary days, when slaves in colonial America petitioned ecclesiastical authorities in Europe to arrange for their emancipation.

These are just some of the connections that this book will allow readers to make. Others deal with the intersectionality of nonviolent campaigns. Gay rights pioneer Frank Kameny, for example, credited the black civil rights movement for providing him with the inspiration and instruction required to politicize the homophile movement of the 1960s. Helen Keller joined other peace advocates during World War I, but she did so because of her unwavering socialist belief in the corruption of U.S. capitalism. And suffragists Elizabeth Cady Stanton and Lucretia Mott first met each other through their mutual work in the abolitionist movement.

We the resisters in the 21st century may sometimes feel as if we're alone or doing something new, something innovative, something unique. But the truth is that a richly interconnected history has birthed us into this moment and offers us resources for resisting today and persisting tomorrow.

Our interconnected history also offers us hope because it shows us that some nonviolent protests can indeed succeed. Drawing from her groundbreaking work with Maria Stephan, Erica Chenoweth has argued that "historically speaking, nonviolent struggle is a more effective technique than violent struggle." When democracy of some form is an intended goal, "nonviolent resistant campaigns are 10 times more likely to usher in democratic institutions than violent ones. Armed resistance actually tends to weaken democracy in previously democratic countries, while nonviolent resistance has no such effect."

Although this book does not always identify the outcomes of the nonviolent protests documented here, just a bit of extra research will show that many of these campaigns were considerably successful in advancing democratic values and the rights to life, liberty, and the pursuit of happiness. For example, the early women's rights movement eventually resulted in the enfranchisement of women, the March on Washington for Jobs and Freedom helped lead to the passage of the Civil Rights Act of 1964, and numerous LGBT protests in recent years eventuated in the repeal of the government's "Don't Ask, Don't Tell" policy.

Of course there were horrific failures along the way. The nonviolent protests of Native Americans did not prevent the government from slaughtering them or forcing them on to barren lands. The nonviolent protests of individual slaves to white Christians did not typically lead to their emancipation. And more than a few of the nonviolent protests of factory workers in the first part of the twentieth century were crushed by industrialists; some of the workers, like many Native Americans and slaves before them, were maimed and murdered. While we herald the effectiveness of nonviolent protests, it's important to recall that nonviolence is not for the weak of heart; it requires courage, and sometimes a willingness to die, in the face of the unspeakable horrors that our government is so capable of sanctioning and committing.

Thanks to the countless nonviolent resisters before us, our government has relented at points in our history. But let's not forget for one moment that state-sanctioned horrors continue to plague us—people of color, immigrants, the LGBT community, people with disabilities, women of all colors, the poor, and others—as well as animals and the environment.

But as the horrors visit us every day, so does our opportunity to stand on the shoulders of the men, women, and children whose nonviolent protests, documented here, have shaped us into the resisters we are today and can be tomorrow. And may we at last stand tall and exercise our constitutional right to resist for the sake of the democracy that still eludes us. All of Us—We the People, We the Resisters.

Notes on the Documents

I tried not to be heavy-handed in changing or correcting the grammar used by authors of the primary sources included here. I deleted outmoded grammar at some points, and in those places where I did retain its use, my purpose was to preserve the historic feel of the written word.

Excerpting historic documents always presents a challenge, and my hope is that I exercised care in doing so. Almost all of the writings here are shortened in some way, some of them quite liberally, and ellipses usually indicate my deletions. In some cases, I relied on the excellent editing done by other scholars who worked on the documents. You can find in the acknowledgments a list of editors whose work helped me to navigate the enormous amount of relevant and available material.

I deleted any notes that might have appeared in some of the original documents and did not add notes to explain particular references in the documents. Only rarely did I employ brackets to add information about references. Keeping or adding notes or bracketed information would have required me to delete some of the documents published here.

The most difficult choices I faced centered on the selection of which texts to include and which to exclude. My choices reflect my desire to show different types of actors, a wide range of nonviolent actions, and a diversity of goals and ends. The uneven quality of the documents reflects the availability of the historic material.

I should note, too, that some big names are missing in the pages ahead—William Sill, Eugene Debs, and Martin Luther King, Jr., come to mind. Also missing are some important protests—the Uprising of the 20,000 led by Clara Lemlich, Lucy Stone's resistance to traditional marriage, and the student sit-in movement in the 1960s are but a few examples. I decided not to include King-authored documents for practical reasons: it is very difficult, and expensive, to secure permission to publish his work. As for Sill, Debs and other prominent peacemakers in U.S. history, as well as those historic protests I do not address, the best I can do in light of their absence here is to remind you that this work is not comprehensive and to encourage you to supplement the pages ahead by consulting the work of my colleagues who write on the increasingly important topic of nonviolent resistance.

ONE

Early Roots of Resistance

We Cannot Condemn Quakers (1657)

Edward Hart

Some of the earliest roots of resistance in U.S. history can be found among Quakers and Baptists and their opposition to political and religious authorities. Quakers arrived in America in 1656, and it did not take long for them to become infamous for beliefs threatening to the social order (their insistence on the equality of women, for example) and for loud preaching in public. Quakers were not quietists, and Peter Stuyvesant, the director-general of New Netherland, did not take kindly to them.

Compared to the Massachusetts Bay Colony, where Puritans enforced their orthodoxy with little mercy, New Netherland was designed to be relatively tolerant in religious matters. There were no religious tests, and the Dutch settlers had mandated that "no one shall be persecuted or investigated because of his religion." But Stuyvesant, the stern son of a Calvinist minister, sought to establish his preference for the Dutch Reformed Church and to prevent non-Reformed colonists from exercising their faith in public.

Stuyvesant was especially determined to banish the brash Quakers, and in 1657 he ordered the public torture of Robert Hodgson for preaching in public. It was a horrific scene. The Dutch authorities dragged Hodgson behind a horse cart, chained him to a wheelbarrow, threw him in a dungeon, hanged him by his hands, and whipped him until he almost died. But Stuyvesant was unsatisfied and soon issued an ordinance that prohibited anyone from housing Quakers.

Edward Hart, the town clerk in Flushing, scoffed at the ordinance, and on December 27 he enlisted about thirty town members, none of whom were Quakers, to sign a petition of protest to be sent to Stuyvesant. The historic petition below, now known as "The Flushing Remonstrance," was remarkably bold in its public opposition to the most powerful leader of New Netherland. It was also an invitation to arrest. Predictably, Stuyvesant ordered the arrest of Hart, as well as three others, and forced the rest of the signatories to recant.

In spite of the ordinance, Quakers continued to practice their faith in Flushing—and to earn Stuyvesant's wrath. In 1662 he ordered the arrest of farmer John Bowne for holding Quaker meetings in his home. Bowne, a determined resister, refused to pay his fine and was shipped off to trial before the West India Company (WIC) in Amsterdam. But the WIC, attuned to the positive economic benefits of religious tolerance, sided with Bowne in April 1663, permitting him to return to Flushing as a free man and ordering Stuyvesant to "allow everyone to have his own belief." With religious tolerance the law of the land, Bowne built the Flushing Quaker Meeting House in 1694. It still stands today as testimony to resistance in colonial America.

Right Honorable,

You have been pleased to send up to us a certain prohibition or command that we should not receive or entertain any of those people called Quakers because they are supposed to be by some seducers of the people. For our part we cannot condemn them in this case, neither can we stretch out our hands against them, to punish, banish, or persecute them, for out of Christ God is a consuming fire, and it is a fearful thing to fall into the hands of the living God.

We desire therefore in this case not to judge lest we be judged, neither to condemn lest we be condemned, but rather let every man stand and fall to his own Master. We are bound by the Law to do good unto all men, especially to those of the household of faith. And though for the present we seem to be insensible of the law and the Lawgiver, yet when death and the Law assault us, if we have our advocate to seek, who shall plead for us in this case of conscience betwixt God and our own souls; the powers of this world can neither attack us, neither excuse us, for if God justify who can condemn and if God condemn there is none can justify.

And for those jealousies and suspicions which some have of them, that they are destructive unto magistracy and ministry, that cannot be, for the magistrate hath the sword in his hand and the minister hath the sword in his hand, as witness those two great examples which all magistrates and ministers are to follow, Moses and Christ, whom God raised up, maintained, and defended against all the enemies both of flesh and spirit; and therefore that which is of God will stand, and that which is of man will come to nothing. And as the Lord hath taught Moses or the civil power to give an outward liberty in the state by the law written in his heart designed for the good of all, and can truly judge who is good, who is evil, who is true, and who is false, and can pass definitive sentence of life or death against that man which rises up against the fundamental law of the States General; so hath he made his ministers a savor of life unto life, and a savor of death unto death.

The law of love, peace, and liberty in the states extending to Jews, Turks, and Egyptians, as they are considered the sons of Adam, which is the glory of the outward state of Holland, so love, peace, and liberty extending to all in Christ Jesus, condemns hatred, war, and bondage. And because our Savior saith it is impossible but that offenses will come, but owe unto him by whom they cometh, our desire is not to offend one of his little ones, in whatsoever form, name, or title he appears in, whether Presbyterian, Independent, Baptist, or Quaker, but shall be glad to see anything of God in any of them, desiring to do unto all men as we desire all men should do unto us, which is the true law both of church and state; for our Savior saith this is the law and the prophets.

Therefore if any of these said persons come in love unto us, we cannot in conscience lay violent hands upon them, but give them free egress and regress unto our town, and houses, as God shall persuade our consciences. And in this we are true subjects both of church and state, for we are bound by the law of God and man to do good unto all men and evil to no man. And this is according to the patent and charter of our town, given unto us in the name of the States General, which we are not willing to infringe, and violate, but shall hold to our patent and shall remain, your humble subjects, the inhabitants of Flushing.

Buy Slaves to Free Them (1693)

George Keith

Another root of resistance in U.S. history emerged from those who fought to abolish slavery. In 1688 four Quakers from Germantown, Pennsylvania—Gerrett Hendricks, Derick Op Den Graeff, Francis Daniell Pastorius, and Abraham Op Den Graef—drafted what historian James G. Basker identifies as "the earliest known expression of public opposition to slavery in the American colonies." In an appeal to their Quaker community, Hendricks and his friends recommended the abolition of slavery among them. "What thing in the world can be done worse towards us," they wrote, "than if men should rob or steal us away & sell us for slaves to strange countries, separating husband from their wife and children." Four years later, George Keith, the headmaster of the Friend's Public School in Philadelphia, presented his own anti-slavery arguments to Quakers in his community. As evident in the writing below, Keith offered not only a detailed theological argument against slavery but also a nonviolent strategy for resisting it, a creative plan adopted by many Quakers in the years to follow.

Seeing our Lord Jesus Christ hath tasted death for every man, and given himself a ransom for all, to be testified in due time, and that his Gospel of peace, liberty, and redemption from sin, bondage, and all oppression is freely to be preached unto all, without exception, and that *Negroes, Blacks* and *Tannies* are a real part of mankind, for whom Christ hath shed his precious blood, and are capable of salvation, as well as *White Men;* and Christ the Light of the World hath (in measure) enlightened them and every man that cometh into the world; and that all such who are sincere *Christians* and true believers in Christ Jesus, and followers of him, bear his image, and are made conformable unto him in love, mercy, goodness, and compassion, who came not to destroy men's lives, but to save them, nor to bring any part of mankind into outward bondage, slavery, or misery, nor yet to detain them, or hold them therein, but to ease and deliver the oppressed and distressed, and bring into liberty both inward and outward.

Therefore we judge it necessary that all faithful Friends should discover themselves to be true *Christians* by having the fruits of the Spirit of Christ, which are *love, mercy, goodness, and compassion* towards all in misery, and that suffer oppression and severe usage, so far as is in them possible to ease and relieve them, and set them free of their hard bondage, whereby it may be hoped that many of them will be gained by their beholding these good works of sincere *Christians,* and prepared thereby, through the preaching the Gospel of Christ, to embrace the true faith of Christ. And for this cause it is, as we judge, that in some places in *Europe* Negroes cannot be bought and sold for money, or detained to be slaves, because it suits not with the mercy, love & clemency that is essential to *Christianity,* nor to the doctrine of Christ, nor to the liberty the Gospel calleth all men unto, to whom it is preached. And to buy souls and bodies of men for money, to enslave them and their posterity to the end of the world, we judge is a great hindrance to the spreading of the Gospel, and is occasion of much war, violence, cruelty, and oppression, and theft & robbery of the highest nature; for commonly the Negroes that are sold to white men are either stolen away or robbed from their kindred, and to buy such is the way to continue these evil practices of man-stealing, and transgresseth that Golden Rule and Law, *To do to others what we would have others do to us.*

Therefore, in true *Christian love,* we earnestly recommend it to all our Friends and Brethren not to buy any Negroes, unless it were on purpose to set them free, and that such who have bought any, and have them at present, after some reasonable time of moderate service they have had of them, or may have of them, that may reasonably answer to the charge of what they have laid out, especially in keeping Negro children born in their house, or taken into their house, when under age, that after a reasonable time of service to answer that charge, they may set them at liberty, and during the time they have them, to teach them to read and give them a Christian education.

Some Reasons and Causes of Our Being Against Keeping of Negroes for Term of Life

First, because it is contrary to the principles and practice of the *Christian Quakers* to buy prize or stolen Goods, which we bore a faithful testimony against in our native country; and therefore it is our duty to come forth in a testimony against stolen slaves, it being accounted a far greater crime under *Moses's* Law than the stealing of goods. . . .

Secondly, because Christ commanded, saying, *All things whatsoever ye would that men should do unto you, do ye even so to them.* Therefore as we and our children would not be kept in perpetual bondage and slavery against our consent, neither should we keep them in perpetual bondage and slavery against their consent, it being such intolerable punishment to their bodies and minds that none but notorious criminal offenders deserve the same. But these have done us no harm; therefore how inhumane is it in us so grievously to oppress them and their children from one generation to another.

Thirdly, because the Lord hath commanded, saying, *Thou shalt not deliver unto his Master the Servant that is escaped from his Master unto Thee, he shall dwell with thee, even amongst you in that place which he shall choose in one of thy Gates, where it liketh him best; thou shalt not oppress him,* Deut. 23. 15, 16. By which it appeareth that those which are at liberty and freed from their bondage should not by us be delivered into bondage again, neither by us should they be oppressed, but being escaped from his master, should have the liberty to dwell amongst us, where it liketh him best. . . .

Fourthly, because the Lord hath commanded, saying, *Thou shalt not oppress an hired Servant that is poor and needy, whether he be of thy Brethren, or of the Strangers that are in thy Land within the Gates, least he cry against thee unto the Lord, and it be sin unto thee; Thou shalt neither vex a stranger nor oppress him, for ye were strangers in the Land of Egypt, Deut.* 24. 14, 15. *Exod.* 12. 21. But what greater oppression can there be inflicted upon our fellow creatures than is inflicted on the poor Negroes! they being brought from their own country against their wills, some of them being stolen, others taken for payment of debt owing by their parents, and others taken captive in war, and sold to merchants, who bring them to the *American* plantations, and sell them for bond-slaves to them that will give most for them; the husband from the wife, and the children from the parents; and many that buy them do exceedingly afflict them and oppress them, not only by continual hard labor, but by cruel whippings, and other cruel punishments, and by short allowance of food.

I am but a poor SLave (1723)

Anonymous Slave

Resistance among slaves in colonial America ranged from nonviolent acts, such as working slowly, faking sickness, stealing food and tools, and running away, to more violent ones, like setting property on fire, carrying out insurrections, killing slave owners, and even committing suicide.

In the early 1720s Virginia saw considerable resistance among its slave population. In 1722 slaves from three different counties conspired to carry out a violent insurrection that would have involved hundreds of slaves. The plan never came to fruition because the plot was discovered, and some of its leaders were imprisoned, while others were shipped to

Barbados. But the harsh repression did not quell the desire for liberation, and in the following year eleven slaves from Virginia were imprisoned for plotting yet another potentially violent insurrection. Fearful for their lives and property, Virginia legislators increased penalties for rebellious slaves and added even more restrictions to slaves' lives.

In 1723 slave resistance also took the form of a letter of protest (below) to Edmund Gibson, the new bishop of London, whose spiritual jurisdiction included Virginia. The letter writer, a slave who wished to remain anonymous for fear of violent reprisal, appeals to the bishop's Christian mercy. It was exactly this type of solicitation that slave owners feared as missionaries converted the slave populations to Christianity. Interpreted from a slave's perspective, Christian beliefs, especially those about Moses leading the slaves out of Egypt, became compelling sources of inspiration to fight for liberation.

to The Right Raverrand father in god my Lord arch Bishop of Lonnd this coms to sattesfie your honour that there is in this Land of verJennia a Sort of people that is Calld molatters which are Baptised and brouaht up in the way of the Christian faith and followes the ways and Rulles of the Chrch of England and sum of them has white fathers and sum white mothers and there is in this Land a Law or act which keeps and makes them and there seed SLaves forever –

and most honoured sir a mongst the Rest of your Charitabell acts and deed wee your humbell and poore partishinners doo beg Sir your aid and assistancce in this one thing which Lise as I doo understand in your LordShips brest which is that your honour will by the help of our Suffvering Lord King George and the Rest of the Rullers will Releese us out of this Cruell Bondegg and this wee beg for Jesus Christs his Sake who has commanded us to seeke first the kingdom of god and all things shall be addid un to us

and here it is to bee notd that one brother is a SLave to another and one Sister to an othe which is quite out of the way and as for mee my selfe I am my brothers SLave but my name is Secrett and here it is to bee notd againe that wee are commandded to keep holey the Sabbath day and wee do hardly know when it comes for our task mastrs are has hard with us as the Egypttions was with the Chilldann of Issarall god be marcifll unto us

here follows our Sevarity and Sorrowfull Sarvice we are hard used up on Every account in the first place wee are in Ignorance of our Salvation and in the next place we are kept out of the Church and matrimony is deenied us

and to be plain they doo Look no more upon us then if wee ware dogs which I hope when these Strange Lines comes to your Lord Ships hands will be Looket in to

and here wee beg for Jesus Christ his Sake that as your honour do hope for the marcy of god att the day of death and the Redemtion of our Savour Christ that when this comes to your Lord Ships hands your honour wll Take Sum pitty of us who is your humble but Sorrowfull portitinors

and Sir wee your humble perticners do humbly beg the favour of your Lord Ship that your honour will grant and Settell one thing upon us which is that our childarn may be broatt up in the way of the Christtian faith and our desire is that they may be Larnd the Lords prayer the creed and the ten commandements and that they may appeare Every Lord's day att Church before the Curatt to bee Exammond for our desire is that godllines Shoulld abbound amongs us and wee desire that our Childarn be putt to Scool and and Larnd to Reed through the Bybell

which is all att prasant with our prayers to god for itts good Success before your honour these from your humbell Servants in the Lord

my Riting is vary bad I whope yr honour will take the will for the deede

I am but a poore SLave that writt itt and has no other time butt Sunday and hardly that att Sumtimes . . .

wee dare nott Subscribe any mans name to this for feare of our masters for if they knew that wee have Sent home to your honour wee Should goo neare to Swing upon the gallass tree

I Have No King (1727)

Loron Sauguaarum

Still another deep root of resistance comes from the original inhabitants of what became colonial America, especially those in the regions of New England. The influx of English colonists in the 1600s virtually decimated coastal New England's Native population. That weakening, coupled with the political fragmentation of the various tribes, made it possible for Puritans to grab land controlled and cultivated by the Native Americans, prompting one violent conflict after another.

The colonists expanded their territory at a rapid rate, and Native Americans resisted as they could, using formal petitions of protest, guerilla warfare, alliances with European nations in their struggles with one another, and peace treaties. The Abenaki, a tribe of Native Americans in what we now know as Maine, were especially adept at guerilla warfare against the English settlers, destroying trading posts and burning down their houses and forts. The English retaliated with force, capturing and enslaving Native Americans and even killing those who approached seeking peace. In 1728 the brutal hostilities ceased for the most part when the provincial government of New York—which had Maine within its legal jurisdiction—signed the Treaty of Casco. The treaty gave the Abenaki sovereignty over the disputed territory but also mandated that the Abenaki recognize English property rights within the territory.

Treaties between Native Americans and the English were especially problematic for Native Americans. Duplicitous English negotiators sometimes took advantage of their lack of mastery over the English language by drafting treaties that did not accurately reflect the substance of actual negotiations and agreements. Loron Sauguaarum, an Abenaki leader at the negotiations for the Casco Treaty, was well aware of the dangers of mistranslation, and in the document below he carefully explains his understanding of the terms of the treaty. Doing so, he emphasizes that his tribe's resistance to English royal powers remains resolute.

I, Panaouamskeyen, do inform ye—ye who are scattered all over the earth take notice—of what has passed between me and the English in negotiating the peace that I have just concluded with them. It is from the bottom of my heart that I inform you; and, as proof that I tell you nothing but the truth, I wish to speak to you in my own tongue.

My reason for informing you, myself, is the diversity and contrariety of the interpretations I receive of the English writing in which the articles of peace are drawn up that we have just mutually agreed to. These writings appear to contain things that are not, so that the Englishman himself disavows them in my presence when he reads and interprets them to me himself.

I begin by informing you; and shall speak to you only of the principal and most important matter.

First, that I did not commence the negotiation for a peace, or settlement, but he, it was, who first spoke to me on the subject, and I did not give him any answer until he addressed me a third time. I first went to Fort St. George to hear his propositions, and afterwards to Boston, whither he invited me on the same business.

We were two that went to Boston: I, Laurance Sagouarrab, and John Ehennekouit. On arriving there I did indeed salute him in the usual mode at the first interview, but I was not the first to speak to him. I only answered what he said to me, and such was the course I observed throughout the whole of our interview.

He began by asking me, what brought me hither? I did not give him for answer—I am come to ask your pardon; nor, I come to acknowledge you as my conqueror; nor, I come to make my submission to you; nor, I come to receive your commands. All the answer I made was that I was come on his invitation to me to hear the propositions for a settlement that he wished to submit to me.

Wherefore do we kill one another? he again asked me. 'Tis true that, in reply, I said to him—You are right. But I did not say to him, I acknowledge myself the cause of it, nor I condemn myself for having made war on him.

He said next to me—Propose what must be done to make us friends. 'Tis true that thereupon I answered him—It is rather for you to do that. And my reason for giving him that answer is that having himself spoken to me of an arrangement I did not doubt but he would make me some advantageous proposals. But I did not tell him that I would submit in every respect to his orders.

Thereupon he said to me—Let us observe the treaties concluded by our Fathers, and renew the ancient friendship that existed between us. I made him no answer thereunto; much less, I repeat, did I become his subject, or give him my land, or acknowledge his King as my King. This I never did, and he never proposed it to me. I say, he never said to me—Give thyself and thy land to me, nor acknowledge my King for thy King, as thy ancestors formerly did.

He again said to me—But do you not recognize the King of England as King over all his states? To which I answered—Yes, I recognize him King of all his lands; but I rejoined, do not hence infer that I acknowledge thy King as my King, and King of my lands. Here lies my distinction—my Indian distinction. God hath willed that I have no King, and that I be master of my lands in common.

He again asked me—Do you not admit that I am at least master of the lands I have purchased? I answered him thereupon that I admit nothing, and that I knew not what he had reference to.

He again said to me—If, hereafter, any one desire to disturb the negotiation of the peace we are at present engaged about, we will join together to arrest him. I again consented to that. But I did not say to him, and do not understand that he said to me, that we should go in company to attack such person, or that we should form a joint league, offensive and defensive, or that I should unite my Brethren to his. I said to him only, and I understand him to say to me, that if any one wished to disturb our negotiation of peace, we would both endeavor to pacify him by fair words, and to that end would direct all our efforts.

He again said to me—In order that the peace we would negotiate be permanent, should any private quarrel arise hereafter between Indians and Englishmen, they must not take justice into their own hands, nor do anything, the one to the other. It shall be the business of us chiefs to decide. I again agreed with him on that article, but I did not understand that he alone should be judge. I understood only that he should judge his people, and that I would judge mine.

Finally he said to me—There's our peace concluded; we have regulated everything.

I replied that nothing had been yet concluded, and that it was necessary that our acts should be approved in a general assembly. For the present, an armistice is sufficient. I again said to him—I now go to inform all my relatives of what has passed between us, and will afterwards come and report to you what they'll say to me. Then he agreed in opinion with me.

Such was my negotiation on my first visit to Boston.

As for any act of grace, or amnesty, accorded to me by the Englishman, on the part of his King, it is what I have no knowledge of, and what the Englishman never spoke to me about, and what I never asked him for.

On my second visit to Boston we were four: I, Laurence Sagourrab, Alexis, Francois Xavier and Migounambe. I went there merely to tell the English that all my nation approved the cessation of hostilities, and the negotiation of peace, and even then we agreed on the time and place of meeting to discuss it. That place was Caskebay, and the time after Corpus Christ.

Two conferences were held at Caskebay. Nothing was done at these two conferences except to read the articles above reported. Everything I agreed to was approved and ratified, and on these conditions was the peace concluded. One point only did I regulate at Caskebay. This was to permit the Englishman to keep a store at St. Georges; but a store only, and not to build any other house, nor erect a fort there, and I did not give him the land.

These are the principled matters that I wished to communicate to you who are spread all over the earth. What I tell you now is the truth. If, then, anyone should produce any writing that makes me speak otherwise, pay no attention to it, for I know not what I am made to say in another language, but I know well what I say in my own. And in testimony that I say things as they are, I have signed the present minute which I wish to be authentic and to remain forever.

The People Are the Proper Judge (1750)

Jonathan Mayhew

Another root of resistance in U.S. history can be found with the colonists who resisted the English crown. One of the most important resisters was Jonathan Mayhew, a Congregational minister who served Boston's West Congregational Church from 1747 to 1766. Mayhew was a theological and political recalcitrant. Theologically, he opposed the fundamental tenets of fashionable Calvinism, including its belief in the Trinity, the divinity of Jesus, and the depravity of humanity. Politically, he dismissed the doctrine of the divine right of kings and the accompanying belief that political subjects must always be subordinate to their rulers. The rebellious colonists, no fans of English royalty, found an intellectual leader in the radical Mayhew, and his sermons fueled the revolutionary flames in Boston and surrounding areas. The document below, originally titled "Discourse Concerning Unlimited Submission and Nonresistance to the Higher Powers," carefully lays out Mayhew's theological and political justification for resisting the throne.

Rulers have no authority from God to do mischief. . . . It is blasphemy to call tyrants and oppressors God's ministers. They are more properly "the messengers of Satan to buffet us." No rulers are properly God's ministers but such as are "just, ruling in the fear of God." When once magistrates act contrary to their office and the end of their institution—when they rob and ruin the public, instead of being guardians of its peace and welfare—they immediately cease to be the ordinance and ministers of God, and no more deserve that glorious character than common pirates and highwaymen. So that, whenever that argument for submission fails which is grounded upon the usefulness of magistracy to civil society—as it always does when magistrates do hurt to society instead of good—the other argument, which is taken from their being the ordinance of God, must necessarily fail also; no person of a civil character being God's minister, in the sense of the apostle, any further than he performs God's will by exercising a just and reasonable authority, and ruling for the good of the subject.

If magistrates are unrighteous—if they are respecters of persons—if they are partial in their administration of justice—then those who do well have as much reason to be afraid as those that do evil: there can be no safety for the good, nor any peculiar ground of terror to the unruly and injurious; so that, in this case, the main end of civil government will be frustrated. And what reason is there for submitting to that government which does by no means answer the design of government? . . .

I now add, further, that the apostle's argument is so far from proving it to be the duty of people to obey and submit to such rulers as act in contradiction to the public good, and so to the design of their office, that it proves the direct contrary. For, please to observe, that if the end of all civil government be the good of society; if this be the thing that is aimed at in constituting civil rulers; and if the motive and argument for submission to government be taken from the apparent usefulness of civil authority—it follows that when no such good end can be answered by submission, there remains no argument or motive to enforce it; and if, instead of this good end's being brought about by submission, a contrary end is brought about, and the ruin and misery of society effected by it, here is a plain and positive reason against submission in all such cases, should they ever happen. And therefore, in such cases, a regard to the public welfare ought to make us withhold from our rulers that obedience and submission which it would otherwise be our duty to render to them. If it be our duty, for example, to obey our king merely for this reason, that he rules for the public welfare (which is the only argument the apostle makes use of), it follows, by a parity of reason, that when he turns tyrant, and makes his subjects his prey to devour and destroy, instead of his charge to defend and cherish, we are bound to throw off our allegiance to him, and to resist; and that according to the tenor of the apostle's argument in this passage. Not to discontinue our allegiance in this case would be to join with the sovereign in promoting the slavery and misery of that society, the welfare of which we ourselves, as well as our sovereign, are indispensably obliged to secure and promote, as far as in us lies. . . .

We may very safely assert these two things in general, without undermining government: One is that no civil rulers are to be obeyed when they enjoin things that are inconsistent with the commands of God. All such disobedience is lawful and glorious; particularly if persons refuse to comply with any *legal establishment of religion,* because it is a gross perversion and corruption—as to doctrine, worship, and discipline—of a pure and divine religion, brought from heaven to earth by the Son of God—the only King and Head of the Christian church—and propagated through the world by his inspired apostles. All commands running counter to the declared will of the Supreme Legislator of heaven and earth are null and void, and therefore disobedience to them is a duty, not a crime. Another thing that may be asserted with equal truth and safety is that no government is to be submitted to at the expense of that which is the sole end of all government—the common good and safety of society. Because to submit in this case, if it should ever happen, would evidently be to set up the means as more valuable and above the end, than which there cannot be a greater solecism and contradiction. The only reason of the institution of civil government, and the only rational ground of submission to it, is the common safety and utility.

Tea Overboard (1773, 1834)

George Hewes

One of the most successful acts of nonviolent resistance carried out by col-onists occurred on December 16, 1773. About two weeks earlier, activists had blanketed Boston with a handbill that read: "Friends! Brethren! Countrymen!—That worst of plagues, the detested tea, shipped for this port by the East India Company, is now arrived in the harbor; the hour of destruction, or manly opposition to the machinations of tyranny, stares you in the face. Every friend to his country, to himself and to posterity, is now called upon to meet at Faneuil Hall, at nine o'clock THIS DAY (at which time the bells will ring), to make united and successful resistance to this last, worst, and most destructive measure of administration."

The citizens who gathered, tired of taxes and the East India Company's monopoly on the tea trade, agreed that they would not allow the tea from three separate ships to be unloaded. As the tea sat on ships moored at Griffin's Wharf, the colonists strategized about their next steps. On December 16 a large crowd gathered at the Old South Meeting House for another public meeting. After learning that the governor would not authorize the ships to return to England before the tea was unloaded, Samuel Adams stood before the colonists and said: "This meeting can do no more to save the country." Someone in the galley let out a war cry, while another shouted, "Boston harbor a teapot tonight!"

A crowd took off for Griffin's Wharf, and sixty men, some of them disguised as Native Americans, including George Hewes, whose account of the event is below, boarded the ships and spent the next three hours dumping 342 chests of tea into the water. It was a quiet act of protest. The crowd was orderly, hushed, and most of all, inspired by the nonviolent act of protest. The Revolution had begun.

The tea destroyed was contained in three ships, lying near each other at what was called at that time Griffin's wharf, and were surrounded by armed ships of war, the commanders of which had publicly declared that if the rebels, as they were pleased to style the Bostonians, should not withdraw their opposition to the landing of the tea before a certain day, the 17th day of December, 1773, they should on that day force it on shore, under the cover of their cannon's mouth.

On the day preceding the seventeenth, there was a meeting of the citizens of the county of Suffolk, convened at one of the churches in Boston, for the purpose of consulting on what measures might be considered expedient to prevent the landing of the tea, or secure the people from the collection of the duty. At that meeting a committee was appointed to wait on Governor Hutchinson, and request him to inform them whether he would take any measures to satisfy the people on the object of the meeting.

To the first application of this committee, the Governor told them he would give them a definite answer by five o'clock in the afternoon. At the hour appointed, the committee again repaired to the Governor's house, and on inquiry found he had gone to his country seat at Milton, a distance of about six miles. When the committee returned and informed the meeting of the absence of the Governor, there was a confused murmur among the members, and the meeting was immediately dissolved, many of them crying out, "Let every man do his duty, and be true to his country"; and there was a general huzza for Griffins wharf.

It was now evening, and I immediately dressed myself in the costume of an Indian, equipped with a small hatchet, which I and my associates denominated the tomahawk, with which, and a club. After having painted my face and hands with coal dust in the shop of a blacksmith, I repaired to Griffin's wharf, where the ships lay that contained the tea. When I first appeared in the street after being thus disguised, I fell in with many who were dressed, equipped and painted as I was, and who fell in with me and marched in order to the place of our destination.

When we arrived at the wharf, there were three of our number who assumed an authority to direct our operations, to which we readily submitted. They divided us into three parties, for the purpose of boarding the three ships which contained the tea at the same time. The name of

The Boston Tea Party, 1773

him who commanded the division to which I was assigned was Leonard Pitt. The names of the other commanders I never knew.

We were immediately ordered by the respective commanders to board all the ships at the same time, which we promptly obeyed. The commander of the division to which I belonged, as soon as we were on board the ship, appointed me boatswain, and ordered me to go to the captain and demand of him the keys to the hatches and a dozen candles. I made the demand accordingly, and the captain promptly replied, and delivered the articles; but requested me at the same time to do no damage to the ship or rigging.

We then were ordered by our commander to open the hatches and take out all the chests of tea and throw them overboard, and we immediately proceeded to execute his orders, first cutting and splitting the chests with our tomahawks, so as thoroughly to expose them to the effects of the water.

In about three hours from the time we went on board, we had thus broken and thrown overboard every tea chest to be found in the ship, while those in the other ships were disposing of the tea in the same way, at the same time. We were surrounded by British armed ships, but no attempt was made to resist us.

We then quietly retired to our several places of residence, without having any conversation with each other, or taking any measures to discover who were our associates; nor do I recollect of our having had the knowledge of the name of a single individual concerned in that affair, except that of Leonard Pitt, the commander of my division, whom I have mentioned. There appeared to be an understanding that each individual should volunteer his services, keep his own secret, and risk the consequence for himself. No disorder took place during that transaction, and it was observed at that time that the stillest night ensued that Boston had enjoyed for many months.

During the time we were throwing the tea overboard, there were several attempts made by some of the citizens of Boston and its vicinity to carry off small quantities of it for their family use. To effect that object, they would watch their opportunity to snatch up a handful from the deck, where it became plentifully scattered, and put it into their pockets.

One Captain O'Connor, whom I well knew, came on board for that purpose, and when he supposed he was not noticed, filled his pockets, and also the lining of his coat. But I had detected him and gave information to the captain of what he was doing. We were ordered to take him into custody, and just as he was stepping from the vessel, I seized him by the skirt of his coat, and in attempting to pull him back, I tore it off; but, springing forward, by a rapid effort he made his escape. He had, however, to run a gauntlet through the crowd upon the wharf nine each one, as he passed, giving him a kick or a stroke.

Another attempt was made to save a little tea from the ruins of the cargo by a tall, aged man who wore a large cocked hat and white wig, which was fashionable at that time. He had slightly slipped a little into his pocket, but being detected, they seized him and, taking his hat and wig from his head, threw them, together with the tea, of which they had emptied his pockets, into the water. In consideration of his advanced age, he was permitted to escape, with now and then a slight kick.

The next morning, after we had cleared the ships of the tea, it was discovered that very considerable quantities of it were floating upon the surface of the water; and to prevent the possibility of any of its being saved for use, a number of small boats were manned by sailors and citizens, who rowed them into those parts of the harbor wherever the tea was visible, and by beating it with oars and paddles so thoroughly drenched it as to render its entire destruction inevitable.

Unjustly Taxed (1774)

Isaac Backus

Isaac Backus, an early Baptist resister, came from a family of dissidents in Connecticut. His grandfather was expelled from the Connecticut legislature for opposing the Saybrook Platform, which mandated a centralized ecclesiastical structure to enforce orthodox Puritanism among Congregationalists, and his mother cut ties with their home church because of its support for this legal ruling. Reared by resisters, Backus joined the emerging Separatist movement and was ordained a minister in April 1748. In this role, he challenged tax laws that provided state funds for Congregational parishes and even refused to pay his own taxes, an act of civil disobedience that landed him in jail for a short period of time.

Encouraged by his wife Susanna, Backus also questioned and then renounced his long-held belief in infant baptism. As a new Baptist minister, he then founded the First Baptist Church of Middleborough, Massachusetts, in 1756, and continued his work of agitation against state laws that established and funded Congregationalism. Backus was so energetic about his cause that he sought to build a religious movement of dissent, and in 1773 he penned an influential pamphlet, An Appeal to the Public for Religious Liberty, in which he argued for civil disobedience against the tax laws pertaining to the establishment of Congregationalism. Acts of civil disobedience, Backus believed, would properly show that church and state should be separate, and that civil rulers have no right to impose religious taxes.

Backus did not convince the Massachusetts legislature of the need for church-state separation in 1773, but he did continue to lobby civil authorities on the issue. For example, in his 1774 letter to Samuel Adams (see below), Backus argues his case by drawing parallels between his religious campaign and Adams's political campaign.

Honored Sir:

As you have long exerted yourself and improved your liberties with great applause for civil liberty, I beg leave, though a stranger to your person, to address you upon the cause of religious freedom. I fully confirm with your grand maxim—That it is essential to liberty that representation and taxation go together. Well then, since people do not vote for representatives in our legislature, from ecclesiastical qualifications, but only by virtue of those which are of a civil and worldly nature, how can representatives thus chosen have any right to impose ecclesiastical taxes? Yet they have assumed and long exercised such a power. For they assumed a power to compel each town and parish in the Province to settle a minister, and have empowered the majority of the inhabitants to give away as much of their neighbors' estates as they please to their minister; and if they refuse to yield it to them, then to take it by force. And I am bold in it that taxes laid by the British Parliament upon America are not more contrary to civil freedom than these taxes are to the very nature of liberty of conscience, which is an essential article in our charter. For certainly the discharge of a good conscience towards God as much concerns the support of his worship as it does the attendance upon it, though modern nations would confine it to the latter. Yea, many take away our money to support a way contrary to our consciences; and after they have got it, reflect upon us for not supporting our own way better. And though many pretend that the case is not as I have now represented, because acts from time to time have been made to exempt our denomination and others, from taxes to the established worship; yet if we examine we shall find that this exemption is just like the proceedings of the power at home in taking off some of the taxes which they had laid upon this country, which they still claim the power to tax us as they please. Two thousand dollars will not make good the damages that the Baptists in this province have sustained within these ten years by being taxed to the other party and by suing for their rights before judges and jurors who were of that party. And now for no other crime than refusing last year to yield any further obedience to that taxing law, which is unjustly called an act to exempt our denomination from taxes, a number of people who have been my steady hearers for twenty years are, by Judge Oliver's direction, taxed to his minister. Our reasons for the above refusal I here send you in print. And as the act aforesaid is now out of date, I hope, sir, that you will give proof both to the court and to the world that you regard the religious as well as the civil rights of your countrymen; that so a large number of as peaceable people and as hearty friends to their country as any in the land may not be forced to carry their complaints before those who would be glad to hear that the Legislature of Massachusetts deny to their fellow servants that liberty which they so earnestly insist upon for themselves. A word to the wise is sufficient.

No Money for the Revolutionary War (1776, 1797)

Job Scott

Job Scott was a highly educated minister who devoted his life to advancing education for the growing population of Quakers. Born in 1751, he taught in a Quaker school before founding the New England Friends' Yearly Meeting Boarding School in Providence. Scott was a controversial figure among Quakers of his generation because his writings resisted Quaker orthodoxy, and he was also looked upon as a radical by the governing authorities of Providence when he refused to pay taxes to support the popular Revolutionary War. Below is his written account of that resistance, published by the Quakers of Providence in 1797, four years after his untimely death during a trip to Ireland.

Much close exercise of mind I had for a considerable length of time, on account of some particular scruples, which from time to time revived with weight, and so pressingly accompanied me, that I could not get rid of them. It being a time of war, and preparations for war between Great Britain and America, and the rulers of America having made a paper currency professedly for the special purpose of promoting or maintaining the war, and it being expected that Friends would be tried by requisitions for taxes, principally for the support of war, I was greatly exercised in spirit, both on the account of taking and passing that money, and in regard to the payment of such taxes, neither of which felt easy to my mind. I believed a time would come when Christians would not so far contribute to the encouragement and support of war and fighting as voluntarily to pay taxes that were mainly, or even in considerable proportion, for defraying the expenses thereof; and it was also impressed upon my mind that if I took and passed money that I knew was made on purpose to uphold war, I should bear a testimony against war that for me, as an individual, would be a faithful one. I knew the people's minds were in a rage against such as, from any motive whatever, said or acted anything tending to discountenance the war. I was sensible that refusing to pay the taxes, or to take the currency, would immediately be construed as a pointed opposition to the present war in particular, even as our refusing to bear arms was, notwithstanding our long and well-known testimony against it. I had abundant reason to expect great censure and some suffering in consequence of my faithfulness, if I should stand faithful in these things, though I knew that my scruples were unconnected with any party considerations, and uninfluenced by any motives but such as respect the propriety of a truly Christian conduct in regard to war at large. I had no desire to promote the opposition to Great Britain; neither had I any desire on the other hand to promote the measures or success of Great Britain. I believed it my business not to meddle with anything from such views; but to let the potsherds of the earth alone in their smiting one against another; but I wished to be clear in the sight of God, and to do all that he might require of me towards the more full introduction and coming of his peaceable kingdom and government on earth. . . .

About the latter end of the sixth month this year [1776], an old acquaintance of mine, being now collector of rates, came and demanded one of me. I asked him what it was for. He said, to sink the paper money. I told him as that money was made expressly for the purpose of carrying on war, I had refused to take it and for the same reason could not pay a tax to sink it, believing it my duty to bear testimony against war and fighting. I informed him that for diverse years past, even diverse years before the war began, and when I had no expectation of being tried in this way, it had been a settled belief with me that it was not right to pay such taxes; at least not right for me, in my apprehension, right in itself, though many sincere brethren may not at present see its repugnancy to the pure and peaceable spirit of the gospel. I let him know I did not wish to put him to any trouble, but would be glad to pay it if I could consistently with my persuasion. He appeared moderate, thoughtful, and rather tender, and after a time of free and pretty full conversation upon the subject, went away in a pleasant disposition of mind, I being truly glad to see him so. Diverse such demands were made of me in those troublesome times for diverse years: I ever found it best to be very calm and candid, and to open, as I was from time to time enabled, the genuine grounds of my refusal; and that if possible, so far as to reach the understandings of those who made the demand.

TWO

The Abolitionist Movement and the Struggle for the Rights of Free African Americans

They Do Not Consider Us as Men (1813)

James Forten

James Forten, a free black man who lived in Philadelphia and earned considerable wealth as an investor and as the owner of a sail-making business, frequently petitioned governing authorities for the abolition of slavery and the better treatment of free African Americans. In 1788 he and others petitioned the U.S. Congress to end the slave trade and undertake measures to protect free African Americans from abduction and enslavement. Congress denied the petition, but Massachusetts Representative George Thatcher spoke in favor of it, earning a letter of gratitude from Forten.

In 1813, when Pennsylvania state senators proposed a bill that would have restricted the rights of free black citizens, Forten penned and published fierce letters of protest, one of which is excerpted below. The senators were not successful in their efforts to pass the bill, and Forten continued his fight. In 1816, when pro-slavery whites were promoting African colonization for free black citizens, largely because they feared that their freedom served as inspiration to slaves to liberate themselves, Forten became an ardent

*opponent of colonization. And in the 1830s he joined forces with white ab-
olitionists, especially William Lloyd Garrison, and provided funds for Garrison to publish his groundbreaking abolitionist newspaper, the Liberator.*

Those patriotic citizens, who, after resting from the toils of an arduous war, which achieved our independence and laid the foundation of the only reasonable Republic upon earth, associated together, and for the protection of those inestimable rights for the establishment of which they had exhausted their blood and treasure, framed the Constitution of Pennsylvania, have by the ninth article declared that "All men are born equally free and independent, and have certain inherent and indefeasible rights, among which are those of enjoying life and liberty." Under the restraint of wise and well-administered laws, we cordially unite in the above glorious sentiment, but by the bill upon which we have been remarking, it appears as if the committee who drew it up mistook the sentiment expressed in this article, and do not consider us as men, or that those enlightened statesmen who formed the constitution upon the basis of experience intended to exclude us from its blessings and protection. If the former, why are we not to be considered as men? Has the God who made the white man and the black left any record declaring us a different species? Are we not sustained by the same power, supported by the same food, hurt by the same wounds, pleased with the same delights, and propagated by the same means? And should we not then enjoy the same liberty, and be protected by the same laws? We would wish not to legislate, for our means of information and the acquisition of knowledge are, in the nature of things, so circumscribed that we must consider ourselves incompetent to the task: but let us, in legislation, be considered men. It cannot be that the authors of our Constitution intended to exclude us from its benefits, for just emerging from unjust and cruel emancipation, their souls were too much affected with their own deprivations to commence the reign of terror over others. They know we were deeper skinned than they were, but they acknowledged us as men and found that many an honest heart beat beneath a dusky bosom.

They felt that they had no more authority to enslave us than England had to tyrannize over them. They were convinced that if amenable to the same laws in our actions, we should be protected by the same laws in our rights and privileges. Actuated by these sentiments they adopted the glorious fabric of our liberties, and declaring "all men" free, they did not particularize white and black, because they never supposed it would be made a question whether we were men or not. . . .

Ye, who should be our protectors, do not destroy. We will cheerfully submit to the laws and aid in bringing offenders against them of every color to justice; but do not let the laws operate so severely, so degradingly, so unjustly against us alone.

Women Overthrowing Slavery (1836)

Angelina Grimke

Angelina Grimke grew up on a wealthy plantation in Charleston, South Carolina, in the early 1800s. She and her older sister Sarah were so horrified by the conditions and treatment of slaves at home and throughout the South that they carried out personal acts of resistance. Sarah taught her own slave to read, which was an act of civil disobedience, and Angelina, thirteen years younger, refused confirmation in the Episcopal church because of its unwavering support for slavery.

Unsettled by slavery, Sarah moved to Philadelphia in 1820, leaving behind the wealth and stability offered by her family's plantation. Angelina gave up the same privileged life when she left to be with Sarah in 1829. Although the sisters became abolitionist Quakers, Angelina desired a more radical approach to slavery than what the Quakers were offering, and in 1835 she wrote a letter to William Lloyd Garrison, the publisher of the Liberator, in which she praised his nonviolent resolve in the face of pro-slavery riots in Boston. Emancipation, Sarah wrote, "is a cause worth dying for."

Publication of her letter in the Liberator took Angelina by surprise—Garrison had not sought her permission—but she stood her ground when friends expressed concern about her association with someone as radical as the Boston publisher. Rather than backing down, Grimke turned her attention to writing Appeal to the Christian Women of the South. The 1836 pamphlet, excerpted below, is remarkable for its demand that women practice civil disobedience in order to overthrow the institution of slavery.

Respected Friends,

It is because I feel a deep and tender interest in your personal and eternal welfare that I am willing thus publicly to address you. . . .

It will be, and that very soon, clearly perceived and fully acknowledged by all the virtuous and the candid that *in principle* it is as sinful to hold a human being in bondage who has been born in Carolina as one who has been born in Africa. All that sophistry of argument which has been employed to prove that although it is sinful to send to Africa to procure men and women as slaves, who have never been in slavery, that still it is not sinful to keep those in bondage who have come down by inheritance, will be utterly overthrown. We must come back to the good old doctrine of our forefathers who declared to the world "this self-evident truth that *all* men are created equal, and that they have certain *inalienable* rights, among which are life, *liberty,* and the pursuit of happiness." It is even greater absurdity to suppose a man can be legally born a slave under our *free Republican* government than under the petty despotisms of barbarian Africa. If, then, we have no right to enslave an African, surely we can have none to enslave an American; if a self-evident truth that *all* men everywhere and of every color are born equal, and have an *inalienable right to liberty,* then it is equally true that *no* man can be born a slave, and no man can ever *rightfully* be reduced to *involuntary* bondage and held as a slave, however fair may be the claim of his master or mistress through wills and title-deeds. . . .

But perhaps you will be ready to query, why appeal to *women* on this subject? We do not make the laws which perpetuate slavery. No legislative power is vested in us; *we* can do nothing to overthrow the system, even if we wished to do so. To this I reply, I know you do not make the laws, but I also know that you *are the wives and mothers, the sisters and daughters of those who do;* and if you really suppose you can do nothing to overthrow slavery, you are greatly mistaken.

Speak on this subject. It is through the tongue, the pen, and the press that truth is principally propagated. Speak then to your relatives, your friends, your acquaintances on the subject of slavery; be not afraid if you are consciously convinced if it is *sinful,* to say so openly, but calmly, and to let your sentiments be known. If you are served by the slaves of others, try to ameliorate their condition as much as possible; never aggravate their faults, and thus add fuel to the fire of anger already kindled, in a master and mistress's bosom; remember their extreme ignorance, and consider them as your Heavenly Father does the less culpable on this account, even when they do wrong things. Discountenance all cruelty to them, all starvation, all corporal chastisement; these may brutalize and break their spirits, but will never bend them to willing, cheerful obedience. If possible, see that they are comfortably and seasonably fed, whether in the house or the field; it is unreasonable and cruel to expect slaves to wait for their breakfast until eleven o'clock, when they rise at five or six. Do all you can to induce their owners to clothe them well, and to allow them many little indulgences which would contribute to their comfort. Above all, try to persuade your husband, father, brothers, and sons that slavery is a crime against God and man, and that it is a great sin to keep human beings in such abject ignorance; to deny them the privilege of learning to read and write. The Catholics are universally condemned for denying the Bible to the common people, but slaveholders must not blame them, for they are doing the same thing, and for the very same reason; neither of these systems can bear the light which bursts from the pages of that Holy Book. And lastly, endeavor to inculcate submission on the part of the slaves, but whilst doing this be faithful in pleading the cause of the oppressed. . . .

Act on this subject. Some of you own slaves yourselves. If you believe slavery is sinful, set them at liberty, "undo the heavy burdens and let the oppressed go free." If they wish to remain with you, pay them wages; if not let them leave you. Should they remain, teach them and have them taught the common branches of an English education; they have minds and those minds ought to be improved. So precious a talent as intellect never was given to be wrapped in a napkin and buried in the earth. It is the duty of all, as far as they can, to improve their own menial faculties, because we are commanded to love God with all our minds, as well as with all our hearts, and we commit a great sin if we forbid or prevent that cultivation of the mind in others, which would enable them to perform this duty. Teach your servants then to read &c, and encourage them to believe it is their duty to learn, if it were only that they might read the Bible.

But some of you will say, we can neither free our slaves nor teach them to read, for the laws of our state forbid it. Be not surprised when I say such wicked laws ought not to be barrier in the way of your duty, and I appeal to the Bible to prove this position. What was the conduct of Shiphrah and Puah when the king of Egypt issued his cruel mandate with regard to the Hebrew children? They feared God, and did not as the King of Egypt commanded them, but saved the men and children alive. Did these women do right in disobeying that monarch? "*Therefore* (says the sacred text) *God dealt well* with them, and made them houses" Ex 1. What was the conduct of Shadrach, Meschach, and Abednego, when Nebuchadnezzar set up a golden image in the plain of Dura, and commanded all people, nations, and languages to fall down and worship it? "Be it known unto thee (said these faithful *Jews*), O king, that we will not serve thy gods, nor worship the image which thou hast set up." Did these men do right in disobeying the law of their sovereign? Let their miraculous delivery from the burning fiery furnace answer, Dan. iii. What was the conduct of Daniel when Darius made a firm decree that no one should ask a petition of any man or God for thirty days? Did the prophet cease to pray? No! "When Daniel knew that the writing was signed, he went into his house, and his windows being opened towards Jerusalem, he kneeled upon his knees three times a day, and prayed and gave thanks before his God, as he did aforetime." Did Daniel do right thus to break the law of his king? Let his wonderful deliverance out of the mouths of the lions answer, Dan. vii. Look, too, at the Apostles Peter and John. When the rulers of the Jews "commanded them not to speak at all, nor teach in the name of Jesus," what did they say? "Whether it be right in the sight of God, to hearken unto you more than unto God, judge ye." And what did they do? "They spoke the word of God with boldness, and with great power gave the Apostles witness of the resurrection of the Lord Jesus"; although this was the very doctrine for the preaching of which they had just been cast into prison, and further threatened. Did these men do right? I leave you to answer, who now enjoy the benefits of their labors and sufferings, in that Gospel they dared to preach when positively commanded *not to teach any more* in the name of Jesus, Acts iv.

But some of you may say, if we do free our slaves, they will be taken up and sold, therefore there will be no use in doing it. Peter and John might just as well have said, we will not preach the gospel, for if we do, we shall be taken up and put in prison, therefore there will be no use in our preaching. *Consequences,* my friends, belong no more to you than they did to these apostles. Duty is ours and events are God's. If you think slavery is sinful, all you have to do is set your slaves at liberty, do all you can to protect them, and in humble faith and fervent prayer, commend them to your common Father. . . .

I know that this doctrine of obeying God rather than man will be considered as dangerous and heretical by many, but I am not afraid openly to avow it, because it is the doctrine of the Bible; but I would not be understood to advocate resistance to any law however oppressive if, in obeying it, I was not obligated to commit *sin*. If, for instance, there was a law which imposed imprisonment or a fine upon me *if* I manumitted a slave, I would on no account resist that law. I would set the slave free and then go to prison or pay the fine. *If* a law commands me to *sin I will break it; if* it calls me to *suffer, I* will let it take its course *unresistingly*. The doctrine of blind obedience and unqualified submission to *any human* power, whether civil or ecclesiastical, is the doctrine of despotism and ought to have no place among Republicans and Christians. . . .

But you may say we are *women,* how can *our* hearts endure persecution? And why not? Have not *women* stood up in all the dignity and strength of moral courage to be the leaders of the people, and to bear a faithful testimony for the truth whenever the providence of God has called them to do so? Are there no *women* in that noble army of martyrs who are now singing the song of Moses and the Lamb? Who led out the women of Israel from the house of bondage, striking the timbrel and singing the song of deliverance on the banks of that sea whose waters stood up like walls of crystal to open a passage for their escape. It was a *woman*: Miriam, the prophetess, the sister of Moses and Aaron. . . .

The *women of the South can overthrow* this horrible system of oppression and cruelty, licentiousness and wrong. Such appeals to your legislature would be irresistible, for there is something in the heart of man which *will bend under moral suasion.* There is a swift witness for truth in his bosom, which will *respond to truth* when it is uttered with calmness and dignity. If you could obtain but six signatures to such a petition in only one state, I would say, send up that petition and be not in the least discouraged by the scoffs and jeers of the heartless, or the resolution of the house to lay it on the table. . . . Slavery must be attacked with the whole power of truth and the sword of the spirit.

Escape on the Pearl (1848, 1855)

Daniel Drayton

On the night of April 15, 1848, seventy-seven slaves from Washington, DC—thirty-eight men, twenty-six women, and thirteen children—boarded a schooner named the Pearl with hopes of escaping to freedom. Some of the slaves came from Washington's elite families; one woman had fled from the home of Dolly Madison.

The escape plan was the brainchild of freedman Daniel Bell, who worried that his wife and children, all slaves, would be sold and taken away from him and separated from one another. Bell had tried to purchase their freedom but could not raise sufficient funds, so he pitched his idea to Daniel Drayton, a white sailor and trader known to have previously transported slaves to freedom. Drayton agreed to help, and on the night of April 15 the hull of the Pearl was filled not only with Bell and his family but also sixty-seven other anxious slaves.

The Pearl set out for Philadelphia just before daybreak but could only reach the mouth of the Potomac before a fierce storm forced Drayton to anchor around St. Mary's County in Maryland. Unknown to Drayton and the slaves was that a group of furious slave owners was on their trail, traveling by a steamer called the Salem. The owners had been tipped off by a former slave, Judson Diggs, who was angry that he had not been paid for driving some of the slaves to the Pearl.

On April 17 the Salem caught up with the Pearl, and the slave owners boarded and commandeered the schooner. The Pearl was towed back to Washington, and the slaves were jailed and then sold to owners in Maryland, Virginia, Louisiana, and Georgia. Drayton was tried, convicted, and imprisoned. Below is his account of the events surrounding the largest nonviolent mass attempt to escape from slavery in U.S. history.

I know it is sometimes said, by those who defend slavery or apologize for it, that the slaves of the South are very happy and contented, if left to themselves, and that this idea of running away is only put into their heads by mischievous white people from the North. This will do very well for those who know nothing of the matter personally, and who are anxious to listen to any excuse. But there is not a waterman who ever sailed in Chesapeake Bay who will not tell you that, so far from the slaves needing and prompting to run away, the difficulty is, when they ask you to assist them, to make them take no for an answer. I have known instances where men have lain in the woods for a year or two, waiting for an opportunity to escape on board some vessel. . . .

Shortly after dark the expected passengers began to arrive, coming stealthily across the fields, and gliding silently on board the vessel. I observed a man near a neighboring brick-kiln, who seemed to be watching them. I went towards him, and found him to be black. He told me that he understood what was going on, but that I need have no apprehension of him. Two white men, who walked along the road past the vessel, and who presently returned back the same way, occasioned me some alarm; but they seemed to have no suspicions of what was on foot, as I saw no more of them. I went on board the vessel several times in the course of the evening, and learned from English that the hold was fast filling up. I had promised him, in consideration of the unusual nature of the business we were engaged in, ten dollars as a gratuity, in addition to his wages.

Something past ten o'clock, I went on board, and directed English to cast off the fastenings and to get ready to make sail. . . . As the sun rose, we passed Alexandria. I then went into the hold for the first time, and there found my passengers pretty thickly stowed. I distributed bread among them, and knocked down the bulkhead between the hold and the cabin, in order that they might get into the cabin to cook. They consisted of men and women, in pretty equal proportions, with a number of boys and girls, and two small children. The wind kept increasing and hauling to the westward. Off Fort Washington we had to make two stretches, but the rest of the way we run before the wind. . . .

As we approached the mouth of the Potomac, the wind hauled to the north, and blew with such stiffness as would make it impossible for us to go up the bay, according to our original plan. Under these circumstances, apprehending a pursuit from Washington, I urged Sayres to go to sea, with the intention of reaching the Delaware by the outside passage. But he objected that the vessel was not fit to go outside (which was true enough), and that the bargain was to go to Frenchtown. Having reached Point Lookout, at the mouth of the river, and not being able to persuade Sayres to go to sea, and the wind being dead in our teeth, and too strong to allow any attempt to ascend the bay, we came to anchor in

Runaway slave traveling by river.

Cornfield Harbor, just under Point Lookout, a shelter usually sought by bay craft encountering contrary winds when in that neighborhood.

We were all sleepy with being up all the night before, and, soon after dropping anchor, we all turned in. I knew nothing more till, waking suddenly, I heard the noise of a steamer blowing off steam alongside of us. I knew at once that we were taken. The black men came to the cabin, and asked if they should fight. I told them no; we had no arms, nor was there the least possibility of a successful resistance. The loud shouts and trampling of many feet overhead proved that our assailants were numerous. One of them lifted the hatch a little, and cried out, "Niggers, by G—d!" an exclamation to which the others responded with three cheers, and by banging the butts of their muskets against the deck. A lantern was called for, to read the name of the vessel; and it being ascertained to be the Pearl, a number of men came to the cabin door, and called for Captain Drayton. I was in no great hurry to stir; but at length rose from my berth, saying that I considered myself their prisoner, and that I expected to be treated as such. While I was dressing, rather too slowly for the impatience of those outside, a sentinel, who had been stationed at the cabin door, followed every motion of mine with his gun, which he kept pointed at me, in great apprehension, apparently lest I should suddenly seize some dangerous weapon and make at him. As I came out of the cabin door, two of them seized me, took me on board the steamer and tied me; and they did the same with Sayres and English, who were brought on board, one after the other. The black people were left on board the Pearl, which the steamer took in tow, and then proceeded up the river.

To explain this sudden change in our situation, it is necessary to go back to Washington. Great was the consternation in several families of that city, on Sunday morning, to find no breakfast, and, what was worse, their servants missing. Nor was this disaster confined to Washington only. Georgetown came in for a considerable share of it, and even Alexandria, on the opposite side of the river, had not entirely escaped. The persons who had taken passage on board the Pearl had been held in bondage by no less than forty-one different persons. Great was the wonder at the sudden and simultaneous disappearance of so many "prime hands," roughly estimated, though probably with considerable exaggeration, as worth in the market not less than a hundred thousand dollars—and all at "one fell swoop" too, as the District Attorney afterwards, in arguing the case against me, pathetically expressed it! There were a great many guesses and conjectures as to where these people had gone, and how they had gone; but it is very doubtful whether the losers would have got upon the right track, had it not been for the treachery of a colored hackman, who had been employed to carry down to the vessel two passengers who had been in hiding for some weeks previous. . . . He turned informer, and described the Pearl as the conveyance which the fugitives had taken; and, it being ascertained that the Pearl had actually sailed between Saturday night and Sunday morning, preparations were soon made to pursue her. A Mr. Dodge, of Georgetown, a wealthy old gentleman, originally from New England, missed three or four slaves from his family, and a small steamboat, of which he was the proprietor, was readily obtained. Thirty-five men, including a son or two of old Dodge, and several of those whose slaves were missing, volunteered to man her; and they set out about Sunday noon, armed to the teeth with guns, pistols, bowie knives, &c., and well provided with brandy and other liquors. . . .

The bearing, manner, and aspect of the thirty-five armed persons by whom we had been thus seized and bound, without the slightest shadow of lawful authority, was sufficient to inspire a good deal of alarm. . . .

Some of them showed a good deal of excitement, and evinced a disposition to proceed to lynch us at once. A man named Houver, who claimed as his property two of the boy passengers on board the Pearl, put me some questions in a very insolent tone; to which I replied that I considered myself a prisoner, and did not wish to answer any questions; whereupon one of the bystanders, flourishing a dirk in my face, exclaimed, "If I was in his place, I'd put this through you!" At Piney Point, one of the company proposed to hang me up to the yard arm, and make me confess. . . .

What the particular provisions were, in the District of Columbia, as to helping slaves to escape, I did not know; but I had heard that, in some of the slave states, they were very severe; in fact, I was assured by Craig that I had committed the highest crime, next to murder, known in their laws. Under these circumstances, I made up my mind that the least penalty I should be apt to escape with was confinement in the penitentiary for life; and it is quite probable that I endeavored to console myself, as these witnesses testified, with the idea that, after all, it might, in a religious point of view, be all for the best, as I should thus be removed from temptation, and have ample time for reflection and repentance. But my apprehensions were by no means limited to what I might suffer under the forms of law. From the temper exhibited by some of my captors, and from the vindictive fury with which the idea of enabling the enslaved to regain their liberty was, I knew, generally regarded at the south, I apprehended more sudden and summary proceedings; and what happened afterwards at Washington proved that these apprehensions were not wholly unfounded. The idea of being torn in pieces by a furious mob was exceedingly disagreeable. Many men, who might not fear death, might yet not choose to meet it in that shape. I called to mind the apology of the Methodist minister, who, just after a declaration of his that he was not afraid to die, ran away from a furious bull that attacked him—"that, though not fearing death, he did not like to be torn in pieces by a mad bull." . . .

On arriving off Fort Washington, the steamer anchored for the night, as the captors preferred to make their triumphant entry into the city by daylight. . . . As we passed Alexandria, we were all ordered on deck, and exhibited to the mob collected on the wharves to get a sight of us, who signified their satisfaction by three cheers. When we landed at the steamboat wharf in Washington, which is a mile and more from Pennsylvania Avenue, and in a remote part of the city, but few people had yet assembled. We were marched up in a long procession, Sayres and myself being placed at the head of it, guarded by a man on each side; English following next, and then the Negroes. As we went along the mob began to increase; and, as we passed Gannon's slave pen, that slave trader, armed with a knife, rushed out, and, with horrid imprecations, made a pass at me, which was very near finding its way through my body. Instead of being arrested, as he ought to have been, this slave dealer was politely informed that I was in the hands of the law, to which he replied, "D—n the law!—I have three Negroes, and I will give them all for one thrust at this d—d scoundrel!" and he followed along, waiting his opportunity to repeat the blow. The crowd, by this time, was greatly increased. We met an immense mob of several thousand persons coming down Four-and-a-half street, with the avowed intention of carrying us up before the Capitol, and making an exhibition of us there. The noise and confusion was very great. It seemed as if the time for the lynching had come. When almost up to Pennsylvania Avenue, a rush was made upon us—" Lynch them! lynch them! the d—n villains!" and other such cries, resounded on all sides. Those who had us in charge were greatly alarmed; and, seeing no other way to keep us from the hands of the mob, they procured a hack, and put Sayres and myself into it. The hack drove to the jail, the mob continuing to follow, repeating their shouts and threats. Several thousand people surrounded the jail, filling up the enclosure about it.

Resistance to Civil Government (1849)

Henry David Thoreau

Henry David Thoreau devoted much of his life to resisting a variety of authorities. In 1837 he quit his job as a public school teacher in his hometown of Concord, Massachusetts, after refusing to abide by the requirement that he use corporal punishment when dealing with unruly children. As an independent thinker, he declined membership in the local Congregationalist church and resisted paying Concord's church taxes. Devoted to simple living, he also spurned the work ethic of capitalism, as well as its material benefits. And when his hometown became an important stop along the Underground Railroad, he assisted slaves escaping to freedom in Canada.

When Thoreau refused to pay his poll tax in order to register his protest against slavery, Samuel Staples, Concord's tax collector and constable, jailed him for nonpayment. Thoreau publicly explained his resistance in a January 1848 lecture he titled "The Relation of the Individual to the State," and it is this lecture that later appeared in print as "Resistance to Civil Government," excerpts of which are below. Although it failed to receive considerable attention during his lifetime, the essay has become one of the most influential writings among nonviolent resisters in the United States and abroad. Mahatma Gandhi, the anti-Nazi movement, Martin Luther King, Jr., anti-Vietnam War activists, and countless other resisters have cited Thoreau's essay as inspiring and instructive.

How does it become a man to behave toward this American government today? I answer that he cannot without disgrace be associated with it. I cannot for an instant recognize that political organization as *my* government which is the *slave's* government also.

All men recognize the right of revolution; that is, the right to refuse allegiance to, and to resist, the government when its tyranny or its inefficiency are great and unendurable. But almost all say that such is not the case now. But such was the case, they think, in the Revolution of '75. If one were to tell me that this was a bad government because it taxed certain foreign commodities brought through its ports, it is most probable that I should not make an ado about it, for I can do without them. All machines have their friction; and possibly this does enough good to counterbalance the evil. At any rate, it is a great evil to make a stir about it. But when the friction comes to have its machine, and oppression and robbery are organized, I say let us not have such a machine any longer. In other words, when a sixth of the population of a nation which has undertaken to be the refuge of liberty are slaves, and a whole country is unjustly overrun and conquered by a foreign army, and subject to military law, I think that it is not too soon for honest men to rebel and revolutionize. What makes this duty the more urgent is the fact that the country so overrun is not our own, but ours is the invading army. . . .

If the injustice is part of the necessary friction of the machine of government, let it go, let it go; perchance it will wear smooth—certainly the machine will wear it out. If the injustice has a spring, or a pulley, or a rope, or a crank, exclusively for itself, then perhaps you may consider whether the remedy will not be worse than the evil; but if it is of such a nature that it requires you to be the agent of injustice to another, then I say break the law. Let your life be a counter friction to stop the machine. What I have to do is to see, at any rate, that I do not lend myself to the wrong which I condemn. . . .

I do not hesitate to say that those who call themselves Abolitionists should at once effectually withdraw their support, both in person and property, from the government of Massachusetts, and not wait till they constitute a majority of one before they suffer the right to prevail through them. I think that it is enough if they have God on their side, without waiting for that other one. Moreover, any man more right than his neighbors constitutes a majority of one already. . . .

I know this well, that if one thousand, if one hundred, if ten men whom I could name—if ten *honest* men only—ay, if *one honest* man, in this State of Massachusetts, *ceasing to hold slaves,* were actually to withdraw from this co-partnership, and be locked up in the county jail therefore, it would be the abolition of slavery in America. For it matters not how small the beginning may seem to be; what is once well done is done forever. . . .

Under a government which imprisons any unjustly, the true place for a just man is also a prison. The proper place today, the only place which Massachusetts has provided for her freer and less desponding spirits, is in her prisons, to be put out and locked out of the State by her own act, as they have already put themselves out by their principles. It is there that the fugitive slave, and the Mexican prisoner on parole, and the Indian come to plead the wrongs of his race should find them; on that separate but more free and honorable ground, where the State places those who are not *with* her, but *against* her—the only house in a slave State in which a free man can abide with honor. . . . If the alternative is to keep all just men in prison, or give up a war and slavery, the State will not hesitate which to choose. If a thousand men were not to pay their tax bills this year, that would not be a violent and bloody measure, as it would be to pay them, and enable the State to commit violence and shed innocent blood. This is, in fact, the definition of a peaceable revolution, if any such is possible. If the tax gatherer, or any public officer, asks me, as one has done, "But what shall I do?" my answer is, "If you really wish to do anything, resign your office." When the subject has refused allegiance, and the officer has resigned his office, then the revolution is accomplished. But even suppose blood should flow. Is there not a sort of blood shed when the conscience is wounded? . . .

When I converse with the freest of my neighbors, I perceive that whatever they may say about the magnitude and seriousness of the question and their regard for the public tranquility, the long and the short of the matter is that they cannot spare the protection of the existing government, and they dread the consequences to their property and families of disobedience to it. For my part, I should not like to think that I ever rely on the protection of the State. But if I deny the authority of the State when it presents its tax bill, it will soon take and waste all my property, and so harass me and my children without end. . . . It costs me less in every sense to incur the penalty of disobedience to the State than it would be to obey. I should feel as if I were worth less in that case. . . .

I have never declined paying the highway tax, because I am as desirous of being a good neighbor as I am of being a bad subject; and as for supporting schools, I am doing my part to educate my fellow countrymen now. It is for no particular item in the tax bill that I refuse to pay it. I simply wish to refuse allegiance to the State, to withdraw and stand aloof from it effectually. I do not care to trace the course of my dollar, if I could, till it buys a man or a musket to shoot one with—the dollar is innocent—but I am concerned to trace the effects of my allegiance. In fact, I quietly declare war with the State, after my fashion, though I will still make what use and get what advantage of her I can, as is usual in such cases.

I Won't Obey It! (1850)

Jermain Wesley Loguen

Arguably the most significant nonviolent resistance to slavery was the Underground Railroad, a system of secret routes for those escaping slavery in the South and traveling, often at night, to Mexico, Cuba, Canada, and free points in the United States. Run by African American and white abolitionists, the railroad was most active between around 1820 and 1861, although evidence of a secret system extends back to the late eighteenth century. The abolitionists sometimes used the language of railroad life to describe their roles and actions. "Conductors" escorted and guided slaves on the passage to freedom, secretly moving them from place to place, and "station masters" provided runaways with food, clothing, and "stations"—including homes and barns with hiding places, secret passageways, and tunnels.

Jermain Wesley Loguen, a fugitive slave and minister in the African Methodist Episcopal Zion Church, was a stationmaster along the section of the Underground Railroad that ran through Syracuse, New York. In his 1859 autobiography, A Stop on the Underground Railroad, Loguen wrote that he had helped more than 1,500 slaves escape to freedom.

Loguen also vigorously resisted the Fugitive Slave Law of 1850, which made it a crime for anyone to hide or assist fugitive slaves. Congress passed the act on September 18, and less than a month later the citizens of Syracuse, a hotbed of abolitionism, held a public discussion on the new law. Below is a copy of the speech that Loguen delivered to his fellow citizens. The public meeting responded to Loguen's plea for civil disobedience by voting overwhelmingly to make Syracuse a place of ongoing refuge for fugitive slaves.

I was a slave; I knew the dangers I was exposed to. I had made up my mind as to the course I was to take. On that score I needed no counsel, nor did the colored citizens generally. They had taken their stand—they would not be taken back to slavery. If to shoot down their assailants should forfeit their lives, such result was the least of the evil. They will have their liberties or die in their defense. What is life to me if I am to be a slave in Tennessee? My neighbors! I have lived with you many years, and you know me. My home is here, and my children were born here. I am bound to Syracuse by pecuniary interests, and social and family bonds. And do you think I can be taken away from you and from my wife and children, and be a slave in Tennessee? Have the President and his Secretary sent this enactment up here, to you, Mr. Chairman, to enforce on me in Syracuse?—and will you obey him? Did I think so meanly of you—did I suppose the people of Syracuse, strong as they are in numbers and love of liberty—or did I believe their love of liberty was so selfish, unmanly, and unchristian—did I believe them so sunken and servile and degraded as to remain at their homes and labors, or, with none of that spirit which smites a tyrant down, to surround a United States marshal to see me torn from my home and family, and hurled back to bondage—I say did I think so meanly of you, I could never come to live with you. Nor should I have stopped, on my return from Troy, twenty-four hours since, but to take my family and movables to a neighborhood which would take fire, and arms, too, to resist the least attempt to execute this diabolical law among them. Some kind and good friends advise me to quit my country, and stay in Canada, until this tempest is passed. I doubt not the sincerity of such counselors. But my conviction is strong, that their advice comes from a lack of knowledge of themselves and the case in hand. I believe that their own bosoms are charged to the brim with qualities that will smite to the earth the villains who may interfere to enslave any man in Syracuse. I apprehend the advice is suggested by the perturbation of the moment, and not by the tranquil spirit that rules above the storm, in the eternal home of truth and wisdom. Therefore I have hesitated to adopt this advice, at least until I have the opinion of this meeting. Those friends have not canvassed this subject. I have. They are called suddenly to look at it. I have looked at it steadily, calmly, resolutely, and at length defiantly, for a long time. I tell you the people of Syracuse and of the whole North must meet this tyranny and crush it by force, or be crushed by it. This hellish enactment has precipitated the conclusion that white men must live in dishonorable submission, and colored men be slaves, or they must give their physical and intellectual powers to the defense of human rights. The time has come to change the tones of submission into tones of defiance—and to tell Mr. Fillmore and Mr. Webster, if they propose to execute this measure upon us, to send on their bloodhounds. Mr. President, long ago I was beset by over-prudent and good men and women to purchase my freedom. Nay, I was frequently importuned to consent that they purchase it, and present it as evidence of their partiality to my person and character. Generous and kind as those friends were, my heart recoiled from the proposal. I owe my freedom to the God who made me, and who stirred me to claim it against all other beings in God's universe. I will not, nor will I consent, that anybody else shall countenance the claims of a vulgar despot to my soul and body. Were I in chains, and did these kind people come to buy me out of prison, I would acknowledge the boon with inexpressible thankfulness. But I feel no chains, and am in no prison. I received my freedom from heaven, and with it came the command to defend my title to it. I have long since resolved to do nothing and suffer nothing that can, in any way, imply that I am indebted to any power but the Almighty for my manhood and personality.

Slave hunters seizing fugitives.

Now, you are assembled here, the strength of this city is here to express their sense of this fugitive act, and to proclaim to the despots at Washington whether it shall be enforced here—whether you will permit the government to return me and other fugitives who have sought asylum among you, to the hell of slavery. The question is with you. If you will give us up, say so, and we will shake the dust from our feet and leave you. But we believe better things. We know you are taken by surprise. The immensity of this meeting testifies to the general consternation that has brought it together, necessarily, precipitately, to decide the most stirring question that can be presented, to wit, whether the government, having transgressed Constitutional and natural limits, you will bravely resist its aggressions, and tell its soulless agents that no slaveholder shall make your city and county a hunting field for slaves.

THE ROAD TO LIBERTY; A STATION ON THE UNDERGROUND RAILROAD.

An Underground Railroad rescue.

Whatever may be your decision, my ground is taken. I have declared it everywhere. It is known over the state and out of the state—over the line in the North, and over the line in the South. I don't respect this law—I don't fear it—I won't obey it! It outlaws me, and I outlaw it, and the men who attempt to enforce it on me. I place the governmental officials on the ground that they place me. I will not live a slave, and if force is used to reenslave me, I shall make preparations to meet the crisis as becomes a man. If you stand by me—and I believe you will do it, for your freedom and honor are involved as well as mine—it requires no microscope to see that—I say that if you will stand with us in resistance to this measure, you will be the saviors of your country. Your decision tonight in favor of resistance will give vent to the spirit of liberty, and it will break the bands of party, and shout for joy all over the North. Your example only is needed to be the type of popular action in Auburn, and Rochester, and Utica, and Buffalo, and all the West, and eventually in the Atlantic cities. Heaven knows that this act of noble daring will break out somewhere—and may God grant that Syracuse be the honored spot, whence it shall send an earthquake voice through the land!

What to the Slave Is the Fourth of July? (1852)

Frederick Douglass

While laboring as a slave in Baltimore during the mid- to late-1820s, Frederick Douglass practiced civil disobedience by teaching himself to read. It was a valuable skill that he thought other slaves should have, and in 1833, while working on Thomas Auld's Eastern Shore plantation, Douglass secretly started a school for slaves, a daring act that local whites crushed upon discovery. When Auld hired out his rebellious slave to a nearby farmer, Douglass began yet another school, and this time he and his students plotted an escape to Pennsylvania. After whites discovered and thwarted the bold plan, Auld hired out Douglass yet again, this time to a Baltimore shipyard, where Douglass planned yet another escape. This time he succeeded, in September 1838, by disguising himself as a sailor, carrying the papers of a freedman acquaintance, and boarding a train and then a steamboat to New York. Shortly after, he married Anna Murray, a free black woman, and the new couple moved to New Bedford, Massachusetts.

Although a fugitive slave at this point, Douglass was public in his resistance to slavery. When his speeches caught the attention of leading abolitionists, the Massachusetts Anti-Slavery Society hired him as a traveling speaker. In 1845, against the advice of friends fearful that he might be captured and returned to Maryland, Douglass published his autobiography, Narrative of the Life of Frederick Douglass, Written by Himself. It became a bestseller, and Douglass carried his fame to England, where he was showered with praise and enough money to purchase his own freedom and to begin his abolitionist newspaper, North Star.

The influential newspaper revealed a growing chasm between Douglass and his mentor and friend, the white abolitionist William Lloyd

Garrison, whose focus on persuasion as the best nonviolent method for abolitionists was insufficient for Douglass. Contrary to Garrison, Douglass turned his attention to political abolitionism—using political parties and their policies to attack slavery. Douglass also began to separate from Garrison's absolute nonviolence, and in 1850 he recommended that abolitionists disobey the Fugitive Slave Act by force if they must, and two years later he penned a novella depicting a violent slave insurrection in a positive light.

But Douglass remained personally nonviolent, even as his rhetoric was incendiary, as is evident in the text below—his July 4, 1852 speech on slaves and the Fourth of July, delivered to the citizens of Rochester, New York.

Fellow citizens, pardon me, allow me to ask, why am I called upon to speak here today? . . .

I am not included within the pale of this glorious anniversary! Your high independence only reveals the immeasurable distance between us. The blessings in which you, this day, rejoice are not enjoyed in common. The rich inheritance of justice, liberty, prosperity, and independence, bequeathed by your fathers, is shared by you, not by me. The sunlight that brought life and healing to you has brought stripes and death to me. This Fourth of July is *yours*, not *mine*. *You* may rejoice, *I* must mourn. To drag a man in fetters into the grand illuminated temple of liberty, and call upon him to join you in joyous anthems, were inhuman mockery and sacrilegious irony. Do you mean, citizens, to mock me, by asking me to speak today? If so, there is a parallel to your conduct. And let me warn you that it is dangerous to copy the example of a nation whose crimes, lowering up to heaven, were thrown down by the breath of the Almighty, burying that nation in irrecoverable ruin! . . .

Fellow citizens; above your national, tumultuous joy, I hear the mournful wail of millions, whose chains, heavy and grievous yesterday, are today rendered more intolerable by the jubilee shouts that reach them. . . . To forget them, to pass lightly over their wrongs, and to chime in with the popular theme, would be treason most scandalous and shocking, and would make me a reproach before God and the world. My subject, then, fellow citizens, is *American slavery*. I shall see this day and its popular characteristics from the slave's point of view. Standing there, identified with the American bondman, making his wrongs mine, I do not hesitate to declare, with all my soul, that the character and conduct of this nation never looked blacker to me than on this 4th of July! Whether we turn to the declarations of the past, or to the professions of the present, the conduct of the nation seems equally hideous and revolting. America is false to the past, false to the present, and solemnly binds herself to be false to the future. Standing with God and the crushed and bleeding slave on this occasion, I will, in the name of humanity which is outraged, in the name of liberty which is fettered, in the name of the constitution and the Bible, which are disregarded and trampled upon, dare to call in question and to denounce, with all the emphasis I can command, everything that serves to perpetuate slavery—the great sin and shame of America! . . .

At a time like this, scorching irony, not convincing argument, is needed. Oh! Had I the ability and could I reach the nation's ear, I would today pour out a fiery stream of biting ridicule, blasting reproach, withering sarcasm, and stern rebuke. For it is not light that is needed, but fire; it is not the gentle shower, but thunder. We need the storm, the whirlwind, and the earthquake. The feeling of the nation must be quickened; the conscience of the nation must be roused; the propriety of the nation must be startled; the hypocrisy of the nation must be exposed; and its crimes against God and man must be proclaimed and denounced.

What to the American slave is your 4th of July? I answer: a day that reveals to him, more than all other days in the year, the gross injustice and cruelty to which he is the constant victim. To him, your celebration is a sham; your boasted liberty, an unholy license; your national greatness, swelling vanity; your sounds of rejoicing are empty and heartless; your denunciations of tyrants, brass-fronted impudence; your shouts of liberty and equality, hollow mockery; your prayers and hymns, your sermons and thanksgivings, with all your religious parade, and solemnity, are to him mere bombast, fraud, deception, impiety, and hypocrisy—a thin veil to cover up crimes which would disgrace a nation of savages. There is not a nation on the earth guilty of practices more shocking and bloody than are the people of these United States at this very hour.

He Took Hold of Me and I Took Hold of the Window Sash (1854)

Elizabeth Jennings

On July 16, 1854, Elizabeth Jennings, a young black schoolteacher and church organist, was running late on her way to First Colored American Congregational Church in Manhattan. She and her friend, Sarah Adams, hopped aboard the first horse-drawn streetcar to arrive at the corner of Pearl and Chatham Streets, but the white conductor immediately demanded that the two get off and wait for a streetcar designated for black riders.

Manhattan in 1854 was hostile to African Americans. Although slavery was illegal, the city's public accommodations, along with its schools, churches, and places of employment, were racially segregated. To avoid interracial travel, select streetcars had signs that read, "Negro Persons Allowed in This Car."

After Jennings resisted the conductor's demands and was forcefully ejected from the streetcar, she detailed the racially charged event in a letter, reprinted below. First Colored American, long known as a church resistant to racial injustice, read the letter aloud the following day and then forwarded it to the New York Daily Tribune and to Frederick Douglass's newspaper, the North Star. Both papers printed her letter in full.

Jennings also relayed her story to her father, Thomas L. Jennings, a middle-class tailor who had helped to found the Abyssinian Baptist Church, which supported political rebellion among African Americans, and he enlisted a young white attorney, Chester Arthur, to bring suit against the Third Avenue Railway Company. Arthur, a future president of the United States, won the case, with the judge ruling that "colored persons if sober, well behaved and free from disease" could not be excluded from public transit "by any rules of the Company, nor by force or violence."

Although the ruling did not result in the immediate and full integration of New York's public transit system, it set legal precedent for future cases. And in 1860, with the precedent successfully tested in court by the Legal Rights Association, founded by Elizabeth Jenning's father, Manhattan streetcars became legally accessible to African Americans.

Sarah E. Adams and myself walked down to the corner of Pearl and Chatham Sts. to take the Third-Av. cars. We got on the platform when the conductor told us to wait for the next car. I told him I could not wait, as I was in a hurry to go to church.

He then told me that the other car had my people in it, that it was appropriated for "my people." I told him I had no people. I wished to go to church and I did not wish to be detained. He still kept driving me off the car; said he had as much time as I had and could wait just as long. I replied, "Very well, we'll see." He waited some minutes, when the driver becoming impatient, he said, "Well, you may go in, but remember, if the passengers raise any objections you shall go out, whether or no, or I'll put you out."

I told him I was a respectable person, born and raised in New York, did not know where he was born, and that he was a good-for-nothing impudent fellow for insulting decent persons while on their way to church. He then said he would put me out. I told him not to lay hands on me. He took hold of me and I took hold of the window sash. He pulled me until he broke my grasp. I took hold of his coat and held onto that. He also broke my grasp from that. He then ordered the driver to fasten his horses and come and help him put me out of the cars. Both seized hold of me by the arms and pulled and dragged me down on the bottom of the platform, so that my feet hung one way and my head the other, nearly on the ground.

I screamed "Murder" with all my voice and my companion screamed out, "You will kill her. Don't kill her." I went again in the car and the conductor said, "You shall sweat for this." Then told the driver to drive until he saw [a police] officer or a Station House. They got an officer on the corner of Walker and Bower.

The officer without listening to anything I had to say thrust me out and then tauntingly told me to get redress if I could. This the conductor also told me. He wrote his name, Moss, and the car, No. 7, but I looked and saw No. 6 on the back of the car. After dragging me off the car, he drove me away like a dog, saying not to be talking there and raising a mob or fight.

When I told the conductor I did not know where he was born, he answered, "I was born in Ireland." I made answer it made no difference where a man was born, provided he behaved himself and did not insult genteel persons.

I would have come myself but am quite sore and stiff from the treatment I received from those monsters in human form yesterday afternoon. This statement I believe to be correct and it is respectfully submitted.

Was John Brown Justified? (1859)

William Lloyd Garrison

On Sunday night, October 16, 1859, abolitionist John Brown led twenty-one men—five African Americans and sixteen white men, two of them Brown's sons—on a raid of the federal arsenal at Harpers Ferry, Virginia, with the hope of sparking a violent revolt of slaves across the South. Brown's plan called for taking control of the arsenal, arming his followers and local slaves, and then heading to a mountainous area to the south, where they would continue to spearhead a massive uprising of slaves.

Brown and his men established control of the armory and arsenal, captured about sixty local residents, and waited for more slaves to join them. But by Monday afternoon a local militia had forced them to re-treat into a fire house on the armory grounds. Pinned there, they were an easy target and eight of them were killed. On the following morning, U.S. Marines, dispatched by President Buchanan and under the command of Colonel Robert E. Lee, stormed the fire house, bayonetting two additional men to death and capturing Brown and five others, with two more to fol-low. Five men escaped during the fierce fighting, and Brown's army killed five people—local residents and a Marine. John Brown and his comrades were tried and executed.

Abolitionists struggled with how best to respond to Brown and his raid. Frederick Douglass stated: "While it shall be considered right to pro-tect oneself against thieves, burglars, robbers, and assassins, and to slay a wild beast in the act of devouring his human prey, it can never be wrong for the imbruted and whip-scarred slaves, or their friends, to hunt, harass, and even strike down the traffickers in human flesh." Douglass had been called a coward for not joining his friend's raid, and the black abolitionist responded by saying, "'The tools to those that can use them.' Let every man work for the abolition of slavery in his own way. I would help all, and hinder none."

Remarkably, also supportive of John Brown's raid was William Lloyd Garrison, whose radical abolitionism was consistently framed by his abso-lute pacifism. His comments are below.

As to his trial, I affirm that it was an awful mockery before heaven and earth! He was not tried in a court of justice. Mark how they crowded the counts together in one indictment—murder, treason, and insurrection! Of what was John Brown convicted? Who knows? Perhaps some of the jury convicted him of treason; others of murder; and others, again, of insurrection. Who can tell? There was no trial on any specific point. John Brown has been judicially assassinated. . . .

Was John Brown justified in his attempt? Yes, if Washington was in his; if Warren and Hancock were in theirs. If men are justified in striking a blow for freedom, when the question is one of a three-penny tax on tea, then I say they are a thousand times more justified when it is to save fathers, mothers, wives, and children from the slave-coffle and the auction-block, and to restore to them their God-given rights. Was John Brown justified in interfering in behalf of the slave population of Virginia, to secure their freedom and independence? Yes, if LaFayette was justified in interfering to help our revolutionary fathers. . . . If you believe in the right of assisting men to fight for freedom who are of your own color—God knows nothing of color or complexion—human rights know nothing of these distinctions—then you must cover, not only with a mantle of charity but with the admiration of your hearts, the effort of John Brown at Harper's Ferry. . . .

I am a nonresistant and I not only desire but have labored unremittingly to effect the peaceful abolition of slavery by an appeal to the reason and conscience of the slaveholder; yet as a peace man—an "ultra" peace man—I am prepared to say, "Success to every slave insurrection at the South, and in every slave country." And I do not see how I compromise or stain my peace profession in making that declaration. Whenever there is a contest between the oppressed and the oppressor, the weapons being equal between the parties, God knows my heart must be with the oppressed, and always against the oppressor. Therefore, whenever commenced, I cannot but wish success to all slave insurrections. I thank God when men who believe in the right and duty of wielding carnal weapons are so far advanced that they will take those weapons out of the scale of despotism, and throw them into the scale of freedom. It is an indication of progress, and a positive moral growth; it is one way to get up to the sublime platform of nonresistance; and it is God's method of dealing retribution upon the head of the tyrant. Rather than see men wear their chains in a cowardly and servile spirit, I would, as an advocate of peace, much rather see them breaking the head of the tyrant with their chains. Give me, as a nonresistant, Bunker Hill, and Lexington, and Concord, rather than the cowardice and servility of a Southern slave plantation.

THREE

Removing Native Americans, Dethroning Hawaiians

First Lords of the Soil (1830)

Theodore Frelinghuysen

President Andrew Jackson signed the Indian Removal Act into law on May 28, 1830. The controversial law authorized the president to arrange for the removal of Native Americans occupying lands within states to unsettled lands west of the Mississippi. The most vigorous dissent in the Senate came from Theodore Frelinghuysen of New Jersey, who delivered a scorching six-hour speech that he spread over three days. Below are excerpts of his plea for recognizing the political and civil rights of Native Americans, as well as the existing treaties that had given them the land from which the government was planning to expel them.

No one branch of the government can rescind, modify, or explain away our public treaties. They are the supreme law of the land, so declared to be by the Constitution. . . . Sir, this was a harsh measure, indeed, to faithful allies, that had so long reposed in confidence on a nation's faith. They had in the darkest hour of trial turned to the aegis which the most solemn pledges had provided for them, and were comforted by the conviction that it would continue to shed upon them a pure and untarnished beam of light and hope. Deep, indeed, must have been their despondency when their political father assured them that their confidence would be presumptuous, and dissuaded them from all expectation of relief. . . .

I now proceed to the discussion of those principles which, in my humble judgment, fully and clearly sustain the claims of the Indians to all their political and civil rights, as by them asserted. And here, Mr. President, I insist that, by immemorial possession, as the original tenants of the soil, they hold a title beyond and superior to the British crown and her colonies, and to all adverse pretensions of our confederation and subsequent Union. God, in his providence, planted these tribes on this Western continent, so far as we know, before Great Britain herself had a political existence. I believe, sir, it is not now seriously denied that the Indians are men, endowed with kindred faculties and powers with ourselves; that they have a place in human sympathy, and are justly entitled to a share in the common bounties of a benignant Providence. And, with this conceded, I ask in what code of the law of nations, or by what process of abstract deduction, their rights have been extinguished?

Where is the decree or ordinance that has stripped these early and first lords of the soil? Sir, no record of such measure can be found. And I might triumphantly rest the hopes of these feeble fragments of once great nations upon this impregnable foundation. However mere human policy, or the law of power, or the tyrant's plea of expediency, may have found it convenient at any or in all times to recede from the unchangeable principles of eternal justice, no argument can shake the political maxim—that where the Indian always has been, he enjoys an absolute right still to be, in the free exercise of his own modes of thought, government, and conduct.

Mr. President: In the light of natural law, can a reason for a distinction exist in the mode of enjoying that which is my own? If I use it for hunting may another take it because he needs it for agriculture? I am aware that some writers have, by a system of artificial reasoning, endeavored to justify, or rather, excuse the encroachments made upon Indian territory; and they denominate these abstractions the law of nations, and, in this ready way, the question is dispatched. Sir, as we trace the sources of this law, we find its authority to depend either upon the conventions or common consent of nations. And when, permit me to inquire, were the Indian tribes ever consulted on the establishment of such a law? Whoever represented them or their interests in any Congress of nations, to confer upon the public rules of intercourse, and the proper foundations of dominion and property? The plain matter of fact is that all these partial doctrines have resulted from the selfish plans and pursuits of more enlightened nations; and it is not matter for any great wonder that they should so largely partake of a mercenary and exclusive spirit towards the claims of the Indians.

It is however admitted, sir, that when the increase of population and the wants of mankind demand the cultivation of the earth, a duty is thereby devolved upon the proprietors of large and uncultivated regions, of devoting them to such useful purposes. But such appropriations are to be obtained by fair contract, and for reasonable compensation. It is, in such a case, the duty of the proprietor to sell—we may properly address his reason to induce him; but we cannot rightfully compel the cession of his lands, or take them by violence if his consent be withheld. . . .

Our ancestors found these people, far removed from the commotions of Europe, exercising all the rights, and enjoying the privileges of free and independent sovereigns of this new world. They were not a wild and lawless horde of banditti; but lived under the restraints of government, patriarchal in its influence. They had chiefs, head men, and councils. The white men, the authors of all their wrongs, approached them as friends—they extended the olive branch, and being then a feeble colony, and at the mercy of the native tenants of the soil, by presents and professions, propitiated their good will. The Indian yielded a slow, but substantial confidence, granted to the colonies an abiding place, and suffered them to grow up to a man's estate beside him. He never raised the claim of elder title—as the white man's wants increased, he opened the hand of his bounty wider and wider. By and by, conditions are changed. His people melt away; his lands are constantly coveted; millions after millions are ceded. The Indian bears it all meekly; he complains, indeed, as well he may; but suffers on; and now he finds that this neighbor, whom his kindness had nourished, has spread an adverse title over the last remains of his patrimony, barely adequate to his wants, and turns upon him, and says: "Away, we cannot endure you so near us. These forests and rivers, these groves of your fathers, these firesides and hunting grounds, are ours by the right of power, and the force of numbers." Sir, let every treaty be blotted from our records, and in the judgment of natural and unchangeable truth and justice, I ask who is the injured, and who is the aggressor? . . . Do the obligations of justice change with the color of the skins? Is it one of the prerogatives of the white man, that he may disregard the dictates of moral principles, when an Indian shall be concerned? No, Mr. President. . . . A few pence of duty on tea . . . awakened in the American colonies a spirit of firm resistance; and how was the tax tea met, sir? . . . We successfully and triumphantly contended for the very rights and privileges that our Indian neighbors now implore us to protect and preserve to them. Sir, this thought invests the subject under debate with most singular and momentous interest. We, whom God has exalted to the very summit of prosperity—whose brief career forms the brightest page in history; the wonder and praise of the world; freedom's hope, and her consolation; we, about to turn traitors to our principles and our fame—about to become the oppressors of the feeble, and to cast away our birthright! Sir, I hope for better things.

The Audacious Practices of Unprincipled Men (1836)

Chief John Ross

In 1827 Cherokees in the South attempted to exert their independence from the U.S. by establishing a constitutional, republican government with a capital in New Echota, Georgia. The following year, the same year that gold was discovered on their land, they elected John Ross as the principal chief of the Cherokee nation. White political leaders in Georgia immediately sought to abolish the Cherokee government and to annex and distribute Cherokee land to Georgia's white citizens. In turn, the Cherokees filed a federal suit, arguing that Georgia had violated Cherokee sovereignty. The suit was rendered moot when in another case, Worcester v. Georgia (1832), the U.S. Supreme Court ruled that Native American nations were "distinct, independent political communities retaining their original natural rights" and that the Cherokee nation was indeed sovereign and that only the federal government retained the right to negotiate with the Cherokees.

But Georgia resisted the ruling and continued its efforts to remove Cherokees from lands it considered its own. President Andrew Jackson subsequently sided with the state and instructed the Cherokees to relocate or become subject to Georgia's jurisdiction. Chief Ross adamantly opposed the demand to relocate, but a dissident faction within the Cherokee nation signed a removal treaty, the Treaty of New Echota, in 1835. In the document below, a letter to the U.S. Senate and House of Representatives, Chief Ross argues against the treaty and the removal of Cherokees from their homelands. Ross's appeal failed, and in 1838 the U.S. Army forcibly relocated the Cherokees to territory in what would become Oklahoma. The horrific forced move, now known as The Trail of Tears, saw hundreds of Cherokees dying along the way from harsh conditions.

It is well known that for a number of years past we have been harassed by a series of vexations, which it is deemed unnecessary to recite in detail, but the evidence of which our delegation will be prepared to furnish. With a view to bringing our troubles to a close, a delegation was appointed on the 23rd of October 1835, by the General Council of the nation, clothed with full powers to enter into arrangements with the government of the United States, for the final adjustment of all our existing difficulties. The delegation failing to effect an arrangement with the United States commissioner, then in the nation, proceeded, agreeably to their instructions in that case, to Washington City, for the purpose of negotiating a treaty with the authorities of the United States.

After the departure of the delegation, a contract was made by the Rev. John F. Schermerhorn and certain individual Cherokees, purporting to be a "treaty, concluded at New Echota, in the State of Georgia, on the 29th day of December, 1835, by General William Carroll and John F. Schermerhorn, commissioners on the part of the United States, and the chiefs, headmen, and people of the Cherokee tribes of Indians." A spurious delegation, in violation of a special injunction of the General Council of the nation, proceeded to Washington City with this pretended treaty, and by false and fraudulent representations supplanted in the favor of the government the legal and accredited delegation of the Cherokee people, and obtained for this instrument, after making important alterations in its provisions, the recognition of the United States government. And now it is presented to us as a treaty, ratified by the Senate and approved by the President, and our acquiescence in its requirements demanded, under the sanction of the displeasure of the United States, and the threat of summary compulsion, in case of refusal. It comes to us, not through our legitimate authorities, the known and usual medium of communication between the government of the United States and our nation, but through the agency of a complication of powers, civil and military.

By the stipulations of this instrument, we are despoiled of our private possessions, the indefeasible property of individuals. We are stripped of every attribute of freedom and eligibility for legal self-defense. Our property may be plundered before our eyes; violence may be committed on our persons; even our lives may be taken away, and there is none to regard our complaints. We are denationalized; we are disfranchised. We are deprived of membership in the human family! We have neither land nor home, nor resting place that can be called our own. And this is effected by the provisions of a compact which assumes the venerated, the sacred appellation of treaty.

We are overwhelmed! Our hearts are sickened, our utterance is paralyzed, when we reflect on the condition in which we are placed, by the audacious practices of unprincipled men, who have managed their stratagems with so much dexterity as to impose on the government of the United States, in the face of our earnest, solemn, and reiterated protestations.

The instrument in question is not the act of our nation; we are not parties to its covenants; it has not received the sanction of our people. The makers of it sustain no office nor appointment in our nation, under the designation of chiefs, head

Chief John Ross, c. 1843.

men, or any other title, by which they hold, or could acquire, authority to assume the reins of government, and to make bargain and sale of our rights, our possessions, and our common country. And we are constrained solemnly to declare that we cannot but contemplate the enforcement of the stipulations of this instrument on us, against our consent, as an act of injustice and oppression, which, we are well persuaded, can never knowingly be countenanced by the government and people of the United States; nor can we believe it to be the design of these honorable and high-minded individuals, who stand at the head of the govt., to bind a whole nation, by the acts of a few unauthorized individuals. And therefore, we, the parties to be affected by the result, appeal with confidence to the justice, the magnanimity, the compassion, of your honorable bodies, against the enforcement, on us, of the provisions of a compact, in the formation of which we have had no agency.

The Return of the Winnebago (1873)

S.

In 1873 and 1874 the U.S. Army forcibly moved about 1,000 Winnebago (now called Ho-Chunk) from their homes and lands in Wisconsin to a reservation in Nebraska. The government had previously tried to move the Winnebago to reservations in Iowa and Minnesota, but each time the Native Americans had resisted—simply by packing their bags and trekking back home to Wisconsin. That is also what they did after the U.S. Army forced them into Nebraska; by the end of 1875, most of the Winnebagoes had returned to their homelands in Wisconsin. Finally, the U.S. government gave up. It was an unusual case of surrender for them, but the nonviolent act of moving back home time and again had proven to be an intractable problem. The relentlessness of the Winnebago led the government not only to surrender but also to allow the Native Americans to homestead in Wisconsin. Below is a December 21, 1873 letter to the editor of the Chicago Times in which the writer defends the resisters.

The people of Columbia County and the state of Wisconsin have been this morning regaled by an exhibition of paternal government that needs but the knout or the bastille to make it complete.

About 100 Winnebagoes, whose only crime has been to wear a blanket, detest an Indian agent, and earn an honest living, have been arrested by men wearing the uniforms of the United States Army . . . and have been driven out with bayonets and shackles like sheep to the slaughter. . . .

What kind of government have we that, after officially promulgating under official date of June 17, 1873, "that in the view of this office, no authority is given in any of the acts of Congress, providing funds for the removal of said Indians, *to employ force against the will of said Indians,*" and in view of the following statute of Wisconsin: "All Indians shall be capable of suing and being sued in any of the courts of this state in like manner and with like effect as other inhabitants thereof, and they shall be entitled to the same judicial rights and privileges," that it dares to invade the state of Wisconsin with troops, and arrest her citizens—for these Indians are citizens to all intents and purposes. Or what kind of people have we become, who quietly submit to such an outrage? But what do they care? They are playing for high stakes, a reservation worth at least $1,000,000, and over $1,000,000 more in the funds (if it has not been stolen), and the handling of millions more wrung from the sweat and toil of those who labor. . . .

How much longer will the people submit to have their food and clothing taxed out of their reach, to be used up by officials (or Indians) whose sole object, from the highest to the lowest, is plunder? And who will provide a remedy?

We Ask to Be Recognized as Men (1879)

Chief Joseph

In 1855 Chief Joseph the Elder worked with Washington's territorial governor to establish a reservation for the Nez Perce. The boundaries of the reservation changed dramatically in 1863, when the federal government reclaimed six million acres as part of its efforts to benefit from a gold rush in the area. But Joseph the Elder refused to sign a treaty that would have squeezed the Nez Perce onto a much smaller reservation in Idaho, and his son, Joseph the Younger, also resisted the forced relocation when he became Chief Joseph in 1871. The Nez Perce resistance turned violent in 1877, and although U.S. soldiers far outnumbered their Native American counterparts during four major battles, the Nez Perce earned high marks for their military strategy and tenacity. Chief Joseph surrendered on October 5, 1877, with the assurance that the Nez Perce could return home. But the federal government reneged on its promise and forcibly moved the Nez Perce to lands in what is now Oklahoma. Chief Joseph continued to protest the government's treatment of his people, and in 1879 he traveled to

Washington, DC, to argue his case before President Rutherford B. Hayes. Below is his account of that trip.

At last I was granted permission to come to Washington and bring my friend Yellow Bull and our interpreter with me. I am glad I came. I have shaken hands with a good many friends, but there are some things I want to know which no one seems able to explain. I cannot understand how the government sends a man out to fight us, as it did General Miles, and then breaks his word. Such a government has something wrong about it. I cannot understand why so many chiefs are allowed to talk so many different ways, and promise so many different things. I have seen the Great Father Chief [President Hayes]; the Next Great Chief [Secretary of the Interior]; the Commissioner Chief; the Law Chief; and many other law chiefs, and they all say they are my friends, and that I shall have justice, but while all their mouths talk right, I do not understand why nothing is done for my people. I have heard talk and talk but nothing is done. Good words do not last long unless they amount to something. Words do not pay for my dead people. They do not pay for my country now overrun by white men. They do not protect my father's grave. They do not pay for my horses and cattle. Good words do not give me back my children. Good words will not make good the promise of your war chief, General Miles. Good words will not give my people a home where they can live in peace and take care of themselves. I am tired of talk that comes to nothing. It makes my heart sick when I remember all the good words and all the broken promises. There has been too much talking by men who had no right to talk. Too many misinterpretations have been made; too many misunderstandings have come up between the white men and the Indians. If the white man wants to live in peace with the Indian, he can live in peace. There need be no trouble. Treat all men alike. Give them the same laws. Give them all an even chance to live and grow. All men were made by the same Great Spirit Chief. They are all brothers. The earth is the mother of all people, and all people should have equal rights upon it. You might as well expect all rivers to run backward as that any man who was born a free man should be contented penned up and denied liberty to go where he pleases. If you tie a horse to a stake, do you expect he will grow fat? If you pen an Indian up on a small spot of earth and compel him to stay there, he will not be contented nor will he grow and prosper. I have asked some of the Great White Chiefs where they get their

Native Americans petitioning U.S. Congress, c. 1860s.

authority to say to the Indian that he shall stay in one place, while he sees white men going where they please. They cannot tell me.

I only ask of the government to be treated as all other men are treated. If I cannot go to my own home, let me have a home in a country where my people will not die so fast. I would like to go to Bitter Root Valley. There my people would be happy; where they are now they are dying. Three have died since I left my camp to come to Washington.

When I think of our condition, my heart is heavy. I see men of my own race treated as outlaws and driven from country to country, or shot down like animals.

I know that my race must change. We cannot hold our own with the white men as we are. We only ask an even chance to live as other men live. We ask to be recognized as men. We ask that the same law shall work alike on all men. If an Indian breaks the law, punish him by the law. If a white man breaks the law, punish him also.

Let me be a free man, free to travel, free to stop, free to work, free to trade where I choose, free to choose my own teachers, free to follow the religion of my fathers, free to talk, think and act for myself—and I will obey every law or submit to the penalty.

Whenever the white man treats the Indian as they treat each other, then we shall have no more wars. We shall be all alike—brothers of one father and mother, with one sky above us and one country around us and one government for all. Then the Great Spirit Chief who rules above will smile upon this land and send rain to wash out the bloody spots made by brothers' hands upon the face of the earth. For this time the Indian race is waiting and praying. I hope no more groans of wounded men and women will ever go to the ear of the Great Spirit Chief above, and that all people may be one people.

Hin-mah-too-yah-lat-kekht has spoken for his people.

My Downtrodden People (1898)

Queen Liliuokalani

In 1887 King David Kalakaua of Hawaii, under threat by an armed militia, signed a constitution favored by the Hawaiian League, a group that sought to safeguard and advance the interests of U.S. businessmen, including Sanford Dole. The "Bayonet Constitution," as its opponents called it, effectively transferred power from the historical monarchy to a legislature controlled by Dole and his cronies.

King Kalakaua died in 1891, and when his successor, Queen Liliuokalani, proposed the restoration of power to the monarchy, Dole and others toppled her from the largely symbolic throne. In the document below, the queen describes her trip to the mainland following the coup, as well as her opposition to the U.S. annexation of Hawaii. Although President Grover Cleveland supported the queen's return to power, coup leaders successfully established the Republic of Hawaii and elected Sanford Dole as president. In 1898 President William McKinley, Cleveland's successor, oversaw the annexation of Hawaii, even as the queen and her supporters continued to resist the colonization of their land.

Miles after miles of rich country went by as we gazed from the windows of the moving train, and all this vast extent of territory which we traversed belonged to the United States; and there were many other routes from the Pacific to the Atlantic with an equally boundless panorama. Here were thousands of acres of uncultivated, uninhabited, but rich and fertile lands, soil capable of producing anything which grows, plenty of water, floods of it running to waste, everything needed for pleasant towns and quiet homesteads, except population. The view and the thoughts awakened brought forcibly to my mind that humanity was the one element needed to open to usefulness and enjoyment these rich tracts of land. Colonies and colonies could be established here, and never interfere with each other in the least, the vast extent of unoccupied land is so enormous. I thought what splendid sugar plantations might here be established, how easily and profitably rice might be grown, and in some other spots with what good returns coffee could be planted. There was nothing lacking in this great, rich country save the people to settle upon it, and develop its wealth.

And yet this great and powerful nation must go across two thousand miles of sea, and take from the poor Hawaiians their little spots in the broad Pacific, must covet our islands of Hawaii Nei, and extinguish the nationality of my poor people, many of whom have now not a foot of land which can be called their own. And for what? In order that another race problem shall be injected into the social and political perplexities with which the United States in the great experiment of popular government is already struggling? In order that a novel and inconsistent foreign and colonial policy shall be grafted upon its hitherto impregnable diplomacy? Or in order that a friendly and generous, yet proud-spirited and sensitive race, a race admittedly capable and worthy of receiving the best opportunities for material and moral progress, shall be crushed under the weight of a social order and prejudice with which even another century of preparation would hardly fit it to cope? . . .

While in Boston I was constantly asked if there was any political significance in my visit to America, and if I expected to see the

President. It seemed wise to say nothing about my purpose at that time, but frankness would now indicate an opposite course. By the first vessel that arrived from Honolulu after I reached San Francisco, documents were sent to me by the patriotic leagues of the native Hawaiian people, those associations of which I have already spoken in full; and these representative bodies of my own nation prayed me to undertake certain measures for the general good of Hawaii. Further messages of similar purport reached me while I was visiting my Boston friends.

All the communications received, whether personally or in form, from individuals or from the above-mentioned organizations, were in advocacy of one desired end. This was to ask President Cleveland that the former form of government unjustly taken from us by the persons who in 1892 and 1893 represented the United States should be restored, and that this restoration should undo the wrong which had been done to the Hawaiian people, and return to them the queen, to whom constitutionally, and also by their own choice, they had a perfect right. . . .

The second package of documents received by me in Boston was addressed to President McKinley, and was similar to the others I already had, only they were addressed to Hon. Grover Cleveland while he was president. Accompanying these papers were other documents, showing that full power was accorded to me, not only as their queen, but individually, to represent the real people of Hawaii, and in so doing to act in any way my judgment should dictate for the good of the Hawaiians, to whom the Creator gave those beautiful islands in the Pacific. . . .

When I speak at this time of the Hawaiian people, I refer to the children of the soil—the native inhabitants of the Hawaiian Islands and their descendants. Two delegations claiming to represent Hawaii have visited Washington at intervals during the past four years in the cause of annexation, besides which other individuals have been sent on to assist in this attempt to defraud an aboriginal people of their birthrights— rights dear to the patriotic hearts of even the weakest nation. Lately these aliens have called themselves Hawaiians.

They are not and never were Hawaiians. . . .

But will it also be thought strange that education and knowledge of the world have enabled us to perceive that as a race we have some special mental and physical requirements not shared by the other races which have come among us? That certain habits and modes of living are better for our health and happiness than others? And that a separate nationality, and a particular form of government, as well as special laws, are, at least for the present, best for us? And these things remained to us, until the pitiless and tireless "annexation policy" was effectively backed by the naval power of the United States.

To other usurpations of authority on the part of those whose love for the institutions of their native land we could understand and forgive we had submitted. We had allowed them virtually to give us a constitution, and control the offices of state. Not without protest, indeed; for the usurpation was unrighteous, and cost us much humiliation and distress. But we did not resist it by force. It had not entered into our hearts to believe that these friends and allies from the United States, even with all their foreign affinities, would ever go so far as to absolutely overthrow our form of government, seize our nation by the throat, and pass it over to an alien power.

And while we sought by peaceful political means to maintain the dignity of the throne, and to advance national feeling among the native people, we never sought to rob any citizen, wherever born, of either property, franchise, or social standing.

Perhaps there is a kind of right, depending upon the precedents of all ages, and known as the "right of conquest," under which robbers and marauders may establish themselves in possession of whatsoever they are strong enough to ravish from their fellows. I will not pretend to decide how far civilization and Christian enlightenment have outlawed it. But we have known for many years that our Island monarchy has relied upon the protection always extended to us by the policy and the assured friendship of the great American republic. If we have nourished in our bosom those who have sought our ruin, it has been because they were of the people whom we believed to be our dearest friends and allies. If we did not by force resist their final outrage, it was because we could not do so without striking at the military force of the United States. Whatever constraint the executive of this great country may be under to recognize the present government at Honolulu has been forced upon it by no act of ours, but by the unlawful acts of its own agents. Attempts to repudiate those acts are vain. . . .

It is not for me to consider this matter from the American point of view; although the pending question of annexation involves nothing less than a departure from the established policy of that country, and an ominous change in its foreign relations. It is enough that I am able to say, and with absolute authority, that the native people of Hawaii are entirely faithful to their own chiefs, and are deeply attached to their own customs and mode of government; that they either do not understand, or bitterly oppose, the scheme of annexation. As a native Hawaiian, reared and educated in close intimacy with the present rulers of the Islands and their families, with exceptional opportunities for studying both native and foreign character, it is easy for me to detect the purpose of each line and word in the annexation treaty, and even to distinguish the man originating each portion of it. . . .

It has been shown that in Hawaii there is an alien element composed of men of energy and determination, well able to carry through what they undertake, but not scrupulous respecting their methods. They doubtless control all the resources and influence of the present ruling power in Honolulu, and will employ them tirelessly in the future, as they have in the past, to secure their ends. This annexationist party might prove to be a dangerous accession even to American politics, both on account of natural abilities, and because of the training of an autocratic life from earliest youth.

Many of these men are anything but ideal citizens for a democracy. . . .

Perhaps I may even venture here upon a final word respecting the American advocates of this annexation of Hawaii. I observe that they have pretty successfully striven to make it a party matter. It is chiefly

Republican statesmen and politicians who favor it. But is it really a matter of party interest? Is the American Republic of States to degenerate, and become a colonizer and a land-grabber?

And is this prospect satisfactory to a people who rely upon self-government for their liberties, and whose guaranty of liberty and autonomy to the whole western hemisphere, the grand Monroe doctrine, appealing to the respect and the sense of justice of the masses of every nation on earth, has made any attack upon it practically impossible to the statesmen and rulers of armed empires? There is little question but that the United States could become a successful rival of the European nations in the race for conquest, and could create a vast military and naval power, if such is its ambition. But is such an ambition laudable? Is such a departure from its established principles patriotic or politic? . . .

Oh, honest Americans, as Christians hear me for my downtrodden people! Their form of government is as dear to them as yours is precious to you. Quite as warmly as you love your country, so they love theirs. . . .

It is for them that I would give the last drop of my blood; it is for them that I would spend, nay, am spending, everything belonging to me. Will it be in vain? It is for the American people and their representatives in Congress to answer these questions. As they deal with me and my people, kindly, generously, and justly, so may the Great Ruler of all nations deal with the grand and glorious nation of the United States of America.

FOUR

Striking Against Industrialists

Petition Against Terrorism (1871)

Colored National Labor Union

After the Civil War, African Americans faced exclusion from the power-ful, and white, National Labor Union (NLU). So they began to organize themselves, and one of the most important events in black labor history occurred with the founding of the Colored National Labor Union (CNLU) in 1869.

The CNLU did not think small, and it wasn't long before it petitioned Congress to make land and loans available to poor black farmers in the South. In 1871 the CNLU also drafted and sent to Congress another peti-tion, excerpted below, which included a stinging indictment of white rac-ism during the Reconstruction Era. The petition is also notable for its ex-planation that black labor issues were inextricably connected to education, the judicial system, law enforcement, and property ownership.

To the Honorable the Senate and the House of Representatives:

The undersigned, a committee appointed by the National Labor Con-vention to memorialize Congress in behalf of the colored people and in their name to ask for the appointment of a commission to inquire into the condition of affairs in the southern states of this Union, would respectfully represent—

That the colored people in the states in which the institution of slavery has lately existed are denied the equal protection of the laws, are deprived of adequate means of education, are cheated out of the earnings of their labor, are menaced, assaulted, and murdered for exercising the rights of citizenship, and in defiance of the principles of justice, of the claims of humanity, and of the interests of civilization, are subjected to a well-understood, widespread, and predetermined system of persecution, cruelty, and outrage, extending into all the corners of their lives, and expressly calculated and intended to keep them poor and ignorant, and thereby easy, if not willing, victims to the arrogance, cupidity, and passions of those who formerly held us in slavery.

The local courts not only fail to redress the wrongs of our people and to punish offenses against them, but they are used as convenient instruments of our oppression. The colored people are frequently charged with crimes never committed, commonly convicted on false or insufficient testimony, and for the most trivial offenses are punished with excessive severity, while offenses committed upon them can scarcely ever be brought to trial; and when they are, such trials are a mockery. As a general statement, we are always punished, our aggressors always acquitted.

The courts of the United States afford us little relief. Being located in cities and large places, our people cannot generally go to them. If they do reach them, through great trial and difficulty, and make complaint or give evidence, they are liable to be murdered upon their return to their homes. To be a complainant or a witness in any court against those who mean to deprive us of the rights guaranteed by the Constitution of our country, is to risk still greater injuries, and commonly, to sacrifice life itself. And in all courts wherein we attempt to seek justice, juries are usually so composed that they fail to agree upon a verdict or openly acquit the guilty parties.

If a colored man resents a wrong, or tries to defend himself from abuse, he is frequently killed outright, and the murder falsely claimed to have been an act done in self-defense, or coolly justified by the allegation that "a Negro has been impudent." If the friends of a colored man who is being outraged come to his assistance, they are charged with making an assault, and under the pretense of preserving law and order, an armed party gathers, or is organized, and at once proceeds to shoot them down, hunt, mutilate, and hang them.

Bands of armed and disguised men sally out from secret lodges to intervals more or less frequent, and especially during and subsequent to a political canvass, and their track is marked with the blood of American citizens, dragged from their humble homes and foully and savagely slain.

In nearly every Southern state the whipping post is erected and the dark backs of republican voters made red with the stripes of democratic animosity.

Some of the most atrocious wrongs perpetrated upon our race are done in the name and under the pretended forms of the law, and these and other outrages are committed at the direct instigation, or with the general understood sanction, of those who are known as respectable citizens, and are usually participated in by them, while, as such citizens, and as magistrates, attorneys, witnesses, and jurors, they shield each other, or deny or pervert the facts, or invent pleas of palliation and excuse, or when circumstances are too palpable for even their contradiction, they cause it to be said that "our best citizens disapprove" the deed, and allege that it was done by lawless persons not resident of the locality. But they never discover, they never seek, they never punish, the perpetrators. They count alike upon insidious sophistries to mislead public judgment, upon bold and persistent denials to avert investigations, and upon intimidation and death to suppress evidence and prevent complaints. So prevalent and continuous is the exercise of terrorism, and so powerful the influences of interest, that many of our friends are induced to contribute their aid in concealing vital facts from public information. And not unfrequently (we say it with humiliation and grief) do those whom our votes have elevated to official station not only fail to use the power we have given them for our protection, but unable to withstand the influences surrounding them, or beguiled by the ever-receding phantom of conservative affiliation, they affect to officially know little cause of complaint.

Most of our people are landless and homeless. This was the condition in which they were left when freed; this is the condition in which it is the deliberate purpose of the owners of the soil that they shall remain. They occupy the cabins of the employer, who thus controls their poor abodes as completely as he does the premises occupied by himself. They cannot keep arms to defend themselves, because their cabins are closely watched, visited, and searched. They cannot organize and act together for similar reasons. It is an offense to sell or give a colored person any weapon; it is a crime for a colored person to keep or carry any weapon. For these and other reasons, our people cannot defend themselves against the arms, the organization, and other facilities of the employer. Without independence, they have little power to control the wages to be paid for their labor—none at all to collect what is due them. Compelled to purchase from the landowner, or to take orders for even such portion of their scanty wages as may be allowed them, they are charged excessive prices for whatever they consume, and so brought into debt, in order that they may not save, no matter how hard they work or how frugally they exist. And this procedure is systematic throughout the Southern states. They cannot accumulate means to buy an acre of land; they would not be permitted to purchase, in general, if they could, and scarcely ever in small quantities.

Most of the states either fail to establish any adequate system of education, or they refuse appropriations for educational purposes. Schools provided by philanthropic persons are broken up and teachers are driven out. Benevolent and self-sacrificing ladies of the North, who come among us to teach our children, are uniformly insulted and the foulest slanders heaped upon their characters, in order to disgrace and dishearten them, and thus prevent them from continuing their work.

Your memorialists desire distinctly to represent to your honorable bodies that in all this, the alleged antagonism of race is no element save that of pretense; that in all the persecutions visited upon us, there is but one motive and one purpose. It is the distinctive motive and purpose of the common enemies of government, of the republic, and of liberty—that motive and that purpose to keep colored people in subjection, in order that they may be used without consideration and abused without responsibility. To preserve this power, resort was had to arms; to regain it, this crusade against all the rights of the colored race has been since maintained and is proposed to be continued.

The pacification of the South is a delusion and a snare. Hostility to the government and to the North is inculcated in babyhood and ends but in the grave.

Your memorialists are painfully aware that the nation at large has no proper conception of the condition of affairs in the South, no adequate apprehension of the designs and purposes which rule that section, and little information of the wrongs continually heaped upon loyal people. In the average computation of probabilities, it is too often assumed that while there may be perhaps some foundation for the occasional statements which appear, of course (thus the reasoning runs) there is much exaggeration, and so, tired of hearing the story of our wrongs, and forgetting that the national interests in fourteen states are committed to our unprotected hands, the subject is dismissed.

We come before you to say, in all that seriousness which the gravity of this occasion commands, that not only is there no exaggeration in published statements, but on the contrary, the thousandth part has never yet been told.

The press of the country is practically shut against us. Again and again have verified statements of actual occurrences been communicated to leading republican journals, the *New York Tribune* and others, and publication has been refused, while perfidious misrepresentations have been permitted to pass current. Comparatively few cases of outrage are ever publicly known, even in the localities where they occur, being told only in the whispers of fear and repeated at the risk of life. Of these few isolated cases, only now and then is one reported in the Southern press, or if so reported, reproduced in Northern journals. No conservative paper in the South will, no republican paper there dare, faithfully state the facts of daily life, the constantly occurring round of wrong.

Four millions of human beings are nearly as dumb now as in the fearful years that are gone. Four millions of citizens of the United States look to the Congress of the American people at least to furnish the country with conclusive information as to their condition. We still will trust the people of the North to grant us justice by the national power and the national will. We only ask that needed information may be spread before the people that they may know the facts, and we leave to Congress, to its wisdom and its judgment, the ways and means of carrying out this, the object of our prayer.

Will You Organize? (1877)

Albert Parsons

During the Long Depression of the early 1870s, railroad workers throughout the United States faced deep cuts to their wages. Railroad work was not only poorly paid but also dangerous and sometimes deadly. Stories about men being crushed between cars or losing limbs were common, and the government failed to establish regulations that would protect workers from owners who put profits above safety.

In Martinsburg, West Virginia, the frustrations of railroad workers erupted after their employer, the Baltimore and Ohio Railroad (B&O), told them to expect a 10 percent reduction in wages. In July 1877 workers uncoupled train cars at the Martinsburg station, returned them to the roundhouse, and declared that the trains would not run again until B&O agreed not to cut their wages. With about 600 trains out of commission, the state militia and federal troops were sent in to crush the strike.

As state and federal troops attacked the Martinsburg strikers, the strike spread to railroad workers in companies across the United States, including Baltimore, Philadelphia, Pittsburgh, Chicago, Kansas City, St.

Louis, and San Francisco. In Chicago, one of the main voices encouraging a general strike was Albert Parsons, a socialist and leader of the pro-labor Workingmen's Party of the United States. Parsons was a veteran resister. After serving with the Confederate Army as a teenager, he had bought a farm in Waco, Texas, and hired African Americans at a fair wage to plant and harvest his fields. Refusing to obey Texas laws that criminalized miscegenation, Parsons also fell in love with and married Lucy Eldine Gonzales, a woman of mixed ethnicities who might have been a former slave. And in the mid- to late-1860s Parsons was shot for attempting to register black citizens to vote in Texas.

In the speech below, delivered on the night of July 23, 1877, Parsons encourages workers to organize themselves into a powerful union and use nonviolent methods to achieve their objectives. As a socialist, Parsons hoped those objectives would include the nationalization of essential industries.

We are assembled here as the grand army of starvation. Fellow workers, let us recollect that in this great republic that has been handed down to us by our forefathers from 1776, that while we have the republic we have hope. A mighty spirit is animating the hearts of the American people today. The American people are bowed down with shame and hunger. When I say the American people, I mean the backbone of the country—the men who till the soil, who guide the machine, who weave the material, and cover the backs of civilized men. We are a portion of that people. Our brothers in the State of Pennsylvania, in New Jersey, in the States of Maryland, New York, and Illinois, have demanded of those who have possession of the means of production—our brothers have made demand that they may be permitted to live, and that those men do not appropriate the life to themselves, and that they be not allowed to turn us upon the earth as vagrants and tramps. While we are sad indeed at our distressed and suffering brothers in the States mentioned, that they had to resort to such extreme measures, fellow workers, we recognize the fact that they were driven to do what they have done.

We are assembled here tonight to consider our condition. We have come together this evening, if it is possible, to find means by which the great gloom that now hangs over our republic can be lifted, and once more the rays of happiness can be shed on the face of this broad land. . . .

There never can come good times in this country until the idle men have employment. What are we going to do with the idle men? Are we to take them and shoot them? Are we to let them drop dead? . . . Fellow workers, there is a way to get over this by peaceful means. Say, for instance, there is work for a hundred men. There are two hundred men to do it. If the one hundred men work for fourteen hours a day, let us reduce the hours to seven, and that will give work to the two hundred. Let us reduce the hours of work to one-half and then form a combination, and then demand the wages we want. In order to do this we have to combine in some kind of a labor organization. And if we can form a combination we can get as much for six hours work as we formerly got for twelve. We have got to make a law on the subject of hours. Every boss and capitalist and monopolist and railway king and every man who is interested in labor will be opposed to us in this movement. And also the idle rich, who live upon our strength.

Let us understand our position. If we reduce our hours of labor, the bosses and capitalists will immediately purchase another machine to replace us. Let us, then, immediately reduce the hours of labor once more, and in that way we can keep pace with them. Let us remember that we can make it possible for the wealth-producing classes to enjoy civilization by reducing the hours. It will then become possible for the working classes to learn something of poetry and pictures, but a man who works for fourteen hours can never be anything else than a downcast, ignorant man. If we become organized we can carry on the struggle successfully. . . .

Let us fight for our wives and children, for us it is a question of bread and meat. Let the grand army of labor say who shall fill the legislative halls of this country. Now if we do this we can go to work and unite as one people; can go to the ballot-box and say that the government of the United States shall be the possessors of all the railway lines in the country. If the people go to work and take possession of the railroads and telegraphs we extract the sting from the mouths of Jay Gould and Tom Scott, and they can no longer sting us to death. We take out of their hands the means by which they now enslave us. Let us not forget the fact that all wealth and civilization comes from labor, and labor alone. Let us not forget that while we work ten hours a day the capitalist puts the value of seven hours of it in his pocket. It rests with you to say whether we shall allow the capitalists to go on, or whether we shall organize ourselves. Will you organize? Well, then enroll your names in the grand army of labor, and if the capitalist engages in warfare against our rights, then we shall resist him with all the means that God has given us.

We Have 4,000 Men (1891)
African American Waterfront Workers of Savannah

In 1891 African American wharf workers in Savannah, Georgia, decided to go on strike against the Central Railroad to demand an increase to their wages. Calling a strike was a bold move in Savannah, where a white political and business structure had established Jim Crow laws and used violence to force African Americans into second-class citizenship. Aware of the potentially deadly nature of their strike, the black wharf workers went to great lengths, as the short document below shows, to announce that their protest would remain nonviolent.

We, the Labor and Protective Association, give notice that we don't want war with anyone, but we want an increase of wages and be sure we will not work for the same price. We want 20 cents for wharf workers, 25 cents for ship's hands, 30 cents for headers. We have twelve committees to wait on the agent that we have to communicate with, and no other arrangement can be made except through the committees. They can be got at any time to wait on the gentleman. We have been engaged in singing and praying all day and expect to continue until we get good or bad news. If it be a month it is all the same to us. We have 4,000 men, and we have the labor, and you have got the money and the guns and the ammunition so we will take God for our ammunition. That is all the war we want. We want to keep peace.

A Petition in Boots (1894)

Jacob Coxey

The first major march on Washington began on March 25, 1894, when Jacob Coxey, an entrepreneur with big ideas, and approximately 100 supporters left Massillon, Ohio, for a 350-mile trek to the nation's capital. Coxey conceived of the march as a way to enlist popular support for his "Good Roads Bill," which called for a federal program that would provide jobs for the unemployed and improve the nation's infrastructures. The program was necessary, Coxey believed, because the government had no successful policies for resolving the hardships caused by the Panic of 1893, a depression that had resulted in pervasive unemployment and widespread hunger.

Coxey hoped to enlist thousands of unemployed workers to descend on the capital and demand that Congress transform his proposal into legislation. As word about the march spread, thousands of desperate workers did indeed try to make their way to Coxey, even commandeering trains as part of their protest movement. Although 20,000 or so joined the march at some point along the way, only about 500 actually made it to Washington.

The marchers, popularly known as "Coxey's Army," camped near Rock Creek Park just before heading to the U.S. Capitol. Although Coxey knew that police officers were preparing to arrest him and his followers, charging them with breaking an obscure law that prohibited assembling on the lawn of the Capitol, he remained undeterred, and on May 1, he and his army marched through the city. A crowd of approximately 10,000 gathered to watch the march, and the supportive audience, many of them African American residents, shouted "Coxey! Coxey! Coxey!" as the ragtag bunch, waving banners and led by Coxey's daughter Mamie on a white Arabian stallion, marched to the Capitol.

Coxey and his main lieutenant, Carl Browne, had concocted a plan for dealing with any police attempt to prevent Coxey from speaking at the Capitol. Once there, Browne would provoke an argument with a police officer and then disappear into the crowd, thereby creating a diversion that would allow Coxey to read his "Good Roads Bill" from the Capitol steps. The plan worked—a bit. As the police chased Browne, Coxey began to read from his bill. But Browne was soon caught and clubbed, and the police then arrested Coxey and used their sticks to beat and disperse the crowd.

Within fifteen minutes, the first march on Washington was over. It seemed like an ignominious defeat. The marchers either stayed in Washington or somehow found their way back home, and Coxey and Browne were sentenced to twenty days of labor in a local workhouse. Members of Congress ridiculed the marchers and ignored their demands.

But the story of Coxey's Army did not end there. Fifty years later, Coxey returned to the Capitol, this time by invitation and to some acclaim. Times were different: Franklin Delano Roosevelt was president, and the New Deal, with its federal jobs program, was official policy of the U.S. government. As Coxey proudly read the "Good Roads Bill" from the steps of the Capitol, his sympathetic audience understood that the businessman from Ohio was a thinker and activist who had been far ahead of his times.

Nor does the story of Coxey's march end in 1944. The "petition in boots," as Coxey called it, set a grand precedent for millions of citizens seeking to take their grievances to the nation's capital. Every march on Washington since 1894 stands on the shoulders of Jacob Coxey and those 500 men and women who were beaten and driven back as they peacefully assembled to demand a decent job and a bit of food. Below is the speech that Coxey had intended to give on May 1, 1894.

The Constitution of the United States guarantees to all citizens the right to peaceably assemble and petition for redress of grievances, and furthermore declares that the right of free speech shall not be abridged. . . .

We stand here to remind Congress of its promise of returning prosperity should the Sherman Act be repealed. We stand here to declare by our march of over 400 miles through difficulties and distress, a march unstained by even the slightest act which would bring the blush of shame to any, that we are law-abiding citizens, and as men our actions speak louder than words. We are here to petition for legislation which will furnish employment for every man able and willing to work; for legislation which will bring universal prosperity and emancipate our beloved country from financial bondage to the descendants of King George. We have come to the only source which is competent to aid the people in their day of dire distress. We are here to tell our representatives, who hold their seats by grace of our ballots, that the struggle for existence has become too fierce and relentless. We come and throw up our defenseless hands, and say, help, or we and our loved ones must perish. We are engaged in a bitter and cruel war with the enemies of all mankind—a war with hunger, wretchedness, and despair, and we ask Congress to heed our petitions and issue for the nation's good a sufficient volume of the same kind of money which carried the country through one awful war and saved the life of the nation.

In the name of justice, through whose impartial administration only the present civilization can be maintained and perpetuated, by the powers of the Constitution of our country upon which the liberties of the people must depend, and in the name of the commonweal of Christ, whose representatives we are, we enter a most solemn and earnest protest against this unnecessary and cruel usurpation and tyranny, and this enforced subjugation of the rights and privileges of American citizenship. We have assembled here in violation of no just laws to enjoy the privileges of every American citizen. We are now under the shadow of the Capitol of this great nation, and in the presence of our national legislators are refused that dearly bought privilege, and by force of arbitrary power prevented from carrying out the desire of our hearts which is plainly granted under the great Magna Carta of our national liberties.

Coxey's Army, Washington, D.C., 1894.

We have come here through toil and weary marches, through storms and tempests, over mountains, and amid the trials of poverty and distress, to lay our grievances at the doors of our national legislature and ask them in the name of Him whose banners we bear, in the name of Him who pleads for the poor and the oppressed, that they should heed the voice of despair and distress that is now coming up from every section of our country, that they should consider the conditions of the starving unemployed of our land, and enact such laws as will give them employment, bring happier conditions to the people, and the smile of contentment to our citizens.

Coming as we do with peace and good will to men, we shall submit to these laws, unjust as they are, and obey this mandate of authority of might which overrides and outrages the law of right. In doing so, we appeal to every peace-loving citizen, every liberty-loving man or woman, everyone in whose breast the fires of patriotism and love of country have not died out, to assist us in our efforts toward better laws and general benefits.

The Wail of the Children (1903)

Mother Jones

Before becoming the famous labor organizer Mother Jones, Mary Harris Jones worked as a teacher, a dressmaker, and owner of a seamstress shop. The early part of her adult life was full of tragedy. Her husband and children died of typhoid fever in 1867, and the Chicago fire of 1871 destroyed her possessions, including the seamstress shop. At that point, after years of making clothes for wealthy women, Jones signed up for the emerging labor rights movement, joining the Knights of Labor and traveling to a variety of cities and states to assist workers in need of better wages and healthier working and living conditions.

In 1890 the newly formed United Mine Workers of America hired Jones as an organizer, and she began traveling to coal regions, giving popular talks, helping workers organize, and establishing ties with socialists, including Eugene Debs. Within a decade her popularity had earned her a spot as a contributor to the International Socialist Review.

Jones excelled not only at organizing mine workers but also at enlisting the support of their spouses and children. One of her most famous acts of resistance occurred in 1903 when she led a march of child workers from a Philadelphia textile mill to the luxurious home of President Theodore Roosevelt in Oyster Bay, New York, to protest their horrible working conditions and demand legislation to regulate child labor. The march began with a rally at City Hall in Philadelphia, where Mother Jones raised the mutilated hands of several children so that the gathered crowd could see firsthand the horrors of child labor practices. "Philadelphia's mansions were built on the broken bones, the quivering ears, and the drooping heads of these children," she said before the marchers took off carrying signs that read "We Want to Go to School" and "We Want Time to Play." Although they didn't gain a meeting with the President, they attracted national attention to the issue and laid a groundwork for future legislative action. Below is one of Mother Jones's speeches from the march of the children.

Women striking against child labor, New York City, c. 1900.

After a long and weary march, with more miles to travel, we are on our way to see President Roosevelt at Oyster Bay. We will ask him to recommend the passage of a bill by Congress to protect children against the greed of the manufacturer. We want him to hear the wail of the children, who never have a chance to go to school, but work from ten to eleven hours a day in the textile mills of Philadelphia, weaving the carpets that he and you walk on, and the curtains and clothes of the people.

Fifty years ago there was a cry against slavery, and the men of the North gave up their lives to stop the selling of black children on the block. Today the white child is sold for $2 a week, and even by his parents, to the manufacturer.

Fifty years ago the black babies were sold *c.o.d.* Today the white baby is sold to the manufacturer on the installment plan. He might die at his tasks and the manufacturer with the automobile and the yacht and the daughter who talks French to a poodle dog, as you can see any day at Twenty-third Street and Broadway when they roll by, could not afford to pay $2 a week for the child that might die, except on the present installment plan. What the President can do is to recommend a measure and send a message to Congress which will break the chains of the white children slaves.

He endorsed a bill for the expenditure of $45,000 to fill the stomach of a Prince who went gallivanting about the country. We will ask in the name of the aching hearts of these little ones that they be emancipated. I will tell the President that I saw men in Madison Square last night sleeping on benches and that the country can have no greatness while one unfortunate lies out at night without a bed to sleep on. I will tell him that the prosperity he boasts of is the prosperity of the rich wrung from the poor.

In Georgia where children work day and night in the cotton mills they have just passed a bill to protect song birds. What about the children from whom all song is gone?

The trouble is that the fellers in Washington don't care. I saw them last winter pass three railroad bills in one hour, and when labor cries for aid for the little ones they turn their backs and will not listen to her. I asked a man in prison once how he happened to get there. He had stolen a pair of shoes. I told him that if he had stolen a railroad he could be a United States senator. One hour of justice is worth an age of praying.

You are told that every American-born male citizen has a chance of being president. I tell you that the hungry man without a bed in the park would sell his chance for a good square meal, and these little toilers, deformed, dwarfed in body, soul, and morality, with nothing but toil before them and no chance for schooling, don't even have the dream that they might someday have a chance at the Presidential chair.

You see those monkeys in the cages. They are trying to teach them to talk. The monkeys are too wise, for they fear that then the manufacturers might buy them for slaves in their factories. In 1860 the workingmen had the advantage in the percentage of the country's wealth.

Today statistics at Washington show that with billions of wealth the wage earners' share is but 10 percent. We are going to tell the President of these things.

Negro Workers! (1912)

Committee of Defense, Brotherhood of Timber Workers

In December 1910 Arthur Lee Emerson and Jay Smith began to organize sawmill workers in parts of Texas and Louisiana into an industrial union known as the Brotherhood of Timber Workers (BTW). When the union demanded fair wages and better living conditions, the Southern Lumber Operators' Association held lock-outs, hired strikebreakers, and shut out pro-union workers. White BTW members, concerned that owners would hire non-union African Americans to replace the white workers, opened the union's membership to black workers. Long mistreated and abused by landowners in Texas and Louisiana, black laborers accepted the invitation to better their lives. In 1912 the BTW also voted to affiliate with the Industrial Workers of the World, known for its embrace of socialism and militant actions. Several months after this vote, a shootout between BTW and strikebreakers resulted in the deaths of three men and the arrest of Emerson and eight other union men on charges of murder. The document below shows that BTW responded to this crisis in part by imploring its black members to remain true to the union and to support efforts to free Emerson and his colleagues.

Don't allow yourselves to be divided by your fellow workers by the vicious Lumber Trust.

To all Negro workers, and especially to the Negro forest and lumber workers of the South, we send this message and appeal:

Fellow Worker:

When the forest slaves of Louisiana and Texas revolted against peonage and began, about two years ago, the organization of the Brotherhood of Timber Workers, an industrial union taking in all the workers in the sawmills and camps, the lumber kings at once recognized the power inherent in such a movement and immediately began a campaign of lying and violence against the union and all persons connected with it or suspected of sympathizing with us.

First among the cries they raised with us was, of course, the bunco cries of "white supremacy" and "social equality" coupled with that other cry: "They are organizing Negroes against whites!" which the capitalists and landlords of the South and their political buzzard and social carrion crows always raise in order to justify the slugging and assassination of white and colored working men who seek to organize and better the condition of their class. From the day you, the Negro workers, were "freed," down to the present hour these cries have been used to cloak the vilest crimes against workers, white and colored, and to hide the wholesale rape of the commonwealth of the South by as soulless and coldblooded a set of industrial scalawags and carpetbaggers as ever drew the breath of life.

For a generation, under these specious cries, they have kept us fighting each other—we to secure the "white supremacy" of a tramp and *you* the "social equality" of a vagrant. Our fathers "feel for it," but we, their children, have come to the conclusion that porterhouse steaks and champagne will look as well on your tables as on those of the industrial scalawags and carpetbaggers; that the "white supremacy" that means starvation wages and child slavery for us and the "social equality" that means the same for you, though they may mean the "high life" and "Christian civilization" to the lumber kings and landlords, will have to go. As far as we, the workers of the South, are concerned, the only "supremacy" and "equality" they have ever granted us is the supremacy of misery and the equality of rags. This supremacy and this equality we, the Brotherhood of Timber Workers, mean to stand no longer than we have an organization big and strong enough to enforce our demands, chief among which is "A man's life for all the workers in the mills and forests of the South." Because the Negro workers comprise one-half or more of the labor employed in the Southern labor industry, this battle cry of ours, "A man's life for all the workers," has been considered a menace and therefore a crime in the eyes of the Southern oligarchy, for they, as well as we, are fully alive to the fact that we can never raise our standard of living and better our conditions so long as they can keep us split, whether in race, craft, religious, or national lines, and they have tried and are trying all these methods of division in addition to their campaign of terror, wherein deeds have been and are being committed that would make Diaz blush with shame, they are so atrocious in their white-livered cruelty. For this reason, that they sought to organize all the workers, A. L. Emerson, president of the Brotherhood, and 63 other union men are now in prison at Lake Charles, La., under indictment, as a result of the Massacre of Grabow where three union men and one association gunman were killed, charged with murder in the first degree, indicted for killing their own brothers, and they will be sent to the gallows, or worse, to the frightful penal farms and levees of Louisiana, unless a united working class comes to their rescue with the funds necessary to defend them and the action that will bring them all free of the grave and levees.

Further words are idle. It is a useless waste of paper to tell you, the Negro workers, of the merciless injustice of the Southern Labor Operators' Association, for *your race* has learned through tears and blood the hyenaism we are fighting. Enough. Emerson and his associates are in prison because they fought for the unity of all the workers.

Will you remain silent, turn no hand to help them in this, their great hour of danger?

Our fight is your fight, and we appeal to you to do your duty by these men, the bravest of the brave! Help us free them all. Join the Brotherhood and help us blaze freedom's pathway through the jungles of the South.

"Workers of the world, unite! You have nothing but your chains to lose! You have a world to gain!"

Wage Slavery (1912)

Textile Workers of Lawrence, Massachusetts

Textile workers in Lawrence, Massachusetts, many of them immigrants, faced difficult lives inside and outside their factories in 1912. The poorly paid workers inhaled dust and lint that led to devastating lung ailments, and unsafe textile machinery ripped off numerous limbs. The workers lived in crowded tenements, and food was scarce. Conditions at work and home were so bad that the workers' life expectancy was less than forty years.

The Massachusetts legislature sought to help by reducing the work week for women and children from 56 to 54 hours. Factory owners across the state protested. The response of Lawrence's textile owners, including those at the America Woolen Company, was to slash wages by 3.5 percent, a devastating cut for workers who were already impoverished.

The textile workers refused to accept the reduction of wages and went on strike demanding, among other things, a 54-hour week and a 15 percent increase in wages. When the strike began on January 11, 1912, some workers damaged machines and smashed windows in a successful effort to make the factories inoperable. By the end of the second day of the strike, about 10,000 workers had walked away from their jobs.

The Industrial Workers of the World stepped in to help organize the strikers, whose numbers were growing rapidly, and the strike attracted national attention when violence broke out in response to the owners' decision to hire replacements. Like many strikes, however, most of the strike was nonviolent.

Violence erupted again when concerned strikers tried to send their children to New York City and other places in order to assure their safety and wellbeing. Lawrence police reacted with force to "the children's exodus" on February 24 when mothers refused the order to disperse before putting their sons and daughters on departing trains. The mothers were beaten by police with clubs and dragged away by their hair.

News of the police assaults on the mothers landed in the national

Striking textile workers in Lawrence, Massachusetts, 1912.

media and provoked a national outcry that resulted in President Taft ordering an investigation of labor conditions. Congress began its own investigation and heard shocking testimony from Carmela Teoli, a four-teen-year-old girl whose scalp had been ripped off by a textile machine. Subsequent pressure from Taft, Congress, and citizens across the nation forced the owners to accept some of the workers' demands, and in the mid-dle of March, after the nine-week strike had enlisted about 23,000 workers, Lawrence's textile owners granted a 15 percent wage increase and agreed to rehire the strikers. There was a considerable ripple effect, and by the end of the month 275,000 textile workers across New England enjoyed increas-es in their wages. Below is one of the strike proclamations delivered by the Lawrence strikers.

We, the 20,000 textile workers of Lawrence, are out on strike for the right to live free from slavery and starvation, free from overwork and underpay, free from a state of affairs that had become so unbearable and beyond our control, that we were compelled to march out of the slave pens of Lawrence in united resistance against the wrongs and injustice of years and years of wage slavery.

In our fight we have suffered and borne patiently the abuse and calumnies of the mill owners, the city government, police, militia, state government, legislature, and the local police court judge. We feel that in justice to our fellow workers we should at this time make known the causes which compelled us to strike against the mill owners of Lawrence. We hold that as useful members of society and as wealth producers we have the right to lead decent and honorable lives, that we ought to have homes and not shacks, that we ought to have clean food and not adulterated food at high prices, that we ought to have clothes suited to the weather and not shoddy garments. That to secure sufficient food, clothing, and shelter in a society made up of a robber class on the one hand and a working class on the other hand, it is absolutely necessary for the toilers to band themselves together and form a union, organizing its powers in such form as to them seem most likely to effect their safety and happiness. . . .

The history of the present mill owners is a history of repeated injuries, all having in direct object the establishment of an absolute tyranny over these textile workers. To prove this let facts be submitted to all right-thinking men and women of the civilized world. These mill owners have refused to meet the committees of the strikers. They have refused to consider their demands in any way that is reasonable or just. They have, in the security of their sumptuous offices, behind stout mill gates and serried rows of bayonets and policemen's clubs, defied the state, city, and public. In fact, the city of Lawrence and the government of Massachusetts have become the creatures of the mill owners. They have declared that they will not treat with the strikers till they return to the slavery against which they are in rebellion. They have starved the workers and driven them to such an extent that their homes are homes no longer, inasmuch as the mothers and children are driven by the low wages to work side by side with the father in the factory for a wage that

Parents sending children to safety during Lawrence strike, 1912.

spells bare existence and untimely death. To prove this to the world the large death rate of children under one year of age in Lawrence proves that most of these children perish because they were starved before birth. And those who survive the starving process grow up the victims of malnutrition.

These mill owners not only have the corrupting force of dollars on their side, but the powers of the city and state government are being used by them to oppress and sweep aside all opposition on the part of those overworked and underpaid textile workers. The very courts, where justice is supposed to be impartial, are being used by the millionaire mill owners. And so serious has this become that the workers have lost all faith in the local presiding judge. Without any attempt at a trial, men have been fined or jailed from six months to a year on trumped-up charges that would be a disgrace even in Russia. This judge is prejudiced and unfair in dealing with the strikers. He has placed all the strikers brought before him under excessive bail. He has dealt out lengthy sentences to the strikers as if they were hardened criminals, or old-time offenders. He has refused to release on bail two of the leaders of the strike, while he released a prisoner charged with conspiracy and planting dynamite, on a thousand dollars' bail. He sentenced, at one morning's session of court, 23 strikers to one year in jail on the fake charge of inciting to riot. This judge has declared he is opposed to the union that is conducting the strike.

The brutality of the police in dealing with the strikers has aroused them to a state of rebellious opposition to all such methods of maintaining order. The crimes of the police during this trouble are almost beyond human imagination. They have dragged young girls from their beds at midnight. They have clubbed the strikers at every opportunity. They have dragged little children from their mothers' arms and with their clubs they have struck women who are in a state of pregnancy. They have placed people under arrest for no reason whatsoever. They have prevented mothers from sending their children out of the city and have laid hold of the children and the mothers violently and thrown the children into waiting patrol wagons like so much rubbish. They have caused the death of a striker by clubbing the strikers into a state of violence. They have arrested and clubbed young boys and placed under arrest innocent girls for no offense at all.

The militia has used all kinds of methods to defeat the strikers. They have bayoneted a young boy. They have beaten up the strikers. They have been ordered to shoot to kill. They have murdered one young man, who died as a result of being bayoneted in the back. They have threatened one striker with death if he did not close the window of his home. They have threatened to stay in this city until the strike is over. They have bayoneted one citizen because he would not move along fast enough. And they have held up at the point of the bayonet hundreds of citizens and Civil War veterans.

The city government has denied the strikers the right to parade through the streets. They have abridged public assemblage by refusing the strikers the use of the city hall and public grounds for public meetings. They have turned the public buildings of the city into so many lodging houses for an army of hirelings and butchers. They have denied the strikers the right to use the Common for mass meetings, and they have ordered the police to take little children away from their parents, and they are responsible for all the violence and brutality on the part of the police.

The Massachusetts Legislature has refused to use any of the money of the state to help the strikers. They have voted $150,000 to maintain an army of 1,500 militiamen to be ready to shoot down innocent men, women, and children who are out on strike for a living wage. They have refused to use the powers of the state for the workers. They have appointed investigation committees, who declare, after perceiving the signs of suffering on the part of the strikers on every side, that there is no trouble with these people. . . .

Outlawed, with their children taken away from them, denied their rights before the law, surrounded by bayonets of the militia, and driven up and down the streets of the city by an overfed and arrogant body of police, these textile workers, sons and daughters of the working class, call upon the entire civilized world to witness what they have suffered at the hands of the hirelings of the mill-owning class. These men and women cannot suffer much longer; they will be compelled to rise in armed revolt against their oppressors if the present state of affairs is allowed to continue in Lawrence.

FIVE

Fighting for Women's Rights

All Men and Women Are Created Equal (1848)

Elizabeth Cady Stanton and Others

The abolitionist movement and the early women's rights movement converged in the life of Elizabeth Cady Stanton. Cady married the abolitionist Henry Stanton in 1840, and the two traveled to the World Anti-Slavery Convention in London. Cady Stanton and other women attendees had planned to be politically active—to speak publicly and cast votes—but when the all-male convention voted on the question of formally admitting women, about 90 percent of the delegates opposed the idea.

The male-dominated convention assigned the women to a roped-off area where the men in attendance could not even see them. While sequestered there, Cady Stanton and Lucretia Mott, an abolitionist who had founded the Philadelphia Female Anti-Slavery Society seven years earlier, decided to organize a meeting focused on women's rights back in the U.S.

Eight years later, Cady Stanton, Mott, Martha Wright, Jane Hunt, and Mary Ann McClintock called together the first women's rights convention in the United States. A public notice announcing the convention stated that it would "discuss the social, civil, and religious conditions and rights of women." Attended by about 300 women and men, many of them abolitionists, the convention took place on July 19th and 20th in Cady Stanton's new hometown of Seneca Falls, New York.

On the first day, when only women were admitted, Cady Stanton read the "Declaration of Sentiments" (see below), a document she and McClintock had penned, based on the Declaration of Independence. The document was accepted by the delegates on the second day, when both women and men were allowed to attend. The second day also saw a debate on the question of whether women should be granted the right to vote. Cady Stanton and Frederick Douglass spoke in favor of the right to vote, and although some of the conventioneers dissented from the radical idea, the convention passed a resolution stating that "it is the duty of the women of this country to secure to themselves their sacred right to the elective franchise." The convention's backing of this resolution is one of the most significant moments in the women's suffrage movement.

We hold these truths to be self-evident: that all men and women are created equal; that they are endowed by their Creator with certain inalienable rights; that among these are life, liberty, and the pursuit of happiness; that to secure these rights governments are instituted, deriving their just powers from the consent of the governed. Whenever any form of government becomes destructive of these ends, it is the right of those who suffer from it to refuse allegiance to it, and to insist upon the institution of a new government, laying its foundation on such principles, and organizing its powers in such form as to them shall seem most likely to effect their safety and happiness. Prudence, indeed, will dictate that governments long established should not be changed for light and transient causes; and accordingly, all experience hath shown that mankind are more disposed to suffer, while evils are sufferable, than to right themselves by abolishing the forms to which they are accustomed. But when a long train of abuses and usurpations, pursuing invariably the same object, evinces a design to reduce them under absolute despotism, it is their duty to throw off such government, and to provide new guards for their future security. Such has been the patient sufferance of the women under this government, and such is now the necessity which constrains them to demand the equal station to which they are entitled.

The history of mankind is a history of repeated injuries and usurpations on the part of man toward woman, having in direct object the establishment of an absolute tyranny over her. To prove this, let facts be submitted to a candid world.

He has never permitted her to exercise her inalienable right to the elective franchise.

He has compelled her to submit to laws, in the formation of which she had no voice.

He has withheld from her rights which are given to the most ignorant and degraded men—both natives and foreigners.

Having deprived her of this first right of a citizen, the elective franchise, thereby leaving her without representation in the halls of legislation, he has oppressed her on all sides.

He has made her, if married, in the eye of the law, civilly dead.

He has taken from her all right in property, even to the wages she earns.

He has made her, morally, an irresponsible being, as she can commit many crimes with impunity, provided they be done in the presence of her husband. In the covenant of marriage, she is compelled to promise obedience to her husband, he becoming, to all intents and purposes, her master—the law giving him power to deprive her of her liberty, and to administer chastisement.

He has so framed the laws of divorce, as to what shall be the proper causes of divorce; in case of separation, to whom the guardianship of the children shall be given; as to be wholly regardless of the happiness of women—the law, in all cases, going upon the false supposition of the supremacy of man, and giving all power into his hands.

After depriving her of all rights as a married woman, if single and the owner of property, he has taxed her to support a government which recognizes her only when her property can be made profitable to it.

He has monopolized nearly all the profitable employments, and from those she is permitted to follow, she receives but a scanty remuneration.

He closes against her all the avenues to wealth and distinction, which he considers most honorable to himself. As a teacher of theology, medicine, or law, she is not known.

He has denied her the facilities for obtaining a thorough education—all colleges being closed against her.

He allows her, in church as well as state, but a subordinate position, claiming apostolic authority for her exclusion from the ministry, and, with some exceptions, from any public participation in the affairs of the church.

He has created a false public sentiment by giving to the world a different code of morals for men and women, by which moral delinquencies which exclude women from society, are not only tolerated but deemed of little account in man.

He has usurped the prerogative of Jehovah himself, claiming it as his right to assign for her a sphere of action, when that belongs to her conscience and her God.

He has endeavored, in every way that he could, to destroy her confidence in her own powers, to lessen her self-respect, and to make her willing to lead a dependent and abject life.

Now, in view of this entire disfranchisement of one-half the people of this country, their social and religious degradation—in view of the unjust laws above mentioned, and because women do feel themselves aggrieved, oppressed, and fraudulently deprived of their most sacred rights, we insist that they have immediate admission to all the rights and privileges which belong to them as citizens of these United States.

In entering upon the great work before us, we anticipate no small amount of misconception, misrepresentation, and ridicule; but we shall use every instrumentality within our power to effect our object. We shall employ agents, circulate tracts, petition the state and national legislatures, and endeavor to enlist the pulpit and the press in our behalf. We hope this convention will be followed by a series of conventions, embracing every part of the country.

Firmly relying upon the final triumph of the Right and the True, we do this day affix our signatures to this declaration.

Keep the Thing Going (1851, 1867)

Sojourner Truth

Two years after the historic convention at Seneca Falls, the first National Women's Rights Convention was held at Worcester, Massachusetts. About 900 delegates from eleven different states attended the first day. Abby Kelley Foster, a leading activist from Worcester, dared to tell delegates that women had a right to resist male domination in the same way that the colonial leaders had rebelled against King George. Another famous speaker at the convention was Sojourner Truth. By this time, Truth had published The Narrative of Sojourner Truth, *which she had dictated, because she could not write, to editor Olive Gilbert. The book revealed the horrors of her life as a slave—and made her the most famous black woman in the United States. Part of Truth's power was her physical embodiment of oppression against not only African Americans but also women and the poor and uneducated, as is evident in this reporter's explanation of a speech Truth delivered at a women's rights convention in Akron, Ohio, in 1851.*

One of the most unique and interesting speeches of the convention was made by Sojourner Truth, an emancipated slave. It is impossible to transfer it to paper, or convey an adequate idea of the effect it produced upon the audience. Those only can appreciate it who saw her powerful form, her whole-souled, earnest gesture, and listened to her strong and truthful tones. She came forward to the platform and addressing the President said with great simplicity:

May I say a few words? Receiving an affirmative answer, she proceeded; I want to say a few words about this matter. I am a woman's rights. I have as much muscle as any man, and can do as much work as any man. I have plowed and reaped and husked and chopped and mowed, and can any man do more than that? I have heard much about the sexes being equal; I can carry as much as any man, and can eat as much too, if I can get it. I am strong as any man that is now.

As for intellect, all I can say is, if woman have a pint and man a quart—why can't she have her little pint full? You need not be afraid to give us our rights for fear we will take too much—for we won't take more than our pint'll hold.

The poor men seem to be all in confusion and don't know what to do. Why children, if you have woman's rights give it to her and you will feel better. You will have your own rights, and they won't be so much trouble.

I can't read, but I can hear. I have heard the Bible and have learned that Eve caused man to sin. Well if woman upset the world, do give her a chance to set it right side up again. The lady has spoken about Jesus, how he never spurned woman from him, and she was right. When Lazarus died, Mary and Martha came to him with faith and love and besought him to raise their brother. And Jesus wept—and Lazarus came forth. And how came Jesus into the world? Through God who created him and woman who bore him. Man, where is your part?

But the women are coming up blessed be God and a few of the men are coming up with them. But man is in a tight place, the poor slave is on him, woman is coming on him, and he is surely between a hawk and a buzzard.

Truth also spoke frequently on the rights of women after Emancipation, and below is the text of a speech she delivered at the first annual meeting of the American Equal Rights Association. Held in New York City in 1867, the meeting sought to align the National Woman Suffrage Association with the American Anti-Slavery Society. The alignment collapsed when Susan B. Anthony and others opposed ratification of the Fifteenth Amendment because, although it granted African American men the right to vote, it failed to enfranchise women.

My friends, I am rejoiced that you are glad, but I don't know how you will feel when I get through. I come from another field—the country of the slave. They have got their liberty—so much good luck to have slavery partly destroyed; not entirely. I want it root and branch destroyed. Then we will all be free indeed. I feel that if I have to answer for the deeds done in my body just as much as a man, I have a right to have just as much as a man. There is a great stir about colored men getting their rights, but not a word about the colored women; and if colored men get their rights, and not colored women theirs, you see the colored men will be masters over the women, and it will be just as bad as it was before. So I am for keeping the thing going while things are stirring; because if we wait till it is still, it will take a great while to get it going again. White women are a great deal smarter, and know more than colored women, while colored women do not know scarcely anything. They go out washing, which is about as high as a colored woman gets, and their men go about idle, strutting up and down; and when the women come home, they ask for their money and take it all, and then scold because there is no food. I want you to consider on that, chil'n. I call you chil'n; you are somebody's chil'n, and I am old enough to be mother of all that is here. I want women to have their rights. In the courts women have no right, no voice; nobody speaks for them. I wish woman to have her voice there among the pettifoggers. If it is not a fit place for women, it is unfit for men to be there.

I am above eighty years old; it is about time for me to be going. I have been forty years a slave and forty years free, and would be here forty years more to have equal rights for all. I suppose I am kept here because something remains for me to do; I suppose I am yet to help to break the chain. I have done a great deal of work; as much as a man, but did not get so much pay. I used to work in the field and bind grain, keeping up with the cradler; but men doing no more, got twice as much pay; so with the German women. They work in the field and do as much work, but do not get the pay. We do as much, we eat as much, we want as much. I suppose I am about the only colored woman that goes about to speak for the rights of the colored women. I want to keep the thing stirring, now that the ice is cracked. What we want is a little money. You men know that you get as much again as women when you write, or for what you do. When we get our rights we shall not have to come to you for money, for then we shall have money enough in our own pockets; and maybe you will ask us for money. But help us now until we get it. It is a good consolation to know that when we have got this battle once fought we shall not be coming to you anymore. You have been having our rights so long that you think, like a slaveholder, that you own us. I know that it is hard for one who has held the reins for so long to give up; it cuts like a knife. It will feel all the better when it closes up again. I have been in Washington about three years, seeing about these colored people. Now colored men have the right to vote. There ought to be equal rights now more than ever, since colored people have got their freedom. I am going to talk several times while I am here; so now I will do a little singing. I have not heard any singing since I came here.

Robbed of Citizenship (1873)

Susan B. Anthony

"Men—their rights and nothing more. Women—their rights and nothing less." This was one of the provocative mottos of the National Woman Suffrage Association, the group that Susan B. Anthony represented when lobbying sympathetic Republican leaders, including Ulysses S. Grant, to include the woman's right to vote in their platform for the upcoming presidential election in 1872. Although she failed in this effort, Anthony still sided with the Republicans in the national election, partly because Horace Greely, the Democratic candidate for president, was openly opposed to enfranchising women.

Anthony continued to lobby for a woman's right to vote, and on a speaking tour in the fall of 1872 she often referred to the country's two new constitutional amendments. Citing the Fourteenth Amendment, Anthony pointed out the obvious—that women born or naturalized within the United States were citizens, and that denying them the right to vote abridged their liberty and defied equal protection of the law. Anthony added that the Fifteenth Amendment also supported women's enfranchisement because of its declaration that "the right of citizens of the United States to vote shall not be denied or abridged by the United States or by any State on account of race, color, or previous condition of servitude." She argued that even though the amendment, despite intense lobbying from suffragists, did not include the word "sex" along with "race" and "color," because women were citizens, states were acting illegally when denying them the right to vote

With her constitutional arguments ready, Anthony sought to cast a vote in the 1872 presidential election. It was not the first time a woman sought to vote—women had tried in New Hampshire and the District of Columbia, and several had actually succeeded in Detroit, Michigan, and in Nyack, New York—but none had offered the level of publicity that Anthony's case would. On November 1, after she had consulted with Henry Selden, a former New York Court of Appeals judge, Anthony and fifteen other women, including her three sisters, strode into a barbershop in Rochester's Eighth Ward, where the local board of registry had based itself. Citing the Fourteenth Amendment, the women demanded to be registered to vote. The board of supervisors was shocked, but in a 2-1 vote, with the only Democrat in opposition, the board agreed to register the activists, an act that earned the wrath of the local newspaper, which published another part of the Fourteenth Amendment in response—"Any person . . . who shall vote without having a legal right to vote; or do any unlawful act to secure . . . an opportunity to vote for himself or any other person . . . shall be deemed guilty of a crime."

Anthony and her fifteen colleagues were undeterred, and on November 5 they showed up early at the Eighth Ward polling station, ready to vote. The three election inspectors—the same three who had earlier voted on their registration—passed out ballots to the women, and all sixteen voted.

The story made national news, and Rochester's governing authorities were not pleased. On Thanksgiving Day, Rochester's deputy marshal, E. J. Keeney, knocked on Anthony's door and shared some troubling news. "You see, Miss Anthony," he said, "I am here on a most uncomfortable errand. The fact is, Miss Anthony . . . I have come to arrest you." Keeney offered to help the arrest remain discreet, but Anthony declined, saying, "I prefer to be arrested like anybody else. You may handcuff me as soon as I get my hat and coat." Warrants were served on all sixteen women that day.

Released on bail, Anthony went on another speaking tour, delivering a lecture titled with a stacked question: "Is It a Crime for a United States Citizen to Vote?" The tour ended when Anthony's trial began on June 17. Covered by the New York Times, the trial quickly became a national spectacle; even former U.S. President Millard Fillmore joined the overflowing crowds.

The presiding judge, Ward Hunt, was a known opponent of the woman's right to vote, and his actions, including a decision to deny Anthony a right to act as a witness, demonstrated as much. Perhaps most shocking was that although an all-male jury had been impaneled, Hunt closed the trial by instructing the jury to find Anthony guilty. Reading from the instructions he wrote before the trial had even begun, Hunt stated: "The question before the jury is wholly a question or questions of law under the 14th Amendment. . . . Miss Anthony was not protected in a right to vote. . . . If I am right in this, this result must be a verdict on your part of guilty, and therefore I direct that you find a verdict of guilty."

The courtroom, including the jurors, was shocked by this miscarriage of justice, but no juror spoke against the judge or the verdict when polled by the clerk. (When asked later, the jurors expressed their frustration with the judge and the likeliness of their voting to acquit.) Hunt's verdict prevailed, and though he was attacked in the national press for violating the right to trial by a jury of one's peers, he proceeded to the sentencing part of the trial the following day. But he made a strategic blunder at that point. He asked Anthony, as he did of all found guilty, whether "the prisoner has anything to say why sentence shall not be pronounced." Anthony had plenty to say, and below are her comments to the angry judge.

Women suffragists, New York City.

The Court: The prisoner will stand up. Has the prisoner anything to say why sentence shall not be pronounced?

Miss Anthony: Yes, your honor, I have many things to say; for in your ordered verdict of guilty, you have trampled underfoot every vital principle of our government. My natural rights, my civil rights, my political rights, are all alike ignored. Robbed of the fundamental principle of citizenship, I am degraded from the status of a citizen to that of a subject; and not only myself individually but all of my sex are, by your honor's verdict, doomed to political subjection under this so-called republican government.

Judge Hunt: The Court cannot listen to a rehearsal of arguments the prisoner's counsel has already consumed three hours in presenting.

Miss Anthony: May it please your honor, I am not arguing the question, but simply stating the reasons why sentence cannot, in justice, be pronounced against me. Your denial of my citizen's right to vote is the denial of my right of consent as one of the governed, the denial of my right of representation as one of the taxed, the denial of my right to a trial by a jury of my peers as an offender against law, therefore, the denial of my sacred rights to life, liberty, property, and—

Judge Hunt: The Court cannot allow the prisoner to go on.

Miss Anthony: But your honor will not deny me this one and only poor privilege of protest against this high-handed outrage upon my citizen's rights. May it please the Court to remember that since the day of my arrest last November, this is the time that either myself or any person of my disfranchised class has been allowed a word of defense before judge or jury—

Judge Hunt: The prisoner must sit down; the Court cannot allow it.

Miss Anthony: Of all my prosecutors, from the 8th Ward corner grocery politician, who entered the complaint, to the United States marshal, commissioner, district attorney, district judge, your honor on the bench, not one is my peer, but each and all are my political sovereigns; and had your honor submitted my case to the jury, as was clearly your duty, even then I should have had just cause of protest, for not one of those men was my peer; but, native or foreign, white or black, rich or poor, educated or ignorant, awake or asleep, sober or drunk, each and every man of them was my political superior; hence, in no sense, my peer. Even under such circumstances, a commoner of England tried before a jury of lords would have far less cause to complain than I, a woman, tried before a jury of men. Even my counsel, the Hon. Henry R. Selden, who has argued my cause so ably, so earnestly, so unanswerably before your honor, is my political sovereign. Precisely as no disfranchised person is entitled to sit upon a jury, and no woman is entitled to the franchise, so none but a regularly admitted lawyer is allowed to practice in the courts, and no woman can gain admission to the bar—hence, jury, judge, counsel, must all be of the superior class.

Judge Hunt: The Court must insist—the prisoner has been tried according to the established forms of law.

Miss Anthony: Yes, your honor, but by forms of law all made by men, administered by men, in favor of men, and against women; and hence, your honor's ordered verdict of guilty, against a United States citizen for the exercise of "that citizen's right to vote," simply because that citizen was a woman and not a man. But yesterday, the same manmade forms of law declared it a crime punishable with $1,000 fine and six months' imprisonment, for you, or me, or any of us, to give a cup of cold water, a crust of bread, or a night's shelter to a panting fugitive as he was tracking his way to Canada. And every man or woman in whose veins coursed a drop of human sympathy violated that wicked law, reckless of consequences, and was justified in so doing. As then the slaves who got their freedom [had to] take it over, or under, or through the unjust forms of law, precisely so now must women, to get their right to a voice in this Government, take it; and I have taken mine, and mean to take it at every possible opportunity.

Judge Hunt: The Court orders the prisoner to sit down. It will not allow another word.

Miss Anthony: When I was brought before your honor for trial, I hoped for a broad and liberal interpretation of the Constitution and its recent amendments, that should declare all United States citizens under its protecting aegis—that should declare equality of rights the national guarantee to all persons born or naturalized in the United States. But failing to get this justice—failing, even, to get a trial by a jury *not* of my peers—I ask not leniency at your hands—but rather the full rigors of the law.

Judge Hunt: The Court must insist—(Here the prisoner sat down.)

Judge Hunt: The prisoner will stand up. (Here Miss Anthony arose again.) The sentence of the Court is that you pay a fine of one hundred dollars and the costs of the prosecution.

Miss Anthony: May it please your honor, I shall never pay a dollar of your unjust penalty. All the stock in trade I possess is a $10,000 debt, incurred by publishing my paper—*The Revolution*—four years ago, the sole object of which was to educate all women to do precisely as I have done, rebel against your manmade, unjust, unconstitutional forms of law that tax, fine, imprison, and hang women, while they deny them the right of representation in the Government; and I shall work on with might and main to pay every dollar of that honest debt, but not a penny shall go to this unjust claim. And I shall earnestly and persistently continue to urge all women to the practical recognition of the old revolutionary maxim, that "Resistance to tyranny is obedience to God."

Marriage and Love Have Nothing in Common (1910)

Emma Goldman

Emma Goldman was arguably the most well known anarchist of the twentieth century. One of her more notorious acts of resistance against capitalism occurred when she assisted fellow anarchist Alexander Berkman in his attempt to assassinate Henry Clay Frick, chair of the Carnegie Steel Company, after he used overwhelming force against steelworkers during the Homestead Steel Strike of 1892. Berkman's failure to kill Frick and thereby spark a workers' revolution served as a catalyst for Goldman to focus on nonviolent acts of resistance for advancing anarchist principles in the years to follow.

Goldman explained her vision of anarchism in positive and negative terms. Negatively, anarchism stood "for the liberation of the human mind from the dominion of religion; the liberation of the human body from the dominion of property; liberation from the shackles and restraint of government." And positively, anarchism advocated "a social order based on the free grouping of individuals for the purpose of producing real social wealth; an order that will guarantee to every human being free access to the earth and full enjoyment of the necessities of life, according to individual desires, tastes, and inclinations."

Goldman was imprisoned many times as she joined in workers' strikes and campaigns for free speech, draft resistance, and women's rights, including the right to access birth control. As the excerpt below shows, Goldman also became a passionate proponent of free love, writing prolifically about marriage as an economic arrangement that institutionalizes male superiority and strips women of their independence and dignity.

Marriage and love have nothing in common; they are as far apart as the poles; are, in fact, antagonistic to each other. No doubt some marriages have been the result of love. Not, however, because love could assert itself only in marriage; much rather is it because few people can completely outgrow a convention. There are today large numbers of men and women to whom marriage is naught but a farce, but who submit to it for the sake of public opinion. At any rate, while it is true that some marriages are based on love, and while it is equally true that in some cases love continues in married life, I maintain that it does so regardless of marriage, and not because of it.

On the other hand, it is utterly false that love results from marriage. On rare occasions one does hear of a miraculous case of a married couple falling in love after marriage, but on close examination it will be found that it is a mere adjustment to the inevitable. Certainly the growing-used to each other is far away from the spontaneity, the intensity, and beauty of love, without which the intimacy of marriage must prove degrading to both the woman and the man.

Marriage is primarily an economic arrangement, an insurance pact. It differs from the ordinary life insurance agreement only in that it is more binding, more exacting. Its returns are insignificantly small compared with the investments. In taking out an insurance policy one pays for it in dollars and cents, always at liberty to discontinue payments. If, however, woman's premium is a husband, she pays for it with her name, her privacy, her self-respect, her very life, "until death doth part." Moreover, the marriage insurance condemns her to lifelong dependency, to parasitism, to complete uselessness, individual as well as social. Man, too, pays his toll, but as his sphere is wider, marriage does not limit him as much as woman. He feels his chains more in an economic sense.

Thus Dante's motto over Inferno applies with equal force to marriage: "Ye who enter here leave all hope behind." . . .

It is this slavish acquiescence to man's superiority that has kept the marriage institution seemingly intact for so long a period. Now that woman is coming into her own, now that she is actually growing aware of herself as a being outside of the master's grace, the sacred institution of marriage is gradually being undermined, and no amount of sentimental lamentation can stay it.

From infancy, almost, the average girl is told that marriage is her ultimate goal; therefore her training and education must be directed towards that end. Like the mute beast fattened for slaughter, she is prepared for that. Yet, strange to say, she is allowed to know much less about her function as wife and mother than the ordinary artisan of his trade. It is indecent and filthy for a respectable girl to know anything of the marital relation. Oh, for the inconsistency of respectability, that needs the marriage vow to turn something which is filthy into the purest and most sacred arrangement that none dare question or criticize. Yet that is exactly the attitude of the average upholder of marriage. The prospective wife and mother is kept in complete ignorance of her only asset in the competitive field—sex. Thus she enters into lifelong relations with a man only to find herself shocked, repelled, outraged beyond measure by the most natural and healthy instinct, sex. It is safe to say that a large percentage of the unhappiness, misery, distress, and physical suffering of matrimony is due to the criminal ignorance in sex matters that is being extolled as a great virtue. Nor is it at all an exaggeration when I say that more than one home has been broken up because of this deplorable fact.

If, however, woman is free and big enough to learn the mystery of sex without the sanction of state or church, she will stand condemned as utterly unfit to become the wife of a "good" man, his goodness consisting of an empty head and plenty of money. Can there be anything more outrageous than the idea that a healthy, grown woman, full of life and passion, must deny nature's demand, must subdue her most intense craving, undermine her health and break her spirit, must stunt her vision, abstain from the depth and glory of sex experience until a "good" man comes along to take her unto himself as a wife? That is precisely what marriage means. How can such an arrangement end except in failure? This is one, though not the least important, factor of marriage, which differentiates it from love. . . .

As to the protection of the woman—therein lies the curse of marriage. Not that it really protects her, but the very idea is so revolting, such an outrage and insult on life, so degrading to human dignity, as to forever condemn this parasitic institution.

It is like that other paternal arrangement—capitalism. It robs man of his birthright, stunts his growth, poisons his body, keeps him in ignorance, in poverty and dependence, and then institutes charities that thrive on the last vestige of man's self-respect.

The institution of marriage makes a parasite of woman, an absolute dependent. It incapacitates her for life's struggle, annihilates her social consciousness, paralyzes her imagination, and then imposes its gracious protection, which is in reality a snare, a travesty on human character. . . .

Love, the strongest and deepest element in all life, the harbinger of hope, of joy, of ecstasy; love, the defier of all laws, of all conventions; love, the freest, the most powerful molder of human destiny; how can such an all-compelling force be synonymous with that poor little state and church-begotten weed, marriage?

Why Women Want to Vote (1913)

Anna Howard Shaw

On March 3, 1913, one day before the presidential inauguration of Woodrow Wilson, the abolitionist and lawyer Inez Milholland, sporting a white cape and a crown, sat atop a white horse as she led 5,000 marchers, most of them women, in the first suffragette march on Washington. It was a colorful and joyous display of nonviolent resistance to disfranchisement—until unruly crowds of men showed up to shout epithets and to trip, grab, and shove the marchers. DC police officers offered no protection, and about 100 marchers ended up in a nearby emergency hospital. But the marchers persisted in their procession from near the Capitol to the Treasury building, where they staged a patriotic pageant advocating for equal treatment under the law.

The march was conceived by Alice Paul during the annual convention of the National American Women Suffrage Association (NAWSA) in November 1912. Armed with a PhD from the University of Pennsylvania, where she wrote her dissertation on the legal rights of women in the state, Paul was an advocate of nonviolent direct action. From 1908 until 1910, she had worked with militant suffragists in the Women's Social and Political Union in England. Jailed for their nonviolent direct action campaigns, Paul and her British colleagues also went on hunger strikes, even to the point of being force-fed by prison officials. Upon her return to the United States, Paul found NAWSA's lobbying tactics to be too gradualist, and at the November 12 convention, she pitched the idea for a march on Washington to take place just before the presidential inauguration. The NAWSA granted her permission to proceed with her plans and named her chair of the organization's congressional committee.

One of the historically significant aspects of the planning for the march involved a battle over the place of African American women. Initial plans included a proposal to segregate the march, with black women marching behind the white women. But when the plan became public,

Suffrage parade, New York City, 1912.

black abolitionist Ida B. Wells and others mounted a vigorous dissent, and according to the Crisis, the main publication of the National Association for the Advancement of Colored People (NAACP), "telegrams and protests poured in and eventually the colored women marched according to the State and occupation without let or hindrance."

Although the march did not secure women the right to vote, it did result in President Wilson granting a meeting with suffragist leaders two weeks into his presidency. Alice Paul headed the group and presented a spirited call for the enfranchisement of women. Wilson's response was non-committal, but he promised that the group's request "will receive my most careful consideration."

Below is a rationale for the historic march penned by NWSA president Anna Howard Shaw, whose longtime companion was Lucy E. Anthony, the niece of Susan B. Anthony. Shaw had received a divinity degree from Boston University and served as an unordained Methodist pastor in Massachusetts from 1878 to 1885. The march's conference book stated that "the fact that, early in her career, a conference of the church refused to ordain her on account of her sex inspired her with a desire to work for a broader recognition for women. She resigned from the pulpit and was chosen lecturer for the Massachusetts Woman's Suffrage Association in 1885."

There are some of us who want to vote just because we do. When asked why we want to vote our answer is: Why should we not want to vote? Show us why not. The burden of proof is on the questioners' side. If this thing called the ballot is good for our brothers, why is it not good for us? We are born of the same parents, educated in the same schools, taxed at the same rate, governed by the same laws. Why should our voice not be heard in the state?

Women who answer thus are women of strong personality. They have not only a vigorous personal ego but they have also the pride of sex. . . .

After having investigated the whole field, they have, with Alice Stone Blackwell, come to the conclusion that women should be allowed to vote for the following reasons:

Because it is right and fair that those who must obey the laws should have a voice in making them.

Because it is just that those who must pay taxes should have a vote as to the size of the tax and the way it should be spent.

Because the moral, educational, and humane legislation desired by women would be secured more easily if women had votes. Colorado women worked in vain for years for a state industrial school until they got the ballot; then the legislature promptly granted it.

Because laws unjust to women would be amended more quickly. It took Massachusetts women fifty-five years without the ballot to secure the law making mothers equal guardians of their children with the fathers. It took Colorado women just one year with the ballot to secure a similar law. Women have agitated for this particular reform for over half a century and yet only sixteen of the forty-eight states give equal guardianship to mothers.

Because disfranchisement helps to keep wages down. The Honorable Carroll D. Wright, National Commissioner of Labor, said: "The lack of direct political influence constitutes a powerful reason why women's wages have been kept at a minimum."

Because equal suffrage would increase the proportion of educated voters. The high schools of every state in the Union are graduating more girls than boys.

Because it would increase the proportion of native-born voters. There are one hundred and twenty-nine men of foreign birth in the United States to every one hundred women.

Because it would increase the moral and law-abiding vote very much, while increasing the vicious and criminal vote very little. Women form a minority of all the criminal and vicious classes, and a majority of all the classes working for human advancement.

Because it leads to fair treatment of women in the public service. In Massachusetts the average pay of a female teacher is about one-third that of a male teacher, and in almost all of the states it is unequal. In Wyoming and Utah, the law provides that they shall receive equal pay for equal work.

Because legislation for the protection of children would be secured more easily. Judge Lindsey, of the Denver Juvenile Court, says: "We have in Colorado the most advanced laws of any state in the Union for the care and protection of the home and the children. These laws, in my opinion, would not exist at this time if it were not for the powerful influence of woman suffrage."

Because it is the quietest, easiest, most dignified, and least conspicuous way of influencing public affairs. It takes much less expenditure of time, labor, and personal presence to go up to the ballot box, drop in a slip of paper, and come away, than to persuade a multitude of miscellaneous voters to vote right.

Because it would make women more broadminded. Professor

Edward H. Griggs says, "The ballot is an education and women will become more practical and more wise in using it."

Because woman's ballot would make it harder for notoriously bad candidates to be nominated or elected. In the equal-suffrage states, both parties have to put up men of respectable character or lose the woman's vote.

Because it would increase women's influence.

Because it would help those women who need help the most. Mrs. Maud Nathan, President of the National Consumers League, says: "My experience in investigating the condition of women wage-earners warrants the assertion that some of the evils from which they suffer would not exist if women had the ballot. In the states where women vote, there is far better enforcement of the laws which protect working girls.

Because it is a maxim in war, "Always do the thing to which your adversary particularly objects." Every vicious interest in the country would rather continue to contend with woman's indirect influence than try to cope with woman's vote.

For the Sake of Consistency (1915)

Mary Church Terrell

Mary Church Terrell was born into a wealthy family in Memphis, Tennessee, on September 23, 1863. After graduating from Oberlin College with bachelor's and master's degrees, she taught at Wilberforce College and then at the M Street Colored High School in Washington, DC. Best known for her leading role in advancing the cause of racial justice for African American women, Terrell helped found the National Association of Colored Women in 1896 and steered the group to focus on education, employment, and work in local communities. Terrell was also a founder of the NAACP, which would become the nation's premier advocate for the advancement of black civil rights. The document below, Terrell's contribution to a symposium sponsored by the NAACP's Crisis magazine, shows that she also supported women's suffrage. During the Woodrow Wilson administration, Terrell even picketed the White House in support of woman suffrage.

Even if I believed that woman should be denied the right of suffrage, wild horses could not drag such an admission from my pen or my lips, for this reason: precisely the same arguments used to prove that the ballot be withheld from women are advanced to prove that colored men should not be allowed to vote. The reasons for repealing the Fifteenth Amendment differ but little from the arguments advanced by those who oppose the enfranchisement of women. Consequently, nothing could be more inconsistent than that colored people should use their influence against granting the ballot to women, if they believe that colored men should enjoy this right which citizenship confers.

What could be more absurd and ridiculous than that one group of individuals who are trying to throw off the yoke of oppression themselves, so as to get relief from conditions which handicap and injure them, should favor laws and customs which impede the progress of another unfortunate group and hinder them in every conceivable way? For the sake of consistency, therefore, if my sense of justice were not developed at all, and I could not reason intelligently, as a colored woman I should not tell my dearest friend that I opposed woman suffrage.

But how can anyone who is able to use reason, and who believes in dealing out justice to all God's creatures, think it is right to withhold from one-half of the human race rights and privileges freely accorded to the other half, which is neither more deserving nor more capable of exercising them?

For two thousand years mankind has been breaking down the various barriers which interposed themselves between human beings and their perfect freedom to exercise all the faculties with which they were divinely endowed. Even in monarchies old fetters which formerly restricted freedom, dwarfed the intellect, and doomed certain individuals to narrow circumscribed spheres, because of the mere accident of birth, are being loosed and broken one by one. In view of such wisdom and experience the political subjection of women in the United States can be likened only to a relic of barbarism, or to a spot upon the sun, or to an octopus holding this republic in its hideous grasp, so that further progress to the best form of government is impossible and that precious ideal its founders promised it would be, seems nothing more tangible than a mirage.

SIX

World War I

I Denounce the Governing Class (1915)

Kate Richards O'Hare

Kate Richards O'Hare was one of the two most popular speakers, writers, and activists in the Socialist Party of America before and during World War I. The other was the party's seasoned presidential candidate, Eugene V. Debs. Like Debs, O'Hare was fiercely opposed to U.S. entry into World War I, and she expressed her dissent in speeches across the country and in a monthly socialist newspaper, National Rip-Saw. She served as a staff writer for the publication, and below is one of her 1915 essays that critiques the war and offers a nonviolent way to halt it.

In 1916, O'Hare's radical politics led her to become the first woman to run for the U.S. Senate, even though women had not yet won the right to vote. When her venture into electoral politics proved unsuccessful, she resumed her antiwar campaign under the ever-watchful eye of the U.S. government. In 1917, after delivering a stirring antiwar speech in Bowman, North Dakota, O'Hare was arrested and charged with sedition under the 1917 Espionage Act. The government convicted her, and she received a sentence of five years. But after she served about fourteen months at Missouri State Penitentiary, President Woodrow Wilson commuted her sentence. Freed in May 1920, the relentless resister toured the country and demanded amnesty for all who had dissented during the war.

Never in all the history of the United States has the thoughtful, intelligent citizenship of our nation had such cause to blush for the petty, sordid, groveling character of our so-called statesmen. Never has the womanhood of the country so great cause for resentment and bitterness.

We are facing now two of the most vital, all-embracing questions of life and death, life and death not only for millions of individuals, but life and death for mankind and civilization itself: the mighty problems of war-cursed Europe and unemployment-cursed America.

All through the bitter ice and snow-cursed months of winter, the grim tragedy of unemployment has dogged the footsteps of millions of American men and women. Vast armies of hungry, poverty-stricken men have drifted from city to city, from North to South and East to West, in the vain search for work. These men have crept into jails, workhouses, and municipal lodging houses like animals to their burrows and whined like famished dogs in breadlines and before soup kitchens.

Hundreds of thousands of girls have lost their six-dollar-a-week jobs and have been driven out on the streets to be used by lustful men and made the victims of police brutality.

Homes have been broken up, babies deserted by desperate parents on doorsteps, and orphan asylums flooded by the children of the jobless men haunting the breadlines.

Suicides are occurring with sickening regularity, while crime waves have flooded every city and proven the police machinery of the United States worse than useless for the protection of life and property.

In Europe already the stench of unburied putrefying corpses that only six months ago were the pick and flower of European young manhood is polluting the air. Agriculture and industry are throttled, the whole life of the continent is given over to the appalling task of completely destroying culture, civilization—the race life.

The very soil of Europe is sodden with human blood, the rivers

Anti-conscription march, New York City, 1916.

of that unhappy continent are contaminated with rotting bodies while famine and pestilence hover like vultures over the battlefields.

Millions of men have been slain, millions more will be slain, tens of thousands of men die every time the sun makes its pilgrimage from east to west. Millions of homes have been destroyed, millions of women and children starved, myriads of women in Europe today bear beneath their anguished hearts the little lives that have been conceived in force, that will be nurtured in blazing hate and will be born to deeds of violence and insanity. In a few months, the raped Belgian women will give life to the hated offspring of German invaders, the outraged Polish women will bear the fruit of the hellish lust of the Russian soldiers, and so the cruel, brutal story runs, involving every warring nation and bearing in its train horrors too frightful for the human mind to grasp.

There is useful work enough in the United States to usefully employ every jobless man in the country, and the money that has been stolen by corrupt officials and . . . wasted on armament and preparation for war would provide funds to give labor to every unemployed man and make possible all manner of public industries. The law-making power of our government that allows it to declare a "war tax" would also allow the declaration of a "peace tax"; the constitutional power to issue money with which to wage a war of destruction could just as readily be invoked to wage a war on poverty and unemployment.

The Congress of the United States has the power to stop the war in Europe almost instantly by forbidding the exportation of food and ammunition.

Only gross ignorance, brutal stupidity, or hellish cupidity can explain the inaction of our President and Congress in this hour of world travail.

In the name of the inarticulate unemployed who cannot speak; in the name of voiceless women of Europe who cannot cry out, *I denounce the present policy of the governing class of the United States; I declare that the blood of the European continent stains their souls, and that the misery and vice and crime of the unemployed pollutes their official robes. Before God and man I denounce them and declare their guilt and I challenge them to answer.*

Strike Against War (1916)

Helen Keller

The deaf and blind activist Helen Keller was a political radical who opposed U.S. participation in World War I, describing it as a capitalist war that slaughtered working men and women. Keller was so radical that she left the Socialist Party because she considered it too moderate and cautious on the Great War and other issues. In the 1916 speech below—which she delivered before the Women's Peace Party at Carnegie Hall in New

York City—Keller calls for women activists to practice civil disobedience against unjust laws related to the government's execution of the war.

Two years later Keller was a full-fledged member of the International Workers of the World (IWW) when she spoke out on behalf of IWW members ("Wobblies") who had been arrested in Chicago and four other cities for their antiwar activities. "Their cause is my cause," she said. "While they are threatened and imprisoned, I am manacled." Perhaps because of her celebrity status, Keller herself avoided arrest and imprisonment, but her IWW colleagues in Chicago received sentences of twenty years in prison.

The future of the world rests in the hands of America. The future of America rests on the backs of 80,000,000 working men and women and their children. We are facing a grave crisis in our national life. The few who profit from the labor of the masses want to organize the workers into an army which will protect the interests of the capitalists. You are urged to add to the heavy burdens you already bear the burden of a larger army and many additional warships. It is in your power to refuse to carry the artillery and the dreadnoughts and to shake off some of the burdens, too, such as limousines, steam yachts, and country estates. You do not need to make a great noise about it. With the silence and dignity of creators you can end wars and the system of selfishness and exploitation that causes wars. All you need to do to bring about this stupendous revolution is to straighten up and fold your arms.

We are not preparing to defend our country. Even if we were as helpless as Congressman Gardner says we are, we have no enemies foolhardy enough to attempt to invade the United States. The talk about attack from Germany and Japan is absurd. . . .

Congress is not preparing to defend the people of the United States. It is planning to protect the capital of American speculators and investors in Mexico, South America, China, and the Philippine Islands. Incidentally this preparation will benefit the manufacturers of munitions and war machines.

Until recently there were uses in the United States for the money taken from the workers. But American labor is exploited almost to the limit now, and our national resources have all been appropriated. Still the profits keep piling up new capital. Our flourishing industry in implements of murder is filling the vaults of New York's banks with gold. And a dollar that is not being used to make a slave of some human being is not fulfilling its purpose in the capitalistic scheme. That dollar must be invested in South America, Mexico, China, or the Philippines. . . .

Every modern war has had its root in exploitation. The Civil War was fought to decide whether slaveholders of the South or the capitalists of the North should exploit the West. The Spanish-American War decided that the United States should exploit Cuba and the Philippines. The South African War decided that the British should exploit the diamond mines. The Russo-Japanese War decided that Japan should exploit Korea. The present war is to decide who shall exploit the Balkans, Turkey, Persia, Egypt, India, China, Africa. And we are whetting our sword to scare the victors into sharing the spoils with us. Now, the workers are not interested in the spoils; they will not get any of them anyway.

The preparedness propagandists have still another object, and a very important one. They want to give the people something to think about besides their own unhappy condition. They know the cost of living is high, wages are low, employment is uncertain and will be much more so when the European call for munitions stops. No matter how hard and incessantly the people work, they often cannot afford the comforts of life; many cannot obtain the necessities.

Every few days we are given a new war scare to lend realism to their propaganda. They have had us on the verge of war over the Lusitania, the Gulflight, the Ancona, and now they want the workingmen to become excited over the sinking of the Persia. The workingman has no interest in any of these ships. The Germans might sink every vessel on the Atlantic Ocean and the Mediterranean Sea, and kill Americans with every one—the American workingman would still have no reason to go to war.

All the machinery of the system has been set in motion. Above the complaint and din of the protest from the workers is heard the voice of authority.

"Friends," it says, "fellow workmen, patriots; your country is in danger! There are foes on all sides of us. There is nothing between us and our enemies except the Pacific Ocean and the Atlantic Ocean. Look at what has happened to Belgium. Consider the fate of Serbia. Will you murmur about low wages when your country, your very liberties, are in jeopardy? What are the miseries you endure compared to the humiliation of having a victorious German army sail up the East River? Quit your whining, get busy, and prepare to defend your firesides and your flag. Get an army, get a navy; be ready to meet the invaders like the loyal-hearted freemen you are."

Will the workers walk into this trap? Will they be fooled again? I am afraid so. The people have always been amenable to oratory of this sort. The workers know they have no enemies except their masters. They know that their citizenship papers are no warrant for the safety of themselves or their wives and children. They know that honest sweat, persistent toil, and years of struggle bring them nothing worth holding on to, worth fighting for. Yet deep down in their foolish hearts they believe they have a country. Oh blind vanity of slaves!

The clever ones up in the high places know how childish and silly the workers are. They know that if the government dresses them up in khaki and gives them a rifle and starts them off with a brass band and waving banners, they will go forth to fight valiantly for their own enemies. They are taught that brave men die for their country's honor. What a price to pay for an abstraction—the lives of millions of young men; other millions crippled and blinded for life; existence made hideous for still more millions of human beings; the achievement and inheritance of generations swept away in a moment—and nobody better off for all the misery! This terrible sacrifice would be comprehensible if the thing you die for and call country fed, clothed, housed, and warmed you, educated and cherished your children. I think the workers are the most unselfish of the children of men; they toil and live and die for other people's country, other people's sentiments, other people's liberties, and other people's happiness! The workers have no liberties of their own; they are not free when they are compelled to work twelve or ten or eight hours a day. They are not free when they are ill paid for their exhausting toil. They are not free when their children must labor in mines, mills and factories or starve, and when their women may be driven by poverty to lives of shame. They are not free when they are clubbed and imprisoned because they go on strike for a raise of wages and for the elemental justice that is their right as human beings.

We are not free unless the men who frame and execute the laws represent the interests of the lives of the people and no other interest....

The kind of preparedness the workers want is reorganization and reconstruction of their whole life, such as has never been attempted by statesmen or governments....

It is your duty to insist upon still more radical measures. It is your business to see that no child is employed in an industrial establishment or mine or store, and that no worker is needlessly exposed to accident or disease. It is your business to make them give you clean cities, free from smoke, dirt, and congestion. It is your business to make them pay you a living wage. It is your business to see that this kind of preparedness is carried into every department in the nation, until everyone has a chance to be well born, well nourished, rightly educated, intelligent and serviceable to the country at all times.

Strike against all ordinances and laws and institutions that continue the slaughter of peace and the butcheries of war. Strike against war, for without you no battles can be fought. Strike against manufacturing shrapnel and gas bombs and all other tools of murder. Strike against preparedness that means death and misery to millions of human beings. Be not dumb, obedient slaves in an army of destruction. Be heroes in an army of construction.

The Darker Races and Avaricious Capitalists (1917)

A. Philip Randolph and Chandler Owen

A. Philip Randolph and Chandler Owen met and became friends in New York City in 1915, and a year later they were among the first African Americans to join the Socialist Party. In 1916, they channeled their shared concern for black workers by organizing the United Brotherhood of Elevator and Switchboard Operators. Although the union did not last long, Randolph and Owen became successful in a publishing venture they undertook together the following year—the founding of the Messenger, which they marketed in the masthead as the "Only Radical Negro Magazine."

The two men also published an antiwar booklet, excerpted below, after the United States entered World War I. Like Helen Keller, Randolph and Owen criticized the war as a capitalist assault on working men and women, but they also added that the war was "a white man's war." When Randolph and Owen published an article titled "Pro-Germanism Among Negroes," in which they criticized the government for trying to make the world safe for democracy while ignoring the absence of democracy for African Americans at home, the U.S. Post Office denied them the right to mail their magazine. And in 1918 the U.S. government arrested them both, charging them with treason under the Espionage Act. Unlike their IWW colleagues in Chicago, Randolph and Owen escaped prosecution and imprisonment when a racist judge freed them because he could not believe they were smart enough to have authored the writings that led to the charges.

The object of war is usually largely economic—manufacturers seeking markets for their goods and capitalists seeking investments for their surplus capital. Munitions makers must sell guns, shot, and shell. Uniform makers must dispense of their immense stores of cotton and wool. Banks must loan idle monies. But after the war has proceeded long enough to make possible the use and sale of these goods, it is to the interests of the capitalists, manufacturers, and bankers to call the soldiers off the field—to call them from their arts of destruction to begin the production anew of more goods for sale when they shall reach a surplus. After the goods produced shall have been used there is no gain in having the war continue, but on the contrary, the war's continuance would be a heavy debt upon the capitalist. The capitalists during the war sell immense amounts of goods. When the war ends, the government owes them huge debts. It is necessary for the soldiers to become laborers now to pay these debts. Hence the object of peace is profit—gain—just as the object of war is. . . .

Herein lies the real bone of contention of the world war—darker peoples for cheap labor and darker peoples' rich lands.

The war to be sure is being fought in Europe very largely, but the thing about which the war is fought lies elsewhere. The cause rests in the grab of territory, on the one hand, and the desire to hold what has been grabbed, or to grab more, on the other hand. . . .

So long as African territory is the object of unstinted avarice, greed, and robbery, while its people with dark skins are considered as just subjects of exploitation—now here and now there is slavery, enforced labor, peonage, and wage slavery—just so long will the conditions smolder and brew which needs must inevitably be prolific in the production of future war. . . .

We propose an International Council on the Conditions of Darker Races. . . .

The work of the Council on the Conditions of Darker Races should be, first, to set minimum wages for labor in different countries where these darker, undeveloped peoples live; to set the maximum hours of work and the conditions of employment. . . .

So long as these darker races are economic footballs for the great capitalists, just so long will wars continue to come. When the wars come, millions of young white men in the very flower of their youth will be sent on the journey of life, armless, legless, maimed, and mutilated.

Dark-skinned soldiers may not be wanted in the beginning of the wars, but when the great white nations are hard pressed, they will always call for dark-skinned soldiers to pull their chestnuts out of the fire. The consequence, then, is that a war between whites means war in which the blacks must also give their lives.

To maintain peace we must remove the conditions which create war. Democracy must be enthroned. White and black workingmen must recognize their common interest in industry, in politics, in society, in peace. Secret diplomacy must go. Universal suffrage must prevail. Universal education must be established everywhere. Wage slavery must be abolished. The means and resources of wealth must be socially owned for the common welfare. This will remove the incentive for war.

The people must always vote on whether they want war and conscription.

Free speech, free press, liberty of thought must be maintained in time of war as in peace.

And now America—the United States of America—to twelve million black souls, always loyal and true, grant that freedom from lynching, Jimcrowism, segregation, and discrimination. Stop the disfranchisement in the South which makes your cry of "making the world safe for democracy" a sham, a mockery, a rape on decency and a travesty on common sense.

Finally, in the words of the Petrograd Council of Workers and Solders' Deputies: Workers of all countries—black and white! "In extending to you our fraternal hand over mountains of corpses of our brothers, across rivers of innocent blood and tears, over smoldering ruins of cities and villages, over destroyed treasures of civilization, we beseech you to reestablish and strengthen international unity without regard to race or color."

Herein lies the only security for peace—permanent, durable, and democratic peace—a peace in which the black and white world will be made safe for democracy.

A Deliberate Violator (1918)

Roger Baldwin

New York pacifists and leftist allies organized the Anti-Militarism Committee in 1915 to resist the growing pro-war sentiment in the United States. In the following year, the group transformed itself into the Anti-Preparedness Committee and lobbied U.S. legislators to vote against preparing for and entering the war. Roger Baldwin, a civil liberties activist, joined the group in 1917, after it had yet again changed its name, this time to the American Union Against Militarism (AUAM), one of the most powerful antiwar groups at the time.

Baldwin organized the Civil Liberties Bureau (CLB), an AUAM group that advised conscientious objectors (COs) and lobbied Congress and the Woodrow Wilson administration to make better options available for COs under the Selective Service Act. In the fall of 1917, in response to AAUM leaders' concerns about alienating political leaders, the CLB broke away from the AAUM to become an independent organization, the National Civil Liberties Bureau (NCLB). Like other antiwar groups, the NCLB was under federal surveillance, and the Department of Justice raided its office in August 1918.

A month later NCLB director Baldwin received notice to register for the draft. He promptly refused to do so, declaring himself a CO. The government convicted him of violating the Selective Service Act and sentenced him to a year in prison. Below is the statement Baldwin delivered in court just before his sentence was pronounced.

I am before you as a deliberate violator of the draft act. On October 9, when ordered to take a physical examination, I notified my local board that I declined to do so, and instead presented myself to the United States attorney for prosecution. I submit herewith for the record the letter of explanation which I addressed to him at the time.

I refused to take bail, believing that I was not morally justified in procuring it, and being further opposed to the institution of bail on principle. I have therefore been lodged in the Tombs Prison since my arraignment on October 10. . . .

The compelling motive for refusing to comply with the draft act is my uncompromising opposition to the principle of conscription of life by the state for any purpose whatever, in time of war or peace. I not only refuse to obey the present conscription law, but I would in future refuse to obey any similar statute which attempts to direct my choice of service and ideals. I regard the principle of conscription of life as a flat contradiction of all our cherished ideals of individual freedom, democratic liberty, and Christian teaching.

Anti-Enlistment League flyer calling for pledges to protest WWI, 1915.

I am the more opposed to the present act, because it is for the purpose of conducting war. I am opposed to this and all other wars. I do not believe in the use of physical force as a method of achieving any end, however good. . . .

My opposition is not only to direct military service, but to any service whatever designed to help prosecute war. I could accept no service, therefore, under the present act, regardless of its character.

Holding such profound convictions, I determined, while the new act was pending, that it would be more honest to make my stand clear at the start and therefore concluded not even to register but to present myself for prosecution. I therefore resigned my position as director of the National Civil Liberties Bureau so as to be free to follow that personal course of action. But on the day my resignation took effect (August 31) agents of the Department of Justice began an examination of the affairs of that organization, and I was constrained to withdraw my resignation and to register in order to stand by the work at a critical moment. With that obligation discharged, I resigned, and took the next occasion, the physical examination, to make my stand clear.

I realize that to some this refusal may seem a piece of willful defiance. It might well be argued that any man holding my views might have avoided the issue by obeying the law, either on the chance of being rejected on physical grounds, or on the chance of the war stopping before a call to service. I answer that I am not seeking to evade the draft; that I scorn evasion, compromise, and gambling with moral issues. It may further be argued that the War Department's liberal provision for agricultural service on furlough for conscientious objectors would be open to me if I obey the law and go to camp, and that there can be no moral objection to farming, even in time of war. I answer first that I am opposed to any service under conscription, regardless of whether that service is in itself morally objectionable; and second, that even if that were not the case and I were opposed only to war, I can make no moral distinction between the various services which assist in prosecuting the war—whether rendered in the trenches, in the purchase of bonds or thrift stamps at home, or in raising farm products under the lash of the draft act. All serve the same end—war. Of course all of us render involuntary assistance to the war in the processes of our daily living. I refer only to those direct services undertaken by choice.

I am fully aware that my position is extreme, that it is shared by comparatively few, and that in the present temper it is regarded either as unwarranted egotism or as a species of feeble-mindedness. I cannot, therefore, let this occasion pass without attempting to explain the foundations on which so extreme a view rests. . . .

I am prepared for court martial and sentence to military prison, to follow the 200-300 objectors already sentenced to terms of 10-30 years for their loyalty to their ideals. I know that the way is easy for those who accept what to me is compromise, hard for those who refuse, as I must, any service whatever. And I know further, in military prison I shall

Women's Peace Parade, New York City, 1914.

refuse to conform to the rules for military salutes and the like, and will suffer a solitary confinement on bread and water, shackled to the bars of a cell eight hours a day—as are men of like convictions at this moment.

I am not complaining for myself or others. I am merely advising the court that I understand full well the penalty of my heresy, and am prepared to pay it. . . .

Though at the moment I am of a tiny minority, I feel myself just one protest in a great revolt surging up from among the people—the struggle of the masses against the rule of the world by the few—profoundly intensified by the war. It is a struggle against the political state itself, against exploitation, militarism, imperialism, authority in all forms. It is a struggle to break in full force only after the war. Russia already stands in the vanguard, beset by her enemies in the camps of both belligerents—the Central Empires break asunder from within— the labor movement gathers revolutionary force in Britain—and in our own country the Nonpartisan League, radical labor, and the Socialist Party hold the germs of a new social order. Their protest is my protest. Mine is a personal protest at a particular law, but it is backed by all the aspirations and ideals of the struggle for a world freed of our manifold slaveries and tyrannies. . . .

Having arrived at the state of mind in which those views mean the dearest things in life to me, I cannot consistently, with self-respect, do other than I have, namely, to deliberately violate an act which seems to me a denial of everything which ideally and in practice I hold sacred.

SEVEN

Workers' Rights and the Great Depression

Industrial Slavery, Murder, Riot, and Unbelievable Cruelty (1919)

W. E. B. Du Bois

In 1895 W. E. B. Du Bois became the first African American to receive a doctorate from Harvard University. Du Bois's dissertation was published as his first book, and it offered groundbreaking studies of slavery and discrimination against African Americans in the United States. More than a scholar, Du Bois was an activist who helped to found the Niagara Movement in 1905 and the NAACP four years later. Both groups, with their focus on achieving civil rights through legislation and the courts, fashioned themselves in opposition to Booker T. Washington's accommodationist approach to civil rights. In the 1919 article below, Du Bois, a keen observer of sociological trends, explains the reasons for the great migration of African Americans to the North as an act of resistance to economic dislocation, violence, and poor living conditions.

Since 1910, the most significant economic development among Negroes has been a large migration from the South. This has been estimated to have involved at least 250,000 and is still going on.

As to the reasons of the migration, undoubtedly the immediate cause was economic, and the movement began because of floods in middle Alabama and Mississippi and because the latest devastation of the boll weevil came in these same districts.

A second economic cause was the cutting off of immigration from Europe to the North and consequently widespread demand for common labor. . . .

The third reason has been outbreaks of mob violence in northern and southwestern Georgia and in western South Carolina.

These have been the three immediate causes, but back of them is, undoubtedly, the general dissatisfaction with the conditions in the South.

A colored man of Sumter, SC, says: "The immediate occasion of the migration is, of course, the opportunity in the North, now at last open to us, for industrial betterment. The real causes are the conditions which we have had to bear because there was no escape."

The full economic result of this migration and its extent in the future cannot be forecast at the present writing, but the chances are that the demand for labor caused by the European war will result in a larger rearrangement of Negro laborers and accelerate all tendencies in the distribution of that labor along lines already noted.

Figures like these are beginning to place the so-called Negro problem beyond the realm of mere opinion and prejudice. Here we see a social evolution working itself out before our eyes. The mass of the freedmen are changing rapidly the economic basis of their social development. They have not given up their close connection with the soil, but they are changing its character tremendously, so that today a fourth of them are peasant proprietors. They are forcing themselves into the trades despite the long opposition of white labor unions. As small businessmen, purveying principally to their own group, they are gaining a foothold in trade. As more or less skilled employees, they form a considerable part of our transportation system and they are rapidly developing a professional class which serves its own group and also serves the nation at large.

Many indications of the effect of this new development are seen in the peculiar incidence of racial prejudice. We hear today less argument about Negro education and more about sumptuary laws to control Negro expenditure, freedom of movement and initiative and residence. Politically handicapped as the colored man is, he is learning to wield economic power, which shows that his political rights cannot long be held back. And finally, in the division of his occupations, there is evidence of forethought and calculation within the group which foreshadows greater cooperation for the future.

Since the above was written, there has been a series of important economic happenings involving the American Negro which ought to be noted.

Severe floods and the cotton boll weevil reduced Negro tenants in many parts of the lower South to great distress during the winter following the declaration of war. They sold their cotton at a low figure or had none to sell. When the price of cotton rose, the plantation owners reaped the benefit and immediately began plans for the next season, calculating on labor at an unusually low price.

Meantime, a great foreign immigration of common laborers was cut off by the war, and there arose in the North an unusual demand for common labor. The Negroes began to migrate. In eighteen months 250,000 left the South and moved into the North. They were chiefly attracted by wages which were from 50 to 200 percent above what they had been used to receiving. And they saw also a chance to escape the lynching and discrimination of the South.

Every effort was made by the South to retain them. They were arrested wholesale, labor agents were taxed $500 to $1,000 or more for licenses, and the daily press of the South began to take on a more conciliatory tone. A slow rise in wages has begun. The migration of Negroes, however, continues, since the demand continues. . . .

To offset this, the labor unions have used every effort. The argument was that these blacks kept down the rate of wages. Undoubtedly they did keep wages from rising as high as they otherwise would have, but if Negroes had been received into the unions and trained into the philosophy of the labor cause (which for obvious reasons most of them did not know), they would have made as staunch union men as any. They are not working for low wages because they want to, but because they have to. Nine-tenths of the unions, however, are closed absolutely against them, either by constitutional provision or by action of the local unions. It is probable, therefore, that the friction will go on in the North. East St. Louis has already been echoed at Chester, Pa., and in other industrial centers.

Thus . . . industrial slavery, murder, riot, and unbelievable cruelty have met the Negro—and this not at the hands of the employers but at the hands of his fellow laborers who have in reality common cause with him.

Organization of the Negro Workers (1925)

A. Philip Randolph

In 1925, the same year A. Philip Randolph published the article below, with its call for organizing African American workers, New York porter Ashley Totten asked him to help organize black porters into a union. The porters were employed by the Pullman Company, whose owner, George Pullman, was known not only for his luxurious sleeping cars but especially for his vicious anti-unionism. Although initially hesitant, Randolph played a leading role in organizing the Brotherhood of Sleeping Car Porters (BSCP), the nation's first all-black labor union. However effective a union leader Randolph proved to be, it would take until 1937 for the Pullman Company to sign a labor agreement with the BSCP.

It is gratifying to note that there is now considerable interest manifest in the organization of Negro workers. Doubtless the real reason is that the white unions are slowly but surely awakening to the serious necessity of unionizing the Negro worker in self-defense. They are beginning to realize that Negro labor is playing an increasingly larger and more significant role in American industry. Especially is this true in the East, West, and North, where large numbers of Negro workers have migrated and are competing in the labor market with organized labor. It is this competition which has jolted the organized white workers out of their state of chronic indifference, apathy, and unconcern.

Of course, even now nothing has been done in the interest of Negro labor by the organized labor movement. Some of its leaders such as Hugh Frayne, Thomas J. Curtis, and Ernest Bohm, are members of the Trade Union Committee for Organizing Negro Workers, but it is not apparent that this committee has [accomplished] anything as yet save the moral goodwill of some of the local unions of New York City. In order for it to succeed in its organization work, however, it must be financed by the white organized workers. . . .

Of course, this work is not new or original. *The Messenger* has been the pioneer in the field advocating the organization of Negro labor. Now the *Crisis* is belatedly taking up the fight for the next three years, and the Negro press generally has become sympathetic and active in advising Negroes to organize into labor unions wherever their white brothers will accept them. We are glad to note that Negro editors are learning their economic lessons slowly but surely.

Let no Negro fail in his duty of advancing the cause of Negro labor without let or hindrance. The time is rotten ripe. Immigration from Europe has been materially cut, which means that the yearly supply of labor is much less than it formerly was. This gives the organized workers an advantage, greater bargaining power by virtue of this limited supply. It also gives the Negro worker a strategic position. It gives him power to exact a higher wage from capitalists, on the one hand, and to compel organized labor to let down the bars of discrimination against him, on the other. Thus it benefits him in two ways. And the Negro workers cannot rely upon anything but the force of necessity, the self-interests of the white unions, and the fear of Negro workers' competition, to give them a union card.

Another potent force in the organization of Negro labor is education and agitation. A certain course of action may be to a group's interest to take, but if it doesn't realize [this], it is not likely to act upon it. Thus the Negro press and the enlightened white labor press have a big task before them. But the task of Negro workers consists in more than merely deciding to organize. They must guard against being lured up blind alleys by irresponsible labor talkers who present them all sorts of wild, impossible dreams such as are advocated by the Communists. No labor movement in America among white or black workers can solve the industrial problems of the American workers, white or black, whose seat of control is outside of the country. This ought to be too obvious to require argument. The Communist movement in America is a menace to the American labor movement. It is a menace to the Negro workers. While healthy, intelligent, constructive criticism is valuable and necessary to the American labor movement, criticism which starts from the premise that the existing labor movement should be disrupted and destroyed must be resolutely opposed.

A Bolshevik Revolution in Lawrence? (1919, 1958)

A.J. Muste

Immigrant textile workers in Lawrence, Massachusetts, were not happy with the leaders of their union, the United Textile Workers (UTW), when they negotiated to reduce the work week from 54 to 48 hours in exchange for a reduction in wages. It was the reduction in income that the financially strapped immigrants resisted, and on February 3, 1919, about 30,000 workers, with assistance from Boston pastors A. J. Muste, Cedric Long, and Harold Rotzel, went on strike for both a 48-hour workweek and a 12.5 percent increase in wages. The strikers also began a boycott of local businesses that did not actively support them. In response, unsympathetic city leaders made it illegal for citizens to congregate in large numbers and instructed the police to keep order. Below are excerpts from Muste's account of police violence and the historic strike's unshakeable commitment to nonviolent tactics. In the end, the strikers' union won both the 48-hour workweek and a 15 percent wage increase.

On this visit, and on later visits, we found terrific tension and excitement. This was partly because of the memory of the clashes between strikers and police, the bitterness, of the 1912 strike. There was much more reason for excitement, however, in the immediate situation. A little over a year before, the Bolshevik Revolution had taken place in Russia. Many believed that in the aftermath of the war that revolution would spread, certainly in Europe, perhaps to America. In Winnipeg, Canada, and in Seattle, Washington, there had been general strikes which had received national and international publicity.

We found that among members of the very conservative Quaker Meeting in Lawrence, for example, and indeed in all middle class and native elements of that predominately proletarian and immigrant section, there was a firm conviction that if a general strike were to break out, it would signal the beginning of the Bolshevik Revolution in America, or at least in Massachusetts; certainly in Lawrence. The workers would seize the city hall, the police station, the mills. . . .

We went to see those officials of the great textile companies who would see us. We did actually see William Wood, Jr., son of the head of the American Woolen Company, which employed 16,000 people in its four huge mills. At the outset the officials had been rather pleased that we were coming to town, because they assumed that as pacifists we would urge the workers not to strike. When it became clear that we did not condone starvation wages and union smashing, and that while we opposed violence we conceived of nonviolence as a form of resistance and not of submission, they changed their attitude toward us.

What we found out about the reasons for the impending strike in Lawrence had to do with very specific and painful actualities on the spot, and only remotely, if at all, with global revolution. The average wage of textile workers in the city was $11.00 for a 54-hour week. Eleven dollars a week was quite a lot more money then than it would be now. But even then it was miserable pay. With the end of the war, employment had set in. The mill owners had proposed to cut hours to 48 per week but not to adjust hour or piece rates; in other words, to institute a more than ten percent reduction in take-home pay. The slogan of the strike had become "54-48," that is, "54 hours' pay for 48 hours' work." Housing conditions were appalling. Moreover, we and our friends dug up the facts about unconscionable war profiteering on the part of the industrialists, facts which in later years became common property. We put these facts into a leaflet and passed it out from house to house. This also did not endear us to the mill owners. There was a story, which was true as to substance, that the American Woolen Company had sold raincoats at a good price to the United States Army. The coats had not kept out the rain, so the division to which they had been sold had returned them. American Woolen had promptly sold the lot again out of the front door at a somewhat stiffer price, to another division of the Army. . . .

I have said something about the tense atmosphere which prevailed in Lawrence. On the Sunday evening before the strike began the commissioner of public safety and the chief of police briefed the police in Lawrence and squads from the surrounding cities which had been called in to quell the revolution. The commissioner instructed them to this effect: "If you do not get these people on the picket-line tomorrow morning first, they will get you."

So there was a blood bath on Monday morning. As the vast picket lines formed before the silent mills in the gray dawn, police, on foot and mounted, waded into the lines, clubbing right and left. In at least a couple of cases police broke into homes near the mills, pulled the covers off women in bed and beat them, alleging that the women had been near the line, had thrown stones at the police, and had then fled home. A score or so of those who had got the worst beating were brought to the little hall belonging to some Polish benefit society which the strike committee had hired as its headquarters. It was after these men and women had been given first aid and reports had been received about other beatings that the strike committee convened to deliberate on the next move.

The reports also showed that the strike was almost 100 percent effective. The decision was to picket the mills again *en masse* that afternoon and the next morning. The next morning and the next, police brutalities were reenacted. . . .

When . . . the strike lasted over a month and there were no signs of a break, conditions again became more tense. One night the police mounted machine guns at the head of the principal streets. This was done in spite of the fact that on the workers' side the strike had been remarkably free of violence. Over a hundred strikers were arrested during the sixteen weeks the struggle lasted. Because these cases were heard during, or after, the close of the strike, no one was sentenced to as much as a day in jail or paid even a one-dollar fine. Bringing in the machine guns was clearly an act of provocation. It was hoped that the strikers would resort to violence and that thereupon the strike could be discredited and broken.

This statement is not based on mere speculation. The morning the machine guns appeared, the strike committee met to discuss the strategy for dealing with this development. One of the members got up and made a heated speech, the import of which was: "The police are only a couple hundred. We are thirty thousand. Let's seize the machine guns this afternoon and turn them on the police." Very likely, this could have been done. Among the strikers and their families were a good many young men who had been taught guerilla tactics during the war, and how to operate machine guns. They were bitter enough over the cut in wages with which they had been confronted as soon as the war was over, without the added provocation of having the quarters of the town where they lived besieged with machine guns, as if they were a conquered people.

The three young pacifist ministers who sat there listening to that speech were inwardly shaken and apprehensive as to what might happen. However, one after another the local members of the committee, ordinary workers in the mills, made remarks to this effect: "The guns were put there to provoke us; why play into the hands of the mill management and the police? It would only discredit the strike. They can't weave wool with machine guns. All we have to do is continue to stand together." This view prevailed. . . .

In the afternoon, about two o'clock, those of the strikers who could crowd into the one hall which would hold fifteen or sixteen hundred people, all standing and packed as closely as possible, met there, as they did every afternoon when the weather did not permit an outdoor meeting. The air was electric, as it is whenever large numbers of men meet in a crisis in the middle of a struggle. Speakers addressed them in several languages. Then it was my turn to try to explain the policy of refraining from violence, refusing to be provoked, which had been decided upon by the strike committee in the morning. They had, of course, to be persuaded that it was a sound policy and to follow it enthusiastically; otherwise their morale would be hopelessly undermined. Men and women who, many of them, had already been clubbed on the picket line, whose savings had long since been used up, whose children no longer had shoes to wear to go to school, had to accept bitter defeat or a split in their ranks which could only lead to early defeat—or else had to embrace nonviolent resistance.

When I began my talk by saying that the machine guns were an insult and a provocation and that we could not take this attack lying down, the cheers shook the frame building. Then I told them, in line with the strike committee's decision, that to permit ourselves to be provoked into violence would mean defeating ourselves; that our real power was in our solidarity and in our capacity to endure suffering rather than give up the fight for the right to organize; that no one could "weave wool with machine guns"; that cheerfulness was better for morale than bitterness and that therefore we would smile as we passed the machine guns and the police on the way from the hall to the picket lines around the mills. I told the spies, who were sure to be in the audience, to go and tell the police and the mill management that this was our policy. At this point the cheers broke out again, louder and louder, and the crowds left, laughing and singing:

Though cowards flinch and traitors sneer,
We'll keep the Red Flag flying here.

Brother, Can You Spare a Dime? (1932)

Yip Harburg and the Bonus Marchers

In 1926 Congress passed the World War Adjusted Compensation Act, also known as the Bonus Act, which called for the payment of a bonus to WWI veterans who had served abroad (no more than $625) and at home (no more than $500). Although veterans lauded the bonus, many resented the condition that the government would not pay it until each veteran's birthday in 1945, almost twenty years hence. The delay was especially troubling to jobless veterans and their families during the Great Depression.

In 1932 veterans in Portland, Oregon, led by Walter Waters, decided they could no longer sit by idly, waiting for a bonus they needed right then, so they organized themselves into the "Bonus Expeditionary Forces," with the purpose of going to Washington, DC, and demanding that Congress earmark funds for early payment. The Bonus Army left Portland on freight trains, and as the media covered the cross-country trip, many more veterans, with no work in sight, joined the expedition, jumping on trains, dilapidated trucks, rickety cars, and old buses.

The first group of marchers reached the capital on May 25, and by the middle of June about 20,000 veterans and their families had moved into an encampment next to the Anacostia River. Populated by tents and shanties, the camp included places to eat, a post office, and even an office that published a newspaper.

Critics decried the camp as a communist plot, and the marchers as a bunch of tramps looking for a handout. But a vigorous defense came from retired Marine Corps General Smedley Butler, whose antiwar book

War is a Racket (1935) had made him popular among social radicals. "I never saw such fine Americanism as exhibited by you people," Butler said. "You have just as much right to have a lobby here as any steel corporation. Makes me so damn mad, a whole lot of people speak of you as tramps. By God, they didn't speak of you as tramps in 1917 and '18." Butler even characterized the protest as patriotic. "Take it from me, this is the greatest demonstration of Americanism we have ever had. Pure Americanism."

Democratic Representative Wright Patman of Texas offered his support for the marchers by introducing and lobbying for a bill that would allow for immediate distribution of the bonuses. Although it passed the House, fiscally conservative senators voted it down on June 17, prompting many frustrated veterans to pack their bags and go home. But about 10,000 protestors remained at the camp.

Then, on July 28, Attorney General William Mitchell ordered city police to remove veterans occupying federal property. A riot broke out as the DC police sought to drive out about 50 veterans who had taken over abandoned properties along Pennsylvania Avenue. The police shot and killed two veterans, and Army troops, under the command of General Douglas MacArthur, showed up to finish the job of removing those on the avenue.

Acting under his own authority, MacArthur also decided to rout the veterans at the Anacostia encampment. Army troops in tanks crossed the Anacostia River, entered the encampment, and fired tear gas to clear the area. Infantrymen followed the tanks, and they set fire to one tent or shanty after another. "The sky was red," recalled photographer John DiJoseph. "You could see the blaze all over Washington." MacArthur was successful, and it wasn't until four long years later that the veterans finally received their bonuses.

Below are the lyrics to a song, "Brother, Can You Spare a Dime," that the Bonus Marchers adopted as their movement anthem, as well as text from a flyer announcing the marchers' return in December 1932.

Bonus Army at the U.S. Capitol, Washington, D.C., 1932.

Brother, Can You Spare a Dime?

They used to tell me I was building a dream
And so I followed the mob
When there was earth to plow or guns to bear
I was always there right on the job

They used to tell me I was building a dream
With peace and glory ahead
Why should I be standing in line
Just waiting for bread?

Once I built a railroad, I made it run
Made it race against time

Once I built a railroad, now it's done
Brother, can you spare a dime?

Once I built a tower up to the sun
Brick and rivet and lime
Once I built a tower, now it's done
Brother, can you spare a dime?

Once in khaki suits, gee we looked swell
Full of that yankee doodly dum
Half a million boots went sloggin' through hell
And I was the kid with the drum

Say, don't you remember, they called me Al
It was Al all the time
Why don't you remember, I'm your pal
Say buddy, can you spare a dime?

Once in khaki suits, ah gee we looked swell
Full of that yankee doodly dum
Half a million boots went sloggin' through hell
And I was the kid with the drum

Oh, say, don't you remember, they called me Al
It was Al all the time
Say, don't you remember, I'm your pal
Buddy, can you spare a dime?

Flyer Text

March to Be Led by Rank and File Veterans
Again, the veterans are going to march to Washington, to demand full cash payment of the Bonus! . . . Why are we going to march? Let us see.

A Winter of Hunger Faces the Veterans
Cold, brutal winter is now on us. Over a million and a half unemployed

veterans are hungry; hundreds of thousands of us have no shelter. And there will be more of us in that fix by the time winter comes. . . .

Heroes in 1917; They Call Us "Criminals" Now

In 1917 the government appealed to the masses: "Shall we be more tender with our dollars than with the lives of our sons?" (Second Liberty Bond poster, 1917)

And now, in 1932: "The bonus marchers are criminals . . ." (Statement of President Hoover) Billions went to the billionaires who in 1917 made huge profits from the war, and today the billions go to the same crowd. The Congress that refused to give the starving veterans the bonus gave through the Reconstruction Finance Corporation four and a half billion dollars for the bankers, the railroads and other big corporations.

We got the bullets and the gas in 1917. Many of us were maimed and crippled for life. In 1932 we get the bullets and the gas of the police, as we did in Washington, and of the troops, which Hoover called out against us.

Because we were demanding the Bonus so that we and our families could have something to eat, the President of the United States orders the army to gas and bayonet us, to burn our meager belongings and to drive our wives and children out into the dark of night.

Down with the Sweatshops! (1933, 1945)

Rose Pesotta

At the beginning of the twentieth century, factory owners in Los Angeles made sure their city was anti-union. The city government passed an ordinance to criminalize picketing in 1911, and factory owners were successful at silencing calls for unionization until 1933.

Garment industrialists were virulently anti-union, and workers suspected of organizing for the purposes of collective bargaining were quickly fired. But in 1933 working conditions were so dismal that a group of women workers led by Rose Pesotta, a Russian Jewish seamstress, dared to take a stand and create a local chapter of the International Ladies' Garment Workers' Union (ILGWU). Like those in other cities, garment workers in Los Angeles labored in dark, poorly ventilated rooms filled with dirt and dust. Most of them worked at abysmal piecework rates and often found themselves waiting for an hour or more in between jobs.

Organizing the labor force was a difficult task. About 75 percent of the workers were Mexican, and the rest—Russians, Italians, and US-born women—neither spoke Spanish nor were familiar with the Mexican neighborhoods where most of their colleagues resided. Bilingual and Spanish-language publications assisted organizers as they traveled to the barrios to visit workers in their homes and explain the benefits of unionizing.

On October 12, 1933, after factory owners refused to recognize the union, the garment workers began a strike that would last three weeks. Owners did what they could to crush it, hiring new workers willing to cross the picket line and enlisting police to intimidate the picketers. Although it was largely nonviolent, the strike saw clashes erupt between workers and "scabs" and the police.

Cracks in the owners' position began to appear two weeks into the strike when two manufacturers made overtures to the union. And on October 26, owners agreed to submit to an arbitration board and to abide by its decisions. Two weeks later, at the arbitration board's direction, the garment workers agreed to return to work in exchange for the owners' concessions: recognition of the union, an increase in wages, regularized work schedules, and the elimination of child labor and home work. Below is Pesotta's account of the strike.

The usual method of a labor organizer in new territory is to ring doorbells in seeking out prospective unionists. But there were no doorbells for me to ring when I went calling in these slums with some of the Spanish-speaking girls.

Yet often the squalid exteriors were deceptive, the interiors, while poorly furnished, being clean and neat. In not a few of the Mexican dwellings were frigidaires, expensive radio sets, large floor lamps, vacuum cleaners, and other luxuries which had been sold on the installment plan by silver-tongued salesmen. In one place I visited a huge refrigerator stood as a showpiece in the center of the living room, unused because the electricity had been shut off for nonpayment. In another house, also a rear shack in the Belvedere section, I saw a baby grand piano, bought on time for $340 for a 12-year-old girl studying music in a public school. The child's father was a pick-and-shovel man, irregularly employed, the mother a dress finisher, eking out a meager living. Her greatest fear was that the piano, her proudest possession, would be taken away if she failed in her payments. Hence she was willing to take work home, any kind and for any length of hours, for her daughter's sake.

International Ladies Garment Workers handbill in support of dressmakers' strike, Los Angeles, 1933.

The chief fear that hung over these immigrants, however, was that of deportation. Many families had no income beyond the meager seasonal wage of a single worker, and were on county relief. Employers, knowing that a complaint to the authorities would lead to deportation of outspoken employees, used this threat to curb the rebellious.

Gradually the Mexicans in the dress factories came to our union headquarters, asking questions timidly but eagerly. Some employers, learning of signed membership cards, scoffed: "They won't stick." Others were plainly worried. Women not yet in our ranks came with the disquieting news that their boss had threatened to report them to the immigration authorities and have them "sent back" if they joined our union. We promised that our attorneys would fight any such underhanded move.

Meanwhile the Cloakmakers' Union, having consolidated its ranks, was trying to reach an agreement with the employers. Negotiations had been going on for weeks, but the employers had used various pretexts to stall for time. They hoped matters would drag along until the end of the season, when they would have the upper hand, for it is usually hard to gain any improvement in conditions while factories are shut for lack of work. . . .

At 3 o'clock on Tuesday, September 25, the city's cloakmakers laid down their tools, walked out of the shops, and marched through the garment district to Walker's Orange Grove Theatre on Grand Street. Quickly the place was filled to capacity and another hall had to be opened for the overflow. . . .

With the cloakmakers' action as a cue, the largest meeting of dressmakers ever held in Los Angeles took place in the same auditorium on the 27th. They discussed their grievances at length, cheered speakers who told of the recent dressmakers' victories in the Eastern cities, and voted unanimously for a general strike if the employers failed to recognize their union and refused to grant their reasonable demands. The leadership was given full power to act. Those demands included union recognition, a 35-hour week, a guaranteed minimum wage for each craft, in accordance with the pending dress code; regular union hours, 8:30 a.m. to 4:30 p.m., with an hour for lunch; a five-day week; shop chairman and price committee to be elected by the workers of each shop; no home work; no worker to punch a timecard except on actually entering or leaving the factory; all disputes to be adjusted by a committee composed of the shop chairman, a representative of the union, and a representative of the employer, and an impartial arbitrator selected by mutual consent, to decide on disputes in the event of a deadlock. . . .

On Thursday at 5 AM everyone was on hand. Ten thousand copies of the strike declaration had been printed. English on one side, Spanish on the other. Each committee member took a bundle of these to distribute in front of the buildings in which dress factories were located.

DRESSMAKERS' GENERAL STRIKE DECLARED TODAY! read the large black-type heading on the leaflet. Addressed to "all our union members and nonmembers, all cutters, operators, pressers, finishers, examiners, drapers, sample-makers, cleaners, pinkers, and all jobless dressmakers," it called upon them not to enter the shops, but to "go in an orderly manner" to strike headquarters at 1108 South Los Angeles Street.

"The bosses have forced this strike upon us," the declaration said, "because they refuse to recognize our organization and have refused to concede our just demands.

"Present working conditions in Los Angeles are unbearable. Never has it been so hard for a dressmaker here to earn a living as it is today. The general depression on the one hand, and the sweatshops on the other, have made it possible to break down all standards and make our jobs more insecure than ever before.

"We must make the 35-hour week universal in order that every dressmaker shall have employment. We must establish the guaranteed minimum wage scale for every worker in the industry to assure us a living wage. We must establish the right to the job.

"We must have a powerful union to enforce union standards in every dress shop every day of the year.

"Down with the sweatshops! On with the strike! On to victory!"

When all the others had dispersed, shortly after 7 o'clock, I proceeded to strike headquarters alone, forgetting about breakfast. I unlocked the door, turned on the lights, and looked around. Everything was in good order.

I stepped outside to wait. Los Angeles Street was deserted and silent. Minutes dragged by, painfully. Once I held my watch to my ear to make sure it hadn't stopped.

The watch hands at last reached 7:30 . . . 7:31. The silence remained unbroken. It pressed down on me. I felt as if I were standing in a vacuum. I could hear my own heart beat. 7:35 . . . Still no one in sight. Doubts assailed me. Suppose something had slipped? Suppose the workers didn't respond? Suppose only a few came out. I knew of other strike efforts where the ground had been well prepared that had failed dismally. What effect had sniping by the Communist-led dual union had upon morale? Had the bosses succeeded in intimidating their employees?

I looked up at the loft building I had rented. It looked so huge, so monstrous—and I had been concerned lest it not be big enough for our needs! Again a chill went up my spine, and I felt very small—much smaller than my five feet two.

The minutes dragged on. I stood still, facing the Broadway corner, a block away. I no longer looked at my watch. I could only wait, numbly.

Suddenly the silence was broken. Several girls turned the corner, then more girls and women, then a throng, laughing and talking excitedly. Some from the Clare Dress Company, all smiles, were waving at me. Soon they were pouring into strike headquarters by the hundreds. The Clare Company's employees had been the first to strike; they were all here.

Workers from each factory assembled for separate shop meetings in the smaller rooms. Hall attendants registered each on an individual shop list which gave the name, address, factory location, price of garments worked on, wages received. Each group elected a shop chairman. A striker's card, to be presented daily at headquarters to be punched, would serve as identification, entitling the holder to meals in the commissary and a weekly cash benefit.

As soon as this necessary clerical job was done, the strikers were sent back into the garment district to swell the picketing.

Reporters came, looked over the crowd at headquarters, asked questions, picked up copies of our leaflets, visited the picket lines, and telephoned stories to their offices. . . .

Mass picketing went on throughout the day in front of all the dress factory buildings, in the heart of the downtown shopping district. Traffic frequently stopped for minutes at a time while crowds of shoppers watched the spectacle.

In the evening, when the demonstrations were ended and the

strikers had left headquarters, I met with the staff. We compared notes and mapped out a schedule for next day. Scanning the list of factories and registered strikers, I was satisfied that we had succeeded in shutting down the Los Angeles dress industry.

Everyone on the staff was tired but happy. The spirit of the strikers was excellent. The Mexican girls and women, who were by far the majority, acted almost like seasoned unionists, bearing out my expectations fully.

Death Watch (1935)

League of the Physically Handicapped

President Franklin D. Roosevelt, a liberal Democrat who was physically disabled, led the way in creating the Works Progress Administration (WPA) to provide employment for workers left jobless in the wake of the Great Depression. Although the job-creating program earned praise from many unemployed workers, people with disabilities, defined by the program as unemployable and ineligible for WPA jobs, grew frustrated. Facing blatant discrimination, a group of six disabled adults, three men and three women, staged a sit-in at New York City's Emergency Relief Bureau (ERB) on May 29, 1935, after they were told that bureau director Oswald Knaught would not immediately meet with them to discuss their grievances and pleas for employment.

The group of six had first met at a recreation center for disabled people. One of the six later recalled that the beginnings of their group started when they discovered "that jobs were available, that the government was handing out jobs . . . everybody was getting jobs: newspaper people, actresses, actors, painters, and only handicapped people weren't worthy of jobs. . . . Those of us who . . . were militant just refused to accept the fact that we were the only people who were looked upon as not worthy, not capable of work."

Twenty-four hours passed before the May 29 sit-in attracted any attention outside the ERB building, but after the wife of one of the activists announced the demonstration at a local communist protest, hundreds of radicals created a picket line outside the ERB as the disabled group remained inside. On the sixth day of the sit-in, Knauth conceded and agreed to meet with the activists. But he did not agree to their demands, which included the immediate granting of fifty jobs to disabled men and women, and the hiring of an additional ten for each following week. After he refused their demands, the demonstrators dug in, continuing their sit-in and picketing of the building.

On the ninth day of the protest, Knauth enlisted help from the police, who arrested eleven protestors and effectively ended the sit-in. But the protests were far from over, and the demonstrators loudly hounded the director at a speech he gave the following day. Agitated and frustrated, Knauth once again met with the protestors, telling them he could offer the assistance of his office only when federal funds became available for doing so.

The group of activists decided to name themselves the League of the Physically Handicapped, and to establish a fully functioning office focused on securing jobs. And in November they struck again, picketing WPA offices in New York City and distributing flyers stating their demand for WPA jobs. After three weeks of picketing, WPA director Victor Ridder agreed to hire forty members of the League. Below is a copy of a flyer that the League handed out after it believed Riddle had reneged on his promises.

Within the next year, thanks to the League's relentless resistance, the WPA provided jobs to about 1,500 disabled workers in New York City. Unsatisfied with just jobs, the League then turned its attention to changing federal policies that legalized discrimination against the disabled. The League wrote a paper describing the need for federal policies that would ensure equal treatment of those with disabilities, and it then submitted the paper to President Roosevelt. In a cover letter attached to the paper, League president Sylvia Flexer wrote: "The members of our organization have learned from grim experience that something is basically wrong in the manner in which our country takes care of their economic and social problems."

"Death Watch"

On December 6th, Mr. Ridder announced to the press that within ten days jobs will be given to the unemployed members of The League for the Physically Handicapped. There was to be no more discrimination against handicapped workers.

We accepted this pledge of the administration. We withdrew our picket lines from WPA headquarters at 111 8th Ave.

But the administration deliberately broke its promise!! We accuse!!! The administration of unjust discrimination against the handicapped. Disregarding the needs of the handicapped even after our problem had been brought to their attention. Assuming a calloused and inhuman attitude toward us. Depriving us of what is rightfully ours—the right to live.

Our needs are desperate!!!

We will honor the dead promises of the administration with a "Death Watch" at 111 8th Ave. starting on Friday, Dec. 20, at 4 PM, and continue through the night.

We will fight until we win—We want jobs!!

Since the Administration has ignored our problem, we appeal now to the highest law of the land—public opinion. Write, wire, or phone your protests, demanding that discrimination be stopped!! That the promised jobs be given!! You and your friends can help us.

The Flint Sit-Down Movement (1937)

United Auto Workers

General Motors (GM), like the Ford Motor Company, was rabidly anti-union in the 1930s and hired individuals to harass, intimidate, and rout out pro-union workers. The absence of a union also meant that wages for GM workers were artificially low and that their working conditions were often dangerous. During a heat wave in the summer of 1936, more than a hundred auto workers in Michigan died from causes related to working in oppressively hot factories.

Frustrated and angry, GM workers in Flint began to clamor more loudly for the right to organize and gain the leverage they needed to combat low wages and unsafe conditions, and on November 12, 1936, they staged a sit-down strike at a GM autobody plant. The strikers also refused to leave the building, a tactic that prevented the strike from being broken by replacement workers. The strike then spread to other GM plants, and at its peak about 200,000 GM workers were on strike.

In mid-January GM turned off heat in the plants as a way to force workers to leave, and when that did not work, police officers and GM security forces fired tear gas and wielded clubs against their supporters outside, resulting in the hospitalization of fourteen workers. In early February GM security forces used tear gas again, and this time the Women's Emergency Brigade broke plant windows so the workers could breathe.

After workers did not obey injunctions to vacate the occupied buildings around this same time, Governor Frank Murphy ordered the National Guard to surround the plants and cut off attempts to provide food to the hungry strikers. The workers would not relent, and they remained surrounded and isolated until February 11 when General Motors, which had seen its car production plummet from 53,000 a week to 1,500, finally agreed to increase wages and to recognize the UAW as the union representing the twenty plants that were striking. In exchange, the workers ended the strike and returned to their jobs.

Below are the early demands of the workers.

1. National conference between responsible heads of GMC and chosen representatives of international union, United Automobile Workers of America. Such conference to discuss and bargain collectively on the following points as a basis for national agreement between General Motors Corporation and its employees, as represented by international union, United Automobile Workers of America.

2. Abolition of all piecework system of pay, and the adoption of straight hourly rate.

3. A 30-hour week and six-hour work day and time and one-half for all time worked over the basic work day and work week.

4. Establishment of a minimum rate of pay commensurate with an American standard of living.

5. Reinstatement of all employees who have been unjustly discharged.

6. Seniority, based upon length of service.

7. Recognition of the international union, United Automobile Workers of America, the sole bargaining agency between General Motors Corporation and its employees, for the establishment of joint tribunals and joint rules of procedure for the adjusting of any and all disputes that may arise from time to time between employees of General Motors Corporation and the management.

8. Speed of production shall be mutually agreed upon by the management and the union committee in all General Motors plants.

Women of the Cotton Fields (1938)

Elaine Ellis

One of the effects of the emancipation of slaves was the creation of share-cropping, a system in which a landowner allowed a tenant to farm the owner's land in exchange for a portion of the crop. Poor whites and former slaves with no money to purchase and run their own farms were subject to this system. It was set up to favor the white landowners, and dishonest ones abused it with impunity by providing credit to tenants in need of seed, tools, and fertilizer, among other things, and then charging high interest fees at the time of harvest. Because the tenants were typically required to sell their crops to their landowner, it was also easy for the owners to buy the crops far under market value. When it was abused, sharecropping put tenants into debt they could never pay off, and thereby tied them for life to the owners and their farms.

Journalist Elaine Ellis wrote the following account of African American women sharecroppers for the NAACP's Crisis magazine in 1938. Ellis refers to the Southern Worker, a newspaper published by Communists in Alabama and Tennessee from 1930 to 1937, and to the Share Croppers Union (SCU), a communist and largely black organization founded in Alabama in 1931, shortly after the collapse of the Croppers and Farm Workers Union (CFWU). The CFWU met its demise in July 1931, when an exchange of gunfire between CFWU members and a white sheriff in Camp Hill, Alabama, resulted in the death of union member Ralph Gray and the subsequent scattering of Gray's colleagues. Reformed as SCU members, African American workers suffered more violence when they sought to prevent white authorities from seizing the property of indebted SCU member Clifford James. A gun battle broke out, leaving James and two other SCU workers dead and several others wounded. In the article below, Ellis refers to both of these violent incidents and to two other unions that sought to organize Southern black farmers.

Another cotton picking season has opened in the South. On the farms and plantations, tenants and croppers are harvesting the gleaming white crop with the hope that this year they will get enough from their share to live through the winter. In the cities, the relief agencies are following their annual custom of commanding thousands of undernourished families to go to the cotton fields and pick for what they can get, or starve.

Scenes showing pickets at work in these fields can be secured on postcards throughout the South. Chambers of Commerce and other civic bodies use such pictures quite often in pamphlets which invite the summer tourist to visit Dixie and learn something about the picturesque region that formed the background for "My Old Kentucky Home" and other folk songs that will never be forgotten. The average tourist will drive through some of these states, visit a few capitols, shake hands with a few governors if he gets a chance to see any, and return home. The cotton fields will cease to be of much interest, for he will have seen too many of them.

Tourists are not told by the big-shot advertising agencies that these cotton fields tell the story of what Norman Thomas calls "probably the most depressed body of workers in America." The men, women, and little children who work in these fields under the blazing Southern sun create the great Cotton Kingdom for which this region is famed. In return for their labor, they receive only poverty, ignorance, and disease.

And it is the woman, Negro and white, on whom the burden is heaviest. In every cotton field one can see her type—a stooped woman dragging a heavy cotton sack. Usually she wears a slatted sunbonnet, and her arms and neck are swathed with rags to protect them from the blistering heat.

This is the woman whom civilization has passed by. But it is from her loins, no less than from the earth itself, that the world's greatest cotton industry has sprung. A slave, and a breeder of slaves, hundreds of thousands of her kind have been crushed in its gigantic and merciless machinery. And as long as the tenant system continues, she must be sacrificed to its greed.

In the past, this woman was compelled to reproduce a large number of children because a large labor supply was in demand. Large families also mean a cheaper form of labor; for children, as well as women, generally represent labor that does not have to be paid. Consequently, the "overhead" falls upon the family instead of the landlord. The landlord himself has enforced this monopoly by letting his farm go to the tenant or cropper having the largest family.

Now the tenant-croppers are charged with "overpopulation" by economists and agriculturists who disregard the unwholesome economic factors that have caused an increase in farm tenancy. This increase has amounted to sixty percent since 1930 despite the fact that the AAA drove approximately 300,000 tenants and sharecroppers from the land.

As one solution to this "overpopulation," proponents of the sterilization racket are endeavoring to work up an agitation for sterilization of these cotton workers. The now ex-governor of Arkansas, J. M. Futrell, and H. L. Mencken, the writer, have expressed themselves highly in favor of such a measure. Sterilization, one of the tenets of fascism, makes women its chief victim. One can readily visualize its vicious application as a means of controlling the labor supply.

On the other hand, birth control information has been denied these women, although in some sections of the South there is a plan to introduce it by means of traveling clinics. Now that there is a surplus labor supply, this method that would be such a boon to women is beginning to be viewed in a most favorable light. But the most simple medical attention is still denied them. Even during pregnancy, a woman must work in the field. The fact that she is carrying a child does not excuse her from dragging and lifting the heavy cotton sack. Frequently, when the child is born, she does not have the assistance of a physician. Women in the neighborhood, or a midwife, must help her through her confinement. Very often she does not have even this inadequate aid. It is a common occurrence for a woman who is pregnant to pick cotton until the labor pangs strike her. She may be able to drag herself to the shade of a tree, or to the wagon or car, to give birth to her child. But sometimes it is born among the cotton plants. After it is a few weeks old, it will be taken by its mother to the field. There it will sleep on a pallet with brothers and sisters too young to pick. As soon as it is old enough to carry a sack, it, too, will go into the field.

The mother, in addition to working in the home field, will "hire out" to a neighboring landlord as soon as this crop is harvested. In addition, she has the upkeep of the house and further outside work. Her hours average from about twelve to fourteen a day, each being one of extreme toil.

There is an equally bad situation existing for young girls. Many have their health ruined for life because they are forced to drag and lift the heavy cotton sacks during puberty. While the landlords' daughters attend universities and join sororities, these daughters of the croppers help to pay the cost of their dinner dances, rush weeks, and dissipations.

In the lives of these illiterate farm women, there is mute evidence of a capacity for creation. During planting time, they will sow the seeds of zinnias along the outer cotton rows. After the day's drudgery, which ends late at night with the housework, they will return with buckets of water for the seeds. Often one of these women can be seen standing idle for a moment during the busiest part of the day to gaze across the even rows to where gaily colored zinnias flame among the white cotton. And the change in her is miraculous. This woman is suddenly straight and clear-eyed, and pushing back her bonnet, she shades her eyes with her hand as she looks across the field shimmering in waves of heat. But just as suddenly, she will droop and turn again to her task. The cotton must be picked!

But the women of the cotton fields are awakening. It began back in 1931 when Estelle Milner, a young Negro girl, brought the tenants and sharecroppers of Camp Hill, Alabama, a little paper called *The Southern Worker.* The organization of the Sharecroppers Union that followed, and the bloody battles of Camp Hill and Reeltown will never be forgotten. In the years that have followed, the Sharecroppers Union, Southern Tenant Farmers Union, and the Farmers Union have organized more than 300,000 tenants and sharecroppers throughout the South.

The bloodshed that planters and deputy sheriffs caused at Camp Hill and Reeltown, when mangled croppers were forced to flee for their lives, marked only the beginning of terrorism that breaks out wherever unions of these workers demand better conditions. But undaunted, they struggle on, frequently chalking up victories to their score.

And the women are standing by their men.

Picketing Is Exercising Free Speech (1940)

Frank Murphy

The rise of industrial unionism is doubtless one of the most important resistance movements of the twentieth century. The movement found an indirect supporter in Governor Frank Murphy of Michigan when he refused to use armed force to break the Flint sit-down strike of 1937. Murphy's support became even more evident shortly after he joined the U.S. Supreme Court as an associate justice.

In 1940 Murphy wrote the majority opinion for Thornhill v. Alabama, a landmark ruling that served to protect union workers as they picketed for their rights. The Thornhill case centered on Byron Thornhill, who had been arrested for and convicted of violating a state statute that prohibited any person who, "without a just cause or legal excuse," loitered around or picketed a business for the purpose of interfering with it or impeding its work (Section 3448 of the Code of Alabama of 1923). At the time of his arrest, Thornhill was peacefully picketing his former employer, Brown Wood Preserving Company, as part of a strike called for by a union affiliated with the American Federation of Labor. Thornhill appealed to the U.S. Supreme Court after the Alabama Court of Appeals upheld his conviction and after the Alabama State Supreme Court refused to hear his appeal. Below is an excerpt of Murphy's opinion, which, by identifying picketing as a constitutionally protected form of free speech, served to advance labor interests for years to come.

The freedom of speech and of the press guaranteed by the Constitution embraces at least the liberty to discuss publicly and truthfully all matters of public concern, without previous restraint or fear of subsequent punishment. The exigencies of the colonial period and the efforts to secure freedom from oppressive administration developed a broadened conception of these liberties as adequate to supply the public need for information and education with respect to the significant issues of these times. . . .

In the circumstances of our times, the dissemination of information concerning the facts of a labor dispute must be regarded as within that area of free discussion that is guaranteed by the Constitution ... It is recognized now that satisfactory hours and wages and working conditions in industry and a bargaining position which makes these possible have an importance which is not less than the interests of those in the business or industry directly concerned. The health of the present generation and of those yet unborn may depend on these matters, and the practices in a single factory may have economic repercussions upon a whole region and affect widespread systems of marketing. The merest glance at state and federal legislation on the subject demonstrates the force of the argument that labor relations are not matters of mere local or private concern. Free discussion concerning the conditions in industry and the causes of labor disputes appear to us indispensable to the effective and intelligent use of the processes of popular government to shape the destiny of modern industrial society. The issues raised by regulations, such as are challenged here, infringing upon the right of employees effectively to inform the public of the facts of a labor dispute, are part of this larger problem. We concur in the observation of Mr. Justice Brandeis, speaking for the Court in *Senn's* case (310 U.S. at 478):

> Members of a union might, without special statutory authorization by a State, make known the facts of a labor dispute, for freedom of speech is guaranteed by the Federal Constitution.
> . . .

The range of activities proscribed by [Statute] 3448, whether characterized as picketing, or loitering, or otherwise, embraces nearly every practicable, effective means whereby those interested—including the employees directly affected—may enlighten the public on the nature and causes of a labor dispute. The safeguarding of these means is essential to the securing of an informed and educated public opinion with respect to a matter which is of public concern.

EIGHT

World War II

Jim Crow and National Defense (1941)

A. Philip Randolph

A. Philip Randolph, a bold thinker devoted to mass nonviolent direct action, was president of the Brotherhood of Sleeping Car Porters, the nation's largest and most powerful union of African American workers. In 1941, as the U.S. tooled up for its entry into World War II, Randolph called for a March on Washington to protest segregation in the military and discrimination against black workers in the national defense industry (see below). President Franklin D. Roosevelt, who feared the possibility of thousands of African Americans marching on the White House, hastily issued an executive order stating "there shall be no discrimination in the employment of workers in defense industries or government because of race, creed, color, or national origin." While the desegregation of the military was not addressed or achieved, a partly victorious Randolph called off the march, but not the struggle for desegregation.

We call upon you to fight for jobs in national defense. We call upon you to struggle for the integration of Negroes in the armed forces. . . .

We call upon you to demonstrate for the abolition of Jim-Crowism in all government departments and defense employment.

This is an hour of crisis. It is a crisis of democracy. It is a crisis of minority groups. It is a crisis of Negro Americans. What is this crisis?

To American Negroes, it is the denial of jobs in government defense projects. It is racial discrimination in government departments. It is widespread Jim-Crowism in the armed forces of the nation.

While billions of the taxpayers' money are being spent for war weapons, Negro workers are finally being turned away from the gates of factories, mines, and mills—being flatly told, "nothing doing." Some employers refuse to give Negroes jobs when they are without "union cards," and some unions refuse Negro workers union cards when they are "without jobs."

What shall we do?

What a dilemma!

What a runaround!

What a disgrace!

What a blow below the belt!

Though dark, doubtful, and discouraging, all is not lost, all is not hopeless. Though battered and bruised, we are not beaten, broken, or bewildered.

Verily, the Negroes' deepest disappointments and direst defeats, their tragic trials and outrageous oppressions in these dreadful days of destruction and disaster to democracy and freedom, and the rights of minority peoples, and the dignity and independence of the human spirit, is the Negroes' greatest opportunity to rise to the highest heights of struggle for freedom and justice in government, in industry, in labor unions, education, social service, religion, and culture.

With faith and confidence of the Negro people in their own power for self-liberation, Negroes can break down the barriers of discrimination against employment in national defense. Negroes can kill the deadly serpent of race hatred in the army, navy, air, and marine corps, and smash through and blast the government, business and labor-union red tape to win the right to equal opportunity in vocational training and retraining in defense employment.

Most important and vital of all, Negroes, by the mobilization and coordination of their mass power, can cause President Roosevelt to issue an executive order abolishing discriminations in all government department, Army, Navy, Air Corps, and national defense jobs.

Flyer for the March on Washington Movement, 1941.

Of course, the task is not easy. In very truth, it is big, tremendous and difficult.

It will cost money.

It will require sacrifice.

It will tax the Negroes' courage, determination, and will to struggle. But we can, must, and will triumph.

The Negroes' stake in national defense is big. It consists of jobs, thousands of jobs. It may represent millions, yes hundreds of millions of dollars in wages. It consists of new industrial opportunities and hope. This is worth fighting for.

But to win our stakes, it will require an "all-out," bold and total effort and demonstration of colossal proportions.

Negroes can build a mammoth machine of mass action with a terrific and tremendous driving and striking power that can shatter and crush the evil fortress of race prejudice and hate, if they will only resolve to do so and never stop, until victory comes.

Dear fellow Negro Americans, be not dismayed by these terrible times. You possess power, great power. Our problem is to harness and hitch it up for action on the broadest, daring, and most gigantic scale.

In this period of power politics, nothing counts but pressure, more pressure, and still more pressure, through the tactic and strategy of broad, organized, aggressive mass action behind the vital and important issues of the Negro. To this end, we propose that ten thousand Negroes march on Washington for jobs in national defense and equal integration in the fighting forces of the United States.

An "all-out" thundering march on Washington, ending in a monster and huge demonstration at Lincoln's Monument, will shake up white America.

It will shake up official Washington.

It will give encouragement to our white friends to fight all the harder by our side, with us, for our righteous cause.

It will gain respect for the Negro people.

It will create a new sense of self-respect among Negroes.

But what of national unity?

We believe in national unity which recognizes equal opportunity of black and white citizens to jobs in national defense and the armed forces, and in all other institutions and endeavors in America. We condemn all dictatorships, Fascist, Nazi, and Communist. We are loyal, patriotic Americans all.

But if American democracy will not defend its defenders; if American democracy will not protect its protectors; if American democracy will not give jobs to its toilers because of race or color; if American democracy will not insure equality of opportunity, freedom, and justice to its citizens, black and white, it is a hollow mockery and belies the principles for which it is supposed to stand. . . .

Today we call on President Roosevelt, a great humanitarian and idealist, to . . . free American Negro citizens of the stigma, humiliation, and insult of discrimination and Jim-Crowism in government departments and national defense.

The federal government cannot with clear conscience call upon private industry and labor unions to abolish discrimination based on race and color as long as it practices discrimination itself against Negro Americans.

I Cannot Honorably Participate (1943)

Robert Lowell

In 1940 a group of eight students from Union Theological Seminary in New York City attracted national attention when they refused to register for the draft, as mandated by the Selective Service and Training Act of 1940, the first peacetime conscription in U.S. history. In a collective statement explaining their decision, they said: "To us, the war system is an evil part of our social order, and we declare that we cannot cooperate with it in any way." Pacifists were permitted to declare conscientious objector status, but the Union Eight believed that becoming COs and participating in Civilian Public Service, the government's work camp system for COs, would be actively supporting the war effort. So they went to jail.

Not all war resisters were as absolutist as the Union Eight. In 1943 Robert Lowell, who would become one of the most significant poets in U.S. history, offered nonsectarian, practical reasons for choosing federal imprisonment over war. He explained his rationale in this September 7, 1943, letter to President Franklin D. Roosevelt.

Orders for my induction into the armed forces on September eighth 1943 have just arrived. Because we glory in the conviction that our wars are won not by irrational valor but through the exercise of moral responsibility, it is fitting for me to make the following declaration which is also a decision.

Like the majority of our people I watched the approach of this war with foreboding. Modern wars have proved subversive to the democracies and history had shown them to be the iron gates to totalitarian slavery. On the other hand, members of my family had served in all our wars since the Declaration of Independence: I thought—our tradition of service is sensible and noble; if its occasional exploitation by Money, Politics and Imperialism is allowed to seriously discredit it, we are doomed.

When Pearl Harbor was attacked, I imagined that my country was in intense peril and come what might, unprecedented sacrifices were necessary for our national survival. In March and August of 1942 I volunteered, first for the Navy and then for the Army. And when I heard reports of what would formerly have been termed atrocities, I was not disturbed: for I judged that savagery was unavoidable in our nation's struggle for its life against diabolic adversaries.

Today these adversaries are being rolled back on all fronts and the crisis of war is past. But there are no indications of peace. In June we heard rumors of the staggering civilian casualties that had resulted from the mining of the Ruhr Dams. Three weeks ago we read of the razing of Hamburg, where 200,000 noncombatants are reported dead, after an almost apocalyptic series of all-out air raids.

This, in a world still nominally Christian, is *news*. And now the Quebec Conference confirms our growing suspicions that the bombings of the Dams and of Hamburg were not mere isolated acts of military expediency, but marked the inauguration of a new long-term strategy, endorsed and coordinated by our Chief Executive.

The war has entered an unforeseen phase: one that can by no possible extension of the meaning of the words be called defensive. By demanding unconditional surrender we reveal our complete confidence in the outcome, and declare that we are prepared to wage a war without quarter or principles, to the permanent destruction of Germany and Japan.

Americans cannot plead ignorance of the lasting consequences of a war carried through to unconditional surrender—our Southern states, three-quarters of a century after their terrible battering down and occupation, are still far from having recovered even their material prosperity.

It is a fundamental principle of our American democracy, one that distinguishes it from the demagoguery and herd hypnosis of the totalitarian tyrannies, that with us each individual citizen is called upon to make voluntary and responsible decisions on issues which concern the national welfare. I therefore realize that I am under the heavy obligation of assenting to the prudence and justice of our present objectives before I have the right to accept service in our armed forces. No matter how expedient I might find it to entrust my moral responsibility to the state,

I realize that it is not permissible under a form of government which derives its sanctions from the rational assent of the governed.

Our rulers have promised us unlimited bombings of Germany and Japan. Let us be honest: we intend the permanent destruction of Germany and Japan. If this program is carried out, it will demonstrate to the world our Machiavellian contempt for the laws of justice and charity between nations; it will destroy any possibility of a European or Asiatic national autonomy; it will leave China and Europe, the two natural power centers of the future, to the mercy of the USSR, a totalitarian tyranny committed to world revolution and total global domination through propaganda and violence.

In 1941 we undertook a patriotic war to preserve *our lives, our fortunes, and our sacred honor* against the lawless aggressions of a totalitarian league: in 1943 we are collaborating with the most unscrupulous and powerful of totalitarian dictators to destroy law, freedom, democracy, and above all, our continued national sovereignty.

With the greatest reluctance, with every wish that I may be proved in error, and after long deliberation on my responsibilities to myself, my country, and my ancestors who played responsible parts in its making, I have come to the conclusion that I cannot honorably participate in a war whose prosecution, as far as I can judge, constitutes a betrayal of my country.

A Racist Charge of Mutiny (1944)

Thurgood Marshall

In October 1944 Thurgood Marshall, an esteemed lawyer and director of the NAACP's Legal Defense Fund, traveled to San Francisco to begin the process of offering civilian counsel to fifty African American sailors on trial for mutiny. The sailors were accused of refusing to obey an order to load ammunition on a ship based at Mare Island. Their refusal had occurred shortly after white Navy officers at Port Chicago staged an ammunition-loading contest among black sailors, in which a case of ammunition fell and sparked multiple explosions that led to the deaths of 327 soldiers, most of them African Americans. News about the explosion had reached the black sailors on Mare Island, who became so concerned about their own safety that they carried out an act of nonviolent protest—they simply refused orders to load ammunition.

Six days before he sent the letter below to Navy Secretary James Forrestal—with its series of devastating questions—Marshall was quoted in an NAACP news release as saying that the fifty sailors were being tried only because of their race. Marshall intended for the questions listed in his letter to highlight the racist conditions that had led to the soldiers' refusal. After all fifty sailors were indicted, Marshall became civilian counsel for the men and eventually helped secure their release.

I have just returned from San Francisco, where for the past twelve days I have been investigating the circumstances leading to the court martial of the fifty Negro seamen charged with mutiny, which is now being conducted on Yerba Buena Island.

As to the trial itself, I am convinced that the accused were advised of their rights to civilian counsel prior to the trial and that they had signified their willingness to accept naval counsel. While attending the trial for several days, I was convinced that defense counsel . . . is doing a splendid job in defending these men and, within the limitations of Navy rules, is doing everything possible toward protecting their rights at the trial as well as the development of the case itself.

In addition to attending the trial, I made an investigation as far as possible into the incidents leading up to the Port Chicago explosion and conditions immediately prior to the alleged refusal to obey orders, resulting in the present trial. I, of course, realize it would be impossible to make a thorough investigation since I am a civilian. There are many factors involved in the working conditions in the Twelfth Naval District which could not be brought out in the court martial. I am convinced that there are sufficient facts involved to warrant a thorough and complete investigation by your office as to the following conditions, which existed in the Twelfth Naval District:

1. Why is it that the only naval personnel loading ammunition regularly were Negroes with the exception of their officers and petty officers?

2. Why is it that Negro seamen, many of whom have had special training in such schools as gunnery schools, were nevertheless relegated to the duty of loading ammunition?

3. Why is it that these men were not given any training whatsoever in the dangers to be found in loading ammunition or the proper methods to be used in loading ammunition?

4. Why is it that men with no prior experience whatsoever were given the duty of handling winches in the loading of ammunition when civilian longshoremen were not permitted to handle winches on ammunition unless they had had several years' experience in winch-handling?

5. Why is it that Negro seamen with no prior experience in ammunition were given the job of hatch tender in the loading of ammunition?

6. Why is it that officers "raced" their gangs in contests in the loading of ammunition?

7. Why is it that one of the accused, Seaman Green, while suffering with a broken wrist, despite the fact that the Navy doctors ordered him on the sick list, was not placed on the sick list, but was ordered to load ammunition?

8. Why is it that the Negro seamen who had been loading ammunition and who were at Port Chicago at the time of the explosion were not given any leave whatsoever as a result of this explosion, but were forced to return to the duty of loading ammunition? A psychiatrist from the United States Navy testified at the court martial proceedings that such an explosion as occurred at Port Chicago

would have a lasting effect upon the minds of the men who were near the explosion.

Practically all of the Negroes at Port Chicago were trained at great length and were led to believe that they were being trained to serve as regular seamen. This they are anxious to do. When these men were assigned to Port Chicago instead of being given an opportunity to serve in whatever branch of the service they might find themselves fitted, they were, solely because of their race or color, restricted to the task of loading ammunition and other menial tasks.

As a result of the action of the Twelfth Naval District in releasing some of the men who allegedly refused to obey orders, shipping 150 of the men to the Pacific around the middle of August, the giving of summary courts to some of the men and the singling out of an even 50 to be charged with mutiny, Negro members of the armed forces, as well as Negro and white civilians, believe that a thorough, complete and impartial investigation by your office is essential at this time.

We have been receiving reports in this office for several months, and my investigation in the Bay area seems to justify all of the complaints we have received concerning the discriminatory policies being practiced by the Twelfth Naval District.

In this request for an impartial investigation, we by no means wish to reflect at all upon the manner in which the actual court martial proceedings are being conducted. It is for that reason we believe the investigation is necessary.

The Internment of Japanese Citizens (1944)

Fred Korematsu and Frank Murphy

Less than a month after the bombing of Pearl Harbor, President Roosevelt signed Executive Order 9066, which authorized the secretary of war and his military commanders "to prescribe military areas . . . from which any or all persons may be excluded." In effect, "any and all persons" really meant Japanese Americans living on the West Coast, including all of California, and other areas. Roosevelt justified the order by stating that "the successful prosecution of the war requires every possible protection against espionage and against sabotage to national-defense material, national-defense premises, and national-defense utilities."

By the end of August 1942 the U.S. government had forced about 110,000 Japanese Americans—men, women, and children, all characterized as threats to U.S. security—from their homes and businesses, and transported them to internment camps. About 4,100 Japanese-Americans were ordered to leave the Oakland area, and though virtually all of them complied, Fred Korematsu, a 23-year-old Japanese American, resisted the roundup and adopted a disguise. According to his daughter and the Korematsu Institute, Korematsu "underwent minor plastic surgery to alter his eyes in an attempt to look less Japanese. He also changed his name to Clyde Sarah and claimed to be of Spanish and Hawaiian descent."

But the U.S. government tracked him down, and Korematsu was arrested and jailed on May 30, 1944. While awaiting transfer to an internment camp, Korematsu received a visit from Ernest Besig, the director of the American Civil Liberties Union (ACLU) office in San Francisco. Besig arrived at the meeting with a pressing question: Would Korematsu allow the ACLU to use his case to file a legal challenge to the internment of Japanese Americans? Korematsu agreed, and his case ended up in the U.S. Supreme Court. In a 6 to 3 decision, the Court ruled in favor of the internment, declaring it a necessity in wartime. Below is a dissent offered by Justice Frank Murphy. The U.S. Supreme Court finally overturned the Korematsu decision on June 26, 2018.

This exclusion of "all persons of Japanese ancestry, both alien and non-alien," from the Pacific Coast area on a plea of military necessity in the absence of martial law ought not to be approved. Such exclusion goes over "the very brink of constitutional power," and falls into the ugly abyss of racism.

In dealing with matters relating to the prosecution and progress of a war, we must accord great respect and consideration to the judgments of the military authorities who are on the scene and who have full knowledge of the military facts. The scope of their discretion must, as a matter of necessity and common sense, be wide. And their judgments ought not to be overruled lightly by those whose training and duties ill-equip them to deal intelligently with matters so vital to the physical security of the nation.

At the same time, however, it is essential that there be definite limits to military discretion, especially where martial law has not been declared. Individuals must not be left impoverished of their constitutional rights on a plea of military necessity that has neither substance nor support. Thus, like other claims conflicting with the asserted constitutional rights of the individual, the military claim must subject itself to the judicial process of having its reasonableness determined and its conflicts with other interests reconciled.

What are the allowable limits of military discretion, and whether or not they have been overstepped in a particular case, are judicial questions. The judicial test of whether the government, on a plea of military necessity, can validly deprive an individual of any of his constitutional rights is whether the deprivation is reasonably related to a public danger that is so "immediate, imminent, and impending" as not to admit of delay and not to permit the intervention of ordinary constitutional processes to alleviate the danger. Civilian Exclusion Order No. 34, banishing from a prescribed area of the Pacific Coast "all persons of Japanese ancestry, both alien and non-alien," clearly does not meet that test. Being an obvious racial discrimination, the order deprives all those within its scope of the equal protection of the laws as guaranteed by the Fifth Amendment. It further deprives these individuals of their constitutional rights to live and work where they will, to establish a home where they choose and to move about freely. In excommunicating them without benefit of hearings, this order also deprives them of all their constitutional rights to procedural due process. Yet no reasonable relation to an "immediate, imminent, and impending" public danger is evident to support this racial restriction, which is one of the most sweeping and complete deprivations of constitutional rights in the history of this nation in the absence of martial law.

It must be conceded that the military and naval situation in the spring of 1942 was such as to generate a very real fear of invasion of the Pacific Coast, accompanied by fears of sabotage and espionage in that area. The military command was therefore justified in adopting all reasonable means necessary to combat these dangers. In adjudging the military action taken in light of the then apparent dangers, we must not erect too high or too meticulous standards; it is necessary only that the action have some reasonable relation to the removal of the dangers of invasion, sabotage, and espionage. But the exclusion, either temporarily or permanently, of all persons with Japanese blood in their veins has no such reasonable relation. And that relation is lacking because the exclusion order necessarily must rely for its reasonableness upon the assumption that all persons of Japanese ancestry may have a dangerous tendency to commit sabotage and espionage and to aid our Japanese enemy in other ways. It is difficult to believe that reason, logic, or experience could be marshalled in support of such an assumption.

That this forced exclusion was the result in good measure of this erroneous assumption of racial guilt, rather than *bona fide* military necessity, is evidenced by the Commanding General's Final Report on the evacuation from the Pacific Coast area. In it, he refers to all individuals of Japanese descent as "subversive," as belonging to "an enemy race" whose "racial strains are undiluted," and as constituting "over 112,000 potential enemies . . . at large today" along the Pacific Coast. In support of this blanket condemnation of all persons of Japanese descent, however, no reliable evidence is cited to show that such individuals were generally disloyal, or had generally so conducted themselves in this area as to constitute a special menace to defense installations or war industries, or had otherwise, by their behavior, furnished reasonable ground for their exclusion as a group. . . .

I dissent, therefore, from this legalization of racism. Racial discrimination in any form and in any degree has no justifiable part whatever in our democratic way of life. It is unattractive in any setting, but it is utterly revolting among a free people who have embraced the principles set forth in the Constitution of the United States. All residents of this nation are kin in some way by blood or culture to a foreign land. Yet they are primarily and necessarily a part of the new and distinct civilization of the United States. They must, accordingly, be treated at all times as the heirs of the American experiment, and as entitled to all the rights and freedoms guaranteed by the Constitution.

Japanese American Draft Resisters (1944)

The Voice of the Nisei

Shortly after the bombing of Pearl Harbor, the Selective Service System classified all Japanese Americans as ineligible for military service, this in spite of the presence of 5,000 Nisei (second-generation Japanese Americans born in the US) already in the Army. But with urging from the Japanese American Citizens League, as well as others who believed that drafting Nisei would help prove Japanese American loyalty to the United States, the government revisited its policy and extended the draft to include Nisei in January 1944.

Not all Nisei complied. Between January 1944 and the middle of 1945, more than 300 Nisei resisted the draft by refusing to report for their pre-induction physicals or for actual induction. Leading the way at the Poston Relocation Center in Arizona—the largest internment camp in the US—was 29-year-old George Fujii. On February 6, 1944, Fujii wrote, copied, and posted the notice below across the camp. Five days later he helped write another notice, this one stating that the government should not force

Nisei to serve in the military until it restored all constitutional rights to Japanese Americans and provided compensation for the time in which their rights were denied. Fujii was arrested and charged with sedition on February 19, but his work had already made a difference. By March 1944 more than 100 Nisei at Poston resisted the draft.

Handbill of demands made by the Voice of the Nisei, Poston, Arizona, 1942.

To the Gentlemen of 17 Years to 38 Years of Age

As you know fellow Americans, at last did they recognize and realize that we are Americans. We are going to be drafted soon, just like Americans outside enjoying the freedom and liberty. But, don't you think that they should reconsider the steps that they had taken?

As we believe that Mr. Roosevelt's speech at the Congress was not merely an excuse to draft us to soldiers and die in vain, we are demanding the following as an American Citizen:

1. Personal apology for Gen. DeWitt regarding his statement "Jap is Jap" and be expelled from his office. . . .
2. Freedom rights and privileges should not be denied in California, militarily, economically, and politically.
3. Open the barbwire and withdraw the guard duty of M.P.
4. Such signs as "No Jap," "You Rat," "No Orientals or Colored Admitted," and etc., which were familiar in California, must be taken down throughout the U.S.A.
5. No discrimination upon the Japanese securing occupations.
6. Every opportunity must be given to the Japanese soldier for advancement in the Air Corps, in the Army, and in the Marine Corps.

7. Japanese soldiers must be mixed with other Caucasian soldiers to fight side by side.

Voice of Nisei

Against Dropping Atomic Bombs on Japan (1945)

Leo Szilard

After fleeing Nazi Germany in 1933, Leo Szilard, a physicist who had studied with Albert Einstein, eventually settled in the United States and accepted a positon at Columbia University. Szilard grew concerned about Germany's growing weapons technology, and in 1939 he convinced Einstein to send President Roosevelt a confidential letter warning that Germany was on its way to developing an atomic bomb, and encouraging the U.S. government to begin securing the uranium needed to develop its own.

Szilard played an instrumental role in building the nation's first nuclear reactor, and after moving to the University of Chicago he continued to develop technology that the government used to help construct the atomic bomb. Szilard was not pleased with the military's use of his research, and in 1945 he authored and distributed a petition (see below) urging President Harry Truman not to drop atomic bombs on Japan. Signed by seventy scientists, the petition arrived at the White House but did not land on Truman's desk before he launched the attacks that obliterated Hiroshima and Nagasaki.

Discoveries of which the people of the United States are not aware may affect the welfare of this nation in the near future. The liberation of atomic power which has been achieved places atomic bombs in the hands of the Army. It places in your hands, as Commander-in-Chief, the fateful decision whether or not to sanction the use of such bombs in the present phase of the war against Japan.

We, the undersigned scientists, have been working in the field of atomic power for a number of years. Until recently we have had to reckon with the possibility that the United States might be attacked by atomic bombs during this war and that her only defense might lie in a counterattack by the same means. Today with this danger averted we feel impelled to say what follows:

The war has to be brought speedily to a successful conclusion and the destruction of Japanese citizens by means of atomic bombs may very well be an effective method of warfare. We feel, however, that such an attack on Japan could not be justified in the present circumstances. We believe that the United States ought not to resort to the use of atomic bombs in the present phase of the war, at least not unless the terms which will be imposed upon Japan after the war are publicly announced and subsequently Japan is given an opportunity to surrender.

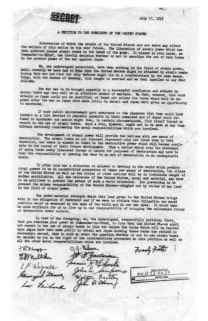

Leo Szilard's petition to President Harry S. Truman, 1945.

If such public announcement gave assurance to the Japanese that they could look forward to a life devoted to peaceful pursuits in their homeland and if Japan still refused to surrender, our nation would then be faced with a situation which might require reexamination of her position with respect to the use of atomic bombs in the war.

Atomic bombs are primarily a means for the ruthless annihilation of cities. Once they were introduced as an instrument of war it would be difficult to resist for long the temptation of putting them to such use.

The last few years show a marked tendency toward increasing ruthlessness. At present our Air Forces, striking at the Japanese cities, are using the same methods of warfare which were condemned by American public opinion only a few years ago when applied by the Germans to the cities of England. Our use of atomic bombs in this war would carry the world a long way further on this path of ruthlessness.

Atomic power will provide the nations with new means of destruction. The atomic bombs at our disposal represent only the first step in this direction and there is almost no limit to the destructive power which will become available in the course of this development. Thus a nation which sets the precedent of using these newly liberated forces of nature for purposes of destruction may have to bear the responsibility of opening the door to an era of devastation on an unimaginable scale.

In view of the foregoing, we, the undersigned, respectfully petition that you exercise your power as Commander-in-Chief to rule that the United States shall not, in the present phase of the war, resort to the use of atomic bombs.

Judgment on Jubilation (1945)

Dorothy Day

Dorothy Day—the founder of the Catholic Worker Movement and publisher of the Catholic Worker, a monthly newspaper that blended Catholic spirituality with social justice themes—advocated nonviolent resistance to the Selective Training and Service Act of 1940 and urged her followers to go to jail rather than become part of the war effort. Day used her newspaper to lament the war's destruction, and she published the following critical essay not long after Truman decided to drop atomic bombs on Japan. She would later become a leading voice in nonviolent campaigns against nuclear weapons.

Mr. Truman was jubilant. President Truman. True man; what a strange name, come to think of it. We refer to Jesus Christ as true God and true Man. Truman is a true man of his time in that he was jubilant. He was not a son of God, brother of Christ, brother of the Japanese, jubilating as he did. He went from table to table on the cruiser which was bringing him home from the Big Three conference, telling the great news; "jubilant" the newspapers said. *Jubilate Deo.* We have killed 318,000 Japanese.

That is, we hope we have killed them, the Associated Press, on page one, column one of the *Herald Tribune* says. The effect is hoped for, not known. It is to be hoped they are vaporized, our Japanese brothers, scattered, men, women and babies, to the four winds, over the seven seas. Perhaps we will breathe their dust into our nostrils, feel them in the fog of New York on our faces, feel them in the rain on the hills of Easton.

Jubilate Deo. President Truman was jubilant. We have created. We have created destruction. We have created a new element, called Pluto. Nature had nothing to do with it. . . .

The papers list the scientists (the murderers) who are credited with perfecting this new weapon. . . .

Scientists, army officers, great universities (Notre Dame included), and captains of industry—all are given credit lines in the press for their work of preparing the bomb—and other bombs, the President assures us are in production now. . . .

Yes, God is still in the picture. God is not mocked. . . . We are held in God's hands, all of us, and President Truman too, and these scientists who have created death, but will use it for good. . . .

And I think, as I think on these things, that while here in the western hemisphere, we went in for precision bombing (what chance of *precision* bombing now?) while we went in for obliteration bombing, Russia was very careful not to bomb cities, to wipe out civilian populations. Perhaps she was thinking of the poor, of the workers, as brothers. . . .

Everyone says, "I wonder what the Pope thinks of it?" How everyone turns to the Vatican for judgment, even though they do not seem to listen to the voice there! But our Lord Himself has already pronounced judgment on the atomic bomb. When James and John (John the beloved) wished to call down fire from heaven on their enemies, Jesus said,

"You know not of what spirit you are. The Son of Man came not to destroy souls but to save." He said also, "What you do unto the least of these my brethren, you do unto me." *(1945)*

NINE

The Civil Rights Movement

BUILDING THE FOUNDATION

Human Holocaust Under the Stars and Stripes (1909)

Ida B. Wells-Barnett

In 1883, at the age of twenty-one, Ida Wells refused to surrender her first-class seat in a car reserved for women on the Chesapeake, Ohio, and Southwestern Railway. In the following year, after trying to sit in first class, she sued the railway for violating her civil rights, and though she lost her case, she won a career. The Living Way, a Baptist weekly, invited her to submit an article about her nonviolent protest, and this invitation led to many others—and to Wells's decision to become a fulltime journalist. By the end of 1889 she was co-owner of a radical black newspaper in Memphis, the Free Speech and Headlight, in which she regularly criticized racial segregation and violence against African Americans.

Racial violence touched her personally when a white mob lynched one of her close friends in March 1892. Writing for her paper, she claimed that the lynching had occurred because whites were fearful that a black-owned grocery cooperative, which her friend had been part of, would have undermined their own businesses. Wells then called on her readers to boycott Memphis trolleys and even to leave the city for the West. Her strong stance led to whites trashing her office and threatening her with death.

Wells moved to New York City and began writing anti-lynching articles for the prestigious New York Age. Her forceful writing prompted black women activists along the northeastern seaboard, including Mary Church Terrell, to join forces and form the National Association of Colored Women in 1896. The new association gave institutional heft to Wells's pioneering campaigns against lynching, as would a major civil rights group founded in 1909 by prominent whites and African Americans, including Wells (now Wells-Barnett), after the lynching of two African Americans in Springfield, Illinois. This new organization—the National Association for the Advancement of Colored People (NAACP)—focused on lobbying members of Congress to pass anti-lynching legislation, an effort that failed time and again. Below are excerpts from a speech that Wells delivered at the NAACP's first annual conference. It includes her assessment of the effectiveness of nonviolent actions on the struggle against lynching.

The lynching record for a quarter of a century merits the thoughtful study of the American people. It present three salient facts:

First: Lynching is color-line murder.

Second: Crimes against women is the excuse, not the cause.

Third: It is a national crime and requires a national remedy. . . .

Just as the lynch-law regime came to a close in the West, a new mob movement started in the South. This was wholly political, its purpose being to suppress the colored vote by intimidation and murder. Thousands of assassins, banded together under the name of Ku Klux Klans, "Midnight Raiders," "Knights of the Golden Circle," et cetera, et cetera, spread a reign of terror by beating, shooting, and killing colored people by the thousands. In a few years, the purpose was accomplished, and the black vote was suppressed. But mob murder continued.

From 1882, in which year fifty-two were lynched, down to the present, lynching has been along the color line. Mob murder increased yearly until in 1892 more than two hundred victims were lynched and statistics show that 3,284 men, women, and children have been put to death in this quarter of a century. During the last ten years from 1899 to 1908 inclusive, the number lynched was 959. Of this number 102 were white,

African Americans march near U.S. Capitol to protest lynching of four African Americans in Georgia, 1946.

while the colored victims numbered 857. No other nation, civilized or savage, burns its criminals: only under the Stars and Stripes is the human holocaust possible. Twenty-eight human beings burned at the stake, one of them a woman and two of them children, is the awful indictment against American civilization—the gruesome tribute which the nation pays to the color line.

Why is mob murder permitted by a Christian nation? What is the cause of this awful slaughter? The question is answered almost daily—always the same shameless falsehood that "Negroes are lynched to protect womanhood." Standing before a Chautauqua assemblage, John Temple Graves, at once champion for lynching and apologist for lynchers, said: "The mob stands today as the most potential bulwark between the women of the South and such a carnival of crime as would infuriate the world and precipitate the annihilation of the Negro race." This is the never-varying answer of lynchers and their apologists. All know that it is untrue. The cowardly lyncher revels in murder, then seeks to shield himself from public execration by claiming devotion to women. But truth is mighty and the lynching record discloses the hypocrisy of the lyncher as well as his crime.

The Springfield, Illinois, mob rioted for two days, the militia of the entire state was called out, two men were lynched, hundreds of people driven from their homes, all because a white woman said a Negro assaulted her. A mad mob went to the jail, tried to lynch the victim of her charge and, not being able to find him, proceeded to pillage and burn the town and to lynch two innocent men. Later, after the police had found that the woman's charge was false, she published a retraction, the indictment was dismissed, and the intended victim discharged. But the lynched victims were dead. Hundreds were homeless and Illinois was disgraced.

As a final and complete refutation of the charge that lynching is occasioned by crimes against women, a partial record of lynchings is cited; 285 persons were lynched for causes as follows:

Unknown cause, 92; no cause, 10; race prejudice, 49; miscegenation, 7; informing, 12; making threats, 11; keeping saloon, 3; practicing fraud, 5; practicing voodooism, 2; bad reputation, 8; unpopularity, 3; mistaken identity, 5; using improper language, 3; violation of contract, 1; writing insulting letter, 2; eloping, 2; poisoning horse, 1; poisoning well, 2; by well caps, 9; vigilantes, 14; Indians, 1; moonshining, 1; refusing evidence, 2; political causes, 5; disputing, 1; disobeying quarantine regulations, 2; slapping a child, 1; turning state's evidence, 3; protecting a Negro, 1; to prevent giving evidence, 1; knowledge of larceny, 1; writing letter to white woman, 1; asking white woman to marry, 1; jilting girl, 1; having smallpox, 1; concealing criminal, 2; threatening political exposure, 1; self-defense, 6; cruelty, 1; insulting language to woman, 5; quarreling with white man, 2; colonizing Negroes, 2; throwing stones, 1; quarrelling, 1; gambling, 1.

Is there a remedy, or will the nation confess that it cannot protect its protectors at home as well as abroad? . . . Education is suggested as preventive, but it is as grave a crime to murder an ignorant man as it is a scholar. True, few educated men have been lynched, but the hue and cry once started stops at no bounds, as was clearly shown by the lynchings in Atlanta and in Springfield, Illinois.

Agitation, though helpful, will not alone stop the crime. Year after year statistics are published, meetings are held, resolutions are adopted, and yet lynchings go on. Public sentiment does measurably decrease the sway of mob law, but the irresponsible bloodthirsty criminals who swept through the streets of Springfield, beating an inoffensive law-abiding citizen to death in one part of the town, and in another torturing and shooting to death a man who for threescore years had made a reputation for honesty, integrity and sobriety, had raised a family and had accumulated property, were not deterred from their heinous crimes by either education or agitation.

The only certain remedy is an appeal to law. Lawbreakers must be made to know that human life is sacred and that every citizen of this country is first a citizen of the United States and secondly a citizen of the state in which he belongs. This nation must assert itself and defend its federal citizenship at home as well as abroad. The strong arm of the government must reach across state lines whenever unbridled lawlessness defies state laws and must give to the individual citizen under the Stars and Stripes the same measure of protection which it gives to him when he travels in foreign lands.

Federal protection of American citizenship is the remedy for lynching.

We March for the Butchered Dead (1917)

Charles Martin and the Negro Silent Protest Parade

On May 8, 1916, Lucy Fryer lay dead, killed with a blunt instrument, and possibly raped. She had lived with her husband on their cotton farm in Waco, Texas, and one of their workers, Jesse Washington, a poor and illiterate black teenager, immediately became a suspect. He initially denied killing Fryer, but allegedly confessed to rape and murder during an interrogation the following morning.

Local authorities held the trial just a week after the murder. It took the all-white jury less than five minutes to find Washington guilty. The crowd of angry whites in the courtroom grabbed Washington, dragged him outside, threw a chain around his neck, doused him in gasoline, and pulled him toward a bonfire as the crowd pummeled him with bricks and shovels. Someone cut off his testicles. Others used the chain to hang him, and for the next two hours they raised and lowered Washington, still alive, over the flames below.

There were about 15,000 in the mob that gathered. Some were smiling, joking, laughing, as if they were at a church picnic. The police were there, and so were local politicians and other community leaders. No one made any sustained effort to stop the mob from burning Washington until only a charred corpse was left, which was then dragged through town.

The lynching of African Americans already had a long history, but violence against black citizens saw a resurgence throughout the South during this time. The lynching of Eli Persons in Memphis was just one more instance, in May 1917. After being beaten into confessing that he had murdered Antoinette Rappel, a 16-year-old white woman, a white mob burned him alive and threw his decapitated head at a group of African Americans in the black section of the city.

Less than two months later, violence also broke out in East St. Louis, Illinois, when a white mob, enraged by African American workers who had replaced them during a strike at a bauxite plant, torched a black neighborhood. With their clothes ablaze, black people ran from their burning homes, only to be shot at or beaten. Hundreds were seriously injured, and about 40 were murdered.

The NAACP, headquartered in Manhattan, struggled with how to respond to all the violence. Vice-president James Weldon Johnson suggested a silent march through New York City streets, and his colleagues agreed that an all-black march would be best. On Saturday, July 28, 1917, about ten thousand African American women, children, and men marched silently down Fifth Avenue. The women and children, clad in white, marched in the front of the parade, and the men, dressed in black suits, followed behind. The silent, somber marchers carried protest signs, and

Children march in the Silent Protest Parade, 1917.

black Boy Scouts quietly handed out flyers about the NAACP—and about the terrifying spectacle of lynching. Below is the text of a flyer, penned by march organizer Charles Martin, distributed by the NAACP shortly before the march.

To the People of African Descent:
Dear Friend:
There will be 10,000 Negroes in line at 1 o'clock Saturday, July 28th, on 59th St. and Fifth Ave. to 23rd Street and Madison Square where the procession will end. . . .

Why Do We March?

We march because by the Grace of God and the force of truth, the dangerous, hampering walls of prejudice and inhuman injustices must fall.

We march because we want to make impossible a repetition of Waco, Memphis, and East St. Louis, by rousing the conscience of the country and bring the murderers of our brothers, sisters, and innocent children to justice.

We march because we deem it a crime to be silent in the face of such barbaric acts.

We march because we are thoroughly opposed to Jim-crow cars, etc., segregation, discrimination, disfranchisement, *lynching,* and the host of evils that are forced on us. It is time that the Spirit of Christ should be manifested in the making and execution of laws.

We march because we want our children to live on a better land and enjoy fairer conditions than have fallen to our lot.

We march in memory of our butchered dead, the massacre of the honest toilers who were removing the reproach of laziness and thriftlessness hurled at the entire race. They died to prove our worthiness to live. We live in spite of death shadowing us and ours. We prosper in the face of the most unwarranted and illegal oppression.

We march because the growing consciousness and solidarity of race coupled with sorrow and discrimination have made us one: a union that may never be dissolved in spite of shallow-brained agitators, scheming pundits, and political tricksters who secure a fleeting popularity and uncertain financial support by promoting the disunion of a people who ought to consider themselves as one.

Be in line on Saturday and show that you have not become callous to the sorrows of your race. May God bless you and every parade.

We Return Fighting (1919)

W. E. B. Du Bois

W. E. B. Du Bois moved to New York City in 1910 to become editor of the Crisis, the main publication of the NAACP. Although Du Bois used the platform to urge young African American men to sign up for the war, he also protested the dissonance between making the world safe for democracy while allowing Jim Crow to roam freely at home. And in 1919 Du Bois and the NAACP led investigations into discrimination against African American soldiers.

In the editorial below, Du Bois describes racism in the United States and assures his readers that returning African American soldiers will fight just as hard for justice at home. Du Bois was right—World War II's military produced a generation of black activists who would use nonviolent resistance to transform America in the post-war years.

We are returning from war! The *Crisis* and tens of thousands of black men were drafted into a great struggle. For bleeding France and what she means and has meant and will mean to us and humanity and against the threat of German race arrogance, we fought gladly and to the last drop of blood; for America and her highest ideals, we fought in far off hope; for the dominant southern oligarchy entrenched in Washington, we fought in bitter resignation, For the America that represents and gloats in lynching, disfranchisement, caste, brutality, and devilish insult—for this, in the hateful upturning and mixing of things, we were forced by vindictive fate to fight, also.

But today we return! We return from the slavery of uniform which the world's madness demanded us to don to the freedom of civil garb. We stand again to look America squarely in the face and call a spade a spade. We sing: This country of ours, despite all its better souls have done and dreamed, is yet a shameful land.

It *lynches.*

And lynching is barbarism of a degree of contemptible nastiness unparalleled in human history. Yet for fifty years we have lynched two Negros a week, and we have kept this up right through the war.

It *disfranchises* its own citizens.

Disfranchisement is the deliberate theft and robbery of the only protection of poor against rich and black against white. The land that disfranchises its citizens and calls itself a democracy lies and knows it lies.

It encourages *ignorance.*

It has never really tried to educate the Negro. A dominant minority does not want Negroes educated. It wants servants, dogs, whores, and monkeys. And when this land allows a reactionary group by its stolen political power to force as many black folk into these categories as it possibly can, it cries in contemptible hypocrisy: "They threaten us with degeneracy; they cannot be educated."

It *steals* from us.

It organizes industry to cheat us. It cheats us out of our land; it cheats us out of our labor. It confiscates our savings. It reduces our wages. It raises our rent. It steals our profit. It taxes us without representation. It keeps us consistently and universally poor, and then feeds us on charity and derides our poverty.

It *insults* us.

It has organized a nationwide and latterly a worldwide propaganda of deliberate and continuous insult and defamation of black blood wherever found. It decrees that it shall not be possible in travel nor residence, work nor play, education nor instruction for a black man to exist without tacit or open acknowledgement of his inferiority to the dirtiest white dog. And it looks upon any attempt to question or even discuss this dogma as arrogance, unwarranted assumption, and treason.

This is the country to which we Soldiers of Democracy return. This is the fatherland for which we fought! But it is *our* fatherland. It was right for us to fight. The faults of our country are our faults. Under similar circumstances, we would fight again. But by the God of heaven, we

W. E. B. Du Bois, second from left in front line, marches in the Silent Protest Parade, New York City, 1917.

are cowards and jackasses if now that that war is over, we do not marshal every ounce of our brain and brawn to fight a sterner, longer, more unbending battle against the forces of hell in our own land.

We *return.*

We *return from fighting.*

We *return fighting.*

Make way for Democracy! We saved it in France, and by the Great Jehovah, we will save it in the United States of America, or know the reason why.

It Brings a Sense of Shame (1947, 1960)

Baltimore Afro-American *and Jackie Robinson*

Jackie Robinson destroyed the color barrier in Major League baseball when he played in his first game as a member of the Brooklyn Dodgers on April 15, 1947. Before signing him, Dodgers president Branch Rickey had sought an assurance from Robinson that he would "turn the other cheek" when confronting racist players, managers, and fans. Robinson agreed, and his presence and success in the otherwise lily-white sport proved inspirational.

Two documents about this historic event are below. The first, an op-ed published by the Baltimore Afro-American shortly after Robinson joined the Dodgers, advises Robinson's fans to remain cool and collected in their stadium seats. In the second document, a newspaper column from 1960, Robinson reflects on his nonviolent strategy in light of the student sit-in movement in Nashville, when more than 150 students were arrested while targeting segregated lunch counters from February to May of that year.

1947 Editorial

Biggest news of last week, as far as many persons are concerned, was the signing of Jackie Robinson to play baseball for the Brooklyn Dodgers.

Robinson thus becomes the first of his race to be signed in the history of modern organized baseball. Before 1900, Moses Walker, a catcher, played with the old Toledo club of the American Association (then a major league) and George Stovey pitched for Newark in the International League.

There were others, too, who played without having their racial identity generally known. But that is all ancient history. What happened in Brooklyn last Friday when Jackie Roosevelt Robinson affixed his signature to a Brooklyn Dodger contract, marks the beginning of a new era.

As this is written, Jackie has played errorless ball. He has contributed most in runs batted in—all of this under terrific pressure. As a member of the Montreal Royals, Robinson, last season, was subjected to every abuse in the book, but he nevertheless led the International League with a batting average of .349, drove in 65 runs, scored 113 more, stole 40 bases, and fielded .985.

Were it not for the color of his skin, there is no question that he would have been signed by Brooklyn long ago. It took a great deal of courage for Branch Rickey, Dodger president, and the now deposed Leo Durocher to meet the challenge which Robinson's performance offered.

Thanks to them and to their faith in an ideal, Robinson is where he is today. In view of the fact that the going will be even tougher than in the International League Jackie's future, while depending in great part upon his own individual performance, also hinges upon the conduct of those who have his interest most at heart.

This means that he should be treated as he would have it—as just another ballplayer, not as a phenomenon. Already there have been indications of excessive enthusiasm on the part of some of his well-wishers—enthusiasm which is definitely embarrassing to Jackie.

There is no cause to cheer every time he comes to bat or upon every occasion when he handles an easy chance. Such immodest and immoderate behavior can do more than anything else to increase his burden.

As a trailblazer, Jackie is well aware that upon his shoulders rests the future of other players of his race in the ranks of organized baseball. All that he wants is a fair chance to demonstrate his ability. He wants no unmerited applause. It is up to us, therefore, to see that his request is granted.

1960 Column by Robinson

CBS is to be congratulated for its thoughtful, enlightening, and arresting report on lunch counter sit-ins, "Anatomy of a Demonstration," shown yesterday over the CBS television network. This, you may recall, is the report a CBS camera crew was filming in Nashville, when Tennessee Governor Ellington charged the network with "instigating" the student sit-ins so they could be filmed for the show, a charge which CBS has denied.

The program documented a workshop in the techniques of nonviolent resistance, the Gandhian method by which Negro Americans in the South are forging a new chapter in the struggle against human indignity. The CBS cameras followed each move, step by step, as a group of Negroes and whites prepared themselves for the antagonisms and possible violence they might meet as they sought service at lunch counters in the downtown area.

The volunteers not only discussed what might happen, but in a greatly interesting sequence, they set up a "sample" lunch counter, split themselves into two groups—the demonstrators and the harassers— and proceeded to test their own principles and personal fortitude by intentionally goading one another in the same manner in which they could expect to be intimidated while on an actual sit-in. The harassing group called the demonstrators vile names, hurled racial insults, blew smoke in their faces, and finally attacked one demonstrator physically by dragging him off his stool. The demonstrators followed the principles of nonviolence—even when beaten—by refusing to fight back.

Actually, this program brought back memories of my own experience in breaking into major league baseball, for this was exactly the principle which Mr. Rickey and I agreed upon for the first tough year with the Dodgers. I can testify to the fact that it was a lot harder to turn the other cheek and refuse to fight back than it would have been to exercise a normal reaction. But it works, because sooner or later it brings a sense of shame to those who attack you. And that sense of shame is often the beginning of progress.

The leader and teacher of the Nashville workshop was a former Vanderbilt University ministerial student, the Rev. James M. Lawson. Though he was scheduled to receive his doctorate from Vanderbilt's Divinity School this summer, he was summarily expelled when his part in the sit-ins was publicized. This has not deterred young Lawson in the least, however, for he has continued to teach the doctrine of peaceful non-cooperation with segregation. Lawson spent three years in India studying the Gandhi precepts first hand, and when accused of preaching a "foreign ideology," he agrees that this concept originated nearly 2,000 years ago in a place called Bethlehem.

The CBS documentary could not have failed to move any thinking viewer, and thus it came as no surprise that a CBS network station in Memphis refused to allow the show on its airwaves. As the old adage goes, there is nothing so dangerous as an idea whose time has come. That these protests and demonstrations are having a telling effect is well demonstrated by the lengths to which desperate segregationists are going to try to curb them—the mass arrests, the tear gas, the fire hoses and the beatings. But still they go on, and they are growing.

The simple reason may be found in the answer Lawson gave to an interviewer during the program. Lawson was asked if Negroes themselves had contributed to the present strife by errors in judgment or strategy. He replied: "Yes. We have sinned by cooperating with the evils of segregation for as long as we have."

Jim Crow in the Armed Forces (1948)

Bayard Rustin

In 1947 Bayard Rustin and his colleague George Houser, both employees of the Fellowship of Reconciliation, an interfaith peace organization headed by A. J. Muste, decided to test the Supreme Court ruling, in Morgan v. Commonwealth of Virginia, that it was unconstitutional for states to apply their segregationist statutes to interstate passengers. Their plan, the "Journey of Reconciliation," called for an interracial group of men to ride buses throughout the Upper South (parts of Virginia, North Carolina, Tennessee, and Kentucky) and to register nonviolent protests when facing bus drivers and companies that demanded segregated seating in spite of the Supreme Court ruling. Eight years before Rosa Parks refused to surrender her seat in Montgomery, Alabama, these first freedom riders attracted national attention and inspired countless others to take their own stance against racial injustice.

Just after the Journey of Reconciliation concluded, Rustin and Houser joined A. Philip Randolph in his public campaign to end segregation in the U.S. military. As the head of the Committee to End Jim Crow in the Military, Randolph testified before the U.S. Senate Armed Services Committee, and in March 1948 he and other African American leaders met with President Harry Truman in the White House. True to form, Randolph did not mince his words when speaking to the president. "Negroes . . . resent the idea of fighting or being drafted into another Jim Crow army," he said. Randolph, Rustin, and others then picketed the White House with signs that read, "If we must die for our country let us die as free men—not as Jim Crow slaves." Randolph even dared to call upon "Negroes and freedom-loving whites in the armed forces . . . to consider laying down their guns in protest."

None of it worked, at least not immediately. On June 24, 1948, President Truman signed a new peacetime draft law that preserved racial segregation in the military. But the campaign continued on. Rustin and Houser organized picket lines and rallies encouraging young men to go to jail rather than serve in the military, and Randolph publicly announced that he was prepared to "oppose a Jim Crow army until I rot in jail."

Truman conceded. On July 26, 1948, the president issued an executive order declaring "that there shall be equality of treatment and opportunity for all persons in the armed services without regard to race, color, religion, or national origin. This policy shall be put into effect as rapidly as possible, having due regard to the time required to effectuate any necessary changes without impairing efficiency or morale." Randolph initially balked, stating that the order did not end segregation, but C. B. Powell, the editor of the New York Amsterdam News, pressured Randolph to abandon his efforts. Below is Rustin's response—he wrote both letters—to Powell's criticism.

To the New York Herald Tribune:
In a recent editorial in the *New York Amsterdam News* Mr. C. B. Powell took issue with A. Philip Randolph on the question of civil disobedience to the new selective service law in an editorial entitled "Reject

Campaign of Civil Disobedience." Since the New York Herald Tribune reprinted the editorial I am sure you will be interested in Mr. Randolph's reply to Mr. Powell, which is enclosed.

> Bayard Rustin, Executive Co-Secretary, League for Nonviolent Civil Disobedience Against Military Segregation. New York, Aug. 2, 1948

Dear Mr. Powell:

Your editorial implies that civil disobedience is contrary to the spirit and tradition of America. On the contrary, the Boston Tea Party is an early example of civil disobedience in American history. You will recall that the thirteen colonies were under the direct rule of England, who determined and levied the taxes. The colonists refused to pay the taxes on the tea, which they then dumped into the sea. This was an outright act of noncooperation and civil disobedience with the established government. Many of the contemporaries of these men called them "agitators" and "traitors"; but today our history books describe them as "defenders of liberty" and "true patriots."

The colonists argued "no taxation without representation." Today Negroes and white people who love freedom say, "no first-class dying for second-class citizenship; no service without equality for all." The underground railroad, which played so great a role in Negro freedom, also was a direct violation of the fugitive slave law.

Later you indicate that "the end result" of our movement "would be the breakdown of law and order." I maintain that those who conscientiously refuse to go along with unjust laws do not destroy but rather defend and maintain real law and order.

Civil disobedience against one law cannot destroy good government. Even if no Negro entered the armed forces there would be a reduction in military strength of only about 10 per cent. But if it did involve the fate of 20 percent, 50 percent, or 80 percent of the army, the responsibility for civil disobedience must rest upon those who pass unjust laws and upon those who support them. If you believe that civil disobedience will destroy government, you in effect are saying that segregation in the armed forces at the present time is necessary to maintain government since the government can eliminate our civil disobedience movement any time by getting rid of racial segregation in the armed forces. The aim of our movement always will be to improve the nature of the government, to urge and counsel resistance to military Jim Crow for the maintenance of the highest law—the principle of equality and justice upon which real community, security, and government in the long run depend.

You imply that our campaign will encourage dangerous groups like the Ku Klux Klan to continue to follow a similar course of noncompliance with law. Civil disobedience cannot logically be so compared. The Ku Klux Klan and other such anti-democratic movements seek to perpetuate injustice through intimidation, fear, hatred, and force of violence; on the other hand, our civil disobedience campaign seeks to gain freedom and to maintain justice by an entirely different method—nonviolent goodwill direct action. This means that the followers of civil disobedience take into themselves whatever suffering is involved in social change, unlike the Ku Klux Klan, which directs suffering into others.

For more than twenty-five years Negro leaders like yourself, white liberals, and trade unionists have waged a campaign to wipe out military Jim Crow. Today, as in the past, we are faced with promises which continually go unkept, an example of which lies in the 1944 Republican party platform, which promised the elimination of military Jim Crow. But last June it was the Republican steering committee which voted to kill Senator Langer's amendments, which would have outlawed segregation in the army. Scarcely a month later, however, at its Philadelphia convention, the Republican party again went on record against military segregation. We are faced with repeated broken promises to outlaw the curse of army segregation by both the Republicans and Democrats. What now are we to do?

All traditional methods should be pursued relentlessly. We should certainly call upon Congress, the President, and the Supreme Court for action and clarification but when these methods fail, as they have, to bring results, we should not be forced into a position where no course of action is open to us except that which has failed us for twenty-five long years. Under the circumstances, are we not duty-bound to find new and challenging methods?

I sincerely believe that those who dislike to see Negro and white youth engage in civil disobedience have a very important task to perform. It is not to deter those who cannot in clear conscience register for or serve in a Jim Crow army. Those who dislike civil disobedience should work now to encourage the Republicans in control of Congress to pass an amendment outlawing segregation in the army. They should urge President Truman to issue an executive order now eliminating segregation in the services.

Only through congressional or executive action outlawing military Jim Crow can the civil disobedience movement be called off. For the civil disobedience movement springs not from my call but from the deep humiliation and resentment that Negro and white youth feel at being forced to serve in a segregated army.

The Courage of These People in Clarendon County (1951)

Thurgood Marshall

On May 16, 1950, the NAACP filed suit in federal district court in Charleston, South Carolina, seeking an injunction that would prohibit the local school board from using race as a factor when offering public education to the children of Clarendon County. The trial began a year later, on May 28, 1951, before a federal panel of three judges—J. Waties Waring, George Timmerman, and John Parker—with Thurgood Marshall and Robert

Carter arguing the case for the NAACP. In a surprise move, the attorney for South Carolina conceded inequality between white and black schools and asked the panel for time to correct the inequality before ruling on the case. Judge Waring countered by saying that the court still had to address the point in Marshall's brief that questioned the constitutionality of segregated education. Marshall then launched into his case by calling a wide range of social scientists, including psychologist Kenneth Clark, to testify about the damaging effects of segregated education on the development of African American children.

Five days after Marshall sent the letter below, the three-judge panel upheld segregation in Clarendon County public schools in a 2-1 ruling. Judge Waring was the dissenting voice, and his opinion held little room for interpretation: "We must face without evasion or equivocation the question as to whether segregation in education in our schools is legal or whether it cannot exist under our American system enunciated in the Fourteenth Amendment. If segregation is wrong, then the place to stop it is in the first grade and not in graduate schools. Segregation is, per se, inequality."

On July 21 Marshall and his colleagues filed a petition for appeal to the Supreme Court, asking the court to rule on the question of whether "racial separation in public elementary and high schools is a constitutionally possible pattern." After initially sending the case back to lower court, the Supreme Court later agreed to review it. The Clarendon County case became one of the landmark cases in the famous Brown decision of 1954.

June 16, 1951

To the Editor:

Regardless of the decision in the Clarendon County school case, the real heroes are the colored people in South Carolina and especially those in Clarendon County.

Many of us who sit in comfortable and safe homes in other sections of the country will never understand the courage of these people in Clarendon County, a rural, prejudiced, Southern community, who dared the risks involved in their bold challenge to white supremacy.

To their aid came the NAACP state conference under the leadership of James M. Hinton, who has never lost his will to fight for human rights, even after having been almost lynched himself.

The nearest one can get to understanding the enormity of the tasks these people took on is to imagine yourself in their position and to ask yourself the question: "Would I have that much courage?" If you are honest with yourself, the answer would most probably be "No!"

The people of Clarendon County and other sections of South Carolina, Georgia and Alabama crowded the courthouse for the trial knowing that only a small proportion of them could get into the small courtroom.

A very few got seats, a few more stood shoulder to shoulder for hours in the courtroom, which was so crowded that they could not even move.

The others stood outside the door and in the hallway. Many had children with them. All of them were extremely well behaved and were living proof of the determination of our people to seek justice in a lawful manner.

These spectators were neither prosperous nor highly educated. Nor did they come from the big cities. For the most part they came from rural communities and made the trip to Charleston to give their support to the people of Clarendon County.

They knew what havoc segregation wreaks. If anyone ever tells you that colored people want segregation, remind him of these people. It was indeed a wonderful experience to be able to be a witness to this display of greatness in human spirit.

Thurgood Marshall
Robert L. Carter

Dogs, Cats, and Colored People (1955)

George Grant

On January 20, 1955, the Baltimore branch of the Congress of Racial Equality (CORE), an interracial group of civil rights activists, held two sit-ins at the Read's Drug Store chain to confront the company's refusal to serve African Americans at its lunch counters. Baltimore NAACP president Ben Everinghim and Dean McQuay Kiah of Morgan State College joined a group of Morgan students for the sit-ins. One was held at the Read's store at the Northwood Shopping Center, which was close to campus, and the other at the store at the corner of Howard and Lexington in the downtown area.

The sit-in at Northwood lasted about a week, prompting an unnamed Read's official to call Morgan State College Dean George Grant. A reporter for the Baltimore Afro-American, B. M. Phillips, reported on the call, and below is his account of the conversation between the Read's official and Dean Grant. About two hours after the phone call, Grant received another call from Read's, this one informing him that the chain would no longer practice racial discrimination at its lunch counters.

Read's official: Please call your students off. They're staging a showdown here in our Northwood store. We're losing business.

Grant: We teach our students here they must practice democracy and help others to understand it. I don't think you want us to tell them what they're doing is wrong.

Read's: Yes, but we're losing business with them sitting at our counters.

Grant: Well, there are several things you can do.

Read's: What's that?

Grant: Why not put a sign up in your store saying dogs, cats, and colored people are not allowed?

Read's: Well, we couldn't do that.

Grant: Well, why not put an ad in the *Afro* saying that Read's wants colored people to shop there but they can't eat there; and you know you have another alternative, you can say to all your customers everyone can be served at our lunch counters.

Read's: Well, we are in sympathy with this thing—we'll see what can be done.

FROM ROSA PARKS TO THE BLACK PANTHERS

Don't Ride the Bus (1955)

Jo Ann Gibson Robinson

Rosa Parks was not the only pioneering agitator for racial justice on the segregated buses of Montgomery, Alabama. So was Jo Ann Gibson Robinson, the hard-driving president of the black community's Women's Political Council (WPC) and English professor at Alabama State College. Almost six years before Parks refused to surrender her bus seat to a white man, Robinson was ejected from a bus for sitting in a row the white driver deemed not available for African Americans, even though the bus was nearly empty. That painful experience helped fuel Robinson's passion to improve conditions for African Americans in the years to follow. With her urging, the WPC implored the Montgomery City Commission to correct the abuses of segregated seating, and in 1954 Robinson told the city's mayor to beware of a bus boycott.

On the night of the arrest of Rosa Parks, Robinson enlisted two Alabama State students and John Cannon, chair of the college's business department, to help mimeograph and distribute more than 50,000 copies of the flyer documented below. (Referenced in the flyer is Claudette Colvin, a young woman whose courageous story of resistance to bus segregation in Montgomery has just recently become widely known.) Robinson's organizing skills led to the first successful nonviolent protest of the modern civil rights movement. The success eventually came in the form of a lawsuit, Gayle v. Browder, filed by the NAACP and supervised by Thurgood Marshall.

This is for Monday, December 5, 1955
Another Negro woman has been arrested and thrown into jail because she refused to get up out of her seat on the bus for a white person to sit down.

It is the second time since the Claudette Colvin case that a Negro woman has been arrested for the same thing. This has to be stopped.

Negroes have rights, too, for if Negroes did not ride the bus, they could not operate. Three-fourths of the riders are Negroes, yet we are arrested, or have to stand over empty seats. If we do not do something to stop these arrests, they will continue. The next time it may be you, or your daughter, or mother.

This woman's case will come up on Monday. We are, therefore, asking every Negro to stay off the buses Monday in protest of the arrest and trial. Don't ride the buses to work, to town, to school, or anywhere on Monday.

You can afford to stay out of school for one day if you have no other way to go except by bus.

You can also afford to stay out of town for one day. If you work, take a cab, or walk. But please, children and grownups, don't ride the bus at all on Monday. Please stay off of all buses.

We Shall Have to Lead Our People to You (1957)

Southern Negro Leaders Conference

By 1957 Martin Luther King, Jr., had come to rely heavily on Bayard Rustin for his organizational abilities and strategic vision. Rustin, along with colleagues Ella Baker and Stanley Levison, was encouraging King to build a long-term movement with a stable structure that would be able to advance civil rights for years to come. King agreed, and in 1957 a new civil rights organization—first called the Southern Negro Leaders conference and later named the Southern Christian Leadership Conference [SCLC]— was born, giving King and his team an institutional base for launching numerous nonviolent civil rights campaigns from 1957 to 1968.

In 1957 SCLC leaders invited President Eisenhower to travel to the South and give a public address condemning racial violence. When Eisenhower refused, King asked Rustin to assume the leading role in organizing a protest rally in Washington, DC. The Prayer Pilgrimage for Freedom took place on May 17, 1957, the third anniversary of the Brown v. Board of Education decision.

About 25,000 demonstrators, most of them African Americans, gathered at the Lincoln Memorial in Washington, DC, to demand that the federal government expedite the implementation of Brown. The highlight of the day was a rousing speech by King. "Give us the ballot," King dared the government, "and we will quietly and nonviolently, without rancor or bitterness, implement the Supreme Court's decision on May seventeenth, 1954." Below is the draft of correspondence written by Rustin and Levison; the SCLC leaders edited it before sending it along to President Eisenhower shortly before the pilgrimage.

Permit us to acknowledge receipt of the White House communications of January 18, 1957, stating your inability to schedule an address in the south to encourage the maintenance of law and order as requested by the Southern Negro Leaders Conference on January 11, 1957.

We pointed out in our letter to you that lawlessness was becoming a deeply disturbing feature of the daily life of our communities. Violence has continued to erupt by night and day. It has grown to alarming proportions. Some of the acts of violence would be unbelievable were the grim ruins not mute testimony. Under the cover of darkness, dynamite bombs have been exploded in our churches and the homes of our ministers and citizens. We have been compelled to post unarmed guards nightly to protect our church property. We are no longer faced with sporadic violence, but with what appears to be an organized campaign of violence and terror.

Against this shocking background, we have met in New Orleans to consider your response to our request.

While we are sensitive to the burden of your responsible office, we are aware that human life and orderly, decent conduct of our communities are at stake. These imperative considerations make it difficult for us to accept as final your message that you cannot make a speech in the south at this time. It is our sincere belief that action on your part at this moment can avert tragic situations by cooling passions fostering reasonableness, and encouraging respect for law. In saying this, we are not unmindful of the immense responsibility of your office in the conduct of our national and international affairs. However, morality, like charity, begins at home. Here at home, as we write, we are confronted with a breakdown of law, order, and morality. This condition is a sinister challenge and a threat to government by law. It calls for drastic and remedial action.

The flouting of the Supreme Court decisions serves not only to deprive a part of our citizenry of its rightful privileges but even more, it weakens the fabric of our democratic society for all people, Negro and white. The unleashing of violence against individuals who peacefully pursue justice, against clergyman, and against the house of God are unspeakable crimes. They arouse the conscience of all honorable Americans to compel an end to those outrages as proof of their devotion to democratic and spiritual ideals.

African Americans turn out to vote in Peachtree, Alabama, 1966.

To this end,

1. We implore you to reexamine your decision not to speak out to the South on the question of law and order.

2. We further urge you to call a White House conference on the maintenance of law and order similar to those held earlier on education and juvenile delinquency. We believe such a conference can help develop in the South and in the nation an orderly growth toward civil rights.

We ask you to do these things because our people, though resolute and courageous, cannot be expected forever to be targets for rifles, shotguns, and for bombs, particularly when our women and children are brought within range of those deadly weapons. We know that if a halt is put to these terrorist practices, our appeals for nonviolent Christian behavior will come into serious question by those whose frustration it has already been difficult to contain.

We believe your inability to come south is a profound disappoint-ment to the millions of Americans, North and South, who earnestly are looking to you for leadership and guidance in this period of inevitable social change.

Mr. President, we urge you to give democratic leadership to the confused citizens of the South and the nation in this critical hour. We implore you to enunciate whether in the North or South an Eisenhower doctrine for democracy at home.

In the absence of some early and effective remedial action, we shall have no moral choice but to lead a pilgrimage of prayer to Washington. If you, our president, cannot come South to relieve our harassed peo-ple, we shall have to lead our people to you in the capitol in order to call the nation's attention to the violence and organized terror directed toward men, women, and children who merely seek freedom and first class citizenship. . . .

Mr. President, we prayerfully urge you to give early and serious consideration to the two requests we have made in this letter, for the violence our people face by day and in the dark of each night, makes it imperative that we hear from you at your earliest convenience.

SNCC and Nonviolence (1960)

Ella Baker and SNCC

Ella Baker, a granddaughter of slaves, was one of the early civil rights movement's most significant and effective leaders. As an NAACP field sec-retary in the 1940s, Baker traveled throughout the South offering work-shops on ways to organize and conduct successful campaigns against ra-cial injustice. Her work instructed thousands of African Americans, and in 1953 she became the first woman to be elected president of the NAACP in New York City. Around this same time, she was also working with Bayard Rustin on developing the structure and strategy of what would become the SCLC. Martin Luther King, Jr. recognized Baker's excellent organizing skills and invited her to lead the Crusade for Citizenship, a program intended to increase the number of African American voters and safeguard their right to vote.

Baker then served as SCLC's acting director but found her work deeply frustrating, partly because King and his inner circle of males proved unwilling to grant her independent decision-making powers. Although frustrated in her own role, Baker was very excited about the 1960 student sit-in at Woolworth lunch counters in Greensboro, North Carolina, and the many subsequent sit-ins. She saw the nonviolent protests as refreshing because they were grassroots in nature, separate from the top-down instruction from King and the SCLC.

With Baker's urging, the SCLC invited student protestors across the South to attend the Southwide Youth Leadership Conference at Shaw University. Held over Easter weekend in 1960, the conference gave birth to the Student Nonviolent Coordinating Committee (SNCC), an organization separate from the SCLC. King had hoped for the students to form an SCLC division, but Baker urged them to avoid tying themselves to the SCLC and its heavy dependence on the charismatic leadership of King. Below is an account that Baker wrote shortly after the historic conference, and following her words is an early draft of SNCC's "statement of purpose."

The Student Leadership Conference made it crystal clear that current sit-ins and other demonstrations are concerned with something much bigger that a hamburger or even a giant-sized Coke.

Whatever may be the difference in approach to their goal, the Negro and white students, North and South, are seeking to rid America of the scourge of racial segregation and discrimination—not only at lunch counters, but in every aspect of life. In reports, casual conversations, discussion groups, and speeches, the sense and the spirit of the following statement that appeared in the initial newsletter of the students at Barber-Scotia College, Concord, NC, were echoed time and again:

We want the world to know that we no longer accept the inferior position of second-class citizenship. We are willing to go to jail, be ridiculed, spat upon, and even suffer physical violence to obtain first-class citizenship.

By and large, this feeling that they have a destined date with freedom was not limited to a drive for personal freedom, or even freedom for the Negro in the South. Repeatedly it was emphasized that the movement was concerned with the moral implications of racial discrimination for the "whole world" and the "human race."

This universality of approach was linked with a perspective and recognition that "it is important to keep the movement democratic and to avoid struggles for personal leadership."

It was further evident that desire for supportive cooperation from adult leaders and the adult community was also tempered by apprehension that adults might try to "capture" the student movement. The students showed willingness to be met on the basis of equality, but were intolerant of anything that smacked of manipulation or domination.

This inclination toward *group-centered leadership,* rather than toward a *leader-centered group pattern of organization,* was refreshing indeed to those of the older group who bear the scars of battle, the frustrations and disillusionment that come when the prophetic leader turns out to have heavy feet of clay.

However hopeful might be the signs in the direction of group-centeredness, the fact that many schools and communities, especially in the South, have not provided adequate experience for young Negroes to assume initiative and think and act independently accentuated the need for guarding the student movement against well-meaning, but nevertheless unhealthy, overprotectiveness.

Here is an opportunity for adults and youth to work together and provide genuine leadership—the development of the individual to his highest potential for the benefit of the group.

Many adults and youth characterized the Raleigh meeting as the greatest or most significant conference of our period.

Whether it lives up to this high evaluation or not will, in large measure, be determined by the extent to which there is more effective training in and understanding of nonviolent principles and practices, in group dynamics, and in the redirection into creative channels of the normal frustrations and hostilities that result from second-class citizenship.

Greensboro sit-in, North Carolina, 1960.

SNCC's Statement of Purpose

Carrying out the mandate of the Raleigh Conference to write a statement of purpose for the movement, the Temporary Student Nonviolent Coordinating Committee submits for careful consideration the following draft. We urge all local, state, or regional groups to examine it closely. Each member of our movement must work diligently to understand the depths of *nonviolence.*

————

We affirm the philosophical or religious ideal of nonviolence as the foundation of our purpose, the presupposition of our faith, and the manner of our action. Nonviolence as it grows from Judaic-Christian traditions seeks a social order of justice permeated by love. Integration of human endeavor represents the crucial first step toward such a society.

Through nonviolence, courage displaces fear; love transforms hate. Acceptance dissipates prejudice; hope ends despair. Peace dominates war; faith reconciles doubt. Mutual regards cancel enmity. Justice for all overthrows injustice. The redemptive community supersedes systems of gross social immorality.

Love is the central motif of nonviolence. Love is the force by which God binds man to himself and man to man. Such love goes to the extreme; it remains loving and forgiving even in the midst of hostility. It matches the capacity of evil to inflict suffering with an even more enduring capacity to absorb evil, all the while persisting in love.

By appealing to conscience and standing on the moral nature of human existence, nonviolence nurtures the atmosphere in which reconciliation and justice become actual possibilities.

Prepared by Rev. J. M. Lawson, Jr., Saturday, May 14, 1960

We're Going to Keep Coming (1961)

Jim Zwerg

Although the first Freedom Riders in the 1947 Journey of Reconciliation had faced threatening situations, their daring resistance to segregation on buses offering interstate travel had not attracted the type of media attention necessary to remediate the unconstitutional discrimination. In response to the ongoing segregation, in 1961 the Congress of Racial Equality (CORE) organized a group of volunteers—Freedom Riders—to put to the test the recent U.S. Supreme Court ruling in Boynton v. Virginia that it was unconstitutional to segregate facilities for interstate travelers, for example, terminals and restrooms.

CORE's plan called for an interracial group of male and female riders to travel on buses through the Deep South. In preparation for this dangerous trip, the volunteers would receive intensive training in nonviolent resistance. According to CORE director James Farmer, the purpose of the rides was "to create a crisis, so that the federal government would be compelled to enforce the law."

The first group of riders, seven African Americans and six whites, left Washington, DC, for New Orleans on May 4, 1961. As the riders made their way through Virginia, they encountered angry whites and police officers waiting to arrest them, but when they entered Rock Hill, South Carolina, violence erupted. Two riders, including John Lewis of the Student Nonviolent Coordinating Committee, were assaulted and badly beaten, and police officers arrested another rider for daring to enter a whites-only restroom. But the ride continued on to Atlanta, where Martin Luther King, Jr. met with the resisters and told a Jet reporter that he thought they would "never make it through Alabama."

Freedom Riders John Lewis, left, and Jim Zwerg, Montgomery, Alabama, 1961.

Freedom Riders depart for Washington, D.C., 1961.

On May 14 the riders, still traveling on two buses, entered Anniston, Alabama, where a white mob of about 100, many of them Ku Klux Klan members, were waiting for them. The driver of the first bus pulled up to the mob and said: "Well, boys, here they are. I brought you some niggers and nigger-lovers." The mob surrounded the bus as it was firebombed and engulfed in flames, forcing the riders out the doors and into the hands of the white mob, which beat them brutally.

When the second bus arrived in Birmingham, angry whites armed with metal pipes struck the riders with impunity. In both Anniston and Birmingham, the local police stood by or were intentionally absent as the beatings took place. Farmer was so concerned that he stopped the ride, and some of the Freedom Riders traveled on to New Orleans by plane.

The Freedom Rides continued in a different form when another inter-racial group, upset with Farmer's decision, boarded a bus in Nashville on May 17 with plans to travel to Birmingham and resume the rides. Led by student Diane Nash, the riders were stranded for a few days in Birming-ham after they were arrested and unable to find a driver to help them continue their journey. But the ride continued when John Seigenthaler, a representative for the Kennedy administration, met with Alabama Gover-nor John Patterson and arranged for a state police escort as the riders took off for Montgomery.

The state police did indeed escort the riders as they left Birmingham, but they also made sure to peel away as soon as the riders crossed the city line. This meant that the Freedom Riders had no police protection when they arrived at the Montgomery terminal on May 21. An awful scene awaited them. Jim Zwerg, a white Freedom Rider, later recalled that the riders were supposed to have been taken from the terminal by waiting cars, and that the plan failed in the face of overwhelming violence. The two documents below are Zwerg's account of the event and an excerpt of the statement he made from his hospital bed.

The nation reacted in horror to the scenes of violence meted out upon the nonviolent riders, leading the Kennedy administration to announce on May 29 that the Interstate Commerce Commission had banned seg-regation in all facilities under its control and that it would ensure imple-mentation of the ban. The ban would take effect in November. Until then, hundreds of Freedom Riders continued to ride buses throughout the Deep South.

Zwerg Remembers the Assault

… But the following morning, ultimately we were able to board a bus for Montgomery. And this leg of the trip, I was the seatmate of John Lewis. John sat by the window, and again I sat by the railing, or the aisle. And we had a police escort all the way. I mean … the squad cars would go by, and we'd see these Thompson sub-machine guns in the back seat. The mo-torcyclists would be going back and forth. There was a plane going over.

And we got to the Montgomery city limits, and they *all* disappeared. We rode into the Montgomery bus terminal, and then, just as we turned in, I pointed out to John that a squad car was pulling off. And when we came to the stop, the doors opened, and we got off. And there was this eerie silence around that bus station. The station was over on this side of us; the bus was here; get off here; he was unloading our luggage. There was a railing … on this side there was another railing and then there was a drop-off of maybe 8 to10 feet to a parking area for a post office. There was one little driveway here where some taxis would come in. There were a couple of black taxis there. Not a sign of anybody from the Montgomery churches. We had tried to arrange the same situation as Birmingham where church members were to meet us so we could disperse into the city.

And over in the other area, where normally there would be the busses parked, was maybe a hundred people that we could see at that point. Men, women and children. You could see baseball bats; you could see hammers; you could see pieces of chain. You knew why they were there. Initially, a fellow came out that was just a barrel-chested kind of a fellow, big old cigar out of one side of his mouth, one of those tank top kind of t-shirts. And he caught one of the media folks that had one of the boom mikes that kind of looked like the dish satellite things; he had been training it on the crowd. This guy went over to him and ripped it out of his hand, just threw it to the ground, and jumped on it. And took a swipe at him.

Another fellow went up to one of the folks with a camera, grabbed that, threw that down, and started in on him. The word was out: "You will not take pictures of what's going to happen. There will be no press coverage of this." There is one picture that made it. I don't know where— it almost looks like it was taken from the top of the bus terminal. And it's a picture of three fellas that are going after William Barbee. It's the only picture that I'm aware of of actual violence. All the pictures of me, all the pictures of John were taken after we'd been beaten and basically sitting around for half an hour, in semi-states of consciousness.

We initially, when we saw that there was nobody from the churches, tried to get the women into one of the black cabs, and the black cabbie was more than willing to take the black female students, refused to take the two white ladies that had joined us—Susan Wilbur, who was from Peabody College and a Southern girl, and Susan Herman, who was another exchange student at Fisk University. They were the two ladies that John Seigenthaler saved when he got beaten.

The three of us that stood on the bus platform and took the beating were myself, John Lewis, and William Barbee. The rest made it over that 8-foot embankment down and into the post office. It happened very quickly. Uh, soon after they'd finished with the media, the screams were, "Get the niggers," "Get the nigger-lover," and all this such. And you knew it was very soon going to happen. At that moment, um, I bowed my head, and I prayed. And I asked God to give me the strength to be nonviolent. I asked God to forgive them for whatever they might do. And I asked Him to be with me.

And I don't know how else to share it with you but to say I immediately felt a presence with me. Not just that presence of my brothers and my sisters, but another presence. And a calm and a peace came over me that I knew if I lived or if I died, it was okay. It was gonna' be all right. And I was basically in that situation with my eyes closed when I got grabbed, thrown over this railing and knocked to the ground. I got up to all fours and got kicked in my spine. I flew forward, rolled on my back, and a foot came down on my face. And that is the last thing I remember, thank God, because, I think, probably my being unconscious is what saved my life. That I was relaxed when I was getting those beatings, and kickings, and so forth. I wasn't tensing, or I would have been more severely hurt.

It ended up where uh, I remember briefly in the back of a car. I don't remember those pictures being taken. John was handing me a wet handkerchief and said, "Jim, you've got blood all over your face. You need to wipe it off." I don't think I was awake five seconds.

I woke up again in the back seat of a car that was moving, and I could hear white, Southern men's voices, and I honestly believed that I was going out to be lynched. Um, luckily I passed out very quickly again, and I woke up in the hospital. It ended up where I was in the back seat of a squad car. One of Floyd Mann's deputies—Floyd was sitting in the front seat, another fellow was sitting in the back seat, and then one of the other fellows was driving—and they're the ones that ended up taking me to the hospital.

Then I didn't wake up for about a day and a half. Uh, by that time all of the situation had happened at the church in Montgomery where, uh, finally the Kennedys called out the National Marshals to protect the people there. And really, instead of just threatening that they were going to take some action in Alabama, *took* some action in Alabama, and some things began to change. And the students then in turn were able to go *on* to Jackson, where they were arrested and put in Parchman State Prison.

I was in the hospital five days.

I knew some of my wounds. I was not told of all of my wounds. I knew my nose was broken. I knew I had a pretty bad concussion. I was told my left thumb was broken. I look at the joint on my right thumb, and I'd have to say I think they did something there, too. My teeth were all fractured. I had three vertebrae broken that they never told me about, and I learned unfortunately about two weeks later, when I made an incorrect move and passed out from the pain.

But as a result of my injuries, I could not go on to jail, prison. I needed to heal.

A Living Petition (1963)

Bayard Rustin

In early May 1963 more than 1,000 African American children and teenagers joined Project C, the SCLC campaign to desegregate Birmingham.

Marching through the city streets and rallying at various points, many of the youths ended up in police paddy wagons and in jail cells they packed to the limit. As tensions grew, Eugene "Bull" Connor, Birmingham's commissioner of public safety, instructed police officers and firefighters to turn their German shepherds and high-pressure hoses on the protesting schoolchildren. The horrific scene, which landed on the pages of newspapers across the world, helped fuel the call for a national march on Washington.

Bayard Rustin faced considerable resistance in the eight-week run-up to the March on Washington for Jobs and Freedom. Even before becoming deputy director of the March—in effect, its main organizer—Roy Wilkins, head of the NAACP, opposed Rustin assuming any leadership role. Wilkins was convinced that opponents of the March would use Rustin's gay sexuality, as well as his youthful ties to communism, as fodder to undermine the March.

He was right. FBI Director J. Edgar Hoover passed along information about Rustin's past to U.S. Senator Strom Thurmond of South Carolina, who promptly went to the Senate floor and publicly denounced Rustin as a pervert and a communist. In spite of the vicious assaults on his character, Bayard Rustin went on to successfully organize the most influential nonviolent march in U.S. history. Below are two related documents that suggest the March was about much more than King's "I Have a Dream" speech.

Plea for Nonviolence

The Washington March of August 28 is more than just a demonstration.

It was conceived as an outpouring of the deep feelings of millions of white and colored American citizens that the time has come for the government of the United States of America, and particularly for the Congress of that government, to grant and guarantee complete equality in citizenship to the Negro minority of our population.

As such, the Washington March is a living petition—in the flesh—of the scores of thousands of citizens of both races who will be present from all parts of our country.

It will be orderly, but not subservient. It will be proud, but not

Labor leader A. Phillip Randolph, center, at the March on Washington for Jobs and Freedom, 1963.

arrogant. It will be nonviolent, but not timid. It will be unified in purposes and behavior, not splintered into groups and individual competitors. It will be outspoken, but not raucous.

In a neighborhood dispute there may be stunts, rough words, and even hot insults, but when a whole people speaks to its government, the dialogue and the action must be on a level reflecting the worth of that people and the responsibility of that government.

We, the undersigned, who see the Washington March as wrapping up the dreams, hopes, ambitions, tears, and prayers of millions who have lived for this day, call upon the members, followers, and well-wishers of our several organizations to make the March a disciplined and purposeful demonstration.

We call upon them all, black and white, to resist provocations to disorder and to violence.

March on Washington for Jobs and Freedom, 1963.

Washington, D.C. march, led by the Congress of Racial Equality, in memory of African American girls murdered in the bombing of Sixteenth Street Baptist Church in Birmingham, Alabama, 1963.

We ask them to remember that evil persons are determined to smear the March and to discredit the cause of equality by deliberate efforts to stir disorder.

We call for resistance to the efforts of those who, while not enemies of the March as such, might seek to use it to advance causes not dedicated primarily to civil rights or to the welfare of our country.

We ask each and every one in attendance in Washington or in spiritual attendance back home to place the Cause above all else.

Do not permit a few irresponsible people to hang a new problem around our necks as we return home. Let's do what we came to do— place the national human rights problem squarely on the doorstep of the national Congress and of the federal government.

Let's win at Washington.

What We Demand*

1. Comprehensive and civil rights legislation from the present Congress—without compromise or filibuster—to guarantee all Americans
   access to all public accommodations
   decent housing
   adequate and integrated education
   the right to vote
2. Withholding of federal funds from all programs in which discrimination exists.
3. Desegregation of all school districts in 1963.
4. Enforcement of the Fourteenth Amendment—reducing congressional representation of states where citizens are disfranchised.
5. A new executive order banning discrimination in all housing supported by federal funds.
6. Authority for the attorney general to institute injunctive suits when any constitutional right is violated.
7. A massive federal program to train and place all unemployed workers—Negro and white—on meaningful and dignified jobs at decent wages.

8. A national minimum wage that will give all Americans a decent standard of living. (Government surveys show that anything less than $2.00 an hour fails to do this.)
9. A broadened Fair Labor Standards Act to include all areas of employment which are presently excluded.
10. A federal Fair Employment Practices Act barring discrimination by federal, state, and municipal governments, and by employers, contractors, employment agencies, and trade unions.

*Support of the March does not necessarily indicate endorsement of every demand listed. Some organizations have not had an opportunity to take an official position on all of the demands advocated here.

I Didn't Try to Register for You (1964)

Fannie Lou Hamer

In 1964, as the nation was gearing up for a presidential election, Mississippi's Democratic Party, full of white segregationists, denied African Americans the opportunity to participate in its state meetings as it always had. This time, the state's black activists resisted the exclusion by creating a parallel organization—the Mississippi Freedom Democratic Party (MFDP)—and electing its own delegates to the Democratic National Convention (DNC). The creation of the MFDP meant that the DNC credentials committee had to decide whether to unseat Mississippi's all-white delegation and admit the MFDP's delegation in its stead. Testifying before the committee on behalf of MFDP was the party co-chair and delegate, Fannie Lou Hamer, who had been working with the Student Nonviolent Coordinating Committee to register African American Voters in Mississippi. Hamer delivered her powerful testimony (below) before a national television audience and wept openly as she concluded it.

But President Johnson and the DNC feared an exodus of southern white voters, so rather than unseating the all-white delegation, they offered

MFDP two at-large seats as well as a commitment to refuse the seating of
any segregated delegation at future conventions. Martin Luther King, Jr.
and Bayard Rustin encouraged the MFDP to accept the compromise, but
the black activists dismissed it. "We didn't come all this way for no two
seats," Hamer said.

Mr. Chairman and to the Credentials Committee,

My name is Mrs. Fannie Lou Hamer, and I live at 626 East Lafayette
Street, Ruleville, Mississippi, Sunflower County, the home of Senator
James O. Eastland and Senator Stennis.

It was the 31st of August in 1962 that eighteen of us traveled twenty-six miles to the county courthouse in Indianola to try to register
to become first-class citizens. We was met in Indianola by policemen,
Highway Patrolmen, and they only allowed two of us in to take the lit-
eracy test at the time.

After we had taken this test and started back to Ruleville, we was
held up by the City Police and the State Highway Patrolmen and carried
back to Indianola where the bus driver was charged that day with driving a bus the wrong color.

After we paid the fine among us, we continued on to Ruleville, and
Reverend Jeff Sunny carried me four miles in the rural area where I had
worked as a timekeeper and sharecropper for eighteen years. I was met
there by my children, who told me the plantation owner was angry because I had gone down—tried to register.

After they told me, my husband came, and said the plantation
owner was raising Cain because I had tried to register. And before he
quit talking the plantation owner came and said, "Fannie Lou, do you
know—did Pap tell you what I said?"

And I said, "Yes, sir."

He said, "Well I mean that."

Said, "If you don't go down and withdraw your registration, you
will have to leave." Said, "Then if you go down and withdraw," said, "you
still might have to go because we're not ready for that in Mississippi."

And I addressed him and told him and said, "I didn't try to register for you. I tried to register for myself."

I had to leave that same night.

On the 10th of September 1962, sixteen bullets was fired into the home of Mr. and Mrs. Robert Tucker for me. That same night two girls were shot in Ruleville, Mississippi. Also, Mr. Joe McDonald's house was shot in.

And June the 9th, 1963, I had attended a voter registration workshop; was returning back to Mississippi. Ten of us was traveling by the Continental Trailway bus. When we got to Winona, Mississippi, which is Montgomery County, four of the people got off to use the washroom, and two of the people—to use the restaurant—two of the people wanted to use the washroom.

The four people that had gone in to use the restaurant was ordered out. During this time I was on the bus. But when I looked through the window and saw they had rushed out I got off of the bus to see what had happened. And one of the ladies said, "It was a State Highway Patrolman and a Chief of Police ordered us out."

I got back on the bus and one of the persons had used the washroom got back on the bus, too.

As soon as I was seated on the bus, I saw when they began to get the five people in a highway patrolman's car. I stepped off of the bus to see what was happening and somebody screamed from the car that the five workers was in and said, "Get that one there." And when I went to get in the car, when the man told me I was under arrest, he kicked me.

I was carried to the county jail and put in the booking room. They left some of the people in the booking room and began to place us in cells. I was placed in a cell with a young woman called Miss Ivesta Simpson. After I was placed in the cell I began to hear sounds of licks and screams. I could hear the sounds of licks and horrible screams. And I could hear somebody say, "Can you say, 'yes, sir,' nigger? Can you say 'yes, sir'?"

And they would say other horrible names.

She would say, "Yes, I can say 'yes, sir.'"

"So, well, say it."

She said, "I don't know you well enough."

They beat her, I don't know how long. And after a while she began to pray, and asked God to have mercy on those people.

And it wasn't too long before three white men came to my cell. One of these men was a State Highway Patrolman and he asked me where I was from. And I told him Ruleville. He said, "We are going to check this." And they left my cell and it wasn't too long before they came back. He said, "You are from Ruleville all right," and he used a curse word. And he said, "We're going to make you wish you was dead."

I was carried out of that cell into another cell where they had two Negro prisoners. The State Highway Patrolmen ordered the first Negro to take the blackjack. The first Negro prisoner ordered me, by orders from the State Highway Patrolman, for me to lay down on a bunk bed on my face. And I laid on my face, the first Negro began to beat me.

And I was beat by the first Negro until he was exhausted. I was holding my hands behind me at that time on my left side, because I suffered from polio when I was six years old.

After the first Negro had beat until he was exhausted, the State Highway Patrolman ordered the second Negro to take the blackjack.

The second Negro began to beat and I began to work my feet, and the State Highway Patrolman ordered the first Negro who had beat to sit on my feet—to keep me from working my feet. I began to scream and one white man got up and began to beat me in my head and tell me to hush.

One white man—my dress had worked up high—he walked over and pulled my dress—I pulled my dress down and he pulled my dress back up.

I was in jail when Medgar Evers was murdered.

All of this is on account of we want to register, to become first-class citizens. And if the Freedom Democratic Party is not seated now, I question America. Is this America, the land of the free and the home of the brave, where we have to sleep with our telephones off of the hooks because our lives be threatened daily, because we want to live as decent human beings, in America?

Thank you.

Our Free Speech Fight (1964)

Mario Savio

In September 1964 Katherine Towle, dean of students at the University of California at Berkeley, informed students that they would no longer be permitted to set up tables with political information for students or to recruit students for off-campus political activities. Not long after this, eight students were suspended for disseminating material about the Student Nonviolent Coordinating Committee (SNCC) and the Congress of Racial Equality (CORE). And a few days later, on October 1, student Jack Weinberg was arrested for setting up a CORE table.

Thousands of students watched as Weinberg sat in the police car, and one of them yelled, "Sit down!" Students then conducted a sit-in around the police car, making it impossible for the officers to take Weinberg to jail. Angry chants of "Release him" and "Let him go" filled the air, and Mario Savio, a graduate student in philosophy who had been active in Freedom Summer, jumped atop the car and delivered a fiery speech denouncing the administration's efforts to squelch political activities within the student body. The sit-in lasted thirty-two hours, and 7,000 students showed up to demonstrate their support. The Free Speech movement had begun.

The movement was still going strong two months later, when students occupied an administrative building. The massive sit-in turned ugly as officers shoved students down stairways, kicking and beating them along the way. The sit-in resulted in about 800 arrests. But it also forced the faculty and administration to halt their efforts to restrict student political activity. The administration also granted amnesty to all students who had participated in the movement. Below are comments Savio made in November 1964.

Last summer I went to Mississippi to join the struggle there for civil rights. This fall I am engaged in another phase of the same struggle, this time in Berkeley. The two battlefields may seem quite different to some observers, but this is not the case. The same rights are at stake in both places—the right to participate as citizens in democratic society and the right to due process of law. Further, it is a struggle against the same enemy. In Mississippi, an autocratic and powerful minority rules, through organized violence, to suppress the vast, virtually powerless, majority. In California, the privileged minority manipulates the University bureaucracy to suppress the students' political expression. That "respectable" bureaucracy masks the financial plutocrats; that impersonal bureaucracy is the efficient enemy in a "Brave New World."

In our free speech fight at the University of California, we have come up against what may emerge as the greatest problem of our nation—depersonalized, unresponsive bureaucracy. We have encountered the organized status quo in Mississippi, but it is the same in Berkeley. Beyond that, we find functionaries who cannot make policy but can only hide behind the rules. We have discovered total lack of response on the part of policy makers. To grasp a situation which is truly Kafkaesque, it is necessary to understand the bureaucratic mentality. And we have learned quite a bit about it this fall, more outside the classroom than in.

As bureaucrat, an administrator believes that nothing new happens. He occupies an ahistorical point of view. In September, to get the attention of this bureaucracy which had issued arbitrary effects suppressing student political expression and refused to discuss its action, we held a sit-in on the campus. We sat around a police car and kept it immobilized for over thirty-two hours. At last, the administrative bureaucracy agreed to negotiate. But instead, on the following Monday, we discovered that a committee had been appointed, in accordance with usual regulations, to resolve the dispute. Our attempt to convince any of the administrators that an event had occurred, that something new had happened, failed. They saw this simply as something to be handled by normal university procedures.

The same is true of all bureaucracies. They begin as tools, means to certain legitimate goals, and they end up feeding their own existence. The conception that bureaucrats have is that history has in fact come to an end. No events can occur now that the Second World War is over which can change American society substantially. We proceed by standard procedures as we are.

The most crucial problems facing the United States today are the problem of automation and the problem of racial injustice. Most people who will be put out of jobs by machines will not accept an end to events, this historical plateau, as the point beyond which no change occurs. Negroes will not accept an end to history here. All of us must refuse to accept history's final judgment that in America there is no place in society for people whose skins are dark. On campus, students are not about to accept it as fact that the university has ceased evolving and is in its final state of perfection, that students and faculty are respectively raw material and employees, or that the University is to be autocratically run by unresponsive bureaucrats.

Here is the real contradiction: the bureaucrats hold history has ended. As a result significant parts of the population both on campus and off are dispossessed, and these dispossessed are not about to accept this ahistorical point of view. It is out of this that the conflict has occurred with the universal bureaucracy and will continue to occur until that bureaucracy becomes responsive or until it is clear the university cannot function.

The things we are asking for in our civil rights protests have a deceptively quaint ring. We are asking for the due process of law. We are asking for our actions to be judged by committees of our peers. We are asking that regulations ought to be considered as arrived at legitimately only from the consensus of the governed. These phrases are all pretty old, but they are not being taken seriously in America today, nor are they being taken seriously on the Berkeley campus.

I have just come from a meeting with the Dean of Students. She noticed that she was aware of certain violations of university regulations by certain organizations. University friends of SNCC, which I represent, was one of these. We tried to draw from her some statement on these great principles: consent of the governed, jury of one's peers, due process. The best she could so was to evade or to present the administration party line. It is very hard to make any contact with the human being who is behind these organizations.

The university is the place where people begin seriously to question the conditions of their existence and raise the issue of whether they can be committed to the society they have been born into. After a long period of apathy during the fifties, students have begun not only to question but, having arrived at answers, to act on those answers. This is part of a growing understanding among many people in America that history has not ended, that a better society is possible, and that it is worth dying for.

This free speech fight points up a fascinating aspect of contemporary campus life. Students are permitted to talk all they want so long as their speech has no consequences.

One conception of the university, suggested by a classical Christian world, is that it be in the world but not of the world. The conception of Clark Kerr [university chancellor], by contrast, is that the university is part and parcel of this particular stage in the history of America society; it stands to serve the need of American industry; it is a factory that turns out a certain product needed by industry or government. Because speech does often have consequences which might alter this perversion of higher education, the university must put itself in a position of censorship. It can permit two kinds of speech: speech which encourages continuation of the status quo, and speech which advocates changes in it so radical as to be irrelevant in the foreseeable future.

Someone may advocate radical change in all aspects of American society, and this I am sure he can with impunity. But if someone advocates sit-ins to bring about changes in discriminatory hiring practices, this cannot be permitted because it goes against the status quo of which the university is a part. And that is how the fight began here.

The administration of Berkeley campus has admitted that external, extra-legal groups have pressured the university not to permit students on campus to organize picket lines, not to permit on campus any speech with consequences. And the bureaucracy went along. Speech with consequences, speech in the area of civil rights, speech which some might regard as illegal, must stop.

Many students here at the university, many people in society, are wandering aimlessly about. Strangers in their own lives, there is no place for them. They are people who have not learned to compromise, who for example have come to the university to learn to question, to grow, to learn—all the standard things that sound like clichés because no one takes them seriously. And they find at point or other that for them to become part of society, to become lawyers, ministers, businessmen, people in government, that very often they must compromise those principles which were most dear to them. They must suppress the most creative impulses that they have; this is a prior condition for being part of the system. The university is well structured, well tooled, to turn out people with all the sharp edges worn off, the well-rounded person. The university is well equipped to produce that sort of person, and this means that the best among the people who enter must for four years wander aimlessly much of the time questioning why they are on campus at all, doubting whether there is any point in what they are doing, and looking toward a very bleak existence afterward in a game in which all of the rules have been made up, which one cannot really amend.

It is a bleak scene, but it is all a lot of us have to look forward to. Society provides no challenge. American society in the standard conception it has of itself is simply no longer exciting. The most exciting things going on in America today are movements to change America. America is becoming ever more the utopia of sterilized, automated contentment. The "futures" and "careers" for which American students now prepare are for the most part intellectual and moral wastelands. This chrome-plated consumers' paradise would have us grow up to be well-behaved children. But an important minority of men and women coming to the front today have shown that they will die rather than be standardized, replaceable, and irrelevant.

The Right to Throw Off Such Government (1966)
Huey Newton and Bobby Seale

In October 1966, in the wake of the Watts riots in Los Angeles and the assassination of Malcolm X, two black students at Merritt Junior College in Oakland, California drafted a document (below) that would serve as the founding statement of a new civil rights organization—the Black Panther Party for Self-Defense (BPP). Bobby Seale and Huey Newton founded an organization that is still primarily known for its willingness to use physical force for self-defense, but most of the BPP's everyday work was nonviolent resistance to the economic oppression of urban African Americans. Under the direction of Seale and Newton, the BPP developed social welfare programs in major cities across the nation—programs that helped black people to access health care, education, transportation, clothing, and food. Perhaps its most important and successful work was the program that provided free breakfast for children.

What We Want Now! What We Believe
To those poor souls who don't know Black history, the beliefs and desires of the Black Panther Party for Self-Defense may seem unreasonable. To Black people, the ten points covered are absolutely essential to survival. We have listened to the riot producing words "these things take time" for 400 years. The Black Panther Party knows what Black people want and need. Black unity and self-defense will make these demands a reality.

1. *We want freedom. We want power to determine the destiny of our Black Community.*

We believe that black people will not be free until we are able to determine our destiny.

2. *We want full employment for our people.*
We believe that the federal government is responsible and obligated to give every man employment or a guaranteed income. We believe that if the white American businessmen will not give full employment, then the means of production should be taken from the businessmen and placed in the community so that the people of the community can organize and employ all of its people and give a high standard of living.

3. *We want an end to the robbery by the white man of our Black Community.*
We believe that this racist government has robbed us and now we are demanding the overdue debt of forty acres and two mules. Forty acres and two mules was promised 100 years ago as restitution for slave labor and mass murder of black people. We will accept the payment in currency which will be distributed to our many communities. The Germans are now aiding the Jews in Israel for the genocide of the Jewish people. The Germans murdered six million Jews. The American racist has taken part in the slaughter of over fifty million black people; therefore, we feel that this is a modest demand that we make.

4. *We want decent housing, fit for shelter of human beings.*
We believe that if the white landlords will not give decent housing to our black community, then the housing and the land should be made into cooperatives so that our community, with government aid, can build and make decent housing for its people.

5. *We want education for our people that exposes the true nature of this decadent American society. We want education that teaches us our true history and our role in the present-day society.*
We believe in an educational system that will give to our people a knowledge of self. If a man does not have knowledge of himself and his position in society and the world, then he has little chance to relate to anything else.

6. *We want all black men to be exempt from military service.*

We believe that Black people should not be forced to fight in the military service to defend a racist government that does not protect us. We will not fight and kill other people of color in the world who, like black people, are being victimized by the white racist government of America. We will protect ourselves from the force and violence of the racist police and the racist military, by whatever means necessary.

7. *We want an immediate end to police brutality and murder of Black people.*

We believe we can end police brutality in our black community by organizing black self-defense groups that are dedicated to de-fending our black community from racist police oppression and brutality. The Second Amendment of the Constitution of the United States gives us a right to bear arms. We therefore believe that all black people should arm themselves for self-defense.

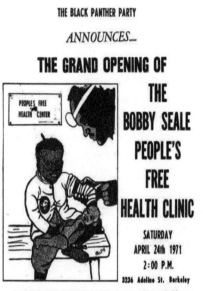

THE BLACK PANTHER PARTY

ANNOUNCES....

THE GRAND OPENING OF THE BOBBY SEALE PEOPLE'S FREE HEALTH CLINIC

SATURDAY
APRIL 24th 1971
2:00 P.M.

3236 Adeline St. Berkeley

A persons' health is their most valuable possession. Improper health care and inadequate facilities can be used to perpetrate genocide on a people. The present facist, racist government used its facilities for that purpose -- the genocide of poor and oppressed people. The people must create institutions within our communities that are controlled and run by the people in order to insure our survival. With this in mind, the Black Panther Party announces the opening of our first Free Health Clinic in the Bay Area.

ALSO.....FREE FOOD & CLOTHING ON OPENING DAY

For further Information contact

Black Panther Party---Berkeley Branch
2230 10th St. Berkeley---Phone 848-7740

SERVING THE PEOPLE BODY AND SOUL

Flyer for Black Panther Party health clinic, Berkeley, California, 1971.

8. *We want freedom for all black men held in federal, state, county, and city prisons and jails.*
We believe that all black people should be released from the many jails and prisons because they have not received a fair and impartial trial.

9. *We want all black people when brought to trial to be tried in court by a jury of their peer group or people from their black communities, as defined by the constitution of the United States.*
We believe that the courts should follow the United States Constitution so that black people will receive fair trials. The 14th amendment of the U.S. Constitution gives a man a right to be tried by his peer group. A peer is a person from a similar economic, social, religious, geographical, environmental, historical, and racial background. To do this the court will be forced to select a jury from the black community from which the black defendant came. We have been and are being tried by all white juries that have no understanding of the "average reasoning man" of the black community.

10. *We want land, bread, housing, education, clothing, justice, and peace.*
When in the course of human events, it becomes necessary for one people to dissolve the political bonds which have connected them with another, and to assume among the powers of the earth, the separate and equal station to which the laws of nature and nature's god entitle them, a decent respect to the opinions of mankind requires that they should declare the causes which impel them to separation.

We hold these truths to be self-evident, that all men are created equal, that they are endowed by their creator with certain inalienable rights, that among these are life, liberty, and the pursuit of happiness. *That to secure these rights, governments are instituted among men, deriving their just powers from the consent of the governed—that whenever any form of government becomes destructive of these ends, it is the right of people to alter or to abolish it, and to institute new government, laying its foundation on such principles and organizing its powers in such form as to them shall seem most likely to effect their safety and happiness. Prudence,* indeed, will dictate that governments long established should not be changed for light and transient causes; and accordingly all experience hath shown, that mankind are more disposed to suffer, while evils are sufferable, than to right themselves by abolishing the forms to which they are accustomed. But when a long train of abuses and usurpations, pursuing invariably the same object, evinces a design to reduce them under absolute despotism, it is their right, it is their duty, to throw off such government, and to provide new guards for their future security.

TEN

The Threat of Atomic Bombs and the Vietnam War

Statement on Omaha Action (1959)

Marjorie Swann

Marjorie Swann was one of the founding members of the Committee for Nonviolent Action, a group of radical pacifists who led direct action campaigns against the nuclear arms race. In 1958 Swann was arrested for criminal trespass after she climbed over a fence at an intercontinental ballistic missiles base near Omaha, Nebraska, to protest nuclear weapons. She was convicted in federal court of trespassing and served six months in jail. In the trial and sentencing period, some of her opponents characterized her as an unfit mother willing to desert her children, and below is Swann's statement about this and other criticisms.

To my fellow Americans—

As a child, I went with my mother—who was rehabilitation chairman of the Legion auxiliary of which I was also a member—to the Hines Veteran Hospital near Chicago. There I saw the horrible physical and psychological results of war—results minor compared to those which will come from a nuclear war with missiles and H-bombs—but still so terrible that even then I could see no way to justify the cause of this damage to the human body and soul.

My father was shell-shocked and gassed in World War I, and even though these injuries were not as serious as those I saw at the hospital, my brother and sisters and I experienced in our own lives the direct effects of war. My brother was in the army in World War II, driving supply trucks from India across the Himalayas into China, and I know the awful tension of waiting and wondering if that final telegram is going to come from the War Department.

As I grew up, I was taught in Sunday school that God is Love, that *all* men are brothers, that we should love our enemies as ourselves. In school I was taught the futility of World War I, and my high school principal organized an international relations club for high school students which emphasized understanding and good will among the people of all nations, and the necessity of settling international conflict without war. I heard my father and his fellow Legionnaires say many times, "Never will *my* son go to war!" I believed all these things and took them seriously.

About the age of 17, I came to understand that the antiwar attitudes of the twenties and thirties was not sufficient; that these laudable sentiments had to be translated into political and economic reality; and that the welfare of each human being *is* the responsibility of every other human being—that we are in truth our brother's keeper . . . our Russian, German, Chinese, African brother as well as those in our own country. So I became a pacifist—not a self-righteous pacifist, I hope, but one who does have sincere disagreement with most of you about how to achieve and maintain peace in this one world of which we are all citizens.

"But," many of you say, including Judge Robinson of the federal district court, "What are we to do; let the Russians walk over us? How can we give up our arms and our missiles if they don't give up theirs? We certainly can't trust them."

There is no simple answer to that question; none of us in Omaha Action would want you to believe we have a blueprint. Many proposals have been made; if you seriously wish to do so, you will have no difficulty in discovering and studying these proposals. A nonviolent alternative to war is admittedly risky, but let me ask you just one question: what kind of risk are we taking now? One hundred percent is the only answer, if we continue in our present direction.

Possibly not 100 percent risk of war, if there is any validity in the deterrent theory, although history and commonsense tell us that an arms race inevitably ends in war. But can you try to imagine what kind of "democracy" we will have if we continue on our present course of military buildup and control? It is not only physical survival with which we must be concerned, but also survival of the human spirit—of the divine right of human beings to think and feel for themselves, to make their own choices and live their own lives, and the divine duty to share, voluntarily, not because we are forced to by a despotic government.

It is part of the law of the universe that ends and means must be consistent. True peace cannot come by means of war. We will have peace when we are ready to pay as much for it as we pay for war. . . .

I know many of you ask why I take this action of deliberately violating an order of the United States government. Particularly, why a mother who has the responsibility of raising four children? Do I not feel guilty in disgracing them by going to prison, and in leaving them without my care for a number of months?

I can only say that the guilt I may feel now, and the pain at leaving my husband and children, is nothing compared to the guilt and pain I will feel—if I am still alive—at seeing my children blasted to death by an H-bomb; die slowly of radiation sickness; wander starving and in rags down a cratered road as did the children of Korea; or become robots in a militarized and totalitarian state which must obliterate freedom in order to survive.

Look at your children and grandchildren. Think what is in store for them. Accept your responsibility for their future. That is what my friends and I ask as we go to prison. If you will try to save the children of all the world, prison is a small price for us to pay.

The Cruel Deception of Civil Defense (1961)

The Civil Defense Protest Committee

The Soviet Union tested a nuclear bomb on August 29, 1949. This threat, and the emergence of the Cold War, led the U.S. government to establish a civil defense program with an aim to convince the public that there were concrete steps individual citizens could take to help them survive a nuclear attack. Beginning in 1955, the civil defense program included "Operation Alert," an annual drill that required everyday citizens to take shelter as if a real nuclear strike was about to happen. Some activists, like the Catholic pacifist Dorothy Day in New York City, registered their dissent by deliberately occupying public space during the drills, an illegal act that led to their arrest. On December 9, 1961, the Civil Defense Protest Committee, with Bayard Rustin as its staff coordinator, ran a full-page protest statement in the New York Times. Below is an excerpted version of the statement.

An Open Letter to President Kennedy
We are deeply disturbed by current developments in the field of civil defense. It appears to us that the prodigious energy of our people is being channeled into wrong directions for wrong reasons; and that continuation of this trend may be extremely dangerous to the nation and to civilization itself.

The Effect of Large Nuclear Weapons
We are now in the era of 50 to 100 megaton bombs. According to the AEC estimate of October 1, a 100 megaton bomb, exploded in the air, would have an 18-mile radius of total destruction of ordinary structures, and would ignite most wooden buildings in a radius of 60 miles. Within that area, a large proportion of the population would be suffocated by lack of oxygen or poisoned by carbon monoxide. Basement shelters under burning buildings would be useless, as would blast shelters without a reserve air supply.

Admittedly it may be possible to design and construct a civil defense capability to permit national survival after a massive attack with such weapons. It would entail, at the very least, permanent, deep underground placement of enough of our economy and communications, and a sufficient decentralization of public activities, to enable operation of vital services immediately after attack. It also would require enough public blast shelters to permit ready access by almost everyone on a few minutes notice, even in the cities. The cost of such a program would be comparable to the entire capital investment of the country—several thousand dollars per person—and would consume a substantial fraction of our gross national product for a number of years. There is a serious question as to whether the Soviet Union would stand idly by while we try to make ourselves really bomb-proof. In addition, we believe that the prospect of living indefinitely in an underground fortress would not appeal to the nation.

The nation has not yet faced up to the real dangers of thermonuclear war. We believe that most of our people do not understand what the world would look like the day after an attack or what problems would be involved in recovering from a war which killed, injured, poisoned, and destroyed on such a large scale. Many of those who do understand have found the prospect too awful and have therefore put the idea from their minds.

The Results of an Inadequate Program

We are aware that our government is trying to deal realistically with the problem of war or peace. Unfortunately, however, government encouragement of shelter construction, as interpreted by the popular press, some local CD officials, and would-be shelter manufacturers, had led to a cruel deception with respect to the protection which would be afforded, especially by individual fallout shelters. These shelters might be adequate in a "minor" atomic war, as could have started in 1950. Such a conservative program has little relevance to the type of largescale attack which might be anticipated in 1962.

It is undoubtedly true that such shelters in areas remote from blast centers might temporarily keep alive a certain number of people. However, the continued survival of those, and of civilization as we know it, also requires the protection of the physical basis of society—the means of production and of distribution, government and communication, etc. A program for doing that is very different from anything now being considered.

The principal danger of the present program is the false sense of security engendered. It is much like a quack cure for cancer. If we are lucky, the "treatment" may not kill us, but in the meantime, while the cancer is growing and becoming incurable, we fail to go to a reputable physician for sensible treatment. By buying a shelter program which does not shelter, and thereby believing that we can survive a thermonuclear war, we are increasing the probability of war. This probability increases both because we may be more willing to "go to the brink" if we think survival is possible and because we are less likely to devise and take any of the constructive steps which may ease tension and secure the peace.

Arguments in Favor of Civil Defense
We recognize that many sincere people support the present civil defense program for what they believe are good reasons. Space is too short to discuss these at length, but we have examined them at length and believe they are wrong.

For example, it is said that civil defense is a deterrent. If it really protected us to the extent necessary for survival it might be; but at present its only deterrent value lies in the demonstration to the Soviet Union that we expect to have a war. Even on this point, it might in fact be argued that this is more likely to precipitate a preemptive attack than to deter one.

It is sometimes said that we should protect ourselves against a limited nuclear war, in which, perhaps, only a few cities on each side would be destroyed. Such a war is highly unlikely. Regardless of the cause of the war, limitation would call for a degree of restraint and mutual agreement between the parties which, if obtainable in peacetime, could prevent war altogether.

There is also the "anything is better than nothing" argument. Of course, every government has responsibilities of trying to protect its citizens, even if only a relatively few of them are likely to survive a disaster. The danger is that the individual man for whom a shelter is made at his home or place of work is being made to feel significantly safer. For any given person this is almost certain to prove false.

The Moral Issues

We have not touched on the moral issues of the shelter program—the question of whether it is right to plan on "losing" our cities and the people in them when decisions of war and peace are made, the question of defending private shelters against intruders, the question of abandoning millions of injured outside while the rest of us hide underground, the question of shelters for the wealthy vs. shelters for the poor or the apartment dweller, the question of the long-term effect of a shelter psychology on the values of a democratic society—these are important issues as well. We have dealt here primarily with the more pressing questions of the adequacy of civil defense and its effect on war and peace. A moral code does not exist in a vacuum. If we lose the structure of society we cannot hope to keep our moral values.

To sum up, we believe that although the present civil defense program, and in particular the construction of fallout shelters, might save a small fraction of the population in a nuclear war, the potential gain is more than offset by the fact that such activity prepares the people for the acceptance of thermonuclear war as an instrument of national policy. We believe that this acceptance would substantially increase the likelihood of war—a war which would be permanently fatal to our democratic society, even if not to all of us. The American people are capable of great effort and sacrifice. We believe this effort should be directed toward a positive program for peace with freedom. This is bound to be at least as difficult and time consuming as any preparation for war, and will require the highest type of leadership for success. At the present time the nation is not ready to consider such a program, largely because of widespread lack of understanding of just how catastrophic war today would be. We call upon you, Mr. President, to make this plain and then lead the nation forward on a race towards peace.

The Cuban Missile Crisis (1962)

Women Strike for Peace

Founded in 1961 at the home of Washington, DC activist Dagmar Wilson, Women Strike for Peace (WSP) used nonviolent direct action to oppose nuclear weapons. "We are dedicated to the purpose of general and complete disarmament," the group declared at its first national conference. "We demand that nuclear tests be banned forever, that the arms race end, and the world abolish all weapons of destruction under United Nations safeguards."

The group's first action was to hold a "Strike for Peace" on November 1, 1961. In New York City, about 400 women and children marched to the Soviet Union's mission to the United Nations and presented a letter calling for the USSR to end all nuclear testing. In Washington, DC, about 800 protestors marched to the White House and the Soviet Embassy, carrying letters for Jacqueline Kennedy and Nina Khrushchev, wife of Soviet premier Nikita Khrushchev.

A year later, it was revealed that U.S. reconnaissance missions over Cuba had discovered the construction of missile sites that held medium-range and intermediate-range ballistic nuclear missiles shipped from the Soviet Union. President Kennedy responded to the discovery by ordering a naval quarantine of Cuba and demanding that the Soviet Union dismantle and remove the missiles. On October 22, Kennedy announced the quarantine to the U.S. public in a nationally televised conference that communicated the urgency of the moment. "It shall be the policy of this nation to regard any nuclear missile launched from Cuba against any nation in the Western Hemisphere as an attack by the Soviet Union on the United States, requiring a full retaliatory response upon the Soviet Union," he said.

Anti-nuclear and peace activists moved into high gear, and WSP called upon its members, in an October 25, 1962 letter (see below), to descend on the Kennedy White House. On October 27 about 1,000 protestors, including WSP members, demonstrated in front of the White House, carrying signs reading, "End This Madness," "Disarm Under World Law," and "Peace, Sí, Stick, No."

While WSP protestors were picketing the White House, the Kennedy administration was at once preparing for war and using diplomatic channels to resolve the crisis. After a tense standoff an agreement was reached with concessions from both sides, and on October 28 Khrushchev announced his plan to dismantle and remove Soviet missiles from Cuba.

In these nightmare days, no one of us can speak for any other. Facing the immediate possibility of annihilation, we react individually—as we die individually, even in mass destruction. Each of us finds in herself unsuspected fears and unexpected strength.

A year ago many of you made an individual decision, not knowing what the consequences might be, to speak out for mankind. Another opportunity, perhaps our last, is at hand.

This Saturday, October 27, we will walk once more to try to tell our President and the world how we feel about our children and all our children.

Women and students from many other cities are joining us—we have no idea yet how many, but we have been receiving calls far into the night, from around the country. . . .

There has been no opportunity to get a consensus on the enclosed statement, so it represents the thinking of only a few of us who have been closely in touch these past few days. We feel, however, that it would be generally the position of the thousands of Women Strikers across the country.

If ever there was a time to strike for peace, this is it! There may not be another. Join us—1:00 and throughout the day—at the White House—Saturday, October 27.

Yours for Tomorrow,
Washington WSP Steering Committee

What Do Women Strikers Think Now?

1. *Is this crisis real?*
Much more so than the general public realizes, because of the awesome power of nuclear weapons and the possibility that they will be set off by accident or design.

2. *Does the Soviet Union really have missile bases in Cuba?*
There is no reason to think the charge false.

3. *What do Women Strikers think of these bases?*
We are opposed to bases in Cuba as provocative and think they should be eliminated.

4. *Does the U.S. have missile bases near the Soviet Union?*
There are NATO missile bases in Turkey and Italy.

5. *What do Women Strikers think of these bases?*
We are opposed to these bases as provocative and think they should be eliminated.

6. *But aren't the NATO bases defensive?*
Our government claims they are, as the Cuban government claims their bases are needed to protect themselves against invasion. Since a wildcat invasion was attempted and there is now talk of an official invasion, they may have reason for fear.

7. *Don't you think we should act to protect our country?*
Indeed we do, and to protect the rest of the world as well. Nuclear destruction of our country and the Soviet Union would not accomplish

this. We risk nuclear war by belligerent acts, as does the Soviet Union. War no longer affords protection for anyone.

8. *But what else can we do?*
We can agree to the request of [United Nations] Secretary General U Thant for a moratorium to negotiate.

9. *But could we trust the Soviets to observe a moratorium?*
No country can trust any country while both are armed to the teeth. But if we can get off this hot spot and have a cooling-off period for all the decision-makers, there is a better chance for reason to prevail.

Hiroshima Day protest, New York City, 1968.

10. *But won't the Soviets back down now that we have a quarantine?*
A quarantine comes close to being a blockade, which is an act of war. Soviet and Cuban leaders are under intense pressure from military circles to become even more belligerent. Neither can back down without losing face.

11. *But won't the Russians take us over if we lay down our arms?*
We are not asking for instant disarmament, but for a moratorium on acts of war until negotiation can permit a lessening of tensions. At that time, worldwide disarmament can and must be started in earnest to prevent a repetition of crises.

12. *What if the Russians and the Cubans refuse to cooperate with the UN?*
This is a question to be faced only if the UN gives up attempts to mediate. We do not believe that Cuba and the Soviet Union will be able to

hold out indefinitely against the combined effort of all countries in the United Nations—any more than the United States could hold out indefinitely against world opinion.

13. *What would we gain by following U Thant's recommendation?*
First, a relaxing of tensions and a face-saving vehicle all around. Second, we might be able to regain moral leadership by proving that we are a law-abiding nation concerned for the welfare of all mankind. We have nothing to lose by following this course, and we may have a world to gain.

14. *But don't we have to leave these decisions to our president?*
Decisions that may end our children's lives should be taken only in consultation with all the people. The ordinary man and woman has no channel of communication comparable to that of the military advisers. Therefore we must call out in every way we can for wisdom and restraint. "We cherish the right and accept the responsibility of the individual in a democratic society to act to influence the course of government." *(1962)*

The March on Washington to End the Vietnam War (1965)

Students for a Democratic Society

During the anti-communist fervor of the 1950s, the Student League for Industrial Democracy faced recruitment difficulties, partly because its name suggested a focus only on labor issues. In 1960, the group gave birth to the Students for a Democratic Society (SDS), which used its founding document, the Port Huron Statement, to give ideological shape to a leftist student movement that was both free of the fierce anticommunism of the Old Left, and also free to establish connections with other leftist movements, particularly the civil rights movement.

University of Michigan student Tom Hayden drafted the Port Huron Statement (PHS) and later stated that its core purpose was "to inspire people to break out of apathy and to join the growing civil rights and student movements in a campaign to shift national priorities from the Cold War to issues of democracy at home and around the world, especially among the Third World bloc of nations just liberating themselves from colonialism." The SDS, like SNCC, also sought to avoid a top-down structure, favoring instead "participatory democracy," a practice that sought to include as many voices as possible in decision-making processes. "The PHS," Hayden added, "was radical in the sense that we wanted to extend democratic participation and regulation to the corporate economy and challenge the military-industrial powers."

Students for a Democratic Society flyer for the March on Washington to End the War in Vietnam, 1965.

SDS's embrace of a participatory democracy that challenged the military-industrial complex came to its boldest expression when the SDS organized an April 17, 1965 student march on Washington to protest President Johnson's escalation of the war in Vietnam. The march attracted about 15,000 protestors who picketed the White House and gathered for speeches at the Washington Monument. On the day of the march, SDS spokesperson Paul Booth said: "We're really not just a peace group. We are working on domestic problems—civil rights, poverty, university reform. We feel passionately and angrily about things in America, and we feel that a war in Asia will destroy what we're trying to do here." Below is SDS's call to the 1965 march.

The current war in Vietnam is being waged in behalf of a succession of unpopular South Vietnamese, not in behalf of freedom. No American-supported South Vietnamese regime in the past few years has gained the support of its people for the simple reason that the people overwhelmingly want peace, self-determination, and the opportunity for development. American prosecution of the war has deprived them of all three.

*The war is fundamentally a *civil* war, waged by South Vietnamese against their government; it is not a "war of aggression." Military resistance from North Vietnam and China has been minimal; most guerilla weapons are homemade or are captured American arms. The areas of strongest guerilla control are not the areas adjacent to North Vietnam. And the people could not and cannot be isolated from the guerillas by forced sentiment in "strategic hamlets"; again and again government military attacks fail because the people tip off the guerillas; the people and the guerillas are inseparable. Each repressive government policy, each napalm bomb, each instance of torture, creates more guerillas. Further, what foreign weapons the guerillas have obtained are small arms, and are no match for the bombers and helicopters operated by the Americans. The U.S. government is the only foreign government that has sent major weapons to Vietnam.

* It is a *losing* war. Well over half of the area of South Vietnam is already governed by the National Liberation Front—the political arm of the "Viet Cong." In the guerillas the peasants see relief from dictatorial government agents; from the United States they get napalm, the jelled gasoline that burns into the flesh. The highly touted "counter insurgency" the U.S. is applying in its "pilot project war" is only new weaponry, which cannot substitute for popular government. Thousands of government troops have defected—the traditional signal of a losing counter-guerilla war. *How many more lives must be lost before the Johnson Administration accepts the foregone conclusion?*

* It is a *self-defeating* war. If the U.S. objective is to guarantee self-determination in South Vietnam, that objective is far better served

University of Michigan students march against Dow Chemical, Ann Arbor, Michigan, 1969.

by allowing the South Vietnamese to choose their own government—something provided for by the 1951 Geneva Agreement but sabotaged in 1956 by the American-supported dictator Ngo Dinh Diem and never allowed since. The Diem government that invited U.S. intervention was thus illegitimate, having violated the agreement that established it. The Vietnamese, North and South, have no taste for Chinese domination—these two countries have fought one another for over a thousand years. Moreover, South Vietnam is *not* a "domino"—the "threat" to it is internal, not Chinese, and the greater threat to stability in other Southeast Asian countries is US-inspired provocation of China, not China's own plans.

* It is a *dangerous* war. Every passing month of hostilities increases the risk of America escalating and widening the war. Since the '50s US-trained South Vietnamese commando teams have been penetrating North Vietnam, considerably provoking the North Vietnamese. We all

know of the presence of American destroyers in the Tonkin Gulf, a body of water surrounded on three sides by North Vietnamese and Chinese territory. How calm would the United States be if Cuban commandoes were being sent into Florida, and Chinese ships were "guarding" Cape Cod Bay?

* It is a war never declared by Congress, although it costs almost two million dollars a day and has cost billions of dollars since the U.S. began its involvement. The facts of the war have been systematically concealed by the U.S. government for years, making it appear as if those expenditures have been helping the Vietnamese people. These factors erode the honesty and decency of American political life, and make democracy at home impossible. We are outraged that two million dollars a day is expended for a war on the poor in Vietnam, while government financing is so desperately needed to abolish poverty at home. *What kind of America is it whose response to poverty and oppression in South Vietnam is napalm and defoliation, whose response to poverty and oppression in Mississippi is . . . silence?*

* It is a hideously *immoral* war. America is committing pointless murder.

But the signs are plain that Americans are increasingly disaffected by this state of affairs. To draw together, express, and enlarge the number of these voices of protest, and to make this settlement visible, Students for a Democratic Society (SDS) is calling for a

March on Washington
to End the War
In Vietnam

We urge the participation of all students who agree with us that the war in Vietnam injures both Vietnamese and Americans, and should be stopped.

The March, to be held on Saturday, April 17, 1965, will include a picketing of the White House, a march down the Mall to the Capitol

Building to present a statement to Congress, and a meeting with both student and adult speakers. Senator Ernest Gruening of Alaska and journalist I. F. Stone have already agreed to address the body.

> *Thousands of us can be heard.*
> *We dare not remain silent. (1965)*

A Draft for the Freedom Fight in the U.S. (1966)
Student Nonviolent Coordinating Committee

Just before midnight on January 3, 1966, Samuel Younge stopped at a gas station in Tuskeegee, Alabama to use the restroom. Marvin Segrest, the 63-year-old white station attendant, had no intention of granting access to the young black man. The bathroom was for whites only.

The two men began to argue. An eyewitness, a white bus driver, reported that Younge then headed toward the bus depot next door and grabbed a golf club from a luggage rack. He was about eighty feet away when Segrest fired his gun at him. Younge started to run away, out of the bus driver's sight, and Segrest aimed and shot again. More than an hour later, the Tuskegee police investigated the incident and discovered Younge lying dead, shot in the back of the head.

Charged with second-degree murder, Segrest claimed at his trial that he had mistaken the golf club for a gun and considered Younge a threat to his life.

It took about seventy minutes for the all-white, all-male jury to find Segrest not guilty. But the case did not end there. Younge had been a student at Tuskegee Institute, and his peers were enraged at the news of Segrest's acquittal. Black students ran into the town square, shattering windows along the way, and when they reached the statue of a Confederate soldier, they painted his face black and his back yellow. The national media reported on the uprising.

Younge had also been a SNCC volunteer who helped register black citizens to vote in Macon County. His mentor was James Forman, SNCC's executive secretary, who made sure to publicize Younge's murder in the national media. Forman and others did so in part by referencing Younge in SNCC's well-publicized position paper on Vietnam (below).

The Student Nonviolent Coordinating Committee has a right and a responsibility to dissent with United States foreign policy on any issue when it sees fit. The Student Nonviolent Coordinating Committee now states its opposition to the United States' involvement in Vietnam on these grounds:

We believe the United States government has been deceptive in its claims of concern for the freedom of the Vietnamese people, just as the government has been deceptive in claiming concern for the freedom of colored people in other countries as the Dominican Republic, the Congo, South Africa, Rhodesia, and in the United States itself.

We, the Student Nonviolent Coordinating Committee, have been involved in the black peoples' struggle for liberation and self-determination in this country for the past five years. Our work, particularly in the South, has taught us that the United States government has never guaranteed the freedom of oppressed citizens, and is not yet truly determined to end the rule of terror and oppression within its own borders.

We ourselves have often been victims of violence and confinement executed by United States governmental officials. We recall the numerous persons who have been murdered in the South because of their efforts to secure their civil and human rights, and whose murderers have been allowed to escape penalty for their crimes.

The murder of Samuel Younge in Tuskegee, Alabama, is no different than the murder of peasants in Vietnam, for both Younge and the Vietnamese sought, and are seeking, to secure the rights guaranteed them by law. In each case, the United States government bears a great part of the responsibility for these deaths.

Samuel Younge was murdered because United States law is not being enforced. Vietnamese are murdered because the United States is pursuing an aggressive policy in violation of international law. The United States is no respecter of persons or law when such persons or laws run counter to its needs or desires.

We recall the indifference, suspicion, and outright hostility with which our reports of violence have been met in the past by government officials.

We know that for the most part, elections in this country, in the North as well as the South, are not free. We have seen that the 1965 Voting Rights Act and the 1966 Civil Rights Act have not yet been implemented with full federal power and sincerity.

We question, then, the ability and even the desire of the United States government to guarantee free elections abroad. We maintain that our country's cry of "preserve freedom in the world" is a hypocritical mask, behind which it squashes liberation movements which are not bound, and refuse to be bound, by the expediencies of United States cold war policies.

We are in sympathy with, and support, the men in this country who are unwilling to respond to a military draft which would compel them to contribute their lives to United States aggression in Vietnam in the name of the "freedom" we find so false in this country.

We recoil with horror at the inconsistency of a supposedly "free" society where responsibility to freedom is equated with the responsibility to lend oneself to military aggression. We take note of the fact that 16% of the draftees from this country are Negroes called on to stifle the liberation of Vietnam, to preserve a "democracy" which does not exist for them at home.

We ask, where is the draft for the freedom fight in the United States?

We therefore encourage those Americans who prefer to use their energy in building democratic forms within this country. We believe that work in the civil rights movement and with other human relations organizations is a valid alternative to the draft. We urge all Americans to seek this alternative, knowing full well that it may cost them their lives—as painfully as in Vietnam.

A Call to Resist Illegitimate Authority (1967)

Marcus Raskin and Arthur Waskow

In 1961 Marcus Raskin and Richard Barnet moved in high-level government circles—Raskin was a White House staffer, and Barnet a State Department employee—but both knew that if they were to change society they needed to operate outside government and work with social movements. Raskin and Barnet left their government positions within two years and founded the Institute for Policy Studies (IPS), a liberal think tank modeled on the conservative Heritage Foundation. Part of IPS's mission was to produce scholarship that would reflect and inform liberal social movements, and in 1965 Raskin helped edit The Vietnam Reader, a popular text that college and university professors used as they held teach-ins to protest the war.

Raskin made another contribution to the antiwar movement in 1967 when he and IPS Fellow Arthur Waskow wrote and published "A Call to Resist Illegitimate Authority." The IPS and its supporters arranged to publish the document in the New York Times Review of Books, the Nation, and other places. The call attracted controversy not merely because of its content but also because those who signed or distributed it could be charged with solicitation to commit a crime—the crime of disobeying the Selective Service Law and Regulations. When the government prosecuted the "Boston Five"—Raskin, Benjamin Spock, William Sloan Coffin, Jr., Mitchell Goodman, and Michael Ferber—for counseling draftees to burn their cards and resist the draft, government attorneys also cited the group's distribution of the call.

To the young men of America, to the whole of the American people, and to all men of goodwill everywhere:

1. An ever growing number of young American men are finding that the American war in Vietnam so outrages their deepest moral and religious sense that they cannot contribute to it in any way. We share their moral outrage.

Marchers protest the draft at Yale University, New Haven, Connecticut, 1968.

2. We further believe that the war is unconstitutional and illegal. Congress has not declared a war as required by the Constitution. Moreover, under the Constitution, treaties signed by the President and ratified by the Senate have the same force as the Constitution itself. The Charter of the United Nations is such a treaty. The Charter specifically obligates the United States to refrain from force or the threat of force in international relations. It requires member states to exhaust every peaceful means of settling disputes and to submit disputes which cannot be settled peacefully to the Security Council. The United States has systematically violated all of these Charter provisions for thirteen years.

3. Moreover, this war violates international agreements, treaties, and principles of law which the United States government has solemnly endorsed. The combat role of the United States troops

in Vietnam violates the Geneva Accords of 1954, which our government pledged to support but has since subverted. The destruction of rice, crops, and livestock; the burning and bulldozing of entire villages consisting exclusively of civilian structures; the interning of civilian noncombatants in concentration camps; the summary executions of civilians in captured villages who could not produce satisfactory evidence of their loyalties or did not wish to be removed to concentration camps; the slaughter of peasants who dared to stand up in their fields and shake their fists at American helicopters—these are all actions of the kind which the United States and the other victorious powers of World War II declared to be crimes against humanity for which individuals were to be held personally responsible even when acting under the orders of their governments and for which Germans were sentenced at Nuremberg to long prison terms and death. The prohibition of such acts as war crimes was incorporated in treaty law by the Geneva Conventions of 1949, ratified by the United States. These are commitments to other countries and to mankind, and they would claim our allegiance even if Congress should declare war.

4. We also believe it is an unconstitutional denial of religious liberty and equal protection of the laws to withhold draft exemption from men whose religious or profound philosophical beliefs are opposed to what in the Western religious tradition have been long known as unjust wars.

5. Therefore, we believe on all these grounds that every free man has a legal right and a moral duty to exert every effort to end this war, to avoid collusion with it, and to encourage others to do the same. Young men in the armed forces or threatened with the draft face the most excruciating choices. For them various forms of resistance risk separation from their families and their country, destruction of their careers, loss of their freedom, and loss of their lives. Each must choose the course of resistance dictated by his conscience and circumstances. Among those already in the armed forces some are

refusing to obey specific illegal and immoral orders, some are attempting to educate their fellow servicemen on the murderous and barbarous nature of the war, some are absenting themselves without official leave. Among those not in the armed forces some are applying for status as conscientious objectors to American aggression in Vietnam, some are refusing to be inducted. Among both groups some are resisting openly and paying a heavy penalty, some are organizing more resistance within the United States, and some have sought sanctuary in other countries.

6. We believe that each of these forms of resistance against illegitimate authority is courageous and justified. Many of us believe that open resistance to the war and the draft is the course of action most likely to strengthen the moral resolve with which all of us can oppose the war and most likely to bring an end to the war.

7. We will continue to lend our support to those who undertake resistance to this war. We will raise funds to organize draft resistance unions, to supply legal defense and bail, to support families and otherwise aid resistance to the war in whatever ways may seem appropriate.

8. We firmly believe that our statement is the sort of speech that under the First Amendment must be free, and that the actions we will undertake are as legal as is the war resistance of the young men themselves. But we recognize that the courts may find otherwise, and that if so we might all be liable to prosecution and severe punishment. In any case, we feel that we cannot shrink from fulfilling our responsibilities to the youth whom many of us teach, to the country whose freedom we cherish, and to the ancient traditions of religion and philosophy which we strive to preserve in this generation.

9. We call upon all men of good will to join us in this confrontation with immoral authority. Especially we call upon the universities to fulfill their mission of enlightenment and religious organizations to honor their heritage of brotherhood. Now is the time to resist.

Our Apologies, Good Friends (1968)

Daniel Berrigan

Daniel Berrigan was a Jesuit priest who devoted his life to writing, teaching, and nonviolent activism for peace and justice. He came to prominence in 1968 when he, his brother Philip, and several other activists (eventually known as the Catonsville 9) protested the Vietnam War by using homemade napalm to destroy hundreds of draft files in the parking lot next to the draft board based in Catonsville, Maryland—an act he reflects on in advance in the document below, a statement he eventually read in court. Berrigan was sentenced to three years' imprisonment for this act of civil disobedience, but he fled before officials could imprison him, and was placed on the FBI's most wanted list before he was captured at the home of a fellow radical Christian—William Stringfellow—and imprisoned shortly thereafter.

Next week nine of us will, if all goes well (ill?), take our religious bodies during this week to a draft center near Baltimore. There we shall, of purpose and forethought, remove the A-1 files, sprinkle them in the public street with homemade napalm and set them afire. For which act we shall, beyond doubt, be placed behind bars for some portion of our natural lives, in consequence of our inability to live and die content in the plagued city, to say peace peace when there is no peace, to keep the poor poor, the homeless homeless, the thirsty and hungry thirsty and hungry.

Our apologies, good friends, for the fracture of good order, the burning of paper instead of children, the angering of the orderlies in the front parlor of the charnel house. We could not, so help us God, do otherwise.

For we are sick at heart, our hearts give us no rest for thinking of the Land of Burning Children. And for thinking of that other Child, of whom the poet Luke speaks. The infant was taken up in the arms of an old man, whose tongue grew resonant and vatic at the touch of that beauty. And the old man spoke: this child is set for the fall and rise of many in Israel, a sign that is spoken against.

Small consolation; a child born to make trouble, and to die for it, the first Jew (not the last) to be subject of a "definitive solution." He sets up the cross and dies on it; in the Rose Garden of the executive mansion, on the DC Mall, in the courtyard of the Pentagon. We see the sign, we read the direction; you must bear with us, for His sake. Or if you will not, the consequences are our own.

For it will be easy, after all, to discredit us. Our record is bad: troublemakers in church and state, a priest married despite his vows, two convicted felons. We have jail records, we have been turbulent, uncharitable, we have failed in love for the brethren, have yielded to fear and despair and pride, often in our lives. Forgive us.

We are no more, when the truth is told, than ignorant beset men, jockeying against all chance, at the hour of death, for a place at the right hand of the dying One.

We act against the law at a time of the Poor People's March; at a time, moreover, when the government is announcing even more massive paramilitary means to confront disorder in the cities. The implications of all this must strike horror in the mind of the thinking person. The war in Vietnam is more and more literally being brought home to us. Its inmost meaning strikes the American ghettoes: one war, one crime against the poor, waged (largely) by the poor, in servitude to the affluent. We resist and protest this crime.

Finally, we stretch out our hands to our brothers and sisters throughout the world. We who are priests, to our fellow priests. All of us who act against the law turn to the poor of the world, to the Vietnamese, to the victims, to the soldiers who kill and die; for the wrong reasons, for no reason at all, because they were so ordered—by the authorities of that public order which is in effect a massive institutionalized disorder.

We say killing is disorder. Life and gentleness and community and unselfishness is the only order we recognize. For the sake of that order, we risk our liberty, our good name. The time is past when good people can remain silent, when obedience can segregate people from public risk, when the poor can die without defense.

We ask our fellow Christians to consider in their hearts a question that has tortured us, night and day, since the war began:

How many must die before our voices are heard, how many must be tortured, dislocated, starved, maddened? How long must the world's resources be raped in the service of legalized murder? When, at what point, will you say no to this war?

We wish also to place in question by this act all suppositions about normal times, longings for an untroubled life in a somnolent church, that neat timetable of ecclesiastical renewal, which in respect to the needs of people amounts to another form of time serving.

Redeem the times! The times are inexpressibly evil. Christians pay conscious—indeed religious—tribute to Caesar and Mars; by approval of overkill tactics, by brinkmanship, by nuclear liturgies, by racism, by support of genocide. They embrace their society with all their heart, and abandon the cross. They pay lip service to Christ and military service to the powers of death.

And yet, and yet, the times are inexhaustibly good, solaced by the courage and hope of many. The truth rules, Christ is not forsaken. In a time of death, some men and women—the resisters, those who work hardily for social change, those who preach and embrace the unpalatable truth—such men and women overcome death, their loves are bathed in the light of the resurrection, the truth has set them free. In the jaws of death, of contumely, of good and ill report, they proclaim their love of the people.

We think of such men and women in the world, in our nation, in the churches, and the stone in our breast is dissolved. We take heart once more.

If the Government Doesn't Stop the War, We'll Stop the Government (1971)

Mayday Tribe

On April 24, 1971, about 500,000 resisters descended on Washington to protest the Vietnam War. This time the protestors shifted their focus from the White House, where President Nixon showed no signs of pulling back from the war, to Congress, where Senators George McGovern of South Dakota and Mark Hatfield of Oregon were advocating for a bill that would eliminate all funds appropriated for the war by the end of the year.

A group of militants at the protest, frustrated by the antiwar movement's lack of success thus far, used the occasion to plan for a series of direct-action protests to take place on May 3, hoping to shut down the government by blocking traffic and access to federal buildings. The group called itself the Mayday Tribe and rallied thousands of others with a straightforward slogan: "If the government doesn't stop the war, we'll stop the government."

On May 1 about 40,000 Mayday protestors were part of an encampment on federal park land next to the Potomac. The protestors had received a government permit for the camp, and in the run-up to the civil disobedience campaign, the campers enjoyed rock concerts, ate organic food supplied by local communes, and received training in civil disobedience. The training reviewed suggestions for civil disobedience that the Mayday Tribe had published and distributed earlier in their Mayday Tactical Manual, a few excerpts of which are below.

The tribe's pledge of nonviolence did not deter the Nixon administration from trying to undermine the civil disobedience campaign. Nixon's Department of Justice arranged to revoke the permit for the encampment and ordered police officers to disperse the campers. It was a surprise early morning attack on May 2, and while many of the groggy campers packed their bags and left, a solid core of 12,000-15,000 remained, regrouping at nearby universities. By the end of the day, more than 200 demonstrators *had been arrested, and paratroopers from the 82d Airborne Division had assumed position just outside the District of Columbia, ready to deploy on a moment's notice.*

On the morning of May 3, the Mayday Tribe activists faced strong opposition: 5100 metropolitan police officers, 500 National Parks police officers, and 1500 National Guard troops, with 10,000 federal troops waiting to help out. When dawn came, the activists did what they could to clog major arteries in the downtown area as well as on the four main bridges linking Virginia with the District. Using a variety of tools—trash cans, cars, tree limbs, cinder blocks, wooden railings, bricks, tires, and even nails—the protesters slowed but did not successfully block government employees making their way to work. Police officers were quick to disperse the activists, and they did so with tear gas, nightsticks, and massive arrests. More than 13,000 activists were arrested that day.

Untitled Mayday Tribe Document

Historically May 1 has been the day of the oppressed. May 1 demonstrations have touched off major changes from reform to revolution and this year should be no exception. On May 1 people in Europe, Asia, Latin America, and Africa will be expressing their solidarity with the Vietnamese people. We should join in that struggle. On May 1 people should mass in Washington and present the government with the peace treaty, demanding that Nixon respond within two days by calling an immediate end to the war. If the government refuses to heed the will of the majority for peace after years and years of patience the people should begin to implement the treaty themselves. Beginning on May 3 and continuing for the rest of the week people who presented the treaty and the thousands that will join them should close down the functioning of the federal government through massive civil disobedience. The demonstrations should be nonviolent but disruptive—blocking streets, marches, strikes at schools and other places of work. To be effective—i.e., to provide the spark that can coalesce the people who oppose the war into activity—we must be willing to do more than march. At the same

Women Strike for Peace die-in, New York City, 1972.

time our tactics should not be seen as provocative even though those sorts of tactics may well be just. Civil disobedience is disruptive but it doesn't force the people involved to make a choice between revolution and the system. Revolution is a necessity, but many people who oppose that war don't yet believe this and they shouldn't be excluded from the movement. Civil disobedience will allow groups as diverse as church and youth groups to take part. It also means that people will be taking some risks, opening themselves to arrest. But mass arrest penalties for white people are still relatively light and the demonstration will not be Gandhi-like. People can and should defend themselves from attack.

Mayday Tactical Manual

This is not a polemic. It is not designed to convince you to become a pacifist or argue against the theory of armed revolutionary struggle or people's war. It is an explanation of the tactic we will be using during the Mayday actions. The tactic is nonviolent civil disobedience. . . .

In brief, the aim of the Mayday action is to raise the social cost of the war to a level unacceptable to America's rulers. To do this we seek to create the spectre of social chaos while maintaining the support or at least toleration of the broad masses of American people. . . . The tactic of nonviolent civil disobedience was chosen because it could be used effectively to disrupt government functions and yet still be interpreted favorably to the broad non-demonstrating masses of Americans. Also by engaging in nonviolent disruptions we severely limit the containment and dispersal options of the government and lessen the likelihood of coming into violent conflict with the GIs who will be ordered to disperse us and who we wish to win to our side. . . .

America is a violent country. We are raised on a diet of violence, and therefore we feel we understand it. Nonviolent civil disobedience on the other hand is widely misunderstood and the extent of most people's knowledge is inaccurate characterizations. We need to be clear that we are not talking about an exercise in martyrdom; we are not talking about negotiated arrests; we are talking about using a tactic to attain an objective. The tactic is nonviolent civil disobedience. The objective is to close down the federal government sections of Washington, DC, by blocking traffic arteries during the early morning rush hours of May 3 and 4.

A working definition of nonviolent civil disobedience in this context would be: A) the actions we engage in are nonviolent, which means we don't trash or street fight; B) we are "civil," which means we will try to express our solidarity and friendship with GIs and attempt to see the rank and file policemen as a member of the working class who's simply on the wrong side; C) we will be disobedient, which means no matter what anyone says, no matter what laws we break, we are going to reach our action target—the roads, bridges, and traffic circles leading

Women Strike for Peace protest against the Vietnam War,
Washington, D.C., 1972.

into the federal areas of Washington—and we will not leave our action targets until we have succeeded in our target objective or until we are arrested. . . .

What comes to mind is thousands of us with bamboo flutes, tambourines, flowers, and balloons moving out in the early light of the morning to paralyze the traffic arteries of the American military repression government nerve center. Creativeness, joy, and life against bureaucracy and grim death. That's nonviolent civil disobedience; That's Mayday. . . .

Troop teach-in. [Some protestors] will encircle troops guarding a circle or lining up several deep along the troop lines protecting bridges. They will establish a one-to-one relationship to GIs and demonstrate solidarity. Food and dope will be passed. If a large group of GIs come over to our side the breech will be filled with demonstrators moving through and sitting in on the target road. The Mayday legal facilities will have special sections to serve troops who join us and a special GI counseling center will be located in Algonquin Peace City. These regions are bringing wire cutters to get through fences to the GIs. Wedges and other formations sent to break up the concentrations of demonstrators will be absorbed amoeba-like and given intensive arguments about why they should join us.

ELEVEN

The Movement Expands

RED, BROWN, AND YELLOW POWER

Fish-Ins (1964, 1967)

Janet McCloud and Robert Casey

When the Washington Territory was established in 1853, Governor Isaac Stevens negotiated treaties with local tribes to redistribute land to the U.S. government and move Native Americans onto reservations. The treaties gave the government about sixty-four million acres, leaving Native American tribes with about six million to divide into reservations, but they also stated that "the right of taking fish at all usual and accustomed grounds and stations is further secured to said Indians in common with all citizens of the territory."

This right came under severe attack in the 1960s when the state of Washington claimed and aggressively asserted jurisdiction over lands, on and off reservations, fished by Native Americans. The state's rationale was that Native Americans were fishing illegally with nets and undermining its conservation efforts, particularly those that sought to protect salmon and steelhead populations.

Native Americans were incensed at the state's encroachment on their

long-held right to fish "at all usual and accustomed grounds and stations."
Nisqually Indians, who fished the Nisqually River near the town of Frank's
Landing, were especially angered when a local judge issued a temporary
injunction halting their net fishing in river areas off the reservation. With
little recourse, they organized themselves into the Survival of the Ameri-
can Indian Association (SAIA), a direct-action group whose purpose was
to defend the fishing rights of Native Americans in Washington. Although
focused on civil disobedience to shore up their fishing rights, the SAIA
also hired NAACP attorney Jack Tanner to assure their rights through the
legal system.

Janet McCloud headed the SAIA, and with help from the NAACP
and the National Indian Youth Council, she organized acts of civil disobe-
dience—fish-ins—at the end of February 1964. On March 2 actor Marlon
Brando joined the fish-ins and was arrested along with Native American
protestors, drawing the attention of national media. Brando and about
one thousand Native Americans and their allies marched on the state cap-
itol in Olympia the following day, attracting even more media attention.
Meanwhile, the NAACP continued to plot legal strategy for safeguarding
the legal rights of Native Americans to fish in Washington—a battle that
was finally won in 1974. Below is Janet McCloud and Robert Casey's ac-
count of the early fish-ins.

The Indians of the Pacific Northwest are engaged in what may be called
the last Indian war. They are taking a stand against the never-ending
encroachment and aggression of their white neighbors within the states
of Washington, Oregon, and Idaho. The Indians' fishing stations on the
rivers of these three states are coveted by politically minded sports-
men's groups, who are pushing the state officials to the get the Indians
off the rivers.

Along the banks of the Nisqually River the spotlight is focused
upon a band of pathetically outnumbered Indians who are waging a series of bitter and blood battles against the police power of the state of
Washington. Equally small bands of Indians are springing up all over

Washington State to fight for the last shred of the rights guaranteed to them thru numerous treaties with the United States Government. . . .

It all began in 1854, when the President of the United States sent his official emissary—Isaac Stevens—to negotiate treaties with the Northwest Indians on behalf of the federal government. . . .

Marlon Brando, left, and Robert Satiacum hold fish-in, Puyallup River, Washington, 1964.

In the Oregon Territory on December 26, 1854, the first treaty was negotiated on the banks of the Medicine Creek with the Nisqually, Sqaxin, Puyallup and allied tribes. The Indians protestingly gave up their homelands—millions of acres, today worth billions of dollars. They were allowed to reserve a small reservation to live upon, more for the purpose of isolating the Indians than as a concession. When the Indians learned that they were going to be confined they became very worried, for these were fisher-people and nomadic in their fishing habits. Stevens assured them over and over that he wanted only the land; he further stated that all the fish and game belonged to the Indians, and would belong to them forever. The right to fish was more important to these northwest Indians than the land. The Indians reserved their fishing rights unrestricted.

The current assault on the Indians who are living a way of life that is natural to them was legally triggered by an injunction prohibiting Indians from fishing in their ancestral fishing stations. Judge John Cochran, Pierce County Superior Court, Tacoma, set aside the hundred-year-old treaty commitment of the federal government and forbade Indians to fish on the Nisqually River in Washington State. This was done at the behest of the state's Game and Fisheries Departments, which in turn are carrying out Governor Evans's program. . . .

Following this injunction a series of clashes occurred between the protesting Indians and the state wardens. To cite a few of the most notable ones: On October 7, 1965, two Indian fishermen, Billy Frank and Alvin Bridges, were tending their nets when state wardens came up the Nisqually River in a big power boat and rammed their frail canoe without any warning. It was a dark, rainy night. One of the fishermen was spilled into the ice-cold, dangerous river. Fortunately, despite being dressed in heavy winter gear he made it safely to shore—right into the arms of the wardens waiting there.

The next clash was more serious. On October 9, 1965, also late at night, wardens cornered two teenage boys on a log jam in the middle of the Nisqually River. Word flew out somehow, and the Nisquallies came flying from every direction. The wardens were now the cornered ones, and the enraged Indians would not let them go. Fights erupted everywhere. Indian war cries cut through the still night air, causing the wardens to suffer paroxysms of fear. They sent out a frightened call for reinforcements. . . . Some cars were busted up as well as some people. . . .

Then, on October 13, 1965, the Survival of American Indians Association held a protest fish-in on the Nisqually River. It was highly publicized and was intended as a protest to the continued night raids of the state wardens against Nisqually Indians. Fish-ins had been used in the past by Indians as a way of protesting the state's encroachment on their treaty fishing rights. It has been a peaceful way to vent the Indians' growing bitterness and hostility at the whites' never-ending invasion of their land and rights. . . .

[This is] the basic difference between the current Negro revolt and the ever-continuing Negro struggle. The Negro faces discrimination which sometimes turns into race hatred as he struggles for assimilation. The Indian on the other hand has always faced unreasoning race hatred from the very first. Indians fight desperately to retain an Indian way of life in the face of all the forced assimilation policies of the United States government. In fact, they despise much of the white culture and the values of an avaricious and aggressive white society.

The Occupation of Alcatraz (1969)

Indians of All Tribes

Native Americans had visited and gathered food on Alcatraz Island for hundreds of years before European explorers arrived in the San Francisco Bay in the sixteenth century. The U.S. government took control of the island in 1850, turning it into a military garrison, a military prison, and then a federal prison from 1934 to 1963, when the government decided it was too costly to operate a prison on the island. In 1964 Richard McKenzie and four other Sioux activists occupied the island for four hours and issued a demand that the prison be converted for use as a Native American university and cultural center and filed papers in federal court to claim the island.

On November 9, 1969, Native American activists from the Bay Area, led by Richard Oakes, returned to the island and reclaimed it for Native Americans for one day. Back on the mainland, the urban Indian community, with the leadership of Adam Fortunate Eagle, then developed plans for a much longer occupation, recruiting Native American students at UCLA, and gathering provisions. They sailed back to the island on November 20, beginning the longest Native American occupation of federal land in U.S. history.

The U.S. government's initial response was to barricade the island and force the activists to leave, but when those measures failed, federal officials agreed to talks. During the negotiations, the occupiers demanded the deed to the land and the conversion of structures into a Native American university, a museum, and a cultural center. The government refused to meet the demands and adopted a "wait and see" approach, directing federal agencies, including the FBI and the Coast Guard, not to intervene or try to remove the protestors.

The occupation soon attracted more than 500 Native American college students and activists, and by the end of 1969 the occupiers had established a governing council, a health clinic, a common kitchen, a grade school, and a security force. Supporters from across the country sent cash, canned goods, and clothes that were transported to the island from San Francisco's Pier 40.

In early 1970, internal divisions began to plague the occupiers, and when Oakes left the island after his stepdaughter died in a tragic fall, the protestors faced even more turmoil within their ranks. Meanwhile, the government tried to cut off access to fresh water and other provisions, and its most decisive action occurred on June 11, 1971, when federal marshals and others seized the island, capturing fifteen unarmed occupiers.

The occupation had not won its goals, but the stage was set for further action. Below is a statement about the occupation of Alcatraz distributed on behalf of the Indians of All Tribes, the name adopted by the group of occupiers.

We, the native Americans, reclaim the land known as Alcatraz Island in the name of all American Indians by right of discovery.

We wish to be fair and honorable in our dealings with the Caucasian inhabitants of this land, and hereby offer the following treaty:

We will purchase said Alcatraz Island for twenty-four dollars ($24) in glass beads and red cloth, a precedent set by the white man's purchase of a similar island about 300 years ago. We know that $24 in trade goods for these 16 acres is more than was paid when Manhattan Island was sold, but we know that land values have risen over the years. Our offer of $1.24 per acre is greater than the 47¢ per acre that the white men are now paying the California Indians for their land. We will give to the inhabitants of this island a portion of that land for their own, to be held in trust by the American Indian Affairs and by the bureau of Caucasian Affairs to hold in perpetuity—for as long as the sun shall rise and the rivers go down to the sea. We will further guide the inhabitants in the proper way of living. We will offer them our religion, our education,

"We will not give up." Indian occupiers moments after the removal from Alcatraz Island on June 11, 1971.

our lifeways, in order to help them achieve our level of civilization and thus raise them and all their white brothers up from their savage and unhappy state. We offer this treaty in good faith and wish to be fair and honorable in our dealings with all white men.

We feel that this so-called Alcatraz Island is more than suitable for an Indian reservation, as determined by the white man's own standards. By this we mean that this place resembles most Indian reservations in that:

1. It is isolated from modern facilities, and without adequate means of transportation.
2. It has no fresh running water.
3. It has inadequate sanitation facilities.
4. There are no oil or mineral rights.
5. There is no industry and so unemployment is very great.

6. There are no health care facilities.
7. The soil is rocky and nonproductive; and the land does not support game.
8. There are no educational facilities.
9. The population has always exceeded the land base.
10. The population has always been held as prisoners and kept dependent upon others.

Further, it would be fitting and symbolic that ships from all over the world, entering the Golden Gate, would first see Indian land, and thus be reminded of the true history of this nation. This tiny island would be a symbol of the great lands once ruled by free and noble Indians.

The Longest Walk (1978)

American Indian Movement

In 1968, four prominent Native Americans—Dennis Banks, Clyde Belle-court, Eddie Benton Banai, and George Mitchell—founded the American Indian Movement (AIM) in Minneapolis, Minnesota. At first, the group focused on the needs of poor Native Americans in urban settings, but it soon transformed into a militant civil rights group that addressed all of the social ills plaguing contemporary Native Americans.

About 2,000 Native American activists and their allies arrived in Washington, DC, on July 22, 1978. They were part of "The Longest Walk," a cross-country march designed in part to derail pending legislation in Congress that would have (1) abolished treaties that had granted Native Americans rights to land, water, and fish and game; and (2) cut many social services for Native Americans on reservations. To counter the legislation and raise public awareness about injustices against Native Americans, AIM cofounder Dennis Banks proposed a 3,000-mile march from San Francisco to Washington.

A couple thousand marchers left San Francisco on February 11,

1978. Not everyone had agreed to walk the entire distance to Washington; children, the elderly, and others drove cars and hopped on trains and buses to make the lengthy journey. But twenty-six protestors endured some rather harsh conditions, wintry and sultry days, to march the whole way to the nation's capital. Whether traveling by foot or in vehicles, the marchers stopped in towns and villages and cities along the way, holding teach-ins to educate the public about Native American culture and government attempts to diminish or eliminate it.

They all reconvened in DC on July 22 for twelve days of demonstrations that attracted nationally prominent figures as well as the national media. Protests were staged at the Supreme Court, with its long history of denying rights to Native Americans, and at the Capitol, where the focus was to pressure Congress to defeat the anti-Native American legislation. Below are some of the demands that the marchers made of the nation's political leaders. The activists left Washington by the end of July, and Congress did not pass any of the controversial bills.

We are the sovereign and free children of Mother Earth. Since before human memory, our people have lived on this land. For countless generations, we have lived in harmony with our relatives, the four-leggeds, the winged beings, the beings that swim, and the beings that crawl. For all time our home is from coast to coast; from pole to pole. We are the original people of this hemisphere. The remains of our ancestors and of our many relatives are a greater part of this land than any other's remains. The mountains and the trees are a part of us—we are the flesh of their flesh. We are the Human Beings of many nations, and we still speak many tongues. We have come from the four directions of this Turtle Island. Our feet have traveled our Mother Earth over many thousands of miles. We are the evidence of the Western Hemisphere, the carriers of the original ways of this area of the world, and the protectors of all life on this Turtle Island.

Today we address you in the language of the oppressor, but the concepts predate the coming of the invaders. The injustice we speak of is centuries old, and has been spoken against in many tongues. We are still the original people of this land. We are the people of the Longest Walk.

For many generations we have been seeking justice and peace from the European refugees and their descendants who have settled on our sacred Turtle Island. It has been an incredibly long struggle. We have entered into many agreements for peace and friendship with the governments of these people, and yet we have received neither peace nor friendship. Most of our original homelands have been illegally taken from us. Our people have been, and continue to be, mercilessly hunted and slaughtered to serve the needs of corporations, governments, and their agents.

Today, the conditions in Central and South America are identical to the conditions in this country during the 19th century. The process of annihilation and destruction are carried on with money, sophisticated weapons, missionaries, widespread sterilization, so-called developmental programs, CIA and FBI organized training of terrorists and provocateurs that are sponsored and provided by the United States. We can find no other words for the description of these acts other than murder and terrorism. . . .

Our people are often forced to leave their beloved homelands and are sent to lands where they greatly suffer. Our grandfathers and grandmothers were forced to walk many times in front of the guns of the invaders. Today we have been forced to walk, again in front of guns and the threat of destruction that comes from words in legislation.

The guns of today are not held by the Seventh Calvary but are in the hands of the FBI, the federal marshals, and other persons who are supposedly upholding the laws of the United States. These guns and many other sophisticated weapons have been used to continue a campaign of legalized murder, terrorism, torture, mutilation, and oppression of our people. All of these weapons have been used in direct violation of international laws concerning the use of weapons against civilian populations.

Our Mother Earth feeds, clothes, and shelters us, as she does all life, but those who have embraced western values do not realize the value of Creation. They are exploiting our Mother Earth and all our relatives who walk and grow with us. This is not right.

For countless generations the cycles of life have been guarded and respected by our people. In the short span of five centuries, the people who invaded these lands have caused an unbelievably massive annihilation of all life forms in the Western Hemisphere. We indigenous people recognize and understand the Natural Balance of these life cycles and assert the right to live within this natural order.

Poster supporting the Wounded Knee occupation, South Dakota, 1973.

Most of our original homelands have been taken from us. We have been allowed access to only a tiny fraction of the land which remains and it, too, is being destroyed against our will. Our lands hold natural resources that are coveted by huge transnational corporations. These organizations are very powerful. In many ways, the United States government has acted as a direct agent of these organizations.

We know that the present attacks on our lands and sovereignty will, unless halted, ultimately benefit the interest of corporations which seek coal, uranium, water, and other parts of our Mother Earth. We understand that the attack on our existence originates with these interests. . . .

As a people we have the right to gather together to give a greeting and thanksgiving to the Creation. We have the right to live in peace and tranquility. We have the right to the fruits of our own lands to feed, shelter, and clothe our people. We have a right to conceive and to give birth according to our natural ways. We have the right to educate our children to our ways of life. We have the right to protect ourselves and our lands against abuses and to settle disputes that arise within our own territories. We have the right to clean air, clean water, and the peaceful usage of our lands. We have the right to be a people. These are inherent rights. All people possess these rights under the laws of the Universe, as well as manmade laws. These are rights that cannot be given to or denied by one group of people over another. As the traditional people, we recognize and understand that these rights came from the Creator and not by actions of humans. . . .

We are not United States citizens. We have treaties with the United States, and the U.S. does not make treaties with its own citizens. We protested the 1924 Citizenship Act. We do not claim U.S. citizenship. Nothing the U.S. has done in relations with us has moved us to change that position. . . .

The original intents are clear. They are part of the western desire to practice forced assimilation. If this is denied by you, then prove it by taking action to end these practices.

We call upon all museums, collectors, and other hobbyists for the return of our sacred items, the remains of our people, and items of our material heritage for proper reinternment. We call for the return of those items not taken from the graves, but from our people, to be returned for their continued use in our ways of life.

We call for the restoration of all lands illegally removed from our protection. We call for the payment of war reparations due to us, for the reconstruction of our nations.

We call for an end to the confusing situation regarding state and federal jurisdiction, and direct America's attention to our treaties and agreements which define the relationship of our countries.

We call upon organized religion to become allies in the process of liberation, and to stop their competition for our "souls."

We are here to make it clear to the American government and the people of the world that there is only one definition of who we are as a people. That definition arises from our religions, governments, and the ways of life that we follow. No one else on the Mother Earth has the right to attempt to define us or our existence.

La Huelga and La Causa Is Our Cry (1966)

Dolores Huerta

Until the mid-1960s, political leaders found it easy to ignore Mexican American farm workers. Many were unable to read or write English, and daily survival was much more of a concern than any thought of voting power. Growers abused and oppressed them with impunity, keeping their wages low and denying them the right to organize, and their living and working conditions were often inhumane.

The lives of migrant workers began to change markedly when Cesar Chavez and Dolores Huerta met each other through their work at the Community Service Organization (CSO), a grassroots organization that developed educational and civic programs to assist Latino Americans in Los Angeles and other urban areas. Huerta and Chavez shared an interest in the plight of farm workers, and when they failed to convince the CSO to devote some of its resources to their cause, they left the organization to begin their own efforts to rally farm workers, holding countless evening meetings to encourage them to join together and fight the injustices they faced on and off the fields.

Their efforts paid off when Huerta and Chavez formed the National Farm Workers Association (NFWA) in September 1961. Chavez became president and Huerta vice-president, and together they led numerous non-violent protests—fasts, boycotts, marches, and strikes—to advance workers' rights. One of their most famous campaigns, in cooperation with the Agricultural Workers Organizing Committee, was on behalf of grape pickers in the San Joaquin Valley. The campaign began in September 1965 and attracted national attention when the NFWA and thousands of Mexican

American workers participated in a 300-mile march from Delano to Sacramento. The march ended with a rally at the state capitol on April 28, 1966, and below is an excerpt of the speech delivered by Huerta. The march and rally led to the first contract signed between the grape industry and farm workers.

Today our farm workers have come to Sacramento. To the governor and the legislature of California we say you cannot close your eyes and your ears to us any longer. You cannot pretend that we do not exist. You cannot plead ignorance to our problems because we are here and we embody our needs for you. And we are not alone. We are accompanied by many friends. The religious leaders of the state, spearheaded by the migrant ministry, the student groups, the civil rights groups that make up the movement that has been successful in securing civil rights for Negroes in this country, right-thinking citizens, and our staunchest ally, organized labor, are all in the revolution of the farm worker. . . .

The day has ended when the farm worker will let himself be used as a pawn by employers, government, and others who would exploit them for their own ends. La huelga and la causa is our cry, and everyone must listen. Viva la huelga! Viva Cesar Chavez!

[He has spent months] giving them the confidence they needed through inspiration and hard work. Educating them for months to realize that no one was going to win their battle for them. That their conditions could be changed by only one group of people, themselves. . . .

He did not solicit money from any area. This was prior to the strike of course. Cesar felt that outside money for organization of farm workers was no good and it would not do the trick. And that the workers had to pay for their own organization, and this was accomplished. Prior to the strike the National Farm Workers Association was supported entirely by its own membership through the dues that they paid. Furthermore . . .

Support has been highlighted by people who have joined us here today. Furthermore, these groups are committing themselves to help us until total victory is achieved. The developments of the past seven

months are only a slight indication of what is to come.
The workers are on the rise.
There will be strikes all over
the state and throughout
the country because Del-
ano has shown what can
be done and the workers
know that they are no longer alone.

The agricultural work-
ers are not going to remain
static. The towns that have
been reached by the pil-
grimage will never be the
same.

On behalf of the Na-
tional Farm Workers As-
sociation, its officers, and
its members, on behalf of

*United Farm Workers and their allies march
from Delano to Sacramento, 1966.*

all of the farm workers of this state, we unconditionally demand that
the governor of this state, Edmund Brown, call a special session of the
legislature to enact a collective bargaining law for the farmer workers of
the state of California. We will be satisfied with nothing less. The governor cannot and the legislature cannot shrug off its responsibilities to the
Congress of the United States.

We are citizens and we are residents of the state of California, and
we want the rules set up to protect us in this state, right here. If the
rules to settle our economic problems are not forthcoming, we will call
a general strike to paralyze the state's agricultural economy. We will call
a general strike to let the legislators and the employers know that we
mean business. We will take economic pressure, strikes, boycotts, to
force recognition and obtain collective bargaining rights. The social and

economic revolution of the farm workers is well underway and it will not be stopped until we receive equality. The farm workers are moving. Nothing is going to stop them. The workers are crying for organization, and we are going to organize them. We may act in strange and unusual ways in our organizing, but we're willing to try new and unused methods to achieve justice for the farm workers.

Blowouts—Baby—Blowouts!! (1968)

Chicano Students in East Los Angeles

In the 1960s, Mexican American students lacked access to a decent education in the public schools of East Los Angeles. Facilities were poor, and school officials often underestimated the students' academic abilities, steering them to vocational or even special-education curriculum. Mexican American students had the highest high-school dropout rate in the area, and when they did graduate, they read on average at an eighth-grade level.

In late 1967 concerned students, teachers, and community leaders came together and decided to increase public awareness about the quality of education for Mexican American students and thereby pressure the Los Angeles Board of Education to make positive changes. The group developed a list of demands that included a decrease in class size, better facilities, instruction in Mexican American history, and an increase in the number of teachers and administrators who lived in their school's community and spoke Spanish.

When the board refused to act on the demands, the high school students, with help from college students and other adults, formed committees to plan walkouts or, as the students called them, "blowouts." The blowouts began on March 1, 1968, and during the next eight days approximately 15,000 students walked out of seven public high schools in East Los Angeles. School administrators sought to block the students from leaving school premises, and police officers also showed up to beat and arrest some of the students. But the protests continued, and one of the highlights was a rally, attended by 10,000-15,000 students, where picket signs reading "Chicano Power" inspired and energized Chicanos with an intensity they had not experienced before.

Board members met in response to the blowouts and claimed that they simply lacked the funds to meet all the demands. The students suffered another defeat at the end of March, when thirteen blowout leaders, including Sal Castro, a teacher popular within the Mexican American communities, were arrested and charged with conspiracy to disturb the peace. As the public attention focused on releasing the thirteen prisoners and reinstating Castro in the classroom, the blowouts decreased and then came to a halt.

Even though the board did not meet most of the student demands, it did eventually begin to hire Chicano teachers and administrators in increasing numbers. More important, the blowouts served to inspire Chicano communities in Los Angeles and elsewhere to organize, flex their own political muscle, and advance their interests. Below is content from a student flyer distributed just after the earliest blowouts.

Student Demands

Blow Outs were staged by us, Chicano students, in the East Los Angeles High Schools protesting the obvious lack of action on the part of the LA School Board in bringing ELA schools up to par with those in other areas of the city. We, young Chicanos, not only protested but at the same time offered proposals for much needed reforms. Just what did we propose?

To begin with, we want assurance that any student or teacher who took part in the *Blow Outs*-----*Will Not* be reprimanded or suspended in any manner. You know the right to protest and demonstrate against injustice is guaranteed to all by the constitution.

We want immediate steps taken to implement bilingual and bicultural education for Chicanos. *We want to bring our carnales home.*

Teachers, administrators, and staff should be educated; they should know our language (Spanish), and understand the history, traditions, and contributions of the Mexican culture. *How can they expect to teach us if they do not know us?* We also want the school books revised to reflect the contributions of Mexicans and Mexican-Americans to the U.S. society, and to make us aware of the injustices that we, Chicanos, as a people have suffered in a "gabacho" dominated society. Furthermore, we want any member of the school system who displays prejudice or who fails to recognize, understand, and appreciate us, our culture, or our heritage removed from ELA schools.

Classes should be smaller in size, say about 20 students to 1 teacher, to insure more effectiveness. We want new teachers and administrators to live in the community their first year and that parents from the community be trained as teacher's aides. We want assurances that a teacher who may disagree politically or philosophically with administrators will not be dismissed or transferred because of it. The school belongs to the community and as such should be made available for community activities under supervision of parents' councils.

There should be a manager in charge of janitorial work and maintenance details and the performance of such duties should be restricted to employees hired for that purpose. *In other words no more students doing janitorial work.*

And more than this, we want *rights—rights—student rights—our rights.* We want a free speech area plus the right to have speakers of our own choice at our club meetings. Being civic-minded students we want to know what the happenings are in our community so we demand the right to have access to all types of literature and to be able to bring it on campus.

The type of dress that we wear should not be dictated to us by "gabachos," but it should be a group of Chicano parents and students who establish dress and grooming standards for Chicano students in Chicano schools.

Getting down to facilities. *We want the buildings open to students at all times,* especially the *heads.* Yeah, we want access to the heads at all times . . . . When you get right down to it, *we only demand what others have.* Things like lighting at all ELA football fields, swimming pools. Sport events are an important part of school activity and we want *free admission* for all students. We, *Chicano students, blew out* in protest. Our proposals have been made. The big question is will the School Board take positive action. If so, when?

    If Not--------Blow Outs—Baby—Blow Outs!!

To Resist with Every Ounce (1969)

Cesar Chavez

As Cesar Chavez and the NFWA worked to advance the cause of farm workers' rights, they were met with considerable resistance from the corporate growers in and around Delano. The growers sprayed toxic insecticides on the protestors, called on police to break up strikes, instructed their own security guards to use force, and hired newly arrived workers from Mexico as strikebreakers. Although Schenley Industries had signed a contract with farmworkers in 1966, another major player, the DiGiorgio Fruit Corporation, resisted demands for a similar contract. The strikes continued, and Chavez worked hard to publicize a national boycott of grapes.

Although pressured at times to adopt violent tactics, Chavez remained firm in his commitment to nonviolence. In 1968 he responded to corporate intransigence by holding a twenty-five-day hunger strike, during which he called upon workers to remain nonviolent in their fight for justice. In a letter to E.L. Barr (below), president of the California Grape and Tree Fruit League, Chavez reaffirms his embrace of "militant nonviolence." The strikes against California's grape owners continued for five years, ending when growers signed contracts to increase wages, offer health care, and to protect farm workers from pesticides.

Dear Mr. Barr:

I am sad to hear about your accusations in the press that our union movement and table grape boycott have been successful because we have used violence and terror tactics. If what you say is true, I have been a failure and should withdraw from the struggle; but you are left with the awesome moral responsibility, before God and man, to come forward with whatever information you have so that corrective action can begin at once. . . .

Today on Good Friday, 1969, we remember the life and the sacrifice of Martin Luther King, Jr., who gave himself totally to the nonviolent struggle for peace and justice. In his *Letter from a Birmingham Jail* Dr. King describes better than I could our hopes for the strike and boycott: "Injustice must be exposed, with all the tensions its exposure creates, to the light of human conscience and the air of national opinion before it can be cured." For our part I admit that we have seized upon every tactic and strategy consistent with the morality of our cause to expose that injustice and thus to heighten the sensitivity of the American conscience so that farmworkers will have, without bloodshed, their own union and the dignity of bargaining with their agribusiness employers. By lying about the nature of our movement, Mr. Barr, you are working against nonviolent social change. Unwittingly perhaps, you may unleash that other force which our union by discipline and deed, censure and education, has sought to avoid, that panacean shortcut: that senseless violence which honors no color, class, or neighborhood.

You must understand—I must make you understand—that our membership and the hopes and aspirations of the hundreds of thousands of the poor and dispossessed that have been raised on our account are, above all, human beings, no better and no worse than any other cross-section of human society; we are not saints because we are poor, but by the same measure neither are we immoral. We are men and women who have suffered and endured much, and not only because of our abject poverty but because we have been kept poor. The colors of our skins, the languages of our cultural and native origins, the lack of

Cesar Chavez leads demonstration for United Farm Workers,
San Francisco, c. 1970s.

formal education, the exclusion from the democratic process, the numbers of our men slain in recent wars—all these burdens generation after generation have sought to demoralize us, to break our human spirit. But God knows that we are not beasts of burden, agricultural implements, or rented slaves; we are men. And mark this well Mr. Barr, we are men locked in a death struggle against man's inhumanity to man in the industry that you represent. And this struggle itself gives meaning to our life and ennobles our dying.

As your industry has experienced, our strikers here in Delano and those who represent us throughout the world are well trained for this struggle. They have been under the gun, they have been kicked and beaten and herded by dogs, they have been cursed and ridiculed, they have been stripped and chained and jailed, they have been sprayed with poisons used in the vineyards; but they have been taught not to lie down and die nor to flee in shame, but to resist with every ounce of human endurance and spirit. To resist not with retaliation in kind but to overcome with love and compassion, with ingenuity and creativity, with hard work and longer hours, with stamina and patient tenacity, with truth and public appeal, with friends and allies, with mobility and discipline, with politics and law, and with prayer and fasting. They were not trained in a month or even a year; after all, this new harvest season will mark our fourth full year of strike and even now we continue to plan and prepare for the years to come. Time accomplishes for the poor what money does for the rich.

This is not to pretend that we have everywhere been successful enough or that we have not made mistakes. And while we do not belittle or underestimate our adversaries—for they are the rich and the powerful and they possess the land—we are not afraid nor do we cringe from the confrontation. We welcome it! We have planned for it. We know that our cause is just, that history is a story of social revolution, and that the poor shall inherit the land.

Once again, I appeal to you as the representative of your industry and as a man. I ask you to recognize and bargain with our union before the economic pressure of the boycott and strike takes an irrevocable toll; but if not, I ask you to at least sit down with us to discuss the safeguards necessary to keep our historical struggle free of violence. I make this appeal because as one of the leaders of our nonviolent movement, I know and accept my responsibility for preventing, if possible, the destruction of human life and property. For these reasons, and knowing of Gandhi's admonition that fasting is the last resort in place of the sword, during a most critical time in our movement last February 1968 I undertook a 25-day fast. I repeat to you the principle enunciated to the membership at the start of the fast: if to build our union required the deliberate taking of life, either the life of a grower or his child, or the life of a farmworker or his child, then I choose not to see the union built.

Mr. Barr, let me be painfully honest with you. You must understand these things. We advocate militant nonviolence as our means for social revolution and to achieve justice for our people, but we are not blind

Dolores Huerta with grape harvesters, California, c. 1969.

or deaf to the desperate and moody winds of human frustration, impatience, and rage that blow among us. Gandhi himself admitted that if his only choice were cowardice or violence, he would choose violence. Men are not angels, and time and tide wait for no man. Precisely because of these powerful human emotions, we have tried to involve masses of people in their own struggle. Participation and self-determination remain the best experience of freedom, and free men instinctively prefer democratic change and even protect the rights guaranteed to seek it. Only the enslaved in despair have need of violent overthrow.

This letter does not express all that is in my heart, Mr. Barr. But if it says nothing else it says that we do not hate you or rejoice to see your industry destroyed; we hate the agribusiness system that seeks to keep us enslaved and we shall overcome and change it not by retaliation or bloodshed but by a determined nonviolent struggle carried on by those masses of farm workers who intend to be free and human.

Hasta La Victoria Siempre! (1970)

Young Lords Party

In January 1969 Puerto Rican students gathered in East Harlem to discuss problems in their communities. By the end of the year, the students and others had organized themselves into an activist group, the New York Young Lords Organization, a charter member of the Young Lords Organization (YLO), based in Chicago. Inspired by the Black Panthers, the New York YLO devoted itself to community-building programs—garbage removal, testing for lead paint and tuberculosis, daycare, clothing exchanges, drug rehabilitation, and free breakfast for children.

In 1970 the New York YLO split from the Chicago YLO and organized itself as the Young Lords Party (YLP). With renewed energy, the YLP expanded into several cities, continued its grassroots work in community-building, and broadened its concerns to include, among other things, the overthrow of U.S. capitalism, patriarchy, and heterosexism. Although the YLP was not a nonviolent group, most of its work, like the Black Panthers', was indeed nonviolent. Below is a 1970 document detailing the YLO's principles and politics.

The Young Lords Is a Revolutionary Political Party Fighting for the Liberation of All Oppressed People.

1. *We want self-determination for Puerto Ricans—liberation on the Island and inside the United States.* For 500 years, first spain and then the united states have colonized our country. Billions of dollars in profits leave our country for the united states every year. In every way we are slaves of the gringo. We want liberation and the Power in the hands of the People, not Puerto Rican exploiters. *Que viva Puerto Rico libre!*

2. We want self-determination for all Latinos. Our Latin brothers and sisters, inside and outside the united states, are oppressed by amerikkkan business. The Chicano people built the Southwest, and we support their right to control their lives and their land. The people of Santo Domingo continue to fight against gringo domination and its puppet generals. The armed liberation struggles in Latino America are part of the war of Latinos against imperialism. *Que Viva La Raza!*

3. We want liberation of all Third World people. Just as Latins first slaved under spain and the yanquis, Black people, Indians, and Asians slaved to build the wealth of this country. For 400 years they have fought for freedom and dignity against racist Babylon. Third World people have led the fight for freedom. All the colored and oppressed peoples of the world are under one nation under oppression. *No Puerto Rican is free until all people are free!*

4. We are revolutionary nationalists and oppose racism. The Latin, Black, Indian, and Asian people inside the u.s. are colonies fighting for liberation. We know that washington, wall street, and city hall will try to make our nationalism into racism; but Puerto Ricans are of all colors and we resist racism. Millions of poor white people are rising up to demand freedom and we support them. They are the ones in the u.s. that are stepped on by rulers and the government. We each organize our power, but our fights are the same against oppression and we will defeat it together. *Power to all oppressed people!*

5. We want equality for women, down with machismo and male chauvinism. Under capitalism, women have been oppressed by both society and our men. The doctrine of machismo has been used by men to take out their frustration on wives, sisters, mothers, and children. Men must fight along with sisters in the struggle for economic and social equality and must recognize that sisters make up over half of the revolutionary army; sisters and brothers are equal fighting for our people. *Forward Sisters in the struggle!*

6. We want community control of our institutions and land. We want control of our communities by our people and programs to guarantee that all institutions serve the needs of our people. People's control of police, health services, churches, schools, housing, transportation, and welfare are needed. We want an end to attacks on our land by urban renewal, highway destruction, universities, and corporations. *Land belongs to all the people!*

7. We want a true education of our Afro-Indio culture and Spanish language. We must learn our long history of fighting against cultural as well as economic genocide by the spaniards and now the yanquis. Revolutionary culture, culture of our people, is the only true teaching. *Jibaro si, Yanqui no!*

8. We oppose capitalists and alliances with traitors. Puerto Rican rulers, or puppets of the oppressor, do not help our people. They are paid by the system to lead our people down blind alleys, just like the thousands of government pimps who keep our communities peaceful for business, or the street workers who keep gangs divided and blowing each other away. We want a society where the people socialistically control their labor. *Venceremos!*

9. We oppose the amerikkkan military. We demand immediate withdrawal of all u.s. military forces and bases from Puerto Rico, Vietnam, and all oppressed communities inside and outside the u.s. No Puerto Rican should serve in the u.s. army against his Brothers and Sisters, for the only true army of oppressed people is the People's Liberation Army to fight all rulers. *U.S. out of Vietnam, Free Puerto Rico now!*

10. We want freedom for all political prisoners and prisoners of war. No Puerto Rican should be in jail or prison, first because we are a nation, and amerikkka has no claim on us; second, because we have not been tried by our own people (peers). We also want all freedom fighters out of jail, since they are prisoners of the war for liberation. *Free all political prisoners and prisoners of war!*

11. We are internationalists. Our people are brainwashed by television, radio, newspapers, schools, and books, to oppose people in other countries fighting for their freedom. No longer will we believe these lies, because we have learned who the real enemy is and who our friends are. We will defend our sisters and brothers around the world who fight for justice and are against the rulers of this country. *Que viva Che Guevera!*

12. We believe armed self-defense and armed struggle are the only means to liberation. We are opposed to violence—the violence of hungry children, illiterate adults, diseased old people, and the violence of poverty and profit. We have asked, petitioned, gone to courts, demonstrated peacefully, and voted for politicians full of empty promises. But we still ain't free. The time has come to defend the lives of our people against repression and for revolutionary war against the businessmen, politicians, and police. When a government oppresses the people, we have the right to abolish it and create a new one. *Arm ourselves to defend ourselves!*

13. We want a socialist society. We want liberation, clothing, free food, education, health care, transportation, full employment, and peace. We want a society where the needs of the people come first, and where we give solidarity and aid to the people of the world, not oppression and racism. *Hasta le Victoria siempre! (1970)*

The Yellow Power Movement (1969)

Amy Uyematsu

Amy Uyematsu, a Japanese poet reared by parents who had been held at internment camps during World War II, penned one of the most influential documents of the Yellow Power movement. "The Emergence of Yellow Power in America" was distributed widely in 1969 and served to instruct and inspire many Asian American students and radicals who played leading and rank-and-file roles in the various groups comprising the Yellow Power movement. Below are excerpts of Uyematsu's formative article.

Asian Americans can no longer afford to watch the black-and-white struggle from the sidelines. They have their own cause to fight, since they are also victims—with less visible scars—of the white institutionalized racism. A yellow movement has been set into motion by the black power movement. Addressing itself to the unique problems of Asian Americans, this "yellow power" movement is relevant to the black power movement in that both are part of the Third World struggle to liberate all colored people. . . .

The yellow power movement has been motivated largely by the problem of self-identity in Asian Americans. The psychological focus of this movement is vital, for Asian Americans suffer the critical mental crises of having "integrated" into American society. . . .

In the process of Americanization, Asians have tried to transform themselves into white men—both mentally and physically. Mentally, they have adjusted to the white man's culture by giving up their own languages, customs, histories, and cultural values. They have adopted the "American way of life" only to discover that this is not enough.

Next, they have rejected their physical heritages, resulting in extreme self-hatred. Yellow people share with black the desire to look white. Just as blacks want to be light-complected with thin lips and un-kinky hair, "yellows" want to be tall with long legs and large eyes. The self-hatred is also evident in the yellow man's obsession with unobtainable white women, and in the yellow female's attempt to gain male approval by aping white beauty standards. . . .

Yellow power advocates self-acceptance as the first step toward strengthening personalities of Asian Americans. . . .

The problem of self-identity in Asian Americans also requires the removal of stereotypes. The yellow people in America seem to be silent citizens. They are stereotyped as being passive, accommodating, and unemotional. Unfortunately, this description is fairly accurate, for Asian Americans have accepted these stereotypes and are becoming true to them. . . .

The silent, passive image of Asian Americans is understood not in

Amy Uyematsu's influential article on Yellow Power, 1969.

terms of their cultural backgrounds, but by the fact that they are scared. The earliest Asians in America were Chinese immigrants who began settling in large numbers on the West Coast from 1850 through 1880. They were subjected to extreme white racism, ranging from economic subordination, to the denial of rights of naturalization, to physical violence. . . .

Racist treatment of "yellows" still existed during World War II, with the unjustifiable internment of 110,000 Japanese into detention camps.
. . .

Today the Asian Americans are still scared. Their passive behavior serves to keep attention on the black people. By being as inconspicuous as possible, they keep pressure off of themselves at the expense of the blacks. . . .

The yellow power movement envisages a new role for Asian Americans:

"It is a rejection of the passive Oriental stereotype and symbolizes the birth of a new Asian—one who will recognize and deal with injustices. The shout of Yellow Power, symbolic of our new direction, is reverberating in the quiet corridors of the Asian community.". . .

Another obstacle to the creation of yellow consciousness is the well-incorporated white racist attitudes which are present in Asian Americans. They take much false pride in their own economic progress and feel that blacks could succeed similarly if they only followed the Protestant ethic of hard work and education. . . . But the fact is that the white power structure allowed Asian Americans to succeed through their own efforts while the same institutions persist in denying these opportunities to black people. . . .

The emerging movement among Asian Americans can be described as "yellow power" because it is seeking freedom from racial oppression through the power of a consolidated yellow people. As derived from the black power ideology, yellow power implies that Asian Americans must control the decision-making processes affecting their lives. . . .

One basic premise of both black power and yellow power is that ethnic political power must be used to improve the economic and social conditions of blacks and yellows. . . .

Although it is true that some Asian minorities lead all other colored groups in America in terms of economic progress, it is a fallacy that Asian Americans enjoy full economic opportunity. If the Protestant ethic is truly a formula for economic success, then why don't Japanese and Chinese who work harder and have more education than whites earn just as much? . . .

The explanation for this discrepancy lies in the continuing racial discrimination toward yellows in upper-wage level and high-status positions. . . . In essence, the American capitalistic dream was never meant to include nonwhites.

The myth of Asian American success is most obvious in the economic and social position of Filipino Americans. . . .

A further example of the false economic and social picture of Asian

Americans exists in the ghetto communities of Little Tokyo in Los Angeles and Chinatown in San Francisco. In the former, elderly Japanese live in run-down hotels in social and cultural isolation. And in the latter, Chinese families suffer the poor living conditions of a community that has the second highest tuberculosis rate in the nation.

Thus, the use of yellow political power is valid, for Asian Americans do have definite economic and social problems which must be improved. By organizing around these needs, Asian Americans can make the yellow power movement a viable political force in their lives.

From Colonies to Communities (1969)

Asian Community Center

Nonviolent protests include not only sit-ins, strikes, fasts, parallel governments, and the like, but also the creation of local community centers designed to counter the violence suffered by community members. An example of this is the Asian Community Center (ACC) organized by young Asian American activists in San Francisco in December 1969, which sought to address the physical and psychological needs of the residents of San Francisco's Chinatown. Its food program provided surplus government food to more than 300 families each month, and its educational programs taught young people such things as Asian American history, carpentry, and kung fu. One of the more popular offerings was the film program, which showed movies about China, Mao Tse Tung, and worldwide liberation struggles. Below is ACC's explanation of its mission and platform.

Third World people are suffering from hunger, disease, unemployment, poor housing, miseducation, and racism and death. Asian and other Third World communities are actually internal colonies which this racist society uses to exploit our manpower and labor for low wages. Our people are caught in these colonies and are forced to suffer. The big businessmen and the rich landlord drain us of our resources, the military drags our young men to fight in imperialist wars to kill other Third World people, the school system operates jails which brainwash our younger brothers and sisters to be ashamed of their cultural and racial heritage, and the universities rob us of the people we need to return to rebuild and to serve the community. To keep us weak and unable to resist effectively, the Man permits disease, corruption, narcotics, subhuman housing, and hunger to flourish throughout the Third World colonies. Every Asian community, whether it is Chinatown, Manilatown, or Japanesetown, are internal colonies of the United States—exploited to the hilt, insulted constantly, and brutalized by the forces of law and order.

In December of 1969, a group of young people from the Chinese community in San Francisco made a move into the old, dark, and shoddy basement of the United States Filipino Association Hall. . . . Its purchase was to provide a base where the youth of the community could serve people of Chinatown to solve its problems and attempt to find cures to the ailments plaguing it; to encourage the people of the community to work collectively for their physical and mental wellbeing and to educate them to the real enemy who is shamelessly exploiting our community and our culture. . . .

The situation and rotten conditions that the people of Chinatown were subjected to demanded that there be an organization such as the Asian Community Center to be established.

We knew that we had to inform the people of the community of our motives and objectives so they can understand and relate to what we were trying to do. We drew up a platform which reflected the needs of the people and relayed our ideas:

Platform of the Asian Community Center

What We See
We see the breakdown of our communities and families.
We see our people suffering from malnutrition, tuberculosis, and high
    suicide rates.

We see destruction of our cultural pride.

We see our elderly forgotten and alone.

We see our youth subjected to racism in the classroom and in the streets.

We see our Mothers and Fathers forced into meaningless jobs to make a living.

We see American society preventing us from fulfilling our needs.

What We Want

We want adequate housing, medical care, employment, and education.

What We Believe

To solve our problems, all Asian people must work together.

Our people must be educated to move collectively for direct action.

We will employ any effective means that our people see necessary.

LGBT RIGHTS, WOMEN'S RIGHTS, AND DISABILITY RIGHTS

Ejected from Dewey's (1965)

Janus Society

In 1965 the Dewey's restaurant at 13th Street in Center City Philadelphia, an area known as the city's "gay ghetto," was an afterhours hangout for LGBT people. But not all of the chain's restaurants were equally welcoming, and in April the staff at Dewey's on 17th Street began to refuse service to would-be customers because of their sexual orientation, gender nonconformity, and choice of attire. News about the discrimination traveled fast through Center City's LGBT communities, and the Janus Society of America, a gay rights group headed by Clark Polak, helped organize a protest.

On April 25 an ethnically diverse group of about 150 demonstrators, most of them gay, lesbian, or transgender, were denied service while conducting a sit-in at the 17th Street location. When three teenaged protestors refused to leave the restaurant, city police officers showed up and arrested all three on charges of disorderly conduct. Polak was also arrested when he approached the car and offered the teenagers help with legal services.

Volunteers from the Janus Society then handed out about 1,500 flyers (see below) explaining the illegality of Dewey's discriminatory practices. A second sit-in occurred on May 2 when three demonstrators refused to leave after being denied service. When the police showed up this time, they read the Janus flyer and consulted with their superiors before heading into the restaurant to tell the demonstrators that they had no authority to arrest them and that they could stay there as long as they wanted. It was the first successful demonstration for LGBT rights in U.S. history.

To the Customers of Dewey's Restaurant, 17th and Chancellor Streets
The management of Dewey's has decided to refuse service to certain persons, and this outline has been prepared in an effort to alert the public to the rights of the various parties involved.

1. Dewey's has the right to refuse service to any individual on any basis it chooses, without explanation or justification, except for reason of race, religion, or nationality. There is no indication that Dewey's is refusing service for any of these three reasons. The Dewey's management invites all persons who are refused service in this store to patronize their store at 13th above Locust.

2. An individual who is denied service has the right to refuse to move from his seat *and no criminal action can be rightfully brought against any individual who so refuses.* Individuals who are refused service, however, always retain the right to leave the premises.

3. Criminal action may be brought against any individual who uses rude, abusive, or loud language, and all persons should be especially careful to avoid such at this time.

4. Dewey's has the right to forcibly remove you from the restaurant and even call the police to assist them in this. In the event the police are called, individuals who have followed the instructions in 3 above are still not rightfully liable for criminal prosecution.

5. Persons ejected from Dewey's by force or who leave willingly are liable for prosecution if they congregate and block the sidewalk, or violate the precautions of 3 above. In the event you choose to remain seated and you are forcibly evicted, in order to avoid rightful prosecution, you must not resist, use loud or abusive language, etc.

6. Picketing and other peaceful protests are within the law and not subject to criminal sanctions.

7. If an individual observes the above cautions and is arrested on a charge of disorderly conduct or something of the like, there are certain remedies available such as suing for false arrest and appealing convictions. It should be noted, however, *that it is extremely difficult to prove a case against the police force or to win an appeal of conviction.*

Special note: The term "rightful prosecution" is used in several places above and should not be guaranteed against any prosecution at all. There are many possible reasons why police officers might bring prosecutions against demonstrators in spite of the fact that the charges are eventually considered improper.

The Janus Society is an organization of citizens, both heterosexual and homosexual, who are concerned with improving the social and legal status of homosexuals. The Society maintains a 24-hour legal referral service for persons who are arrested, conducts public lectures and general information programs, and provides a variety of other services to aid heterosexuals and homosexuals to come to a better understanding of homosexuality in specific and sexuality in general.

Homosexual American Citizens Picket the White House (1965)

Frank Kameny

On April 16, 1965, Jack Nichols and Lige Clarke, members of the Matta-chine Society of Washington (MSW), an organization focused on winning civil rights for "homosexuals," as they called themselves, urged their leader, Frank Kameny, to join them in a march on the White House. Fueling their sense of urgency was a recent news report about Fidel Castro's plans to put homosexuals into labor camps. Kameny was uncertain about picketing the White House. "There's no Cuban embassy," he said later, and "it seemed to stretch logic to picket the White House of the U.S. government to protest an action taken by the Cuban government." But Nichols and Clark would have nothing of it, and Kameny succumbed to their enthusiasm, saying he would support the picketing "if the Cuban issue and our own grievances could be suitably combined."

Nichols and Clark got to work, carefully stenciling picket signs and rounding up fellow MSW members to march on the White House. Then they made history. On April 17, ten protesters—men and women—demonstrated on the sidewalk in front of the White House to protest the persecution of homosexuals and to demand their civil rights. It was the first time a group of gay and lesbian activists marched on the White House. The group continued to demonstrate for their rights, and on October 23 their demonstration included the delivery of the following letter, penned by Kameny and excerpted below, to an official at the White House gate.

October 23, 1965

Dear Mr. President:

A group of homosexual American citizens, and these supporting their cause, is picketing the White House, today, in lawful, dignified, and orderly protest—in the best American tradition—against the treatment being meted out to fifteen million homosexual American citizens by their government—treatment which consistently makes of them second-class citizens, at best.

Our grievances fall into two classes: Specific and General.

I. Specific:

    a. Exclusion from Federal Employment . . .

    b. Discriminatory, Exclusionary, and Harshly Punitive Treatment by the Armed Services . . . Denial of Security Clearances to Homosexuals as a Group or Class

II. General:

    a. There can be no justification for the continuing refusal, through two administrations, and for more than three years, of our presidents and their staffs—as well as many government agencies and departments—to accord to spokesmen for the homosexual community even the common courtesy and decency of acknowledgements—much less meaningful responses—to serious and proper letters written to them in search of their assistance in the solution of serious problems affecting large numbers of citizens.

    b. Equally, there can be no justification for the continuing refusal of most agencies and departments of our government—including the staff of the White House—to meet with representatives of the homosexual community (our nation's largest minority after the Negro) constructively to discuss solutions to the problems besetting them— problems in significant measure created by and reinforced by our government and by its attitudes, policies, and practices.

    c. We find offensive the continuing attitude of hostility, enmity, and animosity—amounting to a state of war—directed by our government toward its homosexual citizens. No group of *our* citizenry should have to tolerate an attitude of the sort upon the part of their government.

Our government chooses to note that homosexual American citizens are homosexuals, but conveniently chooses to disregard that they are also Americans and citizens.

In short, Mr. President, the homosexual citizens of America are being treated as second-class citizens—in a country which claims that it has no second-class citizens. The advantages claimed by our country for all of its citizens—equality, opportunity, fair treatment—are not only denied to our homosexual citizens by society at large, they are denied at the active instigation and with the active cooperation of our government. This is not as it should be.

The right of its citizens to be different and not to conform, without being placed thereby in a status of inferiority or disadvantage, has always been the glory of our country. This right should apply to the homosexual American citizen as well. At present it does not.

You have proposed, and are indeed working vigorously and successfully toward what you have felicitously termed "The Great Society." Mr. President—NO society can be truly great which excludes from full participation and contribution, or relegates to a secondary role, ANY minority of its citizenry. The homosexual citizen, totally without cause, is presently systematically excluded from your Great Society.

We ask, Mr. President, for what all American citizens—singly and collectively—have a right to ask: That our problems be given the fair, unbiased consideration by our government due the problems of all the citizenry—consideration in which we, ourselves, are allowed to participate actively and are invited to do so, as citizens in our country have a right to expect to do.

We ask for a reconsideration of ancient, outmoded approaches to, and policies toward homosexuals and homosexuality—approaches and policies which are unseemly for a country claiming to support the principles and the way of life for which our country stands—approaches and policies which should long ago have been discarded. We ask that on these questions, our President and his government accept and shoulder actively the role properly attributed to them by The Report of the

President's Commission on National Goals (1960): "One role of government is to stimulate changes of attitude."

. . .

Sincerely yours,

Franklin E. Kameny

Christopher Street Liberation Day (1970)

Gay Liberation Front

Not long after the Stonewall Uprising—a series of confrontations between LGBT people and the police at the Stonewall Bar in New York City's Greenwich Village in 1969—Martha Shelley, president of the New York City Daughters of Bilitis (DOB), visited with Dick Leitsch, head of the Mattachine Society of New York (MSNY), to propose that their two organizations work together on organizing a march. Although Leitsch was wary of the idea, he issued a call for interested individuals to convene a march committee. The committee set about its work, and on July 2 about 500 demonstrators participated in the march; some protestors, still riled up about Stonewall, threw bottles and set fires.

A nonviolent march for gay rights was already scheduled for two days later at Independence Hall in Philadelphia. Frank Kameny was in charge of the Annual Reminder March, which was in its fourth year, and he had always mandated that picketers dress in suits and dresses and withhold from public displays of affection. But the orderly and ultra-conventional event took an unexpected turn when Kameny spotted and quickly separated two lesbian picketers who had begun to hold hands.

New York City activist Craig Rodwell, the owner of the Oscar Wilde Memorial Bookshop in Greenwich Village, was not pleased. He had grown tired of Kameny's rigid insistence that gay and lesbian protestors make themselves appear "respectable" to heterosexual America, and he protested the break-up, telling the media that Stonewall had sparked a new militancy and that conservative leaders like Kameny no longer represented the emerging movement. After sharing this message, Rodwell and other New Yorkers defiantly marched in pairs and held hands.

On the train ride home, Rodwell told his New York colleagues that the movement should begin to hold an annual march in New York City, with no dress code, to mark the anniversary of Stonewall. The march would not be a "silent plea for rights," as the Annual Reminder was, but an "overt demand for them."

Rodwell's idea gained traction with the budding gay liberation movement back in New York, and after numerous meetings with various groups and city officials, movement leaders organized a new march for June 28, 1970, exactly one year after Stonewall. On that historic day, thousands of activists marched from Greenwich Village to Sheep Meadow in Central Park, where they held a "gay-in" to protest discrimination and celebrate the new pride among them. Frank Kameny marched, too—without a jacket and tie. Below is a march announcement distributed by the Gay Liberation Front (GLF), one of the many participating groups.

Liberation Day—1970 is more than just the first anniversary of the Stonewall Riots. It celebrates a year in which a new spirit has entered the struggle for homosexual freedom—a new spirit both militant in tone and revolutionary in orientation. Homosexuals at last have realized that they will never be able to be liberated by politely asking the system. Freedom is never given—it must be taken. Also, many homosexuals have come to realize that it is the system itself which persecutes us. This is what Gay Liberation is all about.

During this past year the Gay Liberation Movement has grown from one small group rising out of the members of the Stonewall Riots to many groups, some large, some small, all over the country. There are now GLFs in New York City, Los Angeles, Boston, San Francisco, Philadelphia, Berkeley, Chicago, Seattle, Brunswick (N.J.), San Jose (Calif.), Champaign (Ill.). Each arose spontaneously, driven by the needs and anger of the homosexual community in each area.

What it will all come to no one can tell. It is our hope that the day will come when homosexuals will be an integral part of society—being treated as human beings. But this will not come overnight. It can only be the result of a long, hard struggle against

Gay Activist Alliance at the Christopher Street Liberation Day March, New York City, 1970.

bigotry, prejudice, persecution, exploitation—even genocide. The homosexual who wants to live a life of self-fulfillment in our current society has all the cards stacked against them. Gay liberation is for the homosexual who stands up, and fights back. And, as in the words of Nietzsche, "What doesn't destroy me makes me stronger."

What's On
The big event is, of course, the March and Gay-In on Sunday, June 28th. The assembly will be at Sheridan Square from 12 Noon until 2:00 P.M. At 2 o'clock we will start off—along Christopher Street, then up Sixth Avenue to the Sheep Meadow in Central Park for the Gay-In. The Gay-In will last until sunset.

Underground Abortion (1969)

Jane

Eight years before Roe v. Wade, University of Chicago student Heather Booth heard that a friend's sister was in need of an abortion and that she was suicidal. Booth offered to help find a doctor who would perform the abortion. "I viewed it not as breaking the law, but as acting on the Golden

Rule," she recalled. "Someone was in anguish, and I tried to help her."

Word about Booth's offer of assistance traveled fast, and she soon discovered that many others were in anguish. Hoping to establish "some kind of system," Booth and others founded the Abortion Counseling Service of Women's Liberation in 1969 with the purpose of connecting women seeking an abortion with trustworthy doctors willing to perform them.

The group did not merely wait until women came to them; it also placed advertisements in newspapers run by students and city radicals. A typical advertisement read: "Pregnant? Need Help? Call Jane." Jane was the nickname suggested by a group member who liked "sweet names." The calls came pouring in, and before long Jane was referring about fifty women a week—women from all walks of life.

Jane members escorted their clients, sometimes by blindfold, to safe apartments or hotel rooms where doctors waited to perform their assigned abortions. They also cleaned the rooms and instruments and assured the doctors were properly paid. But Jane volunteers were not altogether satisfied with their efforts, primarily because of the judgmental attitudes expressed by some of the male doctors as well as the $500 to $1000 fees they charged. And so the organization sought to assume control over the entire process.

The shift to offering full services began shortly after the organization discovered that one of its doctors was not a doctor at all. At this point, a Jane member asked the abortion provider to teach her how to perform the procedure, and he agreed. The trained Jane volunteer then taught three others. With referrals no longer necessary Jane soon began offering direct abortion services at the much lower rate of $100 per abortion. To assure the quality of their work, they enlisted the services of a respected Chicago obstetrician to examine the women in follow-up visits.

Working with Jane—an act of civil disobedience—always carried the risk of arrest and imprisonment, and in 1972 Chicago police arrested seven Jane members who were present in an apartment that acted as their base of operations. These women became known as the "Abortion Seven," and although they were indicted, the government dropped charges against them shortly after the U.S. Supreme Court issued its ruling in Roe v. Wade in

1973. Below are excerpts from a 1969 Jane pamphlet titled "Abortion—a woman's decision, a woman's right."

What Is the Abortion Counseling Service?
We are women whose ultimate goal is the liberation of women in society. One important way we are working toward that goal is by helping any woman who wants an abortion to get one as safely and cheaply as possible under existing conditions.

Abortion is a safe, simple, relatively painless operation when performed by a trained person in clean conditions. In fact, it's less complicated than a tonsillectomy. People hear about its horrors because des-

From the Film "Jane: An Abortion Service," 1995.

perate women turn to incompetent people or resort to unsafe methods. Much of our time is spent finding reliable and sympathetic doctors who will perform safe abortions for as little money as possible. You will receive the best medical care we know of.

Although abortions are illegal in Illinois, the state has not brought charges against any woman who has had an abortion. Only those who perform abortions have been prosecuted.

Any information you give your counselor is kept confidential. She will not give your name to anyone or discuss anything you tell her without your permission. It is vitally important that you are completely honest about your medical history with your counselor and the doctor.

Loan Fund
Because abortions are illegal and in such demand, they are exorbitantly expensive. In fact, an abortion frequently costs as much as the

combined doctor and hospital bills for having a baby. The ACS believes that no woman should be denied an abortion because she is unable to pay for it. We have a small and constantly depleted noninterest loan fund for women who would otherwise be unable to have an abortion. It is non-profit and non-discriminatory. Twenty-five dollars of what you pay for an abortion goes toward maintaining this service. If you receive money from this fund, please repay it as promptly as you can so that the money may be used to help other women. An unpaid loan may mean that we cannot lend money to someone else who needs it desperately. . . .

Abortion as a Social Problem

We are giving our time not only because we want to make abortions safer, cheaper, and more accessible for the individual women who come to us, but because we see the whole abortion issue as a problem of society. The current abortion laws are a symbol of the sometimes subtle, but often blatant, oppression of women in our society.

Women should have the right to control their own bodies and lives. Only a woman who is pregnant can determine whether she has enough resources—economic, physical, and emotional—at a given time to bear and rear a child. Yet at present the decision to bear the child or have an abortion is taken out of her hands by governmental bodies which can have only the slightest notion of the problems involved.

Cultural, moral, and religious feelings are largely against abortion, and society does all it can to make a woman feel guilty and degraded if she has one.

The same society that denies a woman the decision not to have a child refuses to provide humane alternatives for women who do have children, such as childcare facilities to permit the mother to work, or role flexibility so that men can share in the raising of children. The same society that insists that women should and do find their basic fulfillment in motherhood will condemn the unwed mother and her fatherless child.

The same society that glamorizes women as sex objects and teaches them from early childhood to please and satisfy men views pregnancy and childbirth as punishment for "immoral" or "careless" sexual activity, especially if the woman is uneducated, poor, or black. The same morality that says "that's what she gets for fooling around" also fails to recognize society's responsibility to the often unwelcome child that results. Punitive welfare laws reflect this view, and churches reinforce it.

Our society's version of equal opportunity means that lower-class women bear unwanted children or face expensive, illegal, and often unsafe abortions, while well-connected middle-class women can frequently get safe and hush-hush "D and Cs" in hospitals.

Only women can bring about their own liberation. It is time for women to get together to change the male-made laws and to aid their sisters caught in the bind of legal restrictions and social stigma. Women must fight together to change the attitudes of society about abortion and to make the state provide free abortions as a human right.

There are currently many groups lobbying for population control, legal abortion, and selective sterilization. Some are actually attempting to control some populations, prevent some births—for instance those of black people or poor people. We are opposed to these or any form of genocide. We are for every woman having exactly as many children as she wants, when she wants, if she wants. It's time the Bill of Rights applied to women. It's time women got together and started really fighting for their rights. Governments have to be made to realize that abortions are part of the health care they must provide for the people who support them.

We Call on All Our Sisters (1969)

Redstockings

On February 13, 1969, Redstockings, a radical women's group founded in New York City earlier that month, interrupted a state legislative committee hearing on abortion reform. At the time New York law permitted abortion only if a woman's life was threatened.

Redstockings member Kathy Amatniek stood up in the middle of the hearing and shouted: "All right, now let's hear from some real experts—the women." Her bold outburst shocked the committee members. "Repeal the abortion law, instead of wasting more time talking about these stupid reforms," she added.

Twelve other Redstockings members also stood and shouted out their own concerns. "Why are fourteen men and only one woman on your list of speakers—and she's a nun?" one asked. Another protestor said: "We've waited and waited while you have held one hearing after another. Meanwhile, the baby I didn't want is 2 years old."

Redstockings continued to protest for a woman's right to abortion, and on March 21, 1969, the radical group hosted the nation's first abortion speak-out. Held at Washington Square United Methodist Church in the West Village, the event offered a panel of eleven women who spoke about their experiences with unwanted pregnancies and illegal abortions.

Although it did not exist in its original form longer than two years, Redstockings played an historic role in the nonviolent protests that led up to the Roe v. Wade ruling, Below is the text of the group's radical manifesto.

1. After centuries of individual and preliminary political struggle, women are uniting to achieve their final liberation from male supremacy. Redstockings is dedicated to building this unity and winning our freedom.

2. Women are an oppressed class. Our oppression is total, affecting every facet of our lives.

    We are exploited as sex objects, breeders, domestic servants, and cheap labor. We are considered inferior beings, whose only purpose is to enhance men's lives. Our humanity is denied. Our prescribed behavior is enforced by the threat of physical violence.

    Because we have lived so intimately with our oppressors, in isolation from each other, we have been kept from seeing our personal suffering as a political condition. This creates the illusion that a woman's relationship with her man is a matter of interplay between two unique personalities, and can be worked out individually. In reality, every such relationship is a *class* relationship, and the conflicts between individual men and women are *political* conflicts that can only be solved collectively.

Women on "Relay for ERA," from Seneca Falls, NY, to Houston, TX, c. 1977.

3. We identify the agents of our oppression as men. Male supremacy is the oldest, most basic form of domination. All other forms of exploitation and oppression (racism, capitalism, imperialism, etc.) are extensions of male supremacy: men dominate women, a few men dominate the rest. All power structures throughout history have been male-dominated and male-oriented. Men have controlled all political, economic, and cultural institutions and backed up this control with physical force. They have used their power to keep women in an inferior position. *All men* receive economic, sexual, and psychological benefits from male supremacy. *All men* have oppressed women.

4. Attempts have been made to shift the burden of responsibility from men to institutions or to women themselves. We condemn these arguments as evasions. Institutions alone do not oppress; they are merely tools of the oppressor. To blame institutions implies that men and women are equally victimized, obscures the fact that men benefit from the subordination of women, and gives men the excuse that they are forced to be oppressors. On the contrary, any man is free to renounce his superior position, provided that he is willing to be treated like a woman by other men.

We also reject the idea that women consent to or are to blame for their own oppression. Women's submission is not the result of brainwashing, stupidity, or mental illness but of continual, daily pressure from men. We do not need to change ourselves, but to change men.

The most slanderous evasion of all is that women can oppress men. The basis for this illusion is the isolation of individual relationships from their political context and the tendency of men to see any legitimate challenge to their privileges as persecution.

5. We regard our personal experience, and our feelings about that experience, as the basis for an analysis of our common situation. We cannot rely on existing ideologies as they are all products of male supremacist culture. We question every generalization and accept none that are not confirmed by our experience.

Our chief task at present is to develop female class consciousness through sharing experience and publicly exposing the sexist foundation of all our institutions. Consciousness-raising is not "therapy," which implies the existence of individual solutions and falsely assumes that the male-female relationship is purely personal, but the only method by which we can ensure that our program for liberation is based on the concrete realities of our lives.

The first requirement for raising class consciousness is honesty, in private and in public, with ourselves and other women.

6. We identify with all women. We define our best interest as that of the poorest, most brutally exploited woman. We repudiate all economic, racial, educational, or status privileges that divide us from other women. We are determined to recognize and eliminate any prejudices we may hold against other women.

We are committed to achieving internal democracy. We will do whatever is necessary to ensure that every woman in our movement has an equal chance to participate, assume responsibility, and develop her political potential.

7. We call on all our sisters to unite with us in struggle.

We call on all men to give up their male privilege and support women's liberation in the interest of our humanity and their own.

In fighting for our liberation we will always take the side of women against their oppressors. We will not ask what is "revolutionary" or "reformist," only what is good for women.

The time for individual skirmishes has passed. This time we are going all the way.

Welfare Is a Women's Issue (1972)

Johnnie Tillmon

Johnnie Tillmon did not have the middleclass or upperclass life enjoyed by so many leaders in the national movement for women's rights. Born into poverty in 1926, she began picking cotton in Arkansas at the age of seven. After World War II, when she worked in a defense plant, she took a laundry job where she organized her coworkers and successfully demanded a raise. Then, in the early 1960s, as a single parent with six children, she landed a unionized laundry job, this one in Los Angeles, and moved her family into a housing project in Watts. With her history in organizing, Tillmon became a union leader.

But in 1963, after developing an illness and discovering that one of her daughters needed additional attention at home, Tillmon enrolled in California's welfare program, Aid to Needy Children (ANC). Relying on ANC gave her an up-close and personal look at the stigma and harassment suffered by welfare recipients in government offices and on the streets. Tillmon decided to protest the abuse by founding a welfare organization— ANC Mothers Anonymous—that advocated on behalf of individual clients and for changes in the state's welfare policies.

Tillmon's creative work and powerful speaking abilities earned her a national reputation, and she captured the attention of George Wiley, one of the leaders of Citizens Crusade Against Poverty (CCAP), a national coalition of antipoverty organizations. The two met in April 1966 when Tillmon spoke at a CCAP conference in Washington, DC, and by the end of the year Tillmon and Wiley founded the National Welfare Rights

Organization (NWRO), with the goal of creating a new social movement led by welfare recipients and changing federal policy to lift welfare recipients out of poverty. Tillmon was elected chair of the advocacy group's national coordinating committee, and in 1972 she replaced Wiley as executive director and penned the following article.

I'm a woman. I'm a black woman. I'm a poor woman. I'm a fat woman. I'm a middle-aged woman. And I'm on welfare.

In this country, if you're any one of these things—poor, black, fat, middle-aged, on welfare—you count less as a human being. If you're all those things, you don't count at all. Except as a statistic.

I am a statistic.

I am 45 years old. I have raised six children.

I grew up in Arkansas, and I worked there for fifteen years in a laundry, making about $20 or $30 a week, picking cotton on the side for carfare. I moved to California in 1959 and worked in a laundry there for nearly four years. In 1963 I got too sick to work anymore. Friends helped me to go on welfare.

They didn't call it welfare. They called it AFDC—Aid to Families with Dependent Children. Each month I get $363 for my kids and me. I pay $128 a month rent; $30 for utilities, which include gas, electricity, and water; $120 for food and non-edible household essentials; $50 for the three children in junior and senior high school who are not eligible for reduced-cost meal programs.

There are millions of statistics like me. Some on welfare. Some not. And some, really poor, who don't even know they're entitled to welfare. Not all of them are black. Not at all. In fact, the majority—about two-thirds—of all the poor families in the country are white.

Welfare's like a traffic accident. It can happen to anybody, but especially it happens to women.

And that is why welfare is a women's issue. For a lot of middle-class women in this country, women's liberation is a matter of concern. For women on welfare it's a matter of survival.

Forty-four percent of all poor families are headed by women. That's bad enough. But the *families* on AFDC aren't really families. Because 99 percent of them are headed by women. That means there is no man around. In half the states there really can't be men around because AFDC says if there is an "able-bodied" man around, then you can't be on welfare. If the kids are going to eat, and the man can't get a job, then he's got to go. So his kids can eat.

The truth is that AFDC is like a super-sexist marriage. You trade in *a* man for *the* man. But you can't divorce him if he treats you bad. He can divorce you, of course, cut you off anytime he wants. But in that case, *he* keeps the kids, not you.

The man runs everything. In ordinary marriage, sex is supposed to be for your husband. On AFDC you're not supposed to have any sex at all. You give up control of your own body. It's a condition of aid. You may even have to agree to get your tubes tied so you can never have more children just to avoid being cut off welfare.

The man, the welfare system, controls your money. He tells you what to buy, what not to buy, where to buy it, and how much things cost. If things—rent, for instance—really cost more than he says they do, it's just too bad for you. . . .

In this country we believe in something called the "work ethic." That means that your work is what gives you human worth. But the work ethic itself is a double standard. It applies to men and to women on welfare. It doesn't apply to all women. If you're a society lady from Scarsdale and you spend all day sitting on your prosperity paring your nails, well, that's okay. . . .

People still believe that old lie that AFDC mothers keep on having kids just to get a bigger welfare check. On the average, another baby means another $35 a month—barely enough for food and clothing. Having babies for profit is a lie that only men could make up, and only men could believe. Men, who never have to bear the babies or have to raise them and maybe send them to war.

There are a lot of other lies that male society tells about welfare mothers; that AFDC mothers are immoral, that AFDC mothers are lazy, misuse their welfare checks, spend it all on booze and are stupid and incompetent. . . .

There's one good thing about welfare. It kills your illusions about yourself, and about where this society is really at. It's laid out for you straight. You have to learn to fight, to be aggressive, or you just don't make it. . . .

Maybe it is we poor welfare women who will really liberate women in this country. We've already started on our welfare plan.

Along with other welfare recipients, we have organized together so we can have some voice. Our group is called the National Welfare Rights Organization (NWRO). We put together our own welfare plan, called Guarantee Adequate Income (GAI), which would eliminate sexism from welfare.

There would be no "categories"—men, women, children, single, married, kids, no kids—just poor people who need aid. You'd get paid according to family size only—$6,500 for a family of four (which is the Department of Labor's estimate of what's adequate), and that would be upped as the cost of living goes up.

If I were president, I would solve this so-called welfare crisis in a minute and go a long way toward liberating every woman. I'd just issue a proclamation that "women's" work is *real* work.

In other words, I'd start paying women a living wage for doing the work we are already doing—child-raising and housekeeping. And the welfare crisis would be over, just like that. Housewives would be getting wages, too—a legally determined percentage of their husband's salary—instead of having to ask for and account for money they've already earned.

For me, women's liberation is simple. No woman in this country can feel dignified, no woman can be liberated, until all women get off their knees. That's what NWRO is all about—women standing together, on their feet.

Sitting Against Nixon (1972)

Judy Heumann

Had the Rehabilitation Act of 1972 become law, it would have established new programs for those suffering from blindness, deafness, spinal cord injuries, and renal diseases. It also would have created an Office for the Handicapped within the Department of Health, Education, and Welfare, and funded non-vocational goods and services to help those with disabilities as they moved into independent living. But President Richard Nixon vetoed the bill, criticizing it as an expensive expansion of social welfare programs.

Judy Heumann was livid—and an activist for those with disabilities. Heumann had graduated with honors from Long Island University (LIU) in 1969. Hoping to become a public school teacher, she took the written and oral examinations required for a teaching license, and although she passed them, the New York Board of Education denied her certification, claiming that her confinement to a wheelchair—she had contracted polio as an infant—prevented her from being able to get herself and her students out of a school building in the event of a fire. Heumann filed—and won—a federal civil rights suit against the board.

As Heumann's story spread through the media, she received numerous inquiries from individuals personally acquainted with disabilities and discrimination. Heumann then contacted several friends and colleagues to strategize about forming a political organization that would address a wide range of disabilities and disability-related issues—"something that had the influence of younger people more, that was more cross-disability and that really dealt more with the issues that we had been discussing since we were kids. The transportation problems, the housing problems, the education problems, the employment problems, the effect of the telephone on our lives, all of those; the sheltered workshops, travel, all of those issues were things that we wanted to deal with."

Using the contact information she had collected from the inquiries, Heumann and her friends called a February 1972 meeting at LIU. About eighty people—more than she had expected—showed up, and together they formed a civil rights organization.

Eight months later Disabled in Action (DIA) staged its first public protest—a demonstration against Nixon's veto of the Rehabilitation Act. DIA protestors, some in wheelchairs and others with braces and crutches, held a sit-in outside the building where the Committee to Reelect the President was headquartered. Below is Heumann's memory of the historic event.

So four days before the election, a group of people from DIA . . . organized the demonstration. We had started to do work with a group of people who were working on closing down Willowbrook State Schools for the "mentally retarded on Staten Island," and we decided we were going to go to the city. We were going to go to the city and have a demonstration, and we wanted to go someplace where we would have exposure.

So we went to the federal building. Well, the federal building, as it turned out, was in this little area . . . where there was hardly any traffic in the middle of the day. We . . . had organized this demonstration with also another group called Pride, and we had brought a coffin. And we had great flyers. . . .

Well, here we were in Manhattan at the federal building, and no one could have cared less about the fact that we were there. Because there was nobody there. I mean, people went into the building, but there was no traffic. There was no one to see us, so we thought, "Okay, we will go sit down and block traffic." So we did, but again it didn't really matter because there weren't a lot of cars coming through.

So the police, who had been sent there to deal with us, said . . . "What do you want?" So we said, "Where's Nixon's headquarters?" They told us where it was so we got back in to whatever we had come up in— vans, transportation services, cars—and we drove to Nixon headquarters, which was on Madison Avenue.

So then we thought, "Okay, what are we going to do . . . to kind of deal with this so we get some attention?" So we decided we'll sit down in Madison Avenue. So we did, and about 4:30 in the afternoon 50 people sat down. First, we did a circle and cut off all four streets, but it was a little bit too scary because some of the trucks were very pissed off. So we backed off and only cut off one, but it was still Madison Avenue.

So [the radio show] *Rambling with Gambling* was on WOR. They had the whirly burly bird that would give information about traffic, and what was basically going out was that the city had been shut down by this group of cruel people who were sitting in Madison Avenue.

So they wanted to know why we were there. We said we wanted a meeting with President Nixon to talk to him about what we

Protesters at the Capitol Crawl, calling for passage of the American Disabilities Act, 1990.

were upset about. So we wanted to speak to someone from his office, so they sent someone down from his office, and we said, "We want a meeting with the president." And we were not going to move until we knew we were going to have a meeting with the president. And he left going, "They're crazy, they're crazy." He just walked away.

Well, I guess we were there for about an hour, and then the traffic was subsiding; we kind of made our point. So we decided we'd go *into* Nixon headquarters, so we went into Nixon headquarters and we took their offices over.

But we didn't get a lot of publicity; we had no Vietnam vets with us. So we decided that we would come back the day before the election and we would do everything we could to get Vietnam vets. So we called the McGovern campaign and we got a couple of vets, a guy named Bobby Muller, who's now very involved in landmine removal and set up a national group called Vietnam Veterans of America.

This time we went to Times Square and we marched against the traffic on Times Square. [And then we went] back up to Nixon headquarters [and] took Nixon headquarters over and actually shut them down the day before the election—shut the headquarters down about, I guess, 5, 6, 7 o'clock at night. And Nixon did not meet with us, did not talk with us, but we got publicity because we had Vietnam vets.

The other thing that was going on at that time in New York was a number of police officers had been shot, and so it turned out that some of the police that were actually with us were friends of people who had been injured. And so when we talked about housing, transportation, health care, employment, these guys all got it, because they were having to transport their friends to rehab services and they were having to deal with many of the issues that we were talking about. And I remember one of the police saying to me, "You keep it up because this is great."

The Vegetables Are Rising (1977)

Edward Roberts

Section 504 of the Rehabilitation Act of 1973 prohibited federally funded programs and activities from discriminating against those with disabilities. The Nixon and Ford administrations spent more than two years writing regulations to assure the successful implementation of 504, but after Jimmy Carter assumed office, Joseph Califano, the new secretary of the Department of Health, Education, and Welfare (HEW), appointed a task force to review them. Disability activists, including Judy Heumann, grew

*concerned that the task force, with no representative from the disability
community, might weaken the regulations. Consequently, the American
Coalition of Citizens with Disabilities (ACCD) announced that if Califano
did not sign the original regulations by April 5, the disability rights group
would protest.*

*Califano let the deadline pass without signing, and disability activists
responded, just as they said they would, by conducting sit-ins at federal
sites in ten cities. Most of these lasted a day or two, but 120 protestors in
San Francisco decided to stay put on the fourth floor of the HEW building.
Using wheelchairs and crutches, they had to maneuver with care around
the mattresses, blankets, and personal care items supplied by their friends.
There were battery chargers to operate, and the personal assistants that
some of the activists relied on for everyday living were absent. Allies in the
community helped out as they could; the Black Panthers played a key role
by providing the activists with their daily meals.*

*Twenty-five days into the sit-in, about 50 activists remained—and
became victorious. On April 28, 1977, Califano signed the 504 regulations
with no changes made by the task force. Ed Roberts, an activist whose victory speech is below, reflected on the event by saying, "We were considered
vegetables a few years ago, but now the vegetables are rising." The sit-in
marked the longest occupation of a federal building in U.S. history up to
that point.*

All Right!

It was just, what, three-and-a-half weeks ago that we got here together
to begin talking about something that we knew that we could do. You
know, we didn't come into this with weakness. We came into this movement to show strength, to show what we really are. Which is people
who have learned, from people with disabilities, from being people considered weak, from people being people who are discriminated against
daily; we've learned how to be strong, and we've demonstrated that to
the people of this country.

We knew it. And now they know it. We have a long way to go. We talk about a long journey. It's now been about 10 years since some of us have been struggling, and for years before that. There are people that will be long remembered for their contributions towards opening society; and you know, I think these next ten years together, and I don't think we're going to get it all done overnight, but we have one fantastic start. 504 is going to help us guarantee our own civil rights. And we have learned that through the struggle we gain tremendous strength. We are much stronger than we were three-and-a-half weeks ago. I hope that not only will this record for a sit-in be in the *Guinness Book of Records* for you all to show your grandchildren, but that you'll remember what you did here, what we did together.

Winston Churchill once said, "Never have so few done so much for so many." And this example, this example of people loving each other, committed to something that is right, is one that I know I will always remember. And you know, there is nothing like building a movement on success. We have never been defeated. You think about it. Whenever we have brought ourselves together, whenever we have joined various disabilities together, we find our strength. Our strength is in our unity. And our strength is in our righteousness. Because this is a cause that we've all invested our life in.

We have to begin to think very clearly, that what we need to do is help raise the consciousness of our fellow Americans with disabilities, to help them come out from behind, from the back wards, from the institutions, from the places, the garbage heaps, of our society. We have to stop the warehousing, the segregation, of our brothers and sisters. We have a long way to go. But we have one giant step ahead.

Together we have achieved something that relatively few people achieve in their lives. We have learned more than anything else, about each other, about how much we love each other, and that commitment, that dedication to each other, will carry through the rest of our lives.

We have begun to ensure a future for ourselves, and a future for the millions of young people with disabilities, who I think will find a new world as they begin to grow up. Who may not have to suffer the kinds of

The 504-sit outside San Francisco's City Hall, 1977.

discrimination that we have suffered in our own lives. But that if they do suffer it, they'll be strong and they'll fight back.

And that's the greatest example, that we, who are considered the weakest, the most helpless people in our society, are the strongest, and will not tolerate segregation, will not tolerate a society which sees us as less than whole people. But that we will together, with our friends, reshape the image that this society has of us.

We are no longer asking for charity. We are demanding our rights!

It's not unusual that a movement like this would have its real heart in this area. There are many committed people in this area—Berkeley, San Francisco, the Peninsula, all of Northern California. People have come together and have shown that in our unity is our strength; that in our division is our weakness; that we are going to see attempts to divide us so that we can easily be conquered. But we will not allow that to happen.

I want to say to all of you that from the beginning I knew we could win this. And I didn't see any of you waiver. We knew that we had set a course that we all were gonna follow. We knew the only thing we could tolerate was victory.

We are victorious. We are strong. And we will march ahead together. And nothing will stop our achieving equal opportunity, and the right to move about freely in this society. We will storm the schools and open them up. We will be sure that each person with a disability who has special needs has the money and the power to gain what they need to move them back into the mainstream of society. And we will assure a future for the millions of people who are not now disabled. You know, you come to think of it, that we are assuring a future for a lot of people we don't know at all, and who don't know that their future may be, very similar to ours.

I couldn't be prouder of us together. And I couldn't be happier. And I cannot think of a better way to go into tomorrow, but with rededicating ourselves to the struggle that's ahead, to enforce 504 regulations, to open up more doors, to create choices for people, not the choice of segregation.

I thank you. I join you. I celebrate with you. I rededicate myself to work with you, to ensure the future.

TWELVE

Environmental Justice and Animal Liberation

Earth Day (1970)

Gaylord Nelson

An oil rig owned and operated by Union Oil burst off the coast of Santa Barbara, California, on January 28, 1969. The spill continued for more than a week, sending about 4.2 million gallons of crude oil into the surrounding ocean. It was the most devastating oil spill in U.S. history at the time. An oil slick covered hundreds of miles of ocean waters, sludge blanketed more than thirty miles of beaches, thousands of gulls and grebes died, and an uncounted number of dolphins and seals suffocated.

Horrifying images of the devastation prompted U.S. Senator Gaylord Nelson of Wisconsin to take action. Hoping to tap into the vibrant student movement, Nelson enlisted his colleague, U.S. Representative Paul McCloskey of California, and the two politicians called for a national teach-in about protection of the environment to take place on April 22, 1970. Nelson and McCloskey served as co-chairs of the event and hired Harvard University student Denis Hayes to coordinate the details.

As Hayes plotted with students across the country, it soon became clear that the day would also include demonstrations, picketing, and rallies. Kent State University students were planning a mock funeral for future children, Wayne State University students were organizing a sit-in at the General Motors Building, and University of Illinois students were lining up recruits to clean a nearby stream. The teach-in morphed into Earth Day 1970. It is estimated that about twenty million people participated in teach-ins, demonstrations, clean-up actions, and more on Earth Day. Like many other members of Congress, Democrats and Republicans, Senator Nelson spent the day giving several speeches about the environment; below are excerpts of the comments he made in Denver.

Coupled with the negative effects of the 1969 oil spill, Earth Day 1970 had positive political effects: it helped fuel the creation of the United States Environmental Protection Agency in December 1970 as well as the passage of additional clean air and clean water legislation. Earth Day has been celebrated annually since 1970.

I congratulate you, who by your presence here today demonstrate your concern and commitment to an issue that is more than just a matter of survival. *How* we survive is the critical question.

Earth Day is dramatic evidence of a broad new national concern that cuts across generations and ideologies. It may be symbolic of a new communication between young and old about our values and priorities.

Take advantage of this broad new agreement. Don't drop out of it. Pull together a new coalition whose objective is to put Gross National Quality on a par with Gross National Product.

Campaign nationwide to elect an "Ecology Congress" as the 92nd Congress—a Congress that will build bridges between our citizens and between man and nature's systems, instead of building more highways and dams and new weapons systems that escalate the arms race.

Earth Day can—and it must—lend a new urgency and a new support to solving the problems that still threaten to tear the fabric of this society . . . the problems of race, of war, of poverty, of modern-day institutions.

Ecology is a big science, a big concept—not a copout. It is concerned with the total ecosystem—not just with how we dispose of our tin cans, bottles, and sewage.

Environment is all of America and its problems. It is rats in the ghetto. It is a hungry child in a land of affluence. It is housing that is not worthy of the name; neighborhoods not fit to inhabit.

Environment is a problem perpetuated by the expenditure of tens of billions of dollars a year on the Vietnam War, instead of on our decaying, crowded, congested, polluted urban areas that are inhuman traps for millions of people. . . .

Winning the environmental war is a whole lot tougher challenge by far than winning any other war in the history of man. It will take $20 to $25 billion more a year in federal money than we are spending or asking for now.

Our goal is not just an environment of clean air and water and scenic beauty. The objective is an environment of decency, quality, and mutual respect for all other human beings and all other living creatures. . . .

Establishing quality on a par with quantity is going to require new national policies that quite frankly will interfere with what many have considered their right to use and abuse the air, the water, the land, just because that is what we have always done. . . .

Earth Day may be a historic turning point in American history. It may be the birthdate of a new American ethic that rejects the frontier philosophy that the continent was put here for our plunder, and accepts the idea that even urbanizing, affluent, mobile societies such as ours are interdependent with the fragile but life-sustaining systems of the air, the water, the land. *(1970)*

Oppose, Resist, Subvert (1981)

Edward Abbey

In the 1970s Edward Abbey published fiction and nonfiction that sketched and advocated for the use of radical means to fight the destruction of the environment. These writings encouraged his friends and colleagues in the environmental movement to form Earth First, a loosely knit group dedicated to using militant action, including civil disobedience and the destruction of property, to protect and defend the earth. The group became known especially for "monkeywrenching"—spiking trees, disabling construction vehicles, and setting fire to structures.

One of the group's earliest public actions was the "cracking" of Glen Canyon Dam on the Colorado River in Arizona. On March 21, 1981, about seventy-five Earth Firsters gathered on the Colorado Bridge to protest the dam's construction. As the protestors yelled "Free the Colorado" and held protest signs, five Earth Firsters left the crowd, scaled the fence around the dam, and headed to the center area, where they unfurled a huge sheet of tapered plastic that made the dam appear as if it had a crack through the middle of it. After the successful cracking of Glen Canyon Dam—the five Earth Firsters completed their job and eluded capture—Edward Abbey stood atop the bed of a truck and delivered a speech that has become iconic among Earth Firsters. Below are excerpts from this speech.

We are gathered here today to celebrate three important occasions: the rising of the full moon, the arrival of the Spring Equinox, and the imminent removal of Glen Canyon Dam.

I do not say that the third of these events will necessarily take place today—although I should warn you that some of my born-again Christian brothers and sisters have been praying, night and day, for one little precision earthquake in this here immediate vicinity, and I do predict that one of these times their prayers will be answered—in fact, even now I think I perceive an ominous-looking black fracture down the face of yonder cement plug—and this earth will shake, and that dam will fall, crumble, and go. Glen Canyon Dam is an insult to God's creation, and if there is a God he will destroy it. And if there isn't we will take care of it, one way or another, and if we don't then Mother Nature most certainly will. Give her a few more centuries and the Colorado River will fill Lake Foul [Lake Powell, formed by the dam's construction] with mud, right to the brim, and plug its penstocks and jam its pressure tubes with sand; then the river will come flowing over the top and Glen Canyon Dam will erode away. . . . The willows and the cottonwoods will return, the rice grass and the cliffrose and the juniper, and the birds will come back, and the deer, and the lion and the bighorn sheep, and then, once again, human beings of some kind. . . .

All very well, you say, but we prefer not to wait. . . . To those, the impatient among you, I say, sign our petition to Congress demanding the prompt dismantling of Glen Canyon Dam. Or—we're reasonable folks, we're willing to compromise, we too believe in balance—they can keep their goddam dam, for the time being, if they open the gates and drain Lake Foul. Drain it, to the dregs, to the bitter dregs. Never mind the sunken cabin cruisers, the skeletons of drowned water skis, the fifty million jars of fish bait, and the five hundred million beer cans—time and the winds and the sun and the floods will scour clean. . . .

Oppose. Oppose the destruction of our homeland by these alien forces. And if opposition is not enough, we must resist. And if resistance is not enough, then subvert. After ten years of modest environmental progress, the powers of industrialism and militarism have become alarmed. *The Empire Strikes Back.* We must continue to strike back at the Empire, by whatever means and every means available to us. Win or lose, it's a matter of honor. . . . Oppose, resist, subvert, delay, until the Empire begins to fall apart.

And until that happens: enjoy! Enjoy our great American West—climb those mountains, run those rivers, hike those canyons, explore those forests, and share in the bounty of wilderness, friendship, love, and the common effort to save what we love. Do this and we will be strong, and bold, and happy, we will outlive our enemies, we will live to piss on their graves. Joy, shipmates, joy.

Earth first, life first, freedom first. God bless America, let's save some of it. Love the land—or leave it alone.

Occupy the Forest (1985)

Earth First

In May 1985 Earth First joined another environmental group, the Cathedral Forest Action Group, in trying to halt the clearcutting of Douglas firs in Willamette National Forest in western Oregon. The groups had employed a number of nonviolent methods, including blocking roads and even sitting on cartons of dynamite used by the loggers, but the cutting continued unabated. The tactics assumed a new form when Mikal Jakubal climbed a Douglas fir, set up a platform about 60 feet off the ground, and conducted a one-person sit-in, an idea he and others had discussed during a campfire meeting a couple days earlier. As he sat on the platform, loggers cut trees all around him, doing their best to intimidate him. Jakubal climbed down from the tree by the end of the day, completing the first time that tree-sitting occurred in the United States. "It was my first direct action," he recalled.

Police officers arrested Jakubal, and loggers cut down his tree the following day. Earth First then called upon its members to continue Jakubal's work (see below for the text of the call), and they responded with enthusiasm, conducting one long sit-in from June 23 to July 20, when Linn County law enforcement officers used a crane bucket to capture and arrest Earth Firster Ronald Huber as he was sitting in a fir eighty feet off the ground. Arresting officers also found forty spikes and screws in the tree where Huber had conducted his sit-in; they made the tree unsaleable.

The logging continued after Huber's arrest, and tree-sitting would continue for years to come. Arguably the most famous tree-sitting

occurred when Julia Butter-
fly Hill occupied a Redwood
for 738 days in 1998 and
1999. She descended from
the massive tree only when
the logging company agreed
that it would not cut red-
woods in a three-mile area
surrounding the tree.

Interspecies Action!

Early tree-sitting by Earth First, c. 1985.

Earth Firsters from across the USA are arriving at the Cathedral Forest Wilderness Sanctuary in the Middle Santiam watershed region of Oregon. They are preparing for what looks to be one of the most hotly contested timber sales in the country.

We are planning an ongoing occupation of the Cathedral Forest, selecting certain old growth stands and causing by our presence a de-facto closure of them to clearcutting operations. While our plan is to engage in nonviolent direct action openly and publicly, the nature of the action, placing our bodies high up the trunks of the forest giants with supplies to last indefinitely, will make it impossible for law enforcers to actually arrest the participants as long as they choose to stay up.

This action is conceived as an interspecies one: the hominid participants will prevent the death of the tree species by being up in them; the tree species' participants will keep the humans safe from arrest and incarceration/citation. There may well be unforeseen consequences to this form of symbiotic interaction in the area of communication with the Gene Pool.

4 or 5 human participants can close an entire timber sale if positioned strategically aboard easily constructed, inexpensive platforms 50 or more feet in the air. The average person can easily and safely ascend to

great height after a brief training in some basic true ascent techniques. Resupply of consumables is projected as feasible.

Materials are being collected in Oregon. Base sites in both Corvallis and the Middle Santiam have been prepared.

Our Only Need Is You.

Rescuing the Monkeys (1981)

People for the Ethical Treatment of Animals

Alex Pacheco was a student at Ohio State University when a visit to a local slaughterhouse compelled him to become a vegetarian and organize the school's first animal rights group. He attracted considerable attention on campus, especially from the school's agricultural science majors ("Aggies"), when he criticized local farmers for castrating cows without using an anesthetic. Several Aggies took the criticism personally, camped outside Pacheco's dorm window, and threatened to castrate him—without an anesthetic.

Pacheco transferred to George Washington University, and when volunteering at a local dog pound in 1980, he met employee Ingrid Newkirk. The two soon discovered their shared militancy and decided to organize a new animal rights group—People for the Ethical Treatment of Animals (PETA). With fewer than twenty members, the new group picketed a local poultry slaughterhouse and protested animal research at the National Institutes of Health.

In the summer of 1981 Pacheco hoped to learn more about animal research and accepted an unpaid position at the Institute for Behavioral Research in Silver Spring, Maryland. Research scientist Edward Taub was pleased with Pacheco's interest and introduced him to neurological experiments on monkeys. The animal rights activist was shocked by what he saw—sixteen macaques and one rhesus monkey, nine of whom had been surgically crippled in operations that severed communications between their brains and their limbs. Held in small cages, the monkeys spent their time spinning, masturbating, and biting their limbs. Pacheco was also disturbed by what he heard—that after experimenting with the monkeys Taub was planning to kill them and operate on their neurological systems yet again.

Pacheco decided to resist. He took pictures of the deformed monkeys and their conditions, and solicited affidavits from individuals he sneaked into the laboratory afterhours. These pro-animal veterinarians and scientists testified that the conditions were "miserable," "poorly maintained," even "a very serious health hazard to humans." Pacheco then took his photos and affidavits to the local police, and on September 11, 1981, Montgomery County police seized all seventeen monkeys and later charged Taub with cruelty to animals.

In the ensuing trial, Taub was found guilty of six of the seventeen counts against him and fined $3,000. PETA called the decision "a landmark victory in the struggle for human rights." Taub saw it differently: "What has happened to my work harks back to the Middle Ages and the period of religious inquisition, when scientists were burned at the stake."

Taub appealed, got a second trial, and this time was found guilty of just one count against him. The Maryland Court of Appeals then overturned that remaining conviction, stating that federally funded animal experiments were not required to follow state animal cruelty laws.

In spite of this, PETA gained national attention, and its membership and finances began growing into the huge organization it is today. Below is a PETA press release about the Silver Spring monkeys.

On Friday, September 11, 1981, a search and seizure warrant is to be served at the Institute for Behavioral Research. . . . Friday's seizure of sixteen crab-eating macaques and one rhesus monkey, "Sarah," will be the first time in history that animals have been seized pursuant to a search warrant for a United States research facility. . . .

Friday's warrant marks the end of a four-month undercover investigation by Alex Pacheco, chairperson of People for the Ethical Treatment of Animals, Inc. (PETA). Pacheco has worked as a volunteer since May 11, 1981.

Photographic and written documentation gathered by Pacheco during his time at the Institute shows a pattern of total disregard for the welfare of the animals in their custody. Forced to live in filthy, barren conditions after their capture as adolescents in the wild, many of the monkeys have had portions of their spines surgically removed, rendering their arms or legs "deafferent" (i.e., obstructing or interfering with nerve impulses being conveyed to the brain). Then the monkeys are "taught" to use their deafferent limbs through the administration of electric shocks from a crude, jury-rigged box and forced to defend themselves from researchers armed with metal poles.

Not part of the experimentation: extreme deprivation, frustration, stress and bizarre burning and tingling sensations in their deafferent limbs have caused the primates to self-mutilate: biting off their own fingers and gouging holes in their arms. Although required by federal and local laws, no veterinary attention has been given injured or ill monkeys. Also the victims of a lack of veterinary medical attention: Billy, the gentlest of the macaques, who is believed to have been suffering from a broken arm since mid-August; Hard Times, a monkey who collapsed from possible malnutrition in June; and Paul, a monkey who has chewed off all five fingers on one of his hands. Veterinarians called in by PETA will be examining the animals and arrangements have been made to hospitalize those in need of emergency medical attention.

Due to their stress-induced neuroses, Dr. Geza Teleki, a world-renowned primatologist, warns that the monkeys—whose emotional requirements parallel our own—must be treated with the same considerations afforded "mentally disturbed patients" during their removal and transportation.

A Necessary Fuss (1984)

Animal Liberation Front

On the night of May 28, 1984, five members of the Animal Liberation Front (ALF)—an animal rights group that had migrated to the United States from Britain—walked onto the campus of the University of Pennsylvania in Philadelphia. On a secret mission, the ALF team broke into the university's head injuries laboratory and stole thirty-two tapes that documented years of experiments on monkeys and baboons. Back at their home base, the ALF watched the tapes—which showed shocking images of conscious monkeys and baboons subjected to brain-injuring experiments involving drills and hammers, and of researchers ridiculing and laughing at the brain-injured primates.

The ALF took the tapes to PETA members, who used them to create and distribute a documentary titled "Unnecessary Fuss." Shown on local television and covered in the national media, the documentary led to the loss of grant money supporting the research and forced the university, as well as the wider field, to tighten regulations governing animal experimentation. ALF's foundational beliefs and guidelines are below.

Credo:

The Animal Liberation Front (ALF) carries out direct action against animal abuse in the form of rescuing animals and causing financial loss to animal exploiters, usually through the damage and destruction of property.

The ALF's short-term aim is to save as many animals as possible and directly disrupt the practice of animal abuse. Their long-term aim is to end all animal suffering by forcing animal abuse companies out of business.

It is a nonviolent campaign, activists taking all precautions not to harm any animal (human or otherwise).

Because ALF actions may be against the law, activists work

Rabbits liberated by the Animal Liberation Front.

anonymously, either in small groups or individually, and do not have any centralized organization or coordination.

The Animal Liberation Front consists of small autonomous groups of people all over the world who carry out direct action according to the ALF guidelines. *Any group of people who are vegetarians or vegans and who carry out actions according to ALF guidelines have the right to regard themselves as part of the ALF.*

Guidelines:

1. To liberate animals from places of abuse, i.e., laboratories, factory farms, fur farms, etc., and place them in good homes where they may live out their natural lives, free from suffering.
2. To inflict economic damage to those who profit from the misery and exploitation of animals.

3. To reveal the horror and atrocities committed against animals be-hind locked doors, by performing nonviolent direct actions and liberations.
4. To take all necessary precautions against harming any animal, hu-man and non-human.
5. To analyze the ramifications of any proposed action and never ap-ply generalizations (e.g., all "blank" are evil) when specific infor-mation is available.

Avon Killing (1989)

People for the Ethical Treatment of Animals

By 1989 Avon Products, Inc., acting under pressure from animal rights groups, had significantly reduced the number of animals it used (rabbits, guinea pigs, mice, and others) for testing cosmetics, experiments that in-cluded pouring or dripping nail polish and deodorants onto the animals' exposed pink skin or into their eyes. But rather than praising the company for its progress, People for the Ethical Treatment of Animals (PETA) in-creased pressure on the company so that it would completely eliminate the use of animals for cosmetics testing.

On March 2, 1989, PETA issued a press release announcing its plans to conduct a campaign to distribute about three million "Avon Killing" door hangers calling for a boycott of the company (see below). The phrase "Avon Killing" was a riff on the company's advertising tag ("Avon Calling"), and using door hangers also mimicked the company's door-to-door sales methods. The pressure succeeded. On the same day PETA announced its campaign, Avon announced that the company would halt all animal test-ing by June 1989.

Washington DC—America's largest animal rights group today (March 2) announced an international campaign to boycott Avon, the world's largest cosmetics company, at a National Press Club news conference.

People for the Ethical Treatment of Animals (PETA) will distribute more than three million "Avon Killing" door hangers door-to-door in the United States, Japan, England, Italy, Germany, Mexico, and Canada throughout March to urge Avon to end cruel and unreliable cosmetics tests on animals.

At the news conference PETA presented expert testimony from Donna Hurlock, M.D., of Alexandria, Va., who explained how unreliable animal test results make product safety evaluations impossible to extrapolate to human use.

"You can never rely on animal test results to determine product safety in humans," said Dr. Hurlock. "Today *in vitro* test methods exist which offer reliable ways to gain information and to keep harmful, even cancer-causing products, off the market. Industry must use them."

Former Avon sales representative Penny Frazee of Henderson, Tenn., told how she turned in her sales kit when she learned that Avon had falsely claimed they did not test on animals. "I'm sure they're lying to other reps," said Frazee. "I've come forward so that other people trying to get into the business won't be misled. Avon kills thousands of animals each year for no legitimate reason and I won't have their blood on my hands."

"Images from my 1996 visit to Avon's laboratory still haunt me," said Susan Rich, Compassion Campaign coordinator for PETA. "I saw rows upon rows of cages and the faces of frightened, sick, and dying animals."

"Annual reports and letters to consumers show that Avon puts out 90 percent of its formulas without testing on animals," said Rich. "But, in 1989, *no* animals should suffer to test yet another shampoo, perfume, or mascara. Superior methods exist to test the toxicity and health hazards of cosmetics. We want Avon to go the last 10 percent and join more than 200 cruelty-free companies who use known-safe ingredients and modern testing methods."

According to Rich, a 1988 PETA undercover investigation of Pennsylvania's Biosearch laboratory exposed Avon's contract use of Biosearch to conduct Draize eye irritancy tests in which live rabbits' sensitive eyes were subjected to products for seven days.

"Avon claims to dilute potentially irritating substances, but their standard operating procedure is to test some of their products at full strength in skin irritancy, oral ingestion, and forced inhalation tests at Biosearch," said Rich.

"It is this kind of deception the public won't stand for. People have been lied to about the kinds of testing that go on and the sales representatives have been lied to about testing being done at all. The boycott is a chance for everyone to make a statement against unnecessary animal tests."

THIRTEEN

Anti-Nukes, The Reagan Years, Anti-Gulf War

ANTI-NUKES

I Can Find No Natural Balance with a Nuclear Plant (1974)

Sam Lovejoy

Sam Lovejoy, a twenty-seven-year-old organic farmer living on a Mas-sachusetts commune, picked the morning of George Washington's birth-day to carry out a jolting act of civil disobedience. On February 22, 1974, Lovejoy grabbed some tools from the commune and headed to a nearby area where Northeast Utilities had erected a 500-foot-high tower to test wind direction. The tower was part of the utility company's larger plan to build a twin nuclear power plant on the site.

Arriving at the site in early morning, Lovejoy used his farm tools to loosen the turnbuckles that created the tension necessary for the cables to stabilize the tower. When the high-tension cables lost their strength, the top 360 feet of the tower crashed to the ground, causing about $45,000 in damage.

Lovejoy then walked to a nearby road, waved down a police car, and asked to be escorted to the police station, where he described and confessed to his crime. He also gave the arresting officer the statement that appears below. Lovejoy was charged with malicious destruction of property and then released on his own recognizance.

The radical historian Howard Zinn agreed to serve as an expert witness at Lovejoy's trial. Zinn testified that Lovejoy's actions followed in the footsteps of the Abolitionists, Thoreau, and Gandhi, and when the presiding judge suggested that civil disobedience required the strict observance of nonviolence, Zinn replied: "Violence has to do with human beings, not property." The judge eventually voided the charge on a technicality and instructed the jury to render a verdict of "not guilty." Northeast Utilities canceled the project.

As a farmer concerned about the organic and the natural, I find irradiated fruit, vegetables, and meat to be inorganic; and I can find no natural balance with a nuclear plant in this or any community.

There seems to be no way for our children to be born or raised safely in our community in the very near future. No children? No edible food? What will there be?

While my purpose is not to provoke fear, I believe that we must act; positive action is the only option left open to us. Communities have the same rights as individuals. We must seize back control of our own community.

The nuclear energy industry and its support elements in government are practicing actively a form of despotism. They have selected the less populated rural countryside to answer the energy needs of the cities. While not denying the urban need for electrical energy (perhaps addiction is more appropriate), why cannot reactors be built near those they are intended to serve? Is it not more efficient? Or are we witnessing a corrupt balance between population and risk?

It is my firm conviction that if a jury of twelve impartial scientists was empaneled, and following normal legal procedure they were given all pertinent data and arguments, then this jury would never give a unanimous vote for deployment of nuclear reactors amongst the civilian population. Rather, I believe they would call for the complete shutdown of all the commercially operated nuclear plants.

Through positive action and a sense of moral outrage, I seek to test my convictions.

Declaration of Nuclear Resistance (1976)

Clamshell Alliance

The success of Sam Lovejoy's campaign proved to be a source of inspiration for local activists who opposed the construction of a nuclear power plant in Seabrook, New Hampshire. The activists initially used the court system in their fight, but when that failed and the Nuclear Regulatory Commission approved the project in July 1976, they formed the Clamshell Alliance, a coalition of antinuclear groups based in New England.

Clamshell organized two nonviolent protests in August 1976; in the second, protestors occupied the site of the future power plant for about seventy-five minutes and planted small trees before facing arrest. More than 2,000 protestors showed up for another demonstration, this one in April 1977, and about 1,400 were arrested for trespassing. The national media covered the direct action campaigns, and when Clamshell hosted yet another on-site demonstration two months later, about 20,000 demonstrators joined a three-day-long protest that saw even more national media coverage. Antinuclear movements across the country took inspiration and instruction from Clamshell's actions and staged their own numerous protests.

The Clamshell protests did not prevent the construction of the plant, but they certainly delayed and obstructed it at points. It took fourteen years for the original plan to be completed, and the project costs exceeded six times the proposed costs. Below is Clamshell's rationale for its resistance to nuclear energy, weapons, and technology.

We, the members of the Clamshell Alliance, demand an immediate and permanent halt to the construction and export of nuclear power plants and facilities, and nuclear weapons and supporting technology.

Nuclear power is dangerous to all living creatures and to their natural environment. The nuclear industry is designed to concentrate profits and the control of energy resources in the hands of a powerful few, undermining basic principles of human liberty.

A nuclear power plant at Seabrook, New Hampshire, could lock our region into a suicidal path. As an affiliation of a wide range of groups and individuals, the Clamshell Alliance is unalterably opposed to the construction of this, and any other, nuclear power plant.

We recognize:

1. that the present direction in energy research and development is based on corporate efforts to maximize profits and recoup past investments rather than on meeting our real energy needs;

2. that there is a direct relationship between nuclear power plants and nuclear weapons. The arms industry has used the "peaceful atom" to legitimize its technology. The export of nuclear reactors makes possible the spread of nuclear bombs to nations all over the world. The possibility of nuclear thievery and sabotage of nuclear facilities poses further danger to our civil liberties and our lives;

3. that the centralized nature of nuclear power takes control of energy from local communities and strengthens the monopoly of the utilities;

4. that a political and economic environment committed to the nuclear age is not conducive to the development of, and implementation of, renewable energy sources. With changes in the regulatory and political climate, renewable sources of energy—such as solar technologies—would become competitive, conservation would flourish, and the alleged "need" for nuclear energy would vanish. Awareness of the fact that we live within a balanced, natural ecosystem necessitates changes in "traditional" economic and social values;

Anti-nuclear march, Seabrook, New Hampshire, 1978.

5. that nuclear power plants have proved to be an economic catastrophe. Expensive, inefficient, and unreliable, they require immense investments of capital, and create fewer jobs, than comparable investments in conservation and solar energy;

6. that the dangers of nuclear power plants are intolerable. They include release of "low-level" radiation—a cause of cancer and genetic disorders; the creation of deadly radioactive waste which must be completely isolated from the environment for 250,000 years; the destruction of our lakes, rivers, and oceans by thermal pollution; and the possibility of a catastrophic meltdown. No material gain, real or imagined, is worth the assault on life itself that atomic energy represents.

We therefore demand:

1. that not one more cent be spent on nuclear power reactors or nuclear weapons, except to dispose of those wastes already created and to decommission those plants and weapons now in existence;

2. that our energy policy be focused on developing and implementing clean and renewable sources of energy in concert with an efficient system of recycling and conservation;

3. that all people who lose jobs through the cancellation of nuclear construction, operation, or weapons production be offered retraining and jobs in the natural energy field at decent, union-level wages;

4. that the supply of energy should, in all cases, be controlled by the people. Private monopoly must give way to public control. In concert with public ownership, power supply should be decentralized so that environmental damage is further minimized, and so that control can revert to the local community.

We have full confidence that when the dangers and expense of nuclear energy are made known to the people, they will reject this tragic experiment which has already cost us so much in health, environmental quality, material resources, labor, and control over our own lives.

The Clamshell Alliance will continue its uncompromising opposition to any and all nuclear construction in New England and elsewhere.

Our stand is in defense of the health, safety, and general wellbeing of ourselves and of future generations of all life on this planet.

We therefore announce that, should construction continue at Seabrook, we will mobilize the citizenry and return to the site to blockade or occupy it until construction has ceased and the project is totally and irrevocably cancelled.

Making the World Truly Safe (1979)

Randall Forsberg

Randall Forsberg's interest in nuclear weapons began while she was work-ing as a typist for the Stockholm International Peace Research Institute. Captivated by the material she was typing, Forsberg moved to Boston in 1974, began pursuing a PhD at the Massachusetts Institute of Technology, and founded the Institute for Defense and Disarmament Studies. Forsberg became a popular speaker with peace groups across the nation, and in the late 1970s her work started to focus on the possibility of a nuclear freeze, which she believed arms-control experts had dismissed or ignored as a viable option.

At the time, peace groups like the Fellowship of Reconciliation and Mobilization for Survival had been backing the idea of a U.S. moratorium on the production and deployment of nuclear weapons. Forsberg found that insufficient, arguing that peace groups would be more politically ef-fective if they called for the United States and the Soviet Union to stop producing new nuclear weapons and to reduce their existing stockpiles. Forsberg's idea of a bilateral moratorium—a nuclear freeze in the U.S. and the USSR—reenergized antinuclear groups, and they encouraged Forsberg to produce a statement explaining her position. Forsberg's "Call to Halt the Nuclear Arms Race" (see below) received support from all major peace groups and became the foundational document of the emerging national campaign for a nuclear freeze.

Forsberg and her colleagues took the campaign across the nation and placed freeze referenda before city councils and state legislatures and on city, county, and state ballots. The national campaign culminated on June 12, 1982, when about 700,000 protestors held a nuclear freeze march and rally in New York City. It was—and remains—the largest antinuclear demonstration in U.S. history.

Proposal for a Mutual US-Soviet Nuclear Weapon Freeze
To improve national and international security, the United States and

the Soviet Union should stop the nuclear arms race. Specifically, they should adopt a mutual freeze on the testing, production, and development of nuclear weapons and of missiles and new aircraft designed primarily to deliver nuclear weapons. This is an essential, verifiable first step toward lessening the risk of nuclear war and reducing the nuclear arsenals.

The horror of a nuclear holocaust is universally acknowledged. Today, the United States and the Soviet Union possess 50,000 nuclear weapons. In half an hour, a fraction of these weapons can destroy all cities in the northern hemisphere. Yet over the next decade, the USA and USSR plan to build over 20,000 more nuclear warheads, along with a new generation of nuclear missiles and aircraft.

The weapon programs of the next decade, if not stopped, will pull the nuclear tripwire tighter. Counterforce and other "nuclear warfighting" systems will improve the ability of the USA and USSR to attack the opponent's nuclear forces and other military targets. This will increase the pressure on both sides to use their nuclear weapons in a crisis, rather than risk losing them in a first strike.

Such developments will increase hair-trigger readiness for a massive nuclear exchange at a time when economic difficulties, political dissension, revolution, and competition for energy supplies may be rising worldwide. At the same time, more countries may acquire nuclear weapons. Unless we change this combination of trends, the danger of nuclear war will be greater in the later 1980s and 1990s than ever before.

Rather than permit this dangerous future to evolve, the United States and the Soviet Union should stop the nuclear arms race.

A freeze on nuclear missiles and aircraft can be verified by existing national means. A total freeze can be verified more easily than the complex SALT I and II agreements. The freeze on warhead production could be verified by the Safeguards of International Atomic Energy Agency. Stopping the production of nuclear weapons and weapon-grade material and applying the safeguards to U.S. and Soviet nuclear programs would increase the incentive of other countries to adhere to the

Nonproliferation Treaty, renouncing acquisition of their own nuclear weapons, and to accept the same Safeguards.

A freeze would hold constant the existing nuclear parity between the United States and the Soviet Union. By precluding production of counterforce weaponry on either side, it would eliminate excuses for further arming on both sides. Later, following the immediate adoption of the freeze, its terms should be negotiated into the more durable form of a treaty.

A nuclear weapons freeze, accompanied by government-aided conversion of nuclear industries, would save at least $100 billion each in U.S. and Soviet military spending (at today's prices) in 1981-1990. This would reduce inflation. The savings could be applied to balance the budget, reduce taxes, improve services, subsidize renewable energy, or increase aid to poverty-stricken third world regions. By shifting personnel to more labor-intensive civilian jobs, a nuclear weapons freeze would also raise employment.

Stopping the US-Soviet nuclear arms race is the single most useful step that can be taken now to reduce the likelihood of nuclear war and to prevent the spread of nuclear weapons to more countries. This step is a necessary prelude to creating international conditions in which:

- further steps can be taken toward a stable, peaceful international order;
- the threat of first use of nuclear weaponry can be ended;
- the freeze can be extended to other nations; and
- the nuclear arsenals on all sides can be drastically reduced or eliminated, making the world truly safe from nuclear destruction.

Nuclear Waste on Our Homeland (1995)

Lower Colorado River Tribes

Native American lands have long been targeted as sites for the testing and storage of nuclear weapons, as well as the dumping of nuclear waste. From 1995 to 1999, activists from the Lower Colorado River tribes banded together with environmental activists to oppose plans by U.S. Ecology, a company specializing in the dumping of hazardous wastes, to build a nuclear waste dump in Ward Valley, California. The Native Americans considered the land sacred (see their resolution below), and the environmentalists, like the Native Americans, were concerned that the site might contaminate the Colorado River.

In 1995 the activists built and occupied encampments at the site proposed for the nuclear waste dump, and in the following year they sought a formal role in the federal government's assessment of the environmental impacts of the project. That effort failed. But the activists continued their protests, and in the following year they blocked entrances when the Department of Interior attempted to survey the proposed site. They also held more marches and vigils, and filed a lawsuit claiming a violation of the civil rights of Native American tribes.

The Department of Interior fought back in early 1998 by issuing an order demanding closure of the protestors' encampments. But the resisters refused to budge and even expanded their occupation. Meanwhile, the three-year-long battle over the nuclear waste dump continued in the courts—until November 2000 when the U.S. Court of Appeals ruled against U.S. Ecology, effectively nuking its plans for the dump.

A United Resolution by the Lower Colorado River Federally Recognized Tribes

Consisting of the Fort Mojave, Chemehuevi, Colorado River, Quechan, and Cocopah First Nations, to state their united positions of opposition in regards to the low-level radioactive waste repository facility proposed for construction in Southeastern California at Ward Valley.

Whereas: The Fort Mojave Tribe, Chemehuevi Tribe, Colorado River Tribes, Quechan Tribe, and the Cocopah Tribe are all considered sovereign nations within the external boundaries of the United States by the federal government; and

Whereas: These Tribal groups have been residing in Native North America prior to the arrival of non-Indians; and

Whereas: These Tribes are the Indigenous People of this region and hold an extreme and solemn relationship with the Land, Animals and Water; and

Whereas: These Tribes were given instruction by their Creator on all aspects of survival and to be caretakers of their Traditional land and use areas where they were placed; and

Whereas: These traditional lands have extreme religious, cultural, and archaeological, nonrenewable sources and resources that relate and tie them spiritually and physically to these areas: and

Whereas: The retention of culture, native language, traditions, and land-based reference areas prominent in native song and oral history is a main objective of these Tribes in order to maintain a distinct identity as individual Tribes: and

Whereas: The United States of America has entered into a government-to-government relationship with the Fort Mojave, Chemehuevi, Colorado River, Quechan, and Cocopah Tribes; and

Whereas: Pursuant to said government-to-government relationship, the Congress of the United States has recognized the obligations of the United States to promote, support, and protect the right of Indian people to govern themselves, preserve and practice their native religions, and preserve and protect their Reservation and traditional homelands: and

Whereas: The Congress of the United States, as embodied in the United States Constitution, hundreds of treaties entered into between the United States and Indian Tribes, and countless federal laws and regulations, has undertaken a solemn obligation and trust towards the Fort Mojave, Chemehuevi, Colorado river, Quechan, and Cocopah Tribes, which trust imposes upon the United States the highest standard and fiduciary duties to preserve and protect their Indian religious cultural sites whether located on or off Reservation lands and to protect their Reservation lands, water, and air from toxic contamination or pollution; and

Whereas: The Secretary of the Interior, Mr. Bruce Babbitt, has breached this trust and the solemn obligations owed to the Fort Mojave, Chemehuevi, Colorado River, Quechan and Cocopah Tribes, by refusing to conduct further hearings on whether the low-level radioactive nuclear facility proposed for the Ward Valley would adversely impact or destroy existing religious and cultural sites of the Fort Mojave, Chemehuevi, Colorado River, Quechan, and Cocopah Tribes in the Ward Valley or contaminate and pollute the existing Reservation lands and waters of said Tribes, knowing that his decision was based upon information provided by technical experts, who in the past have been wrong about similar facilities that they said would be safe and which are now leaking and polluting surrounding lands and waters; and

Whereas: By ignoring the voice of the people that will be affected, Mr. Babbitt has shown his total disregard for Native Americans and has shunned his trust responsibility which is mandated through federal legislation. This further demonstrates his non-recognition of our Tribal Leaders which is contrary to the National Historic Preservation Act as amended, by which trust may have been gained on our part and a real understanding of our religious concerns which was the intent by amending the Act; and

Whereas: We can't take the slightest chance of contamination of ground water of the Colorado River which is the basis of our presence and existence.

Therefore: Be It Resolved That the Signed Tribes Listed Below Commit Their Efforts to the Prevention of This Low-level Radioactive Waste Facility Being Permitted or Constructed Anywhere in the Ward Valley.

THE REAGAN YEARS: UNION BUSTING, APARTHEID, AND WARS IN CENTRAL AMERICA

You Are Not Alone (1981)

Lane Kirkland

President Ronald Reagan showed that he was no friend of organized labor when he fired members of the Professional Air Traffic Controllers Association shortly after they staged a walkout in August 1981, and when he refused to negotiate with the union in talks following the massive firing. Reagan had made other anti-labor decisions by this point. He had reduced funding for agencies that supervised safety and health regulations in the workplace, and his budget had slashed welfare policies that helped the working poor. In addition, Reagan had openly ridiculed the leaders of organized labor, characterizing them as out of touch with the masses of U.S. workers.

In response, Lane Kirkland, president of the American Federation of Labor and Congress of Industrial Organizations (AFL-CIO), decided to flex labor's muscle by calling for workers to attend Solidarity Day, September 19, 1981, in Washington, DC. Inspired by the successful uprising of workers in Poland, Kirkland and his allies planned for Solidarity Day to be a chance for labor and civil rights leaders to voice their discontent with Reagan's anti-labor policies and to show solidarity in a time when many indicators suggested a rapid decline of labor's power and influence in Washington.

About 260,000 protestors showed up for Solidarity Day. The massive crowd gathered at the Washington Monument and then marched to the Capitol. One of the speakers was NAACP executive director Benjamin L. Hooks, who declared, "We will not sit idly by while the bare necessities of life are taken from the needy and given to the greedy." Excerpts from Kirkland's speech are below.

We are here today to reaffirm the great goals that have drawn us together, in solidarity, for a hundred years. We are here to answer a challenge to those goals and to all that we have gained together, in solidarity.

President Reagan has told us that he alone speaks for the working people of this country, and that we do not.

The object of governance in America, we are told, is but to raise armies, to foster and nourish commercial enterprise, and to suppress those forces that might check its rapacity.

If you reject the notion that only the state, through its chief executive, faithfully expresses your will, look about you. You are not alone.

If you believe that governments are raised by the people, not as their enemies but as their instruments, to promote the general welfare, look about you. You are not alone.

You are the people that do the work of America. You run its factories and offices, work its farms, transport its produce, maintain its buildings, teach its children, nurse its sick, clean its streets, and fight in its defense.

When something goes wrong in America, you feel it first—before the politicians or the more securely placed. Something has gone wrong and you know it all too well.

Those who have risen to power in this city have set out to strip our government of any capacity to serve your needs and aspirations. They have set out to cancel and dismantle the safeguard of a humane society and to commit us to the economic jungle.

They are sacrificing the homes, health, and hopes of millions on the altar of crank economic abstractions that defy the laws of simple arithmetic and dismay even their friends on Wall Street, who never allow sentiment to blind them to the bottom line.

Their tax cuts, transferring resources from the common good to the private purses of the rich, are proving the most irresponsible fiscal act in our time—as we said they would.

Their monetary policies are causing record high interest rates— as we said they would. They have attacked Social Security and other covenants between the people and their government—as we said they would.

Their indifference or hostility to social justice threatens voting rights, women's rights, workers' rights, and human rights—and this, too, we warned, would come to pass.

We are out of step with no one but the coldhearted, the callous, the avaricious, and the indifferent. We are out front and we shall not fall back to hide and wait for better political weather.

Today is just a start, but solidarity is more than just a day. As our brothers and sisters in Poland have shown the world, it is a quality of the human spirit that can never be defeated.

Solidarity Day March, Washington, D.C., 1981.

End UM Investments in Apartheid (1977)

Southern Africa Liberation Committee

The Southern Africa Liberation Committee (SALC) was founded in 1975 by African students and their allies at the University of Michigan. The interracial group aligned with the African Students' Association (ASA) in an effort to raise campus awareness about apartheid in South Africa, and part of these efforts included hosting political activists from Nelson Mandela's African National Congress. But after the Soweto Uprising in 1976, in which South African government officials killed black schoolchildren, SALC and ASA focused their efforts on demanding that the university divest its holdings in companies engaged in business with South Africa. Below is a pro-divestment flyer circulated by SALC in 1977. The student-led divestment campaign met resistance from university administrators, and full divestment did not occur until 1988. By that time, SALC, ASA, and similar groups at other universities had served to inspire numerous divestment protests that occurred throughout the Reagan years, while the president sided with pro-apartheid white South Africans.

"By most measures of human and governmental conduct, South Africa has been for years a repressive state, its system of apartheid, or separation of the races, keeping the nation's non-white majority of 21.7 million not only separate but distinctly unequal to its 4.3 million whites."

The New York Times, October 23, 1977

Protest the Recent Crackdown

Two weeks ago South Africa added yet another repressive measure to its long list with its suppression of basic democratic rights through the banning of many black individuals, black organizations, and the major black newspaper, as well as many whites who support demands for change in the system of apartheid. For an organization, banning means being put out of business; for an individual it means house arrest along with the loss of the rights of free speech and assembly. The actual number of persons banned is as yet unknown; the government released a partial list which includes 29 people and 19 organizations. At least 200 people were arrested, which is worse than banning, for under South African security laws a person can be detained for an indefinite period without a trial. *The World*, the principle black newspaper and the country's second largest daily, was also banned; this is the first time in South African history that a daily newspaper has been shut down. *The World's* editor, Percy Qoboza, was arrested, and Donald Woods, a prominent white newspaper editor (*The Daily Dispatch*) was banned for 5 years.

Poster calling for international boycott of South Africa, 1976.

End UM Investments in Apartheid

What does this have to do with us? The University of Michigan has approximately $40 million worth of indirect investment in South Africa, as well as lucrative research contracts, professorial exchanges, and other ties. These investments are instrumental in holding up the Vorster regime and the racist system of apartheid which it embraces. Without American support and financial backing in the form of investments such as these, the apartheid system could never stand up under the weight of its injustice and oppression. Our university is an active participant in this support process; whether the investments are direct or indirect makes little difference, for in either case the money still gets there. If you are a student your tuition payments are involved, and if you are a Michigan resident your tax dollars are in it as well. *Our* money is going to support one of the most racist and repressive regimes on this planet. This clearly makes the problem of UM investments *our* responsibility, and not merely the jurisdiction of administration policymakers and financial "experts." We must demand an immediate end to all UM ties with South Africa, in particular our financial ties.

What Can You Do?

Bring up the issue in classes, write articles or letters to local newspapers, organize forums in your departments. Boycott and protest campus recruitments by corporations with holdings in South Africa. IBM will be here Nov. 1 & 3—turn out to protest their recruiting. In short, take advantage of your own situation and resources to expose the real facts of the situation in South Africa. And above all: *Demand that UM Break All Ties with South Africa Immediately!*

Tonight: Come to Alice Lloyd dorm and hear Mary Wade, recently returned from a tour of the frontline states in Southern Africa. Monday, October 30, 7:30 pm.

Boycotting Shell (1986)

United Mine Workers of America

The Reagan administration earned the wrath of anti-apartheid activists by insisting that diplomacy, rather than sanctions or other penalties, was the best method for dismantling apartheid in South Africa. Randall Robinson, the executive director of TransAfrica, an anti-apartheid lobbying group, also saw another obstructionist at play—the media. "For many years there have been attempts by national black leaders and interested white institutions to get this issue addressed by Congress, the Administration, and the American public," he said. "The media has never given it adequate attention and as a result Reagan, without great political consequence, has warmly embraced the most vicious regime in earth."

The lack of media attention began to change on November 22, 1984, when Randall, Mary Frances Berry, and Walter Fauntroy conducted a sit-in at the South African Embassy in Washington, DC, in an effort to secure the release of thirteen imprisoned black labor leaders in South Africa. Throughout the following week, a steady stream of demonstrators, including Arthur Ashe and Harry Belafonte, picketed outside the embassy, carrying signs reading "U.S. Companies Divest," "End U.S. Support of South Africa," and "One Man, One Vote in Africa."

Yolanda King, the youngest daughter of Martin Luther King, Jr., was arrested at the embassy on November 30. Other members of her prominent family—her mother Coretta, her brother Martin, and her sister

Bernice—also joined the picket line, and they were arrested on June 27, 1985. Between the arrest of Randall, Berry, and Fauntroy on Thanksgiving Eve 1984 and the arrests of the Kings on June 27, more than 2,600 persons were arrested while picketing the South African Embassy.

Sit-ins and picketing also took place at corporations and banks that conducted business with South Africa, and university students across the nation used the same methods to demand that their schools divest any funds invested in the apartheid nation. And in January 1986 the executive council of the AFL-CIO approved a request, made by the International Confederation of Free Trade Unions, to call for a boycott of Shell Oil Company products because of the company's heavy investments in petroleum and mining in South Africa as well as its poor treatment of black South African workers. Below is the text from a boycott flyer issued by the United Mine Workers of the AFL-CIO.

You can do something about slave labor conditions in other countries that both hurt workers there and threaten to undercut our own standard of living.

The AFL-CIO, United Mine Workers, and other organizations have endorsed the Shell boycott.

Apartheid Affects Americans

The "apartheid" system in South Africa forces black workers—who make up 85 percent of the population—to live and work under slave labor conditions.

The concentration camp-style system also has an effect on American workers in both the private and public sectors.

1. Multinational corporations invest in countries like South Africa instead of in American jobs. They take advantage of cheap labor overseas, while failing to maintain and moderate operations in the US.
2. South Africa exports products to the United States. Production costs are cheaper when workers are forced to work for slave wages, often with virtually no rights or benefits.
3. South Africa sells products to countries that normally buy from the US, using apartheid to undercut American workers.

4. Profits made in South Africa can finance corporate attacks on American workers. Companies like Royal Dutch/Shell, Phelps Dodge, and IBM can afford to fight workers' unions in the U.S. in part because of high profits made in countries like South Africa.

5. Lower labor standards in countries like South Africa help create a climate for employers to demand a lower standard of living for Americans as well. Cutbacks and jobs lost in America's private sector mean less funding for public services, which hurts public workers and all Americans.

Why Boycott Shell

South African workers are trying to end the apartheid system. But Royal Dutch/Shell (Shell Oil's parent company) is a key company standing in their way because Royal Dutch/Shell supplies fuel to the South African military and police and to the apartheid economy.

South Africa does not have its own oil supplies. Without fuel from companies like Royal Dutch/Shell, South Africa could not continue to enforce slave labor conditions and assault, arrest, and torture trade unionists and others who protest.

In addition, Royal Dutch/Shell itself co-owns the Rietspruit coal mine where striking South African workers have been forced to work at gunpoint and union supporters have been fired.

South Africa's largest black union—the National Union of Mineworkers—has asked for international action against Royal Dutch/Shell.

Among those who have targeted the company are the World Council of Churches, the Free South Africa Movement, the NAACP, and the International Confederation of Free Trade Unions.

Royal Dutch/Shell sells products through its subsidiaries, including Shell Oil Co. in the U.S. and Shell South Africa. The products of all subsidiaries are targets of the boycott, including Shell gasoline, motor oil, tires, and home products such as flea collars and air fresheners.

Until Royal Dutch Shell Withdraws from South Africa . . . Please Don't Buy Shell Products

We Join in Covenant to Provide Sanctuary (1982)

Bay Area Sanctuary Movement

Virulently anticommunist, the Reagan administration funded and armed rightwing governments fighting leftist insurgencies in El Salvador and Guatemala. The US-trained armies in both countries often acted like death squads, raping, torturing, kidnapping, and killing everyday citizens with impunity. Consequently, hundreds of thousands of Salvadorans and Guatemalans fled their homelands, seeking political asylum in the United States and claiming a fear of persecution in their home countries.

The Reagan administration typically denied their requests, partly because granting asylum meant conceding that the United States did indeed sponsor rightwing governments that oppressed and persecuted their own citizens. The U.S. government also refused to classify the Salvadorans and Guatemalans as refugees, a classification that would have allowed them to stay in the United States until the persecutions in their countries subsided.

Reverend John Fife, pastor of Southside Presbyterian Church in Tucson, Arizona, knew the painful realities of the refugees seeking assistance at his church. "We'd take in people who had torture marks all over their body, and the immigration judge would order them deported the next day," he recalled.

Fife and Southside responded to the crisis by creating a grassroots movement of faith communities that offered their physical facilities as temporary safe havens for immigrants from Central America. The sanctuary movement also provided immigrants with food, medical care, legal counsel, housing, employment, and other basic necessities.

Rather than seeking to hide, the movement publicized its actions on March 24, 1982, when Southside held a coordinated press conference with five faith communities from Berkeley, California, to announce and explain their commitment to providing sanctuary. The Bay Area groups had signed and made public a "sanctuary covenant" that sketched their rationale for becoming part of the sanctuary movement. See below for the covenant's text.

The Reagan administration was not keen on conducting raids on churches and synagogues—more than 200 faith communities would declare themselves sanctuaries—but it was not above planting informants within the movement and using their findings to arrest and convict Fife and several others of felony conspiracy and other charges. Fife and his colleagues were convicted, though none ended up in prison.

The convictions did not stop the movement, and by the time it ended about 2,000 refugees had received sanctuary from faith communities. Equally important, widespread publicity about the movement and the refugee crisis led to legislation in the mid- to late-1980s that made it easier for Central Americans to avoid deportation and become U.S. citizens.

The Bay Area has become a place of uncertain refuge for men, women, and children who are fleeing for their lives from the vicious and devastating conflict in Central America. Many of these refugees have chosen to leave their country only after witnessing the murder of close friends and relatives.

The United Nations has declared these people legitimate refugees of war; by every moral and legal standard, they ought to be received as such by the government of the United States. The 1951 United Nations Convention and the 1967 Protocol Agreements on refugees—both signed by the US—established the rights of refugees not to be sent back to their countries of origin. Thus far, however, our government has been unwilling to meet its obligations under these agreements. The refugees among us are consequently threatened with the prospect of deportation back to El Salvador and Guatemala, where they face the likelihood of severe reprisals, perhaps including death.

This is not the first time religious people have been called to bear witness to our faith in providing sanctuary to refugees branded "illegal" in their flight from persecution. The slaves also fled north in our own country and the Jews who fled Nazi Germany are but two examples from recent history. We believe the religious community is now being called again to provide sanctuary to the refugees among us.

Therefore, we join in covenant to provide sanctuary—support, protection, and advocacy—to the El Salvadoran and Guatemalan refugees who request safe haven out of fear and persecution upon return to their homeland. We do this out of concern for the welfare of these refugees, regardless of their official immigrant status. We acknowledge that legal consequences may result from our action. We enter this covenant as an act of religious commitment.

Sanctuary activist Jose Artiga, left, protesting at U.S. Capitol, 1980s.

Pledge of Resistance (1983)

The Pledge of Resistance Campaign

In early November 1983, not long after the U.S. invasion of Grenada, about thirty-five leaders of the Christian peace movement met at the Kirkridge retreat center in Pennsylvania to study, pray, and share thoughts about the challenges of peace that year. Their attention soon focused on Central America and especially Nicaragua, where the Reagan administration was assisting the rightwing Contra insurgency against the leftist Sandanista government.

Fearing an invasion of Nicaragua, the retreat participants drafted and signed a letter promising nonviolent actions, including traveling to Nicaragua and occupying congressional offices, in order to oppose any such invasion. The "Promise of Resistance" was widely circulated, and in response to interests expressed by numerous faith and secular communities, the letter was revised and secularized, with the result being the "Pledge of Resistance" (POR) that appears below. About 42,000 people signed the pledge by the end of December 1984, and about 60,000 more had signed it by the end of the decade. The POR campaign scheduled nationwide vigils, among other things, and lobbied hard, and successfully, against the appropriation of funds for the Contras.

Civil Disobedience Pledge

If the United States invades, bombs, sends combat troops, or otherwise significantly escalates its intervention in Nicaragua or El Salvador, I pledge to join with others to engage in acts of nonviolent civil disobedience as conscience leads me at U.S. federal facilities, including U.S. federal buildings, military installations, congressional offices, offices of the Central Intelligence Agency, the State Department, and other appropriate places. I pledge to engage in nonviolent civil disobedience in order to prevent or halt the death and destruction which such U.S. military action causes the people of Central America.

*Demonstration against the training of Nicaraguan Contra rebels,
Fort Walton, Florida, 1986.*

Legal Protest Pledge

If the United States invades, bombs, sends combat troops, or otherwise
significantly escalates its intervention in Nicaragua or El Salvador, I
pledge to join with others to engage in acts of legal protest as my conscience leads me, including such actions as participating in demonstrations, vigils, leaflettings, and appeals to Congress and the White House.
I also pledge to demonstrate my support for those who engage in acts of
nonviolent civil disobedience in order to prevent or halt further death
and destruction in Central America.

I Sat on the Tracks (1987, 2011)

S. Brian Willson

The following is an excerpted transcript from an October 2011 interview between "Democracy Now" host Amy Goodman and pacifist S. Brian Willson, whose 1987 protest of the Reagan administration's wars in Central American left him disabled. The interview recounts the details of Willson's life-threatening protest and his reasons for carrying it out.

Goodman: On September 1, 1987, Brian Willson took part in a nonviolent political action outside the Concord Naval Weapons Station in California. He sat down on the train tracks along with two other veterans to try to stop a U.S. government munitions train sending weapons to Central America during the time of the Contra wars. The train didn't stop. Willson suffered 19 broken bones, a fractured skull and lost both of his legs. "Before, I had spent many months in Nicaragua in the war zones, and I had been to El Salvador talking to guerrillas and talking to human rights workers, understanding the incredible extent of murders that were going on and maimings and displacements, because of fear of being murdered," Willson said. He decided, "I have to at least escalate my own nonviolent occupation, if you will, of the tracks." In retrospect, Willson added, "I regret that I lost my legs, but I don't regret that I was there. I did what I said I was going to do. . . . Following orders, I discovered, is not what I'm about." . . .

Willson: It was a Tuesday, September 1st, 1987. And, of course, it was planned by me in advance after spending much time in Nicaragua and El Salvador witnessing the carnage of U.S. policy.

Goodman: What was happening then there? . . .

Willson: Well, of course, President Reagan was—had his war on—war of terror and what he called the terrorists in revolutionary Nicaragua, that was—had overthrown Somoza, and the revolutionary process in El

Salvador, trying to oust a very repressive, feudalistic government. And so . . . Reagan declared there was a Soviet beachhead being formed in Latin America, which of course we all know is absurd, just another excuse for putting down self-determination processes in other countries.

So we knew the weapons were coming from the Concord, California, Naval Weapons Station, 25 miles east of San Francisco, and we decided to go there, after many efforts of trying to get Congress to stop the funding—this whole process of petitioning Congress, which is now pretty much an oligarchic institution representing corporations. We decided we would directly try to obstruct the flow of munitions that move on trucks and trains at Concord to the ships in Sacramento River. And so it's a three-mile track from the bunkers to the ship. It crosses a public right-of-way highway. This is where we were vigiling. We had been vigiling for three months. Many arrests had taken place. I had only been a jail support person. And I decided on September 1st, 1987, which was an anniversary of the Veterans Fast for Life the year before on the steps of the Capitol, that two vets and I would do a 40-day, water-only fast between the rails to obstruct, at least temporarily, the movement of the train.

So I had watched these trains move all summer, with flatbed cars full of crates of white phosphorus rockets, 500-pound bombs, mortars, millions of rounds of ammunition. And it was just getting to the point where I said, I have to at least escalate my own nonviolent occupation, if you will, of the tracks. And we told the base what we were doing, why we were doing it, when we were going to do it, and asked for a meeting with the commander, and he refused.

So at 10 of 12:00 on September 1st, we, the two other veterans and I, took our position on the rails, starting our 40-day, water-only fast, knowing we would probably spend much of that in jail. There was a big sign next to our vigil that said, "Penalty for blocking federal munitions trains is a year in prison and a $5,000 fine." So we knew what the consequences were. I actually—and the first train was coming just before noon, first train that day. And the next thing I know, I woke up in a hospital, four days later.

I have no memory of what happened. Of course, I had 40 friends there who were witnessing it. The other two veterans just barely got out of the way. The train was speeding. The FBI, in looking at the one video, said the train was accelerating to more than three times its five-mile-an-hour speed limit at the point of impact. We found out later that the train crew that day had been ordered not to stop the train, which was an unprecedented—basically an illegal order. Why? Because they said I was going to hijack the train, which of course—there were 350 armed Marines to protect the base. There was usually local police present when we were present on the tracks. I had never envisioned it being a dangerous action.

And then, while I was in the hospital, an FBI agent was fired. And after almost 22 years, he was fired for refusing to investigate me and three other veterans as domestic terrorist suspects. So this was all shocking to me, just shocking that I, this all-American kid that grew up in upstate New York, even though I kind of shifted after Vietnam to being a dissenter, or my father would just say a marginal person—I just never imagined this happening. Of course, this government will do anything. We know that. But I would imagine it doing it to people in other countries, but not to me in this country. So it was a very interesting experience.

Goodman: When you woke up in the hospital four days later, what did you understand happened?

Willson: Well, initially, I saw a lot of plants at the base of my bed, green plants. And my partner at the time was sitting next to me. And I blurted out, according—well, this is what I remember, my first words: "Wow! I'm in a jail cell with plants? And my family is next to the bed?" And my family explained to me, "Honey, you are in a hospital. You got hit by the train." And I couldn't believe it. I just couldn't believe it.

And then I was watching the replay on the wall television for several days. They were playing it on the news, and I was watching myself be run over by the train and was like, "Why just like"—this is what happens to people, of course, all over the world who obstruct the Yankee mad train that's trying to repress people who want to have self-determination or what have you. So it was just another part of the U.S. policy coming home very personally to me viscerally.

And the day I woke up, 9,000 people showed up at the tracks and ripped up 300 feet of the tracks and stacked up the railroad ties in a very interesting sculpture. And from that day, for 28 consecutive months, day and night, 24 hours a day, there was a permanent occupation of the tracks of sometimes 200 people, with tents, blocking every train and every truck. Twenty-one hundred people were arrested. Three people had their arms broken by the police. This was all 24 years ago. Occupation of the tracks. The police were abusive. However, the trains, of course, did stop after that. It's just that they had to stop and wait for massive numbers of arrests. And it was amazing.

Goodman: What did you understand then, as you watched the video of yourself and the train rolling over you? As it rolled over you, it sliced off both your legs?

Willson: It sliced off one of my legs and mangled the other one. I had a huge skull fracture. In fact, I have a plate in my skull right here. A piece of my skull the size of a lemon was completely dislodged from my skull and driven into—and destroyed my right frontal lobe, which was the—which is why the doctors were concerned that I might die in the operating room. . . .

Goodman: Had you talked with people who had been hurt in El Salvador and Nicaragua?

Willson: I talked with hundreds of people in El—

Goodman: Before or after?

Willson: Before and after. Before, I had spent many months in Nicaragua in the war zones, and I had been to El Salvador talking to guerrillas and talking to human rights workers, understanding the incredible extent of murders that were going on and maimings and displacements, because of fear of being murdered. I saw and spent lots of time, and very viscerally moved by what I was finding.

One day, in the spring of '87, before I went to the tracks, I visited 200 amputees in the hospital. And I remember coming out of the hospital and sitting on a stone outside the hospital—this was up in the war zones in Nicaragua—and I said, "Their legs are worth just as much as mine"—not knowing that I was going to lose my legs three months later. . . .

I . . . took my first trip to Nicaragua to study what Reagan was calling the Soviet beachhead and the Marxist-Leninists, which I knew, of course, was a code word for poor people organizing for their own self-determination. And within one week after being in the mountains of Nicaragua my very first trip—I couldn't speak Spanish; I had to have somebody always translating for me—the Contras, Reagan's Contra terrorists, the people he trained and armed to overthrow the Sandinista revolution, attacked three farming cooperatives, killed 11 people. I saw six of them coming in on open caskets on horse-drawn wagons to the cemetery in Estelí, and I just wept. And I knew then that's how all civilization has developed—on exploitation and incredible cruelty and murder and maiming.

And then I really studied the history of civilizations. And so I really became quite a historical—a history student, realizing I knew nothing, really, about history. I did not know context. I didn't know how other people really felt when they're being repressed. And, I mean, I did know, I have a sense of it, but I really wanted to know how extensive this had been for several thousand years, and I wanted to understand the context I grew up in, in this—you know, during my lifetime. And so that experience in Nicaragua led me to take many more trips to Nicaragua, studying U.S. policy and meeting many Nicaraguan—I lost 50 Nicaraguan friends that I had met, and acquaintances, to the Contras. They were killed. And in El Salvador, there were 15 that I had gotten to know who were killed by the death squads. And so it was very—it becomes very personal. It's like your family is being murdered. And when your family is murdered, some kind of a response.

Goodman: And so, ultimately, you sat down on those tracks—

Willson: I sat on the tracks.

THE GULF WAR

I Will Refuse to Fight (1990)

Jeff Paterson

Under orders from President Saddam Hussein, about 80,000 Iraqi soldiers invaded nearby Kuwait on August 2, 1990. The invasion was successful, and Hussein claimed that the occupied nation was now the nineteenth province of Iraq. The United States quickly condemned the invasion and called for "the immediate and unconditional withdrawal of all Iraqi forces."

President George H. W. Bush and his allies strategized about how best to respond to Hussein's newly established control of two-thirds of the earth's oil reserves. They opted to secure UN resolutions imposing an embargo on Iraq and demanding its withdrawal from Kuwait. More ominously, the administration amassed more than 500,000 U.S. troops, in cooperation with 200,000 international troops, along the Kuwait-Saudi Arabia border.

When Hussein refused to the leave the country, the air campaign of Desert Storm—the invasion of Kuwait and Iraq—began on January 17, 1991, followed by a massive ground assault on February 24. It was the largest armored assault undertaken by the U.S. since World War II. U.S. and allied troops defeated the Iraqi army by the end of the third day, and Iraq announced on February 27 that it would comply with UN demands.

On January 14, 1991, three days before the U.S. and Coalition forces launched the air campaign of the Persian Gulf War, Native American protestors had beaten a peace drum while approximately 5,000 protestors marched past the White House. But polls showed that the war enjoyed overwhelming support from the U.S. public, and on January 26 pro-war demonstrations took place across the country. Even in Syracuse, New York, with its rich history of antiwar activism, about 5,000 demonstrators attended a supportive rally. On that same day, 125 tractor-trailers, decorated with U.S. flags and yellow ribbons, formed a convoy on the Massachusetts turnpike.

In spite of the war's popularity, the antiwar movement was able to stage large protests in major cities across the country. As pro-war activists turned out on January 26, so too did about 150,000 antiwar activists in Washington, DC, where they marched from the Mall to the White House and then to the Ellipse, chanting, "No blood for oil" and "Hey, Hey, Uncle Sam, we remember Vietnam." On the other side of the country, in San Francisco, about 95,000 protestors gathered at the Civic Center, marched down Market Street and onto the freeway onramps, blocking access to the Bay Bridge at rush hour.

U.S. troops were not immune to the resistance movement before and during the war, and between 1,500 and 2,000 active-duty troops applied for conscientious objector status. About sixty troops were court-martialed for refusing to deploy, and three cities (San Francisco, Oakland, and Berkeley) and numerous faith communities publicly declared themselves as sanctuaries for troops seeking to avoid the killing fields in Iraq. Below is a statement issued by Jeff Paterson, a soldier refusing to serve in the war.

As we speak tens of thousands of servicemen are being mobilized to defend for the first time in American memory a blatantly imperialistic economic interest stripped of the State Department's beloved specter of international communism. Although the U.S. is facing off against a truly despicable man in Saddam Hussein, the reality is that U.S. foreign policy created this monster.

It was the U.S. who tacitly endorsed the Iraqi invasion of Iran ten years ago.

It was the U.S. and West Germany who sold Hussein chemical weapons throughout the war.

It was the U.S. who remained silent when Hussein used these weapons on his own populations.

And after all of this, it was the U.S. who gave Hussein safe passage through the Persian Gulf and the Strait of Hormuz by shipping Iraqi oil under the flag of Kuwait, thus protecting it from Iranian attack by U.S. escorts.

As usual the world banks were delighted to assist Iraq in its invasion of Iran by handing out blank checks to be payable for by the blood of the people after Iran would be crushed into submission. It was these banks that actually financed the carnage of the half million dead resulting from that war. It was this enormous war debt owed by Iraq that forced Hussein in my opinion to make the following choice:

Impose harsh austerity measures on his people and face the downfall of his regime, or with a little military maneuvering take Kuwait and in one fell swoop double the amount of oil produced by Iraq.

Although there are great differences in this interventionist policy and that of U.S. support for the death squad regimes in El Salvador and Guatemala, there is the underlining motive of corporate profit throughout. Unfortunately the American people have fallen for a big lie—that corporate interests are always in the best interests of the people. This is rarely true. What is the equation that balances human lives and corporate profits?

In my opinion no such equation exists, except in the minds of those that are preparing to fight this war.

The United States has no moral ground to stand on in the Persian Gulf.

We created this monster and pointed him in this direction.

We pour millions into the coffers of the Israel's military to wage a war against stone-throwing youth seeking a country to call their own once again.

I cannot and will not be a pawn in America's power plays for profits and oil in the Middle East. I will resist my scheduled departure, tentatively Sunday, by immediately filing for conscientious objector status, and physically refusing to board the plane. And of course if I am drug out to the Saudi desert, I will refuse to fight.

One Billion Dollars a Day (1991)

June Jordan

Born in Harlem in 1926, June Jordan survived a difficult childhood to become one of the most influential poets and essayists of her time. In addition to writing, Jordan took part in numerous nonviolent campaigns, advocating for women's rights, civil rights, sexual freedom, and liberationist politics. In 1991 she read a poem and an article about the Gulf War at an event titled "Poets and Politicians Against the War." Below is an excerpt of her comments.

On a recent cold Sunday morning in Kennebunkport, Maine, George Bush and his wife, Barbara, apparently seated themselves inside a small country church of God to think about what? Alma Powell, wife of the Joint Chief of Commanders of the United States armed forces, reports that she likes to keep comforting foods like vegetable soup ready on top of the stove for Colin, her certainly hard-working husband. Alma adds that these days she knows that her Colin doesn't want to hear little stories about the children, just the soup, ma'am.

Secretary of Defense Dick Cheney, second only to his boss in blood thirst for arms-length armchair warfare, has never served half an hour even in the Army, the Navy, the Air Force or the Marines. I know, it's not right to pick on him just for that. Last Saturday, at a local antiwar rally, organized by the Middle East Children's Alliance, I noted aloud that the war to date was costing us $56 billion; every 24 hours the cost is $1 billion at least. I therefore proposed the following to the crowd scattered on the grass and under the trees. $1 billion a day for seven

About 200 University of Wisconsin-Madison students marched in early 1991 to protect the Persian Gulf War. The students called for university leaders to devote one school day to education about the war.

days for Oakland. Can you imagine that? $1 billion a day, but to hell with the imagination. This is our city, this is our money, these are our lives. $1 billion a day for seven days for Oakland. Or do we accept that that there is only the will and the wallet when it's about kill or be killed? Do we need this money, or not? Do we need it here? Do we need it now? And so on. When I left the stage, a reporter came up to me. "You meant $1 million, didn't you?" "No," I answered him amazed. "$1 billion. $1 billion a day for seven days for Oakland. That's the bill. That's our bill for housing and drug rehabilitation and books in the public schools and hospital care and all of that good stuff."

$1 billion a day. It's a modest proposal. In less than three months, those maniacs in the White House and the Pentagon have spent $56 billion, in my name and with my taxes, trying to obliterate Iraq and its people and their leaders. I'm saying call home the troops and the bucks. We need these big bucks to make this a homeland, not a desert right here for the troops and for you and for me. What's the problem? It's a bargain. $7 billion of a serious improvement of American life in Oakland versus $56 billion for death and destruction inside Iraq? What's the problem? But the reporter was giving me a weak smile of farewell that let me understand he found my proposal preposterous. $1 million for life okay. Billions for kill or be killed, okay. But really big bucks on us, the people of these United States? $1 billion a day to promote, for example, the safety and educational attainment and communal happiness of 339,000 Americans? I must be kidding. As I walked away from the park, I felt a heavy depression overtaking me. The reporter, a tall, white man with clear eyes, could not contemplate the transfer of his and my aggregate resources from death to life as a reasonable idea. Worse, he could not suppose his and my life to be worth anything close to the value of organized high-tech and boastful murder. But then, other people stopped me to ask how can we do that? Do we write letters or what?

So, as I write this column tonight, I am reassured because not every American has lost her mind or his soul. Not every one of my compatriots who become a plaid-wrapped lunatic, lusting after oil and power, the perversions of kicking ass, preferably via TV. A huge number of Americans has joined with enormous numbers of Arab peoples and European communities in Germany, England, France, Italy, Spain, and Muslim communities throughout India and Pakistan to cry out "stop"! When I say huge, I mean it. If 1,000 Americans contacted by some pollster can be said to represent 250 million people, then how many multi, multimillions do we antiwar movement gatherings of more than 100,000 coast to coast and on every continent, how many do we represent? How come nobody ever does that kind of political math? Tonight, February 2, 1991, when yet again the ruling white men of America despise peace and sneer at negotiations and intensify their arms-length, arm-chair prosecution of this evil war, this display of racist value system that will never allow for any nationalism that is not their own and that will never allow third world countries to control their own natural resources and that will never ever express, let alone feel, regret or remorse or shame or horror at the loss of any human life that is not white.

Tonight, I am particularly proud to be an African-American. By launching the heaviest air assault in history against Iraq on January 15, George Bush dared to desecrate the birthday of Martin Luther King Jr. Tonight, and 83,000 bombing missions later, is the 26th anniversary of the assassination of Malcolm X. On this sorry evening, the world has seen the pathological real deal behind the sanctimonious rhetoric of Bush and Company. The Persian Gulf War is not about Iraqi withdrawal from Kuwait. The war is not about Kuwait at all. Clearly, it's not about international law or respect or United Nations resolutions, since by comparison to Washington and Pretoria, the Butcher of Baghdad is a minor league Johnny-come-lately to the realm of outlaw conduct and contempt for world opinion. What has happened tonight is that the Soviet leader, Mikhail Gorbachev, and the government of Iraq have reached an agreement whereby Iraq will withdraw from Kuwait, and that is a fact regardless of anything else included or omitted by the proposal. This agreement should provide for immediate ceasefire, a cessation to the slaughter of Iraqi men and women, and a halt to the demolition nationwide of their water supply, the access to food and security. What is the response of the number one white man in America? He's gone off to the theater. I guess that means that the nearest church was closed. Or that Colin Powell was busy dipping his spoon into the comfort of a pot of soup somebody else cooked for him. And that Dick Cheney was fit to be tied into any uniform so long as nobody would take away his Patriot missiles and Apache helicopters, and B52 cluster bombers, and black and brown and poor white soldiers and sailors and all of the rest of these toys for a truly bigtime coward. Confronted with the nightmare prospect of peace, Bush goes off to the theater because he will be damned if he will acknowledge that Saddam Hussein is a man, is the head of a sovereign state, is an enemy to be reckoned with, an opponent with whom one must negotiate. Saddam is not a white man. He and his Arab peoples must be destroyed. No peace, no ceasefire, no negotiations. And I am proud tonight to remember Dr. King and Malcolm X and to mourn their actions even as I pursue the difficult challenge of their legacy. Both of these men became the targets of white wrath when they in their different ways developed into global visionaries persisting against racism in Alabama, in Harlem, in South Africa, in Vietnam. Neither of these men could have failed to condemn this current attack against the Arab world. Neither of these men ever condoned anything less than equal justice and equal rights.

Hence, the undeniably racist double standards now levied against Saddam Hussein would have appalled and alienated both of them completely. I am proud to shake hands with the increasing number of African-American conscientious objectors. I am proud to remark the steadfast moral certainty of the United States Congressman Ronald Dylan's opposition to the war. I am proud to hear about the conscientious objections of Congressman Gus Savage, and John Conyers, and Mervin as I am proud to observe that even while African-Americans remain disproportionately represented in the United States armed forces, we as a national community stand distinct, despite and apart from all vagaries of popular opinion. We maintain a proportionately higher level of opposition to this horrible war, this horrendous evasion of domestic degeneration and decay.

I want to say something else specific to you, Mr. President. It's true you can humiliate and you can hound and you can smash and burn and terrify and smirk and boast and defame and demonize and dismiss and incinerate and starve, and yes, you can force somebody—force a people to surrender what happens, what happens to remain of their bloody bowels into your grasping, bony, dry hands—but all of us who are weak, we watch you. And we learn from your hatred, and we do not forget. And we are ready, Mr. President. We are most of the people on this god-forsaken planet.

Demonstrate, Demand, Disobey (1991)

Michael Albert and Stephen Shalom

Michael Albert, a co-founder of Z Magazine and South End Press, is a leading leftist critic of U.S. economic and foreign policy, and Stephen Shalom is a frequent contributor to Z, as well as an author of several books on U.S. domestic and foreign policy. Below is their prescription for resisting the Gulf War.

Why oppose war in the Gulf? It's wrong.

- Some liberals oppose a Gulf war on the grounds it will be too expensive. Usually they mean lost stability, lost resources, or heightened recession. Sometimes they mean lost U.S. lives. Rarely do they mean lost Arab lives. While these costs are real, the best grounds on which to oppose the Gulf War are that it is not just.
- It is not anti-interventionist. It is not pro-national sovereignty. It is not pro-international legality. It is not pro-"a new and more peaceful world order."
- This war is to reinforce U.S. control of Arab oil. It is to crush Arab nationalism.
- It is to establish the U.S. as the world's policeman with the bills paid, whether they like it or not, by whomever we pass them on to.
- This war should be opposed because it is wrong. We have no right controlling oil prices. No right administering the future of the Middle East. And no right becoming the world's Hessian state, sacrificing much of the U.S. population to a Third World existence in the process.
- We should oppose this war because we oppose militarism as a solution to international conflict. What is the logic of our antiwar activism? Raise the social cost.
- Arguments that war is immoral will not deter Bush. Arguments that he isn't seeing the costs will not change his mind.
- Pursuers of war, including Bush, don't care about Iraqi lives,

American lives, or anyone's lives. The same holds, by and large, for U.S. media which has yet to discuss the potential loss of Arab lives as a central cost of war.

- Nor do U.S. warmakers care about subtle concerns of culture or history. They care about advancing the geopolitical interests of the U.S. as they are understood by the White House and Wall Street. That's all.

- To get Bush to reverse his war policies requires that the public raise costs that warmakers don't want to pay.

- Warmakers do not want to endure an end to business as usual. They do not want war to cause a new generation to turn to activism. They dread the escalation of dissent from events that oppose war, to actions that oppose militarism, to projects that oppose capitalism.

- These costs curtailed U.S. militarism in Indochina. They can do the same, and more, in the Gulf.

- Raise the social cost. What should be the focus of our activism? Peace and justice.

- Antiwar activity needs to develop lasting consciousness of the causes and purposes of U.S. war policies including understanding underlying institutions. And it also needs to send a powerful message of dissent.

- Events that focus on ROTC, on campus military centers, such as military bases or the Pentagon, and that demand an end to war are excellent.

- Events that focus on centers of domestic suffering that demand an end to war *and* an end to militarism *and* a reallocation of military resources to social ends, are still more powerful.

- Multi-focused events will reveal and enlarge not only antiwar militance, but militance extending to gender, race, and class policies and institutions that warmakers hold even more dear. Multi-issue events send an even more powerful and threatening message than single issue efforts, and can have that much more impact.

- They also have the capacity to build a movement that can last beyond the Gulf crisis to attack the causes as well as the symptoms of oppressive institutions. Build a movement not just for peace, but for peace and justice too.

- Create a multi-issue focus. What tactics should we use? Demonstrate, demand, disobey.

- A gathering of people at a teach-in to learn about U.S. policies threatens leaders of a country who want people as ignorant as possible. A march with many constituencies threatens the leadership of a country who wants people as passive and divided as possible. A march that includes civil disobedience and says that some people are willing to break laws and, moreover, next time many more will do so, is still more powerful.

- Create a multi-tactic movement.

- But lasting movements also have to develop a positive component that can become a center of organizing energy and a place for learning and support.

- In addition to teach-ins, marches, rallies, and civil disobedience, we need to create lasting coalitions and institutional centers of Peace and Justice in occupied buildings on campuses or in community centers, and/or churches.

- Such student and community centers could be places for people to do peace work: creating leaflets and banners and writing letters to GIs. They could be places from which people could do systematic coordinated canvassing and provide each other with support and help.

- Further, these campus and community centers could be places where people consider how their universities or communities might become centers of peace and conversion rather than militarism. Create a long-term movement.

FOURTEEN

LGBT Rights, AIDS, and Women's Rights

LGBT RIGHTS AND AIDS

I Am Proud to Raise My Voice Today (1979)
Audre Lorde

On October 14, 1979, less than a year after the assassination in San Francisco of Harvey Milk, one of the first openly gay politicians in U.S. history, about 75,000 LGBT individuals and their allies gathered for the National March on Washington for Lesbian and Gay Rights. Organizers issued five demands: a gay and lesbian rights law, an executive order banning the government and federally funded organizations from practicing discrimination based on sexual orientation, the repeal of all anti-gay and anti-lesbian laws, the end of discrimination in lesbian and gay custody cases, and the protection of gay youth from laws that discriminated against them.

Sometimes referred to as the "Great Coming Out Party," the march was the first large-scale national protest staged by the LGBT community. Another historic event also occurred in the immediate context of the march. The National Coalition of Black Lesbians and Gays, founded a

year earlier by Delores Berry and Billy Jones, had organized the first Na-
tional Third World Gay and Lesbian Conference to take place just before
the march. Poet and activist Audre Lorde refers to the conference in her
short speech at the march (below).

Thirty years ago, the first time I came to Washington, my family and I couldn't eat ice cream in a drugstore because we were black. Now since then I have come to Washington many times to demonstrate and to testify to different aspects of myself and my beliefs. And I see many familiar faces from those past marches here today.

Well, lesbians and gay men have always been in the vanguard of struggles for liberation and justice in this country and within our communities. The first National Conference for Third World Lesbians and Gay Men met in Washington over the past four days, and it was an outstanding success. We had Third World lesbians and gay men from over forty states—Third World lesbians and gay men from Mexico, from Canada, and from England.

Now we have all come together to demonstrate as lesbians and gay men in behalf of our rights. And this is the beginning of a new front, where we are saying to the world that the struggle of lesbians and gay men is a real and particular and inseparable part of the struggle of all oppressed people within this country.

I am proud to raise my voice here this day as a black lesbian feminist committed to struggle for a world where all our children can grow free from the diseases of racism, of sexism, of classism, and of homophobia, for these oppressions are inseparable. The question always is, What kind of a world do we want to be a part of? And affirmation and work does not stop with this march in Washington. Each of us has a responsibility to take this struggle back to her and his community, translated into daily action.

The National Conference of Third World Lesbians and Gay Men and this march today were once only visions of what could be. Now all of us have made it our reality. Let us carry this solidarity that we are professing here today back with us into our everyday lives tomorrow and the day after and next week and next year, and let it be reflected in a renewed commitment to struggle for a future where we can all flourish, where not one of us will ever be free until we are all free.

The Right to Lesbian and Gay Sex (1987)
The March on Washington for Lesbian and Gay Rights

On August 2, 1982, one of the most remarkable days in gay rights history, twenty-nine-year-old Michael Hardwick was in his home when a city police officer knocked on his front door. A houseguest answered the door and directed the officer to Hardwick's bedroom. When the officer opened the door, he walked in on a sexual encounter between Hardwick and another man. The officer stated that he was there to serve Hardwick a warrant related to public intoxication, which Hardwick protested, saying he had already settled the matter in court. The officer then proceeded to arrest Hardwick and his sexual partner—on grounds that they had violated a sodomy law.

With encouragement from the American Civil Liberties Union, Hardwick challenged Georgia's sodomy laws in a suit he brought against Michael Bowers, the state's attorney general. Hardwick v. Bowers ended up at the U.S. Supreme Court, where Hardwick and the entire LGBT community were delivered a significant blow. Writing for the majority, Justice Byron White argued that homosexuals did not have a "fundamental right . . . to engage in acts of consensual sodomy."

A little more than a year later, Hardwick was present, along with several hundred thousand others, for the second March on Washington for Lesbian and Gay Rights, which focused on the AIDS crisis and the Hardwick decision. An excerpted document detailing the demands of the march is below. Hardwick also participated in a mass act of civil disobedience that LGBT activists staged in front of the Supreme Court to protest the Hardwick decision and call for the repeal of sodomy laws. About 4,000 attended the demonstration, and about 800 were arrested after walking past police barriers and sitting in circles on the plaza in front of the Court.

Chosen Family and Relationships

Recognizing and celebrating the diversity in family relationships, we demand legal recognition of lesbian and gay male domestic partnerships with all the benefits and entitlements that flow from marriage. These include, but are not limited to, rights of inheritance, extended medical benefits, visitation and custody rights, insurance rights, parenting, foster care, and adoption and immigration, etc.

- Since gay and lesbian youth are often without societal and familial support, we demand funding for a broad range of social services targeted to them, including, but not limited to: alternative housing, foster care, counseling services, legal aid, etc. . . .
- We demand safe sex information and health services for gay and lesbian youth, sexuality and anti-homophobia curriculum in the schools, access to and the freedom to organize and participate in all school and related social activities.

Sodomy Laws

Because the sodomy and related laws form the cornerstone of discrimination against lesbians and gay men, the lesbian and gay community of this nation demands a repeal, through federal and local action, of all laws that violate the right to privacy by criminalizing consensual sex between individuals above the age of consent; that the term "sexual orientation" be added to the Federal Civil Rights Act to prohibit discrimination against lesbians and gay men in employment; that Congress, through any means available to it, prohibit states from regulating private adult consensual activities and that education be done on the definition of sodomy to show that sodomy laws prohibit the majority of consensual sexual activity.

ACT-UP die-in at City Hall, New York City, 1989.

Presidential Action/Executive Order

We demand use of the full presidential authority to eliminate all discrimination based on sexual orientation in all aspects of executive branch employment, programs, and policies. Specifically, we demand:

- Issuing of a presidential executive order banning discrimination based on sexual orientation in federal employment, the military, federally contracted private employment, the granting of security clearances and all federally funded programs.
- Inasmuch as the exclusion of gays and lesbians is not medically or scientifically valid, the public health service shall resume its polity of non-enforcement of the gay/lesbian medical exclusion under the immigration law.
- Repeal of all military regulations discriminating against lesbians and gays, including sodomy regulations, upgrade of all less than

honorable military discharges for reasons of homosexuality with full restoration of benefits, including retirement with no statute of limitations.

- A presidential order banning use of HIV testing or AIDS-related discrimination in federal employment or by federal contractors.
- A presidential order guaranteeing uncensored access to information for gay/lesbian prisoners, equality of visitation rights, and protection from discrimination based on AIDS and/or sexual orientation.
- The Justice Department shall cease and desist from the interpretation of laws in manners which are oppressive and destructive to the civil rights of lesbians and gay men and all other people; including repeal of their interpretation discriminating against workers associated with AIDS.

Discrimination Against People with AIDS and People with ARC [AIDS-Related Complex]
- End discrimination against people with AIDS/ARC, those testing positive for the AIDS virus, or those perceived to be in any of those categories.

Funding for AIDS
- We demand complete federal funding of all health and social services for all people with AIDS/ARC: that the federal government underwrite and insure all research for a cure and a vaccine; that the federal government fund a massive AIDS education and prevention program that is explicit, culturally sensitive, lesbian/gay affirming and sex positive.
- That funding come from the military budget, not already existing appropriations in the social services budget.

We Take That Fire and Make It Our Own (1993)

New York Lesbian Avengers

In 1992 six lesbian activists, initially brought together by Ana Simo, founded a direct-action group focused exclusively on lesbian-related is- sues. Naming themselves the Lesbian Avengers, the activists wanted to adopt methods different from the standard picket lines and sit-ins.

One of their early protests had its origins in the September 26, 1992 firebombing of a basement apartment in Salem, Oregon. Brian Mock, a 45-year-old white gay man, and Hattie Mae Cohens, a 29-year-old black lesbian, were killed in the bombing, and four skinheads were charged with murder, arson, assault—and violation of Oregon's hate crime laws.

One month after the firebombing, the Lesbian Avengers built an en- campment in New York City's West Village that included a shrine com- memorating the deaths of Cohen and Mock. "It stands for our fear," said Lysander Puccio in an evening speech at the shrine. "It stands for our grief. It stands for our rage. And it enshrines our intention to live fully and completely as who we are, wherever we are." She concluded her comments with a ritual that has become virtually synonymous with the Avengers— fire-eating. "We take the fire of action into our hearts, and we take it into our bodies," she explained. "And we stand here and now to make it known that we are here and here we will stay. Our fear does not consume us. The fire will not consume us. We take that fire, and we make it our own."

In the following year, the Avengers also organized the first dyke march in U.S. history. The Avengers opted to use the word "dyke" rather than "lesbian" because, as founder Kelly Cogswell puts it, "dyke" was "big and bold, and a declaration of independence from both the women's and gay movements that had always sidelined us. It also thumbed its nose at the obsequious trend of some LGBT activism: 'Please give us a few crumbs. We're just like you, except for who we sleep with.'"

The Avengers advertised the march in dyke publications and by handing out about 8,000 flyers to activists who were gathering for the

1993 March on Washington for Lesbian, Gay, and Bi-Equal Rights and Liberation, which, with about a million in attendance, was one of the largest marches in U.S. history. On the evening of the massive march, about 20,000 lesbians assembled at Dupont Circle and marched to the White House. "We're dykes, we're out, we're out for power," they chanted. In front of police officers positioned just outside the White House fence, the Avengers ate fire as the crowd erupted in cheers.

Broadsheet for March

CALLING ALL LESBIANS!
WAKE UP!
DYKE MANIFESTO

It's time to get out of the beds, out of the bars and into the streets.
It's time to seize the power of dyke love, dyke vision, dyke anger, dyke intelligence, dyke strategy.
It's time to organize and incite. It's time to get together and fight.
We're invisible, sisters, and it's not safe—not in our homes, not in the streets, not on the job, not in the courts.
Where are the *out* lesbian leaders? It's time for a fierce lesbian movement and that's you:
the role model, the vision, the desire.

WE NEED YOU.
Because: we're not waiting for the rapture. We are the apocalypse.
We'll be your dream and their nightmare.

LESBIAN POWER
Lesbian Avengers believe in creative activism: loud, bold, sexy, silly, fierce, tasty and dramatic.
Arrest optional.
Think demonstrations are a good time and a great place
to cruise women.

First New York City Dyke March, 1993.

Lesbian Avengers don't have patience for polite politics, are
bored with the boys.
Think of stink bombs as all-season accessories. Don't have a
position on fur.
Lesbian Avengers believe confrontation fosters growth
and strong bones.
Believe in recruitment, not by the army; not of straight women.
Don't mind handcuffs at all.
Lesbian Avengers do believe homophobia is a form of misogyny.
Lesbian Avengers are not content with ghettoes: we want your house,
your job,
your frequent flyer miles.
We'll sell your jewelry to subsidize our movement.
Lesbian Avengers don't believe in the feminization of poverty.

We demand universal health insurance and housing.
We demand food and shelter for all homeless lesbians.
Lesbian Avengers are the 13th step.
Lesbian Avengers think girl gangs are the wave of the future.

LESBIAN SEX

Believe in transcendence in all states, including Colorado and Oregon.
Think sex is a daily libation, good energy for actions.
Crave, enjoy, explore, suffer from new ideas about relationships:
slumber parties, polygamy (why get married only once?)
personal ads. Affinity groups.
Are old fashioned: pine, long, whine, stay in bad relationships.
Get married but don't want to domesticate our partners.
Lesbian Avengers like the song "More Madonna, Less Jesus"
Use live action words: lick, waltz, eat, fuck, kiss, play, bite, give it up.
Lesbian Avengers like jingles: subversion is our perversion.

LESBIAN ACTIVISM

Lesbian Avengers scheme and scream.
Think actions must be local, regional, national, global, cosmic.
Lesbian Avengers think closeted lesbians, queer boys and sympathetic straights
should send us money.
Believe direct action is a kick in the face.
Lesbian Avengers plan to target homophobes of every stripe and infiltrate the Christian right.
Lesbian Avengers enjoy litigation. Class action suits fit us very well.
TOP 10 AVENGER QUALITIES
(in descending order)
10. Compassion
9. Leadership
8. No big ego
7. Informed

6. Fearlessness
5. Righteous anger
4. Fighting spirit
3. Pro sex
2. Good dancer
1. Access to resources (Xerox machines)

THE LESBIAN AVENGERS. WE RECRUIT.

Transphobia Is at the Heart of Queerphobia (1993)
Phyllis Randolph Frye

In the summer of 1976, after years of struggling with his gender identity, Houston resident Phillip Frye came out as a transgender woman, Phyllis, and immediately began to lobby for the repeal of her city's ban on cross-dressing, a cause she won in 1980. Frye graduated from the law school at the University of Houston, and with her expertise in law and policy, she founded the International Conference on Transgender Law and Employment Policy. The conference met for six successive years, developing and lobbying for regulations and laws that would advance civil rights for the transgender community. One of the obstacles that Frye and her allies faced was within the mainstream lesbian and gay movement; some leaders believed that including transgender-friendly causes would undermine the credibility of the movement and slow its advances toward first class citizenship for lesbians and gays. In the following speech, which she delivered at the 1993 March on Washington for Lesbian and Gay Rights, Frye criticizes the movement for excluding transgender folks and their cause.

Listen up! I've got something to tell you! Why is it that the first march and the second march and this the third march do not have transgendered in the name of the march?

The transgendered community includes crossdressers and transvestites, passing women and female impersonators, drag queens and male impersonators, and pre-, non- and post-operative transsexuals. We definitely include females-to-males as in Joan of Arc, George Sand, Leslie Feinberg, and the transgendered women who fought bravely as soldiers in our colonial and civil wars. Knowing this, why is it that with two rally stages, all day long, there are no female-to-male transgendered speakers? We embrace all races, sexual orientations, creeds, religions, ethnicities, nationalities, ages, and physical impediment. Why is it, then, that with two rally stages, all day long, there is only one transgendered political speaker?

This, my friends, is a very unforgiving society for transgendered persons and their loved ones. While we were reared in one gender identity, we have a definite, true-but-opposite gender identity which must express itself. The empirical data show that being transgendered is not a matter of mere choice. No, rational people do not take upon themselves such unrelenting and often hate-filled social pressures for a mere fling! Transphobia is at the heart of queerphobia.

We are here today in the grand effort to change law and social understanding. The first International Conference on Transgender Law and Employment revealed that the transgendered have no legal protection and no employment protection. The transgendered require legal protection on the basis of "gender identification." Together, my sisters and brothers, we must seek legal protection from discrimination on the basis of both "sexual orientation *and* gender identification."

Listen to me. One of the ten legal strategies that we will develop at the second Transgender Law Conference this upcoming August in Houston will be to resist those surgeons who demand that heterosexual couples divorce as a condition to transgender surgery, even though both partners wish to remain married. Sex reassignment surgery on one half of an ongoing heterosexual marriage yields a same-sex marriage. Therefore, my lesbian, gay, and bisexual sisters and brothers, it will be the transgendered community who leads you into the legalization of the same-sex marriage. Why, then, is transgendered not in the name of this march?

Our history reveals that the majority of those people who died at the beginning of the Nazi Holocaust while wearing pink triangles were the transgendered of all sexual orientations. Our history reveals that the real heroes in the Stonewall uprising were the transgendered, the leather cultists, and the street hustlers who stood up to the bully cops and presented in-your-face resistance to being pushed around further. Why, then, are the transgendered being omitted and snubbed from the focus of the upcoming Stonewall 25? Sadly, the reward to the transgendered, the leather cultists, and the street hustlers of Stonewall is condescension and stereotyping.

You see, pitting lesbians, gays, and bisexuals against the transgendered is another of the bigots' ploys. It's called division. Many in the lesbian, gay, and bisexual community resent being stereotyped as "crossdressing effeminates" simply because the bigots, the dividers, have successfully cast such with a pejorative label. Others in the transgender community resent being stereotyped as "homosexual/bisexual" simply because the bigots, the dividers, have successfully cast such with another pejorative label. While we quarrel amongst ourselves over stereotypes and labels, the bigots, the dividers that fire us, that resist our marriage, that refuse us our citizen's share, those bastards continue to win hands-down.

In order for us to resist this bigots' ploy, this division, we must today embrace each other's stereotypes. We must embrace each other's labels with pride: we must unite. We must go into Congress and into the state houses speaking for lesbian and gay and bisexual *and transgender*— *and transgender*—say it—*and transgender*—and transgender rights. We must seek legal language that protects us on the basis of both "sexual orientation *and gender identification.*" When you speak to your member of Congress, tell them House Bill 431 needs to be amended to add "and gender identification"—"sexual orientation and gender identification."

And in conclusion, when you see Sam Nunn, tell him that Phyllis Frye is an honorably discharged army officer. [Frye offers a military salute to the crowd.]

Why We Fight (1988)

Vito Russo

Founded in 1987, the AIDS Coalition to Unleash Power (ACT UP) quickly became known as a militant group dedicated to using education and non-violent direct action to draw attention to the AIDS crisis, to protest President Reagan's failure to acknowledge the crisis, and to demand affordable drugs for treating HIV-AIDS. ACT UP activist, writer, and film reviewer Vito Russo delivered the speech excerpted below at two protest rallies. On May 9, 1988, he spoke at a "Nine Days of Rage" event at the state capitol in Albany, New York. The nine-day protest was nationwide, staged by ACT UP chapters in more than fifty U.S. cities, and addressed a wide variety of AIDS-related issues, including AIDS among women and people of color, homophobia, and drug use. Russo also delivered the speech at an October 11 ACT UP protest in which about 1,000 activists blocked entrances to the FDA to protest the agency's refusal to make experimental AIDS drugs available as soon as the agency determined they were safe. (The agency's practices called for labeling the drugs safe and effective before approving them for release.) Images of police officers arresting about 175 activists circulated across the nation.

You know, for the last three years, since I was diagnosed, my family thinks two things about my situation. One, they think I'm going to die, and two, they think that my government is doing absolutely everything in their power to stop that. And they're wrong, on both counts.

So, if I'm dying from anything, I'm dying from homophobia. If I'm dying from anything, I'm dying from racism. If I'm dying from anything, it's from indifference and red tape, because these are the things that are preventing an end to this crisis. If I'm dying from anything, I'm dying from Jesse Helms. If I'm dying from anything, I'm dying from the President of the United States. And, especially, if I'm dying from anything, I'm dying from the sensationalism of newspapers and magazines and television shows, which are interested in me, as a human interest story—only as long as I'm willing to be a helpless victim, but not if I'm fighting for my life.

If I'm dying from anything—I'm dying from the fact that not enough rich, white, heterosexual men have gotten AIDS for anybody to give a shit. You know, living with AIDS in this country is like living in the twilight zone. Living with AIDS is like living through a war which is happening only for those people who happen to be in the trenches. Every time a shell explodes, you look around and you discover that you've lost more of your friends, but nobody else notices. It isn't happening to them. They're walking the streets as though we weren't living through some sort of nightmare. And only you can hear the screams of the people who are dying and their cries for help. No one else seems to be noticing.

And it's worse than a war, because during a war people are united in a shared experience. This war has not united us, it's divided us. It's separated those of us with AIDS and those of us who fight for people with AIDS from the rest of the population.

Two and a half years ago, I picked up *Life Magazine*, and I read an editorial which said, "it's time to pay attention, because this disease is now beginning to strike the rest of us." It was as if I wasn't the one holding the magazine in my hand. And since then, nothing has changed to alter the perception that AIDS is not happening to the real people in this country.

It's not happening to us in the United States, it's happening to them—to the disposable populations of fags and junkies who deserve what they get. . . .

And the days, and the months, and the years pass by, and they don't spend those days and nights and months and years trying to figure out how to get hold of the latest experimental drug, and which dose to take it at, and in what combination with other drugs, and from what source? And, how are you going to pay for it? And where are you going to get it? Because it isn't happening to them, so they don't give a shit.

And they don't sit in television studios, surrounded by technicians who are wearing rubber gloves, who won't put a microphone on you, because it isn't happening to them, so they don't give a shit. And they don't have their houses burned down by bigots and morons. They watch it on the news and they have dinner and they go to bed, because it isn't happening to them, and they don't give a shit.

And they don't spend their waking hours going from hospital room to hospital room, and watching the people that they love die slowly—of neglect and bigotry, because it isn't happening to them and they don't have to give a shit. They haven't been to two funerals a week for the last three or four or five years—so they don't give a shit, because it's not happening to them.

And we read on the front page of the *New York Times* last Saturday that Anthony Fauci now says that all sorts of promising drugs for treatment haven't even been tested in the last two years because he can't afford to hire the people to test them. . . .

How many people are dead in the last two years, who might be alive today, if those drugs had been tested more quickly? . . .

And can somebody please tell me why every single penny allocated for education and prevention gets spent on ad campaigns that are directed almost exclusively to white, heterosexual teenagers—who they keep telling us are not at risk!

Can somebody tell me why the only television movie ever produced by a major network in this country, about the impact of this disease, is not about the impact of this disease on the man who has AIDS, but of the impact of AIDS on his white, straight, nuclear family? Why, for eight years, every newspaper and magazine in this country has done cover stories on AIDS only when the threat of heterosexual transmission is raised?

Why, for eight years, every single educational film designed for use in high schools has eliminated any gay-positive material, before being approved by the Board of Education? Why, for eight years, every single public information pamphlet and videotape distributed by establishment sources has ignored specific homosexual content?

Why is every bus and subway ad I read and every advertisement and every billboard I see in this country specifically not directed at gay men? . . .

If it is true that gay men and IV drug users are the populations at risk for this disease, then we have a right to demand that education and prevention be targeted specifically to these people. And it is not happening. We are being allowed to die, while low risk populations are being panicked—not educated, panicked—into believing that we deserve to die.

Why are we here together today? We're here because it is happening to us, and we do give a shit. And if there were more of us, AIDS wouldn't be what it is at this moment in history. It's more than just a disease, which ignorant people have turned into an excuse to exercise the bigotry they have always felt.

It is more than a horror story, exploited by the tabloids. AIDS is really a test of us, as a people. When future generations ask what we did in this crisis, we're going to have to tell them that we were out here today. And we have to leave the legacy to those generations of people who will come after us.

Someday, the AIDS crisis will be over. Remember that. And when that day comes—when that day has come and gone, there'll be people alive on this earth—gay people and straight people, men and women, black and white, who will hear the story that once there was a terrible disease in this country and all over the world, and that a brave group of people stood up and fought and, in some cases, gave their lives, so that other people might live and be free.

So, I'm proud to be with my friends today and the people I love, because I think you're all heroes, and I'm glad to be part of this fight. But, to borrow a phrase from Michael Callen's song: all we have is love right now, what we don't have is time.

In a lot of ways, AIDS activists are like those doctors out there—they're so busy putting out fires and taking care of people on respirators that they don't have the time to take care of all the sick people. We're so busy putting out fires right now that we don't have the time to talk to each other and strategize and plan for the next wave, and the next day, and next month and the next week and the next year.

And we're going to have to find the time to do that in the next few months. And we have to commit ourselves to doing that. And then, after we kick the shit out of this disease, we're all going to be alive to kick the shit out of this system, so that this never happens again.

Stop the Church (1989, 2009)

Michael Petrelis

On December 10, 1989, gay activist Michael Petrelis was at St. Patrick's Cathedral in Manhattan. But he was not there to take part in mass. His mission was to protest the Catholic Church's stances on homosexuality, AIDS, and abortion.

"We will not be silent," Petrelis shouted during mass. "We will fight O'Connor's bigotry." The 30-year-old activist was referring to St. Patrick's John Cardinal O'Connor, who, like the rest of the Roman Catholic hierarchy, had strongly condemned homosexual acts, condom use, and abortion.

At least several dozen protesters joined Petrelis in disrupting the day's celebration of mass. Some of the resisters chained themselves to the pews, and others held a die-in on the floor. About 4,500 other protesters gathered outside, holding signs, chanting, and handing out free condoms. Below is Petrelis's reflection on the 20th anniversary of the protest.

For many Catholics, and a good number of gays too, December 10, 1989, is a date that will live in infamy. That is when members of ACT UP, the AIDS Coalition to Unleash Power, and WHAM, Women's Health Action Mobilization, invaded the heart of a political organization with nonprofit, tax-exempt status—St. Patrick's Cathedral.

More than 5,000 members and supporters of ACT UP and WHAM were kept behind police barricades that day, unable to get into the church, while inside . . . 43 protesters were arrested and hauled out on stretchers, many refusing to comply with NYPD efforts to restore peace inside the cathedral. Overall number arrested inside and outside the cathedral was 111.

Twenty years ago, when velvet revolutions were spreading across Eastern Europe and massive numbers of people were standing up to tyranny and tearing down dictatorships, a rainbow revolution was happening in the gay community, and it was led by ACT UP.

I was a member of the group at the time, and remember the heated arguments that took place before it was decided to protest at the church. We were upset at the many ways in which the New York archdiocese was abusing its tax-exempt status and a religious bully pulpit to intrude upon good health policies. There also existed deep anger over Cardinal Joseph Ratzinger's disgusting Vatican decree from 1986, adding to centuries of Catholics wrecking homosexuals' lives, declaring gayness an "intrinsic moral evil."

The money and power of the Catholic church were directly hin-

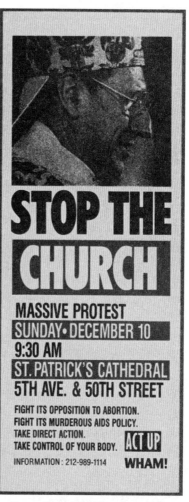

Poster for ACT-UP protest at St. Patrick's Cathedral, New York City, 1989.

dering unfettered access, and in some cases, the very existence of life-saving programs in public schools and municipal health clinics for gays, lesbians, bisexuals, transgenders, women, low-income people, and people of color.

The key culprit behind hateful attacks on wise public health matters at the local and state level was Archbishop John J. O'Connor. His long hand of homophobia reached into too many politicians' offices and how they voted on public service for gays and women. Cardinal O'Connor made no bones about imposing his religious doctrine on people of all faiths or atheists in public education and health care institutions, almost inviting a massive protest at his political base of operations.

As an ACT UP member who was arrested inside St. Patrick's Cathedral twenty years ago today, I remain unapologetic about the demonstrations and being a participant.

With the U.S. Conference of Catholic Bishops agitating against women's health and choice in health care matters now before Congress, many Catholic churches working against gay rights laws, the Vatican's renewed vigor of stigmatizing gay people everywhere, and more sexual abuse scandals involving priests unfolding in several countries, there are valid reasons why we must continue to just say no to the Catholic hierarchy's dangerous influence over public health and demand more accountability from church leaders.

WOMEN'S RIGHTS

Women's Fast for the ERA (1982, 1987)

Sonia Johnson

In the late 1970s Mormon Sonia Johnson of Sterling, Virginia, publicly criticized the Church of Jesus Christ of Latter-Day Saints for its refusal to support passage of the Equal Rights Amendment (ERA). Congress had passed the amendment in 1972, and it initially required ratification in thirty-eight states by the end of 1979. Not long after Johnson organized Mormons for ERA, the church excommunicated her for spreading false doctrine. The excommunication freed Johnson to fully immerse herself in the feminist movement, and she spent the following years on the lecture circuit and taking part in numerous protest movements for the ERA.

Facing defeat, Congress extended the deadline for ratification of the amendment to June 3, 1982. By May, thirty-five states had ratified it and four key battlefields remained: Oklahoma, North Carolina, Florida, and Illinois. Identifying Illinois as their target, Johnson and seven other women held a fast to pressure the Illinois House to vote for the ERA. The fast caught the attention of the national media and lasted for thirty-seven days, threatening the lives of several fasters, but on June 22 the House voted 103 to 72 against ratification. Below is a brief excerpt of Johnson's account of the feminist fast.

By the middle of 1981, the ERA had been in desperate trouble for a long time, and Mary Ann and I were talking seriously about a fast. Zoe Ananda, one of the fasters from California, later expressed to a reporter how we all felt. "I have stuffed one too many envelopes, licked one too many stamps. I have to do something of a deeper nature personally, make some kind of monumental statement."

Several of us had been talking for over a year about how we needed to do something to rivet the attention of the public every day, day after day, upon the ERA, something—like the hostages in Iran—that would make people ask, "What's happening today?" Maybe a fast could accomplish that.

But where were we to do it? Misogynist Virginia, where the ERA had never even gotten out of committee once in nine years? Florida, where Dempsey Barron almost singlehandedly held the amendment hostage?

One night, Maureen Fiedler, a Roman Catholic nun whom I knew from A Group of Women and who decided to join the fast at the last minute, called me and announced, "The place to do it is Illinois. Their rule requiring three-fifths of both houses to ratify a national amendment makes them perfect!" . . .

So Illinois it was. The Land of Lincoln. The only northern industrial state that had not ratified, and the one with the least democratic requirement for ratification. Perfect.

From the moment I realized that I was going to fast, I knew it would be wildly misunderstood—at least on a conscious level—by most people, whether they were for or against the ERA. It was being undertaken by women, after all, and everything women do partakes of our low status. All our acts are devalued simply because we do them; all our strengths are automatically turned into weaknesses. Also, on the surface, women's going without food would appear to be self-punishing and self-destructive, as if we were doing patriarchy's work for it by killing ourselves before they could get around to it, or by allowing their recalcitrance to kill us. In addition, fasting is extreme, and women are sedulously taught to be careful. I knew also that demonstrating so graphically that we were in total control of our lives would enrage practically everybody; it smashes so many icons all at once.

But most intolerably, a fast for women would be courageous. And though women have for centuries been programmed to be courageous in defense of men's happiness, to bear anything for men, we have been taught to look upon such courage on our own behalf as selfish, immature, and—especially—as ridiculous. . . .

At the time I was organizing it, asking dozens of women to participate and being refused by all but seven of them, I felt that eight fasters were pitifully few. Looking back, I am astonished that there were so many who had the courage to say yes. . . .

We were all scared. . . . Mary Barnes, Zoe, and Dina were smokers and caffeine addicts, so they were not only going to give up food, but coffee, diet soft drinks, and cigarettes at the same time. Fasting is hard enough all by itself without trying to become perfect overnight. We all wondered if we would be able to go through with it, we all worried about our health, and each of us confronted the fact that she might die. . . .

We were also worried about our spiritual health. We knew that to have the spiritual power that is possible from fasting we would need to love one another and in general "to purify our hearts." Though it wasn't at all clear how to go about doing this, we nevertheless set about it in earnest those first few days. We told our stories, what had brought each of us to this point; we meditated together; we discussed and tried to work out our differences; we listened to and encouraged one another.

We also talked deep into the night about our purpose in fasting. I confessed that though I obviously wanted ratification of the Equal Rights Amendment and hoped our fast would soften the adamantine heart of the Illinois legislature, I had an equally passionate covert goal. In a discussion we had one night . . . I called this goal "the beginning of the third phase of the women's movement." By this I meant that it was time for women to begin to be active rather than reactive. By fasting, we were defining our own parameters, we were playing our own game and were in total control of it, as we could never be with civil disobedience. We were coming from our place of power, meeting the power-over-others mentality with power-over-ourselves. In this, we met as equals.

In that discussion, what I said most clearly, however, was that it was time for women to begin to understand how worthy we are—how worthy of sacrifice, how worthy of risk. Understanding this is necessary to believing ourselves worthy of justice. Regardless of what we know intellectually, so long as we don't really feel we deserve more than the crumbs society now tosses us, we can't figure out how to get more. Fasting was a symbol that was intended to directly educate the heart, even if the brain denied its significance. It would tell the women in this country how important they are. It would say, there are eight women in Springfield who think your dignity and your human rights are worth giving their lives for. It seemed to me that women desperately needed to hear that. They couldn't possibly hear it too often or in too many ways.

I also wanted to provide women with a model of courage. I thought it was urgent that we begin to identify ourselves with courage, to expect it of ourselves and other women, and to see, in contrast, the bottomless cowardice of men we have trusted to speak for us.

Clarence Thomas, Sexual Harasser (1991)

Anita Hill

On June 8, 1991, seven U.S. Representatives—Barbara Boxer, Nita Lowey, Patsy Mink, Eleanor Holmes Norton, Pat Schroeder, Louise Slaughter, and Jolene Unsoeld—left the House Chambers and marched to the Senate. The idea came from Schroeder, who, like the other six Democratic women, was incensed that the Senate Judiciary Committee was refusing to allow Anita Hill, a professor of law at the University of Oklahoma, to publicly testify at the confirmation hearings for Supreme Court nominee Clarence Thomas. Hill had gone public with claims that Thomas had sexually harassed her numerous times when the two worked together.

Schroeder's plan called for interrupting the Senate Democratic Caucus lunch with the demand that the Judiciary Committee allow Hill to testify. "We all kind of fired ourselves up and went over," she later recalled. "It was a very spontaneous thing."

As they strode up the steps to the Senate, New York Times photographer Paul Hosefros captured the moment of resistance. (His photograph, fondly called "The Female Iwo Jima," now hangs in the offices of each of the surviving women.) The Representatives knocked on the door, expecting the Senators to politely receive them, but they were refused entry. They knocked again, and again they were denied.

As they stewed in the hallway, a Senate staffer arrived to inform them that Democratic leader George Mitchell would meet them in his office. In the meeting, Mitchell encouraged the women to return to the House and lobby the Senators who might be willing to grant Hill a hearing. The women's protest was well-publicized and quickly led to the Judiciary Committee delaying its vote and giving Hill an opportunity to testify. Below is an excerpt from her opening statement.

On October 16, 1991, the Senate voted 52-48 to confirm Thomas as an Associate Justice of the Supreme Court, but Anita Hill's testimony paved the way for an open discussion of workplace sexual harassment, and the need for regulations to address it.

In 1981, I was introduced to now Judge Thomas by a mutual friend. Judge Thomas told me that he was anticipating a political appointment, and he asked if I would be interested in working with him. He was, in fact, appointed as Assistant Secretary of Education for Civil Rights. After he had taken that post, he asked if I would become his assistant, and I accepted that position.

In my early period there, I had two major projects. The first was an article I wrote for Judge Thomas's signature on the education of minority students. The second was the organization of a seminar on high-risk students which was abandoned because Judge Thomas transferred to the EEOC where he became the chairman of that office.

During this period at the Department of Education, my working relationship with Judge Thomas was positive. I had a good deal of responsibility and independence. I thought he respected my work and that he trusted my judgment. After approximately three months of working there, he asked me to go out socially with him.

What happened next and telling the world about it are the two most difficult experiences of my life. It is only after a great deal of agonizing consideration and a great number of sleepless nights that I am able to talk of these unpleasant matters to anyone but my close friends.

I declined the invitation to go out socially with him and explained to him that I thought it would jeopardize what at the time I considered to be a very good working relationship. I had a normal social life with other men outside of the office. I believed then, as now, that having a social relationship with a person who was supervising my work would be ill-advised. I was very uncomfortable with the idea and told him so.

I thought that by saying no and explaining my reasons my employer would abandon his social suggestions. However, to my regret, in the following few weeks, he continued to ask me out on several occasions. He pressed me to justify my reasons for saying no to him. These incidents took place in his office or mine. They were in the form of private conversations which would not have been overheard by anyone else.

My working relationship became even more strained when Judge

Thomas began to use work situations to discuss sex. On these occasions, he would call me into his office for reports on education issues and projects, or he might suggest that, because of the time pressures of his schedule, we go to lunch to a government cafeteria. After a brief discussion of work, he would turn the conversation to a discussion of sexual matters.

His conversations were very vivid. He spoke about acts that he had seen in pornographic films involving such matters as women having sex with animals and films showing group sex or rape scenes. He talked about pornographic materials depicting individuals with large penises or large breasts involved in various sex acts. On several occasions, Thomas told me graphically of his own sexual prowess.

Because I was extremely uncomfortable talking about sex with him at all, and particularly in such a graphic way, I told him that I did not want to talk about these subjects. I would also try to change the subject to education matters or to nonsexual personal matters such as his background or his beliefs. My efforts to change the subject were rarely successful.

Throughout the period of these conversations, he also, from time to time, asked me for social engagements. My reaction to these conversations was to avoid them by eliminating opportunities for us to engage in extended conversations. This was difficult because at the time I was his only assistant at the Office of Education or Office for Civil Rights.

During the latter part of my time at the Department of Education, the social pressures and any conversation of his offensive behavior ended. I began both to believe and hope that our working relationship could be a proper, cordial, and professional one.

When Judge Thomas was made chair of the EEOC, I needed to face the question of whether to go with him. I was asked to do so, and I did. The work itself was interesting, and at that time it appeared that the sexual overtures which had so troubled me had ended. I also faced the realistic fact that I had no alternative job. While I might have gone back to private practice, perhaps in my old firm or at another, I was dedicated to civil rights work, and my first choice was to be in that field. Moreover, the Department of Education itself was a dubious venture. President Reagan was seeking to abolish the entire department.

For my first months at the EEOC, where I continued to be an assistant to Judge Thomas, there were no sexual conversations or overtures. However, during the fall and winter of 1982, these began again. The comments were random and ranged from pressing me about why I didn't go out with him to remarks about my personal appearance. I remember his saying that someday I would have to tell him the real reason that I wouldn't go out with him.

He began to show displeasure in his tone and voice and his demeanor and his continued pressure for an explanation. He commented on what I was wearing in terms of whether it made me more or less sexually attractive. The incidents occurred in his inner office at the EEOC.

One of the oddest episodes I remember was an occasion in which Thomas was drinking a Coke in his office. He got up from the table at which we were working, went over to his desk to get the Coke, looked at the can and asked, "Who has put pubic hair on my Coke?" On other occasions, he referred to the size of his own penis as being larger than normal, and he also spoke on some occasions of the pleasures he had given to women with oral sex.

At this point, late 1982, I began to feel severe stress on the job. I began to be concerned that Clarence Thomas might take out his anger with me by degrading me or not giving me important assignments. I also thought that he might find an excuse for dismissing me.

In January of 1983, I began looking for another job. I was handicapped because I feared that, if he found out, he might make it difficult for me to find other employment and I might be dismissed from the job I had. Another factor that made my search more difficult was that this was during a period of a hiring freeze in the government. In February 1983, I was hospitalized for five days on an emergency basis for acute stomach pain, which I attributed to stress on the job.

Once out of the hospital, I became more committed to find other employment and sought further to minimize my contact with Thomas. This became easier when Allison Duncan became office director, because most of my work was then funneled through her and I had contact with Clarence Thomas mostly in staff meetings.

In the spring of 1983, an opportunity to teach at Oral Roberts University opened up. I taught an afternoon session and seminar at Oral Roberts University. The dean of the university saw me teaching and inquired as to whether I would be interested in pursuing a career in teaching, beginning at Oral Roberts University. I agreed to take the job in large part because of my desire to escape the pressures I felt at the EEOC, due to Judge Thomas.

When I informed him that I was leaving in July, I recall that his response was that now I would no longer have an excuse for not going out with him. I told him that I still preferred not to do so. At some time after that meeting, he asked if he could take me to dinner at the end of the term. When I declined, he assured me that the dinner was a professional courtesy only and not a social invitation. I reluctantly agreed to accept that invitation, but only if it was at the very end of a working day.

On, as I recall, the last day of my employment at the EEOC in the summer of 1983, I did have dinner with Clarence Thomas. We went directly from work to a restaurant near the office. We talked about the work I had done, both at Education and at the EEOC. He told me that he was pleased with all of it except for an article and speech that I had done for him while we were at the Office for Civil Rights. Finally, he made a comment that I will vividly remember. He said that if I ever told anyone of his behavior that it would ruin his career. This was not an apology, nor was it an explanation. That was his last remark about the possibility of our going out or reference to his behavior.

March for Women's Lives (1992)

Sarah Schuster and Jewell Jackson McCabe

In 1992 Pennsylvania Governor Robert Casey, a strict Catholic who op-posed abortion, pushed for legislation that would restrict a woman's access to abortion by requiring a 24-hour waiting period and the notification of her husband if she was married. Women's rights advocates responded to this threat to the right to abortion, as well as others emerging in states across the country, by organizing a massive march and rally in Washington, DC.

About 700,000 protestors marched from the White House to the Mall, where they heard speeches given by, among others, Sarah Schuster, president of the American Association of University Women, and Jewell Jackson McCabe, chair of the Coalition of 100 Black Women. Their comments appear below.

In a 5-4 vote, the Supreme Court ruled against Governor Casey's efforts to restrict access to abortion.

Sarah Schuster

I am proud to be here today on behalf of more than 135,000 college graduate members of the American Association of University Women.

We come from every walk of life, from every heritage in the great American mosaic, and from all 50 states. And we come here with a message for the President, the Congress, and the media. And we're sending that message loud and clear:

We are mainstream Americans, and we're on the march for a mainstream American idea. We're marching for choice; for the simple but powerful idea that women have the inalienable right to make the most personal decisions of our lives—according to the dictates of our own consciences—without any interference from politicians, or judges, or bureaucrats, or bullhorn-wielding fanatics.

And yes, we do believe that women should have the right to consult with medical professionals—doctors, nurses, and counselors—when they make these decisions. And that includes women who visit federally funded family planning clinics.

The Bush Administration's infamous gag rule for the medical professionals at these clinics says they can counsel people on family planning, but they can't mention the dreaded word "abortion." It is the kind of policy that you'd expect from a police state like Romania, not in the good old USA.

Now, it's an election year, so Bush is giving us a kinder, gentler gag rule. If you're a doctor, you can mention abortion; if you're a nurse, you'd better bite your tongue; and if you're a counselor, you'd better check it out with Big Brother in Washington before you open your mouth.

Once again this Administration promotes first-class citizenship for a profession that's mostly male—and second class citizenship for a profession that's mostly female. We're here today to tell the President that we won't settle for anything less than first-class citizenship for the women who are the nurses, the women who are the counselors, and, most of all, for the women who are the patients.

You know, we in AAUW have been called "arch moderates." But we're here to tell the world that there's nothing moderate about our response to the assault on our reproductive rights by the government, the extremists, and the Supreme Court.

We in the pro-choice movement are the mainstream; we are mobilized; and we are mad as hell! Now is not the time to sit on the fence. Now is the time to march in the streets, to march into the offices of our Congress members and Senators, and to march to the polls on primary day and Election Day.

Now is the time to educate, agitate, and lobby as if our lives depended on it—because they do!

Tomorrow, AAUW members will be lobbying our Senators and Congress members to support the Freedom of Choice Act—right now in '92—before the Supreme Court takes away our freedom of choice. We urge you to join us.

We've got a simple message for the Senators and Congress members

Pro-choice march, New York City, 1992.

we're meeting: support the Freedom of Choice Act in '92, if you want to be back in Congress in '93! Because if you think there's an anti-incumbent mood now, wait 'til you see what happens if the House and Senate don't make freedom of choice the law of the land!

Vote with us now, or we'll vote you out in November, because we're going to elect a pro-choice president, and a pro-choice, veto-proof Congress. And to those Senators and Congressmen who still don't get it, we have this message: if your replacement is a pro-choice woman, then we'll be twice as happy to see you go!

For those of us in AAUW—and I'm sure, for most of you who've come here under other banners—this is not just a fight for our personal freedom. It's a fight for our mothers, many of whom didn't enjoy the full freedoms that should have been their birthright as Americans. And it's a fight for our daughters—because, if there's one issue that's of special importance to AAUW, it's making sure that our girls have every opportunity to fulfill their potential.

AAUW just released a major report on sex discrimination in education called "How Schools Shortchange Girls." We're dedicated to tearing down the sexist stereotypes, the discriminatory barriers, and the glass ceilings that hold back girls and women.

But how can we teach girls to liberate their minds if they can't control their bodies? How can we encourage girls to make choices about their education and careers if they can't make the most personal choice of all? How can we win the battle for equity in the schools and lose the war for women's most basic freedom?

When we look in the eyes of your girls—my daughter, who is here today, our granddaughters, our students and nieces and neighbors—we want every one of those girls to be able to go as far as her energy and intelligence and talent and ambition will take her.

That's our dream for every girl. That's a mainstream American dream. And we'll keep marching and lobbying and voting until we can look every American girl in the eye and tell her: the American dream is no lie; you are a first-class citizen; and yes, you can be anything you want to be.

And, until that day, we say, march with us, sister!

Jewell Jackson McCabe
You are a fabulous, fabulous sight to see!

Women, we must watch the Supreme Court, and we must understand that its recent decisions must be seen by all women, especially women of color, for just what they are—assaults on hard-fought freedoms, assaults on victories of principle, assaults on progressive action that has made America great. The Supreme Court is intent on eroding and destroying the civil rights of all of us.

As women, the right to make choices and to control our own lives is the essential issue of our humanity. For women of color, it is not simply a matter of abortion. It is a right to choose, choice being the very essence of our freedom. We need to make it loud and clear that the option in favor of abortion must be there to ensure the quality of life for ourselves and our families. To present this struggle for the right to choose as simply a desire for abortions is an evil and equally brilliant strategy of distortion.

I stand here today and challenge the movement to stand side by side with women of color in a struggle to achieve a broader and wiser reproductive rights agenda.

I challenge the movement to stand side by side with women of color as we demand our active and participatory role in the process of change.

I challenge the movement to stand side by side with women of color as we fight to achieve affordable and available prenatal care for all women; affordable, available childcare for all America's children; affordable, available health services, especially for mothers and children.

As women of color, we cannot afford to be naïve nor passive in the struggle. We must be part of the planning process as we develop strategies for empowerment. We must be informed coequals in the process.

We must watch, and watch, all sinister moves that once again use women of color and the most disenfranchised women of America as guinea pigs. We must watch the state of California as it so sinisterly elects to use Norplant as a punitive measure—Norplant—without knowledge of the long-term effects on a woman's body. We must watch state by state all punitive and coercive methods being used to control our communities. We must choose to control our own bodies and minds in order to control our lives.

And yes, we must work with a vengeance to get Carol Moseley Braun elected as the first African American woman to the United States Senate.

And as we work with that vengeance, we must be proud and continue to support Anita Hill for the historic opportunity she has given us.

We must collectively move forward. Do the deeds that must be done. Show our empowerment either through getting people elected or punishing those who don't.

Women and men of goodwill—Go forth, do good.

Women of color—*This* is our opportunity!

FIFTEEN

The Anti-Globalization Movement

NAFTA Is Economic Hemorrhage (1993)

Jesse Jackson

Reverend Jesse Jackson, Sr., a former member of Martin Luther King's inner circle and director of Operation Breadbasket, founded People United to Serve Humanity (PUSH) in 1971. As PUSH president, Jackson engineered numerous economic boycotts against major companies lacking racial diversity and frequently lobbied for federal policies that would establish economic justice for workers and the poor. Deeply involved in Democratic politics throughout the 1970s, Jackson also ran for the Democratic nomination for president in 1984 and 1988, seeking to align himself with labor unions and their members. In 1993 Jackson joined Ralph Nader in appearing before a U.S. House Committee and publicly criticizing President Bill Clinton for supporting the North American Free Trade Agreement (NAFTA). Before and after offering his testimony (below), Jackson appeared at anti-NAFTA demonstrations across the country.

I am amazed at President Clinton trying to ram down the throats of the American people the policies of the man that he defeated.

The Head of State in Canada, who was one of the architects of this plan, has been defeated, virtually 178 to 2. A co-architect, Mr. Bush, was defeated. And if the people in Mexico could vote and their vote counted, Mr. Salinas would be defeated as well.

The people of Canada, the United States, and Mexico have rejected this proposition. We, as a nation at our best, established several basic principles of foreign policy, international law, and self-determination, human rights, economic justice. Mexico falls short on all four planks.

I am a bit ashamed to see so many Democrats who we thought had changed their character but only changed their politics.

Some of the same Democrats who tolerated, over 1964 and 1965, the horrendous conditions in which blacks and Mexican-Americans lived, are now willing to shift that same toleration south of the Rio Grande. Those who tolerated racial oppression, gender inequality, worker exploitation, changed their behavior only when the law changed in this country. They were . . . often willing to wink at enforcement—and now shift south of the border to Mexico.

I want to make this clear to the foes and the supporters. I believe in the deliberative track with Mexico, not a fast track. A deliberative track will give us time to think it through and work it out. We share 2,000 miles of border with 90 million Mexican neighbors, our allies. Neither of us are going anywhere any time soon. We need a deliberative track, not a fast track, and to build a bridge between the United States and Mexico and not a cliff.

My interests are neither narrow and nationalistic, nor protectionist, nor racist. I want a mutually beneficial fair deal for Mexicans, Americans, and Canadians.

For the record, I believe in free trade and fair trade; but I further want to argue that I would support a United States-Canadian-Mexican common market, not a free trade zone. It does not take into account common market considerations.

If Mexican workers could make just $4.25 an hour, it would improve their conditions. Furthermore, it would enable them to buy what we produce. And, thus, it would be growth for them and expansion for us, a mutually beneficial arrangement.

I can see how most rightwing Republicans can wink their eye at Mexican conditions. They did so in South Carolina where I grew up, in Mississippi, Alabama, and Georgia. I can understand that orientation. But not for this new group of enlightened Democrats in 1993. It is a great source of disappointment as we debate this rather divisive, unnecessarily divisive issue.

There is a great deal of pain in our nation today, perhaps as much as I have ever witnessed. In my work, I travel a good deal and have the opportunity to talk with working people all across the country. They want . . . to have hope, to believe that the future holds promise for themselves and their children. They want a job that pays enough to feed them and their families.

They don't want workfare. They don't need welfare. They just want to work and to get paid. When they work, they want to know that their job will be there as long as they have a chance to be productive. They want to know that if their babies get sick, they can get medical care.

As we approach the 21st century as the wealthiest and the most powerful nation in the history of the world, these wants and needs are all too often not being met.

Among our brothers and sisters in the minority communities, the absence of a good job has become the norm. We have become socially conditioned to high urban unemployment. Sadly, too many of us have come to accept these conditions as a modern fact of life.

In 1992, however, the nation voted overwhelmingly for change. They voted to replace a president who was so far removed from the average American, he proclaimed the discovery of the bar code when he visited the supermarket during his campaign.

The theme of the campaign was "It is the economy, stupid," and the issue, was jobs, jobs, jobs. President Clinton campaigned on a putting-people-first platform and promised high-tech jobs, retraining programs, substantial investment in our nation's future, health care, improved labor relations, indeed, economic stimulus.

NAFTA is economic hemorrhage. Unfortunately, his $200 billion,

4-year investment plan was reduced to $16 billion and then shrunk to only a few hundred million by the deficit hogs.

[T]he wonderful job training program virtually disappeared from the budget. We face a crisis in our cities, plants closing, jobs leaving, tax base eroding, school systems traumatized . . . more police rather than more teachers, more jails rather than more schools, more mandatory sentencing and more ways to electrocute. We need to go another way.

Today there are 16 to 18 million people unemployed or underemployed. We include those who are involuntarily working part time, those who have given up looking.

Official black unemployment is 13 percent, with Hispanic unemployment at 11 percent. Among our young black people, unemployment is over 40 percent; Hispanic teenage unemployment, 30 percent; Native Americans, around 50 percent. These figures for unemployment are shocking.

What is even more shocking is when you look at life for many of those lucky enough to find jobs. . . . [A]ccording to the 1990 census, 14.4 million year-round, full-time workers, 18 percent of the total, earn below the poverty level of $14,000 per year.

So we can see that as we contemplate these numbers that we are failing to create jobs that can support a family. When plants close, manufacturing workers, all too often, are forced on to low-paying, no-benefit jobs in the service industry.

The fact is the workers that will be hurt by this deal—the textile workers, all 600,000 of them, the other workers, electronics workers—there is no promise these workers will get a job when their jobs leave. They are simply being left to be expended and run through. And it is not fair.

In this context, we must view the North American Free Trade Agreement—which I wish were a North American common market, long-term plan; before, we did Europe and Japan, the Marshall and MacArthur Plan—a long-term development plan that was mutually beneficial. It let them grow and let us expand.

Mexicans deserve no less of a development plan than Europeans and the Japanese had. There are two sets of rules on the development of Europe and Japan, over and against Mexico, which is next door.

Let us remember that this agreement was negotiated in secret by the Bush administration. Workers, environmentalists, farmers, and consumer advocates were not at the table; and yet workers, farmers, environmentalists, and consumer advocates are affected by this.

We never voted on this. Nor were our representatives at the table to even deliberate and put forth what was then called a fast-track, trickle-down theory.

It was conceived of as a source of enormous profits for Mr. Bush's friends in high places in multinational corporations: Profits up, wages down, workers busted.

Mr. Clinton understood this as a candidate, made this case, critiqued the shortcomings of Bush's NAFTA in his October 4, speech.

Unfortunately, Mr. Clinton's solutions—namely, the supplemental agreements—fall far short of dealing with the fundamental problem of NAFTA, which is that there cannot be a free trade agreement between nations with such huge disparities in their economies and their political systems.

We share 2,000 miles of border with Mexico. The biggest disparity between two neighbors in the world. And that is why we must end the cliff and create a bridge in that sense to develop them both.

Why do I make the case, Mr. Shays, for common market? It was a sound idea for you to talk about having a common market. But Spain, Greece, and Portugal are substantially below their living stands. If they just signed that deal, all the jobs would have gone rolling over into the poorer countries and the profits in the wealthier ones. They took the time to work out a social contract and build a relationship and reduce the hostilities.

Right now many Americans are screaming that Mexicans are taking our jobs, which is not true. And the more they say it, the more racist it sounds. Racist. Mexicans are not taking jobs from us.

United States corporations are taking jobs to Mexico to exploit them and undercut our own workers. Mexicans are not taking jobs from us.

The U.S. government is greasing the skids for the heavy investors, the high political rollers, to take the plants there. And when these large agribusinesses, ConAgra, Cargrill, are rolling over into Mexico, those Mexican farmers will be put out of business; and they will come dashing across the border to meet other depressed unemployed American family farmers.

Look at how this agreement will affect African Americans. In all these talk shows they have not quite made room to hear our point of view. That is why we tried to get on that debate last night, because we have a point of view different than Mr. Perot's point of view, a point of view different than Pat Buchanan's point of view.

And ours is not narrowly nationalistic. It is not building a wall. It is not racist. It is not protectionist. It is discussing a mutually beneficial arrangement. The hardest hit industries are expected to include the apparel, and automobile manufacturing, food processing, and electronic assembly. All employ large numbers of minorities and women.

Latino workers are more likely to have non-managerial jobs and working in inner cities and rural areas where job loss to Mexico aren't likely to be replaced.

NAFTA contains no language providing financial assistance, job training, or alternative employment for United States workers whose jobs are relocated to Mexico.

Experience clearly illustrates the greater difficulty of black and Latino workers at finding new jobs that pay them comparable wages where they have been displaced from manufacturing jobs. That will be true if this deal goes through.

Close Down the WTO (1999)

Russell Mokhiber and Robert Weissman

The city of Seattle, Washington was rocked by nonviolent and violent protests when it hosted a meeting of the World Trade Organization (WTO) from November 29 to December 3, 1999. About 20,000 demonstrators attended the largest protest rally, hosted by the AFL-CIO, and about 20,000 more participated in marches, sit-ins, die-ins, teach-ins, human chains, and other nonviolent direct actions that disrupted WTO meetings, city traffic, and businesses.

Protestors came from across the country, and their main complaints focused on WTO rulings that favored corporate interests over workers' rights, the environment, endangered species, and consumer health and welfare.

The great majority of demonstraters were nonviolent, but a group of anarchists smashed windows and set fires. In response, the city police fired tear gas, concussion grenades, and rubber bullets at both violent and nonviolent protestors. The mayor also called in the National Guard and set a curfew for the downtown area. By the end of the WTO meeting, more than 500 protestors had been arrested.

Writing for Mother Jones, Russell Mokhiber and Robert Weissman summarized the protesters' main grievances in the document below.

Add a new constituency to the long list of World Trade Organization (WTO) critics which already includes consumers, labor, environmentalists, human rights activists, fair-trade groups, AIDS activists, animal protection organizations, those concerned with Third World development, religious communities, and women's organizations. The latest set of critics includes WTO backers and even the WTO itself.

As the WTO faces crystallizing global opposition—to be manifested in massive street demonstrations and colorful protests in Seattle, where the WTO will hold its Third Ministerial meeting from Nov. 30 to Dec. 3—the global trade agency and its strongest proponents veer between a shrill defensiveness and the much more effective strategy of admitting shortcomings and trumpeting the need for reform.

WTO critics now face a perilous moment. They must not be distracted by illusory or cosmetic reform proposals, nor by even more substantive proposals for changing the WTO—should they ever emerge from the institution or its powerful rich member countries. Instead, they should unite around an uncompromising demand to dismantle the WTO.

Here are 10 reasons why:

1. The WTO prioritizes trade and commercial considerations over all other values. WTO rules generally require domestic laws, rules and regulations designed to further worker, consumer, environmental, health, safety, human rights, animal protection, or other noncommercial interests to be undertaken in the "least trade-restrictive" fashion possible—almost never is trade subordinated to these noncommercial concerns.

2. The WTO undermines democracy. Its rules drastically shrink the choices available to democratically controlled governments, with violations potentially punished with harsh penalties. The WTO actually touts this overriding of domestic decisions about how economies should be organized and corporations controlled. "Under WTO rules, once a commitment has been made to liberalize a sector of trade, it is difficult to reverse," the WTO says in a paper on the benefits of the organization which is published on its web site. "Quite often, governments use the WTO as a welcome external constraint on their policies: 'we can't do this because it would violate the WTO agreements.'"

3. The WTO does not just regulate, it actively promotes, global trade. Its rules are biased to facilitate global commerce at the expense of efforts to promote local economic development and policies that move communities, countries and regions in the direction of greater self-reliance.

4. The WTO hurts the Third World. WTO rules force Third World

Police fire pepper spray at protesters against the World Trade Organization, Seattle, 1999.

countries to open their markets to rich country multinationals, and abandon efforts to protect infant domestic industries. In agriculture, the opening to foreign imports, soon to be imposed on developing countries, will catalyze a massive social dislocation of many millions of rural people.

5. The WTO eviscerates the Precautionary Principle. WTO rules generally block countries from acting in response to potential risk—requiring a probability before governments can move to resolve harms to human health or the environment.

6. The WTO squashes diversity. WTO rules establish international health, environmental and other standards as a global ceiling through a process of "harmonization"; countries or even states and cities can only exceed them by overcoming high hurdles.

7. The WTO operates in secrecy. Its tribunals rule on the "legality" of nations' laws, but carry out their work behind closed doors.

8. The WTO limits governments' ability to use their purchasing

dollar for human rights, environmental, worker rights and other non-commercial purposes. In general, WTO rules state that governments can make purchases based only on quality and cost considerations.

9. The WTO disallows bans on imports of goods made with child labor. In general, WTO rules do not allow countries to treat products differently based on how they were produced—irrespective of whether made with brutalized child labor, with workers exposed to toxics or with no regard for species protection.

10. The WTO legitimizes life patents. WTO rules permit and in some cases require patents or similar exclusive protections for life forms. Some of these problems, such as the WTO's penchant for secrecy, could potentially be fixed, but the core problems—prioritization of commercial over other values, the constraints on democratic decision-making and the bias against local economies—cannot, for they are inherent in the WTO itself.

Because of these unfixable problems, the World Trade Organization should be shut down, sooner rather than later.

That doesn't mean interim steps shouldn't be taken. It does mean that beneficial reforms will focus not on adding new areas of competence to the WTO or enhancing its authority, even if the new areas appear desirable (such as labor rights or competition). Instead, the reforms to pursue are those that reduce or limit the WTO's power—for example, by denying it the authority to invalidate laws passed pursuant to international environmental agreements, limiting application of WTO agricultural rules in the Third World, or eliminating certain subject matters (such as essential medicines or life forms) from coverage under the WTO's intellectual property agreement.

These measures are necessary and desirable in their own right, and they would help generate momentum to close down the WTO.

Students Against Sweatshops (1999)

SOLE

In March 1999 thirty University of Michigan students, supplied with ba-
gels, peanut butter, and beef jerky, held a sit-in at the University president's
office to pressure the school not to sign what they considered to be a weak
code of conduct governing the manufacturing of apparel with the school's
name. The Michigan protest was part of a wider student movement to
force apparel companies to stop manufacturing their products in sweat-
shops—factories that typically paid their workers low wages, required long
workdays and workweeks, used child labor, had unsafe working condi-
tions, or violated other basic worker rights.

The code under protest, developed by the Collegiate Licensing Com-
pany in Atlanta, required apparel companies to follow standard practices
that would ensure their products were not manufactured under sweat-
shop conditions. If the company did not agree to meet the code's stan-
dards, they would be unable to sell to any universities that had adopted
the code. But Michigan students maintained that the code was not strict
enough because, among other things, it did not require manufacturers to
disclose the names and locations of their factories and pay their workers
livable wages.

Conducted by SOLE—Students Organizing for Labor and Economic
Equality—the Michigan sit-in lasted fifty-one hours. The protest enjoyed
widespread support from the student body, the student newspaper, and
eventually school administrators, and by the end of the protest President
Lee Bollinger agreed to create an anti-sweatshop advisory board with stu-
dent representatives (see the excerpted SOLE statement below).

In July 1999 the newly created advisory board informed manufactur-
ers that they had to release the names and locations of their factories that
produced University of Michigan apparel. Bowing to pressure from Michi-
gan and other schools—including the University of North Carolina (Chap-
el Hill), where daring students participated in a rally called "I'd Rather

Go Naked Than Wear Sweatshop Clothes"—Nike disclosed the names and locations of its factories in October 1999.

The No-Sweat 30's Statement Ending the Sit-In
After months of student pressure through educational events, rallies, and direct action such as the past *51 hours*—the University of Michigan has now committed itself to the strongest anti-sweatshop policy of any university and this is *only* because of the continued commitment of students.

It is because of the students the policy now includes an anti-sweatshop advisory board where students are equally represented. Students remain the only voice in this fight that is not tainted by corporate greed.

It is because of the students the policy now includes full disclosure, which means that companies can no longer hide their sweatshops from the rest of the world.

It is because of students the policy now includes full protection of women's rights, including full reproductive freedom. This is especially important because women comprise 90% of sweatshop labor worldwide.

It is because of the students the policy now includes a commitment to implementing a wage that will meet people's basic needs, which the university has until now failed to support.

Students of the University of Michigan are not in this fight alone. We are part of a national student movement that began with successful sit-ins at Duke, Georgetown, and Wisconsin. This movement is now exploding across the country as students demand that their administrations take decisive action on this issue.

But the fight is not over. Sweatshops will not end with this policy. While we have won everything we could through this sit-in, there is still much work to do. At this time the administration refuses to accept a timeline for requiring a wage that meets people's basic needs.

How much longer do these people have to wait?

We are here to tell the university that justice delayed is justice denied.

Defund the Fund! Break the Bank! Dump the Debt! (2000)

Mobilization for Global Justice

After the Seattle WTO protests in 1999, the anti-globalization movement in the United States turned its attention to the April 2000 meetings of the World Bank and the International Monetary Fund (IMF) in Washington, DC. Aiming to disrupt the World Bank and IMF meetings, the movement leaders created the Mobilization for Global Justice (MGJ) and developed plans for almost a week of activities that included training in nonviolence, teach-ins, nonviolent demonstrations, and lobbying.

The MGJ coalition asked about 500 groups to endorse the Mobilization's protest statement and call (below). The groups were diverse in their interests, but they tended to agree that unregulated World Bank and IMF policies saddled poor countries with debt, destroyed the environment, and favored multinational corporations over indigenous populations.

The week of protests began on April 9 with a peaceful march and rally for debt forgiveness. But the culmination occurred a week later. On the morning of April 16, fire marshals showed up at MGJ headquarters, declared it a fire hazard, and with the help of city police, ordered the eviction of hundreds of protestors.

Although the raid delivered a severe blow, protests went ahead as scheduled and thousands of resisters marched through city streets. As they moved toward the bank, city and federal police officers in riot gear hustled them from street to street and used metal barriers to keep them blocks from the bank. By the end of the day, the police had arrested about 600 protestors, charging them with parading without a permit or obstructing traffic.

On April 17 thousands of protestors showed up again to disrupt the WB and IMF meetings, and once again the massive police force used barriers to establish a perimeter that prevented the protestors from getting close to the meetings. As officers stood shoulder to shoulder behind the barriers, protestors blocked traffic at nearby intersections and marched where they could, chanting and carrying signs calling for the end of the World Bank and the IMF. When a few skirmishes broke out, officers used tear gas and clubs against the protestors. The nonviolent demonstrations failed to get close again the following day, when police officers created a twenty-block perimeter.

More than 1000 demonstrators were arrested by the end of the Mobilization, and although the protests did not succeed in shutting down the meetings, they heightened the nation's awareness of the World Bank, the International Monetary Fund, globalization, and its problems. In addition, the Mobilization pushed ahead the anti-globalization movement and fueled future campaigns about social, economic, and political problems in developing countries.

We need your support for the continuing struggle for economic justice. Endorse the Mobilization for Global Justice and join us in our protest against IMF and World Bank policies.

Building on the Energy from Seattle
The movement for global economic justice in the US, which has been building for years, had its coming-out party in Seattle at the World Trade Organization (WTO) ministerial meetings. Our next big opportunity to demand a peaceful, people-centered, and environmentally sound global economic system will be in April 2000 in Washington, DC.

The nation's capital is the home of the International Monetary Fund (IMF) and World Bank Group, whose backing by the wealthy governments of the North has made them the rule-makers for the global economy. The IMF and World Bank, more than any other institutions, are the coercive powers which have created a global economy based on corporate profit derived from exploitation of artificially cheap labor and raw materials. The conditions they created were the foundation for the birth of the WTO. Their semi-annual meetings will be the occasion for a demonstration of our rejection of their rules and their system for imposing them. . . .

We will be demonstrating that activists in the U.S. know about the

Mobilization for Global Justice march against World Bank,
Washington, D.C., 2006.

negative impact of World Bank and IMF programs and stand in solidarity with the people of the global South. We will be demanding an end to the devastation they cause in Africa, Asia, the Caribbean, Latin America, and the countries of Eastern Europe and the former Soviet Union. We will also be exposing the links between the IMF, the World Bank Group, the WTO, and multinational companies and how they work to maximize profits and limit the power of people in both the North and South to protect the environment, determine their economic destiny, and safeguard their human rights.

Endorsement
On the occasion of the first meetings of the governing bodies of the International Monetary Fund and the World Bank in the 21st century, we

call for the immediate suspension of the policies and practices that have caused widespread poverty and suffering among the world's peoples and damage to the world's environment. We assert the responsibility of these institutions, together with the World Trade Organization, for an unjust world economic system.

We issue this call in the name of global justice, in solidarity with the peoples of the Global South struggling for survival and dignity in the face of unjust, imperialistic economic policies. Only when the coercive powers of the international financial institutions are rescinded shall governments be accountable first and foremost to the will of their peoples for equitable economic development. Only when international institutions are no longer controlled by the wealthiest governments for the purpose of dictating policy to the poorer ones shall all peoples and nations be able to forge bonds—economic and otherwise—based on mutual respect and the common needs of the planet and its inhabitants. Only when the well-being of all, including the most vulnerable people and economic systems, is given priority over corporate profits shall we achieve genuine sustainable development and create a world of justice, equality, and peace.

SIXTEEN

The War on Terror

Isn't This Really About Oil? (2002, 2016)

Medea Benjamin

After the Al Qaeda attack on the U.S. of September 11, 2001, President George W. Bush and his administration ramped up efforts to depose Saddam Hussein in Iraq. In its public case against Hussein, the Bush administration claimed he had weapons of mass destruction that posed a clear and present danger to the United States and to stability in the Middle East. On September 19, 2002, Secretary of Defense Donald Rumsfeld testified before Congress that Hussein's offer to allow weapons inspectors to return to Iraq would deter the administration from acting with the speed required to keep the U.S. and the world safe from Iraq's weapons. The secretary added that allies in other countries had promised to assist the United States should it attack Iraq.

Rumsfeld's comments did not go unchallenged. Seated in the gallery were Medea Benjamin, then of Global Exchange, an international human rights organization, and her colleague Diane Wilson, a longtime environmental activist. In the document below, Benjamin recounts her and Wilson's protest at the hearing. Police officers forcibly removed Benjamin and Wilson from the hearing room, and though the officers questioned them about their identities and actions, no arrests were made.

In her comments below, Benjamin recounts that day, and other protests carried out by a group she helped to cofound CODEPINK, which describes itself as a "women-led grassroots organization working to end U.S. wars and militarism, support peace and human rights initiatives, and redirect our tax dollars into healthcare, education, green jobs and other life-affirming programs." One of the organization's earliest protests was an antiwar vigil held in front of the White House from November 17, 2002 to March 8, 2003, International Women's Day, when about 10,000 people, most of them women, held an antiwar rally near the White House.

It was September 18, 2002, the day Secretary of Defense Donald Rumsfeld testified before the House Armed Services Committee about why the U.S. military should invade Iraq. He accused Saddam Hussein of having and hiding weapons of mass destruction, raised the specter of an Iraqi-initiated September 11-style attack, and told the Committee that Iraq under Saddam Hussein was a global threat.

My colleague Diane Wilson and I were in the audience, just behind Rumsfeld and a row of generals. It was the first time we had ever attended a congressional hearing. Shaking, I got up and belted out: "Mr. Rumsfeld, we need weapons inspections, not war. Why are you obstructing the inspections? Isn't this really about oil? How many civilians will be killed? How many Iraqis will be killed?" We unfurled banners that said: "UN Weapons Inspection, Not U.S. War" and repeated that chant over and over until the police came to forcibly remove us.

Once we were out of the room, Rumsfeld joked about us and said: "Of course, the country that threw the inspectors out was not the United States. It was not the United Nations. It was Iraq that threw the inspectors out."

That was a lie. Iraq did not expel the inspectors. In December 1998, the weapons inspectors withdrew for their safety in anticipation of a US-British bombing campaign. But this was just one of so many lies about Saddam Hussein's supposed weapons of mass destruction and his unwillingness to yield to weapons inspections.

In February 2003, just weeks before the U.S. invasion, CODEPINK led a delegation to Iraq. We wanted to see for ourselves what the Iraqis were thinking, particularly the women. We found them terrified at the prospect of a U.S. invasion. Some said to us, in hushed voices, "Yes, Saddam is a dictator, but we don't want the U.S. military to liberate us. That is something we must do ourselves."

We also wanted to meet with the UN weapons inspectors, and we did. They told us there were no weapons of mass destruction and that even if there were, the very presence of so many inspectors in the country guaranteed that they would not be used.

Two weeks after we returned, on March 7, the International Atomic Energy Agency (IAEA) reported to the UN Security Council. Based on more than a hundred visits to suspect sites and private interviews with a number of individual scientists known to have been involved with WMD programs in the past, IAEA leader ElBaradei stated that the IAEA had "to date found no evidence or plausible indication of the revival of a nuclear weapons program in Iraq."

Hans Blix of the UN Special Commission on Iraq (UNMOVIC) said no stockpiles or active programs had been found, but it had not yet been possible to document destruction of all the weapons known to have been produced prior to the 1991 Gulf War. Blitz predicted that months but not years would be needed to complete the job.

The Bush administration dismissed the inspectors' findings because their conclusions contradicted the U.S. government allegations. The next day, President George W. Bush delivered a radio address to the American people, arguing that the inspection teams did not need any more time, because Saddam was "still refusing to disarm." The rest is history.

Iraq posed absolutely no threat to the United States. But the U.S. people, traumatized by the 9/11 attack, were easily duped by the Bush administration's propaganda that Iraq was a terrorist state linked to al-Qaeda, and that it was only minutes away from launching attacks on America with weapons of mass destruction.

Americans were the victims of an elaborate public relations campaign, barraged every day with distortions, deceptions, and lies. By the start of the war in March 2003, 66% of Americans mistakenly thought Saddam Hussein was behind the 9/11 attacks and 79% thought he was close to having a nuclear weapon. Of course, Saddam Hussein had nothing to do with the 9/11 attacks, and had no nuclear weapons and no functional chemical or biological weapons. This massive deception was only achieved with the complicity of the U.S. mainstream press, a press that refused to air the voices of dissenters like us and instead sought to commercialize the Iraq war, embed with the military, and profit from the invasion.

At CODEPINK, we worked furiously to stop the invasion and continued to protest the war after it started. We held a daily vigil in front of the White House in the freezing cold for four months, we went on a month-long hunger strike, we organized massive demonstrations, we protested at the homes of VP Dick Cheney and Secretary of Defense Donald Rumsfeld, as well as the offices and homes of Democratic and Republican congresspeople. We interrupted dozens of congressional hearings to speak out against the war. Over and over again, we were arrested for acts of nonviolent civil disobedience, spending much time in cold, bleak jail cells.

For our work speaking truth to power and confronting an illegal, immoral war, we were attacked viciously for being "unpatriotic" and treated like traitors.

Calling All Americans to Resist War and Repression (2002)

Not in Our Name

After 9/11, as the Bush administration directed a push for the bombing of Afghanistan and began to make a case for war against Iraq, Not in Our

Name (NION) became a prominent voice in the growing antiwar movement. The organization produced the document below and circulated it on the Internet and in advertising space in the nation's major newspapers. With a list of prominent signatories, the "Statement of Conscience" appeared in a full-page advertisement in the New York Times on September 19, 2002. The statement eventually collected more than 65,000 signatures.

Let it not be said that people in the United States did nothing when their government declared a war without limit and instituted stark new measures of repression.

The signers of this statement call on the people of the U.S. to resist the policies and overall political direction that have emerged since September 11, 2001, and which pose grave dangers to the people of the world.

We believe that peoples and nations have the right to determine their own destiny, free from military coercion by great powers. We believe that all persons detained or prosecuted by the United States government should have the same rights of due process. We believe that questioning, criticism, and dissent must be valued and protected. We understand that such rights and values are always contested and must be fought for.

We believe that people of conscience must take responsibility for what their own governments do—we must first of all oppose the injustice that is done in our own name. Thus we call on all Americans to RESIST the war and repression that has been loosed on the world by the Bush administration. It is unjust, immoral, and illegitimate. We choose to make common cause with the people of the world.

We too watched with shock the horrific events of September 11, 2001. We too mourned the thousands of innocent dead and shook our heads at the terrible scenes of carnage—even as we recalled similar scenes in Baghdad, Panama City, and, a generation ago, Vietnam. We too joined the anguished questioning of millions of Americans who asked why such a thing could happen.

But the mourning had barely begun when the highest leaders of the land unleashed a spirit of revenge. They put out a simplistic script of "good vs. evil" that was taken up by a pliant and intimidated media. They told us that asking why these terrible events had happened verged on treason. There was to be no debate. There were by definition no valid political or moral questions. The only possible answer was to be war abroad and repression at home.

In our name, the Bush administration, with near unanimity from Congress, not only attacked Afghanistan but arrogated to itself and its allies the right to rain down military force anywhere and anytime. The brutal repercussions have been felt from the Philippines to Palestine, where Israeli tanks and bulldozers have left a terrible trail of death and destruction. The government now openly prepares to wage all-out war on Iraq—a country which has no connection to the horror of September 11. What kind of world will this become if the U.S. government has a blank check to drop commandos, assassins, and bombs wherever it wants?

In our name, within the US, the government has created two classes of people: those to whom the basic rights of the U.S. legal system are at least promised, and those who now seem to have no rights at all. The government rounded up over 1,000 immigrants and detained them in secret and indefinitely. Hundreds have been deported and hundreds of others still languish today in prison. This smacks of the infamous concentration camps for Japanese-Americans in World War 2. For the first time in decades, immigration procedures single out certain nationalities for unequal treatment.

In our name, the government has brought down a pall of repression over society. The President's spokesperson warns people to "watch what they say." Dissident artists, intellectuals, and professors find their views distorted, attacked, and suppressed. The so-called Patriot Act—along with a host of similar measures on the state level—gives police sweeping new powers of search and seizure, supervised if at all by secret proceedings before secret courts.

Marchers protest war against Iraq, Washington, D.C., 2007.

In our name, the executive has steadily usurped the roles and functions of the other branches of government. Military tribunals with lax rules of evidence and no right to appeal to the regular courts are put in place by executive order. Groups are declared "terrorist" at the stroke of a presidential pen.

We must take the highest officers of the land seriously when they talk of a war that will last a generation and when they speak of a new domestic order. We are confronting a new openly imperial policy towards the world and a domestic policy that manufactures and manipulates fear to curtail rights.

There is a deadly trajectory to the events of the past months that must be seen for what it is and resisted. Too many times in history people have waited until it was too late to resist.

President Bush has declared: "you're either with us or against us."

Here is our answer: We refuse to allow you to speak for all the American people. We will not give up our right to question. We will not hand over our consciences in return for a hollow promise of safety. We say NOT IN OUR NAME. We refuse to be party to these wars and we repudiate any inference that they are being waged in our name or for our welfare. We extend a hand to those around the world suffering from these policies; we will show our solidarity in word and deed.

We who sign this statement call on all Americans to join together to rise to this challenge. We applaud and support the questioning and protest now going on, even as we recognize the need for much, much more to actually stop this juggernaut. We draw inspiration from the Israeli reservists who, at great personal risk, declare "there IS a limit" and refuse to serve in the occupation of the West Bank and Gaza.

We also draw on the many examples of resistance and conscience from the past of the United States: from those who fought slavery with rebellions and the underground railroad, to those who defied the Vietnam war by refusing orders, resisting the draft, and standing in solidarity with resisters.

Let us not allow the watching world today to despair of our silence and our failure to act. Instead, let the world hear our pledge: we will resist the machinery of war and repression and rally others to do everything possible to stop it.

Bring Our Troops Home (2005)

Cindy Sheehan

On April 4, 2004, twenty-four-year-old Army specialist Casey Sheehan was killed in a battle in Baghdad, and two months later President George W. Bush met with Sheehan's family at Fort Lewis in Washington State. In recalling the event, Casey's mother Cindy Sheehan said that the president did not know her son's name, that he disrespectfully called her "Mom," and that he acted as if he were attending a party. Sheehan was hurt and angry—at the president, the war, and the loss of so many innocent lives—and she subsequently joined the antiwar movement and founded an organization called Gold Star Families for Peace. And that was not all.

In early August 2005 Sheehan got in her car and drove to President Bush's 1,600-acre ranch in Crawford, Texas, with plans to meet him and demand that he withdraw U.S. troops from Iraq. When police stopped her a few miles away from the ranch, Sheehan got out of her car and said she would camp there until the president agreed to meet her. Other war protestors joined her.

Conscious of negative publicity and declining support for the war, the Bush team sent National Security adviser Stephen Hadley and deputy White House chief of staff Joe Hagin to meet with Sheehan, but she would not back down from her demand for a one-on-one session with the president. A local farmer offered Sheehan and her friends a pasture for their encampment, and Sheehan remained at "Camp Casey" throughout August, attracting about 10,000 visitors.

Sheehan left Crawford on August 31, ending a twenty-six-day-long antiwar protest that received national and international attention. President Bush ignored her the entire time, but Sheehan was unfazed. "We're going to keep on questioning him, and we're going to keep on until our troops are brought home because there's no noble cause," she said. "And that's why George Bush couldn't come out and talk to me, because he doesn't have a noble cause." Sheehan then boarded a bus for a twenty-five state tour that ended with a September 24 antiwar march in Washington, DC. Below are her comments at the march.

Ahhhh, I love the smell of patriotic dissent in the afternoon!

As we stand here on the grounds of a monument that is dedicated to the father of our country, George Washington, we are reminded that he was well known for the apocryphal stories of never being able to tell a lie. I find it so ironic that there is another man here named George, who stays in this town between vacations, and he seems to never be able to tell the truth. It is tragic for us that our bookend presidents named George have two completely different relationships with honesty.

I also find it ironic and heartbreaking that my son, Casey, who was a brave person, tall and proud, who loved his country and was honest beyond measure, could be sent to his death by someone who is even too cowardly to meet with a brokenhearted mom, let alone go and fight in the illegal and immoral war of his generation. We are losing our best and our brightest in a country that we are destroying, that was no threat to the United States of America. Iraq was and still is no danger to our safety and security, or to our way of life. The weapons of mass destruction and mass deception reside in this town: they are the neocons who pull the strings and the members of Congress who have loosened the purse strings with reckless abandon and have practically given George and company a blank check to run our country into monetary and moral bankruptcy. We are out here in force today to take our country back and restore true democracy and sanity to our political process. The time is now, and we are here because we love our country, and we won't let the reckless maniacs destroy her any further.

We, as a young colony of Great Britain, broke from another tyrant, King George the Third. Well, I wish our George the Third were here today to see us out here in force protesting against his war and against his murderous policies. George is not here, though, because he is out gallivanting around the country somewhere, pretending that he cares about the people who are in the path of hurricane Rita. We know that he cares nothing for the people of America: Katrina, Iraq, and his idiotic response to 9/11 are evidence of that. He is just out and about play-acting like a president whose country is in crisis, just like he pretends to be a commander in chief and a cowboy (I wonder if before he took off to Texas or Colorado or wherever he went, he watched a movie like *Independence Day* to see how that other fake president acted?). The reason he is out today is that his handlers told him that he got a little flak for playing golf and eating birthday cake with Senator McCain while some

Cindy Sheehan sits in front of Daniel Ellsberg speaking at protest calling for withdrawal of U.S. troops from the war against Iraq, Washington, D.C., 2006.

of his employers were hanging off rooftops and treetops in New Orleans. He swaggers around arrogantly like he is a macho dictatorial tyrant who doesn't have to answer to his employers, the people of the United States of America. Those days are over, George. We are here today to tell you that we are a majority and we will never rest until you bring our young people home from the Middle East, and until you start putting money into rebuilding *our* communities: the ones natural disasters destroy with your help, and the ones which your callous and racist war economy are decimating. We won't allow you to take any more money out of social programs to finance Halliburton to rebuild the Gulf States: there is no money. Our bank account is empty. George, this is our rainy day and you have failed us miserably. Stop pouring money into the pockets of the war profiteers and into building permanent bases in Iraq. . . . It is time to bring our billions of dollars home from Iraq too!!!

One thing the Camp Casey movement that hunkered down in Crawford, Texas, this past August taught us is that we the people of America have the power and we can and should name our national policy and make sure it is carried out. I constantly get asked if we are making a difference and if we think (like we're naive boobs) that we will actually stop the war. Well, looking back at how Vietnam was ended and looking back in the history of our country, most notably in the suffragette, union, and civil rights movements, we the people are the only ones who have been able to transform history and affect true and lasting change here in America. So to those people who question if we are making a difference: I tell them to go back to school and read their history books!! And another thing these questioners overlook is that *we are making a difference!!!* And we are here to tell the media, Congress, and this criminal and criminally negligent administration: *We are not going away!!!*

We in the peace movement need to agree on one thing: yes, we need an exit plan, but it is not a strategy, it is a command. The command should be: have all of our military personnel and paid killer mercenaries out of Iraq within 6 months, and the generals carry out the command. Simple, it's not brain surgery, and I think it is so easy even George Bush can sign the order. We can't give the homicidal maniacs any wiggle room or long-term strategy sessions. For one thing, when our leaders strategize, we are put in even more jeopardy—they have proven that they are not too bright or even a little compassionate. But the most important thing is that people die every day in Iraq for absolutely no reason and for lies. We have to say *now* because the people on the other side are saying *never.* We can't compromise, we can't say please, and we can't retreat. If we do, our country is doomed. We have to honor the sacrifices of our loved ones by completing the mission of peace and justice. It is time. Bring our troops home, *now! (2005)*

Eleven Reasons to Close Guantánamo (2015)

Naureen Shah

In 2002 the United States government began to use their migrant deten-
tion facilities at the Guantánamo Bay Naval Base in Cuba to hold de-
tainees from Afghanistan, Pakistan, Iraq, and other areas in the War on
Terror. The government held the detainees—more than 680 by the summer
of 2003—without granting them basic legal rights. In many cases U.S. sol-
diers and CIA operatives humiliated and tortured detainees, allegedly to
extract information to help the United States win the war.

National and international human rights groups galvanized protest
against the government's treatment of the detainees, and liberal politi-
cians joined in the outcry. On January 22, 2009, President Barack Obama
signed an executive order to close the detention facility within one year.
But in 2015, when Naureen Shah, director of Amnesty International USA's
Security and Human Rights Program, wrote the piece below, Guantánamo
was still open. Amnesty International USA served as one of the sponsors
for a January 11, 2015, protest at the White House. Titled "A Promise Still
to Keep: Close Guantánamo, Stop Torture, and End Indefinite Detention,"
the nonviolent protest featured torture survivors and family members of
September 11 victims.

This Sunday, January 11, marks the grim 13th anniversary of the opening of the prison at Guantánamo Bay. With the momentum President
Obama has now, he must make this anniversary Guantánamo's last. Here
are 11 reasons why closing the prison now is a human rights imperative.

1. *They don't know when—if ever—they will be free.*
Imagine if you were in prison. Now imagine you had no idea when, if
ever, you would be charged with a crime or released. For more than *100*
men at Guantánamo, indefinite detention is a cruel reality. They face the
prospect of remaining in limbo—their lives on hold—forever.

2. *We have momentum.*
Six years ago, President Obama ordered Guantánamo closed within a year. In the face of his failure, we have kept up the pressure through protests around the globe. *And we are beginning to see long overdue progress.* In the last year and a half, the government has transferred 39 detainees out of Guantánamo. Compare that to just 4 cleared detainees being transferred between July 2011 and July 2013.

3. *Too many men are in limbo.*
But President Obama must do far more. *More than one hundred detainees still remain in indefinite detention without charge or trial.* Every detainee must either be fairly tried or released.

4. *A history of torture and other inhuman treatment.*
Shackled, hooded and blindfolded, detainees began arriving at Guantánamo in 2002. The place was treated as a "battle lab" for experimental, unproven interrogation techniques, according to a Senate report. Since then, it has been the site of abuses including widespread and prolonged solitary confinement.

Compounding the injustice, at least 28 of those still held at Guantánamo were secretly detained at other U.S. sites, before being sent to Guantánamo. "[T]hey gave me a 'Goodbye Party' at Kandahar and a far worse 'Welcome Party' at Guantánamo," said Shaker Aamer, who was first detained in Afghanistan in 2002 and still languishes at Guantánamo after nearly 13 years—despite being cleared for transfer by the Obama and Bush administrations.

5. *A history of despair: "Death is more desirable than living."*
In 2012, Adnah Latif died at Guantánamo, after being held for more than 10 years without charge—despite a judge's order that he be released. His circumstances, he said, "made death more desirable than living." Latif protested his treatment with a hunger strike and poetry, writing:

> *Where is the world to save us*
> *from torture?*

Where is the world to save us
from the fire and sadness?
Where is the world to save
the hunger strikers?

Nine men have died at Guantánamo since detainee operations began there in January 2002. According to the U.S. military authorities, six of the previous eight deaths were the result of suicide and two from natural causes.

6. Intolerable doublespeak—and the double standard.

With Orwellian overtones, Guantánamo's official slogan is "Honor Bound to Defend Freedom." But the doublespeak goes much further. Every year that Guantánamo has been open, the U.S. has continued to proclaim its commitment to international human rights standards. If an abusive regime was responsible for a place of injustice like Guantánamo, it would surely draw U.S. condemnation. It's long past time for the U.S. authorities to end the doublespeak—and the double standard.

7. We must disrupt the politics of fear.

Members of Congress and pundits have treated Guantánamo like a political football, using it to sustain the politics of fear and ignoring the reality of human beings languishing in detention. That has made the likelihood of human rights obligations being recognized and fully respected by the U.S. even more remote, and fed the possibility that a future president might decide to keep the facility in operation indefinitely.

8. We reject "global war."

To justify the unlawful detentions at Guantánamo, the USA has invoked a vision of "global war" against al-Qa'ida and other armed groups. The Guantánamo detainees held on "law of war" grounds have included people taken into custody far from any battleground as traditionally understood, and not in the territory of a state at war with the United States, including places like Azerbaijan and Thailand. The "global war" theory denies human rights, including the requirement that the U.S. either release or fairly try in federal court every detainee.

9. *Guantánamo is a part of a web of abuse.*
The U.S. is "at a crossroads," President Obama said on May 23, 2013, requiring it to "define the nature and scope of this struggle, or else it will define us." Yes, this "global war" has done just that. Guantánamo, unlawful drone attacks, mass surveillance—they are all part of a web of abuse. Sustained by secrecy and impunity for abuse, this web persists.

10. *The U.S. is damaging human rights globally.*
Why, as we near day 4,749 in the life of this notorious prison camp, is Amnesty International still talking about Guantánamo? As we said on its 10th anniversary, Guantánamo is "a symbol that emboldens predatory states around the world to ignore fundamental human rights . . . and every single one of us is a little less secure as long as Guantánamo remains open."

11. *The debate over Guantánamo and torture is alive and well.*
In his memoir *Decision Points*, President Bush recalled that by his second inauguration in January 2005 he had come to appreciate that Guantánamo had become "a propaganda tool for our enemies, and a distraction for our allies." Yet since President Obama entered office—and especially since last month's release of the summary of the Senate torture report—defenders of abuse have gone on the offensive. In his 2014 memoir, former vice president Dick Cheney wrote: "It's not Guantánamo that does the harm, it is the critics of the facility." Adding he is "happy to note that for President Obama the 'imperative' of closing Guantánamo has evolved into the necessity of keeping it open."

President Obama's delay in closing Guantánamo has provided fodder to those who would revisit the worst detention practices of the "War on Terror." It may even give future administrations an excuse not only to keep Guantánamo open, but to commit other abuses out of alleged "necessity."

Shut Down Creech (2016)

Anti-Drone Activists

Medea Benjamin, the cofounder of CODEPINK, employed the nonviolent practice of heckling when President Obama delivered his first major counterterrorism speech in May 2013. Benjamin repeatedly interrupted the president to demand that he immediately close Guantánamo Bay prison and end drone warfare.

"Can you take the drones out of the hands of the CIA?" Benjamin pleaded. "Can you stop the signature strikes that are killing people on the basis of suspicious activities?"

Obama stopped his speech. "We're addressing that, ma'am," he said.

But Benjamin was unsatisfied. "Will you apologize to the thousands of Muslims that you have killed?" she continued. "Will you compensate the innocent family victims? That will make us safer here at home. I love my country. I love the rule of law. Drones are making us less safe. And keeping people in indefinite detention in Guantánamo is making us less safe. Abide by the rule of law. You're a constitutional lawyer." Benjamin was quieted only when security officials forcibly removed her.

Benjamin played a leading role in focusing CODEPINK and other activists on drone warfare during the Obama administration The majority of the U.S. public approved of Obama's use of drones, but a core of activists carried out nonviolent direct actions throughout his tenure to demonstrate their opposition. In 2016 CODEPINK joined Nevada Desert Experience, Voices for Creative Nonviolence, Veterans for Peace, and others in a weeklong protest at Creech Air Force Base in Indian Springs, Nevada. The text below, a call to participate in the protest, explains the significance of Creech.

On November 10 anti-drone activists blocked the main entrance to the base with a banner reading "Shut Down Creech." Five activists held handcuffs high in the air and announced their plans to conduct a citizen's arrest of the base commander for crimes against humanity. When the *five crossed the police barrier, they were arrested and escorted to jail. On the following day, some of the activists drove to Las Vegas and, holding peace signs, jumped into a Veteran's Day parade before city police forced them out.*

In 2005, Creech Air Force Base secretly became the first U.S. base in the country to carry out illegal, remotely controlled assassinations using the MQ-1 Predator drones, and in 2006, the more advanced Reaper drones were added to its arsenal. Creech drone personnel sit behind computers in the desert north of Las Vegas and kill "suspects" thousands of miles away. Recent independent research indicates that the identity of only one out of 28 victims of U.S. drone strikes is known beforehand. Though officials deny it, the majority killed by drones are civilians.

In 2014, it was leaked that the CIA's criminal drone assassination program, officially a separate operation from the Air Force's, has been piloted all along by Creech's super-secret Squadron 17. In November 2015, four Air Force drone veterans who were based at Creech wrote to President Obama, "We came to the realization that the innocent civilians we were killing only fueled the feelings of hatred that ignited terrorism and groups like ISIS, while also serving as a fundamental recruitment tool similar to Guantánamo Bay. This administration and its predecessors have built a drone program that is one of the most devastating driving forces for terrorism and destabilization around the world."

Since 2009 dozens of activists have been arrested for allegedly trespassing at Creech, while attempting to peacefully interrupt the indiscriminate killing and burning of innocent people by drones.

The U.S. drone program is rapidly proliferating as air bases are being converted to drone bases across the U.S. and abroad, but Creech remains the primary air base in U.S. state-sponsored global terrorism. Creech is where the killer drone program started—it is where we shall end it. We must put an end to this desecration of our Mother Earth and all creatures who inhabit it.

Rize Oliveira of Shut Down Creech protests against U.S.-led drone attacks,
Creech Air Force Base, Clark County Nevada, 2016.

- We must put an end to the dehumanization of lives from Ferguson to Palestine to Syria and Yemen.
- We must close all foreign U.S. military bases. Money for human needs.
- We must put an end to drone murder, drone surveillance, and global militarization.

SEVENTEEN

Emerging Movements in the New Century

MINING, PIPELINES, AND GLOBAL WARMING

Boats Float, Bears Don't (2008)
Greenpeace International

On January 31, 2008, Greenpeace International sponsored a nonviolent protest drawing attention to the negative effects of climate change on polar bears. Scientific studies at the time concluded that polar bears were endangered because climate change was shrinking the Arctic sea ice on which they depended for survival. Some scientists predicted that the shrinking ice would eliminate two-thirds of the polar bear population by the middle of the twenty-first century.

Because of the threat, the U.S. Fish and Wildlife Service had proposed in January 2007 that the government list polar bears as an endangered species, a classification that would require the government to take steps to curb climate change. Two years earlier, environmental groups, including Greenpeace International, had filed a lawsuit demanding that the

Department of Interior consider listing polar bears as an endangered spe-cies. Greenpeace supported the lawsuit with nonviolent actions, including the January 31, 2008 action described below.

On May 14, 2008, the Bush administration announced its decision to list the polar bears as "threatened" rather than "endangered." Although a positive effect of the classification was that U.S. trophy hunters were no longer legally permitted to shoot polar bears, the ruling did nothing to pro-tect the bears from the dangers of shrinking ice caused by climate change.

What's a polar bear to do? Your ice is melting, politicians won't listen, and the government is dragging its feet about listing you as endangered . . . Off to Washington, to start your own floating vigil! Uh oh, here comes the fuzz.

OK, it was one of our activists in a costume—peacefully protesting the Bush Administration's delay in issuing a final Endangered Species Act listing for the polar bear due to global warming. Yesterday, the ac-tivist, dressed in a polar bear suit, sat quietly in a paddleboat in a park pond in front of the Department of Interior. (Until the police took him to jail, where he remains as of this writing.)

Full Steam Ahead for New Oil
While the Department of Interior is dragging their feet on protecting polar bears, they are moving full steam ahead on plans to drill for oil in prime polar bear habitat. New oil leases are opening up in the Chukchi Sea and oil companies are lining up quickly to obtain licenses to drill. A fifth of the remaining Arctic polar bears depend on Chukchi Sea ice in their hunt for food.

In December of 2005, Greenpeace and two other conservation groups sued the Bush Administration when it missed its first legal dead-line to respond to the petition for an endangered species listing. On De-cember 27, 2006, the Service announced its proposal to list the species as "threatened" and had one year to make a final listing decision. The legal deadline for doing so was January 9, 2008.

Greenpeace protest of global warming, U.S. Department of Interior,
Washington, D.C., 2008.

Why Listing Is So Important?
If the polar bears were listed under the United States Endangered Species Act—a safety net for plants and animals on the brink of extinction—they would be granted a broad range of protection. The protection would include a requirement that United States federal agencies ensure that any action carried out, authorized, or funded by the United States government will not "jeopardize the continued existence" of polar bears, or adversely modify their critical habitat.

End Mountaintop Removal (2010)

Appalachia Rising

On September 27, 2010, scientist James Hansen, famous for his early studies of climate warming, joined about 1,000 demonstrators in Washington, DC, for Appalachia Rising, a march and rally protesting mountaintop removal coal mining. The practice entails clear-cutting forests, blasting apart rock, extracting exposed coal, and dumping the leftover earth into nearby valleys and their streams. "The science is clear," Hansen told the activists. "Mountaintop removal destroys historic mountain ranges, poisons water supplies, and pollutes the air with coal and rock dust. Mountaintop removal, providing only a small fraction of our energy, can and should be abolished."

The marchers started at Freedom Plaza and passed the headquarters of the Environmental Protection Agency (EPA) before arriving at PNC Bank, where some of the activists dumped coal waste onto the lobby floors to protest the bank's financing of mountaintop removal. Waiting outside were marchers holding signs that read, "Blowing Up Mountains for Coal Poisons People," "We Are Appalachia," "EPA, Do Your Job," and "Mountain Eco-Systems Won't Grow Back." Appalachian music filled the air.

The activists made their way to Lafayette Park, right across from the White House, and about 100 demonstrators, including Hansen, then walked across the street, past the police line in front of the White House fence, and sat down and linked arms, calling for President Obama to abolish mountaintop removal. The police arrested all of them. Four months later the EPA denied a permit for what would have been the largest mountaintop removal project in the history of Appalachia. Below is an excerpt from the statement issued by Appalachia Rising before the protest.

Appalachia Rising is a mass mobilization in Washington DC on September 27, 2010 calling for the abolition of mountaintop removal and surface mining. It is a culmination of the national movement against surface mining and a foundation upon which to build a pan-Appalachian movement for prosperity and justice. Coalfield citizens and organizers envision a vibrant mobilization of thousands—coalfield residents, students & youth, Christians & people of all faiths, families, celebrities, underground miners, activists, artists, and all who yearn for justice—to converge on Washington DC for a day of nonviolent action and dignified civil disobedience targeting the politicians and agencies who could abolish surface mining with the stroke of a pen. Appalachia Rising declares that we are not a national sacrifice zone. We will not stand idly by as we see our past and future blasted to rubble, our communities and mountains eliminated, and our neighbors poisoned as coal executives and their shareholders grow rich. Appalachians are not, and never will be, collateral damage. We are proud of our coal mining fathers, hardworking neighbors, and Appalachian past, present, and future! Appalachia is endowed with abundant resources too long plundered by outside interests. We call for the abolition of surface mining, a just transition for coalfield communities, and renewed investment in a prosperous and just economy in Appalachia. We invite all who share our vision to join with us on September 27, 2010 in our nation's capital for an end to mountaintop removal, surface mining, and a renewed vision of Appalachia.

The Keystone Pipeline Revolt (2011)

Bill McKibben

One of the largest environmental civil disobedience campaigns in U.S. history took place at the White House from August 20 to September 3, 2011, when 1,253 activists were arrested while protesting plans to build the Keystone XL pipeline. In a letter calling for the campaign, environmentalist and author Bill McKibben wrote, "To call this project a horror is serious understatement. The tar sands have wrecked huge parts of Alberta, disrupting ways of life in indigenous communities—First Nations communities in

Canada, and tribes along the pipeline route in the U.S. have demanded the destruction cease."

The massive disobedience campaign was followed by a November 6 march in Washington, DC, attended by about 5,000 people. The protestors linked arms, formed a human chain, and circled the White House. "Yes, we can, stop the pipeline!" they chanted, adapting candidate Obama's use of "Yes, we can!" McKibben described the nonviolent action as a symbolic way of placing President Obama under house arrest. Referring to the source that the pipeline would draw from, McKibben told the crowd: "That is the second biggest pool of carbon on the planet. If the U.S. government goes ahead and makes it easier to develop that oil-sands project, then there is no credible way to insist that they're working hard on climate change."

On January 18, 2012, Obama denied the permit to build the pipeline, and he rejected the entire proposal on November 6, 2014. Below is an excerpt from McKibben's reflection on the significance of protesting the pipeline.

When we were hauled away from the gates of the White House on the morning of Saturday, August 20th, where 65 of us had been peacefully sitting in for an hour to urge the president to veto the proposed Keystone XL pipeline—a 1,700-mile fuse to the biggest carbon bomb on the continent—we were taken, hands cuffed behind our backs, in paddy wagons to the Park Police headquarters across the river Anacostia. There we sat—hands still cuffed—on a lawn for a couple of hours, until one by one we were called inside, uncuffed and stripped of all but our clothes. . . .

There the District police fingerprinted us and locked us up, two apiece, in four-by-seven cells. No beds, just two stainless-steel slabs without mattress, sheet or pillow. (Shoes made decent pillows, but it's harder than it sounds to sleep on bare steel—my hips were still bruised two weeks later.) We stayed there all night, all the next day and all the next night; baloney sandwiches and a Styrofoam cup of water arrived at 3 a.m. and 3 p.m. The lights never went off, the din was constant and the heat stifling. . . . The hours passed with incredible slowness, especially since the guards, who had taken our watches, kept lying about the time. But on Monday morning at 5 a.m. (we walked past a clock), they shackled us again, this time by the feet—you really do have to put your hand on the next guy's shoulder, and shuffle down the hall, just like in the movies—and took us to the holding cell at the courthouse, where the 45 of us stood, feet cuffed together, in a giant cage with the rest of the District's weekend criminals for about 10 hours. No food, no water—until finally, all of a sudden, they simply called us out and let us go. The judge, apparently, had dismissed all charges, and we were free. . . .

Why were 65 middle-class Americans willing to spend that weekend behind bars? And why were 1,200 others willing to follow us into the paddy wagon over the last week of August and the first of September? This was the largest civil disobedience in this country since at least the nuclear-test protests of the 1980s, and one of the most sustained since the heyday of the civil rights movement, and virtually none of the arrestees were the usual suspects. Plenty of college students showed up, but we'd tried hardest to recruit their elders, arguing that in the fight against global warming it was time for the generation that actually caused the crisis to do a bit of the work. . . .

We were there for a simple reason: because it was time. After two decades of scientists gravely explaining to politicians that global warming is by far the biggest crisis our planet has ever faced, and politicians nodding politely (or, in the case of the Tea Party, shaking their heads in disbelief), it was time to actually do something about it that went beyond reading books, attending lectures, lobbying congressmen or writing letters to the editor. With Texas on fire and Vermont drowning under record rainfall, it wasn't just *our* bodies on the line.

The Keystone XL pipeline wraps up every kind of environmental devastation in one 1,700-mile-long disaster. At its source, in the tar sands of Alberta, the mining of this oil-rich bitumen has already destroyed vast swaths of boreal forest and native land—think mountaintop removal but without the mountain. The biggest machines on earth scrape away the woods and dig down to the oily sand beneath—so far they've only got three percent of the oil, but they've already moved more soil than the Great Wall of China, the Suez Canal, the Aswan Dam and the Pyramid of Cheops combined. The new pipeline—the biggest hose into this reservoir—will increase the rate of extraction, and it will carry that oily sand over some of the most sensitive land on the continent, including the Ogallala aquifer, source of freshwater for the plains. A much smaller precursor pipeline spilled 14 times in the past year.

Even if the oil manages to get safely to the refineries in Texas, it will take a series of local problems and turn them into a planetary one. Because those tar sands are the second-biggest pool of carbon on earth, after the oil fields of Saudi Arabia. Burning up Saudi Arabia is the biggest reason the Earth's temperature has already risen one degree from pre-industrial levels, that epic flood and drought have become ubiquitous, and that the Arctic is melting away. Since we didn't know about climate change when we started in on Saudi Arabia, you can't really blame anyone. But if we do it a second time in Canada, we deserve what we get.

If you do the calculations, explains James Hansen—the planet's most important climate scientist, who was arrested at the White House about halfway through the two weeks of protest—opening up the tar sands to heavy exploitation would mean "it's essentially game over" for the climate. Which is a sentence worth reading twice. Right now, the atmosphere holds 392 parts per million CO_2, already dangerously above the 350 ppm scientists say is the maximum safe level. If you could somehow burn all the tar sands at once, which thank heaven you can't, the atmospheric concentration would rise another 150 parts per million. . . .

Because the pipeline crosses an international border, it requires a presidential "certificate of national interest." In other words, Barack Obama alone will decide, without Congress or anyone else in the way. That means the sides have lined up with all the firepower they can muster. And they are different kinds of firepower. The heavy artillery backing Keystone includes the Chamber of Commerce, the Koch brothers and The Wall Street Journal. They're lobbying hard: TransCanada Corp., which will build the pipeline, spent $160,000 lobbying Congress in 2009, $720,000 last year and $790,000 in the first half of this year. They've wired things the traditional Washington way, hiring Hillary Clinton's former deputy campaign manager as their chief lobbyist. Not, perhaps, because of his expertise on pipelines.

And the opponents? Native people opened up the fight years ago, and still lead it—they were the first to experience the damage, and they found support from some of the big green groups as the pipeline plan began to unfold. Landowners from the high plains organized along the pipeline route; they did so well in swaying public opinion that both the Republican governor and senator from Nebraska have called on Obama to block the pipe. The dramatic civil disobedience over the summer transformed the fight from a regional into a national and emotional one—1,253 people got arrested and 612,000 signed petitions. The head of the NAACP, Ben Jealous, showed up to address the demonstrators, and the Hip Hop Caucus helped headline its closing rally. A few days later, nine Nobel Peace Prize laureates—from the Dalai Lama to Archbishop Desmond Tutu—sent a powerful appeal to the president. *The New York Times* and Robert Redford have also sided with the growing opposition. Only one guy has not tipped his hand—Barack Obama. His people say he'll decide by year's end. The question is: What will sway him most?

If it's money, it's clear who wins. Because the guys supporting this thing have most of the money on earth—the oil industry is the most profitable thing human beings have ever done, by far. ExxonMobil made more money last year than any company in the history of. . .money. If it comes down to money, and it usually does, we'll lose. That was made perfectly clear in early September, when the president, acting at the behest of the Chamber of Commerce, announced he was blocking new clean-air regulations. These are the kind of laws every president approves—even George W. Bush wanted a stricter standard than we have now. But after the Supreme Court decision in *Citizens United*, which allows companies to spend whatever they want on political campaigns, the president's men are so scared of the oil industry's big campaign war chest that they've gotten in the habit of obedience. . . .

To defeat the big money behind the pipeline, we needed to rely on a different currency, one that we possess and they don't. For two weeks, that currency was our bodies, and we spent them well enough to focus national attention on the pipeline. Even international attention—protesters turned out at embassies on every continent. . . . By protest's end, the political world was well aware that this had become Obama's central environmental test between now and next year's election. The odds are still against us, but they're better than they were.

And so the next phase of this campaign unfolds. Groups like Rising Tide are blockading trucks hauling heavy equipment to the tar sands; others geared up for the State Department hearing that were held across the country in late September. But mostly we're targeting Barack Obama, because he's the sole decision-maker. . . .

We're going to target Obama—but we're not going to do him the favor of attacking him. We're not going to say, "We'll never vote for you, you're a corrupt sellout." That's what his aides would like us to do, to marginalize ourselves as the kind of fringe it's politically profitable to defy. Instead, we're going to pay the president the very dangerous compliment of taking his words from the last campaign seriously, and asking him to live up to them.

What words? How about: "At the dawn of the 21st century, the country that faced down the tyranny of fascism and communism is now called to challenge the tyranny of oil."

Or maybe: "Because if we are willing to work for it, and fight for it, and believe in it, then I am absolutely certain that generations from now, we will be able to look back and tell our children. . .this was the moment when the rise of the oceans began to slow and our planet began to heal." . . .

To help nerve Obama up, we'll keep turning people out, by the thousands. On November 6th, exactly one year before the next election, we plan to encircle the White House with protesters, something I'm not sure has ever been done. We won't be getting arrested; instead, it will be like a human Rorschach blot. It's either a giant "O" of hope that he'll do the right thing, or a symbolic house arrest. It's our way of saying: We're not the radicals here. The real radicals run Exxon—they're the people who are willing to *alter the chemical composition of the atmosphere.* (Abbie Hoffman freaked out an entire nation by threatening to dump LSD in a single reservoir—what a small-time thinker he was!) In any reasonable sense of the word, we're conservatives, hoping to preserve something of the world we were born into.

Many of us will also be wearing our Obama '08 pins. But we'll be taking them off, and leaving them in self-addressed, stamped envelopes at the front of the White House, with a note saying: Send this back once you've kept your word. Choose the side you said you were on when you campaigned so beautifully. We see the hideous drought in Texas, the horrible flooding in Vermont, the steadily acidifying ocean—we see the stakes. We understand what kind of world is coming at us unless you decide to lead. And we still want you to do the right thing. Our message will be: *Until you absolutely make us, we refuse to be cynics. But we're not patsies, either.*

Because it really is time. Last year was the warmest on record. This year, before August was over, Americans had endured more billion-dollar weather disasters then we've ever experienced in an entire year. The Texas Forest Service, confronting the blazes that destroyed more than 1 million acres over the summer observes that "no one on the face of this earth has ever fought fires in these extreme conditions." If we ever plan to do something more than talk about the biggest crisis the planet has ever faced, now is the moment to say, "We're going no further down this path." Shutting down Keystone has become the unlikely Lexington and Concord of the climate movement. Revolutions have to start someplace.

LGBTQ RIGHTS

Chained to Serve Openly (2010)

Get EQUAL

On November 15, 2010, thirteen resisters, including Army Lieutenant Dan Choi and longtime gay rights activist Michael Bedwell, handcuffed themselves to the White House fence to protest President Obama's failure to keep his promise to take an active role in the legislative effort to repeal "Don't Ask, Don't Tell," the ban on gay men, lesbians, and bisexuals serving openly in the military. Obama had endorsed repeal during his campaign, but had done nothing more than verbally reiterate his support since his election.

"Barack Obama . . . Silent Homophobia" was one of their loudest chants, and Choi expounded on its significance. "After all his rhetoric, I think we must now conclude that there is truth to the knowledge in homophobia of both sorts: there is a loud homophobia of those with platforms and there is a silent homophobia for those who purport to be our friends and do nothing."

White House spokesman Sin Inouye responded to the protest by stating, "[T]he president remains committed to a legislative repeal," and that the "White House continues to work with Congress towards achieving that comprehensive and lasting legislation." During Senate debate, Senator Ron Wyden of Oregon said, "I don't care who you love. If you love this country enough to risk your life for it, you shouldn't have to hide who you are."

On December 10 2010, Congress approved, and the president signed a bill authorizing repeal. Certification occurred in July 2011, followed by repeal implementation on September 20 of that year.

Below is a letter penned in November 2010 by David Mixner, an activist who had been arrested during a White House protest after the announcement was made that a Department of Defense directive banning gays, lesbians, and bisexuals from military service would be codified into the "Don't Ask, Don't Tell" policy instituted by the Clinton Administration.

Dear friends,

Seventeen years ago, I joined a group of LGBT leaders and activists who were arrested at the White House fence in an effort to lift the unconstitutional . . . military ban. Sadly, 17 years later, GetEQUAL activists *still* have to continue taking action.

This morning, in an effort to pay tribute to one of our own and honor our history, a group of activists gathered at the gravesite of Leonard Matlovich. . . . Sgt. Matlovich's tombstone remains one of the most eloquent summaries of the discrimination the LGBT community faces in the military: Leonard Matlovich.

From there, they went to Senator Reid's office, asking him to show leadership in repealing this discriminatory policy—which now lies squarely on his plate. These activists asked Senator Reid to make good on a promise he made to all of our armed services when he accepted Lt. Dan Choi's West Point ring this summer as a down payment on repeal of the policy this year.

And, right now, veterans, civilians, and activists—including three generations of DADT repeal advocates—have handcuffed themselves to the White House fence to protest inaction and to demand leadership in repealing this discriminatory policy during the "lame-duck" session of Congress.

We don't know whether repeal will happen this year. What we do know is that we shouldn't have to do this—especially when vast majorities of the American public, including Democrats, Republicans, Independents, service members and their families, and many of our elected leaders all agree that the policy should be repealed.

We've been promised by leaders in our own community, the Democratic Party, and the President that "Don't Ask, Don't Tell" would end this year. But we're suffering from a failure in leadership, a failure of courage, and a failure of the moral fortitude to get this done.

I want to see equality in my lifetime. I should *not* have to witness a new generation of activists taking to the same fence that I and others took to decades ago. But I feel more dignified knowing that GetEQUAL will continue to take action to repeal "Don't Ask, Don't Tell," to pass the Employment Non-Discrimination Act, to gain marriage equality, to overcome immigration discrimination, and to fight for the day when we're fully equal under the law.

Our Love Is Equal (2013)

Anthony Kennedy and James Obergefell

LGBT communities in the United States long resisted legal bans against same-sex marriage by entering into, performing, and supporting marriages not legally recognized by the state. Many queer couples considered themselves married even though the state never registered them as such. In the early part of the twenty-first century, resistance also came to expression in marches, rallies, and numerous lawsuits that same-sex couples and their allies filed against states that recognized only heterosexual marriages. The Commonwealth of Pennsylvania encountered such resistance, but it also found itself facing an uncommon resister—a rogue county clerk.

In July 2013, when same-sex marriages were still banned in Pennsylvania, a lesbian couple requested a marriage license from D. Bruce Hanes, the register of wills and clerk of the Orphan's Court in Montgomery County. After receiving conflicting counsel from solicitors and county commissioners, Hanes decided to issue the requested license.

Although the couple chose not to proceed, word about Hanes's decision traveled fast, and on the morning of July 24 Loreen Bloodgood and Alicia Terrizzi, a lesbian couple who had been together for eighteen years, were the first in line at Hanes's office. Hanes issued the state's first same-sex marriage license, as well as 174 more marriage licenses to same-sex couples from July until September 12, 2013, when a Commonwealth Court judge handed down an order requiring him to cease and desist from issuing such licenses. Hanes appealed the decision to the Pennsylvania Supreme Court, but the appeal became moot on May 20, 2014, when in deciding another case U.S. District Judge John Jones III ruled that Pennsylvania's Defense of Marriage Act was unconstitutional.

Hanes's resistance received additional support on June 26, 2016, when the U.S. Supreme Court ruled in Obergefell v. Hodges that the U.S. Constitution guaranteed a nationwide right to same-sex marriage. By the time the Court issued its ruling, most U.S. citizens had already expressed their approval of same-sex marriage and thirty-seven states had legalized it. Justice Anthony Kennedy wrote for the majority in the 5-4 ruling in Obergefell, and below is one of his concluding paragraphs. Following Kennedy's words is the statement that Obergefell made immediately after the announcement of the Supreme Court's ruling. In his comments, Obergefell refers to the recent murder of nine African Americans during an evening prayer service at Emanuel African Methodist Episcopal Church in Charleston, South Carolina. The murderer was white supremacist Dylan Roof.

Anthony Kennedy

No union is more profound than marriage, for it embodies the highest ideals of love, fidelity, devotion, sacrifice, and family. In forming a marital union, two people become something greater than once they were. As some of the petitioners in these cases demonstrate, marriage embodies a love that may endure even past death. It would misunderstand these men and women to say they disrespect the idea of marriage. Their plea is that they do respect it, respect it so deeply that they seek to find its fulfillment for themselves. Their hope is not to be condemned to live in loneliness, excluded from one of civilization's oldest institutions. They ask for equal dignity in the eyes of the law. The Constitution grants them that right.

James Obergefell

Good morning. My name is Jim Obergefell, and I'm from Cincinnati, Ohio. I've lived in Ohio for most of my life.

My husband John and I were together for almost twenty-one years before he passed away as a result of complications of ALS.

I'm here today in front of our nation's highest court because my home state fought the recognition of my marriage to John. And when the man I loved and cared for passed away from one of the cruelest diseases known to humanity, the state of Ohio, the state in which I've lived, worked, and paid taxes for most of my life, continued to fight against my right to list my name on John's death certificate.

No American should have to suffer that indignity. That's why John and I and the thirty plaintiffs who are part of this lawsuit decided to fight.

I know in my heart that John is with me today. That man cared for and loved me for twenty-one years through thick and thin.

Today's ruling from the Supreme Court affirms what millions across this country already know: our love is equal, and that the four words etched unto the front of the Supreme Court—"Equal Justice Under Law"—apply to us, too.

All Americans deserve equal dignity, respect, and treatment when it comes to the recognition of our relationships and families.

Now at last Ohio will recognize our marriage, and, most important, marriage equality will come to every state across our country.

It's my hope that the term "gay marriage" will become a thing of the past, that from this day forward it will simply be "marriage." And our nation will be better because of it.

I also hope that this decision has a profound effect in reducing the stigma, the hurt, the alienation and discrimination that LGBT people all too often feel when we live our lives openly and authentically.

At the same time, while we will celebrate today's victory, my heart is also in Charleston. These past few weeks and months have been a reminder that discrimination in many forms is alive and well in America. It reminds us of the deeply unfortunate reality that progress for some is not progress for all, and that there can be equally significant steps backward as there are forward.

If we're truly dedicated to our democracy and the values that we as a nation cherish, we must be equally committed to ensuring that all citizens are treated equally, that all Americans deserve justice. That's when we're all united. . . .

Most importantly, I'd like to thank John for loving me, for making me a better man, and for giving me something worth fighting for. I love you. This is for you, John.

Thank you.

OCCUPYING WALL STREET AND WASHINGTON

Killing Big Insurance (2009)

Mobilization for Health Care for All

Nataline Sarkisyan, a seventeen-year-old woman, lay dying at the UCLA Medical Center near the end of December 2007. Aggressive treatment for leukemia had resulted in irreparable harm to her liver, and she was in urgent need of a transplant. But the family's health insurer, Cigna Healthcare, denied the procedure, describing it as "experimental." Nataline's doctors vehemently disagreed and sent Cigna a letter pleading for the insurer to review its decision.

About 150 protestors, many of them Sarkisyan's teenage friends, also staged a protest outside Cigna's offices in Glendale. During the well-publicized event, a Cigna representative called Nataline's mother Hilda to let her know that the company had given its permission to proceed with the transplant. But Cigna's reversal of their decision came too late, and Nataline died shortly after.

The Sarkisyan case was a classic example of insurers putting profits before patients, and it helped fuel nationwide protests organized in 2009 and 2010 by the Mobilization for Health Care for All (MHCA). The direct-action campaign, planned by several groups calling for a national single-payer healthcare system, began at the New York City offices of Aetna, a health insurance giant, where seventeen protestors were arrested while

*conducting a sit-in demanding that the insurance provider offer immedi-
ate approval for lifesaving measures requested by medical doctors. Outside
the offices, protestors chanted, "Patients Not Profits." Below is a statement
issued by MHCA in 2009.*

A nonviolent battle to end the private health insurance industry's abuse
of our nation is beginning. On September 29th in New York City, October 8th in Chicago, and in cities across the country on October 15th,
over 100 people, including patients, nurses, and doctors will sit-in at
insurance company offices to demand an end to a system that profits by
denying people care and puts insurance company bureaucrats between
doctors and patients.

The American health care system is broken. We spend far more on
health care than any other nation yet stand alone among industrialized
democracies as the only country that doesn't provide universal health
care. Why? Because our system puts the profits of insurance companies
and their CEOs ahead of the health of the American people.

Thirty cents of every dollar spent on health care in America goes to
insurance company profits and industrial waste. One out of every seven
hundred dollars goes to one CEO alone—Stephen Hemsley of United
Health Group, the largest insurance company in America. While he jets
off to his multimillion dollar vacation home, millions of Americans have
no health insurance at all. And tens of thousands, like Nataline Sarkisyan, . . . who have health insurance, die every year because they can't
get the care they need. Nataline died at 17 while her parents pleaded
with their insurance company to cover a lifesaving liver transplant.

These insurance companies ration care in our country, and they do
it based on one thing—profit. They are the real death panels that hold
the health of our country hostage.

The American people deserve better. That's why we've elected a
new government with a mandate for change. And yet health care reform, even the poor compromise of a weak public option, is in jeopardy. Real reform, a national single-payer plan, has been nearly shut out

of the entire debate. The insurance companies and the right-wing elite are spending millions to kill reform. They spread lies, find scare tactics, and bribe our elected officials with campaign money. Teabagger town hall disruptions and ridiculous lies about government death panels that are going to pull the plug on Grandma have grabbed the headlines and poisoned the debate. And too many politicians, Democrat and Republican, are standing against reform on the side of insurance companies that fund them rather than with the people who elected them.

Many who believed that our chance to win universal health care had finally come are losing hope. But now is not the time to turn back or give up.

Candidate Barack Obama told us change is never easy but the story of America is one of ordinary men and women who struggle against the odds to achieve it. The historic election of 2008 was a big step, but our votes were not enough. The fight is not over.

Years ago the civil rights movement faced a similar challenge after reform legislation to end segregation was blocked by entrenched interests. Even Martin Luther King, Jr. was losing hope for political progress. Then a small group of students changed the course of history. They entered stores where they could shop but couldn't eat because of the color of their skin—and simply sat down. They were dragged out and arrested. This action unleashed a firestorm of nonviolent protests across the South. The students' deep personal sacrifice dramatized the brutal reality of segregation, moved the conscience of a nation, and inspired a movement that went on to win federal civil rights legislation.

We have to do the same thing for the civil rights movement of today. It's time for a campaign of nonviolent civil disobedience to win reform that guarantees the right to health care for all. So beginning on September 29th in New York City . . . over 100 people will put our bodies on the line to take the fight to the real villain in the health care debate. Patients in need of care, nurses, doctors, and people of conscience will enter the offices of major private insurance companies and demand that they cover the care they have denied to their members. We won't leave until they do. . . . The companies will have to decide: admit they're wrong and stop denying care, or have us arrested and show the world how far they will go to protect their obscene profits. If we are arrested, we will embrace it and go to jail.

Occupy, I Love You (2011)

Naomi Klein

Harvard Divinity School student Dave Woessner joined dozens of protestors marching around the bronze bull in Wall Street on September 17, 2011, the first day of Occupy Wall Street (OWS). "When you idealize financial markets as salvific you embrace the idea that profit is all that matters," he said.

The city shut down parts of Wall Street by 10:00 AM, but protestors lined up outside police barricades at Wall Street and Boundary in Lower Manhattan. Line cook Micah Chamberlain of Columbus, Ohio, was at the barriers, holding a sign that read, "End the Oligarchy." The "oligarchy" referred to the nation's wealthiest—the "one percent," as the protestors referred to them. "There are millions of people in this country without jobs," Chamberlain said. "And 1 percent of the people have 99 percent of the wealth."

Organizers referred to themselves as the General Assembly, and their plans called for building an encampment populated indefinitely by protestors who would stage daily demonstrations against corporate corruption. Structurally, the movement sought to avoid investing power in charismatic leaders by making itself radically democratic, lodging decision-making power in the General Assembly, not just the initial organizers but also everyone present for the mass meetings.

On September 29, the New York City General Assembly released an official declaration about the target of its protests. "We come to you at a time when corporations, which place profit over people, self-interest over justice, and oppression over equality, run our governments," it stated. The declaration then listed twenty-three grievances against corporations, the first five of which read: "They have taken our houses through an illegal fore-closure process, despite not having the original mortgage. They have taken bailouts from taxpayers with impunity, and continue to give executives exorbitant bonuses. They have perpetuated inequality and discrimination in the workplace based on age, the color of one's skin, sex, gender identity, and sexual orientation. They have poisoned the food supply through negli-gence, and undermined the farming system through monopolization. They have profited off of the torture, confinement, and cruel treatment of count-less animals, and actively hide these practices." Other grievances faulted corporations for creating debt for students, decreasing the power of unions, blocking alternate forms of energy, hiding oil spills, buying off politicians, controlling the media, sponsoring colonialism at home and abroad, and creating weapons of mass destruction.

The declaration also extended an invitation to "the people of the world": "Exercise your right to peaceably assemble; occupy public space; create a process to address the problems we face and generate solutions to everyone." In response, occupy sites sprouted in minor and major cities across the country, from Occupy Harrisburg in the East to Occupy Oak-land in the West, all of them holding rallies, protests, and sit-ins centered on the movement's famous slogan: "We are the 99 Percent."

Before Occupy Wall Street was evicted from Zucotti Park during an early morning raid on November 15, the national movement had enlisted support from hundreds of thousands of activists and given the nation new terms ("the 99 percent and the 1 percent") for addressing corporate corruption. Occupy also created momentum for unions con-sidering strikes, for a national push for the minimum wage, and for grassroots campaigns seeking to remove corporate influence over politics. Another important legacy of the Occupy Movement was the presidential campaign of Bernie Sanders, a democratic socialist whose economic policies reflected some of Occupy's concerns. Below are comments that writer and activist Naomi Klein delivered at Occupy Wall Street on October 6, 2011.

I love you.

And I didn't just say that so that hundreds of you would shout "I love you" back, though that is obviously a bonus feature of the human microphone. Say unto others what you would have them say unto you, only way louder.

Yesterday, one of the speakers at the labor rally said: "We found each other." That sentiment captures the beauty of what is being created here. A wide-open space (as well as an idea so big it can't be contained by any space) for all the people who want a better world to find each other. We are so grateful.

If there is one thing I know, it is that the 1 percent loves a crisis. When people are panicked and desperate and no one seems to know what to do, that is the ideal time to push through their wish list of pro-corporate policies: privatizing education and social security, slashing public services, getting rid of the last constraints on corporate power. Amidst the economic crisis, this is happening the world over.

And there is only one thing that can block this tactic, and fortunately, it's a very big thing: the 99 percent. And that 99 percent is taking to the streets from Madison to Madrid to say "No. We will not pay for your crisis."

That slogan began in Italy in 2008. It ricocheted to Greece and France and Ireland and finally it has made its way to the square mile where the crisis began.

"Why are they protesting?" ask the baffled pundits on TV. Meanwhile, the rest of the world asks: "What took you so long?" "We've been wondering when you were going to show up." And most of all: "Welcome."

Many people have drawn parallels between Occupy Wall Street and the so-called anti-globalization protests that came to world attention in Seattle in 1999. That was the last time a global, youth-led, decentralized movement took direct aim at corporate power. And I am proud to have been part of what we called "the movement of movements."

But there are important differences too. For instance, we chose

Day 14 of Occupy Wall Street, New York City, 2011.

summits as our targets: the World Trade Organization, the International Monetary Fund, the G8. Summits are transient by their nature, they only last a week. That made us transient too. We'd appear, grab world headlines, then disappear. And in the frenzy of hyper patriotism and militarism that followed the 9/11 attacks, it was easy to sweep us away completely, at least in North America.

Occupy Wall Street, on the other hand, has chosen a fixed target. And you have put no end date on your presence here. This is wise. Only when you stay put can you grow roots. This is crucial. It is a fact of the information age that too many movements spring up like beautiful flowers but quickly die off. It's because they don't have roots. And they don't have long-term plans for how they are going to sustain themselves. So when storms come, they get washed away.

Being horizontal and deeply democratic is wonderful. But these principles are compatible with the hard work of building structures and institutions that are sturdy enough to weather the storms ahead. I have great faith that this will happen.

Something else this movement is doing right: You have committed yourselves to nonviolence. You have refused to give the media the images of broken windows and street fights it craves so desperately. And that tremendous discipline has meant that, again and again, the story has been the disgraceful and unprovoked police brutality. Which we saw more of just last night. Meanwhile, support for this movement grows and grows. More wisdom.

But the biggest difference a decade makes is that in 1999, we were taking on capitalism at the peak of a frenzied economic boom. Unemployment was low, stock portfolios were bulging. The media was drunk on easy money. Back then it was all about start-ups, not shutdowns.

We pointed out that the deregulation behind the frenzy came at a price. It was damaging to labor standards. It was damaging to environmental standards. Corporations were becoming more powerful than governments and that was damaging to our democracies. But to be honest with you, while the good times rolled, taking on an economic system based on greed was a tough sell, at least in rich countries.

Ten years later, it seems as if there aren't any more rich countries. Just a whole lot of rich people. People who got rich looting the public wealth and exhausting natural resources around the world.

The point is, today everyone can see that the system is deeply unjust and careening out of control. Unfettered greed has trashed the global economy. And it is trashing the natural world as well. We are overfishing our oceans, polluting our water with fracking and deepwater drilling, turning to the dirtiest forms of energy on the planet, like the Alberta tar sands. And the atmosphere cannot absorb the amount of carbon we are putting into it, creating dangerous warming. The new normal is serial disasters: economic and ecological.

These are the facts on the ground. They are so blatant, so obvious, that it is a lot easier to connect with the public than it was in 1999, and to build the movement quickly.

We all know, or at least sense, that the world is upside down: we act as if there is no end to what is actually finite—fossil fuels and the atmospheric space to absorb their emissions. And we act as if there are strict and immovable limits to what is actually bountiful—the financial resources to build the kind of society we need.

The task of our time is to turn this around: to challenge this false scarcity. To insist that we *can* afford to build a decent, inclusive society—while at the same time, respect the *real* limits to what the earth can take.

What climate change means is that we have to do this on a deadline. This time our movement cannot get distracted, divided, burned out, or swept away by events. This time we have to succeed. And I'm not talking about regulating the banks and increasing taxes on the rich, though that's important.

I am talking about changing the underlying values that govern our society. That is hard to fit into a single media-friendly demand, and it's also hard to figure out how to do it. But it is no less urgent for being difficult.

That is what I see happening in this square. In the way you are feeding each other, keeping each other warm, sharing information freely, and providing health care, meditation classes, and empowerment training. My favorite sign here says, "I care about you." In a culture that trains people to avoid each other's gaze, to say, "Let them die," that is a deeply radical statement.

A few final thoughts. In this great struggle, here are some things that *don't* matter:

- What we wear.
- Whether we shake our fists or make peace signs.
- Whether we can fit our dreams for a better world into a media soundbite.
    And here are a few things that do matter.
- Our courage.
- Our moral compass.
- How we treat each other.

We have picked a fight with the most powerful economic and political forces on the planet. That's frightening. And as this movement grows from strength to strength, it will get more frightening. Always be aware that there will be a temptation to shift to smaller targets—like, say, the person sitting next to you at this meeting. After all, that is a battle that's easier to win.

Don't give in to the temptation. I'm not saying don't call each other on shit. But this time, let's treat each other as if we plan to work side by side in struggle for many, many years to come. Because the task before us will demand nothing less.

Let's treat this beautiful movement as if it is the most important thing in the world. Because it is. It really is.

Moral Mondays (2013)

William Barber II

As head of the North Carolina NAACP and pastor of Greenleaf Christian Church in Greensboro, William Barber founded the Moral Mondays movement in 2013 to protest the rightwing policies of Governor Pat McCrory and the GOP-controlled state legislature. Barber billed the new religious-left movement as neither Republican nor Democratic but as a "transformational coalition" designed to fight an "immoral agenda"—an agenda that harms prisoners, immigrants, the poor, the unemployed, the sick, people of color, LBGTQ communities, and more.

The coalition established chapters throughout the state and held "Moral Mondays," weekly rallies and protests at the state legislature. The protest movement began with just a couple dozen protestors but soon blossomed into thousands of demonstrators, with more than a thousand, including Barber, arrested for acts of civil disobedience between 2013 and 2014.

A charismatic speaker, Barber resigned as head of the North Carolina NAACP in May 2017 to devote more time and energy into building Moral

Mondays into a national movement. Below are excerpts from comments he made to mark the April 2013 kickoff of the coalition.

We have written to Governor McCrory and to the General Assembly, asking them to reconsider their assault on the poor, the unemployed, our many citizens without healthcare, and our embattled public schools.

They have already voted and passed legislation to:

Deny federal funds for Medicaid to 500,000 poor North Carolinians.

Take unemployment benefits from 165,000 North Carolinians.

Raise taxes on 900,000 of North Carolina's poor and working poor by ending the Earned Income Tax Credit to pay for tax cuts to 23 millionaires. That took over a billion dollars last year from public education, made plans to implement a voucher plan to hand out public money to private schools, and reduce eligibility to preschool for poor children.

To restart the death penalty and repeal the Racial Justice Act that has exposed the racially discriminatory application of the death penalty.

To codify anti-labor language in our state constitution.

To roll back early voting, ban Sunday voting, end same-day registration, and impose an unneeded poll tax disguised as voter ID bill that will cost the state millions, deny student ids from private schools, increase disenfranchisement of formerly incarcerated, charge parents a $2500 tax (poll tax) if their college student votes at college and not at home, and leave us with voting laws more restrictive than Alabama and South Carolina; when you pursue policies that hurt most voters, you can't afford a big turnout.

Many of those pushing this agenda got into public office because of a race-based redistricting plan that is the most discriminatory since the 19th century. . . . They do not want the people to vote.

And this is only the first 50 days of their work, and we haven't even seen the final budget. The policies pursued in these chambers will devastate hundreds of thousands of North Carolinians who are already suffering. The leadership of this Republican "super-majority" are deaf to the cries of those whom Jesus called "the least of these."

Early on just after they were elected we brought thousands of NC Citizens to Jones Street for the seventh annual Historic Thousands on Jones Street Peoples Coalition Assembly and placed before our General Assembly a forward-moving agenda. We lifted up five principles that we believed were bigger than Democrat or Republican but good for the whole:

1) *Economic sustainability and ending poverty* by fighting for full employment, living wages, the alleviation of disparate unemployment, a green economy, labor rights, affordable housing, targeted empowerment zones, strong safety net services for the poor, fair policies for immigrants, infrastructure development, and fair tax reform.

2) *Educational equality* by ensuring every child receives a high quality, well-funded, Constitutional, diverse public education, access to community colleges and universities and equitable funding for minority colleges and universities.

3) *Healthcare for all* by ensuring access to the Affordable Care Act, Medicare and Medicaid, Social Security, and providing environmental protection.

4) *Fairness in the criminal justice system* by addressing the continuing inequalities in the system and providing equal protection under the law for black, brown, and poor white people.

5) *Voting rights* by defending the right to vote and expanding voting rights for all people by standing against suppression tactics, such as voter ID, restriction of early voting, race-based redistricting, or any other effort that undermines equal protection under the law.

Instead they have turned a deaf ear and a defiant posture towards moving forwards and instead have chosen to take our state backwards.

Surely, in the end, the people will rise up and sweep such leaders from office. Even the Republican leadership knows this to be true.

Time to Withdraw Big Money from Politics (2016)

Democracy Spring and Democracy Uprising

Members of Democracy Spring were frustrated that the 2016 elections would prove to be the most expensive in U.S. history, that the Voting Rights Act was no longer as strong as it had been, and that Republican leaders in the U.S. Senate were refusing to act on Judge Merrick Garland, President Obama's nomination to the U.S. Supreme Court. So on April 2 hundreds of Democracy Spring protestors staged a rally at Independence Hall in Philadelphia to protest voter suppression and the presence of "Big Money" in U.S. politics. After the rally, about 100 resisters marched to Washington, DC, where they conducted a sit-in on the Capitol steps from April 11 to April 18.

Joining them was another voting rights group, Democracy Awakening, which held an April 18 march from Union Station to the Capitol. At the head of the march were leaders of the major sponsoring organizations: William Barber II of Moral Mondays, Cornell Brooks of the NAACP, Annie Leonard of Greenpeace, and Aaron Mair of the Sierra Club.

A man dressed in a suit made of fake one-hundred-dollar bills tossed pretend money into the air during the colorful march, and another man used his pink broom to "sweep big money out of politics." Democracy Awakening leaders then met with members of Congress to advocate for passage of legislation that would eliminate Republican-engineered voting impediments and provide funds for the public financing of elections.

March members also joined the sit-in at the Capitol, and over three hundred resisters were arrested on April 19. The number of arrests between April 11 and April 18 totaled about 1,400, making the event one of the largest nonviolent direct action protests in Washington, DC, in the twenty-first century. Although the demonstration was historic, it attracted little attention in the national media. Democracy Spring's complaints and goals are listed in the first document below, followed by Democracy Awakening's call to the April protest.

Democracy Spring

Big Money in Politics. Our political system runs on Big Money. A tiny fraction of the wealthiest 1% fund our politicians' campaigns, making them dependent upon a miniscule economic elite instead of the vast majority of everyday people. The results are predictable: publicly elected officials end up representing the interests of billionaires and corporations at the expense of everyone else.

On issue after issue—from climate change, to healthcare, to wealth and income inequality, to mass incarceration and deportation—big money in politics stands in the way of serious progressive change.

The 2010 Supreme Court decision, *Citizens United v. FEC,* made the problem much worse by permitting unlimited amounts of money in our elections through Super PACS and nonprofits. . . .

Voter Suppression. Every election, millions of Americans are kept from exercising their sacred right to vote due to various laws that make it harder to vote or which disqualify them altogether from the franchise.

Republican politicians who fear being voted out of office use voter suppression laws to keep typically left-leaning populations away from the polls. Voter ID laws, cuts to early voting, elimination of same-day registration and pre-registration, and cuts to the total number of polling places are all voter suppression tactics that disproportionately affect people of color, young people, and poor people. . . .

Fundamental Reform. The sweeping reform agenda we need to solve these problems is simple and straightforward:

1. Guarantee the right to vote for all people.
2. Ban big money in politics and enact publicly funded elections.
3. Overturn *Citizens United.*

Democracy Awakening

In April 2016, more than 200 organizations representing a diverse array of movements and hundreds of thousands of people are coming together to demand a democracy that works for all of us—a nation where our votes are not denied and money doesn't buy access and power. Join us

Democracy Spring sit-in at U.S. Capitol, Washington, D.C., 2016.

as we converge upon Washington, DC for an array of actions, including demonstrations, teach-ins, direct-action trainings, music, a Rally for Democracy, and pressing for a Congress of Conscience through nonviolent direct action and advocacy. Together we will build a nation that is truly of, by, and for the people.

Why. American democracy is premised on the fundamental tenet, "one person, one vote," but since the very beginning, we've had to fight for every voice to be heard and every vote to be counted.

Today, we're fighting for change on many fronts—for action on climate change, racial justice, workers' rights and fair pay, safe food and water, health care, peace, immigration reform, and improvements in education. But an array of barriers is keeping regular Americans shut out of the political process, from restrictive voting laws suppressing the voting rights of people of color, seniors, students, and low-income Americans, to a campaign finance landscape that allows big money to increasingly shape elections and the policy-making process.

For both money in politics and voting rights, the U.S. Supreme Court has eviscerated laws that once protected the voices and votes of everyday Americans. And for both issues, Congress has solutions in front of them, but has so far failed to act. And now the Senate is blocking fair consideration of the nominee to fill the Supreme Court vacancy, including timely hearings and a vote by the full Senate.

It's time for us to come together and claim a democracy where every voice is heard and every vote counts equally—in other words, a democracy that works for all of us.

It's time for a Democracy Awakening.

That's why we are mobilizing. And that's why we need you to *join us*.

Our Demands. We need a Congress that stands up for democracy rather than stands in its way. Here's the agenda we're calling for Congress to pass:

- Fair consideration of the nominee to fill the Supreme Court vacancy, including timely hearings and a vote by the full Senate.
- The Voting Rights Advancement Act, legislation that would restore the protections against voting discrimination that were struck down by the U.S. Supreme Court in its *Shelby County v. Holder* decision, and make additional, critical updates to the Voting Rights Act of 1965.
- The Voter Empowerment Act, legislation to modernize voter registration, prevent deceptive practices that keep people from the ballot box, and ensure equal access to voting for all.
- The Democracy for All Amendment, a constitutional amendment that would overturn U.S. Supreme Court decisions like *Citizens United* and allow elected representatives to set commonsense limits on money in elections.

- The Government by the People Act/Fair Elections Now Act, a small donor empowerment measure that would encourage and amplify small contributions from everyday Americans.

Our reform agenda is aimed at creating a democracy where every voice is heard and every vote counts equally—in other words, a democracy that works for all of us.

PRISON ABOLITION AND BLACK LIVES MATTER

Life Beyond the Prison (2003)

Angela Y. Davis

Angela Y. Davis first came to national attention in 1969, when the University of California at Los Angeles, with support from Governor Ronald Reagan, sought to fire her over her membership in the Communist Party. She landed on the front pages again the following year, when she was indicted on counts of kidnapping, murder, and conspiracy related to the famous Soledad brothers case. Facing arrest, Davis went underground, and FBI Director J. Edgar Hoover placed her on the FBI's most-wanted list. About two months later, on October 13, 1970, FBI agents seized Davis in midtown Manhattan, and she eventually landed in county jail back in California. She was later acquitted on all charges.

Since the 1960s, Davis has been an outspoken proponent of prison abolition, a cause she connected to the "war on drugs" initiated by Richard Nixon and then buttressed by anti-drug policies that dramatically increased sentences for convicted drug offenders, even smalltime users, during the Reagan, Bush, and Clinton administrations. In 1997 Davis and other prison abolitionists breathed new life into the prison abolitionist movement by organizing a September 1998 conference titled "Critical Resistance: Beyond the Prison-Industrial Complex." Held in Berkeley, California, the conference attracted about 3,500 participants from around the world and gave birth to similar conferences in the following years. In May 2001, conference leaders created Critical Resistance National, an umbrella structure that helps direct numerous grassroots campaigns to halt the construction of prisons and jails—and to abolish the prison-industrial complex. Davis continues to play a leading role in articulating the political ideology for the movement, and below is an excerpt from her 2003 book, Are Prisons Obsolete?

When I became involved in antiprison activism during the late 1960s, I was astounded to learn that there were then close to two hundred thousand people in prison. Had anyone told me that in three decades ten times as many people would be locked away in cages, I would have been absolutely incredulous. I imagine that I would have responded something like this: "As racist and undemocratic as this country may be . . . I do not believe that the U.S. government will be able to lock up so many people without producing powerful public resistance. No, this will never happen, unless this country plunges into fascism." That might have been my reaction thirty years ago. The reality is that we are called upon to inaugurate the twenty-first century by accepting the fact that two million people—a group larger than the population of many countries—are living their lives in places like Sing Sing, Leavenworth, San Quentin, and Alderson Federal Reformatory for Women. . . .

In thinking about the possible obsolescence of the prison, we should ask how it is that so many people could end up in prison without major debates regarding the efficacy of incarceration. When the drive to produce more prisons and incarcerate even larger numbers of people occurred in the 1980s during what is known as the Reagan era, politicians argued that "tough on crime" stances—including certain imprisonment and longer sentences—would keep communities free of crime.

However, the practice of mass incarceration during that period has little or no effect on official crime rates. In fact, the most obvious pattern was that larger prison populations led not to safer communities, but, rather, to even larger prison populations. And as the U.S. prison system expanded, so did corporate involvement in construction, provision of goods and services, and use of prison labor. Because of the extent to which prison building and operation began to attract vast amounts of capital—from the construction industry to food and health care provision—in a way that recalled the emergence of the military-industrial complex, we began to refer to a "prison-industrial complex." . . .

The prison has become a black hole into which the detritus of contemporary capitalism is deposited. Mass imprisonment generates profits as it devours social wealth, and thus tends to reproduce the very conditions that lead people to prison. There are thus real and often quite complicated connections between deindustrialization of the economy—a process that reached its peak during the 1980s—and the rise of mass imprisonment, which also began to spiral during the Reagan-Bush era. However, the demand for more prisons was represented to the public in simplistic terms. More prisons were needed because there was more crime. Yet many scholars have demonstrated that by the time the prison construction boom began, official crime statistics were already falling. Moreover, draconian drug laws were being enacted, and "three strikes" provisions were on the agendas of many states. . . .

The prison is one of the most important features of our image environment. This has caused us to take the existence of prisons for granted. The prison has become a key ingredient of our common sense. It is there, all around us. We do not question whether it should exist. It has become so much a part of our lives that it requires a great feat of the imagination to envision life beyond prison.

This is not to dismiss the profound changes that have occurred in the way public conversations about the prison are conducted. Ten years ago, even as the drive to expand the prison system reached its zenith, there were very few critiques of this process available to the public. In fact, most people had no idea about the immensity of this expansion. This was the period during which internal changes—in part through the application of new technologies—led the U.S. prison system in a much more repressive direction. Whereas previous classifications had been confined to low, medium, and maximum security, a new category was invented—that of the super-maximum security prison, or the supermax. The turn toward increased repression, distinguished from the beginning of its history by its repressive regimes, caused some journalists, public intellectuals, and progressive agencies to oppose the growing reliance on prisons to solve social problems that are actually exacerbated by mass incarceration.

In 1990, the Washington-based Sentencing Project published a study of U.S. populations in prison and jail, and on parole and probation, which concluded that one in four black men between the ages of twenty and twenty-nine were among these numbers. Five years later, these numbers have soared to almost one in three (32.2 percent). Moreover, more than one in ten Latino men in this same age range were in jail or prison, or on probation or parole. The second study also revealed that the group experiencing the greatest increase was black women, whose imprisonment increased by seventy-eight percent. According to the Bureau of Justice Statistics, African-Americans as a whole now represent the majority of state and federal prisoners, with a total of 803,400 black inmates—118,600 more than the total number of white inmates. During the late 1990s major articles on prison expansion appeared in *Newsweek, Harper's, Emerge,* and *Atlantic Monthly.* Even Colin Powell raised the question of the rising number of black men in prison when he spoke at the 2000 Republican National Convention, which declared George W. Bush its presidential candidate.

Over the last few years, the previous absence of critical positions on prison expansion in the political arena has given way to proposals for prison reform. While public discourse has become more flexible, the emphasis is almost inevitably on generating the changes that will produce a *better* prison system. In other words, the increased flexibility that has allowed for critical discussion of the problems associated with the expansion of prisons also restricts this discussion to the question of prison reform.

As important as some reforms may be—the elimination of sexual abuse and medical neglect in women's prisons, for example—frameworks that rely exclusively on reforms help to produce the stultifying idea that nothing lies beyond the prison. Debates about strategies of decarceration, which should be the focal point of our conversations on the prison crisis, tend to be marginalized when reform takes the center stage. The most immediate question today is how to prevent the further expansion of prison populations and how to bring as many imprisoned women and men as possible back into what prisoners call "the free world." How can we move to decriminalize drug use and the trade in sexual services? How can we take seriously strategies of restorative rather than exclusively punitive justice? Effective alternatives involve both transformation of the techniques for addressing "crime" and of the social and economic conditions that track so many children from poor communities of color, into the juvenile system and then on to prison. The most difficult and urgent challenge today is that of creatively exploring new terrains of justice, where the prison no longer serves as the major anchor.

Justice for Trayvon! (2012)

Tracy Martin and Sybrina Fulton

On the night of February 26, 2012, Trayvon Martin, a seventeen-year-old African American high school student, left the house of his father's fiancée in a gated community in Sanford, Florida, to go for a snack run at a nearby 7-Eleven. After purchasing a bag of Skittles and a can of Arizona watermelon drink, Martin headed back to the house. George Zimmerman, a twenty-nine-year-old neighborhood watch volunteer, spotted

Martin walking through the gated community and found him so suspicious-looking that he called 911. But moments after asking for the police to call him when they arrived at the community, Zimmerman, carrying a black Kel-Tec 9 mm semi-automatic pistol, crossed paths with Martin. By the time the police arrived, Trayvon Martin was motionless, lying face-down on the ground. His hands were tucked under his body, and he was unarmed.

In his interview at the Sanford Police Department, Zimmerman stated that the shooting was an act of self-defense. The Sanford Police Department chose not to charge Martin, claiming insufficient evidence. With no arrest on the horizon, about 5,000 protestors, many of them wearing hoodies, converged on Union Square in Manhattan on March 21 to demand Zimmerman's arrest. The march was titled "Million Hoodie March" as a way to garner public attention for the organizers' attempts to secure more than one million signatures for an online petition begun by Trayvon's parents, Tracy Martin and Sybrina Fulton. Martin and Fulton also appeared at the Union Square rally, and their comments, as well as the crowd's reactions, all taken from a phone recording of the event, are below.

National outrage at the shooting did not translate into a conviction. State attorney Angela Corey charged Zimmerman with second-degree murder, but there were no witnesses and Corey's team was unsuccessful in proving to the jurors that Zimmerman racially profiled Martin as a criminal, that he instigated a fight, and that, without just cause, he shot an innocent, unarmed young man in the heart. On June 13, 2013, a jury found Zimmerman not guilty. Although Zimmerman escaped a prison sentence, and the U.S. Department of Justice later decided not to bring federal civil rights charges against him, the shooting of Trayvon Martin and its historic protests helped ignite a national conversation on race, racial profiling, police brutality against African Americans, Florida's self-defense ("Stand Your Ground") laws, and injustice in sentencing practices. More important, the shooting and national protests helped fuel the emergence of the Black Lives Matter movement.

Tracy Martin
First of all, I'd like to thank everybody for coming out and supporting my son, for supporting my son. I just want you to know that if Trayvon had been alive, he would be right here on these steps with you guys, rallying for justice.

Trayvon Martin was you. [*Yes!*] Trayvon Martin *did* matter. [*Yes!*]

I just want you to know that we're not gonna stop until we get justice for Trayvon.

Trayvon was . . . your typical teenager, Trayvon being the typical teenager things. Trayvon was *not*—and I repeat, was *not*—a bad person. [*We know that!*]

George Zimmerman took Trayvon's life for *nothing*! [*Nothing!*] George Zimmerman took Trayvon's life *profiling* him. [*That's right!*] My son did not deserve to die. [*No!*]

There's nothing we can say that will bring him back. But I'm here today to assure that justice is served and that no other parents have to go through this again. [*We want justice!*]

Sybrina Fulton
My heart, my heart is in pain.

But to see the support of all of you really makes a difference. [*We love you!*] You probably don't know. You probably don't understand how much you guys mean to us. But it's the support we need. We need this kind of support because our son was not committing any crime. [*No!*]

Our son is *your* son! [*Yes!*]

I want you guys to stand up for justice and stand up for what's right. [*Yes!*] This is not a *black* and *white* thing. [*No!*] This is about a *right* and *wrong* thing! [*Yes!*]

Justice for Trayvon! [*I am Trayvon Martin! Justice for Trayvon! Justice for Trayvon! Justice for Trayvon!*] (2012)

Riding to Ferguson (2014)

Black Lives Matter

Alicia Garza, an Oakland-based advocate for domestic workers, gave birth to the phrase "black lives matter" in 2013, just after the acquittal of George Zimmerman for the murder of Trayvon Martin. Prolific on social media, Garza went on Facebook and typed what she called a "love letter to black people." The letter was short and pointed: "the sad part is, there's a section of America who is cheering and celebrating right now, and that makes me sick to my stomach. We GOTTA get together y'all. stop saying we are not surprised. that's a damn shame in itself. I continue to be surprised by how little Black lives matter. And I will continue that. black people I love you. I love us. Our lives matter."

Patrisse Cullors, Garza's friend and a special-projects director at Oakland's Ella Baker Center for Human Rights, connected those three keywords to a hashtag—#BlackLivesMatter—and another friend, Opal Tometi, built a social media platform that used the hashtag to connect likeminded activists in a new black civil rights movement.

Although it started following Trayvon Martin's murder, the movement really took off after the police killing of Michael Brown in Ferguson, Missouri. The fury around Brown's death led BLM founders and allies to organize about 500 activists from across the country to join the Black Lives Matter Ride, a Labor Day weekend bus trip to Ferguson. In Ferguson the BLM activists participated in community-building activities and protested police brutality. About two hundred marched on the police station.

According to Garza, activists in Ferguson pushed her and her friends in #BlackLivesMatter to create a national organization, structurally modeled after Occupy, with local chapters across the country. As more police shootings and murders of African American men occurred in the following months, the movement gained a national footing, organizing numerous chapters that committed themselves to the movement's mission—"Black Lives Matter is an ideological and political intervention in a world where

Black lives are systematically and intentionally targeted for demise. It is an affirmation of Black folks' contributions to this society, our humanity, and our resilience in the face of deadly protest"—and thirteen guiding principles, including commitments to diversity, the empowerment of black women, and restorative justice. BLM now has chapters in every major region of the United States, and the overall movement has led or participated in more than 1,900 protests.

Below are excerpts of a public service announcement that BLM produced to recruit activists for the Ride to Ferguson, and preceding that is Garza's recollection of the origins of BLM.

Garza

Black Lives Matter began after George Zimmerman was acquitted of the murder of Trayvon Martin. We had been watching the case for a long time, probably over the course of a year, before it actually went to trial and then the jury reached a decision. There was a real disgusting way in which the mainstream respectability narrative—including among black folks and people of color—was looking for a reason that Trayvon was dead, and where they were looking was in his family, in his behavior, you know, they did everything they could to blame that poor child for his murder. But those of us who were watching and following the trial (which was kind of like the O. J. trial for many of us in how riveted we were) I don't think expected that George Zimmerman was not going to be convicted for *something*.

When he was acquitted, it felt like a gut punch. And I remember sitting with friends and talking, and there was nothing to say, but we just wanted to be around each other. A lot of what I was hearing and seeing on social media was that they were never going to charge somebody and convict somebody of killing a black child. My thing was: I'm not satisfied with that. I'm not satisfied with the "I told you so" and I'm not satisfied with the nihilistic "it'll never happen" kind of thing.

I was basically popping off on Facebook saying, "Yes, I'm going to be surprised that this man was not held accountable for the murder of a child." I was basically sending love notes to black people and saying, "We're enough. We are enough, and we don't deserve to die, and we don't deserve to be shot down in the streets like dogs because somebody else is fucking scared of us. And our presence is important, and we matter. Our lives matter, black lives matter." And Patrisse was like, "Oh my god, *black lives matter*." And she put a hashtag in front of it, and that's the origin of it.

BLM Ride Public Service Announcement
The Black Lives Matter Ride . . . was organized . . . to draw attention to the incident that happened in Ferguson but also to the larger and systemic issue of anti-black violence that's often sanctioned by the state, often at the hands of police, and often at the hands of vigilante-type groups. What happened in Ferguson is largely connected to what happens in a lot of places across the country, whether we're in New York City, Los Angeles, Texas, or elsewhere.

The Ride is organized for Labor Day weekend, and what we're intending to do are five things. One, we want to show up and show the families of Mike Brown and the community that we care. We want to also use our bodies as a way to represent solidarity to families across the country who have lost loved ones to police violence.

Secondly, we would like to push for the development of a national policy aimed at specifically addressing and correcting the problem of anti-black violence in the US.

Third, as anyone who's aware who watches the news, a big part of the problem of the peaceful protest that occurred in Missouri had everything to do with the use of militarized instruments by the police, including tear gas, rubber bullets. So we're also pushing for demilitarization of the law enforcement as well.

Fourth, one of the things we like to do is push for the release of the names of all police officers who have been involved in the murdering of black bodies across the country, whether they were on patrol or not.

And fifth, decrease law enforcement spending. And we think that a

March to support Black Lives Matter and boycott of Black Friday, NYC, 2014.

decrease in law enforcement spending could allow for increases in community-directed funds where they're most needed, particularly around jobs, housing, and economic development, and schools.

So we'll get in Ferguson on August 30th in what we hope will be a weekend of community-building with those already on the ground . . . not just to march . . . but also to ensure we all walk away with a national platform, being ready to work in our individual locations, staying connected to each other . . . and figuring out how to turn the tides, how to stop the murdering of black bodies and black people across the country.

We definitely want to ensure that everyone knows that black lives matter and that's why we're riding to Ferguson on Labor Day.

Freeing Slaves in Prison (2016)

Support Prisoner Resistance

On September 9, 2016, about 50,000 prisoners from 24 states began a nationally coordinated strike to mark the 45th anniversary of the Attica Uprising and to protest prison conditions. One of the targets was prison labor wages. At the time, state prisoners nationwide averaged less than $1.00 per hour for their labor. Some states, including Georgia, Arkansas, and Texas, refused to pay their prisoners any wages at all, and in South Carolina the system taxed workers' wages up to ninety percent to help cover the costs of incarceration. Strikers also protested unsafe working conditions, the quality and quantity of food, inadequate health care, overcrowding, and brutality. Complicating matters was the threat of retaliation against the strikers, including threats of solitary confinement, extended sentences, and "bird-feeding," that is, reducing the amount of food. Below is a strike call issued by the Free Alabama Movement and other participating groups.

In one voice, rising from the cells of long term solitary confinement, echoed in the dormitories and cell blocks from Virginia to Oregon, we prisoners across the United States vow to finally end slavery in 2016.

On September 9th of 1971 prisoners took over and shut down Attica, New York State's most notorious prison. On September 9th of 2016, we will begin an action to shut down prisons all across this country. We will not only demand the end to prison slavery, we will end it ourselves by ceasing to be slaves.

In the 1970s the U.S. prison system was crumbling. In Walpole, San Quentin, Soledad, Angola, and many other prisons, people were standing up, fighting, and taking ownership of their lives and bodies back from the plantation prisons. For the last six years we have remembered and renewed that struggle. In the interim, the prisoner population has ballooned and technologies of control and confinement have developed into the most sophisticated and repressive in world history.

The prisons have become more dependent on slavery and torture to maintain their stability.

Prisoners are forced to work for little or no pay. That is slavery. The 13th Amendment to the U.S. constitution maintains a legal exception for continued slavery in U.S. prisons. It states "neither slavery nor involuntary servitude, except as a punishment for crime whereof the party shall have been duly convicted, shall exist within the United States." Overseers watch over our every move, and if we do not perform our appointed tasks to their liking, we are punished. They may have replaced the whip with pepper spray, but many of the other torments remain: isolation, restraint positions, stripping off our clothes, and investigating our bodies as though we are animals.

Slavery is alive and well in the prison system, but by the end of this year, it won't be anymore. This is a call to end slavery in America. This call goes directly to the slaves themselves. We are not making demands or requests of our captors, we are calling ourselves to action. To every prisoner in every state and federal institution across this land, we call on you to stop being a slave, to let the crops rot in the plantation fields, to go on strike and cease reproducing the institutions of your confinement.

This is a call for a nationwide prisoner work stoppage to end prison slavery, starting on September 9th, 2016. They cannot run these facilities without us.

Nonviolent protests, work stoppages, hunger strikes and other refusals to participate in prison routines and needs have increased in recent years. The 2010 Georgia prison strike, the massive rolling California hunger strikes, the Free Alabama Movement's 2014 work stoppage, have gathered the most attention, but they are far from the only demonstrations of prisoner power. Large, sometimes effective hunger strikes have broken out at Ohio State Penitentiary, at Menard Correctional in Illinois, at Red Onion in Virginia, as well as many other prisons. The burgeoning resistance movement is diverse and interconnected, including immigrant detention centers, women's prisons, and juvenile facilities. Last fall, women prisoners at Yuba County Jail in California joined a hunger strike initiated by women held in immigrant detention centers in California, Colorado, and Texas.

Prisoners all across the country regularly engage in myriad demonstrations of power on the inside. They have most often done so with convict solidarity, building coalitions across race lines and gang lines to confront the common oppressor.

Forty-five years after Attica, the waves of change are returning to America's prisons. This September we hope to coordinate and generalize these protests, to build them into a single tidal shift that the American prison system cannot ignore or withstand. We hope to end prison slavery by making it impossible, by refusing to be slaves any longer.

To achieve this goal, we need support from people on the outside. A prison is an easy-lockdown environment, a place of control and confinement where repression is built into every stone wall and chain link, every gesture and routine. When we stand up to these authorities, they come down on us, and the only protection we have is solidarity from the outside. Mass incarceration, whether in private or state-run facilities, is a scheme where slave catchers patrol our neighborhoods and monitor our lives. It requires mass criminalization. Our tribulations on the inside are a tool used to control our families and communities on the outside. Certain Americans live every day under not only the threat of extra-judicial execution—as protests surrounding the deaths of Mike Brown, Tamir Rice, Sandra Bland, and so many others have drawn long overdue attention to—but also under the threat of capture, of being thrown into these plantations, shackled, and forced to work.

Our protest against prison slavery is a protest against the school-to-prison pipeline, a protest against police terror, a protest against post-release controls. When we abolish slavery, they'll lose much of their incentive to lock up our children, they'll stop building traps to pull back those who they've released. When we remove the economic motive and grease of our forced labor from the U.S. prison system, the entire structure of courts and police, of control and slave-catching must shift to accommodate us as humans, rather than slaves.

Prison impacts everyone. When we stand up and refuse on September 9th, 2016, we need to know our friends, families, and allies on the outside will have our backs. This spring and summer will be seasons of organizing, of spreading the word, building the networks of solidarity, and showing that we're serious and what we're capable of.

Step up, stand up, and join us.

Against prison slavery.

For liberation of all.

PROTECTING AND LEGALIZING IMMIGRANTS

Freedom Rides for Immigrant Workers (2003)

Patricia A. Ford

In 2003 immigrant rights groups held an "Immigrant Workers Freedom Ride" to draw attention to the economic plight of immigrants and to call on the federal government to legalize the status of immigrant workers and accord them the rights and privileges due all workers in the United States. Eighteen buses carrying 800 immigrants traveled from 10 different cities, including Los Angeles and San Francisco, to Washington, DC, where immigrants and their allies lobbied members of Congress. During their journeys to the capital, the buses stopped in more than one hundred communities so that the riders could hold local rallies and news conferences explaining the purpose of the Ride. Below is the transcript of a speech delivered by Patricia A. Ford, an executive vice president of the Service Employees International Union, when riders stopped in Alabama.

Hello, brothers and sisters! I am honored to join you here in Alabama on this leg of the Freedom Rides for Immigrant Workers.

I am honored to join so many courageous people who have come out today to show the Freedom Riders that they too care about social justice.

I am honored to be part of a truly important historic moment in the struggle for working people led by SEIU and HERE, the religious community, the civil rights community, black and brown people, and those who have been relegated to the margins of this society.

I am especially honored to be part of this leg of the Freedom Ride—moving across the great state of Alabama.

It is wonderful to be here in the cradle of the civil rights movement to declare yes, we are our brothers and sisters' keepers.

I've been watching news clips of the Freedom Ride as it began on the West Coast, from Seattle, to San Francisco, to Las Vegas, to Portland. Everywhere we could hear that sweet melody "We Shall Overcome."

This is not by accident. It is a sure reminder of the connectedness of our movement and our struggle.

From the days when Dr. Joseph Lowery and Reverend Orange marched with Dr. Martin Luther King, singing "We Shall Overcome," to this time and place, we are reminded that the struggle is long and hard. And many of those crusaders are still with us today, joining us in this new phase of the struggle.

I applaud all of you for understanding the importance of unity and the power of the beautiful rainbow assembled here today. Through our activism and our embrace of immigrant rights, we are bridging the many divides that separate us based on gender, race, and cultural background.

We are all connected to each other in some way, shape, or form. Unity gives us strength.

Truly, we are the changing face of America. We have seen how the rapidly changing demographics make it essential for all of us to guard against falling into that divide-and-rule trap.

Since 9/11 we've endured a new kind of racial profiling.

We still have the traditional garden variety type, like the New Jersey turnpike highway patrol stops or the baseless police harassment of young African-American males in urban centers across the country. But now, under the guise of anti-terrorism, there's also open season on people who look foreign, especially people of color who may happen to be immigrants.

Let there be no mistake, immigration is a civil rights issue! And immigration is a black issue, just as it is a brown issue.

Eleven percent of the black population in this country is immigrants.

The new workforces across this country are largely immigrants from Mexico, Russia, Poland, Haiti, and the Dominican Republic. But most importantly, we are a nation of immigrants.

Undocumented immigrants pay taxes and work hard. A recent study estimates that they contribute at least $300 billion to the U.S. economy annually.

Over 50,000 immigrants are serving in the armed forces, protecting this country.

As we know, immigrants are being rounded up and held for months at a time without charges or access to lawyers.

Some may say it doesn't affect them or their family, because they're not Muslim or Arab or from a foreign country.

Rest assured that whenever they get through fighting their so-called war on terrorism, they won't stop there. Who will be the next target?

History keeps the score card. We need look no further than the 30s, 40s, 50s and 60s to remember a time when our rights and civil liberties were under attack.

Brothers and sisters, please keep in mind that you don't have to be "foreign" to be stamped an enemy of the state.

The organizer of the Sleeping Car Porters, A. Phillip Randolph, was once labeled the most dangerous Negro in the country.

He was targeted, not only because he was organizing exploited sleeping car porters, but because he was uniting black men—isolated because of racism—into a larger movement with whites who also shared the common struggle as workers. Their struggle went beyond the color of their skin.

While the demographics have changed, that reality is no different today. In the larger society, "they" determine who's "colored" when it suits them.

For instance, at one time, Irish and Italian immigrants were not considered white until it became convenient for them to be pitted against the real colored folks.

In the land of the free and the home of the brave, we have seen Africans bought and sold; Native Americans stripped of their ancestral lands; special taxes paid by Chinese immigrants; Japanese Americans locked up in concentration camps; and Jewish refugees from Nazi-occupied Europe denied entry into neighborhoods and social organizations.

Aren't all those immigrant issues?

Uniting people who are similar is easy. What's really hard is uniting people who are different and finding the common links that make us all the same.

No ethnic or racial group has a lock on any issue, especially not injustice.

Blacks, Asians, and Latinos are all struggling for decent wages, adequate health care, and quality schools for their children.

The incarceration rates of black and brown young people are both higher than the percentage of their kids in college. Both groups still experience racial discrimination in housing, employment, and education.

There is no monopoly on racial exploitation. Nor should there be a monopoly on the fight for racial justice!

Yes, we must be our brother and sister's keeper.

As single and separate groups, we cannot achieve victories. Together we are not a minority. We are the majority!

Dr. King understood this. When he left Alabama and went to Chicago, he quickly realized that it was not only about racial justice but it was also about economic justice. That's why he started the Poor People's Campaign and died vowing to amass a new movement of people of all colors connected by the common struggle of economic justice.

That great organizer of farm workers Caesar Chavez also understood this. He united Filipino, Puerto Rican, Mexican, and even Arabic-speaking workers into a great movement.

He always prided himself in seeking "minimum dramatics" to win maximum results. For Caesar Chavez, the struggle was about what he called "winning small victories constantly."

His was a movement that was built on its humility and might. It amounted to giving the poorest people who worked at producing food, food for themselves. Not just bread to eat, but dignity that would allow them to believe in their worth as workers and as human beings.

And Reverend Jesse Jackson understands this. He always reminds us that the majority of poor people in this country are not black or Latino. They are white. And they don't all live in Appalachia.

In closing, to those who may be tired as we continue the long but winnable trudge uphill, I paraphrase the Reverend Joseph Lowery to urge you to not get tired. As we trudge up this very big hill, let's build on our collective strength because we've come too far, fought too hard, marched too long, and died too young to go backwards.

Let freedom ring and justice ride till victory!

We Want a Legalization Process (2006)

Luis Gutierrez, Gloria Romero, and Others

On May Day 2006, hundreds of thousands of immigrants and their allies, most of them Latinos, left their schools, workplaces, homes, and shops to participate in a nationwide protest event called "Day Without an Immigrant." Organizers designed the day as an economic boycott, and numerous businesses in major cities—stores, restaurants, farms, meatpacking companies, and more—closed for the day because of a lack of employees; some even closed to demonstrate solidarity with their immigrant workers. The day also included marches, and one of the favorite targets was a U.S. House bill—referred to below as "Sensenbrenner," shorthand for Wisconsin

Representative Jim Sensenbrenner, the bill's author—that increased bor-
der security and made it a felony to aid "illegal immigrants." But evoking
praise from the protestors was a U.S. Senate plan that offered immigrants
a pathway to citizenship. Below are comments offered on the day by U.S.
Representative Luis Gutierrez of Illinois, California state legislator Gloria
Romero, Los Angeles City Council member William Rosendahl, Gerardo
Lorenz of KTNQ in Los Angeles, and three other demonstrators.

Luis Gutierrez

If we were in Boston and it were 1850, 1860, we would be reading in the
newspaper about the dirty, the uneducated people who were coming to
this country, coming to this country and destroying America, and they
would be referring to Irish immigrants. If it were the turn of the century and it were 1910 and we were in New York City and we picked up
the *New York Times*, we'd read "Only by the rule of law could we hope to
control these people," and they would be referring to Italian immigrants.
You know what? They were wrong in Boston about the Irish. They were
wrong in New York about the Italians. And the Congress and Sensenbrenner was wrong about immigrants across this country today.

What we want—what we want is a legalization process that allows
all of those that work hard, are of good moral character, wishing to raise
their families through sweat and toil to make America a better country,
a road, a pathway to their legalization, so that they can come out of the
shadows of darkness, of discrimination, of bigotry, of exploitation, and
join us fully. I say to the Congress of the United States: You have two
options. Number one, show the political will. Put the resources forward
to deport 12 million people, and if you don't have that, then do the right
thing and legalize 12 million people.

Gloria Romero

It is my honor to march with the people today, constituents that I represent here in Los Angeles. It is a magnificent day in history, and I'm very
proud to present to you, the organizers and the people, a copy of the resolution that was passed by the California State Senate recognizing today

as the great American boycott. And we can look back and see that using a boycott is part of the American tradition, from the Boston Tea Party to Rosa Parks, Dr. Martin Luther King and Cesar Chavez. All we want is fair immigration reform and a recognition of the role of immigrants in this country. Si, se puede!

Bill Rosendahl
This very moment is a defining moment for the United States of America. This is truly a civil rights issue in the 21st century. What the Republican House of Representatives did in calling undocumented immigrants a felon is a disgrace. If there is a crime, it is the crime of leaving 11 million people in the shadows in this great country. We are all Americans! And I say to the Republican-controlled Congress: We want a path to citizenship for all of us. And if you don't see leadership coming from the Republican White House and the Senate and the House of Representatives, throw them out this November. And the last point, it is a crime not to give undocumented immigrants their driver's license. They must be able to have that so we all can be Americans together.

Gerardo Lorenz
I feel very proud of you. I feel proud to live in this nation, and that is why in California we're sending the loudest message, the clearest message, to the Congress of the United States: Here we are. We are asking for legalization. We won't accept anything less.

We need to recognize at all times the work of the women, the work of the men. We have spent decades being stepped on. We need to tell that to the far right of this nation, that we won't take a step backwards. We need to tell the people of Sensenbrenner that you can't use our lives to negotiate federal budgets. This is our presence. When you return to your homes, tell your neighbors that today our boycott was successful, was successful, was successful!

Greg Durandus
My name is Greg Durandus. I'm from Haiti, and I'm here to support

the many Haitian immigrants that live in the U.S. and especially in New York. And I'm here to tell the lawmakers how angry I am, because they don't show respect to the immigrants, and this is an immigrant country.

Margaret Chan

My name is Margaret Chan. I'm from Hong Kong. I came over from Hong Kong with my family when I was seven years old, so I am an immigrant. I am here to support all immigrants, and I'm here to show the people in Washington that it's a stupid idea to make it a felony for people who are undocumented here. I'm an immigration attorney. Does that mean I will be charged with a felony for helping my clients? You know, will doctors have to file, like, their Hippocratic Oath and not help an undocumented person? Is this not the most ridiculous thing you've ever heard of?

Tomiya

My name is Tomiya. I was born in New York, and I'm Japanese American. My family has been here for over a hundred years, and I'm here to support immigrants and immigrant rights. . . . I think that particularly for Asians and people of color, you know, they don't look like they're American, and even though my family has been here for generations, are still treated like foreigners. I certainly understand the racism and discrimination that recent immigrants face, and I'm particularly concerned with the Patriot Act and how that's affecting Arab communities, because I am the descendant of Japanese Americans who were interned. I certainly understand how dangerous the situation is, how it affects all Americans here today.

Stopping Another Deportation (2013)

United We Dream

In December 2010 the U.S. Senate failed to pass the Dream Act, a bipartisan effort to create a pathway to citizenship for undocumented immigrants

Protest against eliminating DACA, New York City, 2017.

who were brought into the United States as children, a group now known as DREAMers. With congressional action stalled, President Obama signed a June 15, 2002 executive memorandum that gave about 800,000 young immigrants protection from deportation and permission to study and work. "People are just breaking down and crying for joy when they found out what the president did," said Lorella Praile of the United We Dream Network, an advocacy group for immigrant youth. But there were limits to the celebration because the executive memorandum—Deferred Action for Childhood Arrivals (DACA)—did not address the outstanding question of citizenship.

United We Dream continued its protests, and on July 10, 2013, about 500 young immigrants and their family members held an "aspirational citizenship ceremony" near the U.S. Capitol as part of their national campaign to pressure the House of Representatives to pass legislation that would create a path to citizenship for 11 million immigrants. Called together by United We Dream, the DREAMers—they named themselves after the Dream Act—recited the "Pledge of Allegiance," sang "The Star-Spangled

Banner," and swore an oath penned for the day. "I hereby pledge to live out the highest values of this land," they said. "I am the future of this nation. I am the American dream." In the following month, DREAMers also carried out acts of civil disobedience. Below is an excerpted press release about an August 21 protest.

Late last night, leaders from United We Dream and the Arizona Dream Coalition, an affiliate of United We Dream, engaged in unprecedented civil disobedience and escalated action to stop a bus in the middle of deportation proceedings at the Phoenix Removal and Detention Facility, the ICE [U.S. Immigration and Customs Enforcement] post in downtown Phoenix. Six heroic DREAMers sat in front of the bus for more than two hours, before the bus finally retreated back into the ICE complex.

Last night's action shone a spotlight on ongoing detentions and deportations and the urgent need for the Obama administration to stop separating our families and for Congress to deliver real immigration reform.

Over one hundred people encircled the ICE facility until well after midnight to shut down operations and ongoing deportations, before local police arrested two leaders. Those arrested included an undocumented youth activist in Arizona, Jose Patino, and Ray Jose, a United We Dream leader and recent DACA recipient from Maryland. After being flooded with phone calls demanding release of the two DREAMers, authorities released both Jose and Patino.

"I am doing this because I am so fed up with people playing games with our lives," said Ray Jose. "My mom and dad are getting tired. My dad cannot do physical labor anymore. It is for the sake of my family, who sacrificed so much for me, that I am ready to do this." . . .

"I did this for my mother, because she works more than anyone in my family, and for my family, because they deserve a chance to fulfill their dreams," said Arizona leader Jose Patino.

This action came only hours after four other heroic DREAM leaders were arrested for chaining themselves to a fence of the ICE complex.

EIGHTEEN

The Trump Era Begins

Not a Legitimate President (January 2017)
John Lewis and Others

Shortly before the inauguration of Donald Trump as the forty-fifth president of the United States, NBC reporter Chuck Todd asked Representative John Lewis of Atlanta, a revered veteran of the civil rights movement, whether he would seek to build a relationship with the incoming president.

"No," Lewis replied. "I believe in forgiveness. I believe in trying to work with people. It's going to be hard. It's going to be very difficult. I don't see this president-elect as a legitimate president."

When Todd pushed for an explanation, Lewis added: "I think the Russians participated in helping this man get elected. And they helped destroy the candidacy of Hillary Clinton."

The congressman then dropped a (nonviolent) bombshell. "I don't plan to attend the inauguration," he said.

Trump exploded on Twitter when he learned of Lewis's planned boycott.

By the time of the inaugural, more than sixty-five Democrats in the House of Representatives announced that they were boycotting the event. Below are some of their announcements; these include references to @realDonaldTrump, the name of Trump's Twitter account.

Virginia Representative Don Beyer
Yes, I treasure the peaceful transfer of power. Yes, I will respect the constitutional prerogatives of the presidency. But I will not be normalizing or legitimizing a man whose election may well have depended on the malicious foreign interference of Russia's leaders, a person who lies profusely and without apology, who mimics the disabilities of others, who insults anyone who dares disagree with him, who would demonize an entire spiritual tradition, and who has demonstrated again and again a profound disrespect for women. His values and his actions are the antitheses of those I hold dear. It would be the height of hypocrisy for me to pretend to be part of this inaugural celebration.

New York Representative Adriano Espaillat
Many have given their lives and dedicated their lives to working to fulfill Dr. King's dream and make it a reality, and it is up to us to preserve his legacy and the legacy of President Barack Obama to ensure that we do not go back in time! President-elect Donald Trump is trying to take us back! And the people Trump is appointing—Steve Bannon, Jeff Sessions—are trying to take us back!

That's why I am not attending the presidential inauguration. Donald Trump and his hate-filled rhetoric that plagued his election simply will continue in his administration. *This* is not Dr. King's Dream!

Illinois Representative Luis Gutierrez
I cannot go to the inauguration of a man who's going to appoint people to the Supreme Court and turn back the clock on women and turn back the clock on immigrants and the safety and freedom that we fought for them.

California Representative Barbara Lee
Inaugurations are celebratory events, a time to welcome the peaceful transition of power and honor the new administration. On January 20th, I will not be celebrating or honoring an incoming president who rode racism, sexism, xenophobia, and bigotry to the White House. . . .

He began his campaign by insulting Mexican immigrants, pledging to build a wall between the United States and Mexico, and then spent a year and a half denigrating communities of color and normalizing bigotry. He called women "pigs," stoked Islamaphobia, and attacked a Gold Star family. He mocked a disabled reporter. . . .

The president-elect has named Steve Bannon, a white nationalist, as his chief strategist. He has nominated Jeff Sessions to the office of attorney general, despite his long career of opposition to civil and human rights. And in perhaps the most damning sign of the chaos to come, the president-elect has expedited the process to repeal the Affordable Care Act and make America sick again.

To make matters worse, after the intelligence community reported Russian interference in our election, Donald Trump frequently and forcefully defended Vladimir Putin. . . . The American people will never forget that when a foreign government violated our democracy, Donald Trump chose the interests of another nation over our own. . . .

On Inauguration Day, I will not be celebrating. I will be organizing and preparing for resistance.

Wisconsin Representative Gwen Moore
When he sees me, I want him to see the resistance.

New York Representative Jerrold Nadler
The rhetoric and actions of Donald Trump have been so far beyond the pale—so disturbing and disheartening—and his continued failure to address his conflicts of interest, to adequately divest or even to fully disclose his financial dealings, or to sufficiently separate himself from the ethical conduct that legal experts on both sides of the aisle have identified, have been so offensive I cannot in good conscience participate in this honored and revered democratic tradition of the peaceful transfer of power.

California Representative Maxine Waters
I never even contemplated attending the inauguration or any activities associated with @realDonaldTrump. I wouldn't waste my time.

Our Pussies Ain't for Grabbing (January 2017)

The Women's March and America Ferrera

On January 21, the first full day of Donald Trump's presidency, more than four million people participated in the Women's March on Washington and its "sister marches." Scholars Erica Chenoweth and Jeremy Pressman describe it as "likely the largest single-day demonstration in recorded U.S. history." There were more than 650 sister marches across the United States, with more than 100,000 attending those in Los Angeles, Oakland, San Francisco, New York City, Chicago, Denver, Seattle, and Boston. Some of the marches took place under very difficult circumstances. Chenoweth and Pressman noted that five people marched in a Los Angeles cancer ward, 2,000 in below-zero temperatures in Fairbanks, and forty in a wind chill of forty below in Unalakleet.

Women and their allies were highly motivated in large part because of the widely publicized revelation that in 2005 Donald Trump had bragged that he could kiss women and grab their genitals without their consent— actions that U.S. laws classify as sexual assault, a chargeable offense. Trump had made other disparaging comments about women through the years, and a former business partner, Jill Harth, publicly accused Trump of sexual harassment and attempted rape. During the campaign, Trump also provoked outrage when he made sexist remarks about news anchor Megyn Kelly and presidential candidates Hillary Clinton and Carly Fiorina.

Fueled by Trump's misogynistic comments and actions, many women, men, and children at the January 21 marches wore "pussyhats," pink knit hats with cat ears, that were intended by their creators to be symbols of "support and solidarity for women's rights and political resistance."

More than 500,000 protestors participated in the Women's March on Washington, dwarfing the number of those who had attended Trump's inauguration. In strategizing about the march's purpose, organizers took direction not only from past women's marches, with their focus on issues such as abortion, sexual violence, and equal pay, but also from the increasing tendency of mass marches to target a wide array of issues. See below for the numerous intersectional principles guiding the march.

Speakers for the day included Faye Wattleton and Gloria Steinem, Janelle Monae and John Lewis, Scarlett Johanssen and Ashley Judd, and America Ferrera and Michael Moore. Ashley Judd drew special attention to Trump's vulgarity by reading a poem penned by nineteen-year-old Nina Donovan from Tennessee. "Our pussies ain't for grabbing," Judd recited. "They are for birthing new generations of filthy, vulgar, nasty, proud, Christian, Muslim, Buddhist, Sikh, you name it, for new generations of nasty women." Ferrera's speech appears below, just after the list of march principles.

March Principles
We believe that Women's Rights are Human Rights and Human Rights are Women's Rights. We must create a society in which women—including Black women, Native women, poor women, immigrant women, disabled women, Muslim women, lesbian, queer, and trans women—are free and able to care for and nurture their families, however they are formed, in safe and healthy environments free from structural impediments.

Ending Violence. Women deserve to live full and healthy lives, free of all forms of violence against our bodies. We believe in accountability and justice in cases of police brutality and ending racial profiling and targeting of communities of color. It is our moral imperative to dismantle the gender and racial inequities within the criminal justice system.

Reproductive Rights. We believe in Reproductive Freedom. We do not accept any federal, state, or local rollbacks, cuts, or restrictions on our ability to access quality reproductive healthcare services, birth control, HIV/AIDS care and prevention, or medically accurate sexuality education. This means open access to safe, legal, affordable abortion, and birth control for all people, regardless of income, location, or education.

LGBTQIA Rights. We firmly declare that LGBTQIA Rights are Human Rights and that it is our obligation to uplift, expand, and protect the rights of our gay, lesbian, bi, queer, trans, or gender non-conforming brothers, sisters, and siblings. We must have the power to control our bodies and be free from gender norms, expectations, and stereotypes.

Worker's Rights. We believe in an economy powered by transparency, accountability, security, and equity. All women should be paid equitably, with access to affordable childcare, sick days, healthcare, paid family leave, and healthy work environments. All workers—including domestic and farm workers, undocumented and migrant workers—must have the right to organize and fight for a living minimum wage.

Civil Rights. We believe Civil Rights are our birthright, including voting rights, freedom to worship without fear of intimidation or harassment, freedom of speech, and protections for all citizens regardless of race, gender, age, or disability. We believe it is time for an all-inclusive Equal Rights Amendment to the U.S. Constitution.

Disability Rights. We believe that all women's issues are issues faced by women with disabilities and Deaf women. As mothers, sisters, daughters, and contributing members of this great nation, we seek to break barriers to access, inclusion, independence, and the full enjoyment of citizenship at home and around the world. We strive to be fully included in and contribute to all aspects of American life, economy, and culture.

Immigrant Rights. Rooted in the promise of America's call for huddled masses yearning to breathe free, we believe in immigrant and refugee rights regardless of status or country of origin. We believe migration is a human right and that no human being is illegal.

Environmental Justice. We believe that every person and every community in our nation has the right to clean water, clean air, and access to and enjoyment of public lands. We believe that our environment and our climate must be protected, and that our land and natural resources cannot be exploited for corporate gain or greed—especially at the risk of public safety and health.

America Ferrera
It's been a heart-wrenching time to be both a woman and an immigrant in this country. Our dignity, our character, our rights have all been under

The Women's March, Washington, D.C., 2017.

attack, and a platform of hate and division assumed power yesterday. But the president is not America. His cabinet is not America. Congress is not America. We are America. And we are here to stay.

We march today for our families and our neighbors, for our future, for the causes we claim, and for the causes that claim us.

We march today for the moral core of this nation, against which our new president is waging a war. He would like us to forget the words—"Give me your tired, your poor, your huddled masses yearning to breathe free"—and instead take up a credo of hate, fear, and suspicion of one another.

But we are gathered here and across the country and around the world to say, "Mr. Trump, we refuse!"

We reject the demonization of our Muslim brothers and sisters. We demand an end to the systemic murder and incarceration of our Black brothers and sisters. We will not give up our right to safe and legal abortions. We will not ask our LGBTQ families to go backwards.

We will not go from being a nation of immigrants to a nation of ignorance. We will not build walls, and we won't see the worst in each other.

And we will not turn our backs on the more than 750,000 young immigrants in this country currently protected by DACA. They are hardworking, upstanding, courageous individuals who refuse to live in the shadow of fear and isolation. They bravely took to the streets to declare themselves and to provide a voice and hope for their community. Today we march with and for them.

Together, we, all of us, will fight, resist, and oppose any single action that threatens the lives and dignity of any and all of our communities.

Together We Rise (March 2017)

Dave Archambault II

Plans for the Dakota Access Pipeline called for the construction of a 1200-milelong pipeline that would transport about 570,000 barrels of crude oil every day from North Dakota to Illinois. When environmental activists learned about this in 2014, they registered their opposition, claiming that fossil fuels should stay underground and that extracting them would most likely add to the negative effects of climate change. The most visible protesters of the pipeline were those in the Standing Rock Sioux tribe, who argued that leaks in the pipeline would contaminate their main water supply, the Missouri River, resulting in major health and economic problems.

The protests began to attract national attention in 2016 when thousands of tribal members and their allies held nonviolent demonstrations at the pipeline's construction sites. The Standing Rock Sioux built a protest camp, where thousands of protestors, including many members of different

Native American tribes, resided in teepees, tents, and temporary buildings. The protests went on for months, and on occasion tensions between the protestors and the local police officers erupted, with the police using attack dogs, pepper spray, rubber bullets, and concussion cannons in their attempt to disperse the protestors.

In light of the concerns expressed by the demonstrators, President Obama declared a temporary halt to the construction in September 2016. But President Trump issued an executive order allowing construction to proceed just after he assumed office in January 2017.

Three months later, members of the Standing Rock Sioux Nation, along with other tribal leaders and their allies, gathered for the Native Nations Rise March in Washington, DC, to demand treaty rights and talks with President Trump. When the marchers reached the Trump International Hotel on Pennsylvania Avenue, they set up a teepee and shouted, "Shame!" The march led to a rally across from the White House, where Standing Rock Sioux Tribal Chairman Dave Archambault II delivered the following remarks.

Let me begin by thanking you all for traveling to be here this week. I know many of you have made great sacrifices to travel to both Standing Rock and now to Washington DC, and let me tell you that without each and every one of these individual sacrifices, we would not have made it as far as we have today.

We have faced one obstacle after another and these obstacles are punctuated by a variety of slights and defeats, but it is not over. We are not defeated. We are not victims. An obstacle is also an opportunity. Together, we confront these obstacles; embrace these opportunities.

Together, we rise.

Today, it is not only we Native Americans that are being ignored and pushed aside in favor of the interests of another. Many of our ally communities are experiencing what we have been for centuries: our ways of life are being destroyed, dictated, limited, and manipulated at the whim of the federal government.

For Natives, treaties were signed and laws were made, but they were summarily destroyed or abrogated when it became merely inconvenient or undesirable to those in charge. For all of us, laws were put in place to respect freedom and equality for all, and each week we see more and more of these basic human rights summarily dismissed by a distant and ruthless administration.

For all American citizens today, and for us Native Americans, for a very long, long, time—the question has been, Why? How? What could possibly justify such treatment and dismissal of basic human respect? They call it the Doctrine of Discovery. In the United States judicial system, the foundational case of not only federal Indian law but property law is based upon the premise that it is not the Native inhabitants of the land who determine its fate. Instead, that decision-making power lies with whichever conquering European nation "possesses" it. Whichever legitimate nation "discovers" it then gains control, and the rights of the Native Nations are "inherently diminished."

There has never been a legitimate legal justification for taking, defining, or diminishing Native Nations. Yet our own legal system is founded upon a hasty, religious-based notion of discovery that distinctly creates two classes of people: those who belong to the conqueror, and those who do not.

From the very beginning, those seeking to build an empire described our ancestors as "limited owners" or mere occupants of the land. They were free to do as they willed. Centuries later, we still see this happening. We see the alleged minority community interests of Bismarck, North Dakota outweighing the interests of our entire tribe. We see corporations being allowed to take shortcuts with the federal government that bypass regulations put in place to protect basic human health.

We see this everywhere. Many tribes across this country and Indigenous Nations around the world are struggling with this very same problem—the imperialistic, conquistador spirit is so deeply embedded in Western and capitalistic society that hundreds of years later, our government is using the exact same arguments to disavow the safety and well-being of entire populations. Not only do they disrespect people of a different origin, they disrespect the treaty rights retained by the original Americans.

Solidarity with Standing Rock march, San Francisco, 2016.

We are in dark and unknown territory. Very real threats to our way of life and our freedom are being issued daily, and we are facing a realistic dismantling of our country as we know it.

Fellow Americans, allies—I stand with you. I hope that you understand that this is the way my fellow Native Americans have felt for centuries. Now we are all in the same boat. We are facing a regime that has no regard for American values, and does not hesitate to fly in the face of the law to benefit the immature antics of an unhinged leader and his moneyed friends.

We are here to resist hate and fear. All around the country we see protests and marches. It is obvious that we are at a tipping point where we must inevitably stand up for what is right. Never before in Indian country have we experienced the level of public awareness and the strength in diverse numbers that we see now. We have reached a critical moment in time where citizens are realizing that we must stand for the core of humanity.

The Standing Rock movement marks a turning point in history not only for tribes, but for every American, because the heart of our movement is now the heart of the resistance. We want and need this movement to live, to build, to resist, and ultimately to succeed. No community should have their interests, public safety, or wellbeing tossed aside because of the interests of corporations or the politically connected. Tribes; immigrants; women; people of color; your average, hard-working American: we are all in this together.

We are in the 21st century. This is no longer a matter of explorers and imperialists versus savages and infidels. We are all Americans, and above all, we are all human. We all deserve to be included, to be respected, and to have our basic rights considered when a corporation seeks to carry out an action that could potentially cause harm to our citizens. At this point in history, we need to be considering our planet and natural resources above all else. We need to ensure the future of our children.

We have fallen prey to this misguided and unfounded system long enough. It is time we stand up and demand our rights and considerations be treated with the respect and deference afforded any other sovereign. We are on the cusp of real change. You stood with Standing Rock and now I ask you to stand with our Indigenous communities around the globe. Together, we rise.

Fearless Girl (April 2017)

Susan Cox

On March 7, 2017, less than two months into the new Trump administration and on the eve of International Women's Day, State Street Global Advisers, a $2.5 trillion asset manager with worldwide offices, installed the statue of "Fearless Girl" directly across from the famous charging bull statue on Wall Street. The girl appears defiant, with her fists on her hips, clad in boots, her eyes staring straight ahead, and her strong chin tilting up, leaning forward. (For a photograph of the statue, see the front cover of this book.)

State Street had installed the statue as part of its campaign to encourage companies to have at least one female board member and to take additional measures to increase gender diversity. At the time of the installation,

Lori Heinel, State Street's deputy global chief investment officer, said, "One of the most iconic images on Wall Street is the charging bull. So the idea of having a female sort of stand against the bull or stand up to the bull just struck us as a very clever but also creative and engaging way to make that statement. Even though it's a little girl, her stance is one of determination, forwardness, and being willing to challenge and take on the status quo."

The Fearless Girl quickly attracted those who were drawn to the statue's apparent stance of opposition. Senator Elizabeth Warren of Massachusetts, Wall Street's (and President Trump's) arch nemesis in Congress, tweeted a photograph of herself standing next to the girl. Thousands of feminists and opponents of unfettered capitalism joined Warren in paying homage to the statue.

State Street Global Advisers pushed back. Lynn Black, an executive vice president, responded to the Resistance's adoption of the statue by saying that Fearless Girl was really "a complement to the charging bull, which represents economic strength." The Fearless Girl was not a mini Elizabeth Warren at all. "She's not raising her fist against the bull," Black said. "She's there to represent her role as a leader, to stand on equal footing, and to play a powerful role in expanding economic prosperity for the world." Kristen Visbal, the sculptor of the statue, supported State Street's interpretation. "She is strong, but not belligerent," Visbal said of her work. "She is proud, but not confrontational." Complicating matters was the not-so-subtle advertisement on the plaque at the base of the statue: "Know the power of women in leadership. SHE makes a difference." The use of "SHE" seemed quite appropriate, given the strength of the little girl, but the public quickly learned that "SHE" was also the ticker symbol for Gender Diversity Index, one of State Street's investment funds.

Leftist publications reacted by identifying the statue as yet another corporate manipulation of the masses. Nick Pinto of the Village Voice described the Fearless Girl as "corporate brand-burnishing"—"not your friend." But the statue continued to attract thousands who didn't care about interpretations from State Street, the sculptor, or even the Village Voice. The reflection below, by writer, feminist, and philosopher Susan

Cox, articulates why the Fearless Girl remains a compelling symbol for the Resistance in the Trump years.

When I first saw an image of the Fearless Girl statue, I was moved. It is rare to see any statue of a woman or girl in New York, let alone one standing in such a bold and defiant pose. . . .

Many of my feminist friends (and social commentators in the media) have argued that the Fearless Girl represents a form of corporate feminism. . . . The stated message behind the statue is that it is advocating for the importance of women in executive leadership positions in male-dominated industries such as finance.

But few will see the statue and come away with that message. In fact, the artist who made the Wall Street "Charging Bull" statue, Arturo Di Modica, agrees with me. At a recent press conference, Di Modica explained that he was unhappy with the Fearless Girl because it changed the meaning of his statue, so that the bull now represents a negative establishment power that is a threat to women and girls. Which is true . . . The two statues together most obviously convey an image of a girl standing up to the forces of male-supremacist capitalism.

Di Modica also claimed that his statue had previously represented "the strength and power of the American people." If "the strength and power of the American people" is the way you prefer to say "American capitalism," sure, that's what it represented. But it certainly didn't just represent some sex-neutral "people." That bull is a raging juggernaut of masculinity, with its huge ball sack, at home in the bro-iest district of the city. . . .

Because of this context, the Fearless Girl also become humorous commentary on the ridiculousness of beastly machismo, which her easy confidence mocks. Mirroring gender dynamics in life, it appears that the more self-assured the girl is, the more the bull rages. Really, there couldn't be a more fun twist on a global icon of masculinity than this defiant little statue.

The Fearless Girl isn't perfect, but *so what?* Isn't having her better than not? Through the eyes of a little girl, will she see the statue and think of corporate boards? Maybe. But mostly she'll see herself represented with a power and confidence that is usually reserved for males alone. So why not champion the Fearless Girl so that she becomes a permanent fixture in New York, where we really could use more female statues?

As feminist writer Caroline Criado-Perez points out, NYC's Central Park has 22 statues of men and *none* of women, other than fictional characters like Alice in Wonderland. . . .

I don't know about you, but I find fighting women's oppression exhausting. We are up against enormous power, and I for one could use a few more symbols in the world that make me smile. When I see that small girl standing in front of that behemoth, I am reminded of Lierre Keith's words:

> We're going to have to match their contempt with our courage. We're going to have to match their brute power with our fierce and fragile dreams. We're going to have to match their endless sadism with a determination that will not bend and will not break and will not stop.

> Take heart, sisters.

And So We Resist Global Warming (June 2017)

Bill McKibben

On April 29, 2017, the hundredth day of the Trump presidency, thousands of protestors at the People's Climate March strode down Pennsylvania Avenue, chanting "Keep it in the soil, can't drink oil!" and "We're here, we're hot, this planet's all we got!" As they circled around the White House, another chant came to the fore: "Resistance is here to stay, welcome to your 100th day!"

The marchers were disturbed by President Trump's pick to head the

Environmental Protection Agency (EPA), Scott Pruitt, an attorney general of Oklahoma, who had actively resisted President Obama's efforts to reduce greenhouse gas emissions from power plants. Equally troubling was Trump's announced plan to eliminate federal spending on climate science and his March 28 executive order instructing the EPA to begin rolling back federal regulations that sought to shut down hundreds of coal-fired plants and prevent the construction of new ones. The most devastating action, however, occurred after the People's Climate March, on June 1, when Trump announced in a press conference that the United States would withdraw from the Paris climate accord, which committed 195 countries to reduce emissions that contribute to the planet's warming.

Trump's decision evoked criticisms from across the globe, and President Emmanuel Macron of France delivered an especially stinging rebuke. "Make our planet great again," he said, referring to Trump's campaign slogan ("Make America Great Again"). In Washington, DC, hundreds shouted "Shame!" as they rallied across from the White House and heard Democratic National Committee Chair Tom Perez claim that clean energy is the path to new jobs in the United States. Another major critic was Bill McKibben, a pioneering and veteran protestor of global warming, whose commentary on Trump's decision appears below.

People say, if all you have is a hammer, then every problem looks like a nail. We should be so lucky. President Trump has a hammer, but all he'll use it for is to smash things that others have built, as the world looks on in wonder and in fear. The latest, most troubling example is his decision to obliterate the Paris climate accord: After nearly 200 years of scientific inquiry and over 20 years of patient diplomacy that united every nation save Syria and Nicaragua, we had this afternoon's big game-show Rose Garden reveal: Count us out.

It's a stupid and reckless decision—our nation's dumbest act since launching the war in Iraq. But it's not stupid and reckless in the normal way. Instead, it amounts to a thorough repudiation of two of the civilizing forces on our planet: diplomacy and science. It undercuts our civilization's chances of surviving global warming, but it also undercuts our civilization itself, since that civilization rests in large measure on those two forces.

Science first. Since the early 1880s we've been slowly but surely figuring out the mystery of how our climate operates—why our planet is warmer than it should be, given its distance from the sun. From Fourier to Foote and Tyndall, from Arrhenius to Revelle and Suess and Keeling, researchers have worked out the role that carbon dioxide and other greenhouse gases play in regulating temperature. By the 1980s, as supercomputers let us model the climate with ever greater power, we came to understand our possible fate. Those big brains, just in time, gave us the warning we required.

And now, in this millennium, we've watched the warning start to play out. We've seen 2014 set a new global temperature record, which was smashed in 2015 and smashed again in 2016. We've watched Arctic sea ice vanish at a record pace and measured the early disintegration of Antarctica's great ice sheets. We've been able to record alarming increases in drought and flood and wildfire, and we've been able to link them directly to the greenhouse gases we've poured into the atmosphere. This is the largest-scale example in the planet's history of the scientific method in operation, the continuing dialectic between hypothesis and skepticism that arrived eventually at a strong consensus about the most critical aspects of our planet's maintenance. Rational people the world around understand. As *Bloomberg Businessweek* blazoned across its cover the week after Hurricane Sandy smashed into Wall Street, "It's Global Warming, Stupid."

But now President Trump (and 22 Republican senators who wrote a letter asking him to take the step) is betting that all of that is wrong. Mr. Trump famously called global warming a hoax during the campaign, and with this decision he's wagering that he was actually right—he's calling his own bluff. No line of argument in the physical world supports his claim, and no credible authority backs him, not here and not abroad. It's telling that he simultaneously wants to cut the funding for the satellites and ocean buoys that monitor our degrading climate. Every piece of data they collect makes clear his foolishness. He's simply insisting that physics isn't real.

But it's not just science that he's blowing up. The Paris accord was a high achievement of the diplomatic art, a process much messier than science, and inevitably involving compromise and unseemly concession. Still, after decades of work, the world's negotiators managed to bring along virtually every nation: the Saudis and the low-lying Marshall Islanders, the Chinese and the Indians. One hundred and ninety-five nations negotiated the Paris accord, including the United States.

The dysfunctional American political process had already warped the process, of course. The reason Paris is a series of voluntary agreements and not a real treaty is because the world had long since understood that no binding document would ever get two-thirds of the vote in our oil-soaked Senate. And that's despite the fact that the agreement asks very little of us: President Barack Obama's mild shift away from coal-fired power and toward higher-mileage cars would have satisfied our obligations.

Those changes, and similar ones agreed to by other nations, would not have ended global warming. They were too small. But the hope of Paris was that the treaty would send such a strong signal to the world's governments, and its capital markets, that the targets would become a floor and not a ceiling; that shaken into action by the accord, we would start moving much faster toward renewable energy, maybe even fast enough to begin catching up with the physics of global warming. There are signs that this has been happening: The plummeting price of solar energy just this spring persuaded India to forgo a huge planned expansion of coal plants in favor of more solar panel arrays to catch the sun. China is shutting coal mines as fast as it can build wind turbines.

And that's precisely the moment President Trump chose to make his move, a bid to undercut our best hope for a workable future in a bizarre attempt to restore the past. A few fossil-fuel barons may be pleased (Vladimir Putin likely among them, since his reign rests on the unobstructed development of Russia's hydrocarbons), but most of the country and the world see this for the disaster it is. Majorities in every single state, red and blue alike, wanted America to stay in the accord.

And so we will resist. As the federal government reneges on its commitments, the rest of us will double down on ours. Already cities and states are committing to 100 percent renewable energy. Atlanta was the latest to take the step. We will make sure that every leader who hesitates and waffles on climate will be seen as another Donald Trump, and we will make sure that history will judge that name with the contempt it deserves. Not just because he didn't take climate change seriously, but also because he didn't take civilization seriously.

Dying for Health Care (June 2017)
ADAPT

On June 22, 2017, U.S. Capitol police arrested forty-three activists during a die-in outside the office of Senate Majority Leader Mitch McConnell of Kentucky. Organized by ADAPT, a disability advocates organization, the die-in protested proposed cuts to Medicaid in the Better Care Reconciliation Act, a health care reform bill designed to replace the Affordable Care Act (ACA), otherwise known as Obamacare. (In the document below, ADAPT's press release about the event, reference is made to the U.S. House bill designed to replace ACA.)

Many of the protestors at McConnell's office were in wheelchairs and connected to lifesaving medical equipment; some of them pulled themselves off their chairs and laid on the floor, and all who were able chanted, "No cuts to Medicaid—save our liberty!" McConnell did not greet his visitors. But the Capitol police showed up, and the protestors shouted even louder as the officers forcibly dragged or carried them away. Images of the event quickly found their way to social media. Republican efforts to repeal and replace ACA failed the following month.

Today, about 60 members of the national disability rights organization ADAPT are staging a die-in at Senate Majority Leader Mitch McConnell's office. Advocates are protesting McConnell's Senate healthcare bill, demanding he bring an end to attacks on disabled people's freedom which are expected in the bill. "The American Health Care Act caps and significantly cuts Medicaid which will greatly reduce access to medical care and home- and community-based services for elderly and disabled Americans who will either die or be forced into institutions," said Brice Darling, an ADAPT organizer taking part in the protest. "Our lives and liberty shouldn't be stolen to give a tax break to the wealthy. That's truly un-American."

Not only will AHCA take away our freedom," said Dawn Russell, an ADAPT organizer from Colorado, "that lost freedom will also cost Americans much more money. The nursing facilities that people will be forced into are much more expensive than community-based services that AHCA would cut." In 2012, the National Council on Disability (an independent federal agency that makes policy recommendations to the President, Congress, and federal agencies) reported that states spent upwards of $300,000 more per person serving disabled people in institutions each year than they would spend providing equivalent services in the community.

The prospect falls on the 18th anniversary of *Olmstead v. LC,* the 1999 Supreme Court ruling which first recognized disabled people's rights to live in the community. ADAPT organizer Nancy Salandra of Pennsylvania was quick to note the connection between that case and the AHCA. "We fought so hard to have our right to live in the community recognized and here we are 18 years later and we are still fighting for our freedom from incarceration."

As they dramatize the deaths AHCA's cuts and forced institutionalization will cause, and as police close in, the advocates who came to McConnell's office from across the country chanted, "I'd rather go to jail than die without Medicaid."

"To say people will die under this law is not an exaggeration," said

Mike Oxford, an ADAPT organizer from Kansas. "Home- and community-based services are what allow us to do our jobs, live our lives, and raise our families. Without these services many disabled and elderly Americans *will* die. We won't let that happen."

On the 15th anniversary of John Dart, the father of the ADA [American Disabilities Act], his words ring true: "Get into politics as if your life depends upon it, 'cause it does."

A White Nationalist Rally in Charlottesville (August 2017)

Brendan Novak

On February 7, 2017, Charlottesville (Virginia) City Council voted in a 3-2 decision to remove a statute of Confederate General Robert E. Lee from Lee Park. Supporters of the measure argued that the statue was a symbol of white supremacy and glorification of Confederate support for slavery. The removal sparked protests, and on Friday, August 11, 2017, white supremacists marched on the campus of the University of Virginia. They gathered again the following day for a "Unite the Right Rally." The Saturday morning rally, which included neo-Nazis and Ku Klux Klan members, attracted counterdemonstrators, and by 11:00 a.m. members of the two groups had physically confronted each other in the park. After city police dispersed the rally, white nationalist James Alex Field drove his car into a crowd of counterdemonstrators celebrating the end of the rally. Field killed 32-year-old paralegal Heather Heyer, who had been there in support of the counterdemonstration, and injured several others; he was later charged with first-degree murder. Brendan Novak, an opinion editor for UVA's student newspaper, reflects on the rally in the column below.

A few weeks ago, I wrote a column in *The Cavalier Daily* explaining the reasoning behind my belief that the alt-right rally should go on. The way I see it, white supremacists, despite their irrefutably toxic ideology, are entitled to the same constitutional liberties as anyone else. I figured, maybe naïvely, that allowing them to assemble in public under the scrutiny of daylight would galvanize public opinion against their hateful beliefs and reveal the rotting foundation on which their ideology rests. It's safe to say that the words and actions of the agitators in town over the weekend have proven how foolish I was. That's not to say I no longer stand by my belief in the sanctity of the First Amendment. I still maintain unconditional support for the right of any individual or group to express themselves, regardless of the message. My concern stems from the fact that the series of demonstrations which unraveled in Charlottesville no longer, and perhaps never did, qualify as protected speech.

Late Friday night we witnessed armed white supremacists marching through Grounds with lit torches, threatening, harassing and physically assaulting students who were organizing peacefully, or trying to go about their business as usual despite the shocking display unfolding in their backyard. On Saturday, the violence only worsened as the white supremacists lashed out against counter-protesters. Three people died, and dozens more were injured as a result of their barbarism. The members of the protest were abundantly clear with their intentions to incite violence in Charlottesville. Their calls for intimidation and agitation are well documented. What I failed to realize before today is that these threats were not overblown rhetoric. The way the ralliers conducted themselves over the weekend is disgusting and inexcusable.

I defended the rights of these white supremacists to assemble based on a belief of open access to the marketplace of ideas, where open discourse allows society to sort through ideologies without the outsize interference of institutions or governments. What I now realize is that the alt-right has no interest in participating in open discourse. Their weekend of demonstrations, and their entire movement, is based on overt and unapologetic intimidation, harassment and threats of violence. I defended the right of the alt-right to peacefully assemble, but they never intended for their assembly to be peaceful. They organized, applied for a

Cornel West, second from right in back, and others protesting "Unite the Right" rally in Charlottesville, Virginia, 2017.

permit and came to town with the full intention of inciting violence and agitating both the community and the national media.

The alt-right is a domestic terrorist organization. Their use of intimidation, terror and violence in the pursuit of their goals more than justify this categorization. They have no interest in engaging in reasoned, mature discourse within the bounds of civil society, and would rather rely on brute force and terrorism to achieve their goals. When the alt-right enters the open marketplace of ideas, they necessarily lose. It is precisely because of this fact that they rely on tactics such as intimidation and terror. Just as I would hesitate to approve of an assembly permit for any other terrorist organization that made consistent, credible threats of violence, I have serious reservations about the claims that this assembly of white supremacists has to protections under the First Amendment.

What is unsettling about recent events is the fact that the protest permit has proven to be mostly irrelevant in the first place. The unsanctioned mass display of intimidation that occurred on Friday is proof enough. I was right to say in my earlier column that "the hateful rhetoric of the alt-right will not simply disappear if the government makes it harder for the ideas to be shared openly." When the Charlottesville City Council ordered the rally be moved to McIntire Park due to concerns of overcrowding, organizers affirmed their intention to disregard the decision and hold the rally in Emancipation Park anyway. Refusing to issue permits to the alt-right doesn't solve any problems; if anything it only creates more. Clearly, these white supremacists will organize either way, and I fear for what could happen if there are more unsanctioned protests without a police presence such as the one on Friday night.

I don't pretend to have the answers for how to properly address the blight which has fallen on Charlottesville, and society as a whole. It is not right to grant assembly permits to groups that openly advertise their intent to commit acts of violence and harassment, but it's no better to allow them to freely and lawlessly pursue their agenda of terror. I still believe true progress and healing can be achieved only through open, honest dialogue, but I'm unsure if it's reasonable to expect the alt-right to come to the table without a fundamental cultural change.

I was wrong about the nature of the alt-right, but I am encouraged by the widespread backlash and denunciation of their ideology. Despite the shocking, gut-wrenching images coming out of my town, the solidarity on display gives me hope that we can work towards a more open and inclusive society.

Targeting Transgender Troops (November 2017)

Jennifer Peace

On July 26, 2017, President Trump took to Twitter to announce a ban on transgender people serving in the U.S. military. "After consultation with my Generals and military experts, please be advised that the United States Government will not accept or allow Transgender individuals to serve in any capacity in the U.S. military," he tweeted. "Our military must be focused on decisive and overwhelming victory and cannot be burdened with the tremendous medical costs and disruption that transgender in the military would entail. Thank you."

Experts immediately questioned Trump's claim about "tremendous medical costs," arguing that predicted costs for gender-transition treatment over a decade ($24 to $84 million) were negligible compared to annual expenditures for erectile dysfunction medicine ($84 million), that allowing gays and lesbians to serve openly in the U.S. military had no significant effect on troop cohesion or readiness, and that about 15,000 transgender soldiers had already served with distinction.

LGBT veterans, advocates, and their allies took to the streets in San Francisco, New York City, and Washington, DC. At the Washington protest, Racheal Deamer of Tyler, Texas, captured the crowd's outrage when she said, "That motherfucker couldn't even serve a day in his life, and he wants to tell other people about whether they should serve?" Below is a protest article penned by Captain Jennifer Peace, an intelligence officer in the U.S. Army.

I can recall where I celebrated every Veterans Day since 2005, during my 13 years of service with the United States Army. One was in Baghdad, Iraq, and another was in Kandahar, Afghanistan. My wife was pregnant and alone the Veterans Day I spent in South Korea, and she was raising our three children by herself the year I was conducting training in the Pacific theater. On four other occasions I was in various training exercises across the country: Sweating in the heat at Fort Huachuca, Arizona. Freezing in the snow at Fort Sill, Oklahoma.

But the most memorable Veterans Day was in 2016. Not because it was spent in some far-off corner of the world, but because I was serving for the first time as my authentic self. The U.S. military had successfully integrated transgender soldiers into its ranks. I could look forward to the rest of my career with the knowledge that I would only be discriminated against based solely on my performance.

As my brigade marched in the local parade I was without fear or anxiety for the first time in many years.

Every November 11 that I have been privileged enough to wake up and put on the uniform has been an honor, and it is on those days that the sound of the bugle at reveille and the raising of the flag seems more ephemeral, a moment that I must somehow capture before the last of my days in service are behind me and I see the flag only as a civilian.

In June 2016, Secretary of Defense Ash Carter announced that transgender service members could serve openly in the armed forces. He determined that trans service members are "talented and trained Americans who are serving their country with honor and distinction. We can't allow barriers unrelated to a person's qualifications to prevent us from recruiting and retaining those who can best accomplish the mission." With those words, I could serve my country authentically.

For over a year after open service, being transgender had nothing to do with my career. I took command of a company. I worked with my first sergeant to develop training plans and led unit runs. I trained my soldiers and they helped develop me as a leader with opportunities and challenges. My company was successful at every assigned mission. As I reflected with pride on the accomplishments of those I served alongside, I was more certain than ever that military service was one of the best choices I had ever made. Being the "transgender soldier" was behind me as I looked to the future.

This summer an announcement by President Donald Trump changed everything. I awoke to the sounds of a phone inundated with texts and alerts, all informing me that the commander in chief had signed a directive that banned transgender military recruits and ordered the discharge of 15,000 service members, myself included, for being transgender, depending on Secretary of Defense James Mattis for recommendations on how to best implement the policy by next March.

I have served for 13 years and deployed to every combat zone of my generation. In 2009, I was the Noncommissioned Officer of the Year, and in 2013 I was the Military Intelligence Career Course Distinguished Honor Graduate. An artillery major wrote on an evaluation that I was the best intelligence officer he had worked with in 20 years, and an infantry colonel rated me as No. 1 of 11 intelligence officers in a combat brigade. I am counted among the ranks of those who, in the words of Carter, can best accomplish the mission. Regardless of my training, qualifications or dedication, I may be discharged.

The recent injunction by a federal judge blocking enforcement of key provisions of the ban is a step in the right direction, but it is far from a decisive victory. The uncertainty still looms in the future and overshadows the cautious optimism generated by the courts.

Aside from my own career, I worry how this will impact the service that I love. If transgender people can be told they are no longer welcome, nothing stops the reversal of other policies: Gays and lesbians, blacks, women—all groups that at one time could not join the military—are now at risk. Will the defense of our nation be secure when one or all of these groups are barred from the armed forces? How do service members continue to trust their leadership? In 2016, Carter said we will no longer discharge transgender soldiers. If, in 2018, the Department of Defense begins to discharge the thousands who have come out as transgender, how can anyone ever again trust the military to hold true to its word?

I do not know what Veterans Day will look like for me in 2018. I do not know if I will still be wearing this uniform or serving our great nation, regardless of my qualification. What I do know is that this Veterans Day I am proud of my service. I have done everything my country has ever asked of me and more, and I am not done yet. This Veterans Day, I stand ready to continue.

Hunger Strike at Guantánamo Bay (December 2017)

Khalid Qassim

In 2002, the U.S. government established a detention camp at the Guantanamo Bay Naval Base in Cuba. The purpose of the camp, known as Gitmo, was to detain and extract information from individuals suspected of being terrorists. Gitmo became a source of public controversy when media outlets revealed that the U.S. government used torture when seeking information from the detainees. Further complicating matters was that the government did not formally charge these individuals, holding them indefinitely and without any means to challenge their detentions.

Shortly after taking office in 2009, President Barack Obama ordered the government to halt the use of torture and to close the detention center within a year. Members of Congress, most of them Republican, protested the order, and nothing ever came of it.

In the document below, Khalid Qassim, a detainee at Guantánamo Bay, explains his reasons for holding a hunger strike in 2017. In spite of the hunger strike, as well as ongoing protests from human rights organizations, on January 30, 2018, President Trump signed an executive order to keep the detention center open.

I've been held at Guantánamo Bay without charge or trial since 2002. Like others here, I'm on hunger strike in protest at my detention without charge. The Trump administration is trying to force us to drop our protest.

I'm currently in solitary confinement—I've been stuck here since 19 October. A "single cell operation," that's what they call it. In fact, it's isolation. It's terrible.

I am in Guantánamo Bay. The U.S. government is starving me to death.

I've twice fallen unconscious in here—a "code yellow." I've also had one "code green." That's when you nearly lose consciousness, but you can still hear people.

I think maybe I will spend two months in solitary. They don't tell you how many days you'll be here.

I feel pain and weakness and dizziness.

The government is claiming that it keeps a close watch on the health of us hunger strikers, but this is nonsense. In the past, the authorities here would weigh the hunger strikers all the time, to ensure we didn't die on their watch. Now, they are refusing even to do basic medical checks. They last did a blood test on me about seven months ago.

On 28 October, I woke up and I couldn't see—everything was blurry. My left eye was hurting a lot. I freaked out. I called out, begging for help. I was terrified that my organs were failing.

Later, I passed out and they called a "code yellow." A lot of people came: the guards, nurses, and one interpreter. When the interpreter saw the condition I was in, he seemed about to cry.

I begged them to do some blood tests. They didn't do anything. I went to a senior medical officer, and asked again. He said no. "You're playing a game," he told me.

I took a deep breath, and replied: "OK. It doesn't matter what you think of me. I'm asking you to take my blood, and to examine it. I'm not asking you to believe me. Just please, take my blood test."

They didn't do it.

That day, I ate to prevent any permanent damage. I ate about 200 calories.

After almost 16 years here, you think you've been through everything. But now it's as though they're sending us back to the old standard operating procedure—from the bad old days, when we first arrived here. They've recently told me: "If you lose some of your organs, it is your choice." We are like lab rats. I can see and feel the results of this experiment on myself.

My lawyers at Reprieve are going through the courts in the US, trying to get us an independent medical examination. When I read the declarations in that case, made by medical experts, it was amazing. They are saying just what we are saying, and what organizations such as Physicians for Human Rights have said: that you cannot coerce someone off his hunger strike, nor deny him medical attention. That it is unethical to force-feed a hunger striker. These things can be hard to understand if you're not in detention in places such as these.

Despite everything, the seeds of hope and faith are still there. I planted these the day I came to Gitmo, before I entered the camp and the blocks. I was ear-muffed and couldn't see anything, then shackled and handcuffed to my belly; chained to the ground, and insulted and beaten with dogs all around. People cursing my mother and cursing me. When I came to Gitmo that day, I planted that faith and that hope. Now it's like a rose—it still lives to this moment, and never dies.

It's not even as though we've just been in Gitmo for a year or two years. It's been nearly 16 years, no charges and no trial. It doesn't make sense. Even in the times of the Inquisition, the dark ages, they had courts.

I always ask the people in charge of the camp: why? If something would happen like this in another country, people would rightly ask, "Why do you put them there for 16 years without a trial?" I will keep asking until they charge or release me.

We Pledge to Resist for Immigrants (2017)

Alison Harrington

When announcing his run for the presidency in June 2015, Donald Trump addressed the issue of Mexicans immigrating to the United States. "When Mexico sends its people, they're not sending their best," he said. "They're bringing drugs. They're bringing crime. They're rapists. And some, I assume, are good people." That same month, Trump proposed building a wall between Mexico and the United States in order to prevent Mexicans from crossing the border.

Trump's candidacy heightened concern among the millions of Mexicans who had entered the United States in the hope of becoming U.S. citizens, but his pledge to deport "millions and millions of undocumented immigrants" set all immigrant communities on edge, fearful of what a Trump presidency might mean for their future.

President Trump began to fulfill his campaign promises not long after he assumed office. His earliest executive orders laid plans for the construction of the infamous wall and expanded the list of immigrants prioritized for deportation. As many immigrants went into hiding, pro-immigration advocates organized marches and rallies across the nation. One movement was already prepared to help immigrants on the run—the sanctuary movement.

In the 1980s hundreds of faith communities—synagogues, mosques, and churches across the nation—had provided safe haven for refugees from war-torn regions in Central America. One of the sanctuary movement's founding leaders was Rev. John Fife of Southside Presbyterian in Tucson, Arizona. Fife's courageous leadership created a lasting legacy at Southside, and the congregation, under the leadership of Rev. Alison Harrington, reactivated the sanctuary movement in 2014 when the Obama administration approved a dramatic increase in the number of deportations. When the Trump administration took power, Harrington continued her efforts, creating a popular online pledge and petition addressed to President Trump. The content of the petition, including its rationale, is below.

Southside reports that before the presidential election of 2016, approximately 400 faith communities identified themselves as part of a national sanctuary network, and that the number has more than doubled since the presidential election. Many of the communities that have signed the pledge have become homes to refugees hiding from U.S. Immigration and Customs Enforcement. Some sanctuary communities, like the East Bay Sanctuary Covenant community in Berkeley, California, also provide immigrants with legal assistance, family support, bail funds, and other basic necessities, while also fighting public policies that criminalize immigrants.

To: President Trump and His Administration

We Pledge to Resist Deportation and Discrimination Through Sanctuary

As people of faith and people of conscience, we pledge to resist the newly elected administration's policy proposals to target and deport millions of undocumented immigrants and discriminate against marginalized communities. We will open up our congregations and communities as sanctuary spaces for those targeted by hate, and work alongside our friends, families, and neighbors to ensure the dignity and human rights of all people.

Why is this important?

Calling upon the ancient traditions of our faiths, which recognized houses of worship as a refuge for the runaway slave, the conscientious objector, and the Central American refugee fleeing the civil wars of the 1980s, Sanctuary is once again growing among communities of faith that are standing in solidarity with immigrants and marginalized communities facing immoral and unjust deportation and discrimination policies.

We find ourselves entering a new phase of U.S. history wherein the politics of fear has stoked an atmosphere of racism and xenophobia across the country. The new Administration has pledged to criminalize, detain, and deport undocumented people at new levels that will tear families and communities apart.

As people of faith and people of conscience, we will take civil initiative out of our moral obligation to embody principles of human rights and dignity, and resist any harmful and unjust policy proposals that further undermine due process and lead to racial profiling and discrimination.

By signing this pledge, we are dedicating ourselves to educate and activate our congregations, to amplify and respond to the voices of immigrant leaders, and to speak out against the discrimination of any and all marginalized people. We are ready to open the doors of our sacred spaces and accompany those facing deportation and discrimination.

We support those answering the call to provide sanctuary at schools, hospitals, college campuses, community centers, and family homes. We will work with partner organizations to create sacred space of sanctuary wherever it is needed.

The Human Impact of the Muslim Ban (December 2017)

Dina El-Rifai

On January 27, 2017, less than a week into his presidency, Donald Trump issued an executive order banning citizens of seven predominately Muslim countries (Iran, Iraq, Libya, Somalia, Sudan, Syria, and Yemen) from entering the United States for ninety days. It was met with immediate and full-throated resistance. When word got out the following day that two Iraqi refugees had been detained at Kennedy International Airport in New York, thousands of protestors converged on the airport to show their support for the detainees and criticize the president. More than forty protests, some of them at airports, erupted across the country over the next few days. In Washington, DC, thousands of protestors rallied across the street from the White House, shouting "Shame!" and "No hate! No fear! Refugees are welcome here!" Walking from the White House to Capitol Hill, the protestors held homemade signs: "Immigrants Make America Great," No Human Being Is Illegal," "Love Trumps Hate," and "Give Me Your Tired, Your Poor, Your Huddled Masses Yearning to Breathe Free." At the Dallas/Fort Worth International Airport, Muslim women prayed with their heads, hands, and knees on the floor. And at San Francisco International Airport, thousands marched while volunteer lawyers offered their services to anyone negatively affected by the ban. Below is commentary offered by Dina El-Rifai of the American Friends Service Committee after the U.S. Supreme Court refused in December 2017 to block the ban while legal challenges continued to mount against it.

Urgent action is needed to protect people in the countries affected by the ban, but instead the U.S. is choosing to follow a dark history of legalized oppression.

Last week, the Supreme Court ruled that the third version of the racist Muslim ban could go into effect while legal challenges against it continue. Until the lower courts make their decisions, the Trump administration can enforce restrictions on travel from eight countries—six of them majority Muslim. This means that the government can now deny visas for people from those countries indefinitely, even if they have a "bona fide" relationship with the US—including grandparents and grandchildren of permanent residents.

Even before last week's decision, communities across the country had already felt the harm inflicted by the Muslim ban, which stoked Islamophobic sentiment, giving power to fear-mongering tactics not unlike those used to justify the internment of Japanese-Americans. In just the past few months, we have seen teachers call the police on an elementary school child with Downs Syndrome, Muslim girls being stripped of their hijab in schools, and countless other ways the Muslim community continues to be violated, assaulted, and demonized in an attempt to rob them of autonomy and agency.

What's significant about Monday's Supreme Court decision is that this is the first time that any version of the ban has been allowed to go into full effect, notes immigration lawyer Hassan Ahmad, a board member of the Virginia Coalition for Immigrant Rights.

And while immigration policy experts and lawyers have pushed back against this ban in the courts, local government, and in the arena of public opinion, we know that this racist policy is just another example of how white supremacy has historically legalized oppression of people of color to maintain systemic power.

Unfortunately, when we read about the Muslim ban, we don't often hear about the scores of individuals and families who will be affected by the policy—and the reasons many of them leave their home countries for the U.S.

Muslim Ban Protest at San Francisco International Airport, 2017.

Here's a look at the human impact of this ban and the conditions individuals face in the Muslim-majority countries affected.

Yemen: Last week, former Yemeni president Ali Abdullah Saleh was assassinated amid an already disturbing humanitarian crisis—a worsening famine that is threatening the lives of millions of Yemeni people. However, instead of working to relieve the increasing turmoil in Yemen, the Trump administration instead is banning those very people who are vulnerable to starvation and conflict.

Libya: A recent CNN report exposed the ongoing enslavement of Black migrants in Libya who are captured, kidnapped, auctioned, and sold into forced labor. Instead of working with the Libyan authorities or publicly denouncing these heinous crimes against humanity—and using this opportunity to begin to rectify the sin and stain of slavery on U.S. history—America has focused on furthering oppression through this ban on Libya.

Chad and Somalia: The U.S. is again feeding into anti-black racism by banning migrants from Chad, the fifth largest country in Africa, as well as from Somalia—a country that is currently experiencing one of the worst droughts in its history and continues to face the devastating and fatal impacts of civil war, food insecurity, and displacement.

Syria: Last week, the Pentagon announced that the U.S. military will stay in Syria indefinitely. With the Syrian refugee crisis being the largest refugee crisis of our time, with millions of Syrians displaced, it's critical that we examine the power dynamics and systems at play that allow for the U.S. military to claim presence in Syria as an occupying and imperialist force while banning the presence of Syrians in the US.

Urgent action is needed to protect the lives of these vulnerable populations, but instead the U.S. is choosing to follow a dark history of legalized oppression.

For numerous individuals from these countries and their families here in the US, the impacts of the Supreme Court decision will be severe and far reaching. That means a refugee family in Somalia with plans to resettle in the U.S. are now barred. A young person from Iran accepted into university in the U.S. would no longer be allowed. A grandfather in Libya would not be allowed to attend his grandchild's wedding in the US.

As a member of the Muslim community, I have seen firsthand the devastation of a mother repeatedly being denied a visa to travel to the U.S. to be with her dying daughter. This ban robs our society of basic humanity, barring 150 million people, the vast majority of them Muslim.

It's important to remember that the Supreme Court decision is not the end of the story. Last week, both the Ninth Circuit Court of Appeals and Fourth Circuit Court of Appeals heard arguments challenging this ban. And both courts' decisions are expected to be appealed to the Supreme Court.

As these cases move forward, we must continue to speak out against this racist ban, and urge Congress to do the same. At AFSC, we will continue to pressure the government to welcome refugees and implement humane immigration policies that respect the dignity of all people. And in cities across the U.S., we're working to end profiling and surveillance programs that target Muslim communities.

All of us deserve to feel safe from hatred and to live and pray in peace. For more resources about how you can oppose Islamophobia—and engage others in our efforts—explore our Communities Against Islamophobia resources.

DACA: Depression, Anxiety, Frustration (January 2018)

Korina Iribe Romo

Beneficiaries of the Deferred Action for Childhood Arrivals (DACA) program grew deeply alarmed when the Trump administration announced on September 5, 2017, that it would begin to phase out the program in March 2018. Created by the Obama administration, DACA made it possible for many "Dreamers"—undocumented people living in the U.S. who had been brought to the country as children—to avoid deportation, receive work permits, and secure an education during a renewable two-year stay. Over 800,000 Dreamers signed up for the DACA program. In announcing the termination of DACA, the Trump administration called upon Congress to take up and resolve the status of Dreamers and address immigration reform. In response, United We Dream, an immigrant youth-led advocacy group, staged numerous nonviolent protests calling upon Congress to pass legislation protecting Dreamers from deportation and allowing them to continue leading productive—and safe—lives in the United States. In the piece below, Arizona State University student Korina Iribe Romo reflects on what DACA means for her life.

Depression, anxiety, frustration: This was my reality as an undocument-ed young woman living in the United States. For many years the love and support of my family were the only thing that sustained me.

In 2012 my life changed with the implementation of the Deferred Action for Childhood Arrivals program. A weight was lifted off my shoulders when I learned I would be able to live a normal life. I immedi-ately began to daydream as I had when I was a little girl, optimistic about my new life in the U.S. My new DACA status would allow me to finally be able to come out of the shadows—not only to survive, but to thrive.

My new-found joy and excitement and that of many others like me sparked attacks from local politicians. In Arizona, the state in which I grew up and call home, a ban on licenses was enacted, and a lawsuit against education access for DACA program recipients immediately fol-lowed. These attacks compelled me to join a local organization and be-come a community organizer. As I integrated myself into the immigrant youth movement, I also continued to live my personal life. The fight for justice brought me many things—confidence, knowledge, and a new perspective on life. But most importantly, it brought me love.

In July 2015, my son was born, instantly bringing light into the world. I had carried him for nine months with mixed emotions of hope and fear. I shared in some of the same fears of most expectant mothers, but I also bore worries in my heart not many did. I thought about how the world would welcome the child of a Dreamer. I cried when I played out all of the "what if" scenarios in my head. What if one day they ended DACA and tried to deport me? The stress was relentless, but I made it through and found ease at the first sight of my baby's smile.

The last two years have been like nothing I've ever experienced on the rollercoaster of motherhood. I remember my heart filling with joy when Iker said "Mamma" for the first time, and I also remember the worry and frustration I felt as he started to fall behind and was di-agnosed with a speech delay. But my son and I have an indescribable bond. He refuses to fall asleep at night unless I am by his side and his little hands can touch my face. Our family is bound by unbreakable love. Still, in the back of my mind the uncertainty about what could happen to our small family has always remained. Recently my concerns have been resurrected. DACA recipients have once again become subjects in a political game after President Trump ended the program in September. Our lives are now in the hands of a Congress whose extreme bipartisanship could threaten our livelihood if a permanent solution is not reached soon.

I find myself thinking about what my family and I will do. How will we financially maintain our new house and be able to put food on our table? What happens to our son if ICE comes to tear our family apart in the middle of the night? These are all painful questions I now have to answer and plan for. There are more than 800,000 DACA youth across the country who face the same complicated questions, many of them also parents. Ending the DACA program is more than just about contributed dollars lost to the economy. It is more than just companies losing employees, and it's more than certain elected officials getting their way to gain political points. Ending DACA means ending the livelihood of real people. It means homes lost, families living in fear and in hunger. It means children like Iker crying as they are torn from the arms of their mothers.

Congress has the opportunity to pass a permanent legislative solution to protect Dreamers by ensuring a DREAM provision is added to the must-pass spending bill in the upcoming weeks. The deadline to pass this new spending bill is Jan. 19. Negotiations have been shared with the public. I strongly believe we cannot justify protection of one group of marginalized people while simultaneously creating policy that will further criminalize and separate families. Ending chain migration, the lottery system and TPS and further militarizing the border will create a multitude of problems for the country and our immigrant communities.

Marching for Our Lives (March 2018)

Patrick Northrup

On Valentine's Day 2018, Nikolas Cruz walked into Marjorie Stoneman Douglas High School (MSDHS) in Parkland, Florida, carrying a black bag that held a .223 caliber AR-15 rifle. Cruz suffered from mental illness and had been expelled for disciplinary reasons. After entering the school with no difficulty, Cruz pulled the fire alarm and opened fire on students and teachers, killing seventeen of them. It was one of the deadliest mass shootings in modern U.S. history. The violence spurred many MSDHS students to lead and participate in a nonviolent gun control rally that took place three days later. Survivors of the MSDHS shooting also helped organize the March for Our Lives in Washington, DC, on March 24, 2018. The march rallied around 80,000 in the nation's capital and hundreds of thousands more in communities across the country. Below is a transcript of the comments delivered by Patrick Northrup, a senior at Millbrook High School, at the March for Our Lives in Winchester, Virginia.

Two years ago I never thought I would be in this position and standing in front of you all today.

I've sat back for far too long and experienced too many senseless killings with nothing changing and I am unable to remain silent on this issue.

Our generation is fed up with the status quo and we're here today demanding a change. For far too long have we turned on the TV only to hear about yet another mass shooting.

For far too long have we gone to school and walked the halls in fear. For far too long have we experienced lockdown drills wondering if we would be the next school, if we would be the next news story. For far too long have we remained silent and failed to use our voices.

But that ends now because the time is up for action!

We are here today because Enough is Enough! We will no longer sit silent and fail to speak out. We are here now using our voices and

standing up to this senseless gun violence happen-
ing all over America!

We are now 12 weeks
into 2018 and there have
already been 17 school
shootings where someone
was injured or killed. That
averages out to about 1.4
school shootings a week!

School shootings have
become so normalized in
our nation and it is truly
sickening. When someone
asks "Did you hear about
the school shooting?" the
answer shouldn't be "which
one?"

*Protesters at March for Our Lives,
Washington, DC, 2018.*

Unfortunately it is the
answer and this is the reality we are facing here in the United States today. Since Columbine, 187,000+ students across the country have been
exposed to gun violence at their school.

Students are anxious and scared on a daily basis in our schools.
This isn't a Republican issue or a Democratic issue. It's our right to live
in a society where we can go to school and focus on our education and
not fear the school lockdown being more than just a drill.

There shouldn't be any "deals" being made. These are student's lives
we are talking about and they're being threatened every day! It is time
to put an end to this normalization madness and daily anxiety felt by
students!

Enough is Enough!

For those who are telling us we are "too young to take a stand and
too young to truly understand what's going on," well, we aren't too young

to go to school with this daily fear and unease. We aren't too young to be shot in our classrooms and hallways. And guess what? In November we won't be too young to go to the polls and vote so we can make the change ourselves if our lawmakers won't.

We are here today fighting for our lives and demanding something be done to prevent these shootings and destroy this normalization.

There are many solutions to this epidemic, most of which are commonsense but let me be very clear. This isn't an attack on anyone's "right to bear arms." We are not fighting to take away people's guns. My late grandfather was a gun owner and a member of the NRA. He was a sportsman and a responsible gun owner. Our goal is not to take away guns from people like him. Our goal is to strengthen the process of purchasing a gun and ensuring people who shouldn't own a gun don't have the opportunity to.

These common sense measures we are fighting for aren't being put into law and I ask those who refuse to do so a few questions.

Why does any teenager need access to an assault rifle? It has been repeatedly demonstrated that the brain does not fully mature until the mid-to-late 20's. According to data collected by the FBI, people under 25 are responsible for nearly half of America's gun homicides.

Why does any gun owner need a bump stock that transforms their weapon into a deadly battlefield machine gun? The only purpose of this is to kill large numbers of people. These accessories do not belong on our streets!

Why can a person who has shown signs of abuse or violence purchase a gun in America?

Why is it easier to buy a gun than it is to buy and drive a car?

Why is it any easier to buy a gun than it is to board an airplane? If someone is too dangerous to step foot onto an airplane, then they are too dangerous to own a gun!

These things don't have to be this way.

Together we say, Enough is Enough!

We must continue to fight for these commonsense measures and demand our lawmakers actually listen to us and hear our voices rather than ignoring us and cashing in on their contributions from the NRA. Are our lives really less valuable than your blood money?

This needs to end. Our lawmakers must start listening to our demands and protect me and my peers.

Enough is enough!

We Do Not Want the Wall (March 2018)

Dulce Garcia

On March 13, 2018, President Trump traveled to San Diego, California, to review prototypes for a wall between the United States and Mexico. While he inspected eight examples, the president indicated that he preferred a cement wall because it seemed most difficult to climb. Hundreds of anti-wall protesters gathered at the San Ysidro port of entry in San Diego and chanted, "No ban! No wall!" After reviewing the prototypes, Trump headed to a fundraiser in Beverly Hills. In a nearby Beverly Hills park, pro-immigration protesters also rallied against the wall. "Say it now, say it clear, immigrants are welcome here," they chanted. Below is an editorial on Trump's San Diego Visit penned by Dulce Garcia, a DACA recipient and immigration attorney.

This week San Diego shows solidarity with our immigrant community, shows love to our neighbors to the south, and love for American values that include compassion, freedom, equality for all, and family values. The purpose of President Donald Trump's visit is to see his prototypes for a wall. He is not here to engage the community and to ask how is it that we may revitalize our border community. Rather, the president is here to create even more fear and division. If he took a good look, he would know the wall is not needed, and if he listened carefully, he would know that we do not want it.

Trump's wall will not stop immigration, it will only make it harder, more dangerous and more costly in terms of money and human life. As long as there are factors driving immigration such as economic conditions in the rest of the world, natural disasters, and fear of persecution, migrants from all over the world will seek entry to the U.S. Trump's wall is but a symbol of hate and division that results in human tragedy, death, and separation of families. It will not stop the smuggling of drugs nor deter human trafficking. Let's make it clear: Trump's wall will serve merely as a physical manifestation of fear and hate of our neighbors to the south. The president continues to attack the image of immigrants by painting us as criminals, in particular those of us that migrated from Mexico.

We already see targeted attacks by ICE and Border Patrol in our communities because Attorney General Jeff Sessions and the president are responding to California's stance as a sanctuary state.

As a Deferred Action for Childhood Arrivals (DACA) recipient, I think his visit is an insult and is hurtful. The president created a crisis by rescinding the DACA program and is using that crisis as an opportunity to negotiate funding for his wall and to push his anti-immigration agenda. The president holds the lives of DACA recipients captive. Unfortunately, there are some activists—unfamiliar with the terror created by this administration in our border communities—who are so fearful for the future of DACA recipients that they have contemplated providing funding for the expensive wall. I hope that others, if not the president, hear our pleas from the border and understand how devastating it would be to add funding for a wall and more funding for DHS without accountability for human life.

As an immigrant, I tend to see the silver lining even in the most difficult situations. Today, that silver lining is that San Diego stands together to resist the threats posed by this administration. Several different press conferences and rallies are scheduled in San Diego County in response to the president's visit. One rally organized by DACA recipients will be in front of the County Administration Building at 5:30 pm. Tuesday. Each rally seems to have a unifying message: We do not want nor need Trump's wall.

#MeToo Is About Restoring Humanity (2018)

Tarana Burke

While working at a youth camp in 1997, Tarana Burke found herself listening to a 13-year-old girl sharing her experience of having been sexually abused by her mother's boyfriend. "I was horrified by her words, the emotions inside of me ran the gamut, and I listened until literally I could not take it anymore ... which turned out to be less than 5 minutes," Burke recalls. Unsure about how to respond, Burke interrupted the girl and directed her to another counselor. As she remembers it,

> *I will never forget the look on her face.*
>
> *I will never forget the look because I think about her all of the time. The shock of being rejected, the pain of opening a wound only to have it abruptly forced closed again—it was all on her face. And as much as I love children, as much as I cared about that child, I could not find the courage that she had found. I could not muster the energy to tell her that I understood, that I connected, that I could feel her pain. I couldn't help her release her shame, or impress upon her that nothing that happened to her was her fault. I could not find the strength to say out loud the words that were ringing in my head over and over again as she tried to tell me what she had endured. ... I watched her walk away from me as she tried to recapture her secrets and tuck them back into her hiding place. I watched her put her mask back on and go into the world like she was all alone and I couldn't even bring myself to whisper . . . **me too.***

Several years later, Burke founded Just BE Inc., a nonprofit dedicated to "the health, well-being, and wholeness of brown girls everywhere," and in 2006 she created the me too movement to help survivors of sexual abuse, especially girls and women of color, access resources for recovery, and to push for policies and research that would benefit survivors.

The me too movement received considerable attention in 2017, when accusations of sexual abuse against movie mogul Harvey Weinstein in-spired actress Alyssa Milano, who did not know of Burke's work, to send the following tweet to her followers: "If you've been sexually harassed or assaulted write 'me too' as a reply to this tweet." Before a full day was over, Milano's tweet was shared in about 12 million posts.

With a hashtag preceding it, "Me Too" became its own movement on numerous social platforms, including Twitter, Facebook, and Snapchat. Burke and Milano joined forces, and the #MeToo movement resulted in numerous marches and rallies for sexual abuse survivors, including a No-vember 12, 2017 march that Burke led in downtown Hollywood. Below are Burke's 2018 remarks on the state and future of the movement.

It's no secret that Hollywood runs off power, privilege and access, and because of that it is important in this moment to also examine the ways that unchecked privilege and power accumulate and are wielded against the most vulnerable. We know this doesn't just happen in Hollywood, so we have to do the same kind of rigorous investigation and analysis of the culture within all our major corporations and communities that consistently allows sexual violence to occur again and again.

What the world recognizes as the #MeToo movement was built on the labor of everyday people who survived sexual violence in a num-ber of forms. Some were harassed, some survived child sexual abuse or other kinds of sexual assault, but all of them endeavored to stand in their truth. All at once starting last October, millions of people raised their hands and voices to be counted among the number of people who had experienced sexual harassment, assault and abuse. More than 12 million in 24 hours on Facebook. Half a million in 12 hours on Twitter. And the numbers kept growing. But as soon as the mainstream media got over the shock of the sheer volume of those who counted themselves in, it immediately pivoted back to what was happening in Hollywood. While that was driven by the dynamic investigative journalism of people like Ronan Farrow of The New Yorker, what was happening around the world was driven by the courage of people from all walks of life. If we don't shift our focus and actually look at the people saying, "Me too," then we are going to waste a really valuable opportunity to change the nature of how we think about sexual violence in this country.

If we could pull back from focusing on the accused and zero in on the ones speaking out, we would see common denominators that bridge the divide between celebrity and everyday citizens: the diminishing of dignity and the destruction of humanity. Everyday people—queer, trans, disabled, men and women—are living in the aftermath of a trauma that tried, at the very worst, to take away their humanity. This movement at its core is about the restoration of that humanity.

This is one reason that the weaponization of #MeToo has been so shocking. Several men and some women, many of whom are rich and powerful, have mischaracterized this movement out of their own fears and inability to hold a nuanced perspective. These same folks are quick to assign blame to the victims of violence based on the media's obsession with who will be "found out" next. So, instead of homing in on the pervasiveness of sexual violence, the focus is on the accused and what's at stake for them: What's going to happen to their careers? What are the consequences for the companies that employed them? What are the consequences for the industry they're in? But how many articles were written about the consequences for the women still working at places like NBC and CBS? The details of those experiences are going to mirror those of so many people. Knowing those stories gives voice to those who survived sexual violence as opposed to the people who perpetrate the violence.

All of the shouting and headlines about who #MeToo is going to take down next creates a kind of careless perception that invalidates the experiences of survivors who risk everything coming forward, whether it's telling their stories, sharing a hashtag or being transparent and vulnerable about some of the worst things that have happened in their lives.

The din of naysayers has, in many regards, severely overshadowed the beauty of what has happened this year. It has been a year of great liberation and empowerment. Every day I meet people who have moved from victim to survivor by simply adding their own "Me too" to the chorus of voices. They have freed themselves from the burden that holding on to these traumas often creates and stepped into the power of release, the power of empathy and the power of truth. They have looked their demons in the face and lived to see another day, and they have become the empirical proof that we can win the fight to end sexual violence.

Moving into 2019, some concrete things must happen in order to build on the momentum we have gained in the last year, starting with changing how we talk about the #MeToo movement. This is a survivors' movement created for and by those of us who have endured sexual violence. The goal is to provide a mechanism to support survivors and move people to action. Any other characterization severely handicaps our ability to move the work forward.

We also need to have a more intentional public dialogue about accountability, and not just the kind that focuses on crime and punishment, but on harm and harm reduction. Narrowing our focus to investigations, firings and prison can hinder the conversation and the reality that accountability and justice look different for different people. We need to refine our approaches for seeking justice to reflect that diversity. Sexual violence happens on a spectrum, so accountability has to happen on a spectrum. And that means various ways of being accountable are necessary. Survivors have to be central to that accountability, and they must be the ones leading and dictating what that accountability looks like. Without that, there's no clear path for people, especially public figures, to regain the trust of those they've harmed and let down. This is playing out publicly as many of the celebrities and entertainers whose behavior was exposed are now attempting comebacks without having made amends to those they harmed, publicly apologizing, or acknowledging how they're going to change their behavior, industries, or communities to help end sexual violence.

Apologies, in and of themselves, are not work. They precede work. The men who are trying to come back have not done any work. Not that

Tarana Burke leading #MeToo March, Hollywood, California, 2017.

I have seen. Oftentimes it's about intent versus impact. So even if you think you're innocent of the actions you're being accused of, human decency dictates that you say, "OK. I want to hear what your experience in that moment was." Terry Crews is a perfect example. He said, "My experience with this thing was that you made me feel that I was humiliated. I was overpowered. You took away my dignity." There is not a plot to excommunicate people for life, but the accused should have the respect, at least, to show that they're committed to change. Show your work.

It is also necessary for us to expand the scope of the movement in the mainstream. In 2006, I launched the #MeToo movement because I wanted to find ways to bring healing into the lives of black women and girls. But those same women and girls, along with other people of color, queer people and disabled people, have not felt seen this year. Whether it was the near abandonment of Lupita Nyong'o when she revealed her experience with Weinstein, or Lena Dunham's support of the man

Aurora Perrineau accused of rape, there was a sharp difference in the response to black women coming forward. Russell Simmons has 18 accusations of rape, sexual assault and sexual misconduct against him, largely by black women, and yet there is no media frenzy around him or his accusers. The depth and breadth of sexual violence in this country can't be quantified, but it definitely doesn't discriminate, and we won't begin to really understand its impact unless we look at the whole story.

I can't stress how critical our next steps are. It's been almost 30 years since Anita Hill testified in front of the Senate Judiciary Committee about the sexual harassment she endured at the hands of now Justice Clarence Thomas. It is so disheartening that we're here again, but it's just another reminder about where we are as a country and how this movement still has to be powered by everyday people who vote, who are vocal, who are active, who are tuned in and aware of how it's bigger than Hollywood, and bigger than politics.

For our part we are building out our work both online with the October launch of our new comprehensive website and on the ground through programming and partnerships. We have also partnered with the New York Women's Foundation to create a #MeToo movement fund that will raise $25 million to put toward working to end sexual violence over the next five years. Our goal is to keep expanding the work and building the movement.

For too long women and others living on the margins have managed to survive without our full dignity intact. It can't continue to be our reality. The work of #MeToo builds on the existing efforts to dismantle systems of oppression that allow sexual violence, patriarchy, racism and sexism to persist. We know that this approach will make our society better for everyone, not just survivors, because creating pathways to healing and restoration moves us all closer to a world where everyone knows the peace of living without fear and the joy of living in your full dignity. I intend to keep doing this work, from within this amazing movement, until we get there.

Resistance Past, Present, and Future

Dolores Huerta

The stories of nonviolent resistance in this book remind me of the grape boycott in New York City. A farmworker called me and excitedly said, "Señora Huerta, they took the grapes out of the store!"

As part of the boycott committee, he had traveled to New York from Delano, a farm labor community in California. His job was to stand outside stores, to explain to people why they should not buy grapes, and to ask owners to remove grapes from their shelves.

"That's great!" I exclaimed and then asked him, "What's the name of the store?"

"I don't know," he said softly.

"Well, what does the sign outside the store say?" I persisted in asking.

He paused.

"I can't tell you," he said. "I don't know how to read."

This story shows the power one person can have when they work with others for a common cause. This is why I love this story. Yes, he was poor, he lacked a formal education, and he couldn't read, yet there he was, advancing the boycott, helping us win basic human rights for farmworkers long denied, and fighting hard so his children—our children—would one day be able to read.

That shows the power of one person, just one person. He didn't need reading skills simply to be uplifted. If he can empower himself to make a difference, so can you.

When Cesar Chavez and I started to organize Mexican farmworkers in California, people said to us, "How are you going to do that? They have no power. They have no assets."

Those naysayers were partly right. The farmworkers did not have bank accounts. They did not have decent wages, or comfortable homes, or good schools. They didn't even have basic access to water, or toilets, in the fields.

But they did have something far more important than all that. They had the power of their own persons, the power of their bodies.

To help beaten-down farmworkers understand that they possessed power was a tremendous challenge. Cesar and I went to their *barrios*. We knocked on their doors. We went into their homes. We sat with them. We ate with them. And, time and time again, no matter what others had told them, we explained to them that they were important, very important, that they had power in their own person, and that if all of us came together, we would even have enough power to secure our rights and to live with justice and dignity.

No one else will make our lives better, we said. The farm owners and corporations sure aren't going to do this for us. So if we want our rights, it's up to us to fight for them and to demand them.

And that's what we did.

We began to believe in ourselves, in our power, in people power, and together we created the United Farm Workers and held rallies, strikes, marches, fasts, and boycotts to secure our rights. As we stood together, our collective power made the difference we had promised. We gained the right to bargain and secured better wages, better working conditions, unemployment compensation, and much more. We paved the way for a better life, and we gave our children the opportunity to read.

We can make a better life today, too. Even now, at this troubling point in our history, when we have a president whose policies hurt workers and immigrants and who encourages hatred toward women, Muslims, people of color, and people with disabilities, we can create a better tomorrow.

One of my favorite sayings comes from the poet Pablo Neruda: "You can cut all the flowers but you cannot keep spring from coming." How powerful and true. They can cut us down, but we will keep coming back. They can even bury us, but we will always push our way through the soil.

That's where revolutionary change starts—from the roots. When we think of all the positive changes made in our country, we can see that they have come from humble backgrounds. Think of the abolitionist movement, the women's movement, the civil rights movement, the workers' movement, and other nonviolent movements documented in this book. Real change, lasting change, positive change, and revolutionary change comes from people empowering women, men, and children shouldering their way up from the bottom.

We need to follow their example because the dirt is really piling up on us right now, trying to bury us. How close are we to the depths of fascism? Pretty close. Our civil liberties are being stripped from us, our prisons are overrunning with people of color, and we have a president who acts like a misogynist bigoted tyrant.

This is no time to be quiet or still. This is an organizing moment, an opportunity rather than a defeat, and we must at once start pushing our way out of the soil as we have never done before.

Look at the DREAMers and what came out of the young people in the Occupy Wall Street, Black Lives Matter, #MeToo, and #NeverAgain movements. Rather than giving in to despair, they have committed their lives to organizing, to building people power, and to showing that power can come from the streets especially with the help of social media. Social media sparks a conversation, but action is implemented when the conversation is brought to the streets. Nonviolent protests on the street, the type carried out by our young folks in the resistance movement, are so important in mobilizing for and creating the justice that still eludes us. I still believe this with every ounce of my being. What we in the farm-workers' movement did in the 1960s—march and rally and boycott and fast—is still vitally important for us today, but so is electoral politics.

Yes, we need to march in the streets and shout at the top of our lungs, but we also need to walk through our neighborhoods, go from door to door and organize ourselves to get everyone out to vote and so we can run for school boards, city councils, and county commissions. That's where we can really change our lives, at the local level, and when we make a difference in our local communities, we can use our grass-roots power to push for justice and equality at the state and federal levels.

We need to start winning local offices right now. Did you vote in the last local election? Did you knock on doors to turn out voters for local elections? Did you plan to run for office? Fighting the revolution from the grassroots level is our main task now. Remember—the most import-ant day of our life together is Election Day, especially election days when we vote for school boards, city councils, and county commissions.

Nonviolence is important to remember, too. Some people today want to take up arms in the fight for justice and equality. They want to carry out the revolution by wielding weapons that maim and kill. I could not disagree more strongly because I still believe in what Cesar and I shared with the farmworkers in the 1960s and 70s—that acting violently only hurts us, that it makes us just like the people who beat us up, and that we don't need to hit back to be strong.

In fact, when we practiced our nonviolent methods in the move-ment, we ended up believing in ourselves all the more and gaining the emotional fortitude required for sustaining and advancing the fight for justice and equality. Nonviolence made us strong. Our nonviolent meth-ods made us feel a strong spiritual power moving within us. It wasn't something that any of us could see, but it was there.

It was also very effective partly because it demanded so much discipline from us. As we in the farmworkers' movement practiced it, nonviolence was an extremely active force that pitted our bodies and souls against the tyranny of the owners and corporations, and it required us to be constantly creative in finding which methods worked best in our collective struggle.

Nonviolence was also effective for us because it allowed many other people to join our movement. This mostly included people who were concerned about justice and equality, but who were put off by calls to carry out a violent revolution. Our unwavering commitment to nonviolence acted as an invitation to the wider public whose support we desperately needed, and our nonviolent power grew all the more as allies joined us in the movement.

Violence isn't nearly as effective as nonviolence. That's what we discovered in the farmworkers' movement, and that's what today's scholars are learning as they look at movements here in the United States and across the world.

But effectiveness aside, there's something personally damaging about violence. Using violent methods, even with the intention of establishing justice, only makes you like the one who's trying to beat you down. People who use violence in today's resistance movements are simply counterparts to the violent alt-right and the violent Nazis. And when you act like them, you hurt yourself and the rest of us.

We live in a culture of violence. I don't mean just the violence of war and terrorism. I also mean the violence of poverty, sexism, racism, homophobia, xenophobia, and so on. We're completely surrounded, and so the last thing we need is for our brothers and sisters in the movement to take up arms and add to the violence that already engulfs us. We can do better than that. We can be better than that.

What we really need is a group of nonviolent activists at the local grassroots level who will not only resist in the streets but also run for political offices with the goal of establishing a peaceful society full of economic justice and free of bigotry.

Do you know that we as a people still do not own our natural resources? *Natural* resources! The gas companies own them. The oil companies own them. The electric companies own them. We *the People* do not. And because we do not control our own natural resources, we don't have the money to pay for the basic goods required for us to survive and flourish. This needs to change!

The exporting of our jobs to countries that allow major corporations to hire poor people for low wages, no benefits, and little protection in the workplace also needs to change. Globalization has crushed our workers, especially the poor and people of color, and it has allowed corporations to exploit the poor in countries that care for their people even less than ours does. This needs to change!

The bigotry we see in our new president and his followers—the bigotry that refers to Mexicans as rapists, that talks of grabbing women's genitals, that makes fun of people with disabilities, that empowers Nazis, that denies housing to the Black community, that kicks transgender folks out of the military, and that slams our doors in the faces of Muslims hoping to become part of our country also needs to change. Is this the kind of president we want? Is this the kind of society we want? This needs to change!

So *can* we change it? Can we create a society with free education, free health care, livable wages, affordable housing, and security in retirement? Can we build a society that believes we all belong to one human family and that does not discriminate against others because of gender, sexual orientation, physical abilities, race or ethnicity, religion, or place of birth?

I know that sometimes the hurdles seem too high. Long ago now, Cesar was doing a 25-day water-only fast in Arizona, and we were trying to organize people to come and support our fight for workers' rights, but it was tough—really tough. The politicians in Arizona had passed a law that made it a crime to say, "strike," "*huelga*," and "boycott." If you said those words, you could go to jail. If you went on strike, you could go to jail for six months.

So Cesar and I were protesting that law, and when I asked some of our professional Latinos to support us and to come to our masses and rallies, they said, "*No se puede*, Dolores. In California, you can do all that, but in Arizona, *no se puede*."

My response was simple: "*Sí se puede!*"

Yes, we can.

Ever since then, *Sí se puede!* has become the rallying cry of the farmworkers' movement, It's our way of resisting despair, hopelessness, and powerlessness. It's our way of expressing our everlasting hope, our belief that power resides with us, and our resolve to wield that power to establish justice and equality.

Sí se puede!

In the deepest recesses of my heart, I believe that we can overcome the bigotry and economic injustice that bury so many of us right now, and that we can finally push our way through the soil and build the beloved community that my friend Martin Luther King, Jr., spoke about—a place full of peace, reconciliation, and economic justice.

Can we build the beloved community right here, right now?

Sí se puede!

The editor is grateful for permission to publish the documents listed below. All good faith efforts have been made to clear permissions for copyrighted material. He will gladly rectify any omissions in a future printing.

ONE

Early Roots of Resistance

We Cannot Condemn Quakers (1657), Edward Hart
Public domain. Flushingfriends.org.

Buy Slaves to Free Them (1693), George Keith
Public domain. George Keith, *An Exhortation & Caution to Friends Concerning Buying or Keeping of Negroes* (New York: William Bradford, 1693); and *American Anti-slavery Writing: Colonial Beginnings to Emancipation,* ed. James G. Basker (New York: The Library of America), 4-8.

I am but a poor SLave (1723), Anonymous Slave
Public domain. Thomas N. Ingersoll, "'Releese Us Out of This Cruell Bondegg': An Appeal from Virginia in 1723," *William and Mary Quarterly,* third series, 51 (October 1994), 776-782; and *Dissent in America: The Voices That Shaped a Nation,* ed. Ralph F. Young (New York: Pearson Longman, 2006), 33-34.

I Have No King (1727), Loron Sauguaarum
Public domain. *Documents Relative to the Colonial History of the State of New York,* vol. 9, ed. E. B. O'Callaghan (Albany: Weed, Parsons & Co., 1855), 966-967; and Young, *Dissent in America,* 38-40.

The People Are the Proper Judge (1750), Jonathan Mayhew
Public domain. *The Pulpit of the American Revolution; or, The Political Sermons of the Period of 1776* (Boston: Gould & Lincoln, 1860); and *Civil Disobedience in America: A Documentary History,* ed. David R. Weber (Ithaca, NY: Cornell University Press, 1978), 39-44.

Tea Overboard (1773; document date, 1834), George Hewes
Public domain. *The Spirit of Seventy-Six: The Story of the American Revolution as Told by Participants* (New York: Harper & Row, 1967), 4-6; and *Voices of a People's History of the United States,* ed. Howard Zinn and Anthony Arnove (New York: Seven Stories Press, 2004), 83-85.

Unjustly Taxed (1774), Isaac Backus
Public domain. Isaac Backus, *An Appeal to the Public for Religious Liberty* (Boston: John Boyle, 1773); and baptiststudiesonline.com.

No Money for the Revolutionary War (1776; document date, 1797), Job Scott
Public domain. *Journal of the Life, Travels, and Gospel Labours of That Faithful Servant and Minister of Christ, Job Scott* (New York, 1797); and *Liberty and Conscience: A History of the Experiences of Conscientious Objectors in America Through the Civil War,* ed. Peter Brock (New York: Oxford University Press, 2002), 52-53.

TWO

The Abolitionist Movement and the Struggle for the Rights of Free African Americans

They Do Not Consider Us as Men (1813), John Fortren

Public domain. *Letters from a Man of Colour on a Late Bill Before the Senate of Pennsylvania* (Philadelphia: s.n., 1813); and Basker, *American Antislavery Writings*, 213-215.

Women Overthrowing Slavery (1836), Angelina Grimke

Public domain. Angelina E. Grimke, *Appeal to Christian Women of the South* (New York: Anti-Slavery Society, 1836); and iath.virginia.edu.

Escape on the Pearl (1848; document date, 1855), Daniel Drayton

Public domain. Daniel Drayton, *Personal Memoir of Daniel Drayton, for Four Years and Four Months a Prisoner (for Charity's Sake) in Washington Jail: Including a Narrative of the Voyage and Capture of the Schooner Pearl* (Boston: Bela Marsh, 1855); and loc.gov.

Resistance to Civil Government (1849), Henry David Thoreau

Public domain. Henry David Thoreau, *The Writings of Henry David Thoreau* (Cambridge, MA: Riverside Press, 1894), vol. 10; and Weber, *Civil Disobedience in America*, 86-89.

I Won't Obey It! (1850), Jermaine Wesley Loguen

Public domain. The Rev. J. W. Loguen, *As a Slave and As a Freeman: A Narrative of Real Life* (Syracuse, NY: J. G. K. Truair & Co., 1859); and *Lift Every Voice: African American Oratory, 1787-1900*, eds. Philip S. Foner and Robert James Branhamer (Tuscaloosa, AL: University of Alabama Press, 1998), 224-226.

What to the Slave Is the Fourth of July? (1852), Frederick Douglass

Public domain. *Oration Delivered in Corinthian Hall, Rochester, by Frederick Douglass, July 5, 1852* (Rochester, NY: Lee, Mann, & Co., 1852); and lib.rochester.edu.

He Took Hold of Me and I Took Hold of the Window Sash (1854), Elizabeth Jennings

Public domain. *New York Tribune*, July 19, 1854; and *A Place at the Table: Struggles for Equality in America*, ed. Maria Fleming (New York: Oxford University Press, 2001), 39.

Was John Brown Justified? (1859) William Lloyd Garrison

Public domain. *Liberator*, December 16, 1859.

THREE

Removing Native Americans, Dethroning Hawaiians

First Lords of the Soil (1830), Theodore Frelinghuysen

Public domain. Theodore Frelinghuysen, *Speech of Mr. Frelinghuysen, of New Jersey, Delivered in the Senate of the United States, April 6, 1830, on the Bill for an Exchange of Lands with the Indians Residing in Any of the States or Territories, and for Their Removal West of the Mississippi* (Washington, DC: The Office of the National Journal), 1830, archive.gov.; and Keith Whittington, *American Political Thought: Readings and Materials* (New York: Oxford University Press, 2016), global.oup.com.

The Audacious Practices of Unprincipled Men (1836), Chief John Ross

Public domain. Chief John Ross to the U.S. Senate and House of Representatives,

September 28, 1836. See *The Papers of Chief John Ross,* vol. 1, ed. Gary E. Moulton (Norman, OK: University of Oklahoma Press, 1985); and Young, *Dissent in America,* 136-137.

The Return of the Winnebago (1873), S.

Public domain. *Chicago Times,* December 21, 1873.

We Ask to Be Recognized as Men (1879), Chief Joseph

Public domain. Chester Anders Fee, *Chief Joseph: The Biography of a Great Indian* (New York: Wilson-Erickson, Inc., 1936), 281-283; and historyisaweapon.com.

My Downtrodden People (1898), Queen Liliuokalani

Public domain. *Hawaii's Story by Hawaii's Queen* (Boston: Lee and Shepard), 1898; digital.library.upenn.edu.

FOUR
Striking Against Industrialists

Petition Against Terrorism (1871), Colored National Labor Union

Public domain. "Memorial of a Committee of the National Labor Council, Praying the Appointment of a Commission to Inquire into the Condition of Affairs in the Southern States," *Index to the Miscellaneous Documents of the Senate of the United States from the Third Session of the Forty-First Congress, 1870-1871* (Washington, DC: Government Printing Office, 1871).

Will You Organize? (1877), Albert Parsons

Public domain. *Inter Ocean,* July 25, 1877; and dhr.history.vt.edu.

We Have 4,000 Men (1891), African American Waterfront Workers of Savannah

Public domain. *Savannah Morning News,* September 29, 1891; and *American Labor: A Documentary Collection,* ed. Melvyn Dubofsky and Joseph A. McCartin (New York: Palgrave Macmillan), 129-130.

A Petition in Boots (1894), James Coxey

Public domain. *Congressional Record: Containing the Proceedings and Debates of the Fifty-Third Congress, Second Session,* vol. 26 (Washington, DC: Government Printing Office, 1894); and historymatters.gmu.edu.

The Wail of the Children (1903), Mother Jones

Public domain. *Brooklyn Daily Eagle,* July 27, 1903; and Jones, "The Wail of the Children," *Mother Jones Speaks: Speeches and Writings of a Working-Class Fighter,* ed. Philip S. Foner (New York: Pathfinder, 1983), 148-149.

Negro Workers! (1912), Committee of Defense, Brotherhood of Timber Workers

Public domain. *Solidarity,* September 28, 1912; and *Let Nobody Turn Us Around: Voices of Resistance, Reform, and Renewal—An African American Anthology,* ed. Manning Marable and Leith Mullings (Lanham, MD: Rowman & Littlefield, 2000), 190-191.

Wage Slavery (1912), Textile Workers of Lawrence, Massachusetts

Public domain. "Proclamation of the Striking Textile Workers of Lawrence," *Report on the Strike of Textile Workers in Lawrence, Massachusetts in 1912,* 62nd Congress, 2nd Session, Senate Document 870, ed. Charles P. Neill (Washington, DC: Government Printing Office, 1912), 503-504; and Zinn and Arnove, *Voices of a People's History,* 272-274.

FIVE
Fighting for Women's Rights
All Men and Women Are Created Equal (1848), Elizabeth Cady Stanton and Others
Public domain. *Proceedings of the Woman's Rights Conventions Held at Seneca Falls and Rochester, N.Y.* (New York: Robert J. Johnston, 1870); and *Women's Rights in the United States: A Documentary History,* ed. Winston E. Langley and Vivian C. Fox (Westport, CT: Praeger, 1994), 82-85.
Keep the Thing Going (1851, 1867), Sojourner Truth
Document 1. Public domain. *Anti-Slavery Bugle,* June 21, 1851; and Marable and Mullings, *Let Nobody Turn Us Around,* 67-68.
Document 2. Public domain. *Proceedings of the First Anniversary of the American Equal Rights Association, Held at the Church of the Puritans, New York, May 9 and 10, 1867* (New York: Robert J. Johnson, 1867), 20-21.
Robbed of Citizenship (1873), Susan B. Anthony
Public domain. Elizabeth Cady Stanton, Susan B. Anthony, Matilda Joslyn Gage, and Ida Husted Harper, *History of Woman Suffrage,* vol. 2 (Rochester, NY: Charles Mann, 1887), 687-689; repr., New York: Arno Press; and Langley and Fox, *Women's Rights in the United States,* 149-151.
Marriage and Love Have Nothing in Common (1910), Emma Goldman
Public domain. Goldman, *Anarchism and Other Essays* (New York: Mother Earth Publishing, third ed., 1917), lib.harvard.edu.
Why Women Want to Vote (1913), Anna Howard Shaw
Public domain. *Official Program: Woman Suffrage Procession, March 13, 1913,* loc.gov.
For the Sake of Consistency (1915), Mary Church Terrell
Public domain. "Women Suffrage and the Fifteenth Amendment," *Crisis,* August 1915. The editor wishes to thank the Crisis Publishing Co., Inc., for the use of this material first published in the August 1915 issue of *Crisis Magazine.* See also *Civil Rights Since 1787: A Reader on the Black Struggle,* eds. Jonathan Birnbaum and Clarence Taylor (New York: New York University Press, 2000), 260-261.

SIX
World War I
I Denounce the Governing Class (1915), Kate Richards O'Hare
Public domain. "I Denounce," *The National Rip-Saw,* 12.1 (March 1915); and marxisthistory.org.
Strike Against War (1916), Helen Keller
Public domain. *New York Call,* January 6, 1916; and *We Who Dared to Say No to War: American Antiwar Writing from 1812 to Now,* ed. Murray Polner and Thomas E. Woods, Jr., (New York: Basic Books, 2008), 140-145.
The Darker Races and Avaricious Capitalists (1917), A. Philip Randolph and Chandler Owen
Public domain. Randolph and Owen, *Terms of Peace and the Darker Races* (New

York: Poole Press Association, 1917); and *Antiwar Dissent and Peace Activism in World War I America,* ed. Scott H. Bennett and Charles F. Howlett (Syracuse, NY: Syracuse University Press, 2014), 163-169.

A Deliberate Violator (1918), Roger N. Baldwin

Public domain. Baldwin, *The Individual and the State: The Problem as Presented by the Sentencing of Roger N. Baldwin* (New York: Graphic Press, 1918); and Bennett and Howlett, *Antiwar Dissent and Peace Activism,* 188-195.

SEVEN
Workers' Rights and the Great Depression
Industrial Slavery, Murder, Riot, and Unbelievable Cruelty (1919), W. E. B. Du Bois

Public domain. Du Bois, "The Economics of the Negro Problem," *The American Labor Year Book, 1917-1918,* ed. Alexander Trachtenberg (New York: The Rand School of Social Science), 180-182; and Birnbaum and Taylor, *Civil Rights Since 1787,* 264-266.

Organization of the Negro Workers (1925), A. Phillip Randolph

Public domain. Randolph, "Negroes and the Labor Movement," *The Messenger* vol. 7 (July 1925): 261, 275; and *African American Political Thought, 1890-1930: Washington, Du Bois, Garvey, and Randolph,* ed. Cary D. Wintz (New York: Routledge, 1996), 300-301.

A Bolshevik Revolution in Lawrence? (1919; document date, 1958), A.J. Muste

No known copyright. Muste, "The Lawrence Strike of 1919," *Liberation,* February-April, 1958; and *Nonviolence in America: A Documentary History* (Maryknoll, NY: Orbis Books, 1995, 1998), 129-141.

Brother, Can You Spare a Dime? (1932), Yip Harburg and Bonus Marchers

Document 1. No known copyright. Harburg, "Brother, Can You Spare a Dime?" (lyrics), 1932; and socialwelfarelibrary.vcu.edu.

Document 2. Public domain. Veteran's Rank and File Committee, *Veterans March to Washington to Arrive at Opening of Congress, December 5th, 1932 to Demand Cash Payment of Bonus* (New York, 1932), loc.gov.

Down with the Sweatshops! (1933; document date, 1945), Rose Pesotta

No known copyright. Pesotta, *Bread upon the Waters* (New York: Dodd, Mead, 1944), 28-40, theanarchistlibrary.org.

Death Watch (1935), League of the Physically Handicapped

Used with permission. Courtesy of Disability Social History Project, "Disability History—The 1930s," disabilityhistory.org.

The Flint Sit-Down Strike (1937), United Auto Workers

No known copyright. *Flint Journal,* Extra, January 4, 1937, dhr.history.vt.edu.

Women of the Cotton Fields (1938), Elaine Ellis

Used with permission. Ellis, "Women of the Cotton Fields," *Crisis* (October 1938): 333, 342. The editor wishes to thank the Crisis Publishing Co., Inc., for the use of this material first published in the October 1938 issue of *Crisis Magazine*; and Marable and Mullings, *Let Nobody Turn Us Around,* 325-327.

Picketing Is Exercising Free Speech (1940), Frank Murphy

Public domain. *Thornhill v. Alabama* 310 U.S. 88 (1940).

EIGHT
World War II
Jim Crow and National Defense (1941), A. Philip Randolph
Public domain. Randolph, *Why Should We March?* (1941), A. Philip Randolph
Papers, Library of Congress, Washington, DC, memory.loc.gov.

I Cannot Honorably Participate (1943), Robert Lowell
Used with permission. "To President Roosevelt," September 7, 1943, "Public Letters
to Two Presidents" from "Appendix" from COLLECTED PROSE by Robert Lowell.
Copyright c 1987 by Caroline Lowell, Harriet Lowell, and Sheridan Lowell. Reprinted by
permissions of Farrar, Straus and Giroux; and *War No More: Three Centuries of American
Antiwar and Peace Writing*, ed. Lawrence Rosenwald (New York: The Library of America,
2016), 252-255.

A Racist Charge of Mutiny (1944), Thurgood Marshall
Public domain. Marshall to Secretary James Forrestal, October 19, 1944, National
Association for the Advancement of Colored People Records, 1842-1999, microfilm edi-
tion, 9, reel 17, 783, Library of Congress, Washington, DC; and *Marshalling Justice: The
Early Civil Rights Letters of Thurgood Marshall*, ed. Michael G. Long (New York: Amistad,
2011), 141-144.

The Internment of Japanese Citizens (1944), Fred Korematsu and Frank Murphy
Public domain. *Korematsu v. United States*, 323 U.S. 214 (1944), law.cornell.edu.

Japanese American Draft Resisters (1944), The Voice of the Nisei
No known copyright. Handbill with List of Demands by the Voice of the Nisei, 1944,
Records of District Courts of the United States, Record Group 21, U.S. National Archives,
Records of the District Courts, College Park, Maryland, recordsofrights.org.

Against Dropping Atomic Bombs on Japan (1945), Leo Szilard
Public domain. *A Petition to the President of the United States*, July 4, 1945, U.S.
National Archives, Record Group 77, Records of the Chief of Engineers, Manhattan Engi-
neer District, Harrison-Bundy File, folder 76; and Rosenwald, *War No More*, 262-263.

Judgment on Jubilation (1945), Dorothy Day
Content from the *Catholic Worker* paper is not copyrighted. Day, "We Go on the
Record: The Catholic Worker Response to Hiroshima," *Catholic Worker*, September 1945,
catholicworker.org.

NINE
The Civil Rights Movement
Building the Foundation
Human Holocaust Under the Stars and Stripes (1909), Ida B. Wells-Barnett
No known copyright. Wells-Barnett, speech delivered at the National Negro Con-
ference, in *Proceedings: National Negro Conference*, 1909, 174-179); and Marable and
Mullings, *Let Nobody Turn Us Around*, 209-212.

We March for the Butchered Dead (1917), Charles Martin and the Negro Silent
Protest Parade
No known copyright. Martin, Negro Silent Protest Parade, flyer, NAACP Records, 7,

The Anti-Lynching Campaign, 1912-1955; Series B: Legislative and Publicity Files, 1916-1955; and nationalhumanitiescenter.org.

We Return Fighting (1919), W. E. B. Du Bois

Used with permission. Du Bois, "Returning Soldiers," *Crisis* (May 1919): 13-14. The editor wishes to thank the Crisis Publishing Co., Inc., for the use of this material first published in the May 1919 issue of *Crisis Magazine*. See also Marable and Mullings, *Let Nobody Turn Us Around*, 244-245.

It Brings a Sense of Shame, (1947, 1960), *Baltimore Afro-American* and Jackie Robinson

Document 1. Used with permission. "Helping Jackie to Make Good," *Baltimore Afro-American,* April 15, 1947.

Document 2. Used with permission. Robinson, "Jackie Robinson," *New York Post,* April 25, 1960.

Jim Crow in the Armed Forces (1948), Bayard Rustin

Used with permission. Rustin to C. B. Powell, August 2, 1948, Records of the League for Nonviolent Civil Disobedience Against Military Segregation, Swarthmore College Peace Collection, Swarthmore, Pennsylvania; and *I Must Resist: Bayard Rustin's Life in Letters*, ed. Michael G. Long (San Francisco: City Lights Books, 2012), 115-118.

The Courage of These People in Clarendon County (1951), Thurgood Marshall

Public domain. Marshall to the Editor of the *Afro-American*, June 16, 1951.

Dogs, Cats, and Colored People (1955), George Grant

Used with permission. "A True Story," *Baltimore Afro-American,* January 1955, crmvet.org.

From Rosa Parks to the Black Panthers

Don't Ride the Bus (1955), Jo Ann Gibson Robinson

No known copyright. Robinson, "This Is for Monday, December 5, 1955," leaflet, kingencyclopedia.stanford.edu.

We Shall Have to Lead Our People to You (1957), Southern Negro Leaders Conference

Used with permission. Southern Negro Leaders Conference to President Dwight D. Eisenhower, Bayard Rustin Papers, microfilm edition, reel 20; and Long, *I Must Resist,* 185-187. Used with permission. Courtesy of the Bayard Rustin Estate, Walter Naegle, executor.

SNCC and Nonviolence (1960), Ella Baker and the Student Nonviolent Coordinating Committee

Document 1. No known copyright. Baker, "Bigger than a Hamburger," *Southern Patriot* 18 (June 1960); and Marable and Mullings, *Let Nobody Turn Us Around,* 398-400.

Document 2. No known copyright. *The Student Voice* 1:1 (June 1960).

We're Going to Keep Coming (1961), Jim Zwerg

Document 1. Used with permission. Jim Zwerg, "One Man's Civil Rights Story," excerpts of lecture, Beloit College, September 18, 2002. Thanks to Ann Bausum, author of *Freedom Riders: John Lewis and Jim Zwerg on the Front Lines of the Civil Rights Movement*

(National Geographic Children's Books, 2005), for providing her transcript of Zwerg's lecture.

A Living Petition (1963), Bayard Rustin

Used with permission. Rustin, *March on Washington for Jobs and Freedom, August 28, 1963, Lincoln Memorial Program,* okra.stanford.edu. Used with permission. Courtesy of the Bayard Rustin Estate, Walter Naegle, executor.

I Didn't Try to Register for You (1964), Fannie Lou Hamer

Public domain. Hamer, "Testimony of Fannie Lou Hamer Before the Credentials Committee of the Democratic National Committee," August 22, 1964, americanradioworks.publicradio.org.

Our Free Speech Fight (1964), Mario Savio

Used with permission from Lynn Hollander Savio. Savio, "An End to History," *Humanity: An Arena of Critique and Commitment,* no. 2 (1964); and historyisaweapon.com.

The Right to Throw Off Such Government (1966), Huey Newton and Bobby Seale

No known copyright. Newton and Seale, *Black Panther,* May 15, 1967; and ucpress. edu.

TEN
The Threat of Atomic Bombs and the Vietnam War

Statement on Omaha Action (1959), Marjorie Swann

Swann, Statement by Marjorie Swann, Participant in Omaha Action, July 21, 1959, Horace Champney Papers, box 4, Swarthmore College Peace Collection; and *Christian Peace and Nonviolence: A Documentary History* (Maryknoll, NY: Orbis Books, 2011), 198-199.

The Cruel Deception of Civil Defense (1961), The Civil Defense Protest Committee

No known copyright. Advertisement, *New York Times,* December 9, 1961.

The Cuban Missile Crisis (1962), Women Strike for Peace

No known copyright. Women Strike for Peace to WSPers and Friends, October 25, 1962; copy in editor's possession. The records of Women Strike for Peace are deposited at the Swarthmore College Peace Collection.

The March on Washington to End the Vietnam War (1965), Students for a Democratic Society

No known copyright. "A Call to All Students to March on Washington to End the War in Vietnam April 17, 1965," *Bulletin* 3.5 (February 1965), sds-1960s.org.

A Draft for the Freedom Fight in the U.S. (1966), Student Nonviolent Coordinating Committee

No known copyright. SNCC, "Statement on American Policy in Vietnam," *Bond v. Floyd,* 251 F. Supp. 336-337 (N. D. Ga. 1966); and Rosenwald, *War No More,* 383-385.

A Call to Resist Illegitimate Authority (1967), Marcus Raskin and Arthur Waskow

Used with permission. "A Call to Resist Illegitimate Authority," *New York Times Review of Books,* October 12, 1967; and vietnamwar.lib.umb.edu. Arthur Waskow has written the following:

At the time of the "Call to Resist," Marc Raskin was co-director and Arthur Waskow was one of the founding Resident Fellows of the Institute for Policy Studies, an important center for the creation of progressive thought and action. Raskin and Waskow had been among the earliest opponents of the U.S. war against Vietnam, in activities ranging from speaking at the first Vietnam Teach-in at the University of Michigan in 1965 (Waskow), to organizing a nationally televised National Teach-in shortly thereafter and later taking responsibility for an anti-war-crimes "Nuremberg-trial" defense as one of the Boston Five who stood trial for actions that included the "Call to Resist" (Raskin), to joining the nonviolent "siege of the Pentagon" in 1967, becoming a leader of the antiwar, anti-racist insurgent DC delegation to the Democratic National Convention in 1968, and helping shape the post-Kent State mass mobilization of antiwar protestors in Washington DC as a member of the steering committee of the New Mobilization Committee to End the War in Vietnam in 1970 (Waskow). Raskin continued as a key thinker and activist at IPS until his death in 2018. Waskow wrote the original multiracial Freedom Seder for the Passover of 1969, became a leader of the movement for political and spiritual renewal of Judaism, became a rabbi, and in 1983 founded The Shalom Center (theshalomcenter.org), a prophetic voice in the Jewish, multireligious, and American worlds. As its director, he continues an active politico-religious life.

Our Apologies, Good Friends (1968), Daniel Berrigan and the Catonsville Nine
Used with permission of the Daniel Berrigan Literary Trust, c 2018. Berrigan, *Night Flight to Hanoi* (New York: Macmillan, 1968), xiii-xix; and Long, *Christian Peace and Nonviolence*, 220-221.

If the Government Doesn't Stop the War, We'll Stop the Government (1971), Mayday Tribe
No known copyright. Mayday Tribe, *Mayday Tactical Manual* (New York: WIN Magazine, 1971); researchdestroy.com.

ELEVEN
The Movement Expands
Red, Brown, and Yellow Power
Fish-Ins (1964; document date, 1967), Janet McCloud and Robert Casey
No known copyright. Janet McCloud and Robert Casey, "The Last Indian War," *Left and Right* 3.1 (Winter 1967): 28-52.

The Occupation of Alcatraz (1969), Indians of All Tribes
No known copyright. See foundsf.org.

The Longest Walk (1978), American Indian Movement
No known copyright. AIM, "Affirmation of Sovereignty of the Indigenous Peoples of the Western Hemisphere," *American Indian Journal*, 4.9 (September 1978): 17-30; and *Say We Are Nations: Documents of Politics and Protest in Indigenous America Since 1887*, ed. Daniel M. Cobb (Chapel Hill: University of North Carolina Press, 2015), 184-188.

La Huelga and La Causa Is Our Cry (1966), Dolores Huerta
Transcript at libraries.ucsd.edu/farmworkermovement.

Blowouts—Baby—Blowouts!! (1968), Chicano Students in East Los Angeles
No known copyright. Copy of flyer at Southern California Library, Los Angeles, CA.

To Resist with Every Ounce (1969), Cesar Chavez
No known copyright. Chavez, "Letter from Delano," farmmovement.org.
Hasta Le Victoria Siempre! (1970), Young Lords Party
No known copyright. *Palente,* 2.15, November 20, 1970; and *The Young Lords: A Reader,* ed. Darrel Enck-Wanzer (New York: New York University Press, 2010), 11-13.
The Yellow Power Movement (1969), Amy Uyematsu
Used with permission. Uyematsu, "The Emergence of Yellow Power in America," *Gidra,* October 1969; and *Roots: An Asian American Reader,* ed. Amy Tachiki, Eddie Wong, Franklin Odo, and Buck Wong (Los Angeles: UCLA Asian American Studies Center, 1971), 9-13.
From Colonies to Communities (1969), Asian Community Center
No known copyright. *Rodan: Northern California Asian American Community News,* 1.5 (November 1970); and Wong and others, *Roots: An Asian American Reader,* 273-275.

Gay and Lesbian Rights, Women's Rights, and Disability Rights
Ejected from Dewey's (1965), Janus Society
Courtesy of the John J. Wilcox, Jr. LGBT Archives, Philadelphia, Pennsylvania. With special thanks to archivist Bob Skiba.
Homosexual American Citizens Picket the White House (1965), Frank Kameny
Public domain. Kameny to the Daughters of Bilitis, June 8, 1965, Franklin Kameny Papers, box 69, Library of Congress, Washington, DC.
Christopher Street Liberation Day (1970), Gay Liberation Front
Courtesy of ONE National Gay & Lesbian Archives, USC Libraries, University of Southern California.
Underground Abortion (1969), Jane
No known copyright. Abortion Counseling Service, *Abortion—a woman's decision, a woman's right,* pamphlet, 1969, cwluherstory.org.
We Call on All Our Sisters (1969), Redstockings
Used with permission. The Redstockings Manifesto was issued in New York City on July 7, 1969. It first appeared as a mimeographed flyer, designed for distribution at women's liberation events. Further information about the Manifesto and other materials from the 1960s rebirth years of feminism is available from the Redstockings Women's Liberation Archives for Action at www.redstockings.org or PO Box 744 Stuyvesant Station, New York, NY 10009.
Welfare Is a Women's Issue (1972), Johnnie Tillmon
No known copyright. Tillmon, "Welfare Is a Women's Issue," *Ms. Magazine* (Spring 1972): 111-116.
Sitting Against Nixon (1972), Judy Heumann
Used with permission. Disabled in Action of Metropolitan New York, "A Discussion with Judy Heumann on Independent Living," disabledinaction.org.
The Vegetables Are Rising (1977), Ed Roberts
No known copyright. Ed Roberts, Speech on 504 Sit-In, April 30, 1977; "Worth Repeating: Ed Roberts' 504 Sit-In Victory Rally Speech," ollibean.com.

TWELVE
Environmental Justice and Animal Liberation
Earth Day (1970), Gaylord Nelson
Public domain. "Partial Text for Senator Gaylord Nelson, Denver, Colo., April 22," nelsonearthday.net.
Oppose, Resist, Subvert (1981), Edward Abbey
Used with permission from Clarke Abbey. Daniel J. Philippon, "Edward Abbey: Remarks at the Cracking of Glen Canyon Dam," *ISLE: Interdisciplinary Studies in Literature and Environment*, 11.2 (July 2004): 161-166.
Occupy the Forest (1985), Earth First
No known copyright. Earth First, flyer, 1985, copy in editor's possession.
Rescuing the Monkeys (1981), People for the Ethical Treatment of Animals
Used with permission. People for the Ethical Treatment of Animals, press release, no date, original at PETA, copy in editor's possession.
A Necessary Fuss (1984), Animal Liberation Front
Used with permission. Animal Liberation Front, "The ALF Credo," no date, animalliberationfront.com.
Avon Killing (1989), People for the Ethical Treatment of Animals
Used with permission. People for the Ethical Treatment of Animals, "'Avon Killing' Boycott Launched in United States, Japan, England, Italy, Germany, Mexico, and Canada: Animal Rights Groups Will Go Door-to-Door with Message," news release, March 2, 1989, original at PETA, copy in editor's possession.

THIRTEEN
Anti-Nukes, The Reagan Years, Anti-Gulf War
Nuclear Power and Nuclear Weapons
I Can Find No Natural Balance with a Nuclear Plant (1974), Sam Lovejoy
Used with permission. "Feb. 22, 1974: Sam Lovejoy Topples Nuclear Plant Tower in Act of Civil Disobedience," in *Teaching a People's History: Zinn Education Project,* zinnedproject.org.
Declaration of Nuclear Resistance (1976), Clamshell Alliance
Used with permission. Clamshell Alliance, "Declaration of Nuclear Resistance," *Win,* June 16 and 23, 1977; and *Nonviolence in America: A Documentary History,* ed. Staughton Lynd and Alice Lynd (Maryknoll: Orbis Books, 1995), 506-508.
Making the World Truly Safe (1979), Randall Forsberg
Used with permission. Randall Forsberg, "Call to Halt the Nuclear Arms Race: Proposal for a Mutual US-Soviet Nuclear-Weapon Freeze," pamphlet, April 1982 (St. Louis, MO: Nuclear Weapons Freeze Campaign, 1982).
Nuclear Waste on Our Homeland (1995), Lower Colorado River Tribes
No known copyright. Colorado River Native Nations Alliance, "A United Resolution by the Lower Colorado River Federally Recognized Tribes," no date, energy-net.org.

Reagan on Unions, South Africa, and Central America
You Are Not Alone (1981), Lane Kirkland
Public domain. "Excerpts from Lane Kirkland Talk at Rally," *New York Times,* September 20, 1991.
End UM Investments in Apartheid (1977), South African Liberation Committee
No known copyright. South African Liberation Committee, "South Africa," flyer, michiganintheworld.history.lsa.umich.edu.
Boycotting Shell (1986), United Mineworkers of America
No known copyright. United Mine Workers of America and Free South Africa Movement, "Why American Workers Have United to Boycott Shell," flyer, undated, Portland Anti-Apartheid Materials, Elizabeth Ussher Groff Collection, Michigan State University Libraries Special Collections.
We Join in Covenant to Provide Sanctuary (1982), Bay Area Sanctuary Movement
No known copyright. Reprinted in Susan B. Coutin, *The Culture of Protest: Religious Activism and the U.S. Sanctuary Movement* (Boulder, CO: Westview, 1993), 230.
Pledge of Resistance Pledge (1983), Pledge of Resistance Campaign
No known copyright. See General Assembly of the Christian Church (Disciples of Christ), "Resolution Concerning the Pledge of Resistance to Prevent the Invasion of Central America," no. 8530, August 1985, disciples.org.
I Sat on the Tracks (1987; document date, 2011), S. Brian Willson
Used with permission. "'Blood on the Tracks': Brian Willson's Memoir of Transformation from Vietnam Vet to Radical Pacifist," interview with Amy Goodman, *Democracy Now,* October 28, 2011.

The Gulf War
I Will Refuse to Fight (1990), Jeff Paterson
Used with permission. Paterson, press conference statement, August 16, 1990; and Lynd and Lynd, *Nonviolence in America,* 481-482.
One Billion Dollars a Day (1991), June Jordan
Used with permission. Jordan, "Poets and Politicians Against the War," speech broadcast, KPFA, Berkeley, CA, distributed by Pacifica Radio Archives, March 1991. Copyright 2017 June Jordan Literary Estate Trust. Reprinted with the permission of the June M. Jordan Literary Estate. www.junejordan.com.
Demonstrate, Demand, Disobey (1991), Michael Albert and Stephen Shalom
Used with permission. Michael Albert and Stephen Shalom, "Gulf War Pullout," *Z Magazine,* February 1991, zcomm.org.

FOURTEEN
LGBT Rights, AIDS, and Women's Rights
I Am Proud to Raise My Voice Today (1979), Audre Lorde
Used with permission. From a speech by Audre Lorde given October 14, 1979. Copyright c 1979 by Audre Lorde. Used herein by permission of the Charlotte Sheedy Literary Agency.

The Right to Lesbian and Gay Sex (1987), The March on Washington for Lesbian and Gay Rights

"Our Demands," courtesy of ONE Archives at the USC Libraries, Los, Angeles, CA, one.usc.edu.

We Take That Fire and Make It Our Own (1993), New York Lesbian Avengers

Used with permission. New York Lesbian Avengers, *Dyke Manifesto,* text from broadside for the 1993 March for Lesbian, Gay and Bi Equal Rights in Washington, DC, Carrie Moyer, designer.

Transphobia Is at the Heart of Queerphobia (1993), Phyllis Randolph Frye

Used with permission. Frye, "Listen Up," speech at the 1993 March on Washington for Lesbian, Gay and Bi Equal Rights and Liberation, The Phyllis R. Frye Collection, 1948-2016, box 1, folder 22, Cushing Library, Texas A&M University, College Station, Texas.

Why We Fight (1988), Vito Russo

No known copyright. Russo, "Why We Fight," speech transcript, May 9, 1988, actupny.org.

Stop the Church (1989; document date, 2009), Michael Petrelis

Used with permission. Petrelis, "20th Anniversary: ACT UP Invaded St. Patrick's Cathedral," mpetrelisblogspot.com.

Women's Rights

Women's Fast for the ERA (1982; document date, 1987), Sonia Johnson

Used with permission. Johnson, *Going Out of Our Mind: The Metaphysics of Liberation* (Freedom, CA: The Crossing Press, 1987), we.riseup.net.

Clarence Thomas, Sexual Harasser (1991), Anita Hill

Public domain. Anita Hill, Testimony, October 11, 1991, *Hearings Before the Committee on the Judiciary, United States Senate, October 11, 12, and 13* (Washington, DC: Government Printing Office, 1993), loc.gov.

March for Women's Lives (1992), Sarah Schuster and Jewell Jackson McCabe

Text of speeches used with permission. See "Pro-Choice Issues: A Rally Was Held in Washington, DC in Support of Abortion Rights for Women," April 5, 1992, c-span.org.

FIFTEEN
The Anti-Globalization Movement

NAFTA Is Economic Hemorrhage (1993), Jesse Jackson

Public domain. Full text of "NAFTA, a Negative Impact on Blue Collar, Minority, and Female Employment? Hearing Before the Employment, Housing, and Aviation Subcommittee of the Committee on Government Operations, House of Representatives, One Hundred Third Congress, first session, November 10, 1993," archive.gov.

Close Down the WTO (1999), Russell Mokhiber and Robert Weissman

Used with permission. Mokhiber and Weissman, "Top 10 Reasons to Shutter the WTO," *Mother Jones,* November 24, 1990, motherjones.com.

Students Against Sweatshops (1999), SOLE

No known copyright. Students Organizing for Labor and Equality, "The No-Sweat 30's Statement Ending the Sit-In," flyer, no date, personal.umich.edu.

Defund the Fund! Break the Bank! Dump the Debt! (2000), Mobilization for Global Justice

No known copyright. Mobilization for Global Justice, "DE-FUND the FUND! BREAK the BANK! DUMP the DEBT!" originally at16.org, now at ratical.org.

SIXTEEN
The War on Terror

Isn't This Really About Oil? (2002; document date, 2016), Medea Benjamin

Used with permission. Benjamin, "Bush's Iraq Lies, Uncontested, Will Haunt Trump," codepink.org.

Calling All Americans to Resist War and Repression (2002), Not in Our Name

No known copyright. Originally posted at notinourname.net, a website archived at loc.gov.

Bring Our Troops Home (2005), Cindy Sheehan

Used with permission. Sheehan, "My Speech at the Anti-War Rally," September 24, 2005, huffingtonpost.com.

Eleven Reasons to Close Guantánamo (2015), Naureen Shah

Used with permission. Shah, "11 Reasons January 11th Must Be Guantánamo's Last Anniversary," January 10, 2015, amnestyusa.org.

Shut Down Creech (2016), Anti-Drone Activists

Used with permission. Shut Down Creech, shutdowncreech.blogspot.com.

SEVENTEEN
The New Century
Mining, Pipelines, and Global Warming

Boats Float, Bears Don't (2008), Greenpeace International

Used with permission from greenpeace.org. Greenpeace, "Polar Bear Paddle Protest," February 1, 2008, greenpeace.org.

End Mountaintop Removal (2010), Appalachia Rising

Used with permission. Appalachia Rising, press release, no date, originally at appalachiarising.org., now accessible at ran.org.

The Keystone Pipeline Revolt (2011), Bill McKibben

Used with permission. "The Keystone Pipeline Revolt: Why Mass Arrests Are Just the Beginning," *Rolling Stone*, September 28, 2011, rollingstone.com.

LGBTQ Rights

Chained to Serve Openly (2010), Get EQUAL

David Mixner to Friends of GetEqual, press release, November 15, 2010, originally at getequal.org. With thanks to Michael Bedwell for providing the release, a copy of which is in the editor's possession, and for assisting with the writing of the introduction to the release.

Our Love Is Equal (2013), Anthony Kennedy and James Obergefell

Document 1. Public domain. *Obergefell* et al. *v. Hodges, Director, Ohio Department of Health*, et al., 2015, supremecourt.gov.

Document 2. Used with permission from Jim Obergefell. "Jim Obergefell Responds to Supreme Court Decision on Same-Sex Marriage," PBS NewsHour, June 26, 2015, youtube.com.

Occupying Wall Street and Washington

Killing Big Insurance (2009), Mobilization for Health Care for All

Mobilization for Health Care for All, "Call to Action," September 24, 2009, youtube.com.

Occupy, I Love You (2011), Naomi Klein

Used with permission. Klein, "Occupy Wall Street: The Most Important Thing in the World Now," *The Nation*, October 6, 2011, thenation.com.

Moral Mondays (2013), William Barber II

Barber, "Why We Are Here Today," news release, April 29, 2013, carolinajustice.typepad.com.

Time to Withdraw Big Money from Politics (2016), Democracy Spring and Democracy Awakening

Document 1. Democracy Spring, "The Problem," no date, democracyspring.org.

Document 2. Used with permission. Democracy Awakening, "April 16-18," no date, democracyawakening.org.

Prison Abolition and Black Lives Matter

Life Beyond the Prison (2003), Angela Y. Davis

Used with permission. Angela Y. Davis, excerpts from *Are Prisons Obsolete?*, pp. 11-12 and 16-21. Copyright c 2003 by Angela Y. Davis. Reprinted with the permission of The Permissions Company.

Justice for Trayvon (2012), Tracy Martin and Sybrina Fulton

No known copyright. "Tracy Martin & Sybrina Fulton Speak at Million Hoodies," March 23, 2012, youtube.com.

Riding to Ferguson (2014), Black Lives Matter

No known copyright. "Black Lives Matter Ride PSA: Call for Riders," August 19, 2014, youtube.com.

Freeing Slaves in Prison (2016), Support Prisoner Resistance

Used with permission. International Workers Organizing Committee and Prisoners, "Call to Action," news release, April 1, 2016, iwoc.noblogs.org.

Protecting and Legalizing Immigrants

Freedom Rides for Immigrant Workers (2003), Patricia A. Ford

No known copyright. Ford, "Freedom Rides for Immigrant Workers," digitized transcript 3, SEIU Executive Vice President's Office: Patricia Ford Records, Walter P. Reuther Library, Archives of Labor and Urban Affairs, Wayne State University.

We Want a Legalization Process (2006), Luis Gutierrez, Gloria Romero, and Others

Used with permission. "Over 1.5 Million March for Immigrant Rights in One of

Largest Days of Protest in U.S. History," May 2, 2006, democracynow.org.

Stopping Another Deportation (2013), United We Dream

Used with permission. United We Dream, "DREAMers Stop Deportation Bus in Ongoing Escalation at ICE Facility in Phoenix," press release, August 22, 2013, unitedwedream.org.

EIGHTEEN
The Trump Era Begins

Not a Legitimate President (January 2017), John Lewis and Others

Comments are in the public domain. Quoted in Eugene Scott and Daniella Diaz, "These Democrats Aren't Attending Trump's Inauguration," January 17, 2017, cnn.com.

Our Pussies Ain't for Grabbing (January 2017), The Women's March and America Ferrera

Document 1. March principles: Women's March, "Unity Principles," no date, womensmarch.com.

Document 2. Ferrera, untitled speech, January 21, 2017, c-span.org.

Together, We Rise (March 2017), Dave Archambault II

Used with permission. "Dave Archambault II Remarks, Native Nations March on Washington, D.C.," press release, March 10, 2017, standwithstandingrock.net.

Fearless Girl (April 2017), Susan Cox

Used with permission. Cox, "Let's Appreciate What the Fearless Girl Represents, Rather than Tearing Her Down," April 20, 2017, *Feminist Current*, feministcurrent.com.

And So We Resist Global Warming (June 2017), Bill McKibben

Used with permission. McKibben, "Trump's Stupid and Reckless Climate Decision," *New York Times*, June 1, 2017.

Dying for Health Care (June 2017), ADAPT

Used with permission. ADAPT, "Disability Advocates Protest Senate Leader Over Cuts to Medicaid for Millions of Elderly and Disabled Americans," press release, June 22, 2017, adapt.org.

A White Nationalist Rally in Charlottesville (August 2017), Brendan Novak

Used with permission. Novak, "I Was Wrong About the 'Alt-Right,'" *Cavalier Daily,* cavalierdaily.com.

Targeting Transgender Troops (November 2017), Jennifer Peace

Used with permission. Peace, "After 13 Years in the Military, This Is My Toughest Veterans Day," November 10, 2017, cnn.com. Jennifer Peace is not responsible for any comments in this book that may be construed as derogatory toward the U.S. government or any of its officials.

Hunger Strike at Guantánamo Bay (December 2017), Khalid Qassim

Qassim, "We Guantánamo Bay Detainees Have the Right to Protest Our Condition," *The Guardian,* December 14, 2017, theguardian.com.

We Pledge to Resist for Immigrants (2017), Alison Harrington

Used with permission. Harrington, "We Pledge to Resist Deportation and Discrimination Through Sanctuary," no date, action.groundswell-mvmt.org.

The Human Impact of the Muslim Ban (December 2017), Dina El-Rifai
Used with permission. El-Rifai, "The Human Impact of the Muslim Ban," December 12, 2017, afsc.org.

DACA: Depression, Anxiety, Frustration (January 2018), Korina Iribe Romo
Used with permission. Romo, "We Need a Permanent Solution for the Dreamers," pennlive.com, January 11, 2018.

Marching for Our Lives (February 2018), Patrick Northrup
Used with permission. Northrup, untitled speech, March 24, 2018, Winchester, Virginia.

We Do Not Want the Wall (March 2018), Dulce Garcia
Used with permission. "San Diego DACA Recipient Says Trump's Border Wall 'Won't Stop Immigration,'" *San Diego Union-Tribune,* March 12, 2018, sandiegouniontribune.com.

#MeToo Is About Restoring Humanity (September 2018), Tarana Burke
Used with permission. Burke, "#MeToo Founder Tarana Burke on the Rigorous Work That Still Lies Ahead," *Variety,* September 2018, *Variety.com.*

FOREWORD
Nonviolent Revolt

"Did you ever ask yourself?": Alexander Berkman, "The Idea of a Thing," in *Life of an Anarchist: The Alexander Berkman Reader,* ed. Gene Fellner (New York: Seven Stories Press, 1995, 2005), 293.

"Because revolution is evolution": Berkman, "The Idea of a Thing," 295.

"What is possible would never have been achieved": Max Weber, "The Vocation of Politics," in *The Essential Weber: A Reader,* ed. Sam Whimster (New York: Routledge, 2004), 269.

"conspiracy of silence": Eric Foner, *Battles for Freedom: The Use and Abuse of American History* (London and New York: I.B. Tauris and the Nation Company, 2017), 201.

"For much of the 1850s": Foner, *Battles for Freedom,* 206.

"Whoever fights monsters": Friedrich Nietzsche, "Aphorism 146," in *Beyond Good and Evil,* ed. Rolf-Peter Horstman and trans. Judith Norman (Cambridge: Cambridge University Press, 2001), 68.

"[M]any ideas, once held to be true": Berkman, "The Idea of a Thing," 294.

INTRODUCTION
We the Resistance

"The politics of dissent": Erica Chenoweth, "People Are in the Streets Protesting Donald Trump. But When Does Protest Actually Work?" *Washington Post,* November 21, 2016.

"a technique of action": See Albert Einstein Institution, "Nonviolent Action," aeinstein.org.

"redeem the soul of America": This was the motto of the Southern Christian Leadership Conference.

"a sit-inner before the sit-ins": Martin Luther King, Jr., "Hall of Famer," *New York Amsterdam News,* August 4, 1962.

"historically speaking, nonviolent struggle": Chenoweth, "People Are in the Streets," November 21, 2016.

ONE
Early Roots of Resistance

We Cannot Condemn Quakers, Edward Hart

"no one shall be persecuted": Kenneth T. Jackson, "A Colony with a Conscience," *New York Times,* December 27, 2007. For the full text of the *Union of Utrecht,* see *The Low Countries in Early Modern Times: A Documentary History,* ed. Herbert H. Rowen (New York: Harper & Row, 1972), 69-74.

"allow everyone": Jackson, "A Colony with a Conscience," December 27, 2007.

Buy Slaves to Free Them, **George Keith**
"the earliest known expression": *American Antislavery Writings: Colonial Beginnings to Emancipation,* ed. James G. Basker (New York: The Library of America, 2012), 1.
"What thing in the world": Gerret Hendricks, Derick Op De Graeff, Francis Daniell Pastorius, and Abraham Op Den Graef, "Resolution of Germantown Mennonites," in Basker, *American Antislavery Writings,* 2.

Tea Overboard, **George Hewes**
"Friends! Brethren! Countrymen!": Boston Tea Party Historical Society, "The Full Description of the Events," no date, boston-tea-party.org.
"This meeting can do no more": Boston Tea Historical Society, "The Full Description of the Events," no date.

TWO
The Abolitionist Movement and the Struggle for the Rights of Free African Americans

Women Overthrowing Slavery, **Angelina Grimke**
"is a cause worth dying for": Carol Berkin, "Angelina and Sarah Grimke: Abolitionist Sisters," The Gilder Lehrman Institute of American History, gilderlehrman.org.

He Took Hold of Me and I Took Hold of the Window Sash, **Elizabeth Jennings**
"colored persons if sober": Katherine Greider, "The Schoolteacher on the Streetcar," *New York Times,* November 13, 2005.

Was John Brown Justified? **William Lloyd Garrison**
"While it shall be considered right": Frederick Douglass to the Editor of the *Rochester Democrat,* October 31, 1859, in *Frederick Douglass: A Life in Documents,* ed. L. Diane Barnes (Charlottesville: University of Virginia Press, 2013), 81.

THREE
Removing Native Americans, Dethroning Hawaiians

The Audacious Practices of Unprincipled Men, **Chief John Ross**
"distinct, independent political communities": *Worcester v Georgia* 31 U.S. 515 (1832), law.cornell.edu.

FOUR
Striking Against Industrialists

A Petition in Boots, **James Coxey**
"Coxey! Coxey! Coxey!": Jon Grinspan, "How a Ragtag Band of Reformers Organized the First Protest March on Washington, DC," *Smithsonian Magazine,* May 1, 2004, smithsonian.com.

The Wail of the Children, **Mother Jones**
"Philadelphia's mansions were built": Thomas Fortuna, "Philadelphia Mill Children March Against Child Labor Exploitation, 1903," October 23, 2011, Global Nonviolent Action Database (nvdatabase.swarthmore.edu).

FIVE
Fighting for Women's Rights

All Men and Women Are Created Equal, **Elizabeth Cady Stanton and Others**
"discuss the social, civil, and religious": Judith Wellman, *The Road to Seneca Falls: Elizabeth Cady Stanton and the First Woman's Rights Convention* (Urbana: University of Illinois Press, 2004), 92.

"it is the duty of the women": Sally G. McMillen, *Seneca Falls and the Origins of the Women's Rights Movement* (New York: Oxford University Press, 2008), 240.

Robbed of Citizenship, **Susan B. Anthony**
"Men—their rights": Godfrey D. Lehman, "Susan B. Anthony Cast Her Ballot for Ulysses S. Grant," *American Heritage,* 37.1 (December 1985), americanheritage.com. All other quotations in this introduction are drawn from this source.

Marriage and Love Have Nothing in Common, **Emma Goldman**
"for the liberation of the human mind": Emma Goldman, *Anarchism and Other Essays,* third edition (New York: Mother Earth Publishing Association, 1917), lib.berkeley. edu.

Why Women Want to Vote, **Anna Howard Shaw**
"telegrams and protests poured in": Sheridan Harvey, "Marching for the Vote: Remembering the Woman Suffrage Parade of 1913," in Library of Congress, *American Memory,* no date, memory.loc.gov.

"will receive my most": Harvey, "Marching for the Vote, *American Memory.*

"the fact that, early in her career": *Official Program, Woman Suffrage Procession, Washington, DC, March 13, 1913,* in Library of Congress, *American Time Capsule: Three Centuries of Broadsides and Other Printed Ephemera,* no date, loc.gov.

SIX
World War I

Strike Against War, **Helen Keller**
"Their cause is my cause": Helen Keller, "In Behalf of the IWW," *Liberator,* March 1918.

SEVEN
Workers' Rights and the Great Depression

Brother, Can You Spare a Dime? **Yip Harburg and Bonus Marchers**
"I never saw such fine Americanism": National Public Radio, "The Bonus Army: How a Protest Led to the GI Bill," broadcast November 11, 2011, npr.org.

"The sky was red": "The Bonus Army," November 11, 2011, npr.org.

Death Watch, **League of the Physically Handicapped**
"that jobs were available": Paul K. Longmore and David Goldberger, "The League of the Physically Handicapped and the Great Depression: A Case Study in the New Disability History," *The Journal of American History* 87. 3 (Dec. 2000): 899.

"The members of our organization": Sylvia Flexer to President Franklin D. Roosevelt, July 31, 1936, President's Official File 836: Physically Handicapped Persons, Franklin D. Roosevelt Presidential Library, Hyde Park, New York.

EIGHT
World War II

Jim Crow and National Defense, A. Philip Randolph
"there shall be no discrimination": Franklin D. Roosevelt, "Executive Order 8802," June 25, 1941, eeoc.gov.

I Cannot Honorably Participate, Robert Lowell
"To us, the war system": Donald Benedict, Joseph J. Bevilacqua, Meredith Dallas, David Dellinger, George M. Houser, William H. Lovell, Howard E. Spragg, and Richard J. Wichlei, *Why We Refused to Register* (New York: The Fellowship of Reconciliation, Keep America Out of War Congress, National Council for Prevention of War, Youth Committee Against War, Young People's Socialist League, and War Resisters League, 1941); and *Nonviolence in America: A Documentary History*, ed. Staughton Lynd and Alice Lynd (Maryknoll, NY: Orbis Books, 1995), 162.

The Internment of Japanese Citizens, Fred Korematsu and Frank Murphy
"to prescribe military areas": Franklin D. Roosevelt, "Executive Order 9066," February 19, 1942, fdrlibrary.org.
"underwent minor plastic surgery": Fred T. Korematsu Institute and Karen Korematsu, "Full Biography," no date, korematsuinstitute.org.

NINE
The Civil Rights Movement

Jim Crow in the Armed Forces, Bayard Rustin
"Negroes … resent the idea": C. P. Trussell, "Congress Told UMT Racial Bars Would Unleash Civil Disobedience," *New York Times,* April 1, 1948.
"If we must die for our country": Quoted in John D'Emilio, *Lost Prophet: The Life and Times of Bayard Rustin* (New York: Free Press, 2003), 152.
"Negroes and freedom-loving whites": Quoted in Cornelius L. Bynum, *A. Philip Randolph and the Struggle for Civil Rights* (Urbana, IL: University of Illinois Press, 2010), 187.
"oppose a Jim Crow army": "Speaker Requests Defiance of Draft," *New York Times,* July 18, 1948.
"that there shall be equality of treatment": Harry S. Truman, "Executive Order 9981," July 26, 1948, trumanlibrary.org.

The Courage of These People in Clarendon County, Thurgood Marshall
"We must face without evasion": Albert J. Dunmore, "Waring Blasts Negro Leadership as Being 'Segregation Profiteers,'" *Pittsburgh Courier,* July 7, 1951.
"racial separation in public": "Public School Segregation Cases," November 26, 1952, NAACP Papers, microfilm edition, 3C, reel 3, 223.

***We Shall Have to Lead Our People to You,* Southern Negro Leaders Conference**
"Give us the ballot": Martin Luther King, Jr., "Give Us the Ballot," May 17, 1957, kingencyclopedia.stanford.edu.

***We're Going to Keep Coming,* Jim Zwerg**
"to create a crisis": Quoted in Henry Hampton, Steve Fayer, and Sarah Flynn, *Voices of Freedom: An Oral History of the Civil Rights Movement from the 1950s through the 1980s* (New York: Bantam Books, 1990), 75.

"never make it through": Quoted in John Lewis and Michael D'Orso, *Walking with the Wind: A Memoir of the Movement* (New York: Simon & Schuster, 2015), 140. See also "Freedom Rides," kingencyclopedia.stanford.edu.

"Well, boys, here they are": Quoted in Raymond Arsenault, *Freedom Riders: 1961 and the Struggle for Racial Justice* (New York: Oxford University Press, 2011), 143. See also "Freedom Rides," kingencyclopedia.stanford.edu.

***I Didn't Try to Register for You,* Fannie Lou Hamer**
"We didn't come all this way": See Jack Hitt, "Party Crasher," *New York Times Magazine,* December 31, 2006.

***Our Free Speech Fight,* Mario Savio**
"Sit down!": Richard Gonzales, "Berkeley's Fight for Free Speech Fired Up Student Protest Movement," npr.org, October 5, 2014.

TEN
The Threat of Atomic Bombs and the Vietnam War

***The Cuban Missile Crisis,* Women Strike for Peace**
"We are dedicated to the purpose": No author listed, "Women Strike for Peace Records, 1961-1996," no date, Swarthmore College Peace Collection, swarthmore.edu.

"It shall be the policy": "Text of Kennedy's Address on Moves to Meet the Soviet Build-Up in Cuba," *New York Times,* October 23, 1962.

"End This Madness": Cabell Phillips, "Pickets Parade at White House," *New York Times,* October 28, 1962.

***The March on Washington to End the Vietnam War,* Students for a Democratic Society**
"to inspire people to break out": Tom Hayden, "Excerpts from the Port Huron Statement of the Students for a Democratic Society," in Hayden, *Writings for a Democratic Society: The Tom Hayden Reader* (San Francisco: City Lights Books, 2008), 35-36.

"We're really not just a peace group": "15,000 White House Pickets Denounce Vietnam War," *New York Times,* April 18, 1965.

***If the Government Doesn't Stop the War, We'll Stop the Government,* Mayday Tribe**
"If the government doesn't stop": See Mayday Collective, *Mayday Tactical Manual* (New York: Win, 1971).

ELEVEN
The Movement Expands

Fish-Ins, Janet McCloud
"the right of taking fish": Quoted in Gabriel Chrisman, "The Fish-in Protests at Frank's Landing," no date, washington.edu.
"at all usual": Chrisman, "The Fish-in Protests," no date.

Homosexuals March on the White House, Frank Kameny
"There's no Cuban embassy": Quoted in *Gay Is Good: The Life and Letters of Gay Rights Pioneer Franklin Kameny,* ed. Michael G. Long (Syracuse, NY: Syracuse University Press, 2014), 91.

Christopher Street Liberation Day, Gay Liberation Front
"silent plea for rights": Quoted in Long, *Gay Is Good,* 193.

Underground Abortion, Jane
"I viewed it not as breaking": Kate Manning, "The Amateur Abortionists," *New York Times,* April 22, 2017. Other quotations in this introduction are drawn from this source.

We Call on All Our Sisters, Redstockings
"All right, now let's hear": Edith Evans Asbury, "Women Break Up Abortion Hearing," *New York Times,* February 14, 1969. Other quotations in this introduction are drawn from this source.

Sitting Against Nixon, Judy Heumann
"something that had the influence": Disabled in Action of Metropolitan New York, "A Discussion with Judy Heumann on Independent Living," no date, disabledinaction. org.

The Vegetables Are Rising, Edward Roberts
"We were considered vegetables": "Disabled in San Francisco Vow to Continue Sit-In," *New York Times,* April 17, 1977.

TWELVE
Environmental Justice and Animal Liberation

Oppose, Resist, Subvert, Edward Abbey
"Free the Colorado": Quoted in Martha F. Lee, *Earth First! Environmental Apocalypse* (Syracuse, NY: Syracuse University Press, 1995), 45.

Occupy the Forest, Earth Firsters
"It was my first direct action": Quoted in Henry Fountain, "Rising Above the Environmental Debate," *New York Times,* June 18, 2006.

Rescuing the Monkeys, People for the Ethical Treatment of Animals
"miserable," "poorly maintained," "a very serious health hazard": Quoted in Peter Carlson, "The Great Silver Spring Monkey Debate," *Washington Post,* February 24, 1991.
"a landmark victory": Carlson, "The Great Silver Spring Monkey Debate," February 24, 1991.

THIRTEEN
Anti-Nukes, The Reagan Years, Anti-Gulf War

I Can Find No Balance with a Nuclear Plant, **Sam Lovejoy**
"Violence has to do with human": Quoted in Zinn Education Project, "Feb. 22, 1974: Sam Lovejoy Topples Nuclear Plant Tower in Act of Civil Disobedience," no date, zinnedproject.org.

You Are Not Alone, **Lane Kirkland**
"We will not sit idly by": Eric Pianin, Warren Brown, Margaret Engel, Mike Sager, and Edward D. Sargent, "250,000 March to Protest Reagan's Policies," *Washington Post,* September 20, 1981.

Boycotting Shell, **United Mine Workers of America**
"For many years": Barbara Gamarekian, "Apartheid Protest Takes Page from 60's History," *New York Times,* November 30, 1984.

We Join in Covenant to Provide Sanctuary, **Bay Area Sanctuary Movement**
"We'd take in people": Clyde Haberman, "Trump and the Battle Over Sanctuary in America," *New York Times,* March 5, 2017.

I Will Refuse to Fight, **Jeff Paterson**
"the immediate and unconditional withdrawal": Michael R. Gordon, "Iraq Army Invades Capital of Kuwait in Fierce Fighting," *New York Times,* August 2, 1990.
"No blood for oil": Tom Bowman, "Antiwar Demonstration Draws 75,000 to Washington," *Baltimore Sun,* January 27, 1991.

FOURTEEN
LGBT Rights, AIDS, and Women's Rights

The Right to Lesbian and Gay Sex, **The March on Washington for Lesbian and Gay Rights**
"fundamental right": *Bowers v. Hardwick* 478 U.S. 186 (1986), law.cornell.edu.

We Take That Fire and Make It Our Own, **The Lesbian Avengers**
"It stands for our fear": In *Lesbian Avengers Eat Fire Too,* directed by Janet Baus and Su Friedrich, produced by The Lesbian Avengers, 1993, lesbianavengers.com.
"big and bold": Kelly Cogswell, "The Dyke March Hits 20!" *Huffington Post,* May 18, 2012.
"We're dykes, we're out": *Lesbians Eat Fire Too,* 1993, lesbianavengers.com.

Stop the Church, **Michael Petrelis**
"We will not be silent": Jason DeParle, "111 Held in St. Patrick's AIDS Protest," *New York Times,* December 11, 1989.

Clarence Thomas, Sexual Harasser, **Anita Hill**
"We all kind of fired ourselves up": Lisa Chase, "An Oral History of the Day Women Changed Congress," September 9, 2014, elle.com.

SIXTEEN
The War on Terror

Isn't This Really About Oil? **Medea Benjamin**
"women-led grassroots organization": No author listed, "What Is CODEPINK?" no date, codepink.org.

Bring Our Troops Home, **Cindy Sheehan**
"Mom": Richard W. Stevenson, "Of the Many Deaths in Iraq, One Mother's Loss Becomes a Problem for the President," *New York Times,* August 8, 2005.
"We're going to keep on questioning": Associated Press, "Antiwar Mom Ends Vigil Near President's Ranch," nbcnews.com, August 31, 2005.

Shut Down Creech, **Anti-Drone Activists**
"Can you take the drones": Amy Goodman with David Goodman and Denis Moynihan, *Democracy Now! Twenty Years Covering the Movements Changing America* (New York: Simon & Schuster, 2016), 46. See also "Medea Benjamin v. President Obama: CodePink Founder Disrupts Speech, Criticizing Drone, Gitmo Policy," democracynow. org, May 24, 2013. Other quotations in this introduction are drawn from this source.

SEVENTEEN
The New Century

End Mountaintop Removal, **Appalachia Rising**
"The science is clear": Dan Lothian, "Protesters Arrested Outside the White House," cnn.com, September 27, 2010.
"Blowing Up Mountains": Frederick J. Frommer, Associated Press, "About 100 Arrested in Mountaintop Mining Protest," *San Diego Union-Tribune,* September 27, 2010. See also Rick Pilz, "Hansen Joins Appalachia Rising Mountaintop Removal Coal Protest, 100 Arrested at White House," climatesciencewatch.org, September 30, 2010.

The Keystone Pipeline Revolt, **Bill McKibben**
"To call this project a horror": Bill McKibben, *Oil and Water: The Education of an Unlikely Activist* (New York: Times Books, 2013), 17-18.
"Yes, we can" and "That is the second biggest": Suzanne Goldenberg, "Thousands Protest at the White House Against Keystone XL Pipeline," *Guardian,* November 6, 2011.

Chained to Serve Openly, **Get EQUAL**
"Barack Obama … Silent Homophobia": Chris Johnson, "13 Arrested at White House in 'Don't Ask' Protest," *Washington Blade,* November 15, 2010.
"I don't care who you love": Carl Hulse, "Senate Repeals Ban Against Openly Gay Military Personnel," *New York Times,* December 18, 2010.

Killing Big Insurance, **Mobilization for Health Care for All**
"experimental": Pauline W. Chen, "When Insurers Put Profits Between Doctor and Patient," *New York Times,* January 6, 2011.
"Patients Not Profits": Colin Moynihan, "17 Held in Protest Outside Health Insurer's Office," *New York Times,* September 29, 2009.

Occupy, I Love You, Naomi Klein
"When you idealize financial markets": Colin Moynihan, "Wall Street Protest Begins, With Demonstrators Blocked," *New York Times,* September 17, 2011.
"We come to you at a time": New York City General Assembly, "Declaration of the Occupation of New York City," occupywallstreet.net, September 29, 2011.

Moral Mondays, William Barber II
"transformational coalition": Alan Bean, "Moral Monday Movement Unleashes 'Linguistic Trauma,'" no date, friendsofjustice.wordpress.com.

Time to Withdraw Big Money from Politics, Democracy Spring and Democracy Uprising
"sweep big money": Zoe Carpenter and Ari Berman, "The Most Important Protest of the 2016 Election," *The Nation,* April 18, 2016.

Riding to Ferguson, Black Lives Matter
"love letter to black people": Wesley Lowery, "Black Lives Matter: Birth of a Movement," *Guardian,* January 17, 2017.
"Black Lives Matter is an ideological": blacklivesmatter.com.

Stopping Another Deportation, United We Dream
"People are just breaking down": Julia Preston and John H. Cushman, Jr., "Obama to Permit Young Migrants to Remain in U.S.," *New York Times,* June 15, 2012.
"I hereby pledge to live out": Julia Preston, "Young Immigrants Stage Citizenship Ceremony at the Capitol," *New York Times,* July 10, 2013.

EIGHTEEN
The Trump Era Begins

Not a Legitimate President, John Lewis and Others
"No. I believe in forgiveness": *Meet the Press,* transcript, nbcnews.com, January 15, 2017.

Our Pussies Ain't for Grabbing, The Women's March and America Ferrera
"likely the largest single-day": Erica Chenoweth and Jeremy Pressman, "This Is What We Learned by Counting the Women's Marches," *Washington Post,* February 7, 2017.
"support and solidarity for women's rights": pussyhatproject.com.
"Our pussies ain't for grabbing," Dana Bruk, "Ashley Judd Gave an Incredibly Fiery Speech at the Women's March," *Harper's Bazaar,* January 21, 2017.

Together We Rise, Dave Archambault II
"Shame!": Joe Heim, "American Indians from Around the U.S. March on White House in Rally for Rights," *Washington Post,* March 10, 2017.

Fearless Girl, Susan Cox
"One of the most iconic images": Rachel Levy, "A $2.5 Trillion Asset Manager Just Put a Statue of a Defiant Girl in Front of the Wall Street Bull," *Business Insider,* March 7, 2017.

"a complement to the charging bull": Nick Pinto, "Fearless Girl Is Not Your Friend," *Village Voice*, April 25, 2017. All following quotations in this introduction are drawn from this source.

And So We Resist Global Warming, Bill McKibben
"keep it in the soil": Chelsea Bailey, "People's Climate March Spurs Thousands to Descend on the White House," nbcnews.com, April 29, 2017.

"We're here, we're hot": Nicholas Fandos, "Climate March Draws Thousands of Protesters Alarmed by Trump's Agenda," *New York Times*, April 29, 2017.

"Make our planet great again": Jon Henley, "'Make Our Planet Great Again': Macron's Response to Trump Is Praised," *Guardian*, June 3, 2017.

Dying for Health Care, ADAPT
"No cuts to Medicaid—save our liberty!": Elise Viebeck, "Protesters Block Hallway Outside McConnell's Office," *Washington Post*, June 22, 2017.

Targeting Transgender Troops, Human Rights Campaign
"After consultation with my generals": Sabrina Siddiqui and Molly Redden, "Donald Trump Says U.S. Military Will Not Allow Transgender People to Serve," *Guardian*, July 26, 2017.

"That motherfucker": John Riley, "Outraged Protests Call Trump's Trans Military Ban 'Bullshit' and 'a Betrayal,'" *Metro Weekly*, July 27, 2017.

We Pledge to Resist for Immigrants, Alison Harrington
"When Mexico sends its people": Katie Reilly, "Here Are All the Times Donald Trump Insulted Mexico," *Time*, August 31, 2016.

The Human Impact of the Muslim Ban, Dina El-Rifai
"Shame": Niraj Chokshi and Nicholas Fandos, "Demonstrators in Streets, and at Airports, Protest Immigration Order," *New York Times*, January 29, 2017.

"Immigrants Make America Great Again": Images of signs can be found in photographs and videos of the march. See, for example, Ben Dreyfuss, "Across the Country, Thousands Protest Trump's 'Muslim Ban,'" motherjones.com, January 29, 2017.

We Do Not Want a Wall, Dulce Garcia
"No ban! No wall!": Julie Watson and Jill Colvin, "Trump Views Designs for Border Wall While Bashing California," Associated Press, March 13, 2018, usnews.com.

#MeToo Is About Restoring Humanity
"I was horrified": Tarana Burke, "The Inception," justbeincwixsite.com.

"the health, well-being, and wholeness": See the home page of justbeincwixsite.com.

"If you've been sexually harassed": Sandra E. Garcia, "The Woman Who Created #MeToo Long Before Hashtags," *New York Times*, October 20, 2017.

ACKNOWLEDGMENTS

Elaine Katzenberger, the publisher of City Lights Books, is really an editor of editors. She guided and strengthened this book—its contents, flow, and framework—in ways I could never imagine, and her rich contributions suggest that her name should appear before mine on the front cover. Thanks, Elaine, for sharing your editorial skills and insight.

I am also deeply grateful to the following individuals and institutions: my dearest friend, Sharon Herr, who proofread the manuscript with her characteristic care and concern; Stacey Lewis, who markets City Lights titles with excitement and passion; archivists at the Library of Congress, the National Archives, and U.S. presidential libraries; Elizabethtown College, especially Kristi Kneas, Fletcher McClellan, Luke Mackey, the High Library staff, and translator Ethan Waugh; scholars whose work I've heavily relied on, including, in no particular order, Herbert Aptheker, Alice Lynd, Staughton Lynd, David R. Weber, Peter Brock, James G. Basker, Ralph F. Young, Howard Zinn, Anthony Arnove, Manning Marble, Leith Mullings, Philip S. Foner, Robert James Branham, Henry Louis Gates, Jr., Evelyn Brooks Higginbotham, Karen Stanford, John Whiteclay Chambers, L. Diane Barnes, Van Gosse, Louis Ruchames, Darrel Enck-Wanzer, Winston E. Langley, Vivian C. Fox, Nancy MacLean, Tom Hayden, Maria Fleming, Pam McAllister, Lila Weinberg, Arthur Weinburg, Scott H. Bennett, Charles F. Howlett, Mari Jo Buhle, Paul Buhle, Harvey J. Kaye, Judith Wellman, Charles Chatfield, Lawrence Rosenwald, Donald W. Whisenhunt, Murray Polner, Thomas E. Woods, Jr., Jonathan Birnbaum, Clarence Taylor, Melvyn Dubofsky, Joseph A. McCartin, Robert Cooney, Helen Michalowski, Daniel M. Cobb, Rosalyn Baxandall, Linda Gordon, David M. Gross, Lionel C. Bascom, David Brion Davis, Steven Mintz, Walter L. Williams, Yolanda Retter, Immanuel Ness, Richard Cahan, Michael Williams, Amy Tachiki, Eddie Wong, Franklin Odo, and Buck Wong; my inspiring students in peace and conflict studies; the Long Resisters, especially Jackson Griffith Long and Nathaniel Finn Long; Robert Thomas Long, Jr. and Karin Frederiksen Long, who found a way out of no way and ushered me through it with fierce love; and, finally, all the courageous, smart, and relentless resisters in U.S. history who inspired me every step along the way.

Michael G. Long is an associate professor of religious studies and peace and conflict studies at Elizabethtown College and is the author or editor of numerous books on civil rights, religion, and politics, including *Jackie Robinson: A Spiritual Biography; Peaceful Neighbor: Discovering the Countercultural Mister Rogers; Gay Is Good: The Life and Letters of Gay Rights Pioneer Franklin Kameny; Beyond Home Plate: Jackie Robinson on Life after Baseball; Martin Luther King, Jr., Homosexuality, and the Early Gay Rights Movement; I Must Resist: Bayard Rustin's Life in Letters; Marshalling Justice: The Early Civil Rights Letters of Thurgood Marshall; First Class Citizenship: The Civil Rights Letters of Jackie Robinson; The Legacy of Billy Graham; Billy Graham and the Beloved Community;* and *Against Us, But for Us: Martin Luther King, Jr. and the State.*